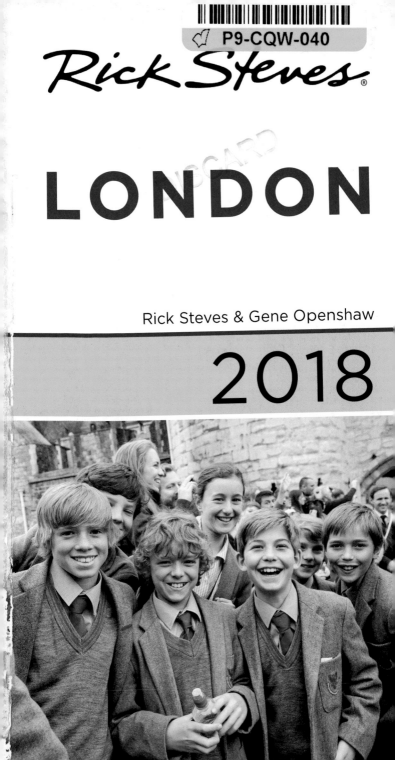

P9-CQW-040

Rick Steves®

LONDON

Rick Steves & Gene Openshaw

2018

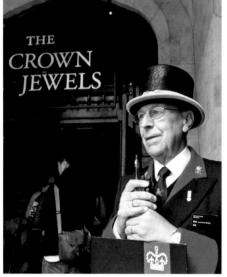

CONTENTS

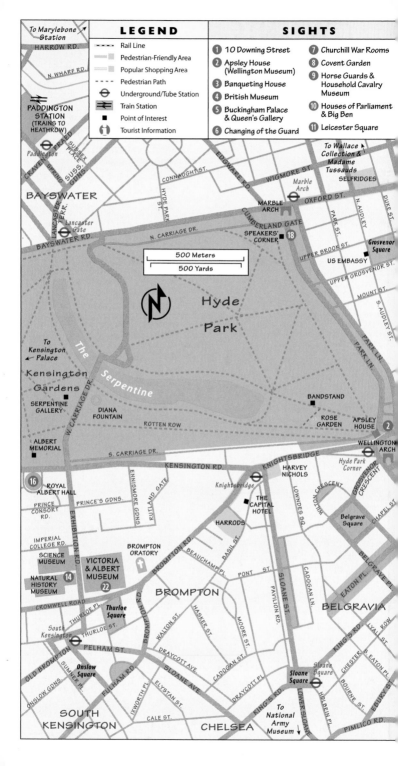

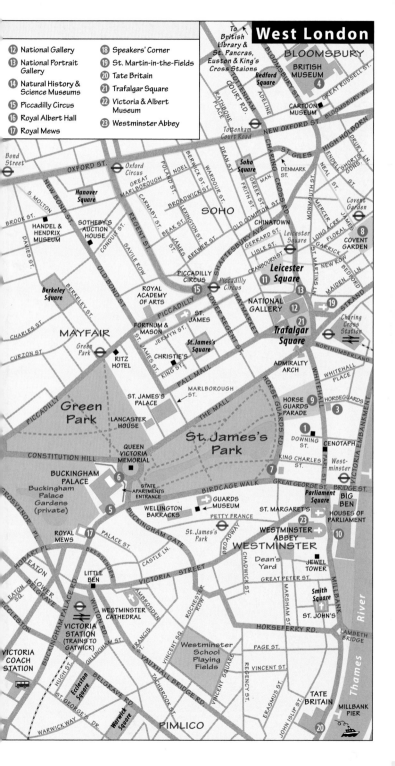

West London

To British Library & St. Pancras, Euston & King's Cross Stations

BLOOMSBURY

- ⑫ National Gallery
- ⑬ National Portrait Gallery
- ⑭ Natural History & Science Museums
- ⑮ Piccadilly Circus
- ⑯ Royal Albert Hall
- ⑰ Royal Mews
- ⑱ Speakers' Corner
- ⑲ St. Martin-in-the-Fields
- ⑳ Tate Britain
- ㉑ Trafalgar Square
- ㉒ Victoria & Albert Museum
- ㉓ Westminster Abbey

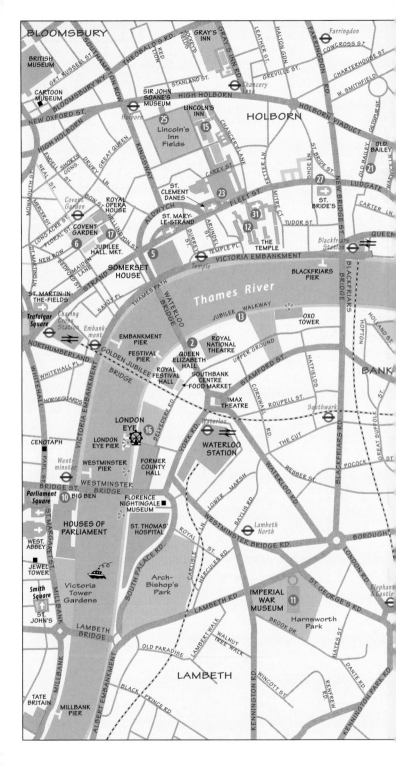

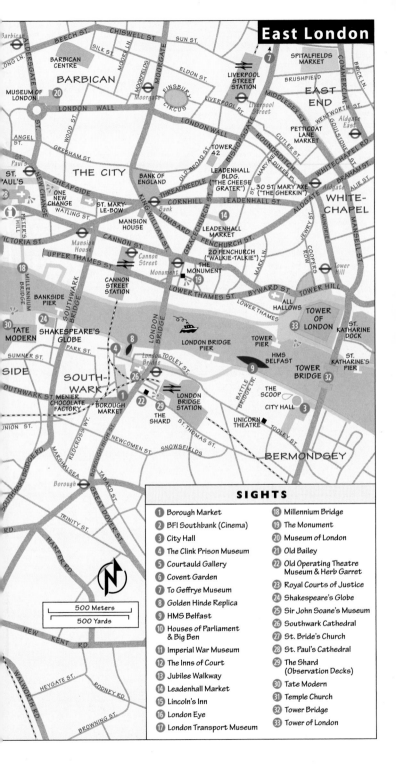

East London

SIGHTS

1. Borough Market
2. BFI Southbank (Cinema)
3. City Hall
4. The Clink Prison Museum
5. Courtauld Gallery
6. Covent Garden
7. To Geffrye Museum
8. Golden Hinde Replica
9. HMS Belfast
10. Houses of Parliament & Big Ben
11. Imperial War Museum
12. The Inns of Court
13. Jubilee Walkway
14. Leadenhall Market
15. Lincoln's Inn
16. London Eye
17. London Transport Museum
18. Millennium Bridge
19. The Monument
20. Museum of London
21. Old Bailey
22. Old Operating Theatre Museum & Herb Garret
23. Royal Courts of Justice
24. Shakespeare's Globe
25. Sir John Soane's Museum
26. Southwark Cathedral
27. St. Bride's Church
28. St. Paul's Cathedral
29. The Shard (Observation Decks)
30. Tate Modern
31. Temple Church
32. Tower Bridge
33. Tower of London

500 Meters
500 Yards

Interchange stations

Step-free access from street to train

Step-free access from street to platform

† Services to/from some stations are subject to variation.
Please search **'TfL stations'** for full details.

Caledonian Road
Station closed temporarily from Spring 2016.

Holland Park
Station closed from Saturday 2 January until early August 2016.

Paddington
Bakerloo line trains will not stop at this station from Saturday 2 April until early August 2016.

Tufnell Park
Station closed until mid-March 2016.

MAYOR OF LONDON

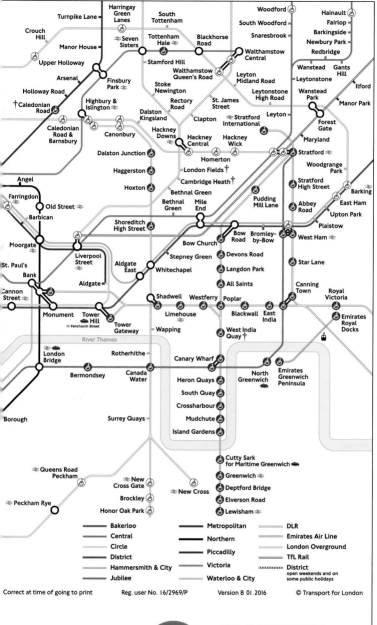

	Bakerloo		Metropolitan		DLR
	Central		Northern		Emirates Air Line
	Circle		Piccadilly		London Overground
	District		Victoria		TfL Rail
	Hammersmith & City		Waterloo & City		District
	Jubilee				open weekends and on some public holidays

Correct at time of going to print   Reg. user No. 16/2969/P   Version B 01.2016   © Transport for London

TRANSPORT FOR LONDON

EVERY JOURNEY MATTERS

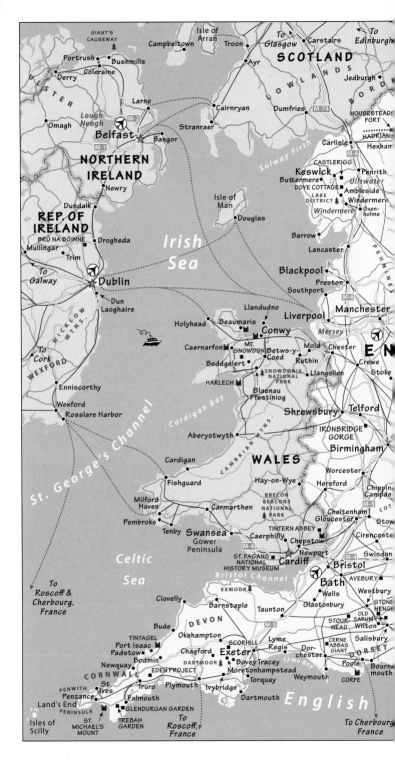

England

LEGEND

⟨A-24⟩	Freeway/Motorway
——	Major Rail Line
✈	Airport
♠	National Park/Natural Wonder
■	Ruin, Museum, Other Point of Interest
⌂	Castle/Monument/Palace

50 Kilometers
50 Miles

Berwick-upon-Tweed
Holy Island
Beal
BAMBURGH CASTLE
S
Alnwick
Newcastle-upon-Tyne
BEAMISH MUSEUM   Durham
YORK SHIRE DALES   A-1   Middlesbrough
Staithes
Grosmont
NORTH YORK MOORS   Whitby
RIEVAULX ABBEY   Goathland   Robin Hood's Bay
Thirsk   Hutton-le-Hole   Pick.
CASTLE HOWARD   EDEN CAMP   Scarborough
York
Bridlington
eeds   Doncaster
I-62
Sheffield   Kingston-upon-Hull
M-1   Grimsby
GLAND
MIDLANDS
Lincoln
Derby   Newark
Nottingham   Boston   Skegness
M-1   The Wash
eicester   Cromer
Stamford   King's Lynn
Coventry   Peterborough   Norwich
Warwick   EAST   Great Yarmouth
Stratford   Ely   ANGLIA
OLDS   Northampton   Cambridge
Moreton
BLENHEIM PALACE   Luton   Ipswich
Oxford   M-1   Stansted   Harwich
Didcot   Hertford   Colchester
M-40   Leavesden
Reading   Thames   M-11
Windsor   London   Southend
HIGH-   Heathrow   City   Southend-on-Sea
CLERE   M-3   Greenwich
Winchester   Gatwick   Whitstable
M-23   M-20   M-2   Ramsgate
Southampton   ARUNDEL   Canterbury
Portsmouth   SISSINGHURST GARDENS   Ashford   WHITE CLIFFS OF DOVER
Battle   Folke-stone   Dover
PEVENSEY   KENT   Calais
ewport   FISHBOURNE ROMAN PALACE   Brighton   Hastings   Rye
Isle of Wight   Newhaven   Alfriston
Eastbourne
BEACHY HEAD

North Sea

To Amsterdam, Netherlands

To Hoek van Holland, Netherlands

Zeebrugge
Ostende   Bruges
Dunkirk   E-40
BELGIUM
E-17
FRANCE
Lille   E-42
A-16   A-26
To St-Malo, France
To Caen (Ouistreham), France
To Dieppe, France
To Paris
To Paris
To Brussels

Channel

N

Rick Steves®

LONDON

2018

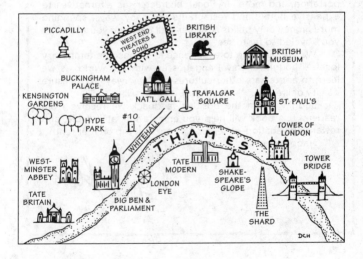

Welcome to Rick Steves' Europe

Travel is intensified living—maximum thrills per minute and one of the last great sources of legal adventure. Travel is freedom. It's recess, and we need it.

I discovered a passion for European travel as a teen and have been sharing it ever since—through my tours, public television and radio shows, and travel guidebooks. Over the years, I've taught thousands of travelers how to best enjoy Europe's blockbuster sights—and experience "Back Door" discoveries that most tourists miss.

Written with my talented co-author, Gene Openshaw, this book offers you a balanced mix of London's blockbuster sights and lesser-known gems. And it's selective—rather than listing a lorry load of museums and galleries, we recommend only the best ones. Our self-guided museum tours and city walks give insight into the city's vibrant history and today's living, breathing culture.

We advocate traveling simply and smartly. Take advantage of our money- and time-saving tips on sightseeing, transportation, and more. Try local, characteristic alternatives to expensive hotels and restaurants. In many ways, spending more money only builds a thicker wall between you and what you traveled so far to see.

We visit London to experience it—to become temporary locals. Thoughtful travel engages us with the world, as we learn to appreciate other cultures and new ways to measure quality of life.

Judging from the positive feedback we receive from readers, this book will help you enjoy a fun, affordable, and rewarding vacation—whether it's your first trip or your tenth.

Happy travels!

Rick Steves

INTRODUCTION

Blow through the city on a double-decker bus, and take a pinch-me-I'm-in-London walk through the West End. Ogle the crown jewels at the Tower of London, hear the chimes of Big Ben, and see the Houses of Parliament in action. Cruise the Thames River, and take a spin on the London Eye. Hobnob with the tombstones in Westminster Abbey, visit with Leonardo, Botticelli, and Rembrandt in the National Gallery, and explore Harry Potter's magical realm at the film studio in Leavesden. Enjoy Shakespeare in a replica of the Globe Theatre and marvel at a glitzy, fun musical at a modern-day theater. Whisper across the dome of St. Paul's Cathedral, then rummage through our civilization's attic at the British Museum. And sip your tea with pinky raised and clotted cream dribbling down your scone.

You can enjoy some of Europe's best people-watching at Covent Garden, and snap to at Buckingham Palace's Changing of the Guard. Just sit in Victoria Station, Piccadilly Circus, or a major Tube station and observe. Tip a pint in a pub with a chatty local, and beachcomb the Thames. Spend one evening at a theater and the other nights catching your breath.

London is more than its museums and landmarks. It's the L.A., D.C., and N.Y.C. of Britain—a living, breathing, thriving organism...a coral reef of humanity. The city has changed dramatically in recent years, and many visitors are surprised to find how "un-English" it is. ESL (English as a second language) seems like the city's first language, as white people are now a minority in major parts of the city that once symbolized white imperialism. London is a city of eight million separate dreams, inhabiting a place that tolerates and encourages them. Arabs have nearly bought out the area north of Hyde Park. Chinese takeouts outnumber fish-and-chips shops. Eastern Europeans pull pints in British pubs, and

Italians express your espresso. Many hotels are run by people with foreign accents (who hire English chambermaids), while outlying suburbs are home to huge communities of Indians and Pakistanis.

But with Britain's recent vote to exit the EU, the British people have decided to pull up the drawbridge. From a practical standpoint, travelers heading to London soon likely won't see much of a post-"Brexit" difference...other than a cheaper pound sterling, and plenty to talk about with your new British friends.

As a beacon of multiculturalism and with huge immigrant populations, London has been a target of terrorism ever since that word entered our lexicon. But its people refuse to be kept down. London is as safe as any American city, and any visitor with a grip on the low statistical risk of being out and about will feel just fine in London town.

London, which has long attracted tourists, seems perpetually at your service, with an impressive slate of sights, entertainment, and eateries, all linked by a great transit system. Come prepared to celebrate all the tradition and fanfare of yesterday while catching the buzz of a city that's trumpeting its future.

ABOUT THIS BOOK

Rick Steves London 2018 is a personal tour guide in your pocket. Better yet, it's actually two tour guides in your pocket: The co-author of this book is Gene Openshaw. Since our first "Europe through the gutter" trip together as high school buddies in the 1970s, Gene and I have been exploring the wonders of the Old World. An inquisitive historian and lover of European culture, Gene wrote most of this book's self-guided museum tours and neighborhood walks. Together, Gene and I keep this book current and accurate (though, for simplicity, from this point "we" will shed our respective egos and become "I").

In this book, you'll find the following chapters:

Orientation to London has specifics on public transportation, helpful hints, local tour options, easy-to-read maps, and tourist information. The "Planning Your Time" section suggests a schedule for how to best use your limited time.

Sights in London describes the top attractions and includes their cost and hours.

Self-Guided Walks cover Westminster (from Big Ben to Trafalgar Square); the West End (it's the thee-ah-ter district, dahling, with restaurants and shops galore, from Leicester Square and Covent Garden to Soho and Piccadilly Circus); The City (the historic financial district—banks, churches, and courts busy with barristers and baristas); Bankside (on the South Bank, through Shakespeare's world to the Tate Modern); and the Docklands (London's new and creatively planned urban district).

Self-Guided Tours lead you through London's most fascinating museums and sights: Westminster Abbey, the Houses of Parliament, the National Gallery, the National Portrait Gallery, the British Museum, the British Library, St. Paul's Cathedral, the Tower of London, the Tate Modern, the Victoria and Albert Museum, and the Tate Britain. The Greenwich Tour ties together the major sights of that London borough.

Sleeping in London describes my favorite hotels, from good-value deals to cushy splurges.

Eating in London serves up a buffet of options, from inexpensive pubs to fancy restaurants.

London with Children includes my top recommendations for keeping your kids (and you) happy in London.

Shopping in London gives you tips on how to enjoy London's celebrated shops, bustling markets, and symbolic souvenirs, without letting it overwhelm your vacation or ruin your budget.

Entertainment in London is your guide to fun, including theater, music, sports, and wintertime activities.

London Connections lays the groundwork for your smooth arrival and departure, covering transportation by train (including the Eurostar to the Continent) and by plane (with detailed information on London's major airports), plus connections to the cruise-ship ports of Southampton and Dover.

Day Trips covers visits to nearby Windsor, Cambridge, and Stonehenge.

Britain: Past & Present gives the background of this country, including a timeline of London history, information about British architecture, and a rundown of contemporary events and current challenges.

Practicalities, near the end of this book, is a traveler's tool kit, with my best advice about money, sightseeing, sleeping, eating, staying connected, and transportation.

The **appendix** has the nuts and bolts: useful phone numbers and websites, a holiday and festival list, books and films, a climate chart, a handy packing checklist, and a fun British-Yankee dictionary.

Throughout this book, you'll find money- and time-saving tips for sightseeing, transportation, and more. Some businesses—especially hotels and walking tour companies—offer special discounts to my readers, indicated in their listings.

Browse through this book and select your favorite sights. Then have a brilliant trip! Traveling like a temporary local, you'll get the absolute most out of every mile, minute, and dollar. As you visit places I know and love, I'm happy you'll be meeting my favorite Londoners.

Planning

This section will help you get started planning your trip—with advice on trip costs, when to go, and things to know before you take off.

TRIP COSTS

Five components make up your trip costs: airfare to Europe, surface transportation in Europe, room and board, sightseeing and entertainment, and shopping and miscellany.

Airfare to Europe: A basic round-trip flight from the US to London can cost, on average, about $1,000-2,000 total, depending on where you fly from and when (cheaper in winter). If London is part of a longer trip, consider saving time and money in Europe by flying into one city and out of another; for instance, into London and out of Paris. Overall, Kayak.com is the best place to start searching for flights on a combination of mainstream and budget carriers.

Transportation in Europe: For a typical one-week visit, allow about $45 for the Tube and buses (for a Seven-Day Travelcard transportation pass). Round-trip train rides to day-trip destinations cost about $20 for Windsor, $35 for Cambridge, and $50 for Salisbury, where you can catch a $20 bus to Stonehenge. You can save money by taking buses instead of trains. Add $60-100 if you plan to take a taxi between London's Heathrow Airport and your hotel (or save money by taking the Tube, train, bus, or airport shuttle).

Room and Board: London is one of Europe's most expensive major capitals. But if you're careful, you can manage comfortably in London on $135 a day per person for room and board. A $135-a-day budget allows $15 for lunch, $30 for dinner, and $90 for lodging (based on two people splitting the cost of a basic $180 double room that includes breakfast). Students and tightwads can do it for as little as $70 a day ($45 for hostel bed, $25 for groceries).

Sightseeing and Entertainment: You'll pay more in London for sights that charge admission than you will anywhere else in Europe. Fortunately, most of London's best sights are free (although many request a donation), including the British Museum, National Gallery, National Portrait Gallery, Tate Britain, Tate Modern, British Library, and the Victoria and Albert Museum. (For a list of free museums—and advice on saving money on sightseeing—see "Affording London's Sights" on page 74.)

Figure on paying roughly $25-40 each for the major sights that charge admission (e.g., Westminster Abbey-$28, Tower of London-$35), $12-20 for guided walks, and $40 for bus tours and splurge experiences (plays range $25-100). An overall average of $50-60 a day works for most people. Don't skimp here. After all,

London Almanac

Population: Approximately 10.3 million people

Currency: British pound (GBP)

City Layout: London is divided into the City of London (the main financial district) and 32 administrative boroughs—12 in inner London.

Tallest Building: The Shard stands at 1,020 feet, making it the tallest building in Western Europe—for now.

Tourist Tracks: Each year London hosts 36 million tourists, most of whom stop to take a photo at Trafalgar Square. London's most popular attraction, the British Museum, sees 6 million visitors annually.

Popular Misconception: "Big Ben" refers not to the clock, but instead to its 13-ton bell.

Culture Count: While the Queen's English is still the language of the land, fewer than half the residents of inner London speak English as their first language. Nearly 300 different languages are spoken in London's schools. About 60 percent of Londoners are white (many of them Continental Europeans rather than Brits), but the incredible diversity of the rest of the population make this city a global melting pot. Some 17 percent of Londoners are Asian (7 percent are Indian and Bangladeshi), and 13 percent are black, including many from African countries (7 percent of Londoners) and the Caribbean (4 percent). Six in 10 Brits call themselves Christian (half of those are Anglican), but in any given week, more Londoners visit a mosque than an Anglican church.

Fun Food Facts: Traditionally, London's most popular takeaway foods were fish-and-chips and minced-meat pie (the pies were originally filled with eels...so minced-meat is an improvement). But it's not all about meat; PETA recently named London the world's most vegan-friendly city. These days you'll find more gourmet sandwich and prepackaged-meal shops than "chippies."

Need a Restroom? Ask for the toilet, loo, lavatory, or bog.

Oldest Pub: The Lamb and Flag in Covent Garden. First licensed in 1623, it was once known as the Bucket of Blood, thanks to rowdy, bare-knuckle fights held there.

Average Londoner: The average Londoner is about 34 years old, has 1.7 children, and will live until the age of 80. He/she earns about 25 percent more than those in other parts of Great Britain, but pays more than twice as much for housing. He/she will drink 75,000 cups of tea in a lifetime and consumes less alcohol per week than the average Brit.

INTRODUCTION

this category is the driving force behind your trip—you came to sightsee, enjoy, and experience London.

Shopping and Miscellany: Figure roughly $2 per postcard, $3 for tea or an ice-cream cone, and $6 per pint of beer. Shopping can vary in cost from nearly nothing to a small fortune. Good budget travelers find that this category has little to do with assembling a trip full of lifelong memories.

WHEN TO GO

July and August are peak season—my favorite time—with long days, the best weather, and the busiest schedule of tourist fun. Prices and crowds don't go up in summer as dramatically in Britain as they do in much of Europe, except for holidays and festivals (see page 581). Still, travelers during "shoulder season" (May, early June, Sept, and early Oct) enjoy lower prices, smaller crowds, decent weather, and the full range of sights and tourist fun spots.

Winter travelers find fewer crowds and soft room prices, but shorter sightseeing hours. The weather can be cold and dreary, and nightfall draws the shades on sightseeing well before dinnertime. While England's rural charm falls with the leaves, London sightseeing is fine in the winter, and is especially popular during the Christmas season. For more on planning a winter holiday visit, read "Winter Diversions" (in the Entertainment in London chapter).

Plan for rain no matter when you go. Just keep traveling and take full advantage of "bright spells." The weather can change several times a day, but rarely is it extreme. As the locals say, "There's no bad weather, only inappropriate clothing." Bring a jacket, and dress in layers. Temperatures below 32°F cause headlines, and days that break 80°F—while more common in recent years—are still infrequent in London. (For more information, see the climate chart in the appendix.) Weather-wise, July and August are not much better than shoulder months. May and June can be lovely. While sunshine may be rare, summer days are very long. The midsummer sun is up from 6:30 to 22:30. It's not uncommon to have a gray day, eat dinner, and enjoy hours of sunshine afterward.

Before You Go

You'll have a smoother trip if you tackle a few things ahead of time. For more information on these topics, see the Practicalities chapter (and www.ricksteves.com, which has helpful travel tips and talks).

Make sure your passport is valid. If it's due to expire within six months of your ticketed date of return, you need to renew it. Allow up to six weeks to renew or get a passport (www.travel.state. gov). Britain's decision to leave the EU will take some time to implement; travelers in 2018 shouldn't see many changes.

Arrange your transportation. Book your international flights. You won't want a car in congested London, but if you'll be touring the countryside beyond, figure out your main form of transportation: You can buy train tickets as you go, get a rail pass, rent a car, or book a cheap flight. (You can wing it in Europe, but it may cost more.) If you'll be taking the **Eurostar train,** consider buying your ticket in advance; for details, see page 472.

Book rooms well in advance, especially if your trip falls during peak season or any major holidays or festivals (see page 581).

Reserve or buy tickets ahead for major sights or shows, saving you from long ticket-buying lines. For simplicity, I **book plays** while in London (but if you have your heart set on a hot show, buying tickets in advance online or by phone is safer). For the current schedule, visit www.officiallondontheatre.co.uk. For more information, see the Entertainment in London chapter.

Advance reservations are advantageous for a few of London's major sights. Booking ahead is not required for **St. Paul's Cathedral,** the **Tower of London,** the **London Eye,** or **Stonehenge,** but it will let you skip a wait of up to 30 minutes in the ticket-buying line. To visit the stones' inner circle, book your visit as soon as you know the date you'll be there.

Consider travel insurance. Compare the cost of the insurance to the cost of your potential loss. Check whether your existing insurance (health, homeowners, or renters) covers you and your possessions overseas.

Call your bank. Alert your bank that you'll be using your debit and credit cards in Europe. Ask about transaction fees, and get the PIN number for your credit card. You don't need to bring pounds for your trip; you can withdraw pounds from cash machines on arrival.

Use your smartphone smartly. Sign up for an international service plan to reduce your costs, or rely on Wi-Fi in Europe instead. Download any apps you'll want on the road, such as maps, translation, transit schedules, and Rick Steves Audio Europe (see sidebar).

Pack light. You'll walk with your luggage more than you think. Bring a single carry-on bag and a daypack. Use the packing checklist in the appendix as a guide.

Travel Smart

If you have a positive attitude, equip yourself with good information (this book), and expect to travel smart, you will.

Read—and reread—this book. To have an "A" trip, be an "A" student. Note opening hours of sights, closed days, crowd-beating tips, and whether reservations are required or advisable. Design an

INTRODUCTION

∩ **Stick This Guidebook in Your Ear!** ∩

My free Rick Steves Audio Europe app makes it easy for you to download my audio tours of many of Europe's top attractions and listen to them offline during your travels. In this book, these include my walks through Westminster and Historic London: The City, and my tours of the British Museum, British Library, and St. Paul's Cathedral. Sights covered by audio tours are marked in this book with this symbol: ∩. The app also offers insightful travel interviews from my public radio show with experts from Great Britain and around the globe. It's all free! You can download the app via Apple's App Store, Google Play, or Amazon's Appstore. For more info, see www.ricksteves.com/ audioeurope.

itinerary that enables you to visit sights at the best possible times. For example, don't visit the historic neighborhood known as The City on a weekend when it's completely dead if you can instead visit on a lively weekday. Check the latest at www.ricksteves.com/ update.

Be your own tour guide. As you travel, get up-to-date info on sights, reserve tickets and tours, reconfirm hotels and travel arrangements, and check transit connections. Visit local tourist information offices (TIs). Upon arrival in a new place, lay the groundwork for a smooth departure; confirm the train, bus, or road you'll take when you leave.

Outsmart thieves. Pickpockets abound in crowded places where tourists congregate. Treat commotions as smokescreens for theft. Keep your cash, credit cards, and passport secure in a money belt tucked under your clothes; carry only a day's spending money in your front pocket. Don't set valuable items down on counters or café tabletops, where they can be quickly stolen or easily forgotten.

Minimize potential loss. Keep expensive gear to a minimum. Bring photocopies or take photos of important documents (passport and cards) to aid in replacement if they're lost or stolen.

Guard your time and energy. Taking a taxi can be a good value if it saves you a long wait for a cheap bus or an exhausting walk across town. To avoid long lines, follow my crowd-beating tips, such as making advance reservations, or sightseeing early or late.

Be flexible. Even if you have a well-planned itinerary, expect changes, strikes, closures, sore feet, bad weather, and so on. Your Plan B could turn out to be even better.

Connect with the culture. Interacting with locals carbonates your experience. Enjoy the friendliness of the British people. Ask questions; most locals are happy to point you in their idea of the right direction. Set up your own quest for the best pub, silly sign, or

chocolate bar. When an opportunity pops up, make it a habit to say "yes."

London...here you come!

ORIENTATION TO LONDON

London is more than 600 square miles of urban jungle—a world in itself and a barrage on all the senses. On my first visit, I felt extremely small. To grasp London more comfortably, see it as the old town in the city center without the modern, congested sprawl. (Even from that perspective, it's still huge.)

The Thames River (pronounced "tems") runs roughly west to east through the city, with most of the visitor's sights on the North Bank. Mentally, maybe even physically, trim down your map to include only the area between the Tower of London (to the east), Hyde Park (west), Regent's Park (north), and the South Bank (south). This is roughly the area bordered by the Tube's Circle Line. This four-mile stretch between the Tower and Hyde Park (about a 1.5-hour walk) looks like a milk bottle on its side (see map on next page), and holds 80 percent of the sights mentioned in this book.

With a core focus and a good orientation, you'll get a sampling of London's top sights, history, and cultural entertainment, and a good look at its ever-changing human face.

The sprawling city becomes much more manageable if you think of it as a collection of neighborhoods.

Central London: This area contains Westminster and what Londoners call the West End. The Westminster district includes Big Ben, Parliament, Westminster Abbey, and Buckingham Palace—the grand government buildings from which Britain is ruled. Trafalgar Square, London's gathering place, has many major museums. The West End is the center of London's cultural life, with bustling squares: Piccadilly Circus and Leicester Square host cinemas, tourist traps, and nighttime glitz. Soho and Covent Garden are thriving people zones with theaters, restaurants, pubs, and boutiques. And Regent and Oxford streets are the city's main shopping zones.

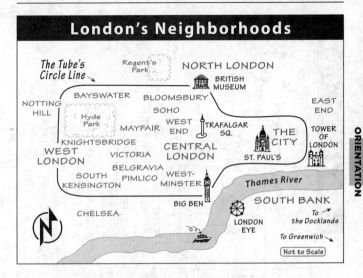

London's Neighborhoods

The Tube's Circle Line

Regent's Park

NORTH LONDON

BRITISH MUSEUM

BAYSWATER BLOOMSBURY

NOTTING HILL

Hyde Park

SOHO

MAYFAIR WEST END

TRAFALGAR SQ.

EAST END

KNIGHTSBRIDGE

CENTRAL LONDON

THE CITY

TOWER OF LONDON

WEST LONDON

VICTORIA

ST. PAUL'S

BELGRAVIA

SOUTH KENSINGTON

PIMLICO

WEST-MINSTER

Thames River

CHELSEA

BIG BEN

SOUTH BANK

LONDON EYE

To the Docklands

To Greenwich

Not to Scale

ORIENTATION

North London: Neighborhoods in this part of town—including Bloomsbury, Fitzrovia, and Marylebone—contain such major sights as the British Museum and the overhyped Madame Tussauds Waxworks. Nearby, along busy Euston Road, is the British Library, plus a trio of train stations (one of them, St. Pancras International, is linked to Paris by the Eurostar "Chunnel" train).

The City: Today's modern financial district, called simply "The City," was a walled town in Roman times. Gleaming skyscrapers are interspersed with historical landmarks such as St. Paul's Cathedral, legal sights (Old Bailey), and the Museum of London. The Tower of London and Tower Bridge lie at The City's eastern border.

East London: Just east of The City is the East End—the former stomping ground of Cockney ragamuffins and Jack the Ripper, and now an increasingly gentrified neighborhood of hipsters, "pop-up" shops, and an emerging food scene.

The South Bank: The South Bank of the Thames River offers major sights (Tate Modern, Shakespeare's Globe, London Eye) linked by a riverside walkway. Within this area, Southwark (SUTH-uck) stretches from the Tate Modern to London Bridge. Pedestrian bridges connect the South Bank with The City, Trafalgar Square, and, perhaps by the end of 2018, Temple Station near Somerset House.

West London: This huge area contains neighborhoods such as Mayfair, Belgravia, Pimlico, Chelsea, South Kensington, and Notting Hill. It's home to London's wealthy and has many trendy shops and enticing restaurants. Here you'll find a range of museums (Victoria and Albert Museum, Tate Britain, and more), my

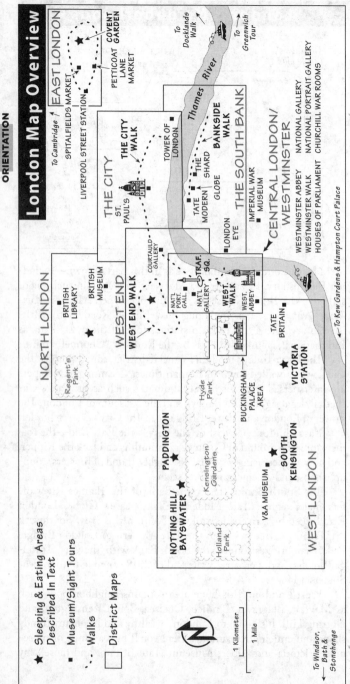

London Map Overview

top hotel recommendations, lively Victoria Station, and the vast green expanses of Hyde Park and Kensington Gardens.

Outside the Center: The Docklands, London's version of Manhattan, is farther east than the East End; Olympic Park is just north of the Docklands. Historic Greenwich is southeast of London and across the Thames. Kew Gardens and Hampton Court Palace are southwest of London. North of London is Hampstead Heath and the Warner Bros. Studio Tour for Harry Potter fans.

ORIENTATION

PLANNING YOUR TIME

London is a super one-week getaway. Its sights can keep even the most fidgety traveler well entertained for seven days. After considering London's major tourist desti-

nations, I've covered just my favorites in this book. You won't be able to see everything, so don't try. You'll keep coming back to London. After dozens of visits myself, I still enjoy a healthy list of excuses to return.

For a one-week visit, buy a 7-Day Travelcard (see page 22) and study up on "Affording London's Sights" (see page 74). Armed with this information and your Travelcard, you'll feel more like a Londoner, forget the high cost of sightseeing, and experience the city with a better attitude.

Here's a suggested schedule for London's best seven days:

London in Seven Days
Day 1

9:00	Tower of London (crown jewels first, then Beefeater tour and White Tower; note that on Sun-Mon, the Tower opens at 10:00).
13:00	Grab a picnic, catch a boat at Tower Pier, and relax with lunch on the Thames while cruising to Westminster Pier.
14:30	Tour Westminster Abbey, and consider their evensong service (usually at 17:00, at 15:00 on Sun and off-season Sat, never on Wed).
17:00 (or after evensong)	Follow my self-guided Westminster Walk. When you're finished, you could return to the Houses of Parliament and possibly pop into see the House of Commons in action (check their schedule first—see page 42).

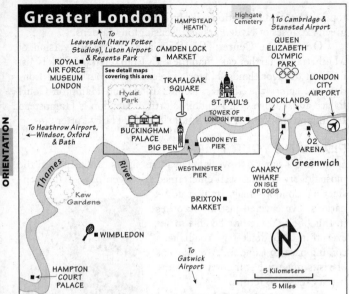

Day 2

8:30   Take a double-decker hop-on, hop-off London sightseeing bus tour (from Victoria Station or Green Park).

10:00   Hop off at Trafalgar Square and walk to Buckingham Palace to secure a spot to watch the Changing of the Guard.

11:00   Buckingham Palace (guards change most days May-July at 11:00, alternate days Aug-April—confirm online).

12:00   Walk through St. James's Park to enjoy London's delightful park scene.

13:00   After lunch, tour the Churchill War Rooms.

16:00   Tour the National Gallery.

Evening   Have dinner—maybe at a pub?—before a play, concert, or evening walking tour. For ideas, see the Entertainment in London chapter; consider these activities for any evening over the following days.

Day 3

9:00   Follow the first two-thirds of my self-guided walk through The City (as far as St. Paul's), then follow my St. Paul's Cathedral Tour.

15:00   Cross London Bridge and follow my self-guided Bankside Walk along the South Bank of the Thames. Tour Shakespeare's Globe or the Tate Modern if you're interested (or, if it's a day that the Tate Modern is open late, circle back here later). Then walk the Jubilee Walkway from the Millennium Bridge to the London Eye.

Evening   Cap your day with South Bank sights and experiences that are open late (a ride on the London Eye—last ascent 20:30 or later in summer; a Shakespeare play at the Globe—usually Tue-Sat at 19:30 and Sun at 18:30 in summer; or a visit to the Tate Modern—open Fri-Sat until 22:00).

Day 4

10:00   Tour the British Museum, then have lunch.

14:00   Tube to Leicester Square to take my self-guided West End Walk to see Covent Garden and Soho, then browse through Regent Street with my Regent Street Shopping Walk.

16:30   Enjoy afternoon tea (at Fortnum & Mason, The Wolseley, Brown's Hotel, or the Orangery at Kensington Palace).

Day 5

Spend the morning exploring a street market (try to make today coincide with the day that your market of choice is busiest—see the Shopping in London chapter for details).

Spend the rest of your day at your choice of major sights: British Library, Tate Britain, Museum of London, Imperial War Museum, or Kew Gardens (consider a cruise to Kew, return to London by Tube).

Day 6

10:00   Cruise from Westminster Pier to Greenwich.

11:15   Tour the salty sights of Greenwich.

16:00   Ride the Docklands Light Railroad (DLR) to the Docklands for my self-guided Docklands Walk and a look at London's emerging "Manhattan."

18:30   Take the DLR or Tube back to London.

Day 7

10:00   Tour the Victoria and Albert Museum.

After lunch (or a picnic in the park), stroll through Hyde Park and visit Kensington Palace. Spend the afternoon at Harrods or other shopping venues.

With More Time

To get a break from big-city London, you can easily spend a day or two side-tripping. Windsor, Cambridge, and Stonehenge each make a satisfying one-day visit.

Overview

TOURIST INFORMATION

It's amazing how hard it can be to find unbiased sightseeing information and advice in London. You'll see "Tourist Information" offices advertised everywhere, but most are private agencies that make a big profit selling tours and advance sightseeing and/or theater tickets; others are run by Transport for London (TFL) and are primarily focused on providing public-transit advice.

The City of London Information Centre next to St. Paul's Cathedral (just outside the church entrance) is the only publicly funded—and impartial—"real" TI (Mon-Sat 9:30-17:30, Sun 10:00-16:00; Tube: St. Paul's, tel. 020/7332-1456, www.visitthecity.co.uk).

While officially a service of The City (London's financial district), this office also provides information about the rest of London. It sells Oyster cards, London Passes (see page 550), advance "Fast Track" sightseeing tickets (described next), and some National Express bus tickets. It also stocks various free publications: *London Planner* (a free monthly that lists all the sights, events, and hours), some walking-tour brochures, the *Official London Theatre Guide,* a free Tube and bus map, the *Guide to River Thames Boat Services,* and brochures describing self-guided themed walks in The City (including Dickens, modern architecture, Shakespeare, and film locations).

The TI gives out a free map of The City and sells several city-wide maps; ask if they have a free map with various coupons for discounts on sights. Skip their room-booking service (charges a commission) and theater box office (may charge a commission).

Visit London, which serves the greater London area, doesn't have an office you can visit in person—but does have an information-packed website (www.visitlondon.com).

Fast Track Tickets: To skip the ticket-buying queues at certain London sights, you can buy Fast Track tickets (sometimes called "priority pass" tickets) in advance—and they can be cheaper than tickets sold right at the sight. They're particularly smart for the Tower of London (a voucher you exchange for a ticket at the Tower's group ticket window), the London Eye, The Shard, and Madame Tussauds Waxworks, all of which get very busy in high season. They're available through various sales outlets (including the City of London TI, souvenir stands, and faux-TIs scattered throughout touristy areas).

ARRIVAL IN LONDON

For more information on getting to or from London, see the London Connections chapter.

By Train: London has nine major train stations, all connected by the Tube (subway). All have ATMs, and many of the larger stations also have shops, fast food, exchange offices, and luggage storage. From any station, you can ride the Tube or taxi to your hotel.

By Bus: The main intercity bus station is Victoria Coach Station, one block southwest of Victoria train/Tube station.

By Plane: London has six airports. Most tourists arrive at Heathrow or Gatwick airport, although flights from elsewhere in Europe may land at Stansted, Luton, Southend, or London City airport. For hotels near Heathrow and Gatwick, see the Sleeping in London chapter.

HELPFUL HINTS

Theft Alert: Wear your money belt. The Artful Dodger is alive and well in London. Be on guard, particularly on public transportation and in places crowded with tourists, who, considered naive and rich, are targeted. The Changing of the Guard scene is a favorite for thieves. And more than 7,500 purses are stolen annually at Covent Garden alone.

Pedestrian Safety: Cars drive on the left side of the road—which can be as confusing for foreign pedestrians as for foreign drivers. Before crossing a street, I always look right, look left, then look right again just to be sure. Most crosswalks are even painted with instructions, reminding foreign guests to "Look right" or "Look left." While locals are champion jaywalkers, you shouldn't try it; jaywalking is treacherous when you're disoriented about which direction traffic is coming from.

Medical Problems: Local hospitals have good-quality 24-hour emergency care centers, where any tourist who needs help can drop in and, after a wait, be seen by a doctor. Your hotel has details. St. Thomas' Hospital, immediately across the river from Big Ben, has a fine reputation.

Getting Your Bearings: London is well-signed for visitors. Through an initiative called Legible London, the city has erected thoughtfully designed, pedestrian-focused maps around town—especially handy when exiting Tube stations. In this sprawling city—where predictable grid-planned streets are relatively rare—it's also smart to buy and use a good map. For suggestions, see page 548.

Wi-Fi: In addition to the Wi-Fi that's likely available at your hotel, many major museums, sights, and even entire boroughs offer free access. For example, **O2 Wifi** hotspots let you connect for free in busy locales such as Trafalgar Square, Leicester Square, and Piccadilly (www.o2wifi.co.uk). Consider a free account with **The Cloud,** a Wi-Fi service found in most London train stations and many museums, coffee shops, cafés, and shopping

Daily Reminder

Sunday: The Tower of London and British Museum are both especially crowded today. Speakers' Corner in Hyde Park rants from early afternoon until early evening. These places are closed: Sir John Soane's Museum, and legal sights (Houses of Parliament, City Hall, and Old Bailey; the neighborhood called The City is dead). Westminster Abbey and St. Paul's are open during the day for worship but closed to sightseers. With all these closures, this morning is a good time to take a bus tour. Most big stores open late (around 11:30) and close early (18:00).

Street markets flourish at Camden Lock, Spitalfields (at its best today), Petticoat Lane, Brick Lane, and Greenwich, but Portobello Road and Brixton markets are closed (though the Brixton farmers market is open 10:00-14:00). Because of all the market action, it's a good day to take the "East End Walk" (see page 78). Theaters are quiet, as most actors take today off. (There are a few exceptions, such as Shakespeare's Globe, which offers Sunday performances in summer, and theaters with family-oriented fare, including *The Lion King,* offered year-round.)

Monday: Nearly all sights are open, except Apsley House, Sir John Soane's Museum, and a few others. The Houses of Parliament may be open as late as 22:30.

Tuesday: Nearly all sights are open, except Apsley House. The British Library is open until 20:00, and the Houses of Parliament may be open as late as 22:00. On the first Tuesday of the month, Sir John Soane's Museum is open until 21:00.

Wednesday: Nearly all sights are open. The British Library is open until 20:00, and the Houses of Parliament may be open as late as 22:00.

centers (though the connection can be slow). When you sign up at www.skywifi.cloud, you'll be asked to enter a street address and postal code; it doesn't matter which one (use your hotel's, or the Queen's: Buckingham Palace, SW1A 1AA). Then use the **Sky WiFi app** to locate hotspots.

Most **Tube stations** and trains have Wi-Fi, but it's free only to those with a British Virgin Media account. However, the Tube's Wi-Fi always lets you access Transport for London's "Plan a Journey" feature (www.tfl.gov.uk), making it easy to look up transit options—and get real-time updates on delays—once you're in a station. To use the Tube's pay Wi-Fi, you can spend £2 for a one-day pass, or £5 for a one-week pass (http://my.virginmedia.com/wifi).

Useful Apps: Mapway's free **Tube Map London Underground** and **Bus Times London** (www.mapway.com) apps show the easiest way to connect tube stations and provide bus stops

Thursday: Nearly all sights are open. The Banqueting House is closed. The British Library is open until 20:00 and the National Portrait Gallery until 21:00.

Friday: All sights are open, except the Houses of Parliament. Sights open late include the British Museum (selected galleries until 20:30), National Gallery (until 21:00), National Portrait Gallery (until 21:00), Victoria and Albert Museum (selected galleries until 22:00), and Tate Modern (until 22:00).

Saturday: Most sights are open, except legal ones (Old Bailey, City Hall; skip The City). The Houses of Parliament are open only with a tour. The Tate Modern is open until 22:00. The Tower of London is especially crowded today. Today's the day to hit the Portobello Road street market; the Camden Lock and Greenwich markets are also good.

Notes: St. Martin-in-the-Fields church offers concerts at lunchtime (Mon, Tue, and Fri at 13:00) and in the evening (several nights a week at 19:30, jazz Wed at 20:00).

Evensong occurs nearly daily at St. Paul's (Sun at 15:15 and Tue-Sat at 17:00), Westminster Abbey (Sun at 15:00, Mon-Tue and Thu-Sat at 17:00 except Sept-April Sat at 15:00), and Southwark Cathedral (Sun at 15:00, Tue-Fri 17:30, Sat at 16:00).

The Original London Sightseeing and Big Bus companies run their last full hop-on, hop-off tours of the day from Victoria Station at about 20:00. See London by Night buses leave Green Park each evening starting at 19:30.

The London Eye spins nightly (last ascent 20:30 or later in summer).

ORIENTATION

and route information. When you are online, the apps provide live updates about delays, closures, and time estimates for your journey. The handy **Citymapper** app for London covers every mode of public transit in the city. **City Maps 2Go** lets you download searchable offline maps; their London version is quite good. And **Time Out London**'s free app has reviews and listings for theater, museums, and movies (download the "Make Your City Amazing" version, which is updated weekly, rather than the boilerplate "Travel Guide" version).

⍥ For free audio versions of some of the self-guided tours in this book (my Westminster Walk, Historic London: The City Walk, and tours of the British Museum, British Library, and St. Paul's Cathedral), get the **Rick Steves Audio Europe** app (see page 8).

Travel Bookstores: Located between Covent Garden and Leicester Square, the very good **Stanfords Travel Bookstore** stocks a huge selection of guidebooks (including current editions of my titles), travel-related novels, maps, and gear (Mon-Sat 9:00-20:00, Sun 11:30-18:00, 12 Long Acre, second entrance on Floral Street, Tube: Leicester Square, tel. 020/7836-1321, www.stanfords.co.uk).

Two impressive **Waterstones** bookstores have the biggest collection of travel guides in town: on Piccadilly (Mon-Sat 9:00-22:00, Sun 12:00-18:30, café, great views from top-floor bar—see sidebar on page 90, 203 Piccadilly, tel. 0843-290-8549) and on Trafalgar Square (Mon-Sat 9:00-21:00, Sun 12:00-18:00, Costa Café on second floor, tel. 020/7839-4411).

Daunts Books, housed in a church-like Edwardian building full of oak accents and stained-glass windows, is a North London staple known for arranging books by geography, regardless of subject or author (Mon-Sat 9:00-19:30, Sun 11:00-18:00, 83 Marylebone High Street, Tube: Baker Street, tel. 020/7724-2295, www.dauntbooks.co.uk).

Baggage Storage: Train stations have replaced lockers with more secure left-luggage counters. Each bag must go through a scanner (just like at the airport). Expect long waits in the morning to check in (up to 45 minutes) and in the afternoon to pick up (each item-£12.50/24 hours, most stations daily 7:00-23:00). You can also store bags at the airports (similar rates and hours, www.left-baggage.co.uk).

GETTING AROUND LONDON

To travel smart in a city this size, you must get comfortable with public transportation. London's excellent taxis, buses, and subway (Tube) system can take you anywhere you need to go—a blessing for travelers' precious vacation time, not to mention their feet. And, as the streets become ever more congested, the key is to master the Tube.

For more information about public transit (bus and Tube), the best single source is the helpful *Hello London* brochure, which includes both a Tube map and a handy schematic map of the best bus routes (available free at TIs, museums, hotels, and at www.tfl.gov.uk). For specific directions on how to get from point A to point B on London's transit, detailed bus maps, updated prices, and general information, check www.tfl.gov.uk or call the automated info line at 0843-222-1234.

Tickets and Cards

London's is the most expensive public transit in the world. While the transit system has six zones, almost all tourist sights are within Zones 1 and 2, so those are the prices I've listed. For more information, visit www.tfl.gov.uk/tickets. A few odd special passes are available, but for nearly every tourist, the answer is simple: Get the Oyster card and use it.

Individual Tickets: Individual paper tickets for the Tube are ridiculously expensive (£5 per Tube ride). Tickets are sold at any Tube station, either at (often-crowded) ticket windows or at easy-to-use self-service machines (hit "Adult Single" and enter your destination). Tickets are valid only on the day of purchase. But unless you're literally taking only one Tube ride your entire visit, you'll save money (and time) by buying an Oyster card.

Oyster Card: A pay-as-you-go Oyster card (a plastic card embedded with a microchip) allows you to ride the Tube, buses, Docklands Light Railway (DLR), and Overground (mostly suburban trains) for about half the rate of individual tickets. To use the card, simply touch the card against the yellow card reader at the turnstile or entrance. It flashes green and the fare is automatically deducted. (You must also tap your card again to "touch out" as you exit.)

Buy the card at any Tube station ticket window, or look for nearby shops displaying the Oyster logo, where you can purchase

a card or add credit without the wait. You'll pay a refundable £5 deposit up front, then load it with as much credit as you'll need. One ride in Zones 1 and 2 during peak time costs £2.90; off peak is a little cheaper (£2.40/ride). The system comes with an automatic price cap that guarantees you'll never pay more than £6.60 in one day for rides within Zones 1 and 2. If you think you'll take more than two rides in a day, £6.60 of credit will cover you, but it's smart to add a little more if you expect to travel outside the city center. If you're staying five or more days, consider adding a 7-Day Travelcard to your Oyster card (details below).

Note that Oyster cards are not shareable among companions taking the same ride; each traveler will need his or her own. If your balance gets low, simply add credit—or "top up"—at a ticket window, machine, or shop. You can always see how much credit remains on your card (along with a list of where you've traveled) by touching it to the pad at any ticket machine.

You'll see advertisements for "contactless payment" using a credit card or mobile device, but that service is intended for residents, not travelers (who would rack up international transaction fees for every ride).

Remember to turn in your Oyster card after your last ride (you'll get back the £5 deposit and unused balance up to £10) at a ticket window or by selecting "Pay as you go refund" on any ticket machine that gives change. This will deactivate your card. For balances of more than £10, you must go to a ticket window for your refund. If you don't deactivate your card, the credit never expires—you can use it again on your next trip.

Passes and Discounts

7-Day Travelcard: Various Tube passes and deals are available. Of these, the only option of note is the 7-Day Travelcard. This is the best choice if you're staying five or more days and plan to use public transit a lot (£33 for Zones 1-2; £60.20 for Zones 1-6). For most travelers, the Zone 1-2 pass works best. Heathrow Airport is in Zone 6, but there's no need to buy the Zones 1-6 version if that's the only ride outside the city center you plan to take—instead you can pay a small supplement to cover the difference. You can add the 7-Day Travelcard to your Oyster card or purchase the paper version at any National Rail train station.

Families: A paying adult can take up to four kids (ages 10 and under) for free on the Tube, Docklands Light Railway (DLR), Overground, and buses. Kids ages 11-15 get a discount. Explore other child and student discounts at www.tfl.gov.uk/tickets or ask a clerk at a Tube ticket window which deal is best.

River Cruises: A Travelcard gives you a 33 percent discount on most Thames cruises (see page 36). The Oyster card gives you roughly a 10 percent discount on Thames Clippers (including the Tate Boat museum ferry).

The Bottom Line

On a short visit (three days or fewer), I'd get an Oyster card and add £20-25 of credit (£6.60 daily cap times three days, plus a little extra for any rides outside Zones 1-2). If you'll be taking fewer rides, £15 will be enough (£2.90 per ride during peak time gets you 5 rides), and if not you can always top up. For a visit of five days or more, the 7-Day Travelcard—either the paper version or on an Oyster card—will likely pay for itself.

By Tube

London's subway system is called the Tube or Underground (but never "subway," which, in Britain, refers to a pedestrian underpass).

The Tube is one of this planet's great people-movers and usually the fastest long-distance transport in town (runs Mon-Sat about 5:00-24:00, Sun about 7:00-23:00; Central, Jubilee, Northern, Piccadilly, and Victoria lines also run

Fri-Sat 24 hours). Two other commuter rail lines are tied into the network and use the same tickets: the Docklands Light Railway (called DLR) and the Overground. The new Crossrail system will eventually cut through central London connecting Heathrow with Paddington, Bond, and Liverpool Street Tube stations on the Elizabeth line before continuing to the city's outlying eastern neighborhoods.

Get your bearings by studying a map of the system. At the front of this book, you'll find a Tube map of the city center, with color-coded lines and names. You can also pick up a free, more extensive Tube map at any station, or download a transit app (described earlier).

Each line has a name (such as Circle, Northern, or Bakerloo) and two directions (indicated by the end-of-the-line stops). Find the line that will take you to your destination, and figure out roughly which direction (north, south, east, or west) you'll need to go to get there.

At the Tube station, there are two ways to pass through the turnstile. With an Oyster card, touch it flat against the turnstile's yellow card reader, both when you enter and exit the station. With a paper ticket or paper Travelcard, feed it into the turnstile, reclaim it, and hang on to it—you'll need it later.

Find your train by following signs to your line and the (general) direction it's headed (such as Central Line: east). Since some

tracks are shared by several lines, double-check before boarding: Make sure your destination is one of the stops listed on the sign at the platform. Also, check the electronic signboards that announce which train is next, and make sure the destination (the end-of-the-line stop) is the direction you want. Some trains, particularly on the Circle and District lines, split off for other directions, but each train has its final destination marked above its windshield.

Trains run about every 3-10 minutes. (The Victoria line brags that it's the most frequent anywhere, with trains coming every 100 seconds at peak time.) A general rule of thumb is that it takes 30 minutes to travel six Tube stops (including walking time within stations), or roughly five minutes per stop.

When you leave the system, "touch out" with your Oyster card at the electronic reader on the turnstile, or feed your paper ticket into the turnstile (it will eat your now-expired ticket). With a paper

Travelcard, it will spit out your still-valid card. Check maps and signs for the most convenient exit.

The system can be fraught with construction delays and breakdowns. Pay attention to signs and announcements explaining necessary detours. Rush hours (8:00-10:00 and 16:00-19:00) can be packed and sweaty. If one train is stuffed—and another is coming in three minutes—it may be worth a wait to avoid the sardine routine. If you get confused, ask for advice from a local, a blue-vested staffer, or at the information window located before the turnstile entry. Online, get help from the "Plan a Journey" feature at www.tfl.gov.uk, which is accessible (via free Wi-Fi) on any mobile device within most Tube stations before you go underground.

Tube Etiquette and Tips

- When your train arrives, stand off to the side and let riders exit before you board.
- When the car is jam-packed, avoid using the hinged seats near the doors of some trains—they take up valuable standing space.
- If you're blocking the door when the train stops, step out of the car and off to the side, let others off, then get back on.
- Talk softly in the cars. Listen to how quietly Londoners communicate and follow their lead.
- On escalators, stand on the right and pass on the left. But note that in some passageways or stairways, you might be directed to walk on the left (the direction Brits go when behind the wheel).
- Discreet eating and drinking are fine (nothing smelly); drinking alcohol and smoking are banned.
- Be zipped up to thwart thieves.
- Carefully check exit options before surfacing to street level. Signs point clearly to nearby sights—you'll save lots of walking by choosing the right exit.

By Bus

If you figure out the bus system, you'll swing like Tarzan through the urban jungle of London (see sidebar for a list of handy routes). Get in the habit of hopping buses for quick little straight shots, even just to get to a Tube stop. However, during bump-and-grind rush hours (8:00-10:00 and 16:00-19:00), you'll usually go faster by Tube.

You can't buy single-trip tickets for buses, and you can't use cash to pay when boarding. Instead, you must have an Oyster card, a paper Travel-card, or a one-day Bus & Tram Pass (£5, can buy on day of travel only—not beforehand, from ticket machine in any Tube station). If you're using your Oyster card, any bus ride in downtown London costs £1.50 (capped at £4.50/day).

The first step in mastering London's bus system is learning how to decipher the bus-stop signs. The accompanying photo shows a typical sign listing the buses (the N91, N68, etc.) that come by here and their destinations (Oakwood, Old Coulsdon, etc.). In the first column, find your destination on the list—e.g., to Paddington (Tube and rail station). In the next column, find a bus that goes there—the #23 (routes marked "N" are night-only). In the final column, a letter within a circle (e.g., "H") tells you exactly which nearby bus stop to use. Find your stop on the accompanying bus-stop map, then make your way to that stop—you'll know it's yours because it will have the same letter on its pole.

O		
Oakwood ⊖	N91	🅐 ⊗
Old Coulsdon	N68	Aldwych
Old Ford	N8	Oxford Circus
Old Kent Road Canal Bridge	53, N381	🅟
	453	🅐 🅟
	N21	🅖
Old Street ⊖ ⇌	243	Aldwych
Orpington ⇌	N47	🅖
Oxford Circus ⊖	Any bus	🅣
	N18	🅢

P		
Paddington ⊖ ⇌	23, N15	🅗 🅙 🅣
Palmers Green ⇌	N29	🅖
Park Langley	N3	🅐 🅜
Peckham	12	🅐 🅟
	N89, N343	🅖
	N136	🅐 🅝
	N381	🅟
Penge Pawleyne Arms	176	🅖
	N3	🅐 🅜
Petts Wood ⇌	N47	🅖
Pimlico Grosvenor Road	24	🅑 🅝
Plaistow Greengate	N15	🅖 🅟
Plumstead ⇌	53	🅟
Plumstead Common	53	🅟

ORIENTATION

When your bus approaches, it's wise to hold your arm out to let the driver know you want on. Hop on and confirm your destination with the driver (often friendly and helpful).

As you board, touch your Oyster card to the card reader, or show your paper Travelcard or Bus & Tram Pass to the driver. Unlike on the Tube, there's no need to show or tap your card when you hop off. On the older heritage "Routemaster" buses without card-readers (used on the #15 route), you simply take a seat, and the conductor comes around to check cards and passes.

To alert the driver that you want to get off, press one of the red buttons (on the poles between the seats) before your stop.

With a mobile phone, you can find out the arrival time of the next bus by texting your bus stop's five-digit code (posted at the stop, above the timetable) to 87287 (if you're using your US phone, text the code to 011-44-7797-800-287). Or try the helpful London Bus Checker app, with route maps and real-time bus info.

By Taxi

London is the best taxi town in Europe. Big, black, carefully regulated cabs are everywhere—there are about 25,000 of them. (While

historically known as "black cabs," London's official taxis are sometimes covered with wildly colored ads.)

I've never met a crabby cabbie in London. They love to talk, and they know every nook and cranny in town. I ride in a taxi each day just to get my London questions answered. Drivers must pass a rigorous test on "The Knowledge" of London geography to earn their license.

If a cab's top light is on, just wave it down. Drivers flash lights when they see you wave. They have a tight turning radius, so you can hail cabs going in either direction. If waving doesn't work, ask someone where you can find a taxi stand. Telephoning a cab will get you one in a few minutes, but costs a little more (tel. 0871-871-8710).

Rides start at £2.60. The regular tariff #1 covers most of the day (Mon-Fri 5:00-20:00), tariff #2 is during "unsociable hours" (Mon-Fri 20:00-22:00 and Sat-Sun 5:00-22:00), and tariff #3 is for nighttime (22:00-5:00) and holidays. Rates go up about 40 percent with each higher tariff. Extra charges are explained in writing on the cab wall. All cabs accept credit and debit cards, including American cards. Tip a cabbie by rounding up (maximum 10 percent).

Connecting downtown sights is quick and easy, and will cost you about £8-10 (for example, St. Paul's to the Tower of London, or between the two Tate museums). For a short ride, three adults in a cab generally travel at close to Tube prices—and groups of four or five adults should taxi everywhere. All cabs can carry five passengers, and some take six, for the same cost as a single traveler.

Don't worry about meter cheating. Licensed British cab meters come with a sealed computer chip and clock that ensures you'll get the correct tariff. The only way a cabbie can cheat you is by taking a needlessly long route. One serious pitfall, however, is taking a cab when traffic is bad to a destination efficiently served by the Tube. On one trip to London, I hopped in a taxi at South Kensington for Waterloo Station and hit bad traffic. Rather than spending 20 minutes and £2 on the Tube, I spent 40 minutes and £16 in a taxi.

If you overdrink and ride in a taxi, be warned: Taxis charge £40 for "soiling" (a.k.a., pub puke). If you forget this book in a taxi, call the Lost Property office and hope for the best (tel. 0845-330-9882).

By Uber

Uber faces legal challenges in London and may not be operating when you visit. If Uber is running, it can be much cheaper than a taxi and is a handy alternative if there's a long line for a taxi or if no cabs are available. Uber drivers generally don't know the city as well as regular cabbies, and they don't have the access to some fast lanes that taxis do. Still, if you like using Uber, it can work great here.

By Car

If you have a car, stow it—you don't want to drive in London. An £11.50 **congestion charge** is levied on any private car entering the city center during peak hours (Mon-Fri 7:00-18:00, no charge Sat-Sun and holidays). You can pay the fee either online or by phone (www.cclondon.com, from within the UK call 0343/222-2222, from outside the UK call 011-44-20/7649-9122, phones answered Mon-Fri 8:00-22:00, Sat 9:00-15:00, be ready to give the vehicle registration number and country of registration). There are painfully stiff penalties for late payments. The system has cut down traffic jams, bolstered London's public transit, and made buses cheaper and more user-friendly. Today, the vast majority of vehicles in the city center are buses, taxis, and service trucks.

By Boat

It's easy to connect downtown London sights between Westminster and the Tower of London by boat (see later).

By Bike

London operates a citywide bike-rental program similar to ones in other major European cities, and new bike lanes are still cropping up around town. Still, London isn't (yet) ideal for biking. Its network of designated bike lanes is far from complete, and the city's many one-way streets (not to mention the need to bike on the "wrong" side) can make biking here a bit more challenging than it sounds. If you're accustomed to urban biking, it can be a good option for connecting your sightseeing stops, but if you're just up for a joyride, stick to London's large parks.

Santander Cycles, in-tended for quick point-to-point trips, are fairly easy to rent and a giddy joy to use, even for the most jaded London tourist. These "Boris Bikes" (as they are affectionately called by locals, after cycle enthusiast and former mayor Boris Johnson) are

ORIENTATION

Handy Bus Routes

The best views are upstairs on a double-decker. Check the bus stop closest to your hotel—it might be convenient to your sightseeing plans. Here are some of the most useful routes:

Route #9: High Street Kensington to Knightsbridge (Harrods) to Hyde Park Corner to Trafalgar Square to Aldwych (Somerset House).

Route #11: Victoria Station to Westminster Abbey to Trafalgar Square to St. Paul's and Liverpool Street Station and the East End.

Route #15: Trafalgar Square to St. Paul's to Tower of London (sometimes with heritage "Routemaster" old-style double-decker buses).

Routes #23 and #159: Paddington Station (#159 begins at Marble Arch) to Oxford Circus to Piccadilly Circus to Trafalgar Square; from there, #23 heads east to St. Paul's and Liverpool Street Station, while #159 heads to Westminster and the Imperial War Museum. In addition, several buses (including #6, #12, and #139) also

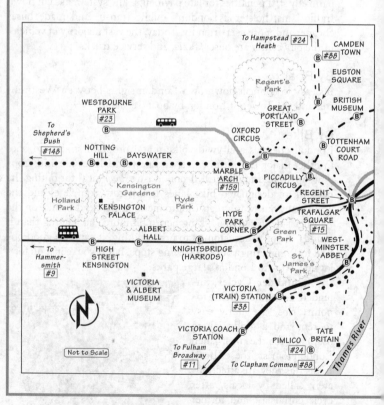

make the corridor run between Marble Arch, Oxford Circus, Piccadilly Circus, and Trafalgar Square.

Route #24: Pimlico to Victoria Station to Westminster Abbey to Trafalgar Square to Euston Square, then all the way north to Camden Town (Camden Lock Market) and Hampstead Heath.

Route #38: Victoria Station to Hyde Park Corner to Piccadilly Circus to British Museum.

Route #88: Tate Britain to Westminster Abbey to Trafalgar Square to Piccadilly Circus to Oxford Circus to Great Portland Street Station (Regent's Park), then north to Camden Town.

Route #148: Westminster Abbey to Victoria Station to Notting Hill and Bayswater (by way of the east end of Hyde Park and Marble Arch).

Route #RV1 (a scenic South Bank joyride): Tower of London to Tower Bridge to Southwark Street (five-minute walk behind Tate Modern/Shakespeare's Globe) to London Eye/Waterloo Station, then over Waterloo Bridge to Aldwych and Covent Garden.

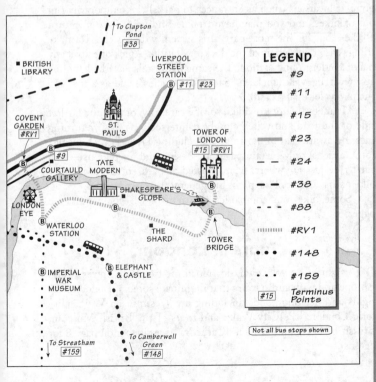

cruisers with big, cushy seats, a bag rack with elastic straps, and three gears.

Approximately 700 bike-rental stations are scattered throughout the city, each equipped with a computer kiosk. To rent a bike, you'll pay an access fee (£2/day). The first 30 minutes are free; if you keep the bike for longer, you'll be charged £2 for every additional 30-minute period.

When you're ready to ride, press "Hire a Cycle" and insert your credit card when prompted. You'll then get a ticket with a five-digit code. Take the ticket to any bike that doesn't have a red light (those are "taken") and punch in the number. After the yellow light blinks, a green light will appear: Now you can (firmly) pull the bike out of the slot.

When your ride is over, find a station with an empty slot, then push your bike in until it locks and the green light flashes.

You can hire bikes as often as you like (which will start your free 30-minute period over again), as long as you wait five minutes between each use. There can be problems, of course—stations at popular locations (such as entrances to parks) can temporarily run out of bikes, and you may have trouble finding a place to return a bike—but for the most part, this system works great. To make things easier, get a map of the docking stations—pick one up at any major Underground station. The same map is also available online at www.tfl.gov.uk (click on "Santander Cycles") and as a free app (http://cyclehireapp.com).

Helmets are not provided, so ride carefully. Stay to the far-left side of the road and watch closely at intersections for *left*-turning cars. Be aware that in most parks (including Hyde Park/Kensington Gardens) only certain paths are designated for bike use—you can't ride just anywhere. Maps posted at park entrances identify bike paths, and nonbike paths are generally clearly marked.

Some bike tour companies also rent bikes—for details, see page 35.

Tours in London

∩ To sightsee on your own, download my free Rick Steves Audio Europe app with **audio tours** that illuminate some of London's top sights and neighborhoods, including my Westminster Walk, Historic London: The City Walk, and tours of the British Museum, British Library, and St. Paul's Cathedral (see sidebar on page 8 for details).

ORIENTATION

▲▲▲ BY HOP-ON, HOP-OFF DOUBLE-DECKER BUS

London is full of hop-on, hop-off bus companies competing for your tourist pound. I've focused on the two companies I like the most: **Original** and **Big Bus.** Both offer essentially the same two tours of the city's sightseeing highlights. Big Bus tours are a little more expensive (£35, cheaper in advance online), while Original tours are cheaper (£26 with this book).

These once-over-lightly bus tours drive by all the famous sights, providing a stress-free way to get your bearings and see the biggies: Piccadilly Circus, Trafalgar Square, Big Ben, St. Paul's, the Tower of London, Marble Arch, Victoria Station, and elsewhere. With a good guide, decent traffic, and nice weather, I'd sit back and enjoy the entire tour. (If traffic is bad or you don't like your guide, you can hop off and try your luck with the next departure.)

Each company offers at least one route with live (English-only) guides, and a second (sometimes slightly different route) with recorded, dial-a-language narration. In addition to the overview tours, both Original and Big Bus include the Thames River boat trip by City Cruises (between Westminster and the Tower of London) and several walking tours. Employees for both companies will try hard to sell you tickets and Fast Track admissions to various sights in London. Review your sightseeing plan carefully in advance so you can take advantage of offers that will save you time or money, but skip the rest.

Pick up a map from any flier rack or from one of the countless salespeople, and study the color-coded system. Sunday morning—when traffic is light and many museums are closed—is a fine time for a tour. Traffic is at its peak around lunch and during the evening rush hour (around 17:00).

Buses run daily about every 10-15 minutes in summer and every 10-20 minutes in winter, starting at about 8:30. The last full loop usually leaves Victoria Station at about 20:00 in summer, and at about 17:00 in winter.

You can buy tickets online in advance, or from drivers or from staff at street kiosks (credit cards accepted at kiosks at major stops such as Victoria Station, ticket valid 24 hours in summer, 48 hours in winter).

Original London Sightseeing Bus Tour

They offer two versions of their basic highlights loop, both marked with a yellow triangle (confirm version with the driver before boarding): **The Original Tour** (live guide) and the **City Sightseeing Tour** (same route but with recorded narration, a kids' soundtrack option, and a stop at Madame Tussauds). Other routes include the orange-triangle **British Museum Tour** (connecting the museum

ORIENTATION

> ## Combining a London Bus Tour and the Changing of the Guard
>
> For a grand and efficient intro to London, consider catching an 8:30 departure of a hop-on, hop-off overview bus tour, riding most of the loop (which takes just over 1.5 hours, depending on traffic). Hop off just before 10:00 at Trafalgar Square (Cockspur Street, stop "S") and walk briskly to Buckingham Palace to find a spot to watch the Changing of the Guard ceremony at 11:00.

and King's Cross neighborhoods with central London), and the blue-triangle **Royal Borough Tour** (high-end shopping and regal hang-outs). The black- and purple-triangle routes act more like shuttles, linking major train stations and Madame Tussauds to the central route. All routes are covered by the same ticket (£32, £6 less with this book, limit four discounts per book, they'll rip off the corner of this page—raise bloody hell if the staff or driver won't honor this discount; also online deals, info center at 17 Cockspur Street sells discounted tickets to Tower of London, St. Paul's Cathedral, and London Eye; Mon-Sat 8:00-18:00, Sun until 17:30; tel. 020/7389-5040, www.theoriginaltour.com).

Big Bus London Tours

For £35 (up to 30 percent discount online—print tickets or have them delivered to your phone), you get the same basic overview tours: Red buses come with a live guide, while the blue route has a recorded narration and a one-hour longer path that goes around Hyde Park. These pricier Big Bus tours tend to have more departures—meaning shorter waits for those hopping on and off (tel. 020/7808-6753, www.bigbustours.com).

BY BUS OR CAR
London by Night Sightseeing Tour

Various companies offer a 1- to 2-hour circuit, but after hours, with no extras (e.g., walks, river cruises), at a lower price. While the narration can be lame, the views at twilight are grand—though note that it stays light until late on summer nights, and London just doesn't do floodlighting as well as, say, Paris. **Golden Tours** buses depart at 19:00 and 20:00 from their offices on Buckingham Palace Road (tel. 020/7630-2028; www.goldentours.com). **See London By Night** buses offer live English guides and daily departures from Green Park (next to the Ritz Hotel) at 19:30, 20:00, 20:30, 21:15, 21:45, and 22:15; October-March at 19:30 and 21:20 only (tel. 020/7183-4744, www.seelondonbynight.com). For a memorable and economical evening, munch a scenic picnic dinner on the top deck. (There are plenty of takeaway options near the various stops.)

Land and Sea Tours

A bright-yellow amphibious WWII-vintage vehicle (the model that ferried supplies and wounded soldiers on Normandy's beaches on D-Day) takes a gang of 30 tourists past some famous sights on land—Big Ben, Trafalgar Square, Piccadilly Circus—then splashes into the Thames for a cruise. The live guide works hard, and it's kid-friendly to the point of goofiness (£27, April-Sept daily, first tour 9:30 or 10:00, last tour usually 17:00-18:00, shorter hours Oct-March, 2-6/hour, 1.25 hours—45 minutes on land and 30 minutes in the river, £3 booking fee by phone or online, departs from Belvedere Road—you'll see the big, ugly vehicle parked near the London Eye, Tube: Waterloo or Westminster, tel. 020/7928-3132, www.londonducktours.co.uk). Note: These tours may not be running by the time you visit—confirm ahead.

Driver-Guides

These guides have cars or a minibus (particularly helpful for travelers with limited mobility), and also do walking-only tours: **Janine Barton** (£390/half-day, £560/day, tel. 020/7402-4600, http://seeitinstyle.synthasite.com, jbsiis@aol.com); cousins **Hugh Dickson** and **Mike Dickson** (£345/half-day, £535/day, overnights also possible, both registered Blue Badge guides; Hugh's mobile 07771/602-069, hughdickson@hotmail.com; Mike's mobile 07769/905-811, michael.dickson5@btinternet.com); and **David Stubbs** (£225/half-day, £330/day, about £50 more for groups of 4-6 people, also does tours to the Cotswolds, Stonehenge, and Stratford, mobile 07775-888-534, www.londoncountrytours.co.uk, info@londoncountrytours.co.uk).

▲▲ON FOOT

Top-notch local guides lead (sometimes big) groups on walking tours through specific slices of London's past. Look for brochures at TIs or ask at hotels. *Time Out,* the weekly entertainment guide, lists some, but not all, scheduled walks. Check with the various tour companies by phone or online to get their full picture.

To take a walking tour, simply show up at the announced location and pay the guide. Then enjoy two chatty hours of Dickens, Harry Potter, the Plague, Shakespeare, street art, the Beatles, Jack the Ripper, or whatever is on the agenda.

London Walks

This leading company lists its extensive and creative daily schedule online, as well as in a beefy *London Walks* brochure (available at hotels and in racks all over town). Just perusing their fascinating lineup opens me up to dimensions of the city I never considered and inspires me to stay longer in London. Their two-hour walks, led by top-quality professional guides (ranging from archaeologists to actors), cost £10 (cash only, walks offered year-round, private tours for groups–£140, tel. 020/7624-3978 for a live person, tel. 020/7624-9255 for a recording of today's or tomorrow's walks and the Tube station they depart from, www.walks.com).

London Walks also offers day trips into the countryside, a good option for those with limited time (£18 plus £36-64 for transportation and admission costs, cash only: Stonehenge/Salisbury, Oxford/Cotswolds, Cambridge, Bath, and so on). These are economical in part because everyone gets group discounts for transportation and admissions.

Sandemans New London "Free Royal London Tour"

This company offers free tours covering the basic London sights in a youthful, light, and irreverent way that can be both entertaining and fun, but it's misleading to call them "free," as tips are expected. Given that London Walks offers daily tours at a reasonable price, taking this "free" tour makes no sense to me (daily at 10:00, 11:00, and 13:00; meet at Covent Garden Piazza by the Apple Store, Tube: Covent Garden). Sandemans also offers guided tours for a charge, including a Pub Crawl (£15, nightly at 19:30, meet at Brewmaster, 37 Cranbourn Street, Tube: Leicester Square, www.newlondon-tours.com).

Beatles Walks

Fans of the still-Fab Four can take one of three Beatles walks (London Walks has two that run 5 days/week; for more on Beatles sights, see page 69).

Jack the Ripper Walks

Each walking tour company seems to make most of its money with "haunted" and Jack the Ripper tours. Many guides are historians and would rather not lead these lightweight tours—but, in tourism as in journalism, "if it bleeds, it leads" (which is why the juvenile London Dungeon is one of the city's busiest sights).

Back in 1888—in the decade of Sherlock Holmes and Dr. Jekyll and Mr. Hyde, when London was still a Dickensian Tale of Two Cities—locals were terrorized by the murder of five prostitutes within a few weeks. In the wee hours, the murderer (who was given his name by local newspapers, which made a fortune on this sensational series of events) slit the throats and cut out the guts of his victims in the poor and wretched side of town. These were desperate women—so desperate they took their customers not to a bed, but up against a wall for a "four-penny knee trembler." While almost no hint of the dark and scary London of that period survives, guides do a good job of spinning the story. Think of this mile-long walk, starting at the Tower of London, as a cheap night out with a few laughs. It's still light out in summer, so the scary factor is limited to the tales of the victims' miserable lot in life and the gory way in which they were killed.

Two reliably good two-hour tours start every night at the Tower Hill Tube station exit. **London Walks** leaves nightly at 19:30 (£10, pay at the start, tel. 020/7624-3978, recorded info tel. 020/7624-9255, www.jacktheripperwalk.com). **Ripping Yarns,** which leaves earlier, is guided by off-duty Yeoman Warders—the Tower of London "Beefeaters" (£8, pay at end, nightly at 18:30, mobile 07813-559-301, www.jack-the-ripper-tours.com). After taking both, I found the London Walks tour more entertaining, informative, and with a better route (along quieter, once hooker-friendly lanes, with less traffic), starting at Tower Hill and ending at Liverpool Street Station. Groups can be huge for both, and one group can be nearly on top of another, but there's always room—just show up.

Private Walks with Local Guides

Standard rates for London's registered Blue Badge guides are about £160-200 for four hours and £260 or more for nine hours (tel. 020/7611-2545, www.guidelondon.org.uk or www.britainsbestguides.org). I know and like five fine local guides: **Sean Kelleher,** an engaging storyteller who knows his history (tel. 020/8673-1624, mobile 07764-612-770, sean@seanlondonguide.com); **Britt Lonsdale** (£250/half-day, £350/day, great with families, tel. 020/7386-9907, mobile 07813-278-077, brittl@btinternet.com); **Joel Reid,** an imaginative guide who specializes in off-the-beaten-track London (mobile 07887-955-720, joelyreid@gmail.com); and two others who work in London when they're not on the road leading my Britain tours: **Tom Hooper** (mobile 07986-048-047, tomh@ricksteves.net), and **Gillian Chadwick** (mobile 07889-976-598, gillychad@hotmail.co.uk). If you have a particular interest, London Walks (see earlier) has a huge selection of guides and can book one for your exact focus (£180/half-day).

BY BIKE

Many of London's best sights can be laced together with a pleasant pedal through its parks.

London Bicycle Tour Company

Three tours covering London are offered daily from their base at Gabriel's Wharf on the South Bank of the Thames. Sunday is the best, as there is less car traffic (**Classic Tour**—£25, daily at 10:30 and 11:00, 6 miles, 3 hours, includes Westminster, Buckingham Palace, Covent Garden, and St. Paul's; **Love London Tour**—£25,

April-Oct daily at 14:30, Nov-March daily at 12:00 if at least 4 people show up, 7 miles, 3 hours, includes Westminster, Buckingham Palace, Hyde Park, Soho, and Covent Garden; **Old Town Tour**—£28.50, April-Oct Sat-Sun at 14:00, Nov-March Sat-Sun at 12:00, 9 miles, 3.5 hours, includes south side of the river to Tower Bridge, then The City to the East End; book ahead for off-season tours). They also rent bikes (£3.50/hour, £20/day; office open daily April-Oct 9:30-18:00, shorter hours Nov-March, west of Blackfriars Bridge on the South Bank, 1 Gabriel's Wharf, tel. 020/7928-6838, www.londonbicycle.com).

Fat Tire Bike Tours

Nearly daily bike tours cover the highlights of downtown London, on two different itineraries (£2 discount with this book): **Royal London** (£22, April-Oct daily at 11:00, mid-May-mid-Sept also at 15:30, Nov-March Thu-Mon at 11:00, 7 miles, 4 hours, meet at Queensway Tube station; includes Parliament, Buckingham Palace, Hyde Park, and Trafalgar Square) and **River Thames** (£30, nearly daily in summer at 10:30, March-Nov Thu-Sat at 10:30, 4.5 hours, reservations required, meet just outside Southwark Tube Station; includes London Eye, St. Paul's, Tower of London, and London Bridge). Their guiding style wears its learning lightly, mixing history with humor. Reservations are easy online, and required for River Thames tours and kids' bikes (off-season tours also available, mobile 078-8233-8779, www.fattirebiketourslondon.com). Confirm the schedule online or by phone. They also offer a range of walking tours that include a fish-and-chips dinner, a beer-tasting pub tour, and theater packages.

▲▲BY CRUISE BOAT

London offers many made-for-tourist cruises, most on slow-moving, open-top boats accompanied by entertaining commentary about passing sights. Several companies offer essentially the same trip. Generally speaking, you can either do a **short city center cruise** by riding a boat 30 minutes from Westminster Pier to Tower Pier (particularly handy if you're interested in visiting the Tower of London anyway), or take a **longer cruise** that includes a peek at the East  End, riding from Westminster all the way to Greenwich (save time by taking the Tube back).

Each company runs cruises daily, about twice hourly, from

ORIENTATION

Thames Boat Piers

Thames boats stop at these piers in the town center and beyond. While Westminster Pier is the most popular, it's not the only dock in town. Consider all the options (listed from west to east, as the Thames flows—see the color maps in the front of this book).

Millbank Pier (North Bank): At the Tate Britain Museum, used primarily by the Tate Boat ferry service (express connection to Tate Modern at Bankside Pier).

Westminster Pier (North Bank): Near the base of Big Ben, offers round-trip sightseeing cruises and lots of departures in both directions (though the Thames Clippers boats don't stop here). Nearby sights include Parliament and Westminster Abbey.

London Eye Pier (a.k.a. **Waterloo Pier,** South Bank): At the base of the London Eye; good, less-crowded alternative to Westminster, with many of the same cruise options (Waterloo Station is nearby).

Embankment Pier (North Bank): Near Covent Garden, Trafalgar Square, and Cleopatra's Needle (the obelisk on the Thames). This pier is used mostly for special boat trips, such as some RIB (rigid inflatable boats) and lunch and dinner cruises.

Festival Pier (South Bank): Next to the Royal Festival Hall, just downstream from the London Eye.

Blackfriars Pier (North Bank): In The City, not far from St. Paul's.

Bankside Pier (South Bank): Directly in front of the Tate Modern and Shakespeare's Globe.

London Bridge Pier (a.k.a. **London Bridge City Pier,** South Bank): Near the HMS *Belfast* and the start of my Bankside Walk.

Tower Pier (North Bank): At the Tower of London, at the east edge of The City and near the East End.

St. Katharine's Pier (North Bank): Just downstream from the Tower of London.

Canary Wharf Pier (North Bank): At the Docklands, London's new "downtown."

Greenwich, Kew Gardens, and Hampton Court Piers: These outer London piers may also come in handy.

morning until dark; many reduce frequency off-season. Boats come and go from various docks in the city center (see sidebar). The most popular places to embark are Westminster Pier (at the base of Westminster Bridge across the street from Big Ben) and London Eye Pier (also known as Waterloo Pier, across the river).

A one-way trip within the city center costs about £10; going all the way to Greenwich costs about £2.50 more. Most companies charge around £4 more for a round-trip ticket. Others sell hop-on, hop-off day tickets (around £19). But I'd rather savor a one-way cruise, then zip home by Tube.

You can buy tickets at kiosks on the docks. A Travelcard can snare you a 33 percent discount on most cruises (just show the card when you pay for the cruise); the pay-as-you-go Oyster card nets you a discount only on Thames Clippers. Because companies vary in the discounts they offer, always ask. Children and seniors generally get discounts. You can purchase drinks and scant, overpriced snacks on board. Clever budget travelers pack a picnic and munch while they cruise.

The three dominant companies are **City Cruises** (handy 45-minute cruise from Westminster Pier to Tower Pier; www.citycruises.com), **Thames River Services** (fewer stops, classic boats, friendlier and more old-fashioned feel; www.thamesriverservices.co.uk), and **Circular Cruise** (full cruise takes about an hour, operated by Crown River Services, www.circularcruise.london). I'd skip the **London Eye**'s River Cruise from London Eye Pier—it's about the same price as Circular Cruise, but 20 minutes shorter. The speedy **Thames Clippers** (described later) are designed more for no-nonsense transport than lazy sightseeing.

To compare all of your options in one spot, head to Westminster Pier, which has a row of kiosks for all of the big outfits.

Cruising Downstream, to Greenwich: Both **City Cruises** and **Thames River Services** head from Westminster Pier to Greenwich. The cruises are usually narrated by the captain, with most commentary given on the way to Greenwich. The companies' prices are the same, though their itineraries are slightly different (Thames River Services makes only one stop en route and takes just an hour, while City Cruises makes two stops and adds about 15 minutes). The **Thames Clippers** boats, described later, are cheaper and faster (about 20-45 minutes to Greenwich), but have no commentary and no up-top seating. To maximize both efficiency and sightseeing, I'd take a narrated cruise to Greenwich one way, and go the other way on the DLR (Docklands Light Railway), with a stop in the Docklands (Canary Wharf station; □ see the Docklands Walk chapter).

Cruising Upstream, to Kew Gardens and Hampton Court Palace: **Thames River Boats** leave for Kew Gardens from Westminster Pier (£13 one-way, £20 round-trip, cash only, discounts with Travelcard, 2-4/day depending on season, 1.5 hours, boats sail April-Oct, about half the trip is narrated, www.wpsa.co.uk). Most boats continue on to Hampton Court Palace for an additional £4 (and another 1.5 hours). Because of the river current, you can save 30 minutes cruising from Hampton Court back into town (depends on the tide—ask before you commit). Romantic as these rides sound, it can be a long trip...especially upstream.

Commuting by Clipper

The sleek, 220-seat catamarans used by **Thames Clippers** are designed for commuters rather than sightseers. Think of the boats as express buses on the river—they zip through London every 20-30 minutes, stopping at most of the major docks en route, including Canary Wharf (Docklands) and Greenwich. They're fast: roughly 20 minutes from Embankment to Tower, 10 more minutes to Docklands, and 15 more minutes to Greenwich. The boats are less pleasant for joyriding than the cruises described earlier, with no commentary and no open deck up top (the only outside access is on a crowded deck at the exhaust-choked back of the boat, where you're jostling for space to take photos). Any one-way ride in Central London (roughly London Eye to Tower Pier) costs £8; a one-way ride to East London (Canary Wharf and Greenwich) is £8.70, and a River Roamer all-day ticket costs £18.50 (discounts with Travelcard and Oyster card, www.thamesclippers.com).

Thames Clippers also offers two express trips. The **Tate Boat** ferry service, which directly connects the Tate Britain (Millbank Pier) and the Tate Modern (Bankside Pier), is made for art lovers (£8 one-way, covered by River Roamer day ticket; buy ticket at kiosks or self-service machines before boarding or use Oyster Card; for frequency and times, see the Tate Britain and Tate Modern tour chapters or www.tate.org.uk/visit/tate-boat). The **O2 Express** runs only on nights when there are events at the O2 arena (departs from London Eye Pier).

Away from the Thames, on Regent's Canal: Consider exploring London's canals by taking a cruise on historic Regent's Canal in north London. Several companies offer trips through Regent's Park, Little Venice, and Camden Lock Market. Check out **London Waterbus Company** (www.londonwaterbus.com), **Jason's Trip** (www.jasons.co.uk), or the good ship *Jenny Wren*, which offers 1.5-hour guided canal boat cruises from Walker's Quay in Camden Town through scenic Regent's Park to Little Venice (£14; 2-3/day April-Oct, weekends only in March, Walker's Quay, 250 Camden High Street, 3-minute walk from Tube: Camden Town; tel. 020/7485-4433, www.walkersquay.com). While in Camden Town, stop by the popular, punky Camden Lock Market to browse through trendy arts and crafts (open daily, busiest on weekends, a block from Walker's Quay, www.camdenlockmarket.com; for more on the market, see page 435).

WEEKEND TOUR PACKAGES FOR STUDENTS

Andy Steves (Rick's son) runs **Weekend Student Adventures** (WSA Europe), offering 3-day and 10-day budget travel packages across Europe including accommodations, skip-the-line sightseeing, and unique local experiences. Locally guided and DIY unguided options are available for student and budget travelers in 13 of Europe's most popular cities, including London (guided trips from €199, see www.wsaeurope.com for details). Check out Andy's tips, resources, and podcast at www.andysteves.com.

SIGHTS IN LONDON

These sights are arranged by neighborhood for handy sightseeing. When you see a 📖 in a listing, it means the sight is covered in much more depth in a self-guided walk or self-guided tour. A 🎧 means the walk or tour is available as a free audio tour (via my Rick Steves Audio Europe app—see page 8). Some walks and tours are available in both formats—take your pick.

Check www.ricksteves.com/update for any significant changes that have occurred since this book was published. For money-saving tips, see "Affording London's Sights" on page 74.

"Voluntary Donations": Some London sights automatically add a "voluntary donation" of about 10 percent to their admission fees. The prices posted and quoted in this book include the donation, though it's perfectly fine to pay the base price without the donation. Some of London's free museums also ask for donations as you enter, but again, it's completely optional.

Central London

WESTMINSTER

These sights are listed in roughly geographical order from Westminster Abbey to Trafalgar Square, and are linked in the 📖 Westminster Walk chapter and my 🎧 Westminster Walk audio tour.

▲▲▲Westminster Abbey

The greatest church in the English-speaking world, Westminster Abbey is the place where England's kings and queens have been crowned and buried since 1066. Like a stony refugee camp huddled outside St. Peter's Pearly Gates, Westminster Abbey has many stories to tell. The steep admission includes a fine audioguide, worthwhile if you have the time and interest. To experience the church

more vividly, take a live tour, or attend evensong or an organ concert.

Cost and Hours: £22, £44 family ticket
(covers 2 adults and 1 child), includes cloister
and audioguide; Mon-Fri 9:30-16:30, Wed
until 19:00 (main church only), Sat 9:30-14:30,
last entry one hour before closing, closed Sun
to sightseers but open for services, guided
tours available; cloister—daily 8:00-18:00;
Tube: Westminster or St. James's Park, tel.
020/7222-5152, www.westminster-abbey.org.

Music: The church hosts evensong performances daily except Wednesday, when it's spoken instead of
sung (Mon-Sat at 17:00 except Sept-April Sat at 15:00, Sun year-
round at 15:00). A free 30-minute organ recital is usually held on
Sunday at 17:45.

📖 See the Westminster Abbey Tour chapter.

▲▲Houses of Parliament (Palace of Westminster)

This Neo-Gothic icon of London, the site of the royal residence
from 1042 to 1547, is now the meeting place of the legislative

branch of government.
Like the US Capitol in
Washington, DC, the
complex is open to visitors.
You can gain access one
of two ways: While Par-
liament is in session, wait
in line to enter for free to
see a couple of the grandest halls and other rooms,
and watch debates in one
or both of the public galleries (either the bickering House of Commons or the sleepy House of Lords). Or, reserve an audioguide or
organized group tour of the historic building—held on Saturdays
year-round, and also on weekdays during parliamentary recess
(generally late July-Sept).

Whichever you choose, your visit will include the cavernous
and historic Westminster Hall, St. Stephen's Hall, and the Central
Lobby—each impressive in its own right.

Cost and Hours: Free when Parliament is in session, otherwise
must visit with a paid tour (see next page); hours for nonticketed
entry to House of Commons—Oct-late July Mon 14:30-22:30, Tue-
Wed 11:30-19:30, Thu 9:30-17:30; for House of Lords—Oct-late
July Mon-Tue 14:30-22:00, Wed 15:00-22:00, Thu 11:00-19:30; last
entry depends on debates; exact schedule at www.parliament.uk.

Tours: Audioguide-£18.50, guided tour-£25.50, Sat year-round 9:00-16:30 and most weekdays during recess (late July-Sept), 1.5 hours. Confirm the tour schedule and book ahead online at www.parliament.uk or by calling 020/7219-4114. The ticket office also sells tour tickets, but there's no guarantee same-day spaces will be available (ticket office open Mon-Fri 10:00-16:00, Sat 9:00-16:30, closed Sun, located in Portcullis House next to Westminster Tube Station, entrance on Victoria Embankment).

Crowd-Beating Tips: For the public galleries, lines tend to be longest at the start of each session, particularly on Wednesdays; for the shortest wait, try to show up later in the afternoon (but don't push it, as things sometimes close down early).

📖 See the Houses of Parliament Tour chapter.

Nearby: Across the street from the Parliament building's St. Stephen's Gate, the **Jewel Tower** is a rare remnant of the old Palace of Westminster, used by kings until Henry VIII. The crude stone tower (1365-1366) was a guard tower in the palace wall, overlooking a moat. It contains a fine exhibit on the medieval Westminster Palace and the tower (£5.20, daily 10:00-18:00, Oct until 17:00; Nov-March Sat-Sun 10:00-16:00, closed Mon-Fri; tel. 020/7222-2219). Next to the tower (and free) is a quiet courtyard with picnic-friendly benches.

Big Ben, the 315-foot-high clock tower at the north end of the Palace of Westminster, is named for its 13-ton bell, Ben. The light above the clock is lit when Parliament is in session. The face of the clock is huge—you can actually see the minute hand moving. For a good view of it, walk halfway over Westminster Bridge.

▲▲▲Churchill War Rooms

This excellent sight offers a fascinating walk through the underground headquarters of the British government's WWII fight against the Nazis in the darkest days of  the Battle of Britain. It has two parts: the war rooms themselves, and a top-notch museum dedicated to the man who steered the war from here, Winston Churchill. For details on all the blood, sweat, toil, and tears, pick up the excellent, essential, and included audioguide at the entry, and dive in. Though you can buy your ticket in advance online, you may still find yourself waiting up to 30 minutes (on busy days) in the security line before entering. Allow 1-2 hours for your visit.

Cost and Hours: £19, includes audioguide, daily 9:30-18:00, last entry one hour before closing; on King Charles Street, 200

SIGHTS

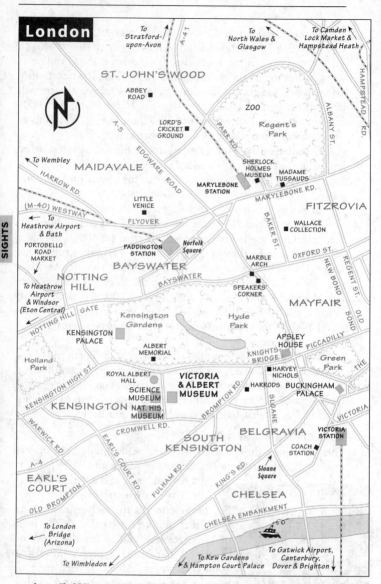

London

To Stratford-upon-Avon

To North Wales & Glasgow

To Camden Lock Market & Hampstead Heath

ST. JOHN'S WOOD

ABBEY ROAD

ZOO

Regent's Park

LORD'S CRICKET GROUND

To Wembley

MAIDAVALE

HARROW RD.

SHERLOCK HOLMES MUSEUM

MADAME TUSSAUDS

MARYLEBONE STATION

MARYLEBONE RD.

FITZROVIA

LITTLE VENICE

(M-40) WESTWAY

FLYOVER

WALLACE COLLECTION

To Heathrow Airport & Bath

PORTOBELLO ROAD MARKET

PADDINGTON STATION

Norfolk Square

BAYSWATER

MARBLE ARCH

OXFORD ST.

NOTTING HILL

BAYSWATER

SPEAKERS' CORNER

MAYFAIR

To Heathrow Airport & Windsor (Eton Central)

NOTTING HILL GATE

Kensington Gardens

Hyde Park

Holland Park

KENSINGTON PALACE

ALBERT MEMORIAL

APSLEY HOUSE

PICCADILLY

Green Park

KNIGHTS-BRIDGE

HARVEY NICHOLS

ROYAL ALBERT HALL

SCIENCE MUSEUM

VICTORIA & ALBERT MUSEUM

HARRODS

BUCKINGHAM PALACE

KENSINGTON

NAT. HIS. MUSEUM

CROMWELL RD.

SOUTH KENSINGTON

BELGRAVIA

VICTORIA STATION

EARL'S COURT

OLD BROMPTON

FULHAM RD.

KING'S RD.

Sloane Square

COACH STATION

CHELSEA

To London Bridge (Arizona)

CHELSEA EMBANKMENT

To Wimbledon

To Kew Gardens & Hampton Court Palace

To Gatwick Airport, Canterbury, Dover & Brighton

yards off Whitehall—follow signs, Tube: Westminster; tel. 020/7930-6961, www.iwm.org.uk/churchill. The museum's gift shop is great for anyone nostalgic for the 1940s.

Cabinet War Rooms: The 27-room, heavily fortified nerve center of the British war effort was used from 1939 to 1945. Churchill's room, the map room, and other rooms are just as they were in 1945. As you follow the one-way route, take advantage of the audioguide, which explains each room and offers first-person

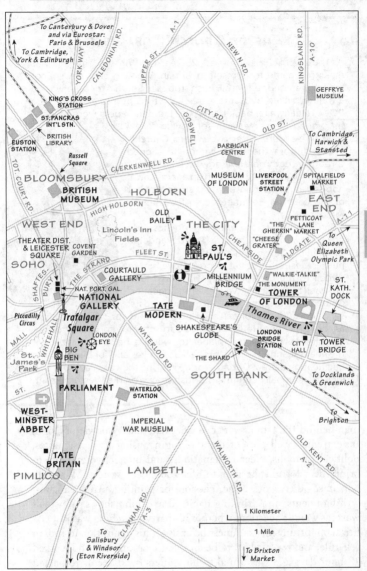

To Canterbury & Dover
and via Eurostar:
Paris & Brussels

To Cambridge,
York & Edinburgh

YORK WAY

CALEDONIAN RD.

UPPER ST.

A-1

NEW N RD.

CITY RD.

KINGSLAND RD.

A-10

KING'S CROSS
STATION

ST. PANCRAS
INT'L STN.

EUSTON
STATION

BRITISH
LIBRARY

Russell
Square

TOT. COURT RD.

GOSWELL

OLD ST.

GEFFRYE
MUSEUM

To Cambridge,
Harwich &
Stansted

CLERKENWELL RD.

BLOOMSBURY

BRITISH
MUSEUM

HOLBORN

HIGH HOLBORN

BARBICAN
CENTRE

MUSEUM
OF LONDON

LIVERPOOL
STREET
STATION

SPITALFIELDS
MARKET

EAST
END

PETTICOAT
LANE
MARKET

A-11

WEST END

THEATER DIST.
& LEICESTER
SQUARE

SOHO

SHAFTES-
BURY

COVENT
GARDEN

OLD
BAILEY

THE CITY

Lincoln's Inn
Fields

FLEET ST.

ST.
PAUL'S

CHEAPSIDE

"THE
GHERKIN"

"CHEESE
GRATER"

ALDGATE

To
Queen
Elizabeth
Olympic Park

COURTAULD
GALLERY

NAT. PORT. GAL.

NATIONAL
GALLERY

THE STRAND

Piccadilly
Circus

Trafalgar
Square

MALL

WHITEHALL

St.
James's
Park

BIG
BEN

LONDON
EYE

PARLIAMENT

WEST-
MINSTER
ABBEY

ST.

WATERLOO RD.

TATE
MODERN

MILLENNIUM
BRIDGE

SHAKESPEARE'S
GLOBE

"WALKIE-TALKIE"

THE MONUMENT

TOWER
OF LONDON

ST.
KATH.
DOCK

Thames River

LONDON
BRIDGE
STATION

THE SHARD

SOUTH BANK

CITY
HALL

TOWER
BRIDGE

To Docklands
& Greenwich

WATERLOO
STATION

IMPERIAL
WAR MUSEUM

WALWORTH RD.

To
Brighton

OLD KENT RD.

A-2

TATE
BRITAIN

PIMLICO

LAMBETH

CLAPHAM RD.

A-3

1 Kilometer

1 Mile

To
Salisbury
& Windsor
(Eton Riverside)

To Brixton
Market

SIGHTS

accounts of wartime happenings here. Be patient—it's well worth
it. While the rooms are spartan, you'll see how British gentility
survived even as the city was bombarded—posted signs informed
those working underground what the weather was like outside, and
a cheery notice reminded them to turn off the light switch to con-
serve electricity.

Churchill Museum: Don't bypass this museum, which occupies a large hall amid the war rooms. It dissects every aspect of the

Winston Churchill (1874-1965)

As the 20th century dawned, 25-year-old Winston Churchill was making a name for himself in Britain. Working as a newspaper reporter embedded with British troops in South Africa, he was on a train attacked by Boers. Churchill was captured and held as a POW. Meanwhile, back home, the London papers were praising

the young man's heroism for saving fellow train passengers. After two weeks, Churchill escaped from the Boer camp—he slipped through a bathroom window, scaled a wall, walked nonchalantly through an enemy town, hopped a freight train, and was smuggled out of the country. He emerged to find himself famous.

Churchill later entered politics. He first followed in his father's (Lord Randolph Churchill) Conservative Party footsteps, but his desire for social reform drove him to switch to the Liberal Party. (He would later flip back to Conservative.) For three decades, Churchill held numerous government posts,

serving as Chancellor of This, Undersecretary of That, and Minister of The Other. He earned praise for prison reform and for developing new-fangled airplanes for warfare; he was criticized for the heavy-handed way he broke labor strikes and for bungling the pacification of Iraq. During World War I, he took a break from politics to personally command British troops on the Western Front.

man behind the famous cigar, bowler hat, and V-for-victory sign. It's extremely well-presented and engaging, using artifacts, quotes, political cartoons, clear explanations, and interactive exhibits to bring the colorful statesman to life. You'll get a taste of Winston's wit, irascibility, work ethic, passion for painting, American ties, writing talents, and drinking habits. The exhibit shows Winston's warts as well: It questions whether his party-switching was just political opportunism, examines the basis for his opposition to Indian self-rule, and reveals him to be an intense taskmaster who worked 18-hour days and was brutal to his staffers (who deeply respected him nevertheless).

A long touch-the-screen timeline lets you zero in on events in his life from birth (November 30, 1874) to his first appointment as prime minister in 1940. Many of the items on display—such as a European map divvied up in permanent marker, which Churchill brought to England from the postwar Potsdam Conference—drive home the remarkable span of history this man influenced. Imagine: Churchill began his military career riding horses in the cavalry

SIGHTS

In 1929, Churchill-the-career-bureaucrat retired from politics. He wrote books *(History of the English-Speaking Peoples)* and spoke out about the growing threat of fascist Germany. When World War II broke out, Prime Minister Chamberlain's appeasement policies were discredited, and—on the day that Germany invaded the Netherlands—the king appointed Churchill prime minister. Churchill guided the nation through its darkest hour (see sidebar on page 270). His greatest contribution may have been his stirring radio speeches that galvanized the will of the British people.

Despite the Allies' victory over the Nazis, Churchill lost the 1945 election. Though considered the ideal man to lead Britain during war, many believed that he and his Conservative Party colleagues were not the best choice to lead the country in peace and during rebuilding. Never one to be idle, he remained active in politics (especially in world affairs) as Leader of the Opposition. In 1946, he gave a speech at a Missouri college, which included the famous Cold War line, "From Stettin in the Baltic to Trieste in the Adriatic, an Iron Curtain has descended across the Continent." In 1951, Churchill was again elected prime minister and served for four years before he retired in 1955. When he died at the age of 90 in 1965, his state funeral in St. Paul's attracted leaders from around the world. Churchill, a legend in his own time, was buried in the family plot at Bladon, a mile from Blenheim Palace, the place of his birth.

and ended it speaking out against nuclear proliferation. It's all the more amazing considering that, in the 1930s, the man who would become my vote for greatest statesman of the 20th century was considered a washed-up loony ranting about the growing threat of fascism.

Eating: Rations are available at the **$$** museum café or, better, get a pub lunch at the nearby **$$** Westminster Arms (food served downstairs, on Storey's Gate, a couple of blocks south of the museum).

Horse Guards

The Horse Guards change daily at 10:30 (9:30 on Sun), and a colorful dismounting ceremony takes place daily at 16:00. The rest of the day, they just stand there—making for boring video (at Horse Guards Parade on Whitehall, directly across from the Banqueting

House, between Trafalgar Square and 10 Downing Street, Tube: Westminster, www.householddivision.org.uk—search "Changing the Guard"). Buckingham Palace pageantry is canceled when it rains, but the Horse Guards change regardless of the weather.

The **Household Cavalry Museum** shows off 350 years of cavalry tradition. Visitors to this little museum see uniforms, weapons, and video clips, and can peek into the stables (£7, includes audioguide, daily 10:00-18:00, Nov-March until 17:00, enter on back side of Horse Guards building). At five minutes after each hour you can see horses return from the changing of the mounted sentries who guard the entrance to Horse Guards Parade.

▲Banqueting House

England's first Renaissance building (1619-1622) is still standing. Designed by Inigo Jones, built by King James I, and decorated by his son Charles I, the Banqueting House came to symbolize the Stuart kings' "divine right" management style—the belief that God himself had anointed them to rule. The house is one of the few London landmarks spared by the 1698 fire and the only surviving part of the original Palace of Whitehall. Today it opens its doors to visitors, who enjoy a restful 10-minute audiovisual history, a 45-minute audioguide, and a look at the exquisite banqueting hall itself. As a tourist attraction, it's basically one big room, with sumptuous ceiling paintings by Peter Paul Rubens. At Charles I's request, these paintings drove home the doctrine of the legitimacy of the divine right of kings. Ironically, in 1649—divine right ignored—King Charles I was famously executed right here.

Cost and Hours: £8, includes audioguide, Fri-Wed 10:00-17:00, closed Thu, may close for government functions—though it stays open at least until 13:00 (call ahead for recorded info), immediately across Whitehall from the Horse Guards, Tube: Westminster, tel. 020/3166-6155, www.hrp.org.uk.

📖 For a brief self-guided tour of the Banqueting House—and more details about its history—see page 124 in the Westminster Walk.

ON TRAFALGAR SQUARE
▲▲Trafalgar Square

London's renovated central square, the climax of most marches and demonstrations, is a thrilling place to simply hang out. Lord Nelson stands atop his 185-foot-tall fluted granite column, gazing out toward Trafalgar, where he lost his life but defeated the French fleet. Part of this 1842 memorial is made from his victims' melted-down cannons. He's surrounded by spraying fountains, giant lions, hordes of people, and—until recently—even more pigeons. A former London mayor decided that London's "flying rats" were a public nuisance and evicted Trafalgar Square's venerable seed salesmen (Tube: Charing Cross).

📖 For more on Trafalgar Square, see page 128 in the Westminster Walk. It's also covered on my 🎧 free Westminster Walk audio tour.

▲▲▲National Gallery

Displaying an unsurpassed collection of European paintings from 1250 to 1900—including works by Leonardo, Botticelli, Ve-

lázquez, Rembrandt, Turner, Van Gogh, and the Impressionists—this is one of Europe's great galleries. The collection is huge; following the route suggested in my self-guided tour will give you the best quick visit. For a more thorough tour, use the gallery's excellent audioguide. Or pick out just one masterpiece or a handful of great artists using the gallery's online "Short of Time" suggestions. Whatever time you spend here is worth it.

Cost and Hours: Free, £5 suggested donation, special exhibits extra, daily 10:00-18:00, Fri until 21:00, last entry to special exhibits 45 minutes before closing; daily free guided tours available, worthwhile audioguide-£4, floor plan-£1; on Trafalgar Square, Tube: Charing Cross or Leicester Square, recorded info tel. 020/7747-2885, switchboard tel. 020/7839-3321, www.nationalgallery.org.uk. The excellent-but-pricey $$$ National Dining Rooms and $$$ National Café, in the museum, are good spots for afternoon tea (see page 418); the museum has cheaper eateries as well.

📖 See the National Gallery Tour chapter.

▲▲National Portrait Gallery

Put off by halls of 19th-century characters who meant nothing to me, I used to call this museum "as interesting as someone else's yearbook." But a selective walk through this 500-year-long *Who's Who* of British history is quick and free, and puts faces on the story of England.

Some highlights: Henry VIII and wives; portraits of the "Virgin Queen" Elizabeth I, Sir Francis Drake, and Sir Walter Raleigh; the only real-life portrait of William Shakespeare; Oliver Cromwell and Charles I with his head on; portraits by Gainsborough and Reynolds; the Romantics (William Blake, Lord Byron, William Wordsworth, and company); Queen Victoria and her era; and the

SIGHTS

London at a Glance

▲▲▲Westminster Abbey Britain's finest church and the site of royal coronations and burials since 1066. **Hours:** Mon-Fri 9:30-16:30, Wed until 19:00, Sat 9:30-14:30, closed Sun to sightseers except for worship. See page 41.

▲▲▲Churchill War Rooms Underground WWII headquarters of Churchill's war effort. **Hours:** Daily 9:30-18:00. See page 43.

▲▲▲National Gallery Remarkable collection of European paintings (1250-1900), including Leonardo, Botticelli, Velázquez, Rembrandt, Turner, Van Gogh, and the Impressionists. **Hours:** Daily 10:00-18:00, Fri until 21:00. See page 49.

▲▲▲British Museum The world's greatest collection of artifacts of Western civilization, including the Rosetta Stone and the Parthenon's Elgin Marbles. **Hours:** Daily 10:00-17:30, Fri until 20:30 (select galleries only). See page 61.

▲▲▲British Library Fascinating collection of important literary treasures of the Western world. **Hours:** Mon-Fri 9:30-18:00, Tue-Thu until 20:00, Sat 9:30-17:00, Sun 11:00-17:00. See page 62.

▲▲▲St. Paul's Cathedral The main cathedral of the Anglican Church, designed by Christopher Wren, with a climbable dome and daily evensong services. **Hours:** Mon-Sat 8:30-16:30, closed Sun except for worship. See page 70.

▲▲▲Tower of London Historic castle, palace, and prison housing the crown jewels and a witty band of Beefeaters. **Hours:** Tue-Sat 9:00-17:30, Sun-Mon 10:00-17:30; Nov-Feb closes one hour earlier. See page 76.

▲▲▲Victoria and Albert Museum The best collection of decorative arts anywhere. **Hours:** Daily 10:00-17:45, Fri until 22:00 (select galleries only). See page 100.

▲▲Houses of Parliament London landmark famous for Big Ben and occupied by the Houses of Lords and Commons. **Hours:** When Parliament is in session, generally open Oct-late July Mon-Thu, closed Fri-Sun and during recess late July-Sept. Guided tours offered year-round on Sat and most weekdays during recess. See page 42.

▲▲Trafalgar Square The heart of London, where Westminster, The City, and the West End meet. **Hours:** Always open. See page 48.

▲▲National Portrait Gallery A *Who's Who* of British history, featuring portraits of this nation's most important historical figures. **Hours:** Daily 10:00-18:00, Thu-Fri until 21:00, first and second floors open Mon at 11:00. See page 49.

▲▲Covent Garden Vibrant people-watching zone with shops, cafés, street musicians, and an iron-and-glass arcade that once hosted a produce market. See page 53.

▲▲Changing of the Guard at Buckingham Palace Hour-long spectacle at Britain's royal residence. **Hours:** May-July daily at 11:00, Aug-April every other day. See page 58.

▲▲London Eye Enormous observation wheel, dominating—and offering commanding views over—London's skyline. **Hours:** Daily June-Aug 10:00-20:30 or later, Sept-May 11:00-18:00. See page 84.

▲▲Imperial War Museum Exhibits examining military conflicts from the early 20th century to today. **Hours:** Daily 10:00-18:00. See page 85.

▲▲Tate Modern Works by Monet, Matisse, Dalí, Picasso, and Warhol displayed in a converted powerhouse complex. **Hours:** Daily 10:00-18:00, Fri-Sat until 22:00. See page 88.

▲▲Shakespeare's Globe Timbered, thatched-roofed reconstruction of the Bard's original "wooden O." **Hours:** Theater complex, museum, and actor-led tours generally daily 9:00-17:30; April-Oct generally morning theater tours only. Plays are also staged here. See page 89.

▲▲Tate Britain Collection of British painting from the 16th century through modern times, including works by William Blake, the Pre-Raphaelites, and J. M. W. Turner. **Hours:** Daily 10:00-18:00. See page 95.

▲▲Natural History Museum A Darwinian delight, packed with stuffed creatures, engaging exhibits, and enthralled kids. **Hours:** Daily 10:00-18:00. See page 100.

▲▲Greenwich Seafaring borough just east of the city center, with *Cutty Sark* tea clipper, Royal Observatory, other maritime sights, and a pleasant market. **Hours:** Most sights open daily, typically 10:00-17:00. See page 104.

▲Wallace Collection One of the finest private family art collections anywhere—free and open to the public—with paintings by such masters as Rembrandt, Rubens, and Velázquez. **Hours:** Daily 10:00-17:00. See page 63.

▲East End Walk Explore the haunt of Jack the Ripper, but also happier locales such as the colorful Spitalfields, Petticoat Lane, and Truman markets, and the curry-scented streets of "Bangla-town." See page 78.

SIGHTS

present royal family, including the late Princess Diana and the current Duchess of Cambridge—Kate.

The collection is well-described, not huge, and in historical sequence, from the 16th century on the second floor to today's royal family, usually housed on the ground floor.

Cost and Hours: Free, £5 suggested donation, special exhibits extra; daily 10:00-18:00, Thu-Fri until 21:00, first and second floors open Mon at 11:00, last entry to special exhibits one hour before closing; excellent audioguide-£3, floor plan-£1; entry 100 yards off Trafalgar Square (around the corner from National Gallery, opposite Church of St. Martin-in-the-Fields), Tube: Charing Cross or Leicester Square, tel. 020/7306-0055, recorded info tel. 020/7312-2463, www.npg.org.uk.

📖 See the National Portrait Gallery Tour chapter.

▲St. Martin-in-the-Fields

The church, built in the 1720s with a Gothic spire atop a Greek-type temple, is an oasis of peace on wild and noisy Trafalgar Square. St. Martin cared for the poor. "In the fields" was where the first church stood on this spot (in the 13th century), between Westminster and The City. Stepping inside, you still feel a compassion for the needs of the people in this neighborhood—the church serves the homeless and houses a Chinese community center. The modern east window—with grillwork bent into the shape of a warped cross—was installed in 2008 to replace one damaged in World War II.

A freestanding glass pavilion to the left of the church serves as the entrance to the church's underground areas. There you'll find the concert ticket office, a gift shop, brass-rubbing center, and the recommended support-the-church Café in the Crypt.

Cost and Hours: Free, donations welcome; hours vary but generally Mon-Fri 8:30-13:00 & 14:00-18:00, Sat 9:30-18:00, Sun 15:30-17:00; services listed at entrance; Tube: Charing Cross, tel. 020/7766-1100, www.stmartin-in-the-fields.org.

Music: The church is famous for its concerts. Consider a free lunchtime concert (£3.50 suggested donation; Mon, Tue, and Fri at 13:00), an evening concert (£9-28, several nights a week at 19:30), or Wednesday night jazz at the Café in the Crypt (£8-15 at 20:00). See the church's website for the concert schedule.

THE WEST END AND NEARBY

📖 The following areas are linked (and further described) in the West End Walk chapter.

▲Piccadilly Circus

Although this square is slathered with neon billboards and tacky

attractions (think of it as the Times Square of London), the surrounding streets are packed with great shopping opportunities and swimming with youth on the rampage.

Nearby Shaftesbury Avenue and Leicester Square teem with fun-seekers, theaters, Chinese restaurants, and street singers. To the northeast is London's Chinatown and, beyond that, the funky Soho neighborhood (described next). And curling to the northwest from Piccadilly Circus is genteel Regent Street, lined with exclusive shops.

SIGHTS

▲Soho

North of Piccadilly, once seedy Soho has become trendy—with many recommended restaurants—and is well worth a gawk. It's the epicenter of London's thriving, colorful youth scene, a fun and funky *Sesame Street* of urban diversity.

Soho is also London's red light district (especially near Brewer and Berwick Streets), where "friendly models" wait in tiny rooms up dreary stairways, voluptuous con artists sell strip shows, and eager male tourists are frequently ripped off. But it's easy to avoid trouble if you're not looking for it. In fact, the sleazy joints share the block with respectable pubs and restaurants, and elderly couples stroll past neon signs that flash *Licensed Sex Shop in Basement*.

▲▲Covent Garden

The centerpiece of this boutique-ish shopping district is an iron-and-glass arcade. The "Actors' Church" of St. Paul, the Royal Opera House, and the London Transport Museum (described next) all border the square, and theaters are nearby. The area is a people-watcher's delight, with cigarette eaters, Punch-and-Judy acts, food that's not good for you (or your wallet), trendy crafts, and row after row of boutique shops and market stalls. For more on this square, see page 191. Bet-

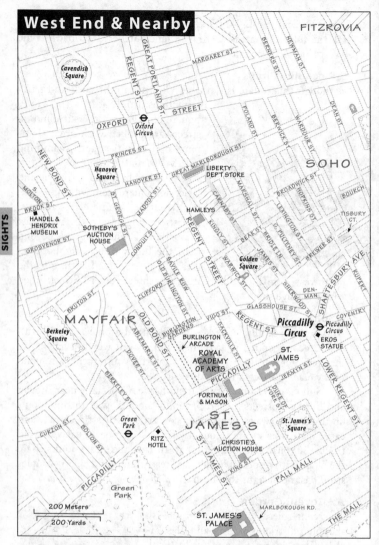

West End & Nearby

FITZROVIA

SOHO

MAYFAIR

ST. JAMES'S

Cavendish Square

Hanover Square

Golden Square

Berkeley Square

Green Park

St. James's Square

HANDEL & HENDRIX MUSEUM

SOTHEBY'S AUCTION HOUSE

LIBERTY DEP'T STORE

HAMLEYS

Piccadilly Circus

EROS STATUE

ST. JAMES

BURLINGTON ARCADE

ROYAL ACADEMY OF ARTS

FORTNUM & MASON

RITZ HOTEL

CHRISTIE'S AUCTION HOUSE

ST. JAMES'S PALACE

Green Park

200 Meters

200 Yards

SIGHTS

ter Covent Garden lunch deals can be found by walking a block or two away from the eye of this touristic hurricane (check out the places north of the Tube station, along Endell and Neal Streets, and see my suggestions on page 404).

▲London Transport Museum

This modern, well-presented museum, located right at Covent Garden, is fun for kids and thought-provoking for adults (if a bit overpriced). Whether you're cursing or marveling at the buses and Tube, the growth of Europe's third-biggest city (after Istanbul and

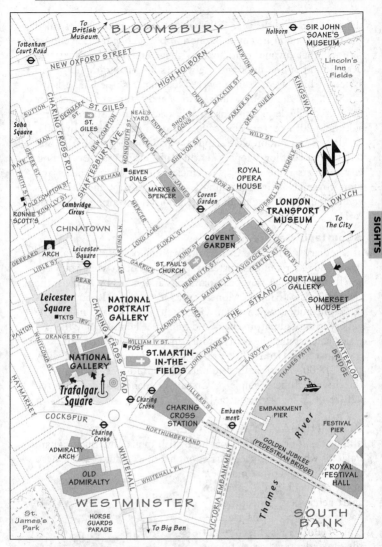

Moscow) has been made possible by its public transit system. Kids enjoy picking up the "stamp card," then punching it with old-fashioned ticket punchers at the different exhibits.

Cost and Hours: £17.50, ticket good for one year, kids under 18 free, Sat-Thu 10:00-18:00, Fri 11:00-18:00, last entry 45 minutes before closing; pleasant upstairs café with Covent Garden view; in southeast corner of Covent Garden courtyard, Tube: Covent Garden, switchboard tel. 020/7379-6344, recorded info tel. 020/7565-7299, www.ltmuseum.co.uk.

Visiting the Museum: After you enter, take the elevator up to the top floor...and the year 1800, when horse-drawn vehicles ruled the road. London invented the notion of a public bus traveling a set route that anyone could board without a reservation. Next, you descend to the first floor and the world's first underground Metro system, which used steam-powered locomotives (the Circle Line, c. 1865). On the ground floor, horses and trains are replaced by motorized vehicles (cars, taxis, double-decker buses, streetcars), resulting in 20th-century congestion. How to deal with it? In 2003, car drivers in London were slapped with a congestion charge, and today, a half-billion people ride the Tube every year. Learn how city planners hope to improve efficiency with better tracks and more coverage of the expanding East End. Finally, an exhibit lets you imagine futuristic modes of transportation waiting to become real.

▲Courtauld Gallery

This gallery, part of the Courtauld Institute of Art, is set to close in mid-2018 for a multiyear renovation. If it's open when you visit, you'll see medieval European paintings and works by Rubens, the Impressionists (Manet, Monet, and Degas), Post-Impressionists (Cézanne and an intense Van Gogh self-portrait), and more. The gallery is located within the grand Somerset House; enjoy the riverside eateries and the courtyard featuring a playful fountain.

Cost and Hours: £7, price can change with exhibit; daily 10:00-18:00, occasionally Thu until 21:00; in Somerset House on the Strand, Tube: Temple or Covent Garden, recorded info tel. 020/7848-2526, www.courtauld.ac.uk.

BUCKINGHAM PALACE AREA

The working headquarters of the British monarchy, Buckingham Palace is where the Queen carries out her official duties as the head of state. She and other members of the royal family also maintain apartments here. The property hasn't always been this grand— James I (1603-1625) first brought the site under royal protection as a place for his mulberry plantation, for rearing silkworms.

Ticketing Options: Three palace sights require admission—the State Rooms (open Aug-Sept only), the Queen's Gallery, and the Royal Mews. You can pay for each separately (prices listed later), or buy a combo-ticket: A £39.50 "Royal Day Out" combo-ticket admits you to all three sights; a £17.70 version covers the Queen's Gallery and Royal Mews. For more information or to book online, see www.royalcollection.

org.uk. Many tourists are more interested in the Changing of the Guard, which costs nothing at all to view.

▲State Rooms at Buckingham Palace

This lavish home has been Britain's royal residence since 1837, when the newly ascended Queen Victoria moved in. When today's Queen is at home, the royal standard flies (a red, yellow, and blue flag); otherwise, the Union Jack flaps in the wind. The Queen opens her palace to the public—but only in August and September, when she's out of town.

Cost and Hours: £23 for lavish State Rooms and throne room, includes audioguide; Aug-Sept only, daily 9:30-18:30, until 19:00 in Aug, last admission 17:15 in Aug, 16:15 in Sept; limited to 8,000 visitors a day by timed entry; come early to the palace's Visitor Entrance (opens at 9:00), or book ahead in person, by phone, or online; Tube: Victoria, tel. 0303/123-7300—but Her Majesty rarely answers.

Queen's Gallery at Buckingham Palace

A small sampling of Queen Elizabeth's personal collection of art is on display in five rooms in a wing adjoining the palace. Her 7,000 paintings, one of the largest private art collections in the world, are actually a series of collections built upon by each successive monarch since the 16th century. The Queen rotates the paintings, enjoying some privately in her many palatial residences while sharing others with her subjects in public galleries in Edinburgh and London. The exhibits change two or three times a year and are lovingly described by the included audioguide.

Because the gallery is small and security is tight (involving lines), I'd suggest visiting this gallery only if you're a patient art lover interested in the current exhibit.

Cost and Hours: £10.30 but can change depending on exhibit, daily 10:00-17:30, from 9:30 Aug-Sept, last entry one hour before closing, Tube: Victoria, tel. 0303/123-7301. Men shouldn't miss the mahogany-trimmed urinals.

Royal Mews

A visit to the Queen's working stables is likely to be disappointing unless you follow the included audioguide or the hourly guided tour (April-Oct only, 45 minutes), in which case it's fairly entertaining—especially if you're interested in horses and/or royalty. You'll see only a few of the Queen's 30 horses (most active between 10:00 and 12:00), a fancy car, and a bunch of old carriages, finishing with the Gold State Coach (c. 1760, 4 tons, 4 mph). Queen Victoria said absolutely no cars. When she died, in 1901, the mews got its first Daimler. Today, along with the hay-eating transport,

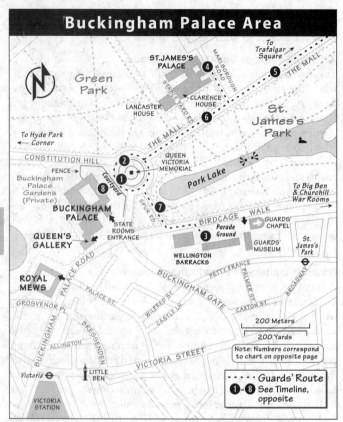

Buckingham Palace Area

To Trafalgar Square

THE MALL

ST. JAMES'S PALACE ④

⑤

MARLBOROUGH ROAD

Green Park

CLARENCE HOUSE

LANCASTER HOUSE

STABLE YARD RD.

⑥

St. James's Park

THE MALL

To Hyde Park Corner

QUEEN VICTORIA MEMORIAL

CONSTITUTION HILL

②

Park Lake

FENCE

Buckingham Palace Gardens (Private)

⑧

Courtyard

①

SPUR RD.

To Big Ben & Churchill War Rooms

BUCKINGHAM PALACE

⑦

STATE ROOMS ENTRANCE

BIRDCAGE WALK

GUARDS' CHAPEL

QUEEN'S GALLERY

③

Parade Ground

GUARDS' MUSEUM

St. James's Park

WELLINGTON BARRACKS

ROYAL MEWS

PALACE ROAD

PALACE ST.

BUCKINGHAM GATE

PETTY FRANCE

PALMER ST.

BROADWAY

GROSVENOR PL.

WILFRED ST.

CASTLE LN.

CAXTON ST.

BRESSENDEN

ALLINGTON

VICTORIA STREET

200 Meters
200 Yards

Note: Numbers correspond to chart on opposite page

Victoria ⊖

LITTLE BEN

VICTORIA STATION

· · · · Guards' Route
①-⑧ See Timeline, opposite

SIGHTS

the stable is home to five Bentleys and Rolls-Royce Phantoms, with at least one on display.

Cost and Hours: £10, April-Oct daily 10:00-17:00, Nov-March Mon-Sat 10:00-16:00, closed Sun; last entry 45 minutes before closing, generally busiest immediately after changing of the guard, guided tours on the hour in summer; Buckingham Palace Road, Tube: Victoria, tel. 0303/123-7302.

▲▲Changing of the Guard at Buckingham Palace

This is the spectacle every visitor to London has to see at least once: stone-faced, red-coated (or in winter, gray-coated), bearskin-hatted guards changing posts with much fanfare, in an hour-long ceremony accompanied by a brass band.

The most famous part takes place right in front of Buckingham Palace at 11:00. But there actually are several different guard-changing ceremonies and parades going on simultaneously, at different locations within a few hundred yards of the palace. All of

Changing of the Guard Timeline

When	What
10:00	Tourists begin to gather. Arrive now for a spot front and center by the ❶ fence outside Buckingham Palace in anticipation of the most famous event—when the "Queen's Guard" does its shift change at 11:00.
10:30	❷ By now, the Victoria Memorial in front of the palace—the best all-purpose viewing spot—is crowded.
10:30-10:45	Meanwhile, at the nearby ❸ Wellington Barracks, the "New Guard" gathers for inspection and the "Old Guard" gathers for inspection at ❹ St. James's Palace.
10:30 (9:30 Sun)	Farther away, along Whitehall, the Horse Guard also changes guard, and begins parading down ❺ the Mall.
10:43	Relieved of duty, the tired St. James's Palace guards march down ❻ the Mall, heading for Buckingham Palace.
10:57	Fresh replacement troops (led by a marching band) head in a grand parade from Wellington Barracks down ❼ Spur Road to Buckingham Palace.
11:00	All guards gradually converge around the Victoria Memorial in front of the palace. The ceremony approaches its climax.
11:00-11:30	Now, the famous Changing of the Guard ceremony takes place ❽ inside the fenced courtyard of Buckingham Palace. Everyone parades around; the guard changes, and they pass the regimental flag (or "colour")—all with much shouting. The band plays a happy little concert and then they march out.
11:40	The tired "Old Guard" (led by a band) heads up Spur Road for Wellington Barracks. The fresh "New Guard" heads up the Mall for St. James's Palace.
11:45	As the fresh "New Guard" takes over at St. James's Palace, there's a smaller changing of the guard ceremony. And with that—"Tourists...d-i-i-s-missed!"

SIGHTS

these spectacles converge around Buckingham Palace in a perfect storm of red-coated pageantry.

To plan your sightseeing strategy (and understand what's going on), see the blow-by-blow account in the "Changing of the Guard Timeline."

Cost and Hours: Free, May-July daily at 11:00, every other day Aug-April, no ceremony in very wet weather; exact schedule subject to change—call 020/7766-7300 for the day's plan, or check www.householddivision.org.uk (search "Changing the Guard"); Buckingham Palace, Tube: Victoria, St. James's Park, or Green Park. Or hop into a big black taxi and say, "Buck House, please."

Sightseeing Strategies: Most tourists just show up and get lost in the crowds, but those who anticipate the action and know where to perch will enjoy the event more. The action takes place in stages over the course of an hour, at multiple locations; see the map. There are several ways to experience the pageantry. Get out your map (or download the official app at www.royalcollection.org.uk) and strategize. Here are a few options to consider:

Watch near the Palace: The main event is in the forecourt right in front of Buckingham Palace (between the palace and the fence) from 11:00 to 11:30. You'll need to get here as close to 10:00 as possible to get a place front and center, next to the fence. The key to good viewing is to get either right up front along the road or fence, or find some raised surface to stand or sit on—a balustrade or a curb—so you can see over people's heads.

Watch near the Victoria Memorial: The high ground on the circular Victoria Memorial provides the best overall view (come before 10:30 to get a place). From a high spot on the memorial, you have good (if more distant) views of the palace as well as the arriving and departing parades along The Mall and Spur Road. The actual Changing of the Guard in front of the palace is a nonevent. It is interesting, however, to see nearly every tourist in London gathered in one place at the same time.

Watch near St. James's Palace: If you don't feel like jostling for a view, stroll down to St. James's Palace and wait near the corner for a great photo-op. At about 11:45, the parade marches up The Mall to the palace and performs a smaller changing ceremony—with almost no crowds. Afterward, stroll through nearby St. James's Park.

Follow the Procession: You won't get the closest views, but you'll get something even better—the thrill of participating in the action. Start with the "Old Guard" mobilizing in the courtyard of St. James's Palace (10:30). Arrive early, and grab a spot just across the road (otherwise you'll be asked to move when the inspection begins). Just before they prepare to leave (at 10:43), march ahead of them down Marlborough Street to The Mall. Pause here to watch them parade past, band and all, on their way to the Buckingham Palace, then cut through the park and head to the Wellington Barracks—where the "New Guard" is getting ready to leave for Buckingham (10:57). March along with full military band and fresh guards from the barracks to the palace. At 11:00 the two guard groups meet in the courtyard, the band plays a few songs, and soldiers parade and finally exchange compliments before returning to Wellington Barracks and St. James's Palace (11:40). Use this time to snap a few photos of the guards—and the crowds—before making your way across the Mall to Clarence House (on Stable Yard Road), where you'll see the "New Guard" pass one last time on their way to St. James's Palace. On their way, the final piece of ceremony takes place—one member of the "Old Guard" and one member of the first-relief "New Guard" change places here.

Join a Tour: Local tour companies such as **Fun London Tours** more or less follow the self-guided route above but add in history and facts about the guards, bands, and royal family to their already entertaining march. These walks add color and good value to what can otherwise seem like a stressful mess of tourists (£17, Changing of the Guard tour starts at Piccadilly Circus at 9:40, must book online in advance, www.funlondontours.com).

North London

▲▲▲British Museum

Simply put, this is the greatest chronicle of civilization...anywhere. A visit here is like taking a long hike through *Encyclopedia Britannica* National Park. The vast British Museum wraps around its Great Court (the huge entrance hall), with the most popular sections filling the ground floor: Egyptian, Assyrian, and ancient Greek, with the famous frieze sculptures from the Parthenon in Athens. The museum's stately Reading Room—famous as the place where Karl Marx hung out while formulating his ideas on communism and writing *Das Kapital*—sometimes hosts special exhibits.

Cost and Hours: Free, £5 donation requested, special exhibits usually extra (and with timed ticket); daily 10:00-17:30, Fri until 20:30 (selected galleries only), least crowded late on weekday afternoons, especially Fri; free guided tours offered, multimedia guide-£6; Great Russell Street, Tube: Tottenham Court Road, ticket desk tel. 020/7323-8181, www.britishmuseum.org.

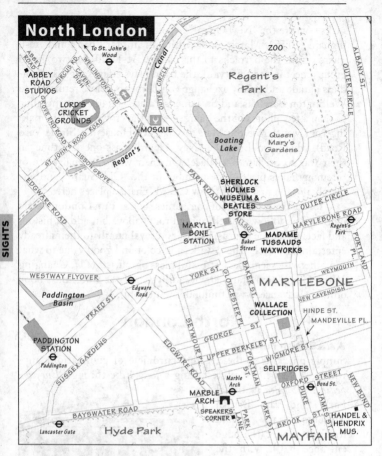

□ See the British Museum Tour chapter or ∩ download my free audio tour.

▲▲▲British Library

Here, in just two rooms, are the literary treasures of Western civilization, from early Bibles to Shakespeare's *Hamlet* to Lewis Carroll's *Alice's Adventures in Wonderland* to the *Magna Carta*. You'll see the Lindisfarne Gospels transcribed on an illuminated manuscript, Beatles lyrics scrawled on the back of a greeting card, and Leonardo da Vinci's genius sketched into his notebooks. The British Empire built its greatest monuments out of paper; it's through literature that England made her most lasting and significant contribution to civilization and the arts.

Cost and Hours: Free, £5 suggested donation, admission charged for special exhibits; Mon-Fri 9:30-18:00, Tue-Thu until 20:00, Sat 9:30-17:00, Sun 11:00-17:00; 96 Euston Road,

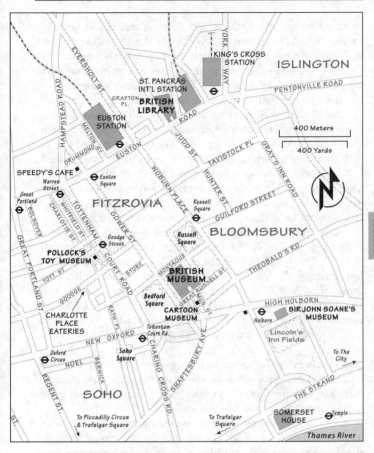

Tube: King's Cross St. Pancras or Euston, tel. 019/3754-6060 or 020/7412-7676, www.bl.uk.

📖 See the British Library Tour chapter or 🎧 download my free audio tour.

▲Wallace Collection

Sir Richard Wallace's fine collection of 17th-century Dutch Masters, 18th-century French Rococo, medieval armor, and as-

sorted aristocratic fancies fills the sumptuously furnished Hertford House on Manchester Square. From the rough and intimate Dutch lifescapes of Jan Steen to the pink-cheeked Rococo fantasies of François Boucher, a

wander through this little-visited mansion makes you nostalgic for the days of the empire. This collection would be a big deal in a midsized city, but here in London it gets pleasantly lost. Because this is a "closed collection" (nothing new is acquired and nothing permanent goes on loan), it feels more like visiting a classic English manor estate than a museum. It's thoroughly enjoyable.

Sir Richard Wallace's biography is as peculiar as the collection. Born the recognized–but-illegitimate son of Richard Seymour-Conway, 4th Marquess of Hertford, Wallace was denied the ancestral title but inherited the family collection at his father's death, became a respected philanthropist, and was eventually knighted by Queen Victoria. Upon his own death his widow bestowed the collection to the people of England under the clever condition that it retain the name Wallace, and not the name of his father.

Cost and Hours: Free, £5 suggested donation, daily 10:00-17:00, audioguide-£4; free guided tours or lectures almost daily at 11:30, 13:00, and 14:30—call or check online to confirm times; just north of Oxford Street on Manchester Square, Tube: Bond Street, tel. 020/7563-9500, www.wallacecollection.org.

Eating: The museum's light-filled atrium contains a **$$$** restaurant serving reasonably priced afternoon tea (£6.50 cream tea, £18.50 English tea, tea served 14:30-16:30, open similar hours as museum).

Visiting the Museum: The manageable collection is displayed on three floors—not much in the basement; fine arts, medieval treasures, and armor on the ground floor; and an even finer painting collection on the top floor.

As you enter the ground floor, on the right you'll find drawing rooms filled with medieval relics, and to the left (through the gift shop) are the collections of Oriental and European armor—one of the finest such collections in Britain. Then head up the red-carpeted grand staircase to the upper floor, packed with paintings.

The Oval Drawing Room is busy with Boucher and Fragonard—pink, giddy, and Rococo. A highlight is the small but symbolism-packed Rococo masterpiece *The Swing* (1767), by Jean-Honoré Fragonard. The woman is being pulled on the swing by her husband. He's on the right, hidden in shadows, literally "in the dark"—unaware that his wife is having an affair with the man hiding in the bushes on the left. The rascal holds his arm erect as he peeps up this swinging lady's skirt and watches her shoe fly off, symbolizing sexual abandon.

The Great Gallery contains paintings by the big names of the 17th century: Rembrandt, Rubens, Velázquez, Titian, Van Dyck, Murillo, and Hals. One of the museum's best-known paintings is *The Laughing Cavalier* (1624) by Frans Hals (see photo). With his hat perched at a jaunty angle, the man smirks enigmatically with unhappy eyes...more of a polite chuckle or a bemused snort.

The Boudoir Cabinet is a tiny room that glitters with exquisite bits of 18th-century French luxury: jeweled snuff boxes, miniatures (a sign of friendship or political allegiance), and spanky pornography for the upper class.

The West Gallery takes you on a trip to 18th-century Venice. It's filled with romantically staged scenes painted by Canaletto and Guardi—purchased as souvenirs by aristocrats on the Grand Tour before the age of postcards. The East Gallery is interesting for its small-scale 17th-century Dutch paintings by Jan Steen and others who could paint quiet, intimate, and rowdy slices of life—usually conveying a folk moral rather than a religious lesson.

Then head back down to the main floor and go out the door behind the staircase, into the building's pretty glassed-in atrium.

SIGHTS

▲Madame Tussauds Waxworks

This waxtravaganza is gimmicky, crass, and crazily expensive, but dang fun...a hit with the kind of tourists who skip the British Museum. The original Madame Tussaud did wax casts of heads lopped off during the French Revolution (such as Marie-Antoinette's). She took her show on the road and ended up in London in 1835. These days, they've dumped anything really historical (except for what they claim is the blade that beheaded Marie-Antoinette) because "there's no money in it and we're a business." Now it's all about hanging with the royals, singing with Lady Gaga, and partying

with Benedict Cumberbatch, the Beckhams, and the Beatles. The gallery, which sprawls through several rooms of a huge building, is one giant photo-op—the whole point is jockeying for position to snap the best picture of your travel buddy with a famous "person." It's extremely crowded and chaotic, as everyone clamors to press the wax with their heroes, while dodging tourist-trinket kiosks and photographers standing by to overcharge you for a print. These wax sculptures are eerily realistic—count how many times you say "excuse me" after bumping into a dummy.

Cost: £35, kids-£30 (free for kids under 5), up to 25 percent discount and shorter lines if you buy tickets in advance on their website; combo-deal with the London Eye, Shrek's Adventure ride, or Sea Life aquarium.

Hours: Roughly July-Aug and school holidays daily 8:30-18:00, Sept-June Mon-Fri 10:00-16:00, Sat-Sun 9:00-17:00, these are last entry times—it stays open roughly two hours later; check website for the latest times as hours vary widely depending on season, Marylebone Road, Tube: Baker Street, tel. 0871-894-3000, www.madametussauds.com.

Crowd-Beating Tips: This popular attraction can be swamped. The ticket-buying line can be an hour or more (believe the posted signs about the wait). Once inside, there can be more waits for some popular exhibits. To avoid the ticket line, buy a Priority Entrance ticket and reserve a time slot at least a day in advance. Or, purchase a Fast Track ticket in advance (available from souvenir stands and shops or at the TI), which gives you access to a dedicated entrance with shorter lines. The place is less crowded (for both buying tickets at the door and for simply enjoying the place) if you arrive after 15:00.

Visiting the Waxworks: First you'll join the paparazzi on the red carpet with A-list stars, then you'll head through several themed sections, featuring Hollywood stars new and old, popular movie characters, sports heroes (including some unfamiliar-to-Americans cricket players and footballers), the royal family (pose with the Queen, Will, and Kate...or settle for Charles and Camilla), scientists, artists, writers, musicians, and world leaders.

Downstairs are exhibits that sometimes have lines—pick and choose if it's worth the wait. A small exhibit explains the casting process and the history of Madame Tussaud and her waxy army. Then you'll board a Disney-type people-mover and cruise through a kid-pleasing "Spirit of London" once-over-very-light history of this city. Finally, you reach a nine-minute-long Marvel Super Heroes "4-D" show—a 3-D movie heightened by wind, "back ticklers," and other special effects. It's totally silly, requires a wait in line, and leaves the crowd buzzing with sensory overload—a fitting finale to the entire Waxworks experience.

▲Sir John Soane's Museum

Architects love this quirky place, as do fans of interior decor, eclectic knickknacks, and Back Door sights. Tour this furnished home on a bird-chirping square and see 19th-century chairs, lamps, wood-paneled nooks and crannies, sculptures, and stained-glass skylights just as they were when the owner lived here. As professor of architecture at the Royal Academy, Soane created his home to be a place of learning, cramming it floor to ceiling with ancient relics, curios, and famous paintings, including several excellent

Canalettos and Hogarth's series on *The Rake's Progress* (which is hidden behind a panel in the Picture Room and opened randomly at the museum's discretion, usually twice an hour). Soane even purchased the Egyptian sarcophagus of King Seti I (Ramesses II's father, on display in the basement) after the British Museum turned it down—at the time, they couldn't afford the £2,000 sticker price.

In 1833, just before his death, Soane established his house as a museum, stipulating that it be kept as nearly as possible in the state he left it. If he visited today, he'd be entirely satisfied by the diligence with which the staff safeguards his treasures. You'll leave wishing you'd known the man.

Cost and Hours: Free, but donations much appreciated; Tue-Sat 10:00-17:00, open and candlelit the first Tue of the month 18:00-21:00 (limited to 250 people), closed Sun-Mon; often long entry lines (especially Sat), knowledgeable volunteers in most rooms, guidebook-£5; £10 guided tour must be booked ahead online and runs Tue and Thu-Sat at 12:00; 13 Lincoln's Inn Fields, quarter-mile southeast of British Museum, Tube: Holborn, tel. 020/7405-2107, www.soane.org.

Cartoon Museum

This humble but interesting museum is located in the shadow of the British Museum. While its three rooms are filled with British cartoons unknown to most Americans, the satirical takeoffs on famous bigwigs and politicians—including Napoleon, Margaret Thatcher, the Queen, and Tony Blair—show the power of parody to deliver social commentary. Upstairs are panels of well-known comics that will interest only diehard fans.

Cost and Hours: £7, Tue-Sun 10:30-17:30, closed Mon, 35 Little Russell Street—go one block south of the British Museum on Museum Street and turn right, Tube: Tottenham Court Road, tel. 020/7580-8155, www.cartoonmuseum.org.

Pollock's Toy Museum

This rickety old house, with glass cases filled with toys and games lining its walls and halls, is a time-warp experience that brings back childhood memories to people who grew up without batteries or computer chips. It also gives a sense of the history of childhood itself, starting from when "childhood" as we know it now first came to be. Though the museum is small, you could spend a lot of time here, squinting at the fascinating toys and well-loved dolls that entertained the children of 19th- and early 20th-century England.

The included information is great. The story of Theodore Roosevelt refusing to shoot a bear cub while on a hunting trip was celebrated in 1902 cartoons, resulting in a new, huggable toy: the Teddy Bear. It was popular for good reason: It could be manufactured during World War I without rationed products; it coincided with the new belief that soft toys were good for a child's development; it was an acceptable "doll for boys"; and it was *the* toy children kept long after they'd grown up.

Cost and Hours: £6, kids-£3, Mon-Sat 10:00-17:00, closed Sun, 1 Scala Street, Tube: Goodge Street, tel. 020/7636-3452, www.pollockstoys.com. A fun retro toy shop is attached.

Handel & Hendrix in London

Coincidentally, two well-known musicians from different eras lived in these two neighboring flats. Touring the rooms, you'll see a few personal effects and period furniture, and learn about their different-yet-similar lives and music. Though the museum brings things to life, little of what's on display was actually owned by either Handel or Hendrix.

Cost and Hours: £10, Mon-Sat 11:00-18:00, closed Sun, in Mayfair in the West End at 25 Brook St, Tube: Bond Street, tel. 020/7495-1685, www.handelhendrix.org.

Visiting the Museum: In 1723, the 38-year-old German composer, George Frideric Handel, moved in and made this flat his home for the next 36 years. You'll see the room where he wrote "Messiah"—a 2.5-hour oratorio created in three weeks—and the kind of harpsichord he might have used. In the dressing room, Handel's servants would get him into his foppish clothes and long, white, and curly powdered wigs. Finally, there's the bedroom, decorated with a canopy bed. It was here that Handel entertained guests, indulged in rich food and drink, got fat, and ultimately died in 1759.

Two centuries later, another long-haired, foreign-born musician with a flair for outrageous fashions and unrestrained decadence, who'd first found fame in London, moved in. It was the summer of '68, and Jimi Hendrix, a rock guitarist from Seattle, unknowingly rented the flat next door to Handel's. He gigged at nearby clubs and afterward invited fellow musicians (George Harrison, Steppenwolf, the Bee Gees, and others) back to his pad. On display, you'll see Hendrix's album collection, including some by Handel. Jimi's bedroom is meticulously reconstructed with period artifacts. Imagine Jimi in his trademark floppy hat, kicking back on the psychedelic bed, cushioned by surrealistic pillows, cradling his guitar, sipping wine, and penning the lyrics to "Voodoo Child."

Beatles Sights

London's city center is surprisingly devoid of sights associated with the famous '60s rock band. To see much of anything, consider taking a guided walk (see page 33).

For a photo op, go to **Abbey Road** and walk the famous crosswalk pictured on the *Abbey Road* album cover (Tube: St. John's Wood, get information and buy Beatles memorabilia at the small kiosk in the station). From the Tube station, it's a five-minute walk west down Grove End Road to the intersection with Abbey Road. The Abbey Road recording studio is the low-key white building to the right of Abbey House (it's still a working studio, so you can't go inside). Ponder the graffiti on the low wall outside, and...imagine. To re-create the famous cover photo, shoot the crosswalk from the roundabout as you face north up Abbey Road. Shoes are optional.

Nearby is **Paul McCartney's current home** (7 Cavendish Avenue): Continue down Grove End Road, turn left on Circus Road, and then right on Cavendish. Please be discreet.

The **Beatles Store** is at 231 Baker Street (Tube: Baker Street). It's small—some Beatles-logo T-shirts, mugs, pins, and old vinyl like you might have in your closet—and has nothing of historic value (open eight days a week, 10:00-18:30, tel. 020/7935-4464, www.beatlesstorelondon.co.uk; another rock memorabilia store is across the street).

Sherlock Holmes Museum

A few doors down from the Beatles Store, this meticulous recreation of the (fictional) apartment of the (fictional) detective sits at the (real) address of 221b Baker Street. The first-floor replica (so to

speak) of Sherlock's study delights fans with the opportunity to play Holmes and Watson while sitting in authentic 18th-century chairs. The second and third floors offer fine exhibits on daily Victorian life, showing off furniture, clothes, pipes, paintings, and chamber pots; in other rooms, models are posed to enact key scenes from Sir Arthur Conan Doyle's famous books.

Cost and Hours: £15, daily 9:30-18:00, expect to wait 15 minutes or more—up to 2 hours in peak season; buy tickets inside the gift shop first, then get in line outside the museum (if you're traveling with a partner, send one person in to buy tickets while the other waits in the entrance line); large gift shop for Holmes connoisseurs, including souvenirs from the BBC-TV series; Tube: Baker Street, tel. 020/7935-8866, www.sherlock-holmes.co.uk.

Nearby: Fans of BBC-TV's "Sherlock" series starring Benedict Cumberbatch—which this museum doesn't cover—may want to grab a bite or snap a photo at Speedy's Café, the filming location for the show's 221b exterior (at 187 North Gower Street, an easy Tube ride to Euston Square).

The City

When Londoners say "The City," they mean the one-square-mile business center in East London that 2,000 years ago was Roman Londinium. The outline of the Roman city walls can still be seen in the arc of roads from Blackfriars Bridge to Tower Bridge. Within The City are 23 churches designed by Sir Christopher Wren, mostly just ornamentation around St. Paul's Cathedral. Today, while home to only 10,000 residents, The City thrives with around 400,000 office workers coming and going daily. It's a fascinating district to wander on weekdays, but since almost nobody actually lives there, it's dull in the evening and on Saturday and Sunday.

📖 Historic London: The City Walk chapter and 🎧 these sights are linked by my free audio tour.

ST. PAUL'S CATHEDRAL AND NEARBY
▲▲▲St. Paul's Cathedral
Wren's most famous church is the great St. Paul's, its elaborate interior capped by a 365-foot dome. Since World War II, St. Paul's has been Britain's symbol of resilience. Despite 57 nights of bombing, the Nazis failed to destroy the cathedral, thanks to St. Paul's volunteer fire watchmen, who stayed on the dome. Today you can climb the dome for a great city view. The crypt (included with admission) is a world of historic bones and memorials, including Admiral Nelson's tomb and interesting cathedral models.

Cost and Hours: £18, £16 if purchased in advance on the website, includes church entry, dome climb, crypt, tour, and audio/videoguide; Mon-Sat 8:30-16:30 (dome opens at 9:30), closed Sun except for worship; book ahead online to skip the line, 15-30-minute wait at busy times, guided tours offered; Tube: St. Paul's, recorded info tel. 020/7246-8348, reception tel. 020/7246-8350, www.stpauls.co.uk.

Music: Evensong services are free (Sun 15:15, Tue-Sat 17:00, not on Mon), but nonpaying visitors are not allowed to linger afterward (see page 261 for details).

Cheap Trick: To get a free cityscape view nearly as good as the expensive view from St. Paul's dome, head for the rooftop terrace at One New Change shopping mall, just behind the church. To reach it, walk through the churchyard (to the left of the church as you face it), cross the busy street, turn right and head toward One New Change. Behind the escalators, you'll find glass elevators where you can ride to the top floor for a fine view of St Paul's and of London.

📖 See the St. Paul's Cathedral Tour chapter or 🎧 download my free audio tour.

SIGHTS

▲Old Bailey

To view the British legal system in action—lawyers in little blond wigs speaking legalese with an upper-crust accent—spend a few minutes in the visitors' gallery at the Old Bailey courthouse, called the "Central Criminal Court." Don't enter under the dome; continue up the block about halfway to the modern part of the building—the entry is at Warwick Passage.

Cost and Hours: Free, generally Mon-Fri 10:00-13:00 & 14:00-17:00 depending on caseload, last entry at 12:40 and 15:40 but often closes an hour or so earlier, closed Sat-Sun, fewer cases in Aug; no kids under 14; 2 blocks northwest of St. Paul's on Old Bailey Street (down a tunnel called Warwick Passage, follow signs to public entrance), Tube: St. Paul's, tel. 020/7248-3277 www.cityoflondon.gov.uk.

Bag Check: Old Bailey has a strictly enforced policy of no bags, mobile phones, cameras, computers, or food. Small purses are OK (but no phones or cameras inside). You can check bags at many nearby businesses, including the Capable Travel agency just down the street at 4 Old Bailey (£5/bag and £1/phone or camera).

The Guildhall

Hiding out in The City, the Guildhall offers visitors a grand medieval hall and a delightful painting gallery for free. This area has been a gathering place since ancient Roman times (on the square, note the circular outline of the Roman amphitheater that once stood here). The meeting spot for guilds in medieval times, it still hosts about 100 professional associations today. The venerable hall, which survived both the Great Fire of 1666 and bombing in World War II, dates from the 15th century and is a rare bit of civil architecture surviving from the Middle Ages.

Adjoining the old hall is the Guildhall Art Gallery, giving

SIGHTS

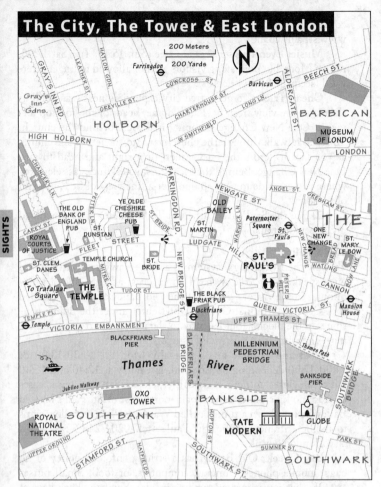

The City, The Tower & East London

insight into old London society with mostly Victorian paintings of numerous London scenes. One of the best Victorian collections in London, it's well-described and organized into themes (home, beauty, faith, leisure, work, love, and imagination), and includes dreamy Pre-Raphaelite works. In the basement is a well-presented exhibit on a Roman amphitheater discovered during a building project in 1988.

Cost and Hours: Free, Mon-Sat 10:00-17:00, Sun 12:00-16:00, 6 blocks northeast of St. Paul's on Gresham Street, Tube: St. Paul's or Bank, tel. 020/7332-3404, www.guildhall.cityoflondon.gov.uk.

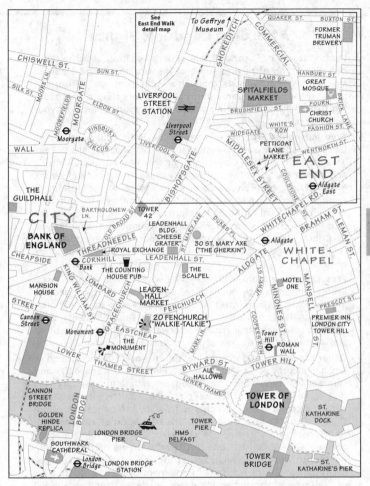

▲Museum of London

This museum tells the fascinating story of London, taking you on a walk from its pre-Roman beginnings to the present. It features London's distinguished citizens through history—from Neanderthals, to Romans, to Elizabethans, to Victorians, to Mods, to today. The displays are chronological, spacious, and informative without being overwhelming. Scale models and costumes help you visualize everyday life in the city at different periods. There are enough whiz-bang multimedia displays (including the Plague and the Great Fire)

Affording London's Sights

London is one of Europe's most expensive cities, with the dubious distinction of having some of the world's steepest admission prices. But with its many free museums and affordable plays, this cosmopolitan, cultured city offers days of sightseeing thrills without requiring you to pinch your pennies (or your pounds).

Free Museums: Free sights include the British Museum, British Library, National Gallery, National Portrait Gallery, Tate Britain, Tate Modern, Wallace Collection, Imperial War Museum, Victoria and Albert Museum, Natural History Museum, Science Museum, National Army Museum, Sir John Soane's Museum, the Museum of London, the Geffrye Museum, the Guildhall, and on the outskirts of town, the Royal Air Force Museum London. About half of these museums request a donation of a few pounds, but whether you contribute is up to you. If you feel like supporting these museums, renting audioguides, using their café, and buying a few souvenirs all help.

Free Churches: Smaller churches let worshippers (and tourists) in free, although they may ask for a donation. The big sightseeing churches—Westminster Abbey and St. Paul's—charge higher admission fees, but offer free evensong services nearly daily (though you can't stick around afterward to sightsee). Westminster Abbey also offers free organ recitals most Sundays.

Other Freebies: London has plenty of free performances, such as lunch concerts at St. Martin-in-the-Fields (see page 453) and summertime movies at The Scoop amphitheater near City Hall (see page 457). For other freebies, check out www.whatsfreeinlondon.co.uk. There's no charge to enjoy the pageantry of the Changing of the Guard, rants at Speakers' Corner in Hyde Park (on Sun afternoon), displays at Harrods, the people-watching scene at Covent Garden, and the colorful streets of the East End. It's free to view the legal action at the Old Bailey and the legislature at work in the Houses of Parliament. You can get into a bit of the Tower of London and Windsor Castle by attending Sunday services in each place's chapel (chapel access only). And, Greenwich is an inexpensive outing. Many of its sights are free, and the DLR journey is cheap.

Good-Value Tours: The London Walks tours with professional guides (£10) are one of the best deals going. (Note that the guides for the "free" walking tours are unpaid by their companies,

to spice up otherwise humdrum artifacts. This regular stop for the local school kids gives the best overview of London history in town.

Cost and Hours: Free, daily 10:00–18:00, last entry one hour before closing, see the day's events board for special talks and tours, café, baggage lockers, 150 London Wall at Aldersgate Street, Tube:

and they expect tips—I'd pay up front for an expertly guided tour instead.) Hop-on, hop-off big-bus tours, while expensive (around £30), provide a great overview and include free boat tours as well as city walks. (Or, for the price of a transit ticket, you could get similar views from the top of a double-decker public bus.) A one-hour Thames ride to Greenwich costs about £12 one-way, but most boats come with entertaining commentary. A three-hour bicycle tour is about £25.

Pricey...but Worth It? Big-ticket sights worth their hefty admission fees (£15-30) are the Tower of London, Kew Gardens, Shakespeare's Globe, and the Churchill War Rooms. The London Eye has become a London must-see—but you may feel differently when you see the prices (£25). St. Paul's Cathedral (£18) becomes more worthwhile if you climb the dome for the stunning view. While Hampton Court Palace is expensive (£23), it is well-presented and a reasonable value if you have an interest in royal history. The Queen charges royally for a peek inside Buckingham Palace (£23, open Aug-Sept only) and her fine art gallery and carriage museum (adjacent to the palace, £10 each). Madame Tussauds Waxworks is pricey but still hard for many to resist (£35, see page 65 for info on discounts). Harry Potter fans gladly pay the Hagrid-sized £39 fee to see the sets and props at the Warner Bros. Studio Tour (but those who wouldn't know a wizard from a Muggle needn't bother).

Totally Pants (Brit-speak for Not Worth It): The London Dungeon, at £28, is gimmicky, overpriced, and a terrible value...despite the long line. The cost of the wallet-bleeding ride to the top of The Shard—£31—is even more breathtaking than the view from Western Europe's tallest skyscraper.

Theater: Compared with Broadway's prices, London's theater can be a bargain. Seek out the freestanding TKTS booth at Leicester Square to get discounts from 25 to 50 percent on good seats (and full-price tickets to the hottest shows with no service charges; see page 447). Buying directly at the theater box office can score you a great deal on same-day tickets, and even the most popular shows generally have some seats under £20 (possibly with obstructed views)—ask. A £5 "groundling" ticket for a play at Shakespeare's Globe is the best theater deal in town (see page 452). Tickets to the Open Air Theatre at north London's Regent's Park start at £25 (see page 453).

Barbican or St. Paul's plus a 5-minute walk, tel. 020/7001-9844, www.museumoflondon.org.uk.

Visiting the Museum: The first part of the tour zips quickly through a half-million years, when Britain morphed from peninsula to island, Neanderthals speared mammoths, and Stone Age humans huddled in crude huts on the South Bank of the Thames.

In 54 B.C., Julius Caesar invaded, and the Romans built "Londinium" on the north bank. The settlement quickly became the hub of Britain and a river-trade town, complete with arenas, forums, baths, a bridge across the Thames, and a **city wall.** That wall—arcing from the present Tower of London to St. Paul's—defined the city's boundaries for the next 1,500 years. The Museum of London sits on the northwest perimeter of the city wall—look out the windows to see a crumbling remnant along the street, now called "London Wall."

When Rome could no longer defend the city (A.D. 410), it fell to the Saxons (becoming "Lundenburg") and, later, the Normans (in 1066), who built the Tower of London. Medieval London was devastated by the Black Death plague of 1348. As the city recovered and grew even bigger, it became clear to wannabe kings that whoever controlled London controlled Britain.

Downstairs, the next millennium of London unfolds. When Queen Elizabeth I brought peace to the land, London thrived as a capital of theaters (the Globe and Rose), arts, and ideas. Then, just when things were going so well, the Great Fire of 1666 destroyed the city, leaving London a blank slate.

Take a stroll through a re-created Georgian **"pleasure garden"** to experience a day in the life of 18th-century high society. The **"Victorian walk"** re-creates a London street and life in the world's greatest city. The interesting costume section helps humanize all the history.

Two world wars and the car changed 20th-century London into a concrete jungle. But it remained a cultural capital of elegance (see an Art Deco elevator from Selfridge's) and a global trendsetter (Beatles-era memorabilia). In the last room, you'll see a touching memorial to the victims of the July 7, 2005 terrorist bombings.

The Monument

Wren's 202-foot-tall tribute to London's 1666 Great Fire was recently restored. Climb the 311 steps inside the column for a monumental view of The City.

Cost and Hours: £4.50, £11 combo-ticket with Tower Bridge, cash only, daily 9:30-18:00, until 17:30 Oct-March, junction of Monument Street and Fish Street Hill, Tube: Monument, tel. 020/7626-2717, www.themonument.info.

TOWER OF LONDON AND NEARBY
▲▲▲Tower of London

The Tower has served as a castle in wartime, a king's residence in peacetime, and, most notoriously, as the prison and execution site of rebels. You can see the crown jewels, take a witty Beefeater tour, and ponder the executioner's block that dispensed with troublesome heirs to the throne and a couple of Henry VIII's wives.

Note that lines can be long; see page 274 for tips on getting in quicker. After your visit, consider taking the boat to Greenwich from here (see cruise info on page 36).

Cost and Hours: £28, family-£70, save time and money with a voucher purchased in advance—see page 274; Tue-Sat 9:00-17:30, Sun-Mon 10:00-17:30; Nov-Feb closes one hour earlier; free Beefeater tours available, skippable audioguide-£4, Tube: Tower Hill, tel. 0844-482-7788, www.hrp.org.uk.

📖 See the Tower of London Tour chapter.

Tower Bridge

The iconic Tower Bridge (often mistakenly called London Bridge) was built in 1894 to accommodate the growing East End. While fully modern and hydraulically powered, the drawbridge was designed with a retro Neo-Gothic look.

The bridge is most interesting when the drawbridge lifts to let ships pass, as it does a thousand times a year (best viewed from the Tower side of the Thames). For the bridge-lifting schedule, check the website or call.

You can tour the bridge at the **Tower Bridge Exhibition,** with a history display and a peek at the Victorian-era engine room that lifts the span. Included in your entrance is the chance to cross the bridge—138 feet above the road along a partially see-through glass walkway. As an exhibit, it's overpriced, though the adrenaline rush and spectacular city views from the walkway may help justify the cost.

Cost and Hours: £9, £11 combo-ticket with Monument, daily 10:00-18:00 in summer, 9:30-17:30 in winter, enter at northwest tower, Tube: Tower Hill, tel. 020/7403-3761, www.towerbridge.org.uk.

Nearby: The best remaining bit of London's **Roman Wall** is just north of the Tower (at the Tower Hill Tube station). The chic **St. Katharine Dock,** just east of Tower Bridge, has private yachts and mod shops. Across the bridge, on the South Bank, is the upscale Butlers Wharf area, as well as City Hall, museums, the Jubilee Walkway, and, towering overhead, the Shard. Or you can head north to Liverpool Street Station and follow my **"East End Walk."**

East London

Every great city needs an "East End"—the downwind-from-industry, poor workers' quarter where rents are cheap, immigrants with different religions and customs can find comfort in numbers, and the everyday people who power the economic engine of that city find a humble home.

London's East End has a long history as the city's poorer side of town—even in medieval times, this was the less desirable end, in part because it was downwind from the noxious hide-tanning district. London's east/west disparity was exacerbated in Victorian times, when the wind carried the pollution of a newly industrialized London. These days, there's a new energy in the East End, and it's well worth exploring.

▲East End Walk: Markets, Banglatown, and Jack the Ripper

This one-hour walk through a bit of the East End neighborhood is basically a big rectangle—from Liverpool Street Station to Brick Lane and back. We'll dip into several colorful markets: Spitalfields, Petticoat Lane, and Truman. We'll pass by several grim Jack-the-Ripper sights (fascinating history, though frankly there's not much to see today). We'll stroll through the curry-scented streets of "Banglatown," the Bangladeshi neighborhood. With a buffet of tempting eateries along or near our route, you could turn this walk into a progressive meal (for recommendations, see page 414). The walk works best on weekends, when the markets thrive (for more on these markets, see page 436).

This neighborhood is in transition—a battle zone between the 19th century and the 21st century. We'll see old brick buildings alongside glassy new offices, and trendy restaurants amid the clamor of new construction projects. The East End Preservation Society is working overtime to protect and preserve what it can of the old East End.

❍ **Self-Guided Walk:** Ride the Tube to the Liverpool Street stop, go upstairs to the train station, then exit to Bishopsgate Street. Liverpool Street Station essentially marks the boundary of The City—you have now entered the "East End."

• *Cross Bishopsgate Street, and turn left. Walk two blocks to the glassy, modern RBS building, then turn right on Brushfield Street. Head toward the steeple of Christ Church, but half a block or so before you get there, detour left (through some arcaded shops) into...*

Spitalfields Market: This lively, inviting, modern-feeling market hall boasts a combination of colorful restaurants, shops, and—on many days—market stalls selling upscale crafts, designer clothes, collectables, and vintage curiosities. Like so many markets,

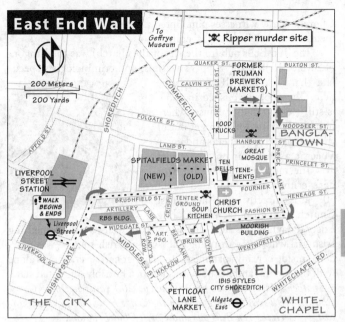

East End Walk

To Geffrye Museum

☒ Ripper murder site

N

200 Meters
200 Yards

QUAKER ST.   FORMER   BUXTON ST.
              TRUMAN
CALVIN ST.   BREWERY
              (MARKETS)

SHOREDITCH   COMMERCIAL   GREY EAGLE ST.   BRICK LANE

FOLGATE ST.   WOODSEER ST.
                FOOD   BANGLA-
ARFOLD ST.   TRUCKS   TOWN
              HANBURY ST.

LAMB ST.   GREAT   PRINCELET ST.
SPITALFIELDS MARKET   TEN   MOSQUE
                      BELLS TENE-
LIVERPOOL   (NEW)   (OLD)   MENTS   FOURNIER
STREET   HENEAGE ST.
STATION   CHRIST
WALK   BRUSHFIELD ST. CHURCH   FASHION ST.
BEGINS   TENTER
& ENDS   ARTILLERY GROUND
Liverpool RBS BLDG. LANE SOUP
Street   CRISPIN KITCHEN
                            MOORISH
WIDEGATE ST. ART   BUILDING
              PSG.   BELL LANE
LIVERPOOL ST. SANDY'S BRUNE TOYNBEE WENTWORTH ST.
BISHOPSGATE   ROW
              MIDDLESEX ST.
              HARROW   EAST END
THE CITY   PETTICOAT IBIS STYLES
              LANE   CITY SHOREDITCH WHITECHAPEL RD.
              MARKET   Aldgate
                       East   WHITE-
                                CHAPEL

it's liveliest on Sunday. That tradition dates back to when it was a Jewish market closed Saturday for the Sabbath.

· *Exit the market at the east end, where you'll find Christ Church.*

Christ Church: This stony church, with its towering 225-foot steeple, has a mysterious heritage. Many find occult symbol-

ism in its curious design (without a cross on top). The interior of the church dates to 1711. That's when Queen Anne decided to build a place for the "God-less thousands who had no place to worship"—meaning to give immigrants a proper Protestant place to worship. It's stripped-down design suited Protestant tastes: simple wood paneling and pure whitewashed walls and columns (the fine 19th-century windows were added during the "Romantic Age"). Above the altar is the coat of arms of the UK: the lion and unicorn and motto *Dieu et Mon Droit*—"God and my right." Downstairs in the crypt is a modern café (with clean WCs).

· *Christ Church was ground zero for London's most famous serial killer, Jack the Ripper.*

Jack the Ripper "Sights": In the autumn of 1888, several gruesome murders were committed within a few blocks of Christ

Church. Many witnesses pinpointed the time of the crimes by remembering the church bells' chimes.

The Ten Bells pub (to the left of the church) was the hangout of several of Jack the Ripper's victims, and criminologists speculate that Jack himself likely came here. The pub, established in 1753, is still a classic public house, where humble working folk can get out of their cramped apartments and enjoy a beer in a fancy living room setting.

The most heinous of the Ripper's crimes was committed about 50 yards directly opposite Christ Church (though no actual building exists today). It was here that Mary Jane Kelly—a 20-something Irish girl who loved drinking and singing Irish songs—was murdered inside her tiny apartment. The Ripper had several hours alone with the victim, and her body was left in a horribly mutilated state.

• *Another Ripper murder occurred about 200 yards north of Christ Church. We'll pass by there later in the walk. For now, start walking east, between the Ten Bells pub and Christ Church, down...*

Fournier Street: The street still looks much like it did in Jack's day: lined with old lantern-like lampposts and brick apartment

buildings. These are classic "tenements." Though the word "tenement" now carries a negative connotation, it originally described any urban apartment building. These were home to many Huguenots—French-Protestant religious refugees who settled here in the 1700s

as weavers. It's not hard to imagine how this gas-lit street would have looked on a foggy night in Jack the Ripper's time. Back then, most of London resembled this street—built of brick. The city's bricks were manufactured in factories right here in this gritty neighborhood, near the street called...Brick Lane.

• *Follow this line of former weaving houses to the end of the street, marked by the modern metal minaret of a mosque. You reach the intersection with Brick Lane, where you're suddenly immersed in...*

"Banglatown," Along Brick Lane: The neighborhood around Brick Lane has been dubbed "Banglatown" for its high concentration of Bangladeshi residents. The neighborhood mosque, Jamme Masjid, is housed in a classic old brick building topped with a modern minaret. This building has a history as dynamic as London itself: It was built as a French Huguenot chapel, became a Methodist chapel, was used as a Jewish synagogue, and was converted into a mosque in 1976.

Turn left and wander north down Brick Lane. It's a world of Indian restaurants and exotic food markets catering to locals. This stretch of road has been called "the curry capital of Europe." Neon signs advertise cheap specials, and awards hang in the windows proclaiming "best," "master," and "champion." Out front, pitchmen jockey for your business. The slightest hesitation on your part will result in an offer of a 20 percent

discount. This is a great place to sample "Ruby Murray"—Cockney rhyming slang for "curry" (see page 256). Just like the US has its mash-up of cuisines called "Tex-Mex," England has "Balti." This is "Indian" food adapted to suit English tastes. It's so popular here that chicken tikka masala has replaced fish-and-chips as the national dish.

• *Continue two blocks down Brick Lane until you reach the complex of brick buildings of the former...*

Truman Brewery: The brewery, established in 1666, now houses the Truman Markets (on weekends), as well as trendy shops, and a creative and colorful food hall. There's no specific "market" location, so browse around—the action spreads across several buildings and streets. There's an open-air courtyard (to reach it, turn left just past the brick sky bridge) with several funky food trucks surrounded by famous works of street art. A half-block farther north on Brick Lane, you'll find the original old brewery smokestack. This is the epicenter of a youthful, trendy scene with several lively pub/café/nightclubs.

• *Now turn around and backtrack (south) up Brick Lane. Turn right on Hanbury Street and find #29. Though the original building here was replaced by a modern structure, the buildings directly across the street at #28 are 19th century, and give you a feel of the times.*

29 Hanbury Street—Another Ripper Murder: This was where the murder took place that started Ripper-mania. On the

night of September 8, 1888, a 40-something flower seller and sometime-prostitute named Annie Chapman was murdered behind the tenement that once stood here. Her throat was slit and her body mutilated. The MO seemed curiously similar to another murder a week before, committed a half-mile from here. It was now clear that London had a crazed serial killer in its midst. The newspapers sensationalized the crime and dubbed the killer "Jack the Ripper." Scotland Yard was called in to examine #29 and interview witnesses—ushering in the era of forensic science and analytical detective work. In all, Jack the Ripper would kill five (and maybe as many as 10) women in a span of three months, most within the sound of the Christ Church bells. Jack was never caught.

• *Return to Brick Lane and continue backtracking up Brick Lane, passing Fournier Street (where we entered). Continue another block and turn right (west) on Fashion Street. We're on the home stretch, heading west toward Liverpool Street Station.*

More Industrial Age Ambience: Stroll down Fashion Street past a long century-old building with a fanciful Moorish (Islamic) design. It now houses a trendy fashion-design school.

Cross busy Commercial Street (there are crosswalks nearby), go a few more steps, and turn left on Toynbee Street. You'll pass a hair salon called "Jack the Clipper."  Turn right on Brune Street, where you'll see more old tenements (on the left) that are still used to house the neighborhood poor. On the right (at #9) is the former "Soup Kitchen for the Jewish Poor." Continue on, turning right onto Tenter Ground, the street where weavers once dried cloth "on tenterhooks," giving us the phrase that means "uneasy." Look up to see the iron racks still rigged to the building.

• *At the end of Tenter Ground, turn left and head toward the building with a* Women *sign. This was where poor women entered to start their shift at a Victorian-era workhouse. Continue straight ahead, entering the very narrow street called...*

Artillery Passage: Henry VIII (around 1500) used this as a practice zone for his artillery. By the 19th century, this narrow lane was typical of streets in this densely packed neighborhood of grimy-faced factory workers. Jack the Ripper films always use this characteristic street. These days, it's lined with trendy, atmospheric eateries.

At the intersection with Sandy's Row is a bollard—a big black metal stake in the pavement. This boundary marker alerts you that you are now officially leaving the East End and re-entering the City of London. Consider the juxtaposition: The City is the richest "One Square Mile" on earth. Its gleaming skyscrapers tower nearby, while far below, in the East End, people still scrummage for "pants, three for a tenner."

• *Our walk is over. From here, you could continue straight ahead to Liverpool Street Station. Or, consider a detour to visit...*

Petticoat Lane Market: To reach the market, turn left on Sandy's Row, then go three blocks (down Sandy's Row and then Middlesex Street) to Wentworth Street, which leads left into the market. One of the oldest markets in Britain, Petticoat Lane has been selling cheap stuff to poor working people for 400 years. It's fun daily and packed on Sunday; enticing food stalls line Goulston Street. To reach Liverpool Street Station, just follow Middlesex Street.

Back at Liverpool Street Station, take a moment to recall the events of July 7, 2005. At 8:45, a Tube train had just pulled out of the station when it was rocked by a terrorist bomb—the first of four to hit London that day. But the next day, Londoners were back on the Tube.

SIGHTS

▲Geffrye Museum

This low-key but well-organized museum—housed in an 18th-century almshouse—is located north of Liverpool Street Station. It's a strip of 11 rooms, each furnished as a living room from a different age and each very well-described. It's an intimate peek at the middle class as its comforts evolved from 1600 to 2000. In summer, explore the fragrant herb garden.

Cost and Hours: Free, £3 suggested donation, Tue-Sun 10:00-17:00, closed Mon, garden open April-Oct, 136 Kingsland Road, tel. 020/7739-9893, www.geffrye-museum.org.uk.

Getting There: Take the Tube to Liverpool Street, then ride the bus 10 minutes north (bus #149 or #242—leave station through Bishopsgate exit and head left a few steps to find stop; hop off at the Pearson Street stop, just after passing the brick museum on the right). Or take the East London line on the Overground to the Hoxton stop, which is right next to the museum (Tube tickets and Oyster cards also valid on Overground).

The South Bank

The South Bank of the Thames is a thriving arts and cultural center, tied together by the riverfront Jubilee Walkway. For fun lunch options in this area, consider one of the nearby street food markets (see page 438).

▲Jubilee Walkway

This riverside path is a popular pub-crawling pedestrian promenade that stretches all along the South Bank, offering grand views of the Houses of Parliament and St. Paul's. On a sunny day, this is the place to see Londoners out strolling. The Walkway hugs the river except just east of London Bridge, where it cuts inland for a couple of blocks. It has been expanded into a 60-mile "Greenway" circling the city, including the 2012 Olympics site.

▲▲London Eye

This giant Ferris wheel, towering above London opposite Big Ben, is one of the world's highest observational wheels and London's answer to the Eiffel Tower. Riding it is a memorable experience, even though London doesn't have much of a skyline, and the price is borderline outrageous. Whether you ride or not, the wheel is a sight to behold.

Designed like a giant bicycle wheel, it's a pan-European undertaking: British steel and Dutch engineering, with Czech, German, French, and Italian mechanical parts. It's also very "green," running extremely efficiently and virtually silently. Twenty-eight people ride in each of its 32 air-conditioned capsules (representing the boroughs of London) for the 30-minute rotation (you go around only once). From the top of this 443-foot-high wheel—the second-highest public viewpoint in the city—even Big Ben looks small. Built to celebrate the new millennium, the Eye has become a permanent fixture on the London skyline.

After buying your ticket inside, you'll be aggressively ushered into the *London Eye 4-D Experience,* a brief (four-minute) and engaging show combining a 3-D movie with wind and water effects. This bombastic ad for the attraction you already bought a ticket for, in some ways, is more exciting than riding the Eye itself. You can politely skip the show if you just want to get on the wheel, and you have the option of coming back after your ride to watch the movie.

Cost: £24.95, about 10 percent cheaper if bought online. Combo-tickets save money if you plan on visiting Madame Tussauds, Shrek's Adventure ride, or Sea Life aquarium. Buy tickets in advance at www.londoneye.com or try in person at the box office (in the corner of the County Hall building nearest the Eye), though day-of tickets are often sold out.

Hours: Daily June-Aug 10:00-20:30 or later, Sept-May generally 11:00-18:00, check website for latest schedule, these are last-ascent times, closed Dec 25 and a few days in Jan for maintenance, Tube: Waterloo or Westminster. Thames boats come and go from London Eye Pier at the foot of the wheel.

Crowd-Beating Tips: The London Eye is busiest between 11:00 and 17:00, especially on weekends year-round and every day in July and August. You may wait up to 30 minutes to buy your ticket, then another 30-45 minutes to board your capsule—it's best to prebook your ticket during these times. Print your advance ticket at home, retrieve it from an onsite ticket machine (bring your payment card and confirmation code), or stand in the "Ticket Collection" line. Even if you buy in advance, you may wait a bit to board the wheel. You can pay an extra £8 for a Fast Track ticket, but since you still may wait up to 30 minutes, it's probably not worth the expense.

By the Eye: The area next to the London Eye has developed a cotton-candy collection of kitschy, kid-friendly attractions. There's a game arcade, an aquarium, and the Shrek's Adventure amusement ride.

▲▲Imperial War Museum

This impressive museum covers the wars and conflicts of the 20th and 21st centuries—from World War I biplanes, to the rise of fascism, the Cold War, the Cuban Missile Crisis, the Troubles in Northern Ireland, the wars in Iraq and Afghanistan, and terrorism. Rather than glorify war, the museum encourages an understanding of the history of modern warfare and the wartime experience, including the effect it has on the everyday lives of people back home. The museum's coverage never neglects the human side of one of civilization's more uncivilized, persistent traits.

Allow plenty of time, as this powerful museum—with lots of artifacts and video clips—can be engrossing. The highlights are the new WWI galleries (renovated to commemorate the 100-year anniversary of that conflict), the WWII area, the "Secret War" section, and the Holocaust exhibit. War wonks love the place, as do general history buffs who enjoy patiently reading displays. For the rest, there are enough interactive experiences and multimedia exhibits and submarines for the kids to climb in to keep it interesting.

The museum (in a kid-friendly, inviting park with an equally inviting café) is housed in what had been the Royal Bethlam Hospital. Also known as "the Bedlam asylum," the place was so wild that it gave the world a new word for chaos. Back in Victorian times, locals—without reality shows and YouTube—paid admission to visit the asylum on weekends for entertainment.

Cost and Hours: Free, £5 suggested donation, special exhibits extra, daily 10:00-18:00, last entry one hour before closing, Tube: Lambeth North or Elephant and Castle; buses #3, #12, and #159 from Westminster area; tel. 020/7416-5000, www.iwm.org.uk.

Visiting the Museum: Start with the atrium to grasp the massive scale of warfare as you wander among and under notable battle machines, then head directly for the museum's latest pride

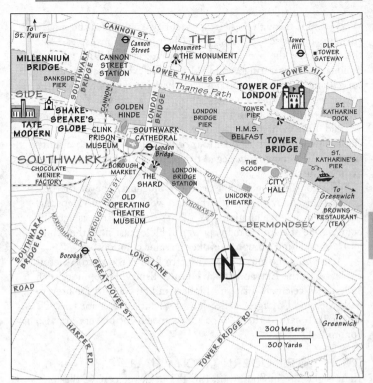

and joy: the recently renovated WWI galleries. Here firsthand accounts connect the blunt reality of a brutal war with the contributions, heartache, and efforts of a nation. Exhibits cover the various theaters and war at sea, as well as life on the home front.

As you escape unscathed, pause to ponder the irony of how different this museum would be if the war to end all wars had lived up to its name. Instead, the museum, much like history, builds on itself. Ascending to the first floor, you'll find the permanent **Turning Points** galleries progressing up to and through World War II and including sections explaining the Blitzkrieg and its effects (see an actual Nazi parachute bomb like the ones that devastated London).

For a deeper understanding of life during these decades, visit the **Family in Wartime** exhibit to see London through the eyes of an ordinary family.

The second floor houses the **Secret War** exhibit, which peeks into the intrigues of espionage in World

SIGHTS

Wars I and II through present-day security. You'll learn about MI5 (Britain's domestic spy corps), MI6 (their international spies—like the CIA), and the Special Operations Executive (SOE), who led espionage efforts during World War II. The exhibit features actual surveillance equipment and poses challenging questions about the role of secrecy in government.

The third floor houses various (and often rotating) temporary art and film exhibits speckled with military-themed works including (when not on its own tour of duty) **John Singer Sargent**'s *Gassed* (1919), showing besieged troops in World War I, and other giant canvases.

The fourth-floor section on the **Holocaust,** one of the best on the subject anywhere, tells the story with powerful videos, artifacts, and fine explanations. While it's not the same as actually being at one of Europe's many powerful Holocaust sites, the exhibits are compelling enough to evoke the same emotions.

Crowning the museum on the fifth floor is the Lord Ashcroft Gallery and the **Extraordinary Heroes** display. Here, more than 250 stories celebrate Britain's highest military award for bravery with the world's largest collection of Victoria Cross medals. Civilians who earned the George Cross medal for bravery are also honored.

FROM TATE MODERN TO CITY HALL

These sights are in Southwark (SUTH-uck), the core of the tourist's South Bank. Southwark was for centuries the place Londoners would go to escape the rules and decency of the city and let their hair down. Bearbaiting, brothels, rollicking pubs, and theater—you name the dream, and it could be fulfilled just across the Thames. A run-down warehouse district through the 20th century, it's been gentrified with classy restaurants, office parks, pedestrian promenades, major sights (such as the Tate Modern and Shakespeare's Globe), and a colorful collection of lesser sights. The area is easy on foot and a scenic—though circuitous—way to connect the Tower of London with St. Paul's.

📖 You'll find more information on these sights in the Bankside Walk chapter.

▲▲Tate Modern

Dedicated in the spring of 2000, the striking museum fills a derelict old power station across the river from St. Paul's—it opened the new century with art from the previous one. Its powerhouse collection includes Dalí, Picasso, Warhol, and much more. Of equal interest are the many temporary exhibits featuring more current, cutting-edge art and the new Blavatnik Building (a.k.a. the Switch House). Each year, the main hall features a different monumental installation by a prominent artist.

Cost and Hours: Free, £4 donation appreciated, fee for special exhibits; open daily 10:00-18:00, Fri-Sat until 22:00, last entry to special exhibits 45 minutes before closing, especially crowded on weekend days (crowds thin out Fri and Sat evenings); free guided tours available, multimedia guide-£4.75, view restaurant on top floor, across the Millennium Bridge from St. Paul's; Tube: Southwark, London Bridge, St. Paul's, Mansion House, or Blackfriars plus a 10-15-minute walk; or connect by Tate Boat museum ferry from Tate Britain—see page 39; tel. 020/7887-8888, www.tate.org.uk.

◻ See the Tate Modern Tour chapter.

SIGHTS

▲Millennium Bridge

The pedestrian bridge links St. Paul's Cathedral and the Tate Modern across the Thames. This is London's first new bridge in a century. When it opened, the $25 million bridge wiggled when people walked on it, so it promptly closed for repairs; 20 months and $8 million later, it reopened. Nicknamed the "blade of light" for its sleek minimalist design (370 yards long, four yards wide, stainless steel with teak planks), its clever aerodynamic handrails deflect wind over the heads of pedestrians.

▲▲Shakespeare's Globe

This replica of the original Globe Theatre was built, half-timbered and thatched, as it was in Shakespeare's time. (This is the first

thatched roof constructed in London since they were outlawed after the Great Fire of 1666.) The Globe originally accommodated 2,200 seated and another 1,000 standing. Today, slightly smaller and leaving space for reasonable aisles, the theater holds 800 seated and 600 groundlings.

Its promoters brag that the theater melds "the three A's"—actors, audience, and architecture—with each contributing to the play. The working theater hosts authentic performances of Shakespeare's plays with actors in period costumes, modern interpretations of his works, and some works by other playwrights.

The Globe complex has four parts: the Globe theater itself, the box office, a museum (called the Exhibition), and the Sam Wanamaker Playhouse (an indoor Jacobean theater around back).

London's Best Views

Though London is a height-challenged city, you can get lofty perspectives on it from several high-flying places. For some viewpoints, you need to pay admission, and at the bars or restaurants, you'll need to buy a drink; the only truly free spots are Primrose Hill, the rooftop terrace of One New Change shopping mall (behind St. Paul's Cathedral), the Sky Garden at 20 Fenchurch, and the viewpoint in front of Greenwich's Royal Observatory.

London Eye: Ride the giant Ferris wheel for stunning London views. See page 84.

St. Paul's Dome: You'll earn a striking, unobstructed view by climbing hundreds of steps to the cramped balcony of the church's cupola. See the St. Paul's Cathedral Tour chapter.

One New Change Rooftop Terrace: Get fine, free views of St. Paul's Cathedral and surroundings—nearly as good as those from St. Paul's Dome—from the rooftop terrace of the One New Change shopping mall just behind and east of the church. See page 70.

Tate Modern: Take in a classic vista across the Thames from the restaurant/bar on the museum's sixth level and from the new Blavatnik Building (a.k.a. the Switch House). See page 304.

20 Fenchurch (a.k.a. "The Walkie-Talkie"): Get 360-degree views of London from the mostly enclosed Sky Garden, complete with a thoughtfully planned urban garden, bar, restaurants, and lots of locals. It's free to access but you'll need to make reservations in advance and bring photo ID (Mon-Fri 10:00-18:00, Sat-Sun 11:00-21:00, 20 Fenchurch Street, Tube: Monument, www.skygarden.london). If you can't get a reservation, try arriving before 10:00 (or 11:00 on weekends) and ask to go up. Once in, you can stay as long as you like.

National Portrait Gallery: A mod top-floor restaurant peers over Trafalgar Square and the Westminster neighborhood. See the

The Playhouse, which hosts performances through the winter, is horseshoe-shaped, intimate (seating fewer than 350), and sometimes uses authentic candle-lighting for period performances. The repertoire focuses less on Shakespeare and more on the work of his contemporaries (Jonson, Marlow, Fletcher), as well as concerts. (For details on attending a performance, see page 452.)

Cost: £16 for adults, £9 for kids 5-15, free for kids 5 and under, family ticket available; ticket includes Exhibition, audioguide, and 40-minute tour of the Globe; when theater is in use, you can tour the Exhibition only for £6.

Hours: The complex is open daily 9:00-17:30. Tours start every 30 minutes; during Globe theater season (late April-mid-Oct), last tour Mon at 17:00, Tue-Sat at 12:30, Sun at 11:30—it's safest to arrive for a tour before noon; located on the South Bank

National Portrait Gallery Tour chapter.

Waterstones Bookstore: Its hip, low-key, top-floor café/bar has reasonable prices and sweeping views of the London Eye, Big Ben, and the Houses of Parliament (see page 17, on Sun bar closes one hour before bookstore, www.5thview.co.uk).

OXO Tower: Perched high over the Thames River, the building's upscale restaurant/bar boasts views over London and St. Paul's, with al fresco dining in good weather (Barge House Street, Tube: Blackfriars or Southwark, tel. 020/7803-3888, www.harveynichols.com/restaurants/oxo-tower-london).

London Hilton, Park Lane: You'll spot Buckingham Palace, Hyde Park, and the London Eye from Galvin at Windows, a 28th-floor restaurant/bar in an otherwise nondescript hotel (22 Park Lane, Tube: Hyde Park Corner, tel. 020/7208-4021, www.galvinatwindows.com).

The Shard: The observation decks that cap this 1,020-foot-tall skyscraper offer London's most commanding views, but at an outrageously high price. See page 94.

Primrose Hill: For dramatic 360-degree city views, head to the huge grassy expanse at the summit of Primrose Hill, just north of Regent's Park (off Prince Albert Road, Tube: Chalk Farm or Camden Town, www.royalparks.org.uk/parks/the-regents-park).

The Thames River: Various companies run boat trips on the Thames, offering a unique vantage point and unobstructed, ever-changing views of great landmarks (see page 36).

Royal Observatory Greenwich: Enjoy sweeping views of Greenwich's grand buildings in the foreground, the Docklands' skyscrapers in the middle ground, and The City and central London in the distance.

over the Millennium Bridge from St. Paul's, Tube: Mansion House or London Bridge plus a 10-minute walk; tel. 020/7902-1400, box office tel. 020/7401-9919, www.shakespearesglobe.com.

Visiting the Globe: You browse on your own in the **Exhibition** (with the included audioguide) through displays of Elizabethan-era costumes and makeup, music, script-printing, and special effects (the displays change). There are early folios and objects that were dug up on site. Videos and scale models help put Shakespearean theater within the context of the times. (The Globe opened in 1599, eleven years after England mastered the seas by defeating the Spanish Armada. The debut play was Shakespeare's *Julius Caesar*.) You'll also learn how they built the replica in modern times, using Elizabethan materials and techniques. Take advantage of the touch screens to delve into specific topics.

SIGHTS

Crossing the Thames on Foot

You can cross the Thames on any of the bridges that carry car traffic over the river, but London's pedestrian bridges are more fun. The **Millennium Bridge** (see photo) connects the sedate St. Paul's Cathedral with the great Tate Modern. The **Golden Jubilee Bridge,** well-lit and with a sleek, futuristic look, links bustling Trafalgar Square on the North Bank with the London Eye and Waterloo Station on the South Bank. Work on a third pedestrian bridge

connecting Temple Station to the South Bank is under way. By the end of 2018, the new **Garden Bridge** should offer a park-like crossing midway between the two existing pedestrian bridges.

You must **tour the theater** at the time stamped on your ticket, but you can come back to the Exhibition museum afterward. A guide (usually an actor) leads you into the theater to see the stage and the various seating areas for the different classes of people. You take a seat and learn how the new Globe is similar to the old Globe (open-air performances, standing-room by the stage, no curtain) and how it's different (female actors today, lights for night performances, concrete floor). It's not a backstage tour—you don't see dressing rooms or costume shops or sit in on rehearsals—but the guides are energetic, theatrical, and knowledgeable, bringing the Elizabethan period to life.

Eating: The **$$$$ Swan at the Globe** café offers a sit-down restaurant (for lunch and dinner, reservations recommended, tel. 020/7928-9444), a drinks-and-plates bar, and a sandwich-and-coffee cart (Mon-Fri 8:00-closing, depends on performance times, Sat-Sun from 10:00).

The Clink Prison Museum

Proudly the "original clink," this was, until 1780, where law-abiding citizens threw Southwark troublemakers. Today, it's a low-tech torture museum filling grotty old rooms with papier-mâché gore. There are storyboards about those unfortunate enough to be thrown in the Clink, but little that seriously deals with the fascinating problem of law and order in Southwark, where 18th-century Londoners went for a good time.

Cost and Hours: Overpriced at £7.50 for adults, £5.50 for kids 15 and under, family ticket available; July-Sept daily 10:00-21:00; Oct-June Mon-Fri 10:00-18:00, Sat-Sun until 19:30; 1 Clink Street, Tube: London Bridge, tel. 020/7403-0900, www.clink.co.uk.

Golden Hinde Replica

This full-size replica of the 16th-century warship, in which Sir Francis Drake circumnavigated the globe from 1577 to 1580, may be closed during your visit—call ahead. Commanding the original ship (now long gone), Drake earned his reputation as history's most successful pirate. This replica, however, has logged more than 100,000 miles, including a voyage around the world. While the ship is fun to see, its interior is not worth touring.

Cost and Hours: £6, daily 10:00-17:30, Tube: London Bridge, ticket office just up Pickfords Wharf from the ship, tel. 020/7403-0123, www.goldenhinde.com.

▲Southwark Cathedral

While made a cathedral only in 1905, this has been the neighborhood church since the 13th century, and comes with some interesting history. The enthusiastic docents give impromptu tours if you ask.

Cost and Hours: Free, £1 map serves as photo permit, Mon-Fri 8:00-18:00, Sat-Sun 8:30-18:00, guidebook-£4.50, Tube: London Bridge, tel. 020/7367-6700, www.cathedral.southwark.anglican.org.

Music: The cathedral hosts evensong Sun at 15:00, Tue-Fri at 17:30, and some Sat at 16:00; organ recitals are Mon at 13:15 and music recitals Tue at 15:15 (call or check website to confirm times).

▲Old Operating Theatre Museum and Herb Garret

Climb a tight and creaky wooden spiral staircase to a church attic where you'll find a garret used to dry medicinal herbs, a fascinating exhibit on Victorian surgery, cases of well-described 19th-century medical paraphernalia, and a special look at "anesthesia, the defeat of pain." Then you stumble upon Britain's oldest operating theater, where limbs were sawed off way back in 1821. (See page 295 for a full description.)

Cost and Hours: £6.50, borrowable laminated descriptions, daily 10:30-17:00, closed Dec 15-Jan 5, at 9a St. Thomas Street, Tube: London Bridge, tel. 020/7188-2679, http://oldoperatingtheatre.com.

SIGHTS

The Shard

Rocketing dramatically 1,020 feet above the south end of the London Bridge, this addition to London's skyline is by far the tallest building in Western Europe. Designed by Renzo Piano (best known as the co-architect of Paris' Pompidou Center), the glass-clad pyramid shimmers in the sun and its prickly top glows like the city's nightlight after dark. Its uppermost floors are set aside as public viewing galleries, but the ticket price is as outrageously high as the building itself, especially given that it's a bit far from London's most exciting landmarks. The Aqua Shard bar on the 31st floor offers views from half the height for the price of a fancy drink (free to ride up, but if they're at capacity they can turn you away, bar open 12:00-24:00; no sportswear, shorts, or flip-flops; access the bar from separate entrance on St. Thomas Street, www.aquashard.co.uk). For a list of cheaper view opportunities in London, see the sidebar on page 90.

Cost and Hours: £31 (cheaper if booked online at least a day in advance); book as soon as you have reasonable chance of assuring decent weather, least crowded on weekday mornings, but perhaps better photo opportunities in the early evening (less haze); daily 10:00-22:00, shorter hours Oct-March; Tube: London Bridge—use London Bridge exit and follow signs, tel. 0844-499-7111, www.theviewfromtheshard.com.

Visiting the Shard: From the entrance on Joiner Street (just off St. Thomas Street) you'll take a two-part elevator ride up to the 68th floor, then climb up one story to the main observation platform. It's equipped with cool telescopes that label major landmarks, and even let you see how the view from here would appear at other times of the day. From here you've got great views of St. Paul's, the Tower of London, Southwark Cathedral (straight down), and, in the distance, the 2012 Olympic stadium in one direction, and the Houses of Parliament in the other (find Buckingham Palace, just left of the Eye). On the clearest days, you can see 40 miles out, and a few people say they've been able to make out ships on the North Sea. Even in bad weather it's mesmerizing to watch the constant movement of the city's transit system, which looks like a model-train set from this height. Ascending to the 72nd floor gets you to the open-air deck, where the wind roars over the glass enclosure. As you look up, try to picture Prince Andrew rappelling off the very top, which he and 40 others did in 2012 as a charity fundraising stunt.

HMS *Belfast*

This former Royal Navy warship, a veteran of World War II that took part in the D-Day invasion, clogs the Thames just upstream from the Tower Bridge. The huge vessel—now manned with wax sailors—thrills kids who always dreamed of sitting in a turret shooting off their imaginary guns. If you're into WWII warships, this is the ultimate. Otherwise, it's just lots of exercise with a nice view of the Tower Bridge.

Cost and Hours: Adult-£16, kids 5-15-£8, family ticket for 2 adults and up to 3 kids-£41, kids under 5-free, includes audioguide, daily March-Oct 10:00-18:00, Nov-Feb until 17:00, last entry one hour before closing, Tube: London Bridge, tel. 020/7940-6300, www.iwm.org.uk/visits/hms-belfast.

City Hall

The glassy, egg-shaped building near the south end of Tower Bridge is London's City Hall, designed by Sir Norman Foster, the

architect who worked on London's Millennium Bridge and Berlin's Reichstag. Nicknamed "the Armadillo," City Hall houses the office of London's mayor—it's here that the mayor consults with the Assembly representatives of the city's 25 districts. An interior spiral ramp allows visitors to watch and hear the action below in the Assembly Chamber—ride the lift to floor 2 (the highest visitors can go) and spiral down. On the lower ground floor is a large aerial photograph of London and a handy cafeteria. Next to City Hall is the outdoor amphitheater called The Scoop (see page 456 for info on performances).

Cost and Hours: Free, open to visitors Mon-Thu 8:30-18:00, Fri until 17:30, closed Sat-Sun; Tube: London Bridge station plus 10-minute walk, or Tower Hill station plus 15-minute walk; tel. 020/7983-4000, www.london.gov.uk.

West London

▲▲Tate Britain

One of Europe's great art houses, Tate Britain specializes in British painting from the 16th century through modern times. The recently renovated museum has a good representation of William Blake's religious sketches, the Pre-Raphaelites' naturalistic and detailed art,

Gainsborough's aristocratic ladies, and the best collection anywhere of J. M. W. Turner's swirling works.

Cost and Hours: Free, £4 donation suggested, admission fee for special exhibits; daily 10:00-18:00, last entry 45 minutes before closing; free tours generally daily; on the Thames River, south of Big Ben and north of Vauxhall Bridge, Tube: Pimlico, Tate Boat museum ferry goes directly to the museum from Tate Modern—see page 39; switchboard tel. 020/7887-8888, www.tate.org.uk.

☐ See the Tate Britain Tour chapter.

Victoria Station

From underneath this station's iron-and-glass canopy, trains depart for the south of England and Gatwick Airport. While Victoria Station is famous and a major Tube stop, few tourists actually take trains from here—most just come to take in the exciting bustle. It's a fun place to be a "rock in a river" teeming with commuters and services. The station is surrounded by big red buses and taxis, travel agencies, and lousy eateries. It's next to the main intercity bus station (Victoria Coach Station) and some of the best moderately priced lodgings in town.

Westminster Cathedral

This cathedral, the largest Catholic church in England and just a block from Victoria Station, is strikingly Neo-Byzantine, but not very historic or important to visit. Opened in 1903, the church has an unfinished interior, with a spooky, blackened ceiling waiting for the mosaics that are supposed to be placed there. While it's definitely not Westminster Abbey, half the tourists wandering around inside seem to think it is. Take the lift to the top of the 273-foot bell tower for a view of the glassy office blocks of Victoria Station.

Cost and Hours: Free entry, £6 for the lift; church—daily 7:00-19:00; tower—daily 9:30-17:00, Sat-Sun until 18:00; 5-minute walk from bus terminus in front of Victoria Station, just off Victoria Street at 42 Francis Street, Tube: Victoria, www.westminstercathedral.org.uk.

▲National Army Museum

This museum tells the story of the British army from 1415 through the Bosnian conflict and Iraq, and how it influences today's society. The five well-signed galleries are neatly arranged by theme—"Army," "Battle," "Soldier," "Society," and "Insight"—with plenty of interactive exhibits for kids. History buffs appreciate the carefully displayed artifacts that bring school lessons to life, from 17th-century uniforms to Wellington's battle cloak. Other highlights of the collection include the skeleton of Napoleon's horse, Lawrence

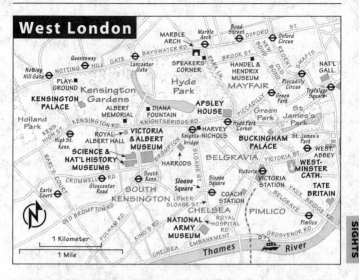

West London

MARBLE ARCH · Marble Arch · Bond Street · OXFORD ST. · Oxford Circus

Queensway · BAYSWATER RD. · BROOK ST. · NEW BOND · OLD BOND · REGENT · SHAFTS.

Notting Hill Gate · NOTTING HILL GATE · Lancaster Gate · SPEAKERS' CORNER · HANDEL & HENDRIX MUSEUM · NAT'L GALL.

PLAY-GROUND · Kensington Gardens · Hyde Park · MAYFAIR · Piccadilly Circus · Trafalgar Square

KENSINGTON PALACE · ALBERT MEMORIAL · DIANA FOUNTAIN · APSLEY HOUSE · Green Park · St. James's Park

Holland Park · KENSINGTON RD. · KNIGHTSBRIDGE RD. · HARVEY · Hyde Park Corner · Green Park · BUCKINGHAM PALACE · St. James's Park

KENS. HIGH ST. · High St. Kens. · ROYAL ALBERT HALL · VICTORIA & ALBERT MUSEUM · Knights-bridge · Knights-Nichols · BELGRAVIA · Victoria St. · WEST. ABBEY

SCIENCE & NAT'L HISTORY MUSEUMS · HARRODS · WEST-MINSTER CATH.

EARL'S COURT · CROMWELL RD. · South Kens. · Victoria · VICTORIA STATION · TATE BRITAIN

Earls Court · Gloucester Road · SOUTH KENSINGTON · Sloane Square · Sloane Square · COACH STATION · Pimlico

OLD BROMPTON RD. · FULHAM RD. · KING'S RD. · LOWER SLOANE ST. · CHELSEA · PIMLICO · Pimlico · GROSVENOR RD.

NATIONAL ARMY MUSEUM · ROYAL HOSPITAL RD. · CHELSEA EMBANKMENT · VAUX BRIDGE RD. · BELGRAVE

1 Kilometer · 1 Mile · Thames River

SIGHTS

of Arabia's silk robe, and Burberry's signature Trench coat (originally designed for WWI soldiers).

Cost and Hours: Free, £5 suggested donation, daily 10:00-17:30, Wed until 20:00, free tours daily at 11:00 and 14:00, Royal Hospital Road, Chelsea, Tube: 10 minute walk from Sloane Square, exit the station and head south on Lower Sloan Street, turn right on Royal Hospital Road, the museum is two long blocks ahead on the left, tel. 020/7730-0717, www.national-army-museum.ac.uk.

HYDE PARK AND NEARBY

A number of worthwhile sights border this grand park, from Apsley House on the east to Kensington Palace on the west.

▲Apsley House (Wellington Museum)

Having beaten Napoleon at Waterloo, Arthur Wellesley, the First Duke of Wellington, was once the most famous man in Europe.

He was given a huge fortune, with which he purchased London's ultimate address, Number One London. His refurbished mansion offers a nice interior, a handful of world-class paintings, and a glimpse at the life of the great soldier and two-time prime minister. Those who

know something about Wellington ahead of time will appreciate the place much more than those who don't, as there's scarce biographical background. The place is well-described by the included audioguide, which has sound bites from the current Duke of Wellington (who still lives at Apsley).

Cost and Hours: £10.30, Wed-Sun 11:00-17:00, closed Mon-Tue, no photos, 20 yards from Hyde Park Corner Tube station, tel. 020/7499-5676, www.english-heritage.org.uk.

Visiting the House: An 11-foot-tall marble statue of Napoleon, clad only in a fig leaf, greets you. Napoleon commissioned the sculptor Canova to make it for him but didn't like it, and after Napoleon's defeat, Wellington acquired it as a war trophy. It's one of several images Wellington acquired of his former foe to have in his home. The two great men were polar opposites—Napoleon the daring general and champion of revolution, Wellington the play-it-safe strategist and conservative politician—but they're forever linked in history.

The core of the collection is a dozen first-floor rooms decorated with fancy wallpaper, chandeliers, a few pieces of furniture, and wall-to-wall paintings from Wellington's collection. You'll see fancy dinnerware and precious objects given to the Irish-born general by the crowned heads of Europe, who were eternally grateful to him for saving their necks from the guillotine. The highlight is the large ballroom, the Waterloo Gallery, decorated with Anthony van Dyck's *Charles I on Horseback* (over the main fireplace), Diego Velázquez's earthy *Water-Seller of Seville* (to the left of Van Dyck), and Jan Steen's playful *Dissolute Household* (to the right). Just outside the door, in the Portico Room, is a large portrait of the Duke of Wellington by Francisco Goya—the original subject is said to have been Napoleon's brother, but when Wellington prevailed Goya deftly adjusted the face.

Downstairs is a small gallery of Wellington memorabilia, including a pair of Wellington boots, which the duke popularized—Brits today still call rubber boots "wellies".

Nearby: Hyde Park's pleasant rose garden is picnic-friendly. **Wellington Arch,** which stands just across the street, is open to the public but not worth the £5.50 charge (or £12.50 combo-ticket with Apsley House; elevator up, lousy views and boring exhibits).

▲Hyde Park and Speakers' Corner

London's "Central Park," originally Henry VIII's hunting grounds, has more than 600 acres of lush greenery, Santander Cycles rental stations, the huge man-made Serpentine Lake (with rental boats and a lakeside swimming pool), the royal Kensington Palace (described next), and the ornate Neo-Gothic Albert Memorial across from the Royal Albert Hall (for more about the park, see www. royalparks.org.uk/parks/hyde-park). The western half of the park is known as Kensington Gardens. The park is huge—study a Tube map to choose the stop nearest to your destination.

On Sundays, from just after noon until early evening, **Speakers' Corner** offers soapbox oratory at its best (northeast corner of

the park, Tube: Marble Arch). Characters climb their stepladders, wave their flags, pound emphatically on their sandwich boards, and share what they are convinced is their wisdom. Regulars have resident hecklers who know their lines and are always ready with a verbal jab or barb. "The grass roots of democracy" is actually a holdover from when the gallows stood here and the criminal was allowed to say just about anything he wanted to before he swung. I dare you to raise your voice and gather a crowd—it's easy to do.

The **Princess Diana Memorial Fountain** honors the "People's Princess," who once lived in nearby Kensington Palace. The low-key circular stream, great for cooling off your feet on a hot day, is in the south-central part of the park, near the Albert Memorial and Serpentine Gallery (Tube: Knightsbridge). A similarly named but different sight, the **Diana, Princess of Wales Memorial Playground,** in the park's northwest corner, is loads of fun for kids (Tube: Queensway).

Kensington Palace

For nearly 150 years (1689-1837), Kensington was the royal residence, before Buckingham Palace became the official home of

the monarch. Sitting primly on its pleasant parkside grounds, the palace gives a barren yet regal glimpse into royal life—particularly that of Queen Victoria, who was born and raised here. It's strange to think that, in this city that was so shaped by Victoria, this relatively paltry exhibit is London's first and only museum that's

SIGHTS

truly *about* Victoria. (For more on Victoria's life and times, see the sidebar on page 102.)

After Queen Victoria moved the monarchy to Buckingham Palace, lesser royals bedded down at Kensington. Princess Diana lived here both during and after her marriage to Prince Charles (1981-1997). More recently, Will and Kate moved in. However—as many disappointed visitors discover—none of these more recent apartments are open to the public. The palace hosts a revolving series of temporary exhibits, some great, others not so. To see what's on during your visit, check online.

Cost and Hours: £19, daily 10:00-18:00, Nov-Feb until 16:00; a long 10-minute stroll through Kensington Gardens from either High Street Kensington or Queensway Tube stations, tel. 0844-482-7788, www.hrp.org.uk.

Outside: Garden enthusiasts enjoy popping into the secluded Sunken Garden, 50 yards from the exit. Consider afternoon tea at the nearby Orangery (see page 418), built as a greenhouse for Queen Anne in 1704.

▲▲▲Victoria and Albert Museum

The world's top collection of decorative arts encompasses 2,000 years of art and design (ceramics, stained glass, fine furniture, clothing, jewelry, carpets, and more), displaying a surprisingly interesting and diverse assortment of crafts from the West, as well as Asian and Islamic cultures. There's much to see, including Raphael's tapestry cartoons, five of Leonardo da Vinci's notebooks, the huge Islamic Ardabil Carpet (4,914 knots in every 10 square centimeters), a cast of Trajan's Column that depicts the emperor's conquests, and pop culture memorabilia, including the jumpsuit Mick Jagger wore for the Rolling Stones' 1972 world tour.

Cost and Hours: Free, £5 donation requested, extra for some special exhibits, daily 10:00-17:45, some galleries open Fri until 22:00, free tours daily, on Cromwell Road in South Kensington, Tube: South Kensington, from the Tube station a long tunnel leads directly to museum, tel. 020/7942-2000, www.vam.ac.uk.

📖 See the Victoria and Albert Museum Tour chapter.

▲▲Natural History Museum

Across the street from the Victoria and Albert, this mammoth museum is housed in a giant and wonderful Victorian, Neo-Romanesque building. It was built in the 1870s specifically for the huge collection (50 million specimens). Exhibits are wonderfully explained, with lots of creative, interactive displays. It covers everything from life ("creepy crawlies," human biology, our place in evolution, and awe-inspiring dinosaurs) to earth science (meteors, volcanoes, and earthquakes).

Cost and Hours: Free, £5 donation requested, fees for (optional) special exhibits, daily 10:00-18:00, open later last Fri of the month, helpful £1 map, long tunnel leads directly from South Kensington Tube station to museum (follow signs), tel. 020/7942-5000, exhibit info and reservations tel. 020/7942-5011, www.nhm.ac.uk. Free visitor app available via the "Visit" section of the website.

Visiting the Museum: Enter by the main Cromwell Road entrance (in the middle of the long building), which is easiest for

getting oriented. You step into Hintze Hall, with a big *Diplodocus* skeleton (if it's on loan, a blue-whale skeleton will greet you instead) bookended by a massive slice of sequoia tree and Charles Darwin sitting as if upon a throne overseeing it all. Review the "What's on Today" board for special events and tours, and note which sections are closed. For more information, ask one of the many helpful guards scattered throughout the museum.

The building is organized into several color-coded "zones." The Blue Zone (to the left) has the biggest animals and biggest crowds: dinosaurs, a life-size blue whale model, and other stuffed-and-mounted mammals.

Straight ahead, up the stairs behind Darwin, is the Cadogan Treasures Gallery, housing a rotating display of the museum's greatest hits, including a dodo skeleton, moon rock, stuffed specimen of the extinct great auk, fossil of the earliest known bird *(Archaeopteryx)*, and the *Iguanodon* tooth that kicked off human awareness of dinosaurs.

To the right are the Red and Green zones, with a dramatic escalator ride up to experience an earthquake, and rooms tracing the evolution of the earth and its creatures. Don't miss a room called "The Vault" that contains rare and precious stones, including a meteorite from Mars, the Aurora Pyramid of Hope—displaying 296 diamonds showing their full range of natural colors—and this description of some microscopic cosmic diamonds: "These are the oldest things you will ever see."

Keep exploring. The Orange Zone (far left) lets you see today's scientists at work in their labs, and the newly opened gallery overlooking the central hall contains some of the museum's oldest pieces.

Even with limited time to spend here, pop in, if only for the dinosaur collection—including a realistic animatronic *T. rex*—and to hear English children exclaim, "Oh, my goodness!"

SIGHTS

Queen Victoria (1819-1901)

Plump, pleasant, and not quite five feet tall, Queen Victoria, with her regal demeanor and 64-year reign, came to symbolize the global dominance of the British Empire during its greatest era.

Born in Kensington Palace, Victoria was the granddaughter of "Mad" King George III, the tyrant who sparked the American Revolution. Her domineering mother raised her in sheltered seclusion, drilling into her the strict morality that would come to be known as "Victorian." At 18, she was crowned queen. Victoria soon fell madly, deeply in love with Prince Albert, a handsome German nobleman with mutton-chop sideburns. They married and set up house in Buckingham Palace (the first monarchs to do so) and at Windsor Castle. Over the next 17 years, she and Albert had nine children, whom they eventually married off to Europe's crowned heads. Victoria's royal descendants include Kaiser Wilhelm II of Germany (who started World War I); the current monarchs of Spain, Norway, Sweden, and Denmark; and England's Queen Elizabeth II, who is Victoria's great-great-granddaughter.

Victoria and Albert promoted the arts and sciences, organizing a world's fair in Hyde Park (1851) that showed off London as *the* global capital. Just as important, they were role models for an entire nation; this loving couple influenced several generations with their wholesome middle-class values and devoted parenting. Though Victoria is often depicted as dour and stuffy—she supposedly coined the phrase "We are not amused"—in private she was warm, easy to laugh, plainspoken, thrifty, and modest, with a talent for sketching and journal writing.

In 1861, Victoria's happy domestic life ended. Her mother's death was soon followed by the sudden loss of her beloved Albert to typhoid fever. A devastated Victoria dressed in black for the funeral—and for her remaining 40 years never again wore any other color. She hunkered down at Windsor with her family. Critics complained she was an absentee monarch. Rumors swirled that her kilt-wearing servant, John Brown, was not only her close friend but also her lover. For two decades, she rarely appeared in public.

▲Science Museum

Next door to the Natural History Museum, this sprawling wonderland for curious minds is kid-perfect, with themes such as measuring time, exploring space, climate change, the evolution of modern medicine, and the Information Age. It offers hands-on fun, with trendy technology exhibits, a state-of-the-art IMAX

Over time, Victoria emerged from mourning to assume her role as one of history's first constitutional monarchs. She had inherited a crown with little real power. But beyond her ribbon-cutting ceremonial duties, Victoria influenced events behind the scenes. She studiously learned politics from powerful mentors (especially Prince Albert and two influential prime ministers) and kept well-informed on what Parliament was doing. Thanks to Victoria's personal modesty and honesty, the British public never came to disdain the monarchy, as happened in other countries.

Victoria gracefully oversaw the peaceful transfer of power from the nobles to the people. The secret ballot was introduced during her reign, and ordinary workers acquired voting rights (though this applied only to men—Victoria opposed women's suffrage). The traditional Whigs and Tories morphed into today's Liberal and Conservative parties. Victoria personally promoted progressive charities, and even paid for her own crown.

Most of all, Victoria became the symbol of the British Empire, which she saw as a way to protect and civilize poorer peoples. Britain enjoyed peace at home, while its colonial possessions included India, Australia, Canada, and much of Africa. Because it was always daytime someplace under Victoria's rule, it was often said that "the sun never sets on the British Empire."

The Victorian era saw great changes. The Industrial Revolution was in full swing. When Victoria was born, there were no trains. By 1842, when she took her first train trip (with much fanfare), railroads crisscrossed Europe. The telegraph, telephone, and newspapers further laced the world together. The popular arts flourished—it was the era of Dickens novels, Tennyson poems, Sherlock Holmes stories, Gilbert and Sullivan operettas, and Pre-Raphaelite paintings. Economically, Britain saw the rise of the middle class. Middle-class morality dominated—family, hard work, honor, duty, and sexual modesty.

By the end of her reign, Victoria was wildly popular, both for her personality and as a focus for British patriotism. At her Golden Jubilee (1887), she paraded past adoring throngs to Westminster Abbey. For her Diamond Jubilee (1897), she did the same at St. Paul's Cathedral. Cities, lakes, and military medals were named for her. When she passed away in 1901, it was literally the end of an era.

theater (shows-£11, £9 for kids, £27/£30 for families of 3 or 4), the Garden—a cool play area for children up to age seven, plus several other pay-to-enter attractions, including a virtual-reality spacecraft descent to Earth (£7) and Wonderlab kids area (£8 for adults, £6 for kids). Look for the family "What's On" brochure and ask about tours and demonstrations at the info desk.

Cost and Hours: Free, £5 donation requested, daily 10:00-18:00, until 19:00 during school holidays, last entry 45 minutes before closing, Exhibition Road, Tube: South Kensington, tel. 0333-241-4000, www.sciencemuseum.org.uk.

Greater London

EAST OF LONDON
▲▲Greenwich

This borough of London—an easy boat trip or DLR (light rail) journey from downtown—combines majestic, picnic-perfect parks; the stately trappings of Britain's proud nautical heritage (the restored *Cutty Sark* clipper, the over-the-top-ornate retirement home for sailors at the **Old Royal Naval College,** and the comprehensive **National Maritime Museum**); and the **Royal Observatory Greenwich,** with a fine museum on how Greenwich Mean Time came to be and a chance to straddle the eastern and western hemispheres at the prime meridian. An affordable jaunt from central London, and boasting several top-notch museums (including some free ones), Greenwich is worth considering and easy to combine with a look at the Docklands (described next).

    ☐ See the Greenwich Tour chapter.

▲▲The Docklands

Once the primary harbor for the Port of London, the Docklands has been transformed into a vibrant business center, with ultra-tall skyscrapers, subterranean supermalls, trendy pubs, and peaceful parks with pedestrian bridges looping over canals. It also boasts the very good **Museum of London Docklands,** which illuminates the gritty and fascinating history of the port. While not full of the touristy sights that many are seeking in London, the Docklands offers a refreshing look at the British version of a 21st-century city. It's best at the end of the workday, when it's lively with office workers. It's ideal to see on your way back from Greenwich, since both line up on the same train tracks.

    ☐ See The Docklands Walk chapter.

Queen Elizabeth Olympic Park

London refashioned this park—the biggest new park to open in the city in a century—from the site of the 2012 Olympic Games. You'll find miles of parkland trails and waterways, kids' play areas, an array of sporting venues (London Aquatics Centre, Lee Valley VeloPark, Copper Box Arena), quirky sculpture, and places to eat. The park is huge—bigger than Hyde Park/Kensington Gardens. It's also quite beautiful, laced with canals and tributaries of the Lea River.

Cost and Hours: Free and always open, toll-free tel. 0800-0722-110, www.queenelizabetholympicpark.co.uk.

Getting There: From central London by Tube, it's a 30-minute ride to the Stratford station. Follow exits toward Queen Elizabeth Olympic Park and Westfield Stratford City. Outside the Tube exit, take another escalator up to "The Street" (which is actually the outdoor part of the Westfield shopping center), bear left at the digital fountain past the line of restaurants, cross the street at The Cow pub, and the park is directly ahead of you, across the road.

Visiting the Park: The best overview of the park is along a 500-yard-long berm called the **Greenway,** which sits at the park's southern perimeter, or at the **Knight's Bride** (toward the park's northern edge), looking south back over the buildings. The easiest landmark to head for is the **View Tube,** just outside the park—a covered shelter with a free lookout tower, café, WC, and maps. There's also the hard-to-miss red, 350-foot viewing tower called the **Orbit,** which was designed as an Eiffel-Tower-like landmark and has been compared to a giant hookah. In 2016, the Orbit added a new feature that makes it feel even more like an amusement park: the world's longest, tallest, and transparent tunnel slide (£16.50 includes Orbit entrance, plus one ride). For help in planning your visit, drop by the "Information Point" near the Aquatics Centre, where you can also ask about a tour with a Blue Badge guide (£10, Wed and Sat at 11:00).

WEST OF LONDON
▲▲Kew Gardens

For a fine riverside park and a palatial greenhouse jungle to swing through, take the Tube or the boat to every botanist's favorite escape, Kew Gardens. While to most visitors the Royal Botanic Gardens of Kew are simply a delightful opportunity to wander among 33,000 different types of plants, to the hardworking organization that runs them, the gardens are a way to promote the understanding and preservation of the botanical diversity of our planet.

Cost and Hours: £16.50, June-Aug £11 after 16:00, kids 4-16-£3.50, kids under 4-free; April-Aug Mon-Thu 10:00-18:30, Fri-Sun 10:00-19:30, closes earlier Sept-March—check schedule online, glasshouses close at 17:30 in high season—earlier off-season, free one-hour walking tours daily at 11:00 and 13:30, Tube: Kew Gardens, boats run April-Oct between Kew Gardens and

Westminster Pier—see page 36, tel. 020/8332-5000, recorded info tel. 020/8332-5655, www.kew.org.

Getting There: From the Tube station, cross the footbridge over the tracks, which drops you in a little community of plant-and-herb shops, a two-block walk from Victoria Gate (the main garden entrance).

Visiting the Gardens: Pick up a map brochure and check at the gate for a monthly listing of the best blooms. Garden lovers could spend days exploring Kew's 300 acres. For a quick visit, spend a fragrant hour wandering through three buildings: the Palm House, a humid Victorian world of iron, glass, and tropical plants that was built in 1844; a Waterlily House that Monet would swim for; and the Princess of Wales Conservatory, a meandering modern greenhouse with many different climate zones growing countless cacti, bug-munching carnivorous plants, and more. With extra time, check out the Xstrata Treetop Walkway, a 200-yard-long scenic steel walkway that puts you high in the canopy 60 feet above the ground. Young kids will love the Climbers and Creepers indoor/outdoor playground and little zip line, as well as a slow and easy ride on the hop-on, hop-off Kew Explorer tram (adults-£5, kids-£2 for nar-rated 40-minute ride, departs Victoria Gate, ask for schedule when you enter).

Eating: For a sun-dappled lunch or snack, walk 10 minutes from the Palm House to the **$$ Orangery Cafeteria** (Mon-Thu 10:00-17:30, Fri-Sun 10:00-18:30, until 15:15 in winter, closes early for events).

▲Hampton Court Palace

Fifteen miles up the Thames from downtown, the 500-year-old palace of Henry VIII is worth ▲▲ for palace aficionados. Actu-

ally, it was originally the palace of his minister, Cardinal Wolsey. When Wolsey, a clever man, realized Henry VIII was experiencing a little pal-ace envy, he gave the mansion to his king. The Tudor palace was also home to Elizabeth I and Charles I. Sections were updated by Christopher Wren for William and Mary. The stately palace stands overlooking the Thames and in-cludes some fine Tudor rooms, includ-ing a Great Hall with a magnificent hammer-beam ceiling. The industrial-strength Tudor kitchen was capable of keeping 600 schmoozing courtiers thoroughly—if not well—fed. The sculpted garden features a rare Tudor tennis court and a popular maze.

The palace tries hard to please, but it doesn't quite sparkle. From the information center in the main courtyard, you can pick up audioguides for self-guided tours of various wings of the palace (free but slow, aimed mostly at school-age children). For more in-depth information, strike up a conversation with the costumed characters or docents posted in each room. The Tudor portions of the castle, including the rooms dedicated to the young Henry, are most interesting; the Georgian rooms are pretty dull. The maze in the nearby garden is a curiosity some find fun (maze free with palace ticket, otherwise £4.70).

Cost and Hours: £23, family-£57; online discounts, daily April-Oct 10:00-18:00, Nov-March until 16:30, last entry one hour before closing, café, tel. 0844-482-7777 or 020/3166-6000, www.hrp.org.uk.

Getting There: From London's Waterloo Station, take a South West train. The train will drop you on the far side of the river from the palace—just walk across the bridge (2/hour, 35 minutes, Oyster cards OK). Consider arriving at or departing from the palace by boat (connections with London's Westminster Pier, see page 36); it's a relaxing and scenic three- to four-hour cruise past two locks and a fun new/old riverside mix.

Kew Gardens/Hampton Court Blitz: Because these two sights are in the same general direction (about £20 for a taxi between the two), you can visit both in one day. Here's a game plan: Start your morning at Hampton Court, tour the palace and garden, and have a Tudor-style lunch in the atmospheric dining hall. After lunch, take bus #R68 from Hampton Court Station to Richmond (40 minutes), then transfer to bus #65, which will drop you off at the Kew Gardens gate (5 minutes). After touring the gardens, have tea in the Orangery, then Tube or boat back to London.

NORTH OF LONDON
Royal Air Force Museum London

A hit with aviation enthusiasts, this huge aerodrome and airfield contain planes from World War II's Battle of Britain up through the Gulf War. You can climb inside some of the planes, try your luck in a cockpit, and fly with the Red Arrows in a flight simulator.

Cost and Hours: Free, £3 suggested donation, flight simulator-£3, daily 10:00-18:00, café, shop, parking-£3 for up to 3 hours, Grahame Park Way, 30-minute ride from downtown London plus another 15 minutes by foot, Tube: Colindale—top of Northern Line Edgware branch, tel. 020/8205-2266, www.rafmuseum.org.uk.

Hampstead Heath

This surprisingly vast expanse of greenery sprawls over a square mile and a quarter at the northern edge of downtown London.

It features rolling, scrubby pastures ("heath") as well as tranquil wooded areas. Its most popular viewpoint, Parliament Hill, offers distant views of London's fast-growing skyline. At the northeast corner of the park is a chunk of land owned by English Heritage, where a stately palace called Kenwood House overlooks a pasture, pond, and gentle wood; inside is a fine art collection, plus an inviting café (and WCs). Maps posted at each entrance to the park help get you oriented. On a sunny day, the park is crammed with Londoners communing with nature—relieved to escape from their bustling burg. The adjoining village of Hampstead is quaint and cute; a stroll through here is almost as pleasant as the park itself.

Getting There: Hampstead Heath is just a 20-minute Tube ride from downtown London. The handiest Tube stop is the one called Hampstead (on the convenient Northern line/Edgware branch, which runs north-to-south through London's city center). This stop is in the middle of the charming village of Hampstead, from which it's about a 10-minute walk to the park (turn left out of the station to head one block down Hampstead High Street, then turn left on Flask Walk and follow it until it becomes Well Walk and eventually runs into East Heath Road; the park is in front of you, with Parliament Hill still a ways in and to the right). The station called Hampstead Heath, directly at the southern tip of the park and closer to Parliament Hill, is on the less convenient Overground line; however, bus #24 easily (though slowly) connects Victoria Station and downtown London (including Trafalgar Square) with the Hampstead Heath stop.

Hampstead Heath combines well with a visit to the fun and funky Camden Lock Market (see page 435), which is on both the Northern Tube line and the bus #24 route.

Highgate Cemetery

Located in the tea-cozy-cute village of Highgate, north of the city, this Victorian cemetery represents a fascinating, offbeat piece of London history. Built as a private cemetery, this was the fashionable place to bury the wealthy dead in the late 1800s. It has themed mausoleums, professional mourners, and several high-profile residents in its East Cemetery, including Karl Marx, George Eliot, and Douglas Adams. The tomb of "Godfather of Punk" Malcolm McLaren (former manager of the Sex Pistols) is often covered with rotten veggies.

Cost and Hours: East Cemetery—£4, Mon-Fri 10:00-17:00, Sat-Sun 11:00-17:00; older, creepier West Cemetery—viewable by £12 guided tour only, price includes entrance to East Cemetery, Mon-Fri at 13:45—must book in advance; Sat-Sun 2/hour, 11:00-15:00, no reservations taken but space is limited; Tube: Archway on the Northern Line/High Barnet branch or—slower—bus #C2 from Victoria Station or Oxford Circus, tel. 020/8340-1834, www.highgatecemetery.org.

SIGHTS

The Making of Harry Potter:
Warner Bros. Studio Tour London

While you can visit several real-life locations in Britain where the Harry Potter movies were filmed (see sidebar on page 110), there's only one way to see imaginary places like Hogwarts' Great Hall, Diagon Alley, Dumbledore's office, and #4 Privet Drive: Visit the Warner Bros. Studio in Leavesden, where Daniel Radcliffe and company brought the tale of the boy wizard to life.

Attractions include the actual sets used for the films (Hogwarts bridge, Hagrid's hut), several familiar costumes and props (such as the Nimbus 2000, the Sorting Hat, the Sword of Gryffindor, Hagrid's motorcycle, and a Hogwarts Express attraction), video interviews with the actors and filmmakers, and exhibits about how the films' special effects were created.

Your visit starts with an intro film and brief overview by a live guide. Then you're free to wander through large halls with the sets, props, and costumes. You may be impressed by the level of detail the super-enthusiastic designers put into even the simplest of props. The visit culminates with a stroll down Diagon Alley and a room-sized 1:24-scale model of Hogwarts.

As this attraction is understandably popular, it's essential to reserve your visit online far in advance (entry possible only with reserved time slot). Allowing about three hours at the studio, plus nearly three hours to get there and back, this experience will eat up the better part of a day.

Cost and Hours: £39, kids ages 5 to 15-£31, family ticket for 2 adults and 2 kids-£126; opening hours flex with season—first tour at 9:00 or 10:00, last tour as early as 14:30 or as late as 18:30, if you miss your assigned entry time you'll be admitted

Harry Potter's London

Harry Potter's story is set in a magical Britain, and the places mentioned in the books, except London, are fictional, but you can visit many real film locations. Many locations are closed to visitors, though, or are an unmagical disappointment in person, unless you're a huge fan. For those die-hards, here's a sampling.

Spoiler Warning: The information below will ruin surprises for the three of you who haven't yet read or seen the Harry Potter series.

Harry's story begins in suburban London, in the fictional town of Little Whinging. In *The Sorcerer's Stone* (2001), the gentle giant Hagrid touches down on his flying motorcycle at #4 Privet Drive. There, baby Harry—orphaned by the murder of his wizard parents—is left on the doorstep of his antimagic aunt and uncle. The scene was shot in **Bracknell** (pop. 50,000, 10 miles west of Heathrow) on a street of generic brick rowhouses called Picket Close.

Later, 10-year-old Harry first realizes his wizard powers when talking with a boa constrictor, filmed at the **London Zoo's Reptile House** in Regent's Park (Tube: Great Portland Street).

Big Ben and **Parliament,** along the Thames, welcome Harry to the modern city inhabited by Muggles (nonmagic folk). London bustles along oblivious to the parallel universe of wizards. Hagrid takes Harry shopping: They enter the glass-roofed **Leadenhall Market** (Tube: Bank) and approach the **storefront** at 42 Bull's Head Passage—the entrance to The Leaky Cauldron pub (which, in the books, is placed among the bookshops of Charing Cross Road). The pub's back wall parts, opening onto the magical Diagon Alley, where Harry shops for wands, cauldrons, and wizard textbooks. He pays for them with gold Galleons from goblin-run Gringotts Wizarding Bank, filmed in the marble-floored Exhibition Hall of **Australia House** (Tube: Temple), home of the Australian Embassy.

Harry catches the train to Hogwarts at **King's Cross Sta-**

with the next group; audio/videoguide-£5, café, still photography allowed, tel. 0845-084-0900, www.wbstudiotour.co.uk.

Getting There: Leavesden is about 20 miles northwest of London. Reaching the studio is easy, requiring a **train and shuttle bus** connection. Give yourself at least 90 minutes to get from your central London hotel to the studio for your appointed time.

tion. (The fanciful exterior shown in the 2002 *Chamber of Secrets* was actually shot in nearby **St. Pancras International Station.**) Inside the glass-roofed train station, on a **pedestrian sky bridge** over the tracks, Hagrid gives Harry a train ticket. Harry heads to platform 9¾, where he and his new buddy Ron magically push their luggage carts through a brick pillar between the platforms, emerging onto a hidden platform. (For a fun photo-op, head to King's Cross Station's track 9 to find the *Platform 9¾* sign, the luggage cart that looks like it's disappearing into the wall, a Harry Potter gift shop, and a 30-minute wait in line to snap a photo.)

A red steam train—the Hogwarts Express—speeds the boys through the (Scottish) countryside to Hogwarts, where Harry will spend the next seven years. The steam engine used in filming is on display at a Platform 9¾ exhibit at the **Harry Potter Warner Bros. Studio Tour.**

In *The Prisoner of Azkaban* (2004), Harry careens through London's lamp-lit streets on a purple three-decker bus (also on display at the Harry Potter Warner Bros. Studio Tour) that dumps him at The Leaky Cauldron pub. In this film, the pub's exterior was shot on rough-looking Stoney Street at the southeast edge of **Borough Market,** by The Market Porter pub, with trains rumbling overhead (Tube: London Bridge).

In *The Order of the Phoenix* (2007), the Order takes to the night sky on broomsticks, zooming down the Thames and over London, passing over plenty of identifiable landmarks, including the **Tower Bridge, London Eye, Big Ben,** and **Buckingham Palace.** They arrive at Sirius Black's home at "Twelve Grimmauld Place," filmed at a parklike square called Lincoln's Inn Fields, near Sir John Soane's Museum (Tube: Holborn).

The **Millennium Bridge** is attacked by Death Eaters and collapses into the Thames in the dramatic finale to *The Half-Blood Prince* (2009). For *Order of the Phoenix* and *Deathly Hallows: Part 1* (2010), the real government offices of **Whitehall** serve as exteriors for the Ministry of Magic. Also for *Deathly Hallows,* Harry, Ron, and Hermione fight off disguised Death Eaters in a Muggle café, filmed in the West End's bustling **Piccadilly Circus.** Other London settings, like Diagon Alley, only exist at Warner Bros. Studio in Leavesden (20 miles north of London), where most of the films' interiors were shot.

First, take the frequent train from London Euston (platforms 8-11) to Watford Junction (about 5/hour, 20 minutes). At Watford Junction, exit the station and look left to find the bus stop. Catch the Mullany's Coaches shuttle bus (instantly recognizable by its bright paint job) to the studio tour (2-4/hour, 15 minutes, £2 one-way, £2.50 round-trip, buy ticket from driver).

SIGHTS

More direct (and more expensive), Golden Tours runs multiple daily **buses** between their office near Victoria Station and the studio (price includes round-trip bus and studio entrance: adults-£60-70, kids-£55-65; generally leaves London as early as 7:30, then throughout the day until around 16:00, tour begins 1.5-2 hours after bus departs, reserve ahead at www.goldentours. com).

WESTMINSTER WALK

From Big Ben to Trafalgar Square

Just about every visitor to London strolls along historic Whitehall from Big Ben to Trafalgar Square. This quick nine-stop walk gives meaning to that touristy ramble. Under London's modern traffic and big-city bustle lie 2,000 fascinating years of history. You'll get a whirlwind tour as well as a practical orientation to London.

Orientation

Length of This Walk: Allow one hour for a leisurely walk, and add more time if you tour the Churchill War Rooms (1-2 hours) and the Banqueting House (30-60 minutes). Other nearby sights include the Houses of Parliament, Westminster Abbey, National Gallery, National Portrait Gallery, and St. Martin-in-the-Fields.

Getting There: Take the Tube to Westminster, then take the Westminster Pier exit. The walk ends at Trafalgar Square (nearest Tube stop: Charing Cross).

Churchill War Rooms: £19, daily 9:30-18:00, last entry one hour before closing.

Supreme Court: Free, Mon-Fri 9:30-16:30, closed Sat-Sun, £1 guidebooklet, requires security check, tel. 020/7960-1900, www.supremecourt.uk.

Banqueting House: £8, includes audioguide, Fri-Wed 10:00-17:00, closed Thu, may close for government functions—though it always stays open at least until 13:00.

Horse Guards: It's free to watch the Horse Guards change at Horse Guards Parade on Whitehall (Mon-Sat at 10:30, Sun at 9:30, dismounting ceremony daily at 16:00).

Tours: ∩ Download my free Westminster Walk audio tour.

Services: WCs along this walk are at Westminster Pier (pay), in

Supreme Court (free), at the intersection of Bridge Street and Whitehall (underground, pay), and at Trafalgar Square (free, in square, at National Gallery, and downstairs at St. Martin-in-the-Fields).

Eateries: See page 405 for recommendations near Trafalgar Square, and page 131 for places near Westminster Abbey.

The Walk Begins

• *Start halfway across Westminster Bridge.*

❶ Westminster Bridge
Views of Big Ben and Parliament
• *First look upstream, toward the Parliament.*

Ding dong ding dong. Dong ding ding dong. Yes, indeed, you are in London. **Big Ben** is actually "not the clock, not the tower, but the bell that tolls the hour." However, since the 13-ton bell is not visible, everyone just calls the whole works Big Ben. Named for a fat bureaucrat, Ben is scarcely older than my great-grandmother, but it has quickly become the city's symbol. The

tower—officially named the "Elizabeth Tower" in honor of Queen Elizabeth II's Diamond Jubilee—is 315 feet high. The clock faces are 23 feet across, and the 13-foot-long minute hand sweeps the length of your body every five minutes. For fun, call home from near Big Ben at about three minutes before the hour to let your loved one hear the bell ring. (If the bell is silent during your visit, it's due to a multiyear renovation of the tower and clock mechanism.)

Big Ben hangs out in the north tower of the Houses of Parliament (still known to Brits as the "Palace of Westminster"), which stretches along the Thames. Britain is ruled from this long building, which for five centuries was the home of kings and queens. Then, as democracy was foisted on tyrants, a parliament of nobles was allowed to meet in some of the rooms. Soon, commoners were elected to office, the neighborhood was shot, and the royalty moved to Buckingham Palace. While most of the current building looks medieval with its prickly flamboyant spires, it was actually reconstructed in the "Neo-Gothic" style after an 1834 fire destroyed the palace (which itself had been rebuilt following a fire in 1512).

Today, the House of Commons meets in one end of the building. The House of Lords debates and advises in the other end of

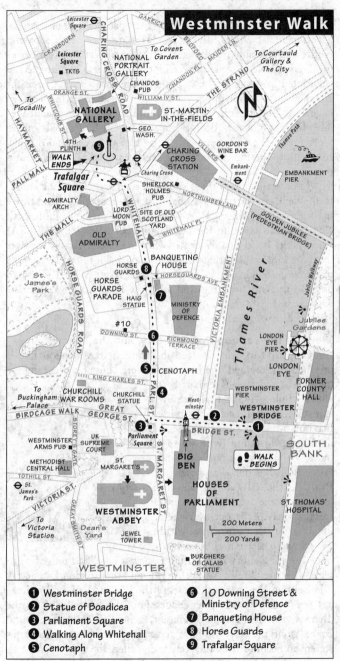

Westminster Walk

1. Westminster Bridge
2. Statue of Boadicea
3. Parliament Square
4. Walking Along Whitehall
5. Cenotaph
6. 10 Downing Street & Ministry of Defence
7. Banqueting House
8. Horse Guards
9. Trafalgar Square

this 1,000-room complex, providing a tempering effect on extreme governmental changes. The two houses are very much separate: Notice the riverside tea terraces with the color-coded awnings—royal red for lords, common green for commoners. Alluding to the traditional leanings of the two chambers, locals say, "Green for go...red for stop" (for tips on visiting the Houses of Parliament, see page 143). The modern Portcullis Building (with the black tube-like chimneys), across Bridge Street from Big Ben, holds offices for many of the 650 members of the House of Commons. They commute to the Houses of Parliament by way of an underground passage.

Looking south, in the distance beyond the Houses of Parliament, you'll see the huge Vauxhall district—redeveloped and thriving today after being a WWII bomb-site wasteland until about 1990. It's also home to the headquarters of MI6 (the local CIA) where James Bond would check in when in London. Across the river from the Houses of Parliament is St. Thomas Hospital. Three of its five brown-and-cream buildings survived World War II. The two bombed sections were replaced with the hospital's towering new wing.

• *Now look north (downstream).*

Views of the London Eye, The City, and the Thames

Built in 2000 to celebrate the millennium, the London Eye—originally nicknamed "the London Eyesore," but now generally appreciated by locals—is a giant Ferris wheel standing 443 feet tall. It slowly spins 32 capsules, each filled with a maximum of 28 visitors, up to London's best viewpoint (with up to 40 miles' visibility on a rare clear day). Aside from Big Ben, Parliament, St. Paul's Cathedral (not visible from here), and the wheel itself, central London's skyline is not overwhelming; it's a city that wows from within.

Next to the wheel sprawls the huge former County Hall building, now a hotel and tourist complex (with the Shrek's Adventure ride and the London Dungeon). The London Eye marks the start of the Jubilee Walkway, a pleasant one-hour riverside promenade along the South Bank of the Thames, through London's vibrant, gentrified arts-and-cultural zone. Along the way, you have views across the river of St. Paul's stately dome and the financial district, called The City.

London's history is tied to the **Thames,** the 210-mile river linking the interior of England with the North Sea. The city got its start in Roman times as a trade center along this watery highway. As recently as a century ago, large ships made their way upstream to the city center to unload. Today, the major port is 25 miles downstream, and tourist cruise boats ply the waters.

Look for the **boat piers** on either bank of the Thames. Several tour-boat companies offer regular cruises from Westminster

Pier (on the left) or London Eye Pier (on the right). This is an efficient, scenic way to get from here to the Tower of London or Greenwich (downstream) or Kew Gardens (upstream). For details, see page 36.

Lining the embankment, beneath the lampposts, are little green copper **lions' heads** (just about 2 feet tall) with rings for tying up boats. Before the construction of the Thames Barrier in 1982 (the world's second-largest movable flood barrier, downstream near Greenwich), high tides from the nearby North Sea made floods a recurring London problem. The police kept an eye on these lions: "When the lions drink, the city's at risk."

Notice how pedestrians are protected from bridge traffic. In 2017, a terrorist used a vehicle as a weapon to kill four pedestrians on this bridge. A few months later, after another similar attack on London Bridge, the government installed security barriers on eight Thames bridges. Londoners appreciate this pragmatic approach to keeping people safe—they know that when politicians and media overreact to a terrorist attack it only rewards and encourages the evil.

Until 1750, only London Bridge crossed the Thames. Then a bridge was built here. Early in the morning of September 3, 1802, William Wordsworth stood where you're standing and described what he saw:

> *This City now doth, like a garment, wear*
> *The beauty of the morning; silent, bare,*
> *Ships, towers, domes, theatres, and temples lie*
> *Open unto the fields, and to the sky;*
> *All bright and glittering in the smokeless air.*

• *Near Westminster Pier is a big statue of a lady on a chariot (nicknamed "the first woman driver"...no reins).*

❷ Statue of Boadicea, Queen of the Iceni

Riding in her two-horse chariot, daughters by her side, this Celtic Wonder Woman leads her people against Roman invaders. Julius Caesar was the first Roman general to cross the Channel, but even

WESTMINSTER

he was weirded out by the island's strange inhabitants, who worshipped trees, sacrificed virgins, and went to war painted blue. Later, Romans would subdue and civilize them, naming this spot on the Thames "Londinium" and building roads that turned it into a major urban center.

But Boadicea refused to be Romanized. In A.D. 60, after Roman soldiers raped her daughters, she rallied her people and "liberated" London, massacring its 60,000 Romanized citizens. However, the brief revolt was snuffed out, and she and her family took poison to avoid surrender.

• *There's a civilized public WC down the stairs behind Boadicea. Cross the street to just under Big Ben and continue one block inland to the busy intersection of Parliament Square. Pause here to survey the square.*

❸ Parliament Square

To your left are the sandstone-hued **Houses of Parliament.** If Parliament is in session, the entrance (midway down the building) is likely lined with tourists, enlivened by political demonstrations, and staked out by camera crews interviewing Members of Parliament (MPs) for the evening news. Only the core part, Westminster Hall, survives from the circa-1090s original. While the Houses of Parliament are commonly described as Neo-Gothic (even in this book), this uniquely English style is more specifically called Neo-Perpendicular Gothic. For a peek at genuine Perpendicular Gothic (the fanciest and final stage of that style), simply look across the street at the section of Westminster Abbey closest to the Houses of Parliament—it dates from 1484.

Kitty-corner across the square, the two white towers of **Westminster Abbey** rise above the trees. The broad boulevard of Whitehall (here called Parliament Street) stretches to your right up to Trafalgar Square.

Parliament Square is the heart of what was once a suburb of London—the medieval City of Westminster. Like Buda and Pest (later Budapest), London is two cities that grew into one. In Roman and medieval times, the city was centered farther east, around St. Paul's Cathedral. But in the 11th century, King Edward the Confessor moved his court here, and the center of political power shifted to this area. Edward built a palace and a church (minster) here in the west, creating the city of "West Min-

WESTMINSTER

ster." Over time, the palace evolved into a meeting place for debating public policy—a parliament. Today's Houses of Parliament sit atop the remains of Edward's original palace.

Across from Parliament, the cute little church with the blue sundials, snuggling under the Abbey "like a baby lamb under a ewe," is **St. Margaret's Church.** Since 1480, this has been *the* place for politicians' weddings, including Winston and Clementine Churchill's.

The expanse of green between Westminster Abbey and Big Ben is filled with statues that honor famous statesmen for their contributions to Britain and to mankind. The statue of **Winston Churchill,** the man who saved Britain from Hitler, shows him in the military overcoat he was fond of wearing. According to tour guides, the statue has a current of electricity running through it to honor Churchill's wish that if a statue were made of him, his

head wouldn't be soiled by pigeons. At the opposite corner of the square from Churchill stands **Nelson Mandela,** who battled South African apartheid. Nearby is the robed statue of **Mahatma Gandhi,** who helped liberate India from the British. And behind them

(across the street) stands the man who liberated America's slaves, **Abraham Lincoln** (erected in 1920, patterned after a similar statue in Chicago's Lincoln Park).

The white building (flying the Union Jack) at the far end of the square houses Britain's **Supreme Court.** You can wander the building after going through security, see a small exhibit on this recently sanctioned legal body, and observe any courts currently in session (it also has a café and WCs).

In 1868, the world's first traffic light was installed on the corner where Whitehall now spills double-decker buses into the square. Another reminder of a bygone era is the little yellow "Taxi" lantern atop the fence on the street corner closest to Parliament. In pre-mobile phone days, when an MP needed a taxi, this lit up to hail one. And here's one more ancient artifact: Along the north side of Parliament Square are some nearly obsolete remnants of 20th-century technology—red phone booths, mainly used today by tourists wanting a photo-op with Big Ben.

• *Consider touring Westminster Abbey (*📖 *see the Westminster Abbey Tour chapter). Otherwise, turn right (north), walk away from the Houses of Parliament and the Abbey, and continue up Parliament Street, which becomes Whitehall.*

❹ Walking Along Whitehall

Today, Whitehall is choked with traffic, but imagine the effect this broad street must have had on out-of-towners a little more than a century ago. In your horse-drawn carriage, you'd clop along a tree-lined boulevard past well-dressed lords and ladies, dodging street urchins. Gazing left, then right, you'd try to take it all in, your eyes dazzled by the bone-white walls of this man-made marble canyon.

Whitehall is now the most important street in Britain, lined with the ministries of finance, treasury, and so on. You may see limos and camera crews as important dignitaries enter or exit. Political demonstrators wave signs and chant slogans—sometimes about issues foreign to most Americans (Britain's former colonies still resent the empire's continuing influence), and sometimes about issues very familiar to us (the wars in the Middle East and the economy). Notice the security measures. Iron grates seal off the concrete ditches between the buildings and sidewalks for protection against explosives. And concrete balustrades and black bollards protect key government departments and pedestrians alike.

The black ornamental arrowheads topping the iron fences were once colorfully painted. In 1861, Queen Victoria ordered them all painted black when her beloved Prince Albert ("the only one who called her Vickie") died. Possibly the world's most determined mourner, Victoria wore black for the standard two years of mourning—and then tacked on 38 more. (For more on Victoria, see the sidebar on page 102.)

• *Continue down Whitehall. On your right is a colorful pub, the **Red Lion**. (It's known for its bell that gave an eight-minute warning, calling MPs back for votes.) Across the street, a long one-block detour down King Charles Street leads to the **Churchill War Rooms**, the underground bunker of 27 rooms that was the nerve center of Britain's campaign against Hitler (see page 43 for details). Farther along, you reach a tall, square stone monument in the middle of the boulevard.*

❺ Cenotaph

This monument honors those who died in World Wars I and II. The monumental devastation of these wars led to the drastic decline of the British Empire.

The actual cenotaph is the slab that sits atop the pillar—an empty tomb. You'll notice no religious symbols on this memorial. The dead honored here came from many creeds and all corners of Britain's empire. It looks lost in a sea of noisy cars, but on each

Remembrance Sunday (closest to November 11), Whitehall is closed to traffic, the royal family fills the balcony overhead in the foreign ministry, and a memorial service is held around the cenotaph.

The year 2014 marked the centennial of the start of what Brits call "the Great War"— World War I. It's hard for an American to understand the war's long-term impact on Europe. On a single day (at the Battle of the Somme, 1916), the British suffered roughly as many casualties as the US did in the entire Vietnam War—nearly 60,000. It's said that if the roughly one million WWI dead from the British Empire were to march four abreast past the cenotaph, the sad parade would last for seven days.

• *Just past the cenotaph is a crosswalk. On the other (west) side of Whitehall is a black iron security gate guarding the entrance to Downing Street.*

❻ 10 Downing Street and the Ministry of Defence

Britain's version of the White House is where the prime minister and her husband live, at #10. It's the black-brick building 100 yards down the blocked-off street, on the right; there's a lantern and usually a security guard.

Like the White House's Rose Garden, the black door marked #10 is a highly symbolic point of power, popular for photo ops to mark big occasions. This is where suffragettes protested in the early 20th century, where Neville Chamberlain showed off his regrettable peace treaty with Hitler, and where Winston Churchill made famous the V-for-Victory sign. It's where President Barack Obama came to discuss global economic issues with Gordon Brown, and where David Cameron suffered his stunning Brexit defeat—which resulted in the appointment of a new prime minister, Theresa May.

It looks modest, but #10's entryway does open up into fairly impressive digs—the prime minister's offices (downstairs), her residence (upstairs), and two large formal dining rooms. The PM's staff has offices here. Many on the staff are permanent bureaucrats, staying on to serve as prime ministers come and go. The cabinet meets at #10 on Tuesday mornings. This is where foreign dignitaries come for official government dinners, where the prime minister receives honored schoolkids and victorious soccer teams, and where she gives monthly addresses to the nation. Next door, at #11, the chancellor of the exchequer (finance minister) lives with his family, and #12 houses the PM's press office.

This has been the traditional home of the prime minister since the position was created in the early 18th century. But even before that, the neighborhood (if not the building itself) was a center of power, where Edward the Confessor and Henry VIII had palaces. The facade is, frankly, quite cheap, having been built as part of a middle-class cul-de-sac of homes by American-born George Downing in the 1680s. When the first PM moved in, the humble interior was combined with a mansion in back. During a major upgrade in the 1950s, they discovered that the facade's black bricks were actually yellow—but had been stained by centuries of Industrial Age soot. To keep with tradition, they now paint the bricks black.

The guarded metal gates were installed in 1989 to protect against Irish terrorists. Even so, #10 was hit and partly damaged in 1991 by an Irish Republican Army mortar launched from a van. These days, there's typically not much to see unless a VIP happens to drive up. Then the bobbies snap to and check credentials, the gates open, the car is inspected for bombs, the traffic barrier midway down the street drops into its bat cave, the car drives in, and... the bobbies go back to mugging for the tourists.

The huge building across Whitehall from Downing Street is the **Ministry of Defence** (MOD), the "British Pentagon." This bleak place looks like a Ministry of Defence should. In front are statues of illustrious defenders of Britain. At the far right (in the beret, hands behind his back) stands "Monty"—**Field Marshal Bernard Law Montgomery** of World War II—who beat the Nazis in North Africa (defeating Erwin "The Desert Fox" Rommel at El Alamein), which gave the Allies a jumping-off point to retake Europe. Along with Churchill, Monty breathed confidence back into a

THE WOMEN OF WORLD WAR II

demoralized British army, persuading them they could ultimately beat Hitler. A **memorial** honoring the women who fought and died in World War II stands in the middle of the street. Its empty uniforms evoke the often-overlooked sacrifices of Britain's female war heroes.

You may be enjoying the shade of London's **plane trees.** They do well in polluted London: roots that thrive in clay, waxy leaves

Whitehall of the Victorian Era

It was in the mid-1800s that Westminster and its main street, Whitehall, really came into their own.

Queen Victoria's 64-year reign was a time of unparalleled progress, peace, and expansion—both of the British Empire and the British middle class. One-fifth of the globe fell under British colonial rule. The Industrial Revolution was booming, churning out new products in textile factories, moving people and goods on steam trains, and lighting the streets with gas lamps. By the end of the century, electricity and telephones joined the world's first subway.

Whitehall ruled that empire. The Royal Navy was head-quartered in the Old Admiralty Complex, and the army was by the Horse Guards (before later moving across the street to the new Ministry of Defence).

The police headquarters was at Scotland Yard. It got its

name from a former Scottish palace that once stood there. Then in 1829, London's newly formed Metropolitan Police force moved in. Because they were directed by Sir Robert "Bob" Peel, the police came to be known as "bobbies." Originally, these police only arrested criminals actually caught in the act. But during Victoria's reign, Scotland Yard also opened a detective wing. They used forensics and intellectual know-how to investigate past crimes. (CSI: Whitehall?) That work inspired Arthur Conan Doyle's stories of the fictional private detective Sherlock Holmes, who used logic and science to solve crimes that baffled even Scotland Yard. These days, London's police force—popularly known as "The Met"—is headquartered at "New" Scotland Yard. It's located not far from here, a few blocks west of Westminster Abbey.

Scotland Yard's most famous case was trying to find Jack the Ripper—a serial killer of the 1880s. He brutally murdered several prostitutes in East London, east of St. Paul's Cathedral. The case came to symbolize the tale of two cities that London had become by the Victorian Era. Here in Westminster, the police were headquartered in a clean neighborhood of shiny new marble buildings. Meanwhile, across town, the old city was in decay—a dirty den of criminals and Oliver Twist-type street urchins. Wealthy ladies and gentlemen were fleeing west. Westminster boomed while The City crumbled. For the next century, the western half turned its face away from its former city center.

Oh, and Jack the Ripper was never caught by Scotland Yard. Not even Sherlock Holmes could crack that case.

that self-clean in the rain, and bark that sheds and regenerates so pollution doesn't enter the trees' vascular systems.

Farther up Whitehall, flanked by the Welsh and Scottish government offices and (I hope) eternally pondering the cenotaph is an equestrian statue. **Field Marshal Douglas Haig** (marked with his honorary title, *Earl Haig*) was commander in chief of the British army from 1916 to 1918. He was responsible for ordering so many brave and not-so-brave British boys out of the trenches and onto the killing fields of World War I.

• *At the corner (same side as the Ministry of Defence), you'll find the...*

❼ Banqueting House

This two-story building is just about all that remains of what was once the biggest palace in Europe—Whitehall Palace, which

once stretched from Trafalgar Square to Big Ben. Henry VIII started building it when he moved out of the Palace of Westminster (now the Parliament) and into the residence of the archbishop of York. Queen Elizabeth I and other monarchs added on as England's worldwide prestige grew.

Today, the exterior of Greek-style columns and pediments looks rather ho-hum, much like every other white marble building in London. But in 1620 it was a one-of-a-kind wonder—a big white temple rising above small half-timbered huts. Built by architect Inigo Jones, it sparked London's interest in the classical style. Within a century, London was awash in Georgian-style architecture, the English version of Neoclassical.

Facing the Banqueting House, look at the first-floor windows (with the balustrade)—the site of one of the pivotal events of English history. On January 30, 1649, a man dressed in black appeared at one of the windows and looked out at a huge crowd that surrounded the building. He stepped out the window and onto a wooden platform. It was King Charles I. He gave a short speech to the crowd, framed by the magnificent backdrop of the Banqueting House. His final word was "Remember." Then he knelt and laid his neck on a block as another man in black approached. It was the executioner—who cut off the king's head.

Plop—the concept of divine monarchy in Britain was decapitated. But there would still be kings after Oliver Cromwell, the Protestant antimonarchist who brought about Charles I's death and then became England's leader. Soon after Cromwell's death, royalty was restored, and Charles' son, Charles II, got his revenge here

The Banqueting House Through History

Imagine the many events this place has hosted over the centuries. Originally built as the royal dining hall for the sprawling Whitehall Palace, the Banqueting House also served as its de facto throne room. Picture ambassadors arriving here and walking the length of this hall lined with courtiers to pay homage to the king on his canopied throne. Loyal subjects knelt here to be made knights and nobles.

In the 1600s, the hall was famous throughout Europe as an occasional theater. Plays called "masques" were performed by torchlight and featured mask-wearing actors, singers and dancers, and elaborate costumes, sets, and special effects.

Picture the scene in 1622, when the brand-new Banqueting House was inaugurated with a performance of *The Masque of Augurs*, by Shakespeare protégé Ben Jonson (with set design by the hall's architect, Inigo Jones). King James and his courtiers crowded the balcony and tiered seats, and watched in awe as a parade of goofy commoners in masks entered the hall, singing and reveling, accompanied by two dancing bears. The comic chaos was suddenly interrupted by Greek gods who descended magically from the ceiling, eventually bringing harmony to the realm—just as a wise king does. And behind one of the masks, one of the actors was none other than 21-year-old Prince "I just can't wait to be king" Charles.

In 1649, the Banqueting House served a much more serious purpose—as an execution site for the public beheading of Charles I. Oliver Cromwell subsequently used this symbolic spot to legitimize his own leadership as Lord Protector. When Charles' son, Charles II, restored the monarchy in 1660, it was here that they celebrated.

In 1698, a massive fire destroyed Whitehall Palace, leaving only the name and the Banqueting House. The monarchs moved their residence elsewhere, eventually to Buckingham Palace. The Banqueting House became the Royal Chapel, complete with organ and pews.

Today, besides being a museum, the Banqueting House still functions much as it did in its heyday—hosting government receptions for foreign dignitaries or for Parliament. World-renowned classical musicians perform for the paying public. And it's a rent-a-hall for parties and dinners: You could rent the venue for a wedding for as little as $24,000.

in the Banqueting Hall...by living well. But, from then on, every king knew that he ruled by the grace of Parliament.

• *You can pop into the Banqueting House, following the self-guided tour below. Otherwise, skip to "Horse Guards."*

Banqueting House Interior

Start with the 10-minute video on the history of the House, which shows the place in banqueting action. History buffs might consider the included 45-minute audioguide. The low-ceilinged ground floor, a.k.a. the Undercroft, was King James I's personal wine cellar and tasting room. Climb to the first floor to find a portrait of the doomed king.

The main hall is impressive—two stories high, white with gold trim, full of light, and topped with colorful paintings in a gold-coffered ceiling. At 55 feet wide, 55 feet high, and 110 feet long, it's a perfect double cube. The chandeliers can be raised and lowered to accommodate any event. The throne is a modern reconstruction, but it gives an idea of the king's canopied throne that once stood here.

Ceiling Paintings: Charles I, who inherited the Banqueting House from his father, commissioned the famed Peter Paul Rubens to complete the decor. The paintings glorify Charles' dad, James I, the man who built the Banqueting House and who once told Parliament: "Kings are called gods...even by God himself."

To view the large oval painting in the center, *The Apotheosis of James I,* approach from the entrance, like a visiting ambassador, and watch the scene unfold. King James I (in red robe, with gray beard) rests his foot on a globe, as king of the whole world. Lady Faith (with a torch) and Miss Justice (with scales) lead him up into heaven, where baby angels blow trumpets and the goddess Minerva crowns him with the laurel wreath of wisdom. Minerva sticks her foot in our face, a triumph of illusion three centuries before 3-D glasses.

The painting above the throne, *The Peaceful Reign of King James,* shows wise King James seated on his throne, flanked by corkscrew columns from the temple of wise King Solomon. To the left, Peace embraces Plenty. Two angels swoop down at dramatic angles to adorn James with laurels, while a cherub holds his royal crown. Below, the Roman gods—Mercury, Mars, Minerva—arrive to help James subdue the serpents of rebellion.

In the painting above the entrance, *The Union of the Crowns,* James points his scepter at two ladies—England and Scotland—warning them to get along. James united the two bickering countries, having been crowned both King of Scots (in 1567) and King of England (1603). Smoke clouds of peace rise in the background as Cupid (bottom left corner) torches the weapons of war. The ladies place a crown on a baby's head and lead him to the throne. It's James' son, the future Charles I. When Charles grew up, he had this painting hung so that he could see it (right-side up) while seated on the Banqueting House throne.

• *When you're finished ogling the paintings, head back outside. Continue up Whitehall on the left (west) side, where you'll see (and smell) the building known as Horse Guards, guarded by traditionally dressed soldiers—who are also called Horse Guards.*

❽ Horse Guards

For 200 years, soldiers in cavalry uniforms have guarded this arched entrance along Whitehall that leads to Buckingham Palace and one of its predecessors as royal residence, St. James's Palace.

Two different squads alternate, so depending on the day you visit, you'll see soldiers in either red coats with white plumes in their helmets (the Life Guards), or blue coats with red plumes (the Blues and Royals). Together, they constitute the Queen's personal bodyguard. Besides their ceremonial duties here in old-time uniforms, these elite troops have fought in Iraq and Afghanistan. Both Prince William and Prince Harry have served in the Blues and Royals.

Stroll between the two guards, into the courtyard. The Horse Guards building was the headquarters of the British army from the time of the American Revolution until the Ministry of Defence was created in World War II. Back when this archway was the only access point to The Mall (the street leading to Buckingham Palace), it was a security checkpoint. Anyone on horseback had to dismount before passing through. Today, by tradition, you must dismount

WESTMINSTER

your bicycle, Vespa, or Segway and walk it through. During the 2012 Olympics, the broad expanse of Horse Guards Parade was covered in sand to host beach volleyball.

The Household Cavalry Museum (through the arch and to the right) offers a glimpse at the stables and a collection of uniforms and weapons (for details, see page 48).

• *Continue up Whitehall, passing the Old Admiralty (#26, on left), headquarters of the British navy that once ruled the waves. Across the street, behind the old Clarence Pub, stood the original Scotland Yard, headquarters of London's crack police force in the days of Sherlock Holmes. Finally, Whitehall opens up into the grand, noisy, traffic-filled Trafalgar Square.*

Marking the top of Whitehall (on the closest side of the square) is a small but proud statue of Charles I, erected here after the Restoration of the monarchy. The king, who was beheaded in 1649, looks all the way down the grand boulevard to the Houses of Parliament, which to this day symbolizes the people power that (under the leadership of Oliver Cromwell) made him a foot shorter at the top.

To reach the center of the square, cross a few streets at the crosswalks.

❾ Trafalgar Square

London's central meeting point bustles around the world's biggest Corinthian column, where **Admiral Horatio Nelson** stands 170 feet off the ground, looking over London in the direction of one of the greatest naval battles in history. Nelson saved England at a time as dark as World War II. In 1805, Napoleon was poised on the other side of the Channel, threatening to invade. Meanwhile, more than 900 miles away, the one-armed, one-eyed, and one-minded Lord Nelson attacked the French fleet off the coast of Spain at Trafalgar. The French were routed, Britannia ruled the waves, and the once-invincible French army was slowly worn down, then defeated at Waterloo. Nelson, while victorious, was shot by a sniper in the battle. He died, gasping, "Thank God, I have done my duty."

At the top of Trafalgar Square (north) sits the domed **National Gallery** with its grand staircase, and, to the right, the steeple of **St. Martin-in-the-Fields,** built in 1722, inspiring the steeple-over-the-entrance style of many town churches in New England (free lunch concerts—see page 453).

At the base of Nelson's column are bronze reliefs cast from melted-down enemy cannons, and four huggable lions dying to

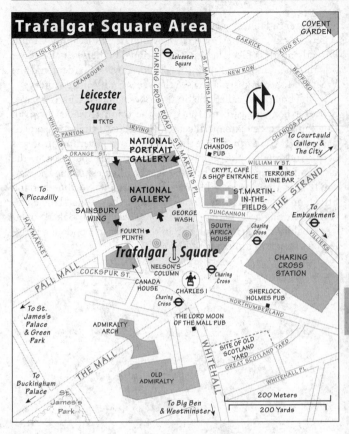

Trafalgar Square Area

Leicester Square

Leicester Square

TKTS

NATIONAL PORTRAIT GALLERY

THE CHANDOS PUB

CRYPT, CAFÉ & SHOP ENTRANCE

TERROIRS WINE BAR

NATIONAL GALLERY

ST. MARTIN-IN-THE-FIELDS

SAINSBURY WING

GEORGE WASH.

DUNCANNON

SOUTH AFRICA HOUSE

Charing Cross

To Embankment

FOURTH PLINTH

Trafalgar Square

NELSON'S COLUMN

CHARING CROSS STATION

CANADA HOUSE

Charing Cross

CHARLES I

Charing Cross

SHERLOCK HOLMES PUB

PALL MALL

COCKSPUR ST.

NORTHUMBERLAND

To St. James's Palace & Green Park

ADMIRALTY ARCH

THE LORD MOON OF THE MALL PUB

SITE OF OLD SCOTLAND YARD

GREAT SCOTLAND YARD

To Buckingham Palace

THE MALL

OLD ADMIRALTY

WHITEHALL PL.

St. James's Park

To Big Ben & Westminster

200 Meters

200 Yards

To Courtauld Gallery & The City

WILLIAM IV ST.

THE STRAND

To Piccadilly

LISLE ST.

CRANBOURN

WHITCOMB

PANTON

ORANGE ST.

STREET

HAYMARKET

CHARING CROSS ROAD

ST. MARTIN'S PL.

ST. MARTINS LANE

NEW ROW

GARRICK

KING ST.

BEDFORD

CHANDOS PL.

VILLIERS

WHITEHALL

COVENT GARDEN

IRVING

To Embankment

WESTMINSTER

have their photo taken with you. Of the many statues that dot the square, the pedestal on the northwest corner (the "fourth plinth") is periodically topped with contemporary art. The fountains, lit by colored lights, can shoot water 80 feet in the air.

Trafalgar Square is the center of modern London, connecting Westminster, The City, and the West End. Spin clockwise 360 degrees and survey the city:

To the south (down Whitehall) is the center of government, Westminster. Looking southwest, through the Admiralty Arch and down the broad boulevard called The Mall, you can see Buckingham Palace in the distance. (Down Pall Mall is St. James's Palace and Clarence House, where Prince Charles lives when in London.) A few blocks northwest of Trafalgar Square is Piccadilly Circus. Directly north (a block behind the National Gallery) sits Leicester Square, the jumping-off point for Soho, Covent Garden, and the West End theater district (☐ see the West End Walk chapter).

The boulevard called the Strand takes you past Charing Cross Station, then eastward to The City, the original walled town of London and today's financial center. In medieval times, when people from The City met with the Westminster government, it was here. And finally, Northumberland Street leads southeast to the Golden Jubilee pedestrian bridge over the Thames. Along the way, you'll pass the Sherlock Holmes Pub (just off Northumberland Street, on Craven Passage), housed in Sir Arthur Conan Doyle's favorite watering hole, with an upstairs replica of 221b Baker Street.

Soak it in. You're smack-dab in the center of London, a thriving city atop two millennia of history.

WESTMINSTER ABBEY TOUR

Westminster Abbey is more than just an "abbey"—it's the most famous English church in Christendom, where royalty has been wedded, crowned, and buried since the 11th century. Indeed, the histories of Westminster Abbey and England are almost the same. A thousand years of English history—3,000 tombs, the remains of 29 kings and queens, and hundreds of memorials to poets, politicians, scientists, and warriors—lie within its stained-glass splendor and under its stone slabs.

Orientation

Cost: £22, £44 family ticket (covers 2 adults and 1 child), cheaper if you book online, includes fine audioguide and entry to the cloister. Praying is free, thank God. It's also free to enter just the cloister (through Dean's Yard, around the right side as you face the main entrance), but if it's too crowded inside, the marshal at the cloister entrance may not let you in.

Hours: Abbey—Mon-Fri 9:30-16:30, Wed until 19:00 (main church only), Sat 9:30-14:30, last entry one hour before closing, closed Sun to sightseers but open for services; cloister—daily 8:00-18:00. Special events can shut down all or part of the Abbey.

Information: Tel. 020/7222-5152, www.westminster-abbey.org

Renovation: In the summer of 2018, the Abbey will open the **Queen's Diamond Jubilee Galleries** in a medieval balcony above the main floor of the church. This new church museum will also have breathtaking views of the Abbey's interior. To enter, it's likely that you'll need a timed-entry ticket; see the website for the latest information.

When to Go: The place is most crowded every day at midmorning and all day Saturdays and Mondays. Visit early, during lunch, or late to avoid tourist hordes. Weekdays after 14:30—especially Wed—are less congested; come late and stay for the 17:00 evensong (but keep in mind the Wed 17:00 evensong is generally spoken, not sung). The main entrance, on the Parliament Square side, often has a sizable line. You can skip it by booking tickets in advance via the Abbey's website. Show your ticket to the marshal at the entrance; only tickets bought directly through the Abbey's website qualify.

Dress Code: None, even for services.

Getting There: Near Big Ben and the Houses of Parliament (Tube: Westminster or St. James's Park).

Visitor Information: Because special events and services can shut out sightseers, check the website or call ahead to confirm that the Abbey is open, and get the latest schedule for guided tours, concerts, or services. If you have questions about the cathedral, ask any marshal in red or volunteer verger in green. There's surprisingly little posted information on the Abbey's sights, so you must rely on the audioguide, the vergers, or this book.

Church Services and Music: Mon-Fri at 7:30 (prayer), 8:00 (communion), 12:30 (communion), 17:00 evensong (except on Wed, when the evening service is generally spoken—not sung); **Sat** at 8:00 (communion), 9:00 (prayer), 15:00 (evensong; May-Aug it's at 17:00); **Sun** services generally come with more music: at 8:00 (communion), 10:00 (sung Matins), 11:15 (sung Eucharist), 15:00 (evensong), 18:30 (evening service). Services are free to anyone, though visitors who haven't paid church admission aren't allowed to linger afterward. Free **organ recitals** are usually held Sun at 17:45 (30 minutes). For a schedule of services or recitals on a particular day, look for posted signs with schedules or check the Abbey's website.

Tours: The included **audioguide** is excellent, taking some of the sting out of the steep admission fee. The Westminster Abbey Official Tour **app** includes an audio tour narrated by Jeremy Irons. To add to the experience, you can take an entertaining **guided tour** from a verger—the church equivalent of a museum docent (£5, schedule posted both outside and inside entry, up to 6/day in summer, 2-4/day in winter, 1.5 hours).

Length of This Tour: Allow 1.5 hours. If you have less time, focus on the main part of the church, skipping the cloister.

Visitor Services: WCs are in the cloister next to the café. Outside the Abbey, the nearest public pay WCs are in front of Methodist Central Hall, the grand domed building across the street from the Abbey's west entrance.

Eating: The Abbey's cellar has a **$$ café** with table service and simple fare (salads and sandwiches, £17.50 afternoon tea); enter through the cloister. Other options are nearby: **$ Wesley's Café,** the cafeteria in the basement of Methodist Central Hall across the street, serves cheap breakfast and lunch (Mon-Fri 8:00-16:00, Sat-Sun from 9:00, good free WC). The Supreme Court building on Parliament Square has a basic basement **$ café** and free WCs (must go through security checkpoint to enter; Mon-Fri 9:30-16:30, closed Sat-Sun). **$$ The Westminster Arms** pub is just past the Methodist Central Hall on Storey's Gate (pub grub including fish-and-chips served daily 12:00-20:00, eat downstairs). Picnickers can find benches at the nearby Jewel Tower, a half-block south of the Abbey.

Starring: Edwards, Elizabeths, Henrys, Annes, Marys, and poets.

The Tour Begins

You'll have no choice but to follow the steady flow of tourists through the church, along the route laid out for the audioguide. It's all one-way, and most days the crowds are a real crush. Here are the Abbey's top 10 (plus one) stops.

• *Walk straight in, entering the north transept. Pick up the map flier that locates the most illustrious tombs and borrow the included audioguide. Follow the crowd flow to the right, passing through* **"Scientists' Corner,"** *with memorials to Isaac Newton (to the left of the choir entrance), Michael Faraday, Charles Darwin (on the floor), and others. Enter the spacious...*

❶ Nave

Look down the long and narrow center aisle of the church. Lined with the raying hands of the Gothic arches, glowing with light from the stained glass, this is more than a museum. With saints in stained glass, heroes in carved stone, and the bodies of England's greatest citizens under the floor stones, Westminster Abbey is the religious heart of England.

The Abbey was built in 1065. Its name, Westminster, means Church in the West (west of St. Paul's Cathedral). The king who built the Abbey was Edward the Confessor. Find him in the stained glass windows on the left side of the nave ("left" as you face the altar). He's in the third bay from the end (marked *S: Edwardus rex...*), with his crown, scepter, and ring. Take some time to thank him for this Abbey.

For the next 250 years, the Abbey was redone and remodeled to become essentially the church you see today, notwithstanding an extensive resurfacing in the 19th century. Thankfully, later archi-

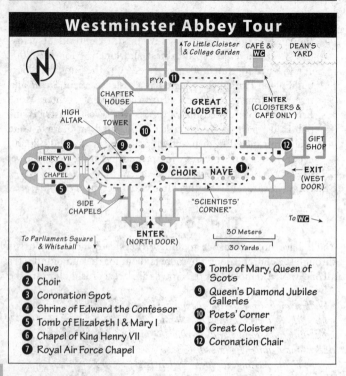

Westminster Abbey Tour

1. Nave
2. Choir
3. Coronation Spot
4. Shrine of Edward the Confessor
5. Tomb of Elizabeth I & Mary I
6. Chapel of King Henry VII
7. Royal Air Force Chapel
8. Tomb of Mary, Queen of Scots
9. Queen's Diamond Jubilee Galleries
10. Poets' Corner
11. Great Cloister
12. Coronation Chair

tects—ignoring building trends of their generation—honored the vision of the original planner, and the building was completed in one relatively harmonious style.

The Abbey's 10-story nave is the tallest in England. The chandeliers, 10 feet tall, look small in comparison (16 were given to the Abbey by the Guinness family).

On the floor near the west entrance of the Abbey is the flower-lined **Grave of the Unknown Warrior,** one ordinary WWI soldier buried in soil from France with lettering made from melted-down weapons from that war. Take time to contemplate the million-man army from the British Empire, and all those who gave their lives. Their memory is so revered that, when Kate Middleton walked up the aisle on her wedding day, by tradition she had to step around the tomb (and her wedding bouquet was later placed atop this tomb, also in accordance with tradition). Hanging on a column next to the tomb is the US Medal of Honor, presented by General John J. Pershing in 1921 to honor England's WWI dead. Closer to the door, also on the floor, is a memorial to a hero of World War II, Winston Churchill.

• *Now walk straight up the nave toward the altar. This is the same route every future monarch walks on the way to being crowned. Midway up the nave, you pass through the colorful screen of an enclosure known as the...*

❷ Choir

These elaborately carved wood and gilded seats are where monks once chanted their services in the "quire"—as it's known in British churchspeak. Today, it's where the Abbey boys' choir sings the evensong. You're approaching the center of a cross-shaped church.

The **"high" (main) altar**—which usually has a cross and candlesticks atop it—sits on the platform up the five stairs in front of you.

• *It's on this platform that the monarch is crowned.*

❸ Coronation Spot

The area immediately before the high altar is where every English coronation since 1066 has taken place. Imagine the day when Prince William becomes king. (Or you can picture Prince Charles, who'll come first if his mother doesn't manage to outlive him.)

The nobles in robes and powdered wigs look on from the carved wooden stalls of the choir. The Archbishop of Canterbury stands at the high altar. The coronation chair (which we'll see later) is placed before the altar on the round, brown pavement stone representing the earth. Surrounding the whole area are temporary bleachers for 8,000 VIPs, going halfway up the rose windows of each transept, creating a "theater."

Long silver trumpets hung with banners sound a fanfare as the monarch-to-be enters the church. The congregation sings, "I will go into the house of the Lord," as William parades slowly down the nave and up the steps to the altar. After a church service, he sits in the chair, facing the altar, where the crown jewels are placed. William is anointed with holy oil, then receives a ceremonial sword, ring, and cup. The royal scepter is placed in his hands, and—dut, dutta dah—the archbishop lowers the Crown of St. Edward the Confessor onto his royal head. Finally, King William V stands up, descends the steps, and is presented to the people. As cannons roar throughout the city, the people cry, "God save the king!"

Royalty are also given funerals here. Princess Diana's coffin was carried to this spot for her funeral service in 1997. The "Queen Mum" (mother of Elizabeth II) had her funeral here in 2002. This is also where most of the last century's royal weddings have taken place, including the unions of Queen Elizabeth II and Prince Philip (1947), her parents (1923), her sister Princess Margaret (1960), and her son Prince Andrew (to Sarah Ferguson, 1986). Most recently, in April 2011, Prince William and Kate Middleton strolled up the nave, passed through the choir, climbed the five steps to the high altar, and became husband and wife—and the future King and Queen of the United Kingdom and its Commonwealth. Though royal marriages and funerals can happen anywhere, only one church can hold a coronation—the Abbey.

• *Now veer left and follow the crowd. You'll walk past the statue of Robert ("Bob") Peel, the prime minister whose policemen were nicknamed "bobbies." Stroll a few yards into the land of dead kings and queens. Use the audioguide to explore the* **side chapels**—*the Chapel of St. John the Baptist and Chapel of St. Michael. There you'll see effigies of the dead lying atop their tombs of polished stone. They lie on their backs or recline on their sides. Dressed in ruffed collars, they relax on pillows, clasping their hands in prayer, many buried side by side with their spouses.*

After exploring the chapels, pause at the wooden staircase on your right.

❹ Shrine of Edward the Confessor

The holiest part of the church is the raised area behind the altar (where the wooden staircase leads—sorry, no tourist access except with verger tour). Step back and peek over the dark coffin of Edward I to see the tippy-top of the green-and-gold wedding-cake tomb of King Edward the Confessor—the man who built Westminster Abbey.

God had told pious Edward to visit St. Peter's Basilica in Rome. But with the Normans thinking conquest, it was too dangerous for him to leave England. Instead, he built this grand church and dedicated it to St. Peter. It was finished just in time to bury Edward and to crown his foreign successor, William the Conqueror, in 1066. After Edward's death, people prayed at his tomb, and, after getting good results, Pope Alexander III canonized him. This elevated, central tomb—which lost some of its luster when Henry VIII melted down the gold coffin-case—is surrounded by the tombs of eight kings and queens.

• *Continue on. At the top of the stone staircase, veer left into the private burial chapel of Queen Elizabeth I.*

❺ Tomb of Queens Elizabeth I and Mary I

Although only one effigy is on the tomb (Elizabeth's), there are actually two queens buried beneath it, both daughters of Henry VIII (by different mothers). Bloody Mary—meek, pious, sickly, and Catholic—enforced Catholicism during her short reign (1553-1558) by burning "heretics" at the stake.

Elizabeth—strong, clever, and Protestant—steered England on an Anglican course. She holds a royal orb symbolizing that she's queen of the whole globe. When 26-year-old Elizabeth was crowned in the Abbey, her right to rule was questioned (especially by her Catholic subjects) because she was considered the bastard seed of Henry VIII's unsanctioned marriage to Anne Boleyn. But

Elizabeth's long reign (1559-1603) was one of the greatest in English history, a time when England ruled the seas and Shakespeare explored human emotions. When she died, thousands turned out for her funeral in the Abbey. Elizabeth's face on the tomb, modeled after her death mask, is considered a very accurate take on this hook-nosed, imperious "Virgin Queen" (she never married).

The two half-sisters disliked each other in life—Mary even had Elizabeth locked up in the Tower of London for a short time. Now they lie side by side for eternity. The Latin inscription ends, "Here we lie, two sisters in hope of one resurrection."

• *Continue into the ornate, flag-draped room up a few more stairs, directly behind the main altar.*

❻ Chapel of King Henry VII (The Lady Chapel)

The light from the stained-glass windows; the colorful banners overhead; and the elaborate tracery in stone, wood, and glass give this room the festive air of a medieval tournament. The prestigious Knights of the Bath meet here, under the magnificent ceiling studded with gold pendants. The ceiling—of carved stone, not plaster (1519)—is the finest English Perpendicular Gothic and fan vault-

ing you'll see (unless you're going to King's College Chapel in Cambridge). The ceiling was sculpted on the floor in pieces, then jigsaw-puzzled into place. It capped the Gothic period and signaled the vitality of the coming Renaissance.

The knights sit in the wooden stalls with their coats of arms on the back, churches on their heads, their banner flying above, and the graves of dozens of kings beneath their feet. When the Queen worships here, she sits in the southwest corner chair under the carved wooden throne with the lion crown (immediately to the left as you enter).

Behind the small altar is an iron cage housing tombs of the old warrior Henry VII of Lancaster and his wife, Elizabeth of

York. Their love and marriage finally settled the Wars of the Roses between the two clans. The combined red-and-white rose symbol decorates the top band of the ironwork. Henry VII, the first Tudor king, was the father of Henry VIII and the grandfather of Elizabeth I. This exuberant chapel heralds a new optimistic postwar era as England prepares to step onto the world stage.

• *Go to the far end of the chapel and stand at the banister in front of the modern set of stained-glass windows.*

❼ Royal Air Force Chapel

Saints in robes and halos mingle with pilots in parachutes and bomber jackets. This tribute to WWII flyers is for those who earned their angel wings in the Battle of Britain (July-Oct 1940). Hitler's air force ruled the skies in the early days of the war, bombing at will, and threatening to snuff Britain out without a fight. But while determined Londoners hunkered down underground, British pilots in their Spitfires and Hurricanes took advantage of newly invented radar to get the jump on the more powerful Luftwaffe. These were the fighters about whom Churchill said, "Never...was so much owed by so many to so few."

The Abbey survived the Battle and the Blitz, but this window did not. As a memorial, a bit of bomb damage has been preserved—the little glassed-over hole in the wall below the windows in the lower left-hand corner. The book of remembrances lists each of the 1,497 airmen (including one American) who died in the Battle of Britain.

You're standing on the grave of Oliver Cromwell, leader of the rebel forces in England's Civil War. Or, rather, what had been his grave, when Cromwell was buried here from 1658 to 1661. Then his corpse was exhumed, hanged, drawn, quartered, and decapitated, and the head displayed on a stake as a warning to anarchists.

• *Exit the Chapel of Henry VII. Turn left into a side chapel with the tomb (the central one of three in the chapel).*

❽ Tomb of Mary, Queen of Scots

Historians get dewy-eyed over the fate of Mary, Queen of Scots (1542-1587). The beautiful, French-educated queen was held under house arrest for 19 years by Queen Elizabeth I, who considered her a threat to her sovereignty. Elizabeth got wind of an assassination plot, suspected Mary was behind it, and had her first cousin (once removed) beheaded. When Elizabeth died

childless, Mary's son—James VI, King of Scots—also became King James I of England and Ireland. James buried his mum here (with her head sewn back on) in the Abbey's most sumptuous tomb.

• *Exit Mary's chapel. Ahead of you, again, is the tomb of the church's founder, Edward the Confessor. Continue on, until you emerge in the south transept. Look for the doorway that leads to a stairway and elevator to the...*

❾ Queen's Diamond Jubilee Galleries

In the summer of 2018, the Abbey will open a space that has been closed off for 700 years—an internal gallery 70 feet above the main floor known as the triforium. This balcony will house the new Queen's Diamond Jubilee Galleries, a small museum where you'll see exhibits covering royal coronations, funerals, and much more from the Abbey's 1,000-year history. There will also be stunning views of the nave straight down to the Great West Door. Because of limited access to the galleries, it's likely visitors will need a timed-entry ticket (see the Abbey website for details).

• *After touring the Queen's Galleries, return to the main floor. You're in...*

❿ Poets' Corner

England's greatest artistic contributions are in the written word. Here the masters of arguably the world's most complex and expressive language are remembered. (Many writers are honored with plaques and monuments; relatively few are actually buried here.)

• *Start with Chaucer, buried in the wall under the blue windows, marked with a white plaque reading* Qui Fuit Anglorum...

Geoffrey Chaucer (c. 1343-1400) is often considered the father of English literature. Chaucer's *Canterbury Tales* told of earthy people speaking everyday English, not French or Latin. He was the first great writer buried in the Abbey (thanks to his job as a Westminster clerk). Later, it became a tradition to bury other writers here, and Poets' Corner was built around his tomb. The blue windows have blank panels awaiting the names of future poets.

• *The plaques on the floor before Chaucer are gravestones and memorials to other literary greats.*

Lord Byron, the great lover of women and adventure: "Though the night was made for loving, / And the day returns too soon, / Yet we'll go no more a-roving / By the light of the moon."

Dylan Thomas, alcoholic master of modernism, with a Romantic's heart: "Oh as I was young and easy in the mercy of his means, / Time held me green and dying / Though I sang in my chains like the sea."

W. H. Auden, Brit-turned-American modernist on love, politics, and religion: "He was my North, my South, my East and West / My working week and Sunday rest / My noon, my midnight, my talk, my song / I thought that love would last forever: I was wrong."

Lewis Carroll, creator of *Alice's Adventures in Wonderland* and *Through the Looking-Glass:* "'Twas brillig, and the slithy toves / Did gyre and gimble in the wabe..."

T. S. Eliot, American-turned-British author of the influential *Waste Land:* "April is the cruellest month, breeding / Lilacs out of the dead land, mixing / Memory and desire, stirring / Dull roots with spring rain."

Alfred, Lord Tennyson, conscience of the Victorian era: "'Tis better to have loved and lost / Than never to have loved at all."

Robert Browning: "Oh, to be in England / Now that April's there."

• *Farther out in the south transept, you'll find a statue of...*

William Shakespeare: Although he's not buried here, this greatest of English writers is honored by a fine statue that stands near the end of the transept, overlooking the others: "Life's but a walking shadow, a poor player that struts and frets his hour upon the stage and then is heard no more."

George Frideric Handel: High on the wall opposite Shakespeare is the German immigrant famous for composing the *Messiah* oratorio: "Hallelujah, hallelujah, hallelujah." The statue's features are modeled on Handel's death mask. Musicians can read the vocal score in his hands for "I Know That My Redeemer Liveth." His actual tomb is on the floor, next to...

Charles Dickens, whose serialized novels brought literature to the masses: "It was the best of times, it was the worst of times."

On the floor near Shakespeare, you'll also find the tombs of **Samuel Johnson** (who wrote the first English dictionary) and the great English actor **Laurence Olivier.** (Olivier disdained the "Method" style of acting—experiencing intense emotions in order to portray them. When co-star Dustin Hoffman stayed up all night in order to appear haggard for a scene, Olivier said, "My dear boy, why don't you simply try acting?")

And finally, near the center of the transept, find the small, white floor plaque of **Thomas Parr** (marked *THO: PARR*). Check the dates of his life (1483-1635) and do the math. In his (reputed) 152 years, he served 10 sovereigns and was a contemporary of Columbus, Henry VIII, Elizabeth I, Shakespeare, and Galileo. Famous simply for supposedly being an "Old, Old, Very Old Man," as poet John Taylor dubbed him in 1635, Parr is mentioned in works by celebrated writers such as Charles Dickens, Henry David Thoreau, Bram Stoker, Robert Graves, and James Joyce.

• *Exit the church (temporarily) at the south door, which leads to the...*

⓫ Great Cloister

The buildings that adjoin the church housed the monks. (The church is known as the "abbey" because it was the headquarters of the Benedictine Order until Henry VIII kicked them out in 1540.)

Cloistered courtyards gave them a place to meditate on God's creations.

The **Chapter House** is where the monks had daily meetings. It features fine architecture and stained glass, some faded but well-described medieval paintings and floor tiles, and—in the corridor—Britain's oldest door. A few steps farther down the hall is the **Pyx Chamber.** This old, thick-walled room once safeguarded the coins used to set the silver standard of the realm (a pyx is a small box that held gold and silver coins).

As you return to the church, look back through the cloister courtyard to the church exterior, and meditate on the **flying buttresses.** These stone bridges that push in on the church walls allowed Gothic architects to build so high.

If you need a bite or drink, or the WC, head for the abbey café.

• *Go back into the church for the last stop.*

⓬ Coronation Chair

A gold-painted oak chair waits here under a regal canopy for the next coronation. For every English coronation since 1308 (except two), it's been moved to its spot before the high altar to receive the royal buttocks. The chair's legs rest on lions, England's symbol. The space below the chair originally held a big sandstone

rock from Scotland called the Stone of Scone (pronounced "skoon"), symbolizing Scotland's unity with England's monarch. But in the 1990s, Britain gave Scotland more sovereignty, its own Parliament, and the Stone, which Scotland has agreed to loan to

Britain for future coronations (the rest of the time, it's on display in Edinburgh Castle).

Next to the chapel with the chair hangs a 600-year-old portrait of King Richard II. The boy king is holding the royal orb and scepter, wearing the crown, and seated upon this very chair.

Finally, take one last look down the nave. Listen to and ponder this place, filled with the remains of the people who made Britain a world power—saints, royalty, poets, musicians, scientists, soldiers, politicians. Now step back outside into a city filled with the modern-day poets, saints, and heroes who continue to make Britain great.

HOUSES OF PARLIAMENT TOUR

With an epic history, the Houses of Parliament (home to the House of Commons and the House of Lords) remains the site of fierce verbal tussles among members of the UK's Conservative, Labour, and smaller parties. "Westminster" (as Brits call the place) appears almost nightly on TV, as the impressive backdrop to the latest political news. A visit here gives both UK residents and foreign tourists alike a chance to tour a piece of living history and see the British government in action.

The Houses are open and free to the public when Parliament is in session (check online). You can stroll through the building's majestic rooms and watch Parliament give speeches and debate policy. When Parliament is recessed, and on Saturdays year-round, you can still visit by paying for a guided tour or audioguide. In fact, recess is the best time for touring the lavish palace itself, as you have more freedom to roam and view additional rooms. My self-guided tour covers the main rooms you'll see with either option.

Orientation

Cost: Free when Parliament is in session; otherwise must visit with a paid tour or audioguide (see below).

Hours: Open for nonticketed entry when Parliament is in session, generally from October to late July, Monday through Thursday (House of Commons—Mon 14:30-22:30, Tue-Wed 11:30-19:30, Thu 9:30-17:30; House of Lords—Mon-Tue 14:30-22:00, Wed 15:00-22:00, Thu 11:00-19:30; last entry depends on debates; exact schedule at www.parliament.uk). When Parliament is not in session, you can visit by booking a tour or renting an audioguide (see next page).

Information: Tel. 020/7219-4272 or 020/7219-3107, www. parliament.uk.

When to Go: Expect lines—it may take 20-30 minutes to get through security, then another 20-60 minutes to be admitted to the House chambers. You'll have the best chance of viewing both chambers if you arrive at around 14:00. Lines are longest at the start of each day's session, but that's when the most fiery debates often occur (and it's almost impossible to enter on Wed, when the prime minister normally attends). The later in the day you enter, the less crowded (and less exciting) it is. Avoid going at 16:00, when parliamentary functions make things extra busy. Visiting after 18:00 is risky, as sessions can end well before their official closing time, and visitors aren't allowed in after the politicians call it a day.

Getting There: You can't miss this gigantic riverside Neo-Gothic temple of government—it's London's most recognized symbol. The visitors entrance is around the back side (away from the river) on Cromwell Green, facing the buttresses of Westminster Abbey. Tube: Westminster.

Choosing a House: As you line up to enter the building, the guard may ask if you want to visit the House of Commons or the House of Lords. The House of Lords is less important politically, but they meet in a more ornate room, and the wait time is shorter (likely less than 30 minutes). The House of Commons is where major policy is made, but the room is sparse, and wait times are longer (30-60 minutes or more).

I choose "Lords" (because the line is shorter), but it really doesn't matter. Once inside the building, you'll be able to sightsee the public spaces described in this tour as you make your way to the chamber you intend to visit.

Visitor Information: To see what it's like when Parliament is in session, visit www.parliamentlive.tv. To preview a debate from home, tune into "Prime Minister's Questions"; in the US, the broadcast airs live Wed mornings on C-SPAN2 and repeats Sun evenings on regular C-SPAN (www.c-span.org).

Tours: On Saturdays and whenever Parliament is in recess (late July-Sept), you can only enter by taking a behind-the-scenes **tour** with a live guide or by paying for an **audioguide** which lets you sightsee on your own. There are advantages to visiting during a recess: It may be less crowded, you have access to additional palatial rooms, and you can see the interior of both chambers without a wait—all while learning about the history of Britain's political system (audioguide tour-£18.50, guided tour-£25.50, 1.5 hours, both tours depart every 15-20 minutes on a timed-entry system, Sat 9:00-16:30 and most weekdays

during recess—days and times vary, confirm schedule at www.
parliament.uk).

    Book ahead online or by calling 020/7219-4114 to secure
a time slot, or try booking on the spot at Portcullis House, near
Westminster Bridge and Big Ben (ticket office open Mon-Fri
10:00-16:00, Sat 9:00-16:30, closed Sun, enter from Victoria
Embankment). For either a guided tour or an audioguide, arrive at the visitors entrance on Cromwell Green 30 minutes
before your tour time to clear security.

Length of This Tour: Once you clear the security rigmarole, it
takes less than an hour to tour the interior and drop in—brief-
ly—on a parliamentary session.

Starring: A grand building and a gaggle of chattering parliamentarians.

BACKGROUND

The Palace of Westminster has been the center of political power
in England for nearly a thousand years. Around 1050, King Edward the Confessor moved here to be next to his newly constructed
"minster" (church) in the "west"—Westminster Abbey. The Palace became the monarch's official residence, the meeting place
of his noble advisors, and the supreme court of the land. In the
1500s, Henry VIII moved down the block to Whitehall Palace
(now destroyed, see page 125), and later monarchs chose to live at
Kensington and Buckingham Palaces. But Westminster Palace remained home to the increasingly powerful advisors, or Parliament.

    In 1834, a horrendous fire gutted the Palace. It was rebuilt in
a retro Neo-Gothic style that recalled England's medieval Christian roots—pointed arches, stained-glass windows, spires, and
saint-like statues. At the same time, Britain was also retooling its
government. Democracy was on the rise, the queen became a constitutional monarch, and Parliament emerged as the nation's ruling body. The Palace of Westminster became a symbol—a kind of
cathedral—of democracy.

The Tour Begins

• *Enter midway along the west side of the building (across the street from
Westminster Abbey), where a tourist ramp leads to the...*

❶ Visitors Entrance

Line up for the airport-style security check. You'll be given a visitor
badge. If you have questions, the attendants are extremely helpful.

• *Once past security, you pass through an open-air courtyard in the shadow of Big Ben, and enter Westminster Hall. Here (through the door to*

the right), you'll find the WCs, gift shop, and the Jubilee Café (which has live video feeds of Parliament in session). Now take in the cavernous...

❷ Westminster Hall

This vast hall—covering 16,000 square feet—survived the 1834 fire, and is one of the oldest and most important buildings in England. In some ways, this hall is where modern democracy was born.

Begun in 1097, the hall first served as the heart of the monarch's residence, the Palace of Westminster. It was the glorious throne room. The king would preside from the far (south) end, atop a raised platform—dispensing justice, welcoming ambassadors, hosting his coronation banquet, toasting revelers. By the late-1200s, the hall had also become the place where nobles would occasionally gather with the king to address their concerns and simply talk (or *"parler"*)—the first Parliament.

The hall was extensively remodeled around 1390 by Richard II, who made it the grandest space in Europe. His self-supporting oak-timber roof (1397) wowed everyone. Unlike earlier roofs that spanned the hall with long beams, this "hammer-beam" roof uses short beams that jut horizontally out from the walls. They're part of a complex system of curved braces and arches that distribute the weight of the roof outward to the walls, not downward to the floor, so there's no need for supporting pillars. The 26 carved angels also do their part to hold up the 650-ton roof and tirelessly support the chandeliers with their necks.

Stroll the room to read various information displays and plaques (in the pavement) about the hall's history. In the 1300s, the hall began hosting not only assemblies of nobles (or "Lords") but gatherings of knights, mayors, and businessmen from towns and shires across England—what would become the "Commons." England's vaunted legal system was invented in this hall, as this was the major court of the land for 700 years. In 1305, the Scottish patriot William ("Braveheart") Wallace was tried here. In 1483, Richard ("Now is the winter of our discontent") III had his coronation after-party here. King Charles I was tried and sentenced to death here. Guy Fawkes was condemned for plotting to blow up the Halls of Parliament in 1605. (He's best remembered today for the sly-smiling "Guy Fawkes mask"—now the symbol of 21st-century anarchists.)

In more recent times, this hall has hosted the lying-in-state of

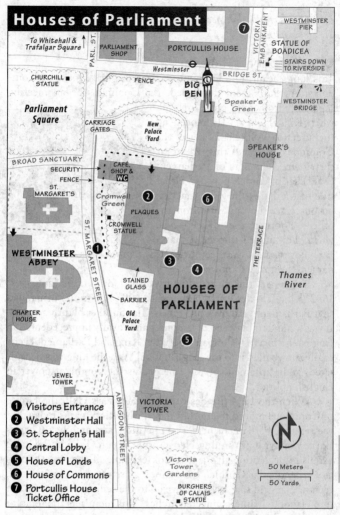

Houses of Parliament

To Whitehall &
Trafalgar Square

PARL. ST.

PARLIAMENT
SHOP

PORTCULLIS HOUSE

WESTMINSTER
PIER

VICTORIA EMBANKMENT

STATUE OF
BOADICEA

Westminster

BRIDGE ST.

STAIRS DOWN
TO RIVERSIDE

CHURCHILL
STATUE

FENCE

BIG
BEN

Speaker's
Green

WESTMINSTER
BRIDGE

**Parliament
Square**

CARRIAGE
GATES

New
Palace
Yard

SPEAKER'S
HOUSE

BROAD SANCTUARY

SECURITY
FENCE

CAFÉ,
SHOP &
WC

ST.
MARGARET'S

*Cromwell
Green*

❷

❻

PLAQUES

CROMWELL
STATUE

**WESTMINSTER
ABBEY**

ST. MARGARET STREET

❶

❸

❹

THE TERRACE

*Thames
River*

STAINED
GLASS

BARRIER

*Old
Palace
Yard*

**HOUSES OF
PARLIAMENT**

CHAPTER
HOUSE

❺

JEWEL
TOWER

ABINGDON STREET

VICTORIA
TOWER

*Victoria
Tower
Gardens*

BURGHERS
OF CALAIS
STATUE

N

50 Meters

50 Yards

❶ Visitors Entrance
❷ Westminster Hall
❸ St. Stephen's Hall
❹ Central Lobby
❺ House of Lords
❻ House of Commons
❼ Portcullis House
   Ticket Office

HOUSES OF PARLIAMENT

Winston Churchill, George VI, and the Queen Mother. In 2011, Britain's bigwigs gathered here for a speech by then-President Barack Obama.

At the far end of the hall, ascend the stairs to the landing, called "St. Stephen's Porch." The huge stained-glass window (with the UK's lion-and-unicorn coat of arms in the center) is relatively new, having replaced bomb damage from World War II. To the left of the window, above the doorway, find the circle of colorful medallions—an art installation celebrating women's suffrage.

• *Take one more look back over Westminster Hall, with a king's-eye view of this cradle of democracy. Now continue up the stairs, and enter St. Stephen's Hall.*

❸ St. Stephen's Hall

This long, beautifully lit room was the original House of Commons. As Parliament developed, the Commons began meeting separately from the Lords. In 1530, when King Henry VIII moved up the street to Whitehall Palace, the Commons claimed this room as their own. Members of Parliament (MPs) sat in church pews on either side of the hall—the ruling faction on one side, the opposition on the other—a format they'd keep even when they moved into new chambers. For the next three centuries, this room was the center of Parliament, as it rose to power.

It was here that British history turned forever. On January 4, 1642, King Charles I marched in with 400 soldiers and demanded that Parliament turn over five rebels. The Speaker bluntly refused. It was a standoff between commoners and royalty unprecedented in English history. This impasse between King and Parliament eventually snowballed into the English Civil War, the king was decapitated, and Parliament finally emerged as the dominant power in English politics.

When the 1834 fire destroyed St. Stephen's Hall, the House of Commons moved to another room, where it remains today. For the rebuild, Parliament held a competition, and architect Charles Barry won with a stunning Neo-Gothic design. Take in the hall's exquisite decoration. It's a textbook example of the style known as Perpendicular Gothic. The stained-glass windows form a tall, rectangular grid that leads the eye up to the ceiling, which fans out into elaborately interconnected arches. This room sets the tone for the Perpendicular style we'll see throughout the palace.

The room's decorations emphasize the proud spirit that helped create modern democracy. The mosaic over the entrance depicts King Edward III, who ratified the House of Commons in the 1300s. The windows feature England's towns and boroughs which gained a voice through the Commons. The statues that line the room honor distinguished parliamentarians, including Robert Walpole (England's first prime minister), as well as Edmund Burke and William Pitt, both of whom supported the democratic ideals of the American Revolution.

The room's murals depict major events in English history. It starts (on the left wall) in the year 877 with the English people rallying to drive off the Danes to preserve their independence. Next up is the almost-legendary 12th-century king, Richard the Lion-heart. Then it's 1215, and the nobles force the tyrant King John to sign the Magna Carta—a charter that limited absolute monarchy and started the whole concept of a parliament. Next, English people read the Wycliffe Bible, which put the word of God in the hands of ordinary citizens. The mural on the opposite wall shows the courageous Speaker of the House Thomas More, standing up to a cardinal representing King Henry VIII, even though it would eventually cost More his life.

• *Now, put your camera away, and continue into the next room, the...*

❹ Central Lobby

This ornate, octagonal, high-vaulted room is often called the "heart of British government," because it sits in the geographical center of the Palace, midway between the House of Commons (to the left) and the House of Lords (right). Clerks bustle about. Constituents come to this lobby to petition, or "lobby," their MPs (from which the term may derive). Television newscasters interview MPs here for the evening news, with this magnificent Neo-Gothic backdrop. Video monitors list the schedule of meetings and events going on in this 1,100-room governmental hive.

This is the best place to admire the Palace's interior decoration—carved wood, chandeliers, statues, and floor tiles. Long, slender columns rise from the floor and fan out into a dazzling gilded ceiling studded with bosses, where Gothic ribs create a kaleidoscope effect. Architect Barry and his partner, Augustus Pugin, designed every detail inside and out, from the symbolism of the statues to the color of the upholstery.

The room's decor trumpets the enlightenment of the British governing system. The colorful mosaics over the four doors represent the countries of the United Kingdom. There's England's St. George and the dragon (to the right), Scotland's St. Andrew, Wales' St. David, and Ireland's St. Patrick. The room's many statues—of kings, queens, and 19th-century politicians—symbolize how the Crown and Parliament both have their place in British history.

• *This lobby marks the end of the public space where you can wander freely. To see the House of Lords or House of Commons you must wait in line. You must also check your belongings—bag, camera, phone, even this guidebook—so read the following section before entering.*

When Parliament is not in session, you may have access to additional rooms: The Divisions Corridor (used for counting MPs votes), the vast Royal Gallery (where visiting heads of state are feted), the sumptuous Robing Room (where monarchs are dressed for special occasions), and more.

HOUSES OF PARLIAMENT

❺ House of Lords

When you're called, you'll walk to the Lords Chamber by way of the long **Peers' Corridor.** Paintings on the corridor walls depict the antiauthoritarian spirit brewing under the reign of Charles I: You'll see Parliament rebuffing Charles' demands for the five MPs, and the freedom-seeking Pilgrims (third panel on left) leaving England for America on the Mayflower.

Passing through the mahogany-ceilinged **Peers Lobby,** you reach the **House of Lords Chamber,** where you'll watch the proceedings from the upper-level visitors gallery. Each day opens with a 30-minute session where four questions are posed to the government, usually followed by legislation and then debate.

The House of Lords consists of around 800 members, called "Peers." They are not elected by popular vote. Some are nobles who've inherited the position, or bishops whose seat comes with the job. Others are appointed by the Queen. These days, their role is largely advisory. They can propose, revise, and filibuster laws, but they have no real power to pass laws on their own. On any typical day, only a handful of the lords actually shows up to debate. But despite (or because of) their lack of real power, the Lords are often considered less partisan and more objective, so people really do pay attention.

The Lords Chamber is church-like and impressive, with stained glass and intricately carved walls that suggest cathedral choir stalls. The benches where the Lords sit are always upholstered red (the ones in the House of Commons are green). At the far end is the Queen's huge gilded throne, with three seats—originally for Queen Victoria, Prince Albert, and their son. Today's Queen is the only one who may sit there, and only once a year, when she gives a speech to open Parliament. Above the throne, the mural depicts a scene appropriate to this traditional chamber: the first Christian king of England kneeling before a bishop to be baptized.

In front of the throne sits the woolsack—a cushion stuffed with wool. Here the Lord Speaker presides, with a ceremonial mace behind the backrest. To the Lord Speaker's right (our left) are the members of the ruling party (a.k.a. "government"). The first two rows in the seats closest to the woolsack are filled with bishops. To the Lord Speaker's left (our right) are the members of the opposition (the Labour Party, currently the largest opposition party in both houses). Unaffiliated Crossbenchers sit in between. All around the chamber, there are dangling microphones, high-def cameras, and video monitors, to amplify the Lords' messages to the world.

❻ House of Commons

The **corridor** leading to the House of Commons is lined with murals celebrating Parliament's final triumph over monarchy in the 1600s. Heroic citizens hide patriots and defy the tyrannical King James II. Eventually, Parliament would emerge supreme, empowered with choosing the monarchs who would govern the country—the "Glorious Revolution" of 1688.

Pass through the relatively modest **Members Lobby,** with its statues of prime ministers who have strolled these corridors: Goateed Disraeli (Queen Victoria's favorite), Winston Churchill, and the "Iron Lady" Margaret Thatcher. You may see office boxes where MPs can get their messages, though these are becoming obsolete in a paperless world.

The **Commons Chamber**—with its green carpet and cushions—may be much less grandiose than the Lords', but this is where the sausage gets made. The House of Commons is as powerful as the Lords, prime minister, and Queen combined.

This seat of power is surprisingly small—barely 3,000 square feet. The chamber was destroyed in the Blitz, and Churchill rebuilt it with the same cube-shaped floor plan. Of today's 650-plus MPs, only 450 can sit—the rest have to stand at the ends. On any given day, most MPs are in their offices, located elsewhere in the complex or in nearby modern buildings.

As in the House of Lords, the ruling party sits on the right of the Speaker (our left), opposition on the left (our right). Television screens on the wall show the topic and who is speaking; the press box is to the left, above the government MPs. Members stand when they want to speak, waiting patiently to be called on by the Speaker.

Keep an eye out for two red lines on the floor, which must not be crossed when debating the other side. (They're supposedly

two sword-lengths apart, to prevent a literal clashing of swords.) Between the benches is the canopied Speaker's Chair, for the chairman who keeps order and chooses who can speak next. A green bag on the back of the chair holds petitions from the public. The clerks sit at a central table that holds the ceremonial mace, a symbol of the power given Parliament by the monarch. Also on the table are the two "dispatch boxes"—old wooden chests that serve as lecterns, one for each side.

The Queen is not allowed in the Commons Chamber. The last monarch to enter a Commons Chamber was Charles I, and you know what happened to him. When the prime minister visits, she speaks from one of the boxes. Her ministers (or cabinet) join her on the front bench, while lesser MPs (the "backbenchers") sit behind.

It's often a fiery spectacle, as the prime minister defends her policies, while the opposition grumbles and harrumphs in displeasure. It's not unheard-of for MPs to get out of line and be escorted out by the Serjeant at Arms (who calls in to his doorkeepers—think of them as Parliamentary bouncers—for the heavy lifting). One furious MP even grabbed the Serjeant's hallowed mace and threw it to the ground. His career was over.

• *And so is our tour. Heading back out of the sprawling complex, be sure to get a good look at—if you haven't already—the Houses of Parliament's best-known symbol, its giant clock tower. For a full description of what tourists call "Big Ben," see the start of the* 📖 *Westminster Walk. Big Ben is also covered on my* 🎧 *free Westminster Walk audio tour.*

NATIONAL GALLERY TOUR

The National Gallery lets you tour Europe's art without ever crossing the Channel. With so many exciting artists and styles, it's a fine overture to art if you're just starting a European trip, and a pleasant reprise if you're just finishing. The "National Gal"—with Britain's greatest collection of paintings—is always a welcome interlude from the bustle of London sightseeing.

This tour gives you a quick chronological sweep through art history: medieval holiness, Renaissance realism, Dutch detail, Baroque excess, British restraint, and the colorful French Impressionism that leads to the modern world. Cruise like an eagle with wide eyes for the big picture, seeing how each style progresses into the next. As with all museums, expect a few changes. Most likely, 80 percent of the paintings will be where we say they are, 10 percent will be found nearby, and 10 percent will be out on loan or in restoration. Enjoy the biggies quickly, leaving yourself with enough time to circle back and browse.

Orientation

Cost: Free, but £5 suggested donation (collection boxes are happy to receive your loose change); special exhibits extra.

Hours: Daily 10:00-18:00, Fri until 21:00, last entry to special exhibits 45 minutes before closing.

Getting There: It's as central as can be, overlooking Trafalgar Square, a 15-minute walk from Big Ben and 10 minutes from Piccadilly. The closest Tube stop is Charing Cross or Leicester Square. Handy buses #9, #11, #15, and #24 (among others) pass by.

Information: Info tel. 020/7747-2885, switchboard tel. 020/7839-3321, www.nationalgallery.org.uk.

Visitor Information: The information desk in the lobby has a £1 floor plan (similar to this book's map, but with a few masterpieces highlighted) and a schedule of upcoming events and lunchtime lectures. The National Gallery loans out many paintings, so some canvases mentioned in this tour may not be on display. If you can't find a particular piece, ask the attendants stationed in each room.

Tours: Free one-hour **overview tours** leave from the Sainsbury Wing info desk daily at 11:30 and 14:30, plus Fri at 19:00. Ask the info desk about 10-minute talks on individual paintings, Mon-Fri at 16:00.

The **audioguides** are excellent. Choose from the one-hour highlights tour, several theme tours, or an option that lets you dial up info on any painting in the museum (£4).

The museum is surprisingly family-friendly (especially on Sunday mornings). Check their website for a variety of **kids' activities** or look for the "Family Fun" brochure at the information desk.

Length of This Tour: Allow 1.5 hours. If you have less time, the can't-miss pieces are Van Eyck's *Arnolfini Portrait,* Leonardo's *Virgin and Child with St. Anne and St. John the Baptist,* Rembrandt's *Belshazzar's Feast* and self-portraits, Velázquez's *Rokeby Venus,* Turner's *Fighting Téméraire,* the Impressionists, and Van Gogh's *Sunflowers.*

Cloakroom: Cloakrooms are at each entrance (£1 for bags). You can take a small bag into the museum.

Cuisine Art: There are three eateries in the Gallery. The **$$$ National Dining Rooms,** located on the first floor of the Sainsbury Wing, has a classy table-service restaurant menu, cheaper **$$ bakery section,** and offers afternoon tea (see page 419). The **$$$ National Café,** located near the Getty Entrance, has a table-service restaurant, also offering tea service, and an adjoining **$ sandwich/soup/salad/pastry café.** Seek out the **$ Espresso Bar,** near the Portico and Getty entrances, for sandwiches, pastries, and soft couches. Outside the Gallery, several options are on or near Trafalgar Square (see page 405).

Starring: You name it—Leonardo, Raphael, Titian, Rembrandt, Monet, and Van Gogh.

The Tour Begins

The National Gallery has three entrances facing Trafalgar Square: The main Portico Entrance (under the dome, in the center), the low-key Getty Entrance (to the right as you face the building), and the Sainsbury Entrance (in the smaller building to the left of the main entrance).

• *Enter through the Sainsbury Entrance. Pick up the handy map (£1) and climb the stairs. At the top, turn left, then left again through Room 51, and enter Room 52.*

MEDIEVAL AND EARLY RENAISSANCE
(1200s-Early 1400s)

In Rooms 52 and 53, shiny gold paintings of saints, angels, Madonnas, and crucifixions float in an ethereal gold never-never

land. One thing is very clear: Medieval heaven was different from medieval earth. The holy wore gold plates on their heads. Faces were serene and generic. People posed stiffly, facing either directly out or to the side, never in between. Saints are recognized by the symbols they carry (a key, a sword, a book), rather than by their human features. Art in the Middle Ages was religious, dominated by the Church. The illiterate faithful could meditate on an altarpiece and visualize heaven. It's as though they couldn't imagine saints and angels inhabiting the dreary world of rocks, trees, and sky they lived in.

• *One of the finest medieval altarpieces is in a glass case in Room 53.*

❶ Anonymous, *The Wilton Diptych*, c. 1395-1399

Two saint/kings and St. John the Baptist present King Richard II (left panel) to the Virgin Mary and her rosy-cheeked baby (right

panel), who are surrounded by angels with flame-like wings. Despite the gold-leaf background, a glimmer of human realism peeks through. The kings have distinct, down-to-earth faces. And the outside shows not a saint, not a god, but a real-life deer lying down in the grass of this earth.

But the anonymous artist is struggling with reality. John the Baptist is holding a "lamb of God" that looks more like a Chihuahua. Nice try. Mary's exquisite fingers hold an anatomically impossible little foot. The figures are flat, scrawny, and sinless, with cartoon features—far from flesh-and-blood human beings. Still, Richard II himself (king of England from 1377 to 1399) knelt before this portable altarpiece to inspire his personal devotions to the Virgin.

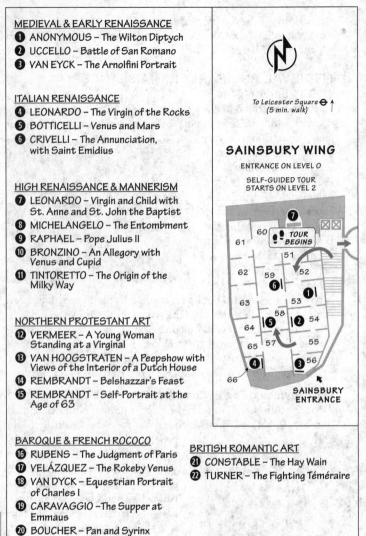

MEDIEVAL & EARLY RENAISSANCE
1 ANONYMOUS – The Wilton Diptych
2 UCCELLO – Battle of San Romano
3 VAN EYCK – The Arnolfini Portrait

ITALIAN RENAISSANCE
4 LEONARDO – The Virgin of the Rocks
5 BOTTICELLI – Venus and Mars
6 CRIVELLI – The Annunciation, with Saint Emidius

HIGH RENAISSANCE & MANNERISM
7 LEONARDO – Virgin and Child with St. Anne and St. John the Baptist
8 MICHELANGELO – The Entombment
9 RAPHAEL – Pope Julius II
10 BRONZINO – An Allegory with Venus and Cupid
11 TINTORETTO – The Origin of the Milky Way

NORTHERN PROTESTANT ART
12 VERMEER – A Young Woman Standing at a Virginal
13 VAN HOOGSTRATEN – A Peepshow with Views of the Interior of a Dutch House
14 REMBRANDT – Belshazzar's Feast
15 REMBRANDT – Self-Portrait at the Age of 63

BAROQUE & FRENCH ROCOCO
16 RUBENS – The Judgment of Paris
17 VELÁZQUEZ – The Rokeby Venus
18 VAN DYCK – Equestrian Portrait of Charles I
19 CARAVAGGIO – The Supper at Emmaus
20 BOUCHER – Pan and Syrinx

BRITISH ROMANTIC ART
21 CONSTABLE – The Hay Wain
22 TURNER – The Fighting Téméraire

To Leicester Square (5 min. walk)

SAINSBURY WING

ENTRANCE ON LEVEL 0

SELF-GUIDED TOUR STARTS ON LEVEL 2

TOUR BEGINS

SAINSBURY ENTRANCE

NATIONAL GALLERY

• *Continuing into Room 54, you'll leave this gold-leaf peace and find...*

2 Uccello, *Battle of San Romano*, c. 1438-1440

This colorful battle scene shows the victory of Florence over Siena in 1432—and the battle for literal realism on the canvas. It's an early Renaissance attempt at a realistic, nonreligious, three-dimensional scene.

Uccello challenges his ability by posing the horses and soldiers at every conceivable angle. The background of farmyards, reced-

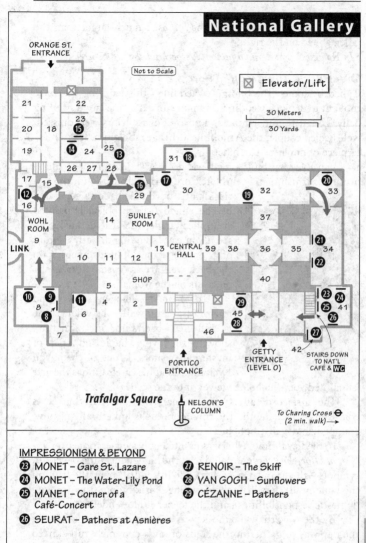

National Gallery

ORANGE ST. ENTRANCE

Not to Scale

⊠ Elevator/Lift

30 Meters
30 Yards

21
22
23
20 18
15
19 14 24 25 13
26 27 28
17 15 12 16 29
16 31 18
17
30 32 33 20
WOHL ROOM 14 SUNLEY ROOM 37 19
9
LINK 13 CENTRAL HALL 39 38 36 35 34 21
10 11 12 22
5 SHOP 40
10 9 11 23 24
8 4 2 29 25 41
8 45 26
6 28 27
7 46 42

STAIRS DOWN TO NAT'L CAFÉ & **WC**

GETTY ENTRANCE (LEVEL 0)

PORTICO ENTRANCE

Trafalgar Square

NELSON'S COLUMN

To Charing Cross ⊖ (2 min. walk)→

IMPRESSIONISM & BEYOND

23 MONET – Gare St. Lazare
24 MONET – The Water-Lily Pond
25 MANET – Corner of a Café-Concert
26 SEURAT – Bathers at Asnières

27 RENOIR – The Skiff
28 VAN GOGH – Sunflowers
29 CÉZANNE – Bathers

NATIONAL GALLERY

ing hedges, and tiny soldiers creates an illusion of distance. The artist actually constructs a grid of fallen lances in the foreground, then places the horses and warriors within it. Still, Uccello hasn't quite worked out the bugs—the figures in the distance are far too

big, and the fallen soldier on the left isn't much larger than the fallen shield on the right.

• *In Room 56, you'll find a famous Netherlandish masterpiece.*

❸ Van Eyck, *The Arnolfini Portrait,* 1434

Called by some "The Shotgun Wedding," this painting was once thought to depict a wedding ceremony forced by the lady's swelling belly. Today it's understood as a portrait of a solemn, well-dressed, well-heeled couple, the Arnolfinis of Bruges, Belgium. It is a masterpiece of down-to-earth details.

Van Eyck has built a medieval dollhouse, inviting us to linger over the furnishings. Feel the texture of the fabrics, count the ter-

rier's hairs, trace the shadows generated by the window. Each object is painted at an ideal angle, with the details you'd see if you were standing directly in front of it. So the strings of beads hanging on the back wall are as crystal clear as the bracelets on the woman.

To top it off, look into the round mirror on the far wall—the whole scene is reflected backward in miniature, showing the loving couple and a pair of mysterious visitors. Is one of them Van Eyck himself at his easel? Or has the art-

ist painted you, the home viewer, into the scene?

The surface detail is extraordinary, but the painting lacks true Renaissance depth. The tiny room looks unnaturally narrow, cramped, and claustrophobic.

In medieval times (this was painted only a generation after *The Wilton Diptych*), everyone could read the hidden meaning of certain symbols—the chandelier with its one lit candle (love), the fruit on the windowsill (fertility), the dangling whisk broom (the woman's domestic responsibilities), and the terrier (Fido—fidelity).

By the way, the woman likely is not pregnant. The fashion of the day was to gather up the folds of one's extremely full-skirted dress. At least, that's what they told her parents.

• *Return to Room 55, turn left into Room 57, and enter the...*

ITALIAN RENAISSANCE (Late 1400s)

The Renaissance—or "rebirth" of the culture of ancient Greece and Rome—was a cultural boom that changed people's thinking about every aspect of life. In politics, it meant democracy. In religion, it meant a move away from Church dominance and toward the assertion of man (humanism) and a more personal faith. Science and secular learning were revived after centuries of superstition and ignorance. In architecture, it was a return to the balanced columns and domes of Greece and Rome. In painting, the Renaissance meant realism. Artists rediscovered the beauty of nature and the human body. With pictures of beautiful people in harmonious 3-D surroundings, they expressed the optimism and confidence of this new age.

❹ Leonardo, *The Virgin of the Rocks,* c. 1491-1508

In this painting, Mary, the mother of Jesus, plays with her son and little John-ny the Baptist (with cross, at left) while an androgynous angel looks on. Leon-ardo brings this holy scene right down to earth by setting it among rocks, sta-lactites, water, and flowering plants. But looking closer, we see that Leonardo has deliberately posed his people into a pyra-mid shape, with Mary's head at the peak, creating an oasis of maternal stability and serenity amid the hard rock of the earth. Leonardo, who was born illegitimate, may have sought in his art the young mother he never knew. Freud thought so.

• *In Room 58 is...*

❺ Botticelli, *Venus and Mars,* c. 1485

Mars takes a break from war, succumbing to the delights of love (Venus), while impish satyrs play innocently with the discarded tools of death. In the early spring of the Renaissance, there was an optimistic mood in the air—the feeling that enlightened Man could solve all problems, narrowing the gap between mortals and the Greek gods. Artists felt free to use the pagan Greek gods as symbols of human traits, virtues, and vices. Venus has sapped man's medieval stiffness; the Renaissance has arrived.

• *Continue to Room 59.*

❻ Crivelli, *The Annunciation, with Saint Emidius,* 1486

Mary, in green, is visited by the dove of the Holy Spirit, who beams down from the distant heavens in a shaft of light.

Like Van Eyck's wedding, this is a brilliant collection of realistic details. Notice the hanging rug, the peacock, the architectural minutiae that lead you way, way back, then bam!—you have a giant pickle in your face.

It combines meticulous detail with Italian spaciousness. The floor tiles and building bricks recede into the distance. We're sucked right in, accelerating through the alleyway, under the arch, and off into space. The Holy Spirit spans the entire distance, connecting heavenly background with earthly foreground. Crivelli creates an Escheresque labyrinth of rooms and walkways that we want to walk through, around, and into—or is that just a male thing?

Renaissance Italians were interested in—even obsessed with—portraying 3-D space. Perhaps they focused their spiritual passion away from heaven and toward the physical world. With such restless energy, they needed lots of elbow room. Space, the final frontier.

• *Continue into Room 60, then turn right into Room 51, where we first entered. In an adjoining room, find a chalk drawing labeled* The Leonardo Cartoon, *and enter the...*

HIGH RENAISSANCE (1490s-Early 1500s)

The Renaissance was born in Florence, but it flowered in Venice and Rome, before spreading north to the rest of Europe. The "Big Three" of the High Renaissance—Leonardo (whom we saw earlier), Michelangelo, and Raphael—were all Florence-trained. Like Renaissance architects (which they also were), they carefully composed their figures on canvas, "building" them into geometrical patterns that reflected the balance and order they saw in nature.

In Venice—a city grown wealthy by trading with the luxurious and exotic East—artists forged a happy-go-lucky art style that shows a taste for the finer things in life. Madonnas and saints were replaced by smooth-skinned, sexy, golden centerfolds. Venetian artists revived the classical world in all its pagan glory, creating beautiful scenes of sensuous Nature.

❼ Leonardo, *Virgin and Child with St. Anne and St. John the Baptist,* c. 1499-1500

At first glance, this chalk cartoon (a full-size preparatory drawing for a painting) looks like a simple snapshot of two loving moms and two playful kids. The two children play—oblivious to the violent deaths they'll both suffer—beneath their mothers' Mona Lisa smiles.

But follow the eyes: Shadowy-eyed Anne turns toward Mary, who looks tenderly down to Jesus, who blesses John, who gazes back dreamily. As your eyes follow theirs, you're led back to the literal and psychological center of the composition—Jesus—the Alpha and Omega. Without resorting to heavy-handed medieval symbolism, Leonardo drives home a theological concept in a natural, human way. Leonardo the perfectionist rarely finished paintings. This sketch—pieced together from two separate papers (see the line down the middle)—gives us an inside peek at his genius.

• *From Room 51, cross to the main building (the West Wing) and enter the large Room 9, filled with big, colorful canvases. Turn right and exit at the far end into Room 8.*

❽ Michelangelo, *The Entombment*, c. 1500-1501

Michelangelo, the greatest sculptor ever, proves it here in this "painted sculpture" of the crucified Jesus being carried to the tomb.

Florentine artists like Michelangelo were inspired by ancient statues of balanced, anatomically perfect, nude Greek gods. Like a chiseled Greek god, this musclehead in red ripples beneath his clothes. Christ's naked body, shocking to the medieval Church, was completely acceptable in the Renaissance world, where classical nudes were admired as an expression of the divine.

Renaissance balance and symmetry reign. Christ is the center of the composition, flanked by two people leaning equally, who support his body with strips of cloth. They, in turn, are flanked by two others.

The painting is not damaged, but it is unfinished. Michelangelo, 25 years old at the time, moved on to other projects before he got around to adding crucial details, even leaving a blank space in the lower right where Mary would have been.

Regardless of the lack of detail, Michelangelo lets the bodies do the talking. The two supporters strain to hold up Christ's

NATIONAL GALLERY

Painting: From Tempera to Tubes

The technology of painting has evolved over the centuries.

1400s: Artists used tempera (pigments dissolved in egg yolk) on wood.

1500s: Still painting on wood, artists mainly used oil (pigments dissolved in vegetable oil, such as linseed, walnut, or poppy).

1600s: Artists applied oil paints to canvases stretched across wooden frames.

1850: Paints in convenient, collapsible tubes are invented, making open-air painting feasible.

The Frames: Although some frames are original, having been chosen by the artist, most are selected by museum curators. Some are old frames from other paintings, others are Victorian-era reproductions in wood, and still others are recent reproductions made of a composite substance to look like gilded wood.

body, and in their tension we, too, feel the great weight and tragedy of their dead god. Michelangelo expresses the divine through the human form.

❾ Raphael, *Pope Julius II,* 1511

The new worldliness of the Renaissance even reached the Church. Pope Julius II, who was more a swaggering conquistador than a

pious pope, set out to rebuild Rome in Renaissance style, hiring Michelangelo to paint the ceiling of the Vatican's Sistine Chapel.

Raphael gives a behind-the-scenes look at this complex leader. On the one hand, the pope is an imposing pyramid of power, with a velvet shawl, silk shirt, and fancy rings boasting of wealth and success. But at the same time, he's a bent and broken man, his throne backed into a corner, with an expression that seems to say, "Is this all there is?"

• *And now for something completely different, still in Room 8.*

NATIONAL GALLERY

MANNERISM (1520s-1600)

Mannerism, developed in reaction to the High Renaissance, subverts the balanced, harmonious ideal of the previous era with exaggerated proportions, asymmetrical compositions, and decorative color.

❿ Bronzino, *An Allegory with Venus and Cupid,* c. 1545

You may not recognize this painting, but you might recognize a foot. Look closely at the figure of boy Cupid, on the left. His right foot became famous on TV in the 1970s and 1980s in the comedy show *Monty Python's Flying Circus.* As the show opened and circus music played, the credits would come to an end on the last note, with Cupid's giant foot coming down from above to squash the scene with a flatulent *ffft!* The Pythons used collage-style graphics to end sketches abruptly (rather than fumble for a punch line), thus making a seamless (if surreal) transition to the next bit.

• *From Room 8, pass through Room 7 and enter Room 6 for...*

⓫ Tintoretto, *The Origin of the Milky Way,* c. 1575

In this scene from a classical myth, the god Jupiter places his illegitimate son, baby Hercules, at his wife's breast. Juno says, "Wait a minute. That's not my baby!"

Her milk spurts upward, becoming the Milky Way.

Tintoretto places us right up in the clouds, among the gods, who swirl around at every angle. Jupiter appears to be flying almost right at us. An X composition unites it all—Juno slants one way while Jupiter tilts the other.

• *Backtrack into the big Room 9. Exit this room at the far end and immediately turn left into Room 16.*

NORTHERN PROTESTANT ART (1600s)

We switch from CinemaScope to a tiny TV—smaller canvases, subdued colors, everyday scenes, and not even a bare shoulder.

Money shapes art. While Italy had wealthy aristocrats and the powerful Catholic Church to purchase art, the North's patrons were middle-class, hardworking, Protestant merchants. They wanted simple, cheap, no-nonsense pictures to decorate their homes and offices. Greek gods and Virgin Marys were out, hometown folks and hometown places were in—portraits, landscapes, still lifes, and slice-of-life scenes. Painted with great attention to detail, this is art meant not to wow or preach at you, but to be enjoyed and lingered over. Sightsee.

NATIONAL GALLERY

⑫ Vermeer, *A Young Woman Standing at a Virginal,* c. 1670

Inside a simple but wealthy Dutch home, a prim virgin plays an early piano called a "virginal." We've surprised her, and she pauses to look up at us.

By framing off such a small world to look at—from the blue chair in the foreground to the wall in back—Vermeer forces us to appreciate the tiniest details, the beauty of everyday things. We can meditate on the tiles lining the floor, the subtle shades of the white wall, and the pale, diffused light that seeps in from the window. Amid straight lines and rectangles, the woman's billowing dress adds a soft touch. The painting of a nude cupid on the back wall only strengthens this virgin's purity.

• *Exit Room 16, cut across Room 15, and enter the long Room 29 (with forest-green wallpaper). Midway through Room 29, turn left and find Room 25.*

⑬ Van Hoogstraten, *A Peepshow with Views of the Interior of a Dutch House,* c. 1655-1660

Look through the open end of this ingenious device to make the painting of a house interior come to three-dimensional life. Compare the twisted curves of the painting with the illusion it creates and appreciate the painstaking work of the dedicated artist. Painted on the top of the box is another anamorphic projection.

• *Enter the adjoining Room 24.*

⑭ Rembrandt, *Belshazzar's Feast,* c. 1635

Belshazzar, the wicked king of Babylon, has been feasting with God's sacred dinnerware when the meal is interrupted. The king turns to see the hand of God, burning an ominous message into the wall that Belshazzar's number is up. As he turns, he knocks over a goblet of wine. We see the jewels and riches of his decadent life.

Rembrandt captures the scene at the most ironic moment. Belshazzar is about to be ruined. We know it, his guests know it, and, judging by the look on his face, he's coming to the same conclusion.

Rembrandt's flair for the dramatic is accentuated by the strong

NATIONAL GALLERY

contrast between light and dark. Most of his canvases are a rich, dark brown, with a few crucial details highlighted by a bright light.

Before leaving this room, notice the self-portrait of Rembrandt at age 34, just to the left. Remember this face.

• *Nearby (either in Room 24 or in the adjoining Room 23), you'll find...*

⓯ Rembrandt, *Self-Portrait at the Age of 63,* 1669

Rembrandt throws the light of truth on...himself. He made this craggy self-portrait in the year he would die, at age 63. Contrast

it with one done three decades earlier (which we just saw in the previous room). Rembrandt, the greatest Dutch painter, started out as the successful, wealthy young genius of the art world. But he refused to crank out commercial works. Rembrandt painted things that he believed in but no one would invest in—family members, down-to-earth Bible scenes, and self-portraits like these.

Here, Rembrandt surveys the wreckage of his independent life. He was bankrupt, his mistress had just died, and he had also buried several of his children. We see a disillusioned, well-worn, but proud old genius.

• *Backtrack to the long, forest-green Room 29.*

BAROQUE (1600s)

This room holds big, colorful, emotional works by Peter Paul Rubens and others from Catholic Flanders (Belgium). While artists in Protestant and democratic Europe painted simple scenes, those in Catholic and aristocratic countries turned to the style called Baroque. Baroque art took what was flashy in Venetian art and made it flashier, what was gaudy and made it gaudier, what was dramatic and made it shocking.

⓰ Rubens, *The Judgment of Paris,* c. 1636-1639

Rubens painted anything that would raise your pulse—battles, miracles, hunts, and, especially, fleshy women with dimples on all four cheeks. For instance, *The Judgment of Paris* (one of two versions by Rubens in this museum) is little more than an excuse for a study of the female nude, showing front, back, and profile all on one canvas.

• *Exit Room 29 at the far end. In Room 30 (with red wallpaper), on the left-hand wall, you'll find...*

⓱ Velázquez, *The Rokeby Venus,* c. 1647-1651

Like a Venetian centerfold, Venus lounges diagonally across the canvas, admiring herself, with flaring red, white, and gray fabrics to highlight her rosy white skin and inflame our passion. Horny Spanish kings loved Titianesque nudes despite Spain's strict Inquisition, the Church tribunal that rooted out bad behavior. This work by the king's personal court painter is a rare Spanish nude from that ultra-Catholic country. The sole concession to Spanish modesty is the false

reflection in the mirror—if it really showed what the angle should show, Velázquez would have needed two mirrors...and a new job.

In 1914, the painting was slashed seven times by a knife-wielding vandal. She claimed she'd attacked "the most beautiful woman in mythological history" to protest the arrest of "the most beautiful character in modern history"—a fellow suffragette.

• *From Room 30, turn left into the big, red Room 31, where you'll see a large canvas.*

⓲ Van Dyck, *Equestrian Portrait of Charles I,* c. 1637-1638

King Charles sits on a huge horse, accentuating his power. The horse's small head makes sure that little Charles isn't dwarfed.

Charles was a soft-on-Catholics king in a hardcore Protestant country until England's Civil War (1648), when his genteel head was separated from his refined body by Cromwell and company.

Kings and bishops used the grandiose Baroque style to impress the masses with their power. Van Dyck's portrait style set the tone for all the stuffy, boring portraits of British aristocrats who wished to be portrayed as sophisticated gentlemen—whether they were or not.

• *Return to Room 30 and turn left, exiting at the far end, and entering Room 32. On the right wall, find...*

⓳ Caravaggio, *The Supper at Emmaus,* 1601

After Jesus was crucified, he rose from the dead and appeared without warning to some of his followers. Jesus just wants a quiet meal, but the man in green, suddenly realizing who he's eating with, is about to jump out of his chair in shock. To the right, a man spreads his hands in amazement, bridging the distance between Christ and us by sticking his hand in our faces.

The Baroque took reality and exaggerated it. Most artists amplified prettiness, but Caravaggio exaggerated grittiness, using real, ugly, unhaloed people in Bible scenes. Caravaggio's paintings look like how a wet dog smells. Reality.

We've come a long way since the first medieval altarpieces that wrapped holy people in gold foil. From the torn shirts to the five o'clock shadows, from the blemished apples to the uneven part in Jesus' hair, we are witnessing a very human miracle.

• *Leave Room 32 at the far end, and enter Room 33.*

FRENCH ROCOCO (1700s)

As Europe's political and economic center shifted from Italy to France, Louis XIV's court at Versailles became its cultural hub. Every aristocrat spoke French, dressed French, and bought French paintings. The Rococo art of Louis' successors was as frilly, sensual, and suggestive as the decadent French court. We see their rosy-cheeked portraits and their fantasies: lords and ladies at play in classical gardens, where mortals and gods cavort together.

• *One of the finest examples is the tiny...*

⓴ Boucher, *Pan and Syrinx,* 1759

Curious Pan seeks a threesome, but to elude him, Syrinx eventually changes into reeds, leaving him all wet.

Rococo art is like a Rubens that got shrunk in the wash—smaller, lighter pastel colors, frillier, and more delicate than the Baroque style. Same dimples, though.

• *Enter Room 34. The most eye-catching painting is of **Whistlejacket**, the famous racehorse of a late 18th-century prime minister, captured on a blank background by George Stubbs. Mentally hop on and prance around Room 34, taking in the English country-garden ambience.*

BRITISH ROMANTIC ART (Early 1800s)

❷❶ Constable, *The Hay Wain,* 1821

The reserved British were more comfortable cavorting with nature than with the lofty gods. Come-as-you-are poets like Wordsworth found the same ecstasy just in being outside.

John Constable set up his easel out-of-doors, making quick sketches to capture the simple majesty of billowing clouds, spread-ing trees, and everyday rural life.  Even British portraits (by Thomas Gainsborough and others) placed re-fined lords and ladies amid idealized greenery.

This simple style—believe it or not—was considered shocking in its day. The rough, thick, earth-toned paint and crude country settings scandalized art lovers used to the highfalutin, prettified sheen of Baroque and Rococo.

❷❷ Turner, *The Fighting Téméraire,* 1839

Constable's landscape was about to be paved over by the Industrial Revolution. Soon, machines began to replace humans, factories belched smoke over Constable's hay cart, and cloud-gazers had to punch the clock. Romantics tried to resist it, lauding the forces of nature and natural human emotions in the face of technological "progress." But alas, here a modern steamboat symbolically drags a famous but obsolete sailing battleship off into the sunset to be destroyed.

Turner's messy, colorful style gives us our first glimpse into the modern art world—he influenced the Impressionists. Turner takes an ordinary scene (like Constable), captures the play of light with messy paints (like Impressionists), and charges it with mystery (like, wow).

• *To view more Constables, Stubbs' horses, an enormous collection of Turners, and other British art, visit London's Tate Britain (📖 see the Tate Britain Tour). For now, continue ahead to Room 41.*

IMPRESSIONISM AND BEYOND (1850-1910)

For 500 years, a great artist was someone who could paint the real world with perfect accuracy. Then along came the camera, and, click, the artist was replaced by a machine. But unemployed artists refused to go the way of *The Fighting Téméraire.*

They couldn't match the camera for painstaking detail, but they could match it—even beat it—in capturing color, the fleet-ing moment, the candid pose, the play of light and shadow, the

NATIONAL GALLERY

quick impression. A new breed of artists burst out of the stuffy confines of the studio. They donned scarves and berets and set up their canvases in farmers' fields or carried their notebooks into crowded cafés, dashing off quick sketches in order to catch a momentary... impression.

• *The Impressionist paintings are scattered throughout Rooms 41-46. Here are a few of my favorites. Start with the misty Monet train station.*

㉓ Monet, *Gare St. Lazare*, 1877
Claude Monet, the father of Impressionism, was more interested in the play of light off his subject than the subject itself. He uses smudges of white and gray paint to capture how sun filters through the glass roof of the train station and is refiltered through the clouds of steam.

㉔ Monet, *The Water-Lily Pond*, 1899
In his Giverny home, near Paris, Monet planned an artificial garden, rechanneled a stream, built a bridge, and planted water lilies. Various paintings in the Gallery collection show scenes from Monet's garden—a living work of art, an oasis of order and calm in a hectic world.

㉕ Manet, *Corner of a Café-Concert*, 1878-1880
Imagine just how mundane (and therefore shocking) Manet's quick "impression" of this café must have been to a public that was raised on Greek gods, luscious nudes, and glowing Madonnas.

㉖ Seurat, *Bathers at Asnières*, 1884
Viewed from about 15 feet away, this is a bright, sunny scene of people lounging on a riverbank. Up close it's a mess of dots, showing the Impressionist color technique taken to its logical extreme. The "green" grass is a shag rug of green, yellow, red, brown, purple, and white brushstrokes. The boy's "red" cap is a collage of red, yellow, and blue.

Seurat has "built" the scene dot by dot, like a newspaper photo, using small points of different bright colors. Only at a distance do

NATIONAL GALLERY

the individual brushstrokes blend. Impressionism is all about color. Even people's shadows are not dingy black, but warm blues, greens, and purples.

• *In Room 42, you'll find...*

㉗ Renoir, *The Skiff,* 1875

It's a nice scene of boats on sun-dappled water. Now move in close. The "scene" breaks up into almost random patches of bright colors. The "blue" water is actually separate brushstrokes of blue, green, pink, purple, gray, and white. The rower's hat is a blob of green, white, and blue. Up close, it looks like a mess, but when you back up to a proper distance, *voilà!* It shimmers. This kind of rough, coarse brushwork (where you can actually see the brushstrokes) is one of the telltale signs of Impressionism. Renoir was not trying to paint the water itself, but the reflection of sky, shore, and boats off its surface.

• *In Room 45, you'll see...*

㉘ Van Gogh, *Sunflowers,* 1888

In military terms, Van Gogh was the point man of his culture. He went ahead of his cohorts, explored the unknown, and caught

a bullet young. He added emotion to Impressionism, infusing life even into inanimate objects. These sunflowers, painted with characteristic swirling brushstrokes, shimmer and writhe in either agony or ecstasy—depending on your own mood.

Van Gogh painted these during his stay in southern France, a time of frenzied creativity, when he hovered between despair and delight, bliss and madness. A year later, he shot himself.

In his day, Van Gogh was a penniless nobody, selling only one painting in his whole career. In 1987, a different *Sunflowers* painting (he did a half-dozen versions) sold for $40 million (a salary of about $2,500 a day for 45 years), and could probably fetch five times that today.

㉙ Cézanne, *Bathers,* c. 1894-1905

We've traveled from medieval spirituality to Renaissance realism to Baroque elegance and Impressionist colors. Before you spill out into the 21st-century hubbub of London, relax for a second with this gaggle of bathing nudes. These bathers are arranged in strict triangles à la Leonardo—the five nudes on the left form one tri-

NATIONAL GALLERY

angle, the seated nude on the right forms another, and even the background trees and clouds are triangular patterns of paint.

Cézanne uses the Impressionist technique of building a figure with dabs of paint (though his "dabs" are often larger-sized "cube" shapes) to make solid, 3-D geometrical figures in the style of the Renaissance. In the process, his cube shapes helped inspire a radical new style—Cubism—bringing art into the 20th century.

• *Our tour is over, and the 21st century beckons. Exiting Room 45, you find yourself in the stairwell of the Gallery's main entrance (under the dome) on Trafalgar Square. Stepping back outside, the National Portrait Gallery is just around the corner. You're in the heart of London, surrounded by a lifetime of sights yet to enjoy.*

NATIONAL PORTRAIT GALLERY TOUR

Rockstar groupies, book lovers, movie fans, gossipmongers, and even historians all can find at least one favorite celebrity here. From Elizabeth I to Elizabeth II, Byron to Bowie, Keats to Kate, the National Portrait Gallery puts a face on 500 years, making "history" the simple story of flesh-and-blood people. Consider that, for the most part, these portraits were painted in the presence of their subjects—providing us with a tangible link to the real person in the painting. The Gallery is a great rainy-day museum for serious students, or a quick (and free) peek at the eccentric inhabitants of the British Isles.

Orientation

Cost: Free, £5 suggested donation; fee for optional special exhibits.

Hours: Daily 10:00-18:00, Thu-Fri until 21:00—often with music and drinks offered in the evening, first and second floors open Mon at 11:00, last entry to special exhibits one hour before closing.

Information: Tel. 020/7306-0055, recorded info tel. 020/7312-2463, www.npg.org.uk.

Getting There: It's at St. Martin's Place, 100 yards off Trafalgar Square (around the corner from the National Gallery and opposite the Church of St. Martin-in-the-Fields). The closest Tube stops are Charing Cross and Leicester Square.

Visitor Information: A floor plan costs £1. The first-floor mezzanine level (just up the stairs from the main lobby) houses a bookshop and computer kiosks.

Tours: The £3 audioguide—highly recommended—lets you choose from several theme tours, or lets you dial up any of 300 individual works. Look for "Portrait Explorer" computers that give info on virtually any portrait or artist in the extensive collection.

Length of This Tour: Allow 1.5 hours. If you're in a rush, focus on your favorite Brits through history.

Services: WCs are in the basement and on the third floor. Pay lockers and coat check (£2 donation) are both in the basement.

Cuisine Art: The elegant **$$$ Portrait Restaurant** on the top floor is pricey for lunch or dinner but offers afternoon tea, and has a fine view over the rooftops of Westminster (reservations wise, tel. 020/7312-2490); you can also enjoy a drink at the bar with the same view. The **$$ Portrait Café** in the basement is cheaper and offers sandwiches, salads, and pastries. For more eateries near Trafalgar Square, see page 405.

Starring: Royalty (Henry VIII, Elizabeth I, Victoria), writers (Shakespeare, the Brontës), scientists (Newton, Darwin), politicians (Churchill), and musicians (Handel, McCartney).

OVERVIEW

The Gallery covers 500 years of history from top to bottom—literally. Start on the second floor and work chronologically down to modern times on the ground floor. Historians should linger at the upper floor; celebrity hunters will lose elevation quickly and head to the contemporary section. The portraits include many, many famous people from all walks of life, so use this chapter as an overview, then follow your interests, either with an audioguide or by reading the museum's informative labels.

The Tour Begins

• *From the lobby (which is up on the first floor), ride the long escalator up to the second floor and start in Room 1, marked The Tudors.*

Second Floor

1500s—DEBUT

The small, isolated island of Britain (pop. four million) enters the world stage. The Tudor kings—having already settled family feuds (the Wars of the Roses), balanced religious factions, and built England's navy—bring wealth from abroad.

• *Find the large black-and-white sketch (cartoon) of Henry VIII with his hands on his hips.*

❶ Henry VIII (1491-1547), The Whitehall Mural Cartoon

Young, athletic, intense, and charismatic, with jeweled hands, gold dagger, and bulging codpiece (the very image of kingly power),

NATIONAL PORTRAIT GALLERY

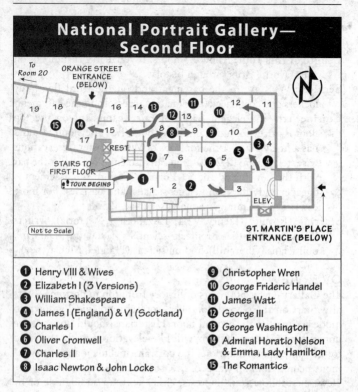

National Portrait Gallery— Second Floor

1. Henry VIII & Wives
2. Elizabeth I (3 Versions)
3. William Shakespeare
4. James I (England) & VI (Scotland)
5. Charles I
6. Oliver Cromwell
7. Charles II
8. Isaac Newton & John Locke
9. Christopher Wren
10. George Frideric Handel
11. James Watt
12. George III
13. George Washington
14. Admiral Horatio Nelson & Emma, Lady Hamilton
15. The Romantics

Henry VIII carried England on his broad shoulders from political isolation to international power.

In middle age, he divorced his older, dull-eyed, post-childbearing queen, **Catherine of Aragon** (see her portrait on the nearby wall), for the younger, shrewd, sparkling-eyed **Anne Boleyn** (near Catherine; see photo, next page), in search of love, sex, and a male heir. Nine months later, the future Elizabeth I was born, and the pope excommunicated adulterous Henry. Defiant, Henry started the (Protestant) Church of England, sparking a century-plus of religious strife between the country's Protestants and Catholics.

By the time Henry died—400 pounds of stinking, pus-ridden paranoia—he had wed six wives (see the sixth, sweet young **Catherine Parr**, opposite her predecessors), executed several of them (including Anne Boleyn), killed trusted advisors, and pursued costly wars (for more on Henry, see the sidebar, later).

NATIONAL PORTRAIT GALLERY

After all that, he'd produced only one male heir—**Edward VI** (see an image of him nearby). Nine-year-old Edward (son of Henry's third wife, Jane Seymour) ruled for only six years (1547-1553) before dying young, leaving England in religious and economic turmoil. (One of the Edward VI portraits often on display is an optical illusion. View it through the hole at the right end to put the enigmatic boy king into perspective.)

• *Go to Room 2, with portraits of the next generation of Tudors. Among them, you'll always find at least one image of...*

❷ Elizabeth I (1533-1603)

Elizabeth I was pale, stern-looking, red-haired (like her father, Henry VIII), and wore big-shouldered power dresses. During her

reign, she kept Protestant/Catholic animosity under control and made England a naval power and cultural capital.

Three different portraits (the displays change) depict the span of her life. The one with the most elaborate frame (with a crown on the top) shows her coronation at age 26, with the crown, scepter, and orb. At age 42 (see photo), she exudes a regal bearing. The largest painting *(The Ditchley Portrait)* captures her standing on a map of England, age 60. She looks ageless, always aware of her public image, resorting to makeup, dye, wigs, showy dresses, and pearls to dazzle courtiers.

The "Virgin Queen" was married only to her country, but she flirtatiously wooed opponents to her side. ("I know I have the body of a weak and feeble woman," she'd coo, "but I have the heart and stomach of a king.") When England's navy sank 72 ships of the Spanish Armada in a single power-shifting battle (1588), Britannia ruled the waves, feasting on New World spoils. Elizabeth surrounded herself with intellectuals, explorers, and poets.

• *Pass through Room 3, through the stairwell, and into Room 4.*

❸ William Shakespeare (1564-1616)

Though Shakespeare was famous in his day, his long hair, beard, earring, untied collar, and red-rimmed eyes make him look less the celebrity and more the bohemian barfly he likely was (for more on Shakespeare's life and influence, see the sidebar on page 232).

Henry VIII (1491-1547)

The notorious king who single-handedly transformed England was a true Renaissance Man—six feet tall, handsome, charismatic, well-educated, and brilliant. He spoke English, Latin, French, and Spanish. A legendary athlete, he hunted, played tennis, and jousted with knights and kings. He played the lute and wrote folk songs; his "Pastime with Good Company" is still being performed. When 17-year-old Henry, the second monarch of the House of Tudor, was crowned king in Westminster Abbey, all of England rejoiced.

Henry left affairs of state in the hands of others, and filled his days with sports, war, dice, women, and the arts. But in 1529, Henry's personal life became a political atom bomb, and it changed the course of history. Henry wanted a divorce, partly because his wife had become too old to bear him a son, and partly because he'd fallen in love with Anne Boleyn, a younger woman who stubbornly refused to be just the king's mistress. Henry begged the pope for an annulment, but—for political reasons, not moral ones—the pope refused. Henry went ahead and divorced his wife anyway, and he was excommunicated.

The event sparked the English Reformation. With his defiance, Henry rejected papal authority in England. He forced monasteries to close, sold off some church land, and confiscated everything else for himself and the Crown. Within a decade, monastic institutions that had operated for centuries were left empty and gutted (many ruined sites can be visited today, including the abbeys of Glastonbury, St. Mary's at York, Rievaulx, and Lindisfarne). Meanwhile, the Catholic Church was reorganized into the (Anglican) Church of England, with Henry as its head. Though Henry himself basically adhered to Catholic doctrine, he discouraged the veneration of saints and relics, and commissioned an English translation of the Bible. Hard-core Catholics had to assume a low profile. Many English welcomed this break from Italian religious influence, but others rebelled. For the next few generations, England would suffer through bitter Catholic-Protestant differences.

Henry famously had six wives. The issue was not his love life (which could have been satisfied by his numerous mistresses), but the politics of royal succession. To guarantee the Tudor family's dominance, he needed a male heir born by a recognized queen.

Henry's first marriage, to Catherine of Aragon, had been arranged to cement an alliance with her parents, Ferdinand and Isabel of Spain. Catherine bore Henry a daughter, but no sons. Next came Anne Boleyn, who also gave birth to a daughter. After a turbulent few years with Anne and several miscarriages, a frustrated Henry had her beheaded at the Tower of London. His next wife, Jane Seymour, finally had a son (but Jane died soon after giving birth). A blind marriage with Anne of Cleves ended quickly when she proved to be both politically useless and ugly—the "Flanders Mare." Next, teen bride Catherine Howard ended up cheating on Henry, so she was executed. Henry finally found comfort—but no children—in his later years with his final wife, Catherine Parr.

In 1536 Henry suffered a serious accident while jousting. His health would never be the same. Increasingly, he suffered from festering boils and violent mood swings, and he became morbidly obese, tipping the scales at 400 pounds with a 54-inch waist.

Henry's last years were marked by paranoia, sudden rages, and despotism. He gave his perceived enemies the pink slip in his signature way—charged with treason and beheaded. (Ironically, Henry's own heraldic motto was "Coeur Loyal"—true heart.) Once-wealthy England was becoming depleted, thanks to Henry's expensive habits, which included making war on France, building and acquiring palaces (he had 50), and collecting fine tapestries and archery bows.

Henry forged a large legacy. He expanded the power of the monarchy, making himself the focus of a rising, modern nation-state. Simultaneously, he strengthened Parliament—largely because it agreed with his policies. He annexed Wales, and imposed English rule on Ireland (provoking centuries of resentment). He expanded the navy, paving the way for Britannia to soon rule the waves. And—thanks to Henry's marital woes—England would forever be a Protestant nation.

When Henry died at age 55, he was succeeded by his nine-year-old son by Jane Seymour, Edward VI. Weak and sickly, Edward died six years later. Next to rule was Mary, Henry's daughter from his first marriage. A staunch Catholic, she tried to brutally reverse England's Protestant Reformation, earning the nickname "Bloody Mary." Finally came Henry's daughter with Anne Boleyn—Queen Elizabeth I, who ruled a prosperous, expanding England, seeing her father's seeds blossom into the English Renaissance.

London abounds with "Henry" sights. He was born in Greenwich (at today's Old Royal Naval College) and was crowned in Westminster Abbey. He built a palace along Whitehall and enjoyed another at Hampton Court. At the National Portrait Gallery, you can see portraits of some of Henry's wives, and at the Tower you can see where he executed them. Henry is buried alongside his third wife, Jane Seymour, at Windsor Castle.

This unassuming portrait captures 45-year-old Shakespeare just before he retired from his career as actor, poet, and world's greatest playwright. The shiny, domed forehead is a beacon of intelligence. (I suspect Shakespeare liked this plain-spoken portrait.)

The museum attributes this portrait to a Shakespeare contemporary, John Taylor, and claims it's the only one that could have been painted during the Bard's lifetime. But other scholars insist it was done long after the writer's death. Compare this version with the one you can see in the British Library (see page 233.) One recently discovered portrait (not in the museum) depicts a 46-year-old Shakespeare looking like a matinee idol, with a full head of hair. The search goes on for the "real" Will.

• *Also in Room 4, find the portrait of James I that marks the end of the Elizabethan Age and the beginning of the...*

1600s—RELIGIOUS AND CIVIL WARS

Catholic kings bickered with an increasingly vocal Protestant Parliament until the English Civil War erupted (1642-1651), killing thousands, decapitating the king, and eventually establishing Parliament as the main power.

❹ James I of England and VI of Scotland (1566-1625)

When the "Virgin Queen" died childless, her cousin—an arrogant Scotsman—moved to genteel London and donned the royal robes. Deeply religious, he launched the "King James" translation of the Bible, but he alienated Anglicans (Church of England), harder-line Protestants (Puritans), and democrats everywhere

by insisting that he ruled by divine right, directly from God. He passed on this attitude to his son, Charles.

• *Turn left and enter Room 5, with portraits of Civil War veterans.*

❺ Charles I (1600-1649)

Picture Charles' sensitive face (with scholar's eyes and artist's long hair and beard) severed from his elegant body (in horse-riding finery), and you've arrived quickly at the heart of the Civil War.

NATIONAL PORTRAIT GALLERY

The short, shy, stuttering Charles angered Protestants and democrats by dissolving Parliament, raising taxes, and marrying a Catholic. Parliament formed an army, fought the king's supporters, arrested and tried Charles, and—outside the Banqueting House on Whitehall—beheaded him.

• *The man responsible was...*

❻ Oliver Cromwell (1599-1658)

Cromwell, with armor, sword, command baton, and a determined look, was the Protestant champion and military leader. The Civil

War pitted Parliamentarians (Parliament, Protestant Puritans, industry, and urban areas) against Royalists (King, Catholics, nobles, traditionalists, and rural areas). After Charles' execution, Cromwell led kingless England as "Lord Protector."

Stern Cromwell hated luxury and ordered a warts-and-all portrait (see wart on his left temple and scar between his eyebrows). He has a simple, bowl-cut hairstyle adorning his 82-ounce brain (49 is average). Speaking of heads, three years after Cromwell's death, vengeful Royalists exhumed his body, cut off the head, stuck it on a stick, and placed it outside Westminster Abbey, where it rotted publicly for 24 years.

• *Pass through Room 6 and into Room 7. Facing you is...*

❼ Charles II (1630-1685)

After two decades of wars, Cromwell's harsh rule, and Puritanical excesses (no dancing, theater, or political incorrectness), Parliament welcomed the monarchy back (with tight restrictions) under Charles II. England was ready to party.

Looking completely ridiculous, with splayed legs, puffy face, big-hair wig, garters, and ribbons on his shoes, Charles II became a king with nothing to do, and he did it with grace and a sense of humor. Charles' picture is sandwiched between portraits of his devoted wife, Catherine of Braganza, and one of his well-known mistresses, the actress Nell Gwyn.

• *Make a U-turn right, entering Room 8. In the right corner are the bewigged and unamused...*

❽ Isaac Newton (1642-1727) and John Locke (1632-1704)

The 1600s, the Age of Enlightenment, saw scientific discoveries suggesting that the world operates in an orderly, rational way. Isaac Newton explained the universe's motion with the simplest of formulas (f=ma, etc.), and John Locke used human reason to plan a democratic utopia, coining phrases like "life, liberty..." that would inspire America's revolutionaries.

• *Walk straight ahead (through Room 9) to Room 10. Along the right wall, find...*

❾ Christopher Wren (1632-1723)

Christopher Wren—leaning on blueprints with a compass in hand—designed St. Paul's Cathedral, a glorious demonstration of mathematics in stone.

• *In Room 11, make a U-turn left, entering Room 12, with painters, writers, actors, and musicians of the 1700s.*

1700s—DOMESTIC STABILITY, WARS WITH FRANCE

Blossoming agriculture, the first factories, overseas colonization, and political stability from German-born kings (George I, II, III) allowed the arts to flourish. Overseas, England financed wars against Europe's No. 1 power, France.

❿ George Frideric Handel (1685-1759)

In London, an old form of art became something new—modern theater. Handel, a German who wrote Italian operas in England, had several smash hits in London (especially with the oratorio *Messiah*, on his desk), making musical theater popular with ordinary folk. Hallelujah.

• *Walk on to Room 13 for the portrait of...*

⓫ James Watt (1736-1819)

Deep-thinking Watt pores over plans to turn brainpower into work power. His steam engines (with a separate condenser to capture formerly wasted heat energy) soon powered gleaming machines, changing the focus of England's economy from grain and ships to iron and coal.

• *Head to Room 14, where you'll find George III over your left shoulder and George Washington along the right wall.*

⓬ George III (1738-1820) and
⓭ George Washington (1732-1799)

Just crowned at 23, King George III gives little hint in this portrait that he will lead England into the drawn-out, humiliating "American War" (Revolutionary War) against a colony demanding independence. George III, perhaps a victim of an undiagnosed disease, closed out the stuffy "Georgian" era (in Percy Shelley's words) "an old, mad, blind, despised, dying king."

Perhaps it was the war that drove him mad, or perhaps it was that his enemy, George Washington (portrait nearby), had the same hairdo. Washington was born in British-ruled Virginia and fought for Britain in the French and Indian War, but sided with the colonies in what the British called the "American War." This famous portrait of Washington is one of several versions of a 1796 portrait by Gilbert Stuart.

1800s—COLONIAL AND INDUSTRIAL GIANT

Britain defeated France (Napoleon) and emerged as the world's top power. With natural resources from overseas colonies (Australia, Canada, India, West Indies, China), good communications, and a growing population of seven million, Britain became the first industrial powerhouse, dotted with smoke-belching factories and laced with railroads.

• *Exit Room 14 into Room 8 and turn right, ending up in the bright aqua Room 17, featuring a red-jacketed man flanked by portraits of brave Brits who battled Napoleon.*

⓮ Admiral Horatio Nelson (1758-1805) and Emma, Lady Hamilton (1761-1815)

While the Duke of Wellington fought Napoleon on land (the final victory at Waterloo, near Brussels, 1815), Admiral Nelson battled France at sea (Battle of Trafalgar, off Spain, 1805).

Often displayed near Nelson is a portrait of Emma, Lady Hamilton, dressed in white, with her famously beautiful face turned coyly. She first met dashing Nelson on his way to fight the French in Egypt. She used the influence of her husband, Lord Hamilton, to restock Nelson's ships. Nelson's daring victory at the Battle of the Nile made him an instant celebrity, though the battle cost him an arm and an eye. The hero—a married man—returned home to woo, bed, and impregnate Lady H., with sophisticated Lord Hamilton's patriotic tolerance.

• *Step into Room 18.*

⓯ The Romantics

Not everyone worshipped industrial progress. Romantics questioned the clinical detachment of science, industrial pollution, and the personal restrictions of modern life. They reveled in strong emotions, non-Western cultures, personal freedom, opium, and the beauties of nature.

• *Scattered around the room, you may see...*

John Keats (1795-1821) broods over his just-written "Ode to a Nightingale." ("My heart aches, and a drowsy numbness pains / My sense, as though of hemlock I had drunk.")

Samuel Taylor Coleridge (1772-1834), at 23, is open-eyed, open-mouthed, and eager. ("And all should cry, Beware! Beware! / His flashing eyes, his floating hair! / ...For he on honey-dew hath fed, / And drunk the milk of Paradise." —"Kubla Khan")

Mary Wollstonecraft Shelley (1797-1851), in telling ghost stories with husband Percy Shelley and friend Lord Byron, conceived a tale of science run amok—*Frankenstein*—imitated by many. ("Ahhhhhhh, sweet mystery of life, at last I've found you!")

William Wordsworth (1770-1850): "The world is too much with us... / Little we see in Nature that is ours; / We have given our hearts away, a sordid boon!"

Percy Bysshe Shelley (1792-1822), political radical, sexual explorer (involving Mary and Claire Clairmont), traveler, and poet. ("O wild West Wind, thou breath of Autumn's being,... / If Winter comes, can Spring be far behind?")

George Gordon, **Lord Byron** (1788-1824), was athletic, exotic, and passionate about women and freedom. Famous and scandalous in his day, he became a Kerouacian symbol of the Romantic movement. ("She walks in beauty, like the night / Of cloudless climes and starry skies...")

Jane Austen (1775-1817) wrote of the landed-gentry class that surrounded her—its manners, love lives, and lifestyle. ("The person, be it gentleman or lady, who has not pleasure in a good novel, must be intolerably stupid.")

• *After browsing Rooms 19 and 20, backtrack to Room 15 and head downstairs one flight to the **first floor**. Turn right at the bottom of the stairs, pass through the long hall lined with busts (Room 22), and enter Room 21.*

First Floor

1837-1901—THE VICTORIANS

As the wealthiest nation on earth with a global colonial empire, Britain during Queen Victoria's long reign embraced modern tech-

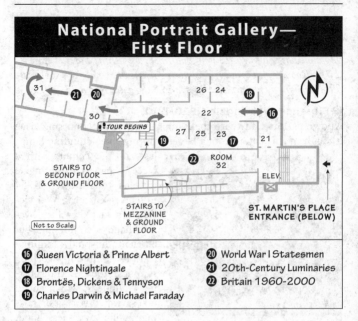

National Portrait Gallery— First Floor

Not to Scale

STAIRS TO SECOND FLOOR & GROUND FLOOR

TOUR BEGINS

STAIRS TO MEZZANINE & GROUND FLOOR

ROOM 32

ELEV.

ST. MARTIN'S PLACE ENTRANCE (BELOW)

16 Queen Victoria & Prince Albert
17 Florence Nightingale
18 Brontës, Dickens & Tennyson
19 Charles Darwin & Michael Faraday
20 World War I Statesmen
21 20th-Century Luminaries
22 Britain 1960-2000

nology, contributing to the development of power looms, railroads, telephones, motorcars, and electric lights. It was a golden age of science, literature, and middle-class morality, though pockets of extreme poverty and vice lurked in the heart of London itself.

• *Find a statue of a happy couple, titled Queen Victoria and Prince Albert in Anglo-Saxon Dress. Flanking the statue are paintings of...*

16 Queen Victoria (1819-1901) and Prince Albert (1819-1861)

Crowned at 18, the short (4'11"), plump, bug-eyed, quiet girl inherited a world empire. The next year, she proposed marriage (the custom) to the German Prince Albert. They were a perfect match—lovers, friends, and partners—a model for middle-class couples. (See the white statue of the pair as genteel knight and adoring lady.) Albert co-

ruled, especially when "Vickie" was pregnant with their nine kids. "Bertie" promoted education, science, public works, and the Great Exhibition of 1851 in Hyde Park. When Albert died at 42, a heart-

NATIONAL PORTRAIT GALLERY

broken Victoria moped for 40 years. (For more on Victoria, see the sidebar on page 102.)

• *Double back through the long hall lined with stuffy busts of starched shirts (Room 22), browsing around the rooms branching off, which are filled with many prominent Victorians. Start with Room 23 and...*

⓱ Florence Nightingale (1820-1910)

Known as "the Lady with the Lamp" for her nightly nursing visits (though in this detail from a larger painting, she's standing lamp-

less, in the center, with a piece of paper), Nightingale traveled to Turkey in 1854 to tend to Crimean War victims. In fact, her forte was not hands-on nursing but efficient hospital administration (sanitation, keeping supplies stocked, transporting wounded), which ended up saving lives and raising public awareness about health issues. To learn more about her, you can visit the Florence Nightingale Museum, just across the Thames from Big Ben (in Gassiot House at 2 Lambeth Palace Road, Tube: Westminster, Waterloo, or Lambeth North).

• *Across the hall, in Room 24, you'll find several...*

⓲ Writers

Anne, Emily, and Charlotte Brontë (left to right, youngest to oldest, painted by brother Branwell), three teenage country girls, grew up to write novels such as *Wuthering Heights* (Emily, 1818-1848) and *Jane Eyre* (Charlotte, 1816-1855), about the complex family and love lives of England's rural gentry.

To the left of the Brontës is a youthful **Charles Dickens** (1812-1870). He was only 12 years old when his dad was sent to a debtor's prison, forcing young Charles to work in a factory. The experience gave him a working-class perspective on British society. He became phenomenally successful writing popular novels *(Oliver Twist, A Tale of Two Cities, A Christmas Carol)* for Britain's educated middle-class.

Nearby is **Alfred, Lord Tennyson** (1809-1892), the poet laureate of Victorian earnestness. ("Theirs not to reason why, /

NATIONAL PORTRAIT GALLERY

Theirs but to do and die; / Into the Valley of Death / Rode the six hundred.")
• *Head to Room 27.*

⑲ Science and Technology
Charles Darwin (1809-1882), with basset-hound eyes and long white beard, looks tired after a lifetime of reluctantly defending his controversial theory of evolution, which shocked an entire generation.

 Michael Faraday (1791-1867), across from Darwin, shocked himself from time to time, harnessing electricity as the work force of the next century.
• *The long hall (Room 22) leads into Room 30, dedicated to World War I, and Room 31.*

1900s—WORLD WARS
Two devastating world wars and an emerging US superpower shrank Britain from global empire to island nation. But the country remained a cultural giant, producing writers, actors, composers, painters, and Beatles.

⑳ World War I Statesmen
Fighting Germans from trenches in France and Belgium, the British Army lost nearly a million men. In the big group portrait titled *Some Statesmen of the Great War*, find a bored-looking Winston Churchill.
• *The large Room 31 contains 20th-century portraits of writers, politicians, generals, and socialites. The display unfolds roughly chronologically (working clockwise around the room), but these exhibits change frequently; some portraits mentioned here may not be on view during your visit. Be prepared to put the book aside and browse.*

㉑ 20th-Century Luminaries

George Bernard Shaw (1856-1950)—playwright, critic, and political thinker—brought socialist ideas into popular discussion with plays such as *Man and Superman* and *Major Barbara*. **Virginia Woolf** (1882-1941) wrote feminist essays ("A woman must have money and a room of her own if she is to write fiction.") and experimental novels (*Mrs. Dalloway* jumps back and forth in time) before filling her pockets with stones and drowning herself in a river to silence the voices in her head.

The **Duchess of Windsor** (see photo) caught the eye of **Edward, Duke of Windsor.** The Duchess' smug smile tells us she got her man.

Edward VIII (1894-1972), great-grandson of Queen Victoria, became king in 1936 as a bachelor dating a common-born

(gasp), twice-divorced (double gasp) American (oh no!) named Wallis Simpson (1896-1986). Rather than create a constitutional stink, Edward quietly abdicated, married Wallis, and moved to the Continent with her, living happily ever after. They hosted cocktail parties, played golf, and listened to servants call them "Your Majesty"—though they were now just plain Duke and Duchess of Windsor. (His brother "Bertie" took over as King George VI, and George VI's daughter became Queen Elizabeth II. Elizabeth—and all the other royals—essentially snubbed their disgraced aunt and uncle for the rest of their lives.)

In the darkest days at the beginning of World War II, with Nazi bombs raining on a wounded London, Sir **Winston Churchill** (1874-1965) rallied his people with stirring speeches from the Houses of Parliament. ("We shall fight on the beaches...We shall never surrender!") Britain's military chief, Field Marshall **Bernard Montgomery, 1st Viscount** (1887-1976, known as "Monty") points out the D-Day beaches of the decisive Allied assault.

Sir **Laurence Olivier** (1907-1989), movie and stage actor, played everything from romantic leads and Shakespeare heavies to character parts with funny accents. Sir **Noel Coward** (1899-1973) continued the British tradition of writing witty, sophisticated comedies about the idle rich. **Henry Moore** (1898-1986), the most famous 20th-century sculptor, combined the grandeur of Michelangelo, the raw stone of primitive carvings, and the simplified style of abstract art. **Dylan Thomas** (1914-1953) wrote abstract

NATIONAL PORTRAIT GALLERY

imagery with a Romantic's heart ("Do not go gentle into that good night..."). American-born poet **T. S. Eliot** (1888-1965; see photo) captured the quiet banality of modern life: "This is the way the world ends / Not with a bang but a whimper."

• *Backtrack to the staircase. Before going downstairs, continue past the stairwell into the long Room 32, filled with an exhibit on...*

㉗ Britain 1960-2000

This ever-changing collection highlights the relationship between portraitist and subject. Often included in this section are contemporary royals (including Queen Elizabeth II, Prince Charles, and the late Princess Di), politicians (Margaret Thatcher), and fixtures of British popular culture (Sir Paul McCartney and Mick Jagger, among others).

• *Now head down to the **ground floor**. Just past the ticket desk are rooms set aside for temporary exhibits. At other times they display portraits covering...*

2000 TO THE PRESENT

London since the Swinging '60s has been a major exporter of pop culture. The contemporary collection, located in Rooms 32-42, changes often depending on who's hot, but you may find royal youngsters (William and Harry, plus a famously creepy-looking Kate), politicians (Tony Blair), entrepreneurs (Sir Richard Branson), classic-rock geezers (Sir Elton John, David Bowie), and actors (Sir Michael Caine, Dame Judi Dench), as well as those in lower-profile professions—writers (Sir Salman Rushdie, Doris Lessing, Germaine Greer), scientists (Stephen Hawking), composers, painters, and intellectuals.

We've gone from battles to Beatles, seeing Britain's history in the faces of its major players.

WEST END WALK

From Leicester Square to Piccadilly Circus

The West End, the area just west of the original walled City of London, is London's liveliest neighborhood. It's easy to get caught up in fantasies of jolly olde England, but the West End is where you'll feel the pulse of the living, breathing London of today. Theaters, pubs, restaurants, bookstores, ethnic food, markets, and boutiques attract rock stars, punks, tourists, and ladies and gentlemen stepping from black cabs for a night on the town.

Most of this book's walks and tours focus on history, art, and museums. But this walk is about appreciating the London lifestyle: the entertainment energy at Leicester Square; the thriving popular hum of Covent Garden; the rock-and-roll history of Denmark Street; the bohemian, creative, hedonistic groove of Soho; and the bustling neon hub of Piccadilly Circus. Use the walk to get the lay of the land, then go explore—especially in the evening, when the neon glitters and London sparkles.

Orientation

Length of This Walk: Allow two hours to lace together these highlights.

When to Go: Take your pick—sightseeing by day, or nightlife after dark. Early evenings are ideal, since most pubs and squares are carbonated with locals enjoying a post-work pint. After that, join the bustle of people who should probably be grabbing a cab home.

Getting There: Take the Tube to the Leicester Square stop, which is a block from the square itself.

Finding Your Way: A more detailed map than the one provided here may help you find your way more quickly through the maze of irregular streets.

The Walk Begins

• *Start at Leicester Square. Stand at the top of the square and take in the scene.*

❶ Leicester Square

Leicester (LESS-ter) Square is a small park surrounded by glitzy cinema houses. This space was modernized and spiffed up in anticipation of the 2012 Olympics crowds. It sits smack in the middle of the theater district—ground zero for London's enticing offerings of flashy musicals, intimate plays starring big-name actors, and much more (for details, see the Entertainment in London chapter). Here, at the entertainment center of London, a statue of Shakespeare looks out, as if pondering the quote chiseled into his pedestal: "There is no darkness but ignorance."

The square's **movie theaters**—the Odeon (Britain's largest cinema), Empire, and Vue—are famous for hosting red-carpet

movie premieres. When Bradley Cooper, Benedict Cumberbatch, Keira Knightley, or Jennifer Lawrence needs a publicity splash, it'll likely be here. (Search online for "London film premieres" to find upcoming events.) On any given night, this entire area is a mosh-pit of clubs and partying teens in town from the suburbs.

Leicester Square is the central clearinghouse for daytime theater ticket sales. Check out the **TKTS booth** (see page 447) and ignore all the other establishments that bill themselves as "half-price" (they're just normal booking agencies). It's often cheaper still to buy tickets directly from one of the theaters we'll pass on this walk.

Global Studios, former home of **Capital Radio London** (next to the Odeon), played a role in rock-and-roll history. Back in the

1960s, the British Invasion was in full swing—Beatles, Rolling Stones, The Who—but Brits couldn't hear much of it. The BBC was the only radio station in town, and it was mostly talk and Bach, with only a smattering of pop. Rock fans had to resort to "pirate" radio stations, beamed from Luxembourg or from ships at sea. Capital Radio was one of the first commercial stations allowed to play rock and roll—and that was in 1973! Ironically, within a few years, Capital had

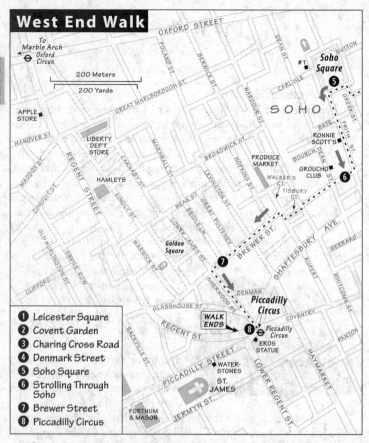

West End Walk

OXFORD STREET

To
Marble Arch
Oxford Circus

200 Meters
200 Yards

APPLE STORE

LIBERTY DEP'T STORE

HANOVER ST.

REGENT STREET

HAMLEYS

CONDUIT ST.

MADDOX ST.

SAVILE ROW

OLD BURLINGTON ST.

CLIFFORD ST.

GREAT MARLBOROUGH ST.

BERWICK ST.

FOUBERT ST.

CARNABY ST.

KINGLY ST.

MARSHALL ST.

BROADWICK ST.

LEXINGTON ST.

HOPKINS ST.

BEAK ST.

BRIDLE LN.

GREAT PULTENEY ST.

LOWER JAMES ST.

Golden Square

WARWICK ST.

SHERWOOD ST.

SACKVILLE ST.

GLASSHOUSE ST.

REGENT ST.

WALK ENDS

PICCADILLY STREET

ST. JAMES

FORTNUM & MASON

JERMYN ST.

DEAN ST.

SUTTON

CARLISLE

Soho Square

#1

5

S O H O

WARDOUR ST.

PRODUCE MARKET

WALKER'S CT.

GREEK ST.

FRITH ST.

RONNIE SCOTT'S

BOURCH. DEAN ST.

GROUCHO CLUB

6

TISBURY CT.

BREWER ST.

DENMAN

7

Piccadilly Circus

8 Piccadilly Circus

EROS STATUE

WATER-STONES

COVENTRY

SHAFTESBURY AVE.

GERRARD

RUPERT ST.

WHITCOMB ST.

PANTON

HAYMARKET

LOWER REGENT ST.

1. Leicester Square
2. Covent Garden
3. Charing Cross Road
4. Denmark Street
5. Soho Square
6. Strolling Through Soho
7. Brewer Street
8. Piccadilly Circus

WEST END

itself become mainstream. (The Clash struck back with their song "Capital Radio," which starts, "Yes, it's time for the Dr. Goebbels Show...") Today, Capital is owned by Global (a British radio conglomerate) and FM 95.8 carries on as a major top-40 broadcasting power.

• *Exit Leicester Square from its top corner, heading east (past the Vue cinema) on Cranbourn Street. Cross Charing Cross Road and continue along Cranbourn to the six-way intersection.*

Pause here to notice two things: traffic and chain outlets. London's "Congestion Zone" pricing fights downtown traffic by charging regular vehicles big bucks to enter the center. Sure there's still lots of traffic, but it could be far worse. The traffic you do see is limited to residents, taxis, service vehicles, city buses...and those willing to pay that fee to drive here. Also, take a moment to survey the various eateries. London keeps countless restaurants busy, and the vast majority are chains. Most places that look like one-offs are just chain outlets dressed up to look like one-offs. In our globalized, corporate

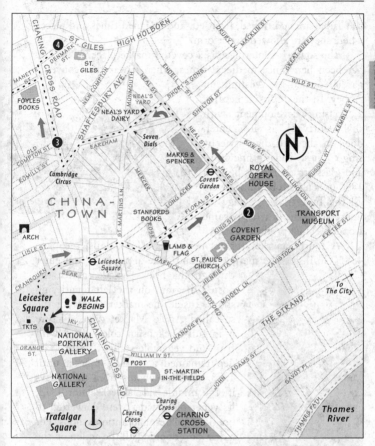

world, the economy of scale is hard to compete with, and London's food scene (like its hotel scene) is brutal on the mom-and-pop shop. If you don't factor in the intangible social issues, they have simply a better economic value.

• *Now, angle right onto Garrick Street. Shortly afterward, turn left onto calm, brick-lined Floral Street. Soon you'll see (on the left) the back door of Stanfords, an excellent travel book and map shop—pop in (see page 19). A few steps farther, across the street and down the tiny lane called Lazenby Court, is the convivial old Lamb & Flag pub. Farther along Floral Street, you'll be immersed in a scintillating array of fashion boutiques. When Floral Street opens onto traffic-free James Street, turn right and head for...*

❷ Covent Garden

Covent Garden (only tourists pluralize the name) is a large square teeming with people and street performers—jugglers, sword swallowers, and guitar players. London's buskers (including those in

WEST END

the Tube) are auditioned, licensed, and assigned times and places where they are allowed to perform.

The square's centerpiece is a covered marketplace. A market has been here since medieval times, when it was the "convent" garden owned by Westminster Abbey. In the 1600s, it became a housing development with this courtyard as its center, done in the Palladian style by Inigo Jones. Today's fine iron-and-glass structure was built in 1830 (when such buildings were all the Industrial Age rage) to house the stalls of what became London's chief produce market.

A tourist market thrives here today (for details, see page 438). Go inside the market hall and poke around. As you enter

through the brick passage, notice the posted diagram on the left identifying shops. Inside the market, you'll hit the so-called Apple Market zone. Picture it in full Dickensian color, lined with fruit and vegetable stalls. Covent Garden remained a produce market until 1973 (look for photos from these days in the middle side aisles). After 1973, its venerable arcades were converted to boutiques, cafés, and antique shops. For a drink overlooking all the action on the square below, The Punch & Judy pub has a view terrace on the rooftop.

Back outside, across from the west end of the market hall, stands **St. Paul's Church** (not the famous cathedral), with its Greek temple-like facade and blue clock face (irregular hours, pay WCs just to the left). Known as the Actors' Church, it's long been a favorite of nervous performers praying for success. To go inside, pass through one of the gates on either side of the facade, and find the entrance around back. If the gates are closed, you can duck down the streets on either side of the church and look for the passage leading to the tranquil churchyard—a nice escape from the busker bustle on Covent Garden. Inside, the walls are lined with memorials to theater folk, some of whom (Chaplin, Karloff) you might recognize.

At the bottom (southeast) corner of the square is the **London Transport Museum,** which gives a well-presented look at the evolution of this city's famously well-planned mass transit system (see page 54).

Tucked into the top (northeast) corner of the square is the **Royal Opera House,** which showcases top-notch opera and ballet.
• *Backtrack two blocks up St. James Street and continue straight up narrow Neal Street (alongside the Marks & Spencer department store), browsing your way northwest along the lively and colorful streets.*

❸ From Covent Garden to Charing Cross Road

Two blocks up Neal Street, you'll pass through an up-and-coming shopping zone. Turn left on Short's Gardens, where Neal's Yard Dairy (at #17) sells a wide variety of cheeses from the British Isles. This is the original shop of what is now a thriving chain. Everything is well-described, and they'll slice off a sample if you ask nicely.

Continue along Short's Gardens to the next intersection—called **Seven Dials**—where seven sundials atop a pole mark the meeting of seven small streets. Built in 1694, this once served the time-keeping needs of this busy merchants' quarter. Continue straight ahead onto Earlham Street.

Then, bearing left, you'll spill out into **Cambridge Circus**—the busy intersection of Shaftesbury Avenue and Charing Cross Road—with its fine red-brick Victorian architecture and classic theaters. **Charing Cross Road** is the traditional home of London's bookstores. Turn right up Charing Cross and walk two blocks to reach one of the biggest, **Foyles Books,** which puts on free events several nights a week—from book signings to jazz in their gallery (usually around 18:00, bookstore is on left at 107 Charing Cross Road, café and WCs, www.foyles.co.uk).
• *A few steps up from Foyles, turn right onto...*

❹ Denmark Street

This seemingly nondescript little street is a musician's mecca. In the 1920s, it was known as "Britain's Tin Pan Alley"—the center of the UK's music-publishing industry, when songwriters here cranked out popular tunes printed as sheet music.

Later, in the 1960s, Denmark Street was ground

zero for rock and roll's British Invasion, which brought so much great pop music to the US. Regent Sound Studio (at #4, half a block down on the right, now a guitar store with a similar name) was a low-budget recording studio. It was here in 1964 that the Rolling Stones recorded the song that raised them from obscurity, "Not Fade Away." Other acts that recorded on Denmark Street include The Who ("Happy Jack"), The Kinks (who wrote a song called "Denmark Street"), the Beatles ("Fixing a Hole"), David Bowie, and Black Sabbath (who made their first two records here—including the track "Iron Man"). Today, Regent is a music store, and the former studio's walls are lined with a wonderland of guitars.

The storefront at #20 (on the left, now Wunjo Guitars) was formerly a music publishing house that employed a lowly office boy named Reginald Dwight. In 1969, on the building's rooftop, he wrote "Your Song" and went on to become famous as Sir Elton John. In the 1970s, the Sex Pistols lived in apartments above #6. The 12 Bar Café at #25, on the left (now closed), helped launch the careers of more recent acts: Damien Rice, KT Tunstall, Jeff Buckley, and Keane.

Today, Denmark Street offers one-stop shopping for the modern musician. Without leaving this short street, you could buy a vintage Rickenbacker guitar, get your sax repaired, take piano lessons, lay down a bass track, have a few beers, or tattoo your name across your knuckles like Ozzy Osbourne. Notice the bulletin board in the alley alongside the 12 Bar Café (through doorway #27). If you're a musician looking for a band to play in, this could be your connection.

• *From Denmark Street, go back across Charing Cross Road and head down Manette Street. After a short block, on the right (down the lane called Orange Yard) you'll see The Borderline, where R.E.M. and Oasis have played. Continue down Manette Street and under the "Pillars of Hercules" passage, then turn right up Greek Street to...*

❺ Soho Square

The Soho neighborhood is London's version of New York City's Greenwich Village. It's a ritzy, raffish, edgy, and colorful area. Because of its eccentric 1970s landlord, porn publisher Paul Raymond, the Soho district escaped late-20th-century development. So, rather than soulless office towers, it retains its characteristic charm. And because the square has no real through-roads, it's almost traffic-free—strangely quiet and residential-feeling for being in the center of such a huge city.

Soho Square Gardens is a favorite place for a nap or picnic on a sunny afternoon (pick up picnic goodies from nearby shops). The little house in the middle of the square is the gardener's hut. History plaques at each entrance tell the area's story, which dates back to 1731. Originally a "key garden," this was once a yard shared by the wealthy people who lived on this square. And speaking of wealthy people, at #1, on the west (left) side of the square, the MPL building (McCartney Publishing Limited) houses offices of Britain's richest musician, Sir Paul McCartney.

• *At the bottom of the square, wander down Frith Street (which runs parallel to Greek Street).*

❻ Strolling Through Soho

The restaurants and boutiques here and on adjoining streets (such as Greek, Dean, and Wardour streets) are trendy and creative, the kind that attract high society when they feel like slumming it. Bars with burly, well-dressed bouncers abound. Private clubs, like the low-profile **Groucho Club** (a block over, at 45 Dean Street), cater to the late-night rock crowd.

Ronnie Scott's Jazz Club (at 47 Frith Street) has featured big-name acts for more than 50 years. In 1970, Jimi Hendrix jammed here with Eric Burdon and War; it was the last performance before his death in a London apartment a few days later. Even today Ronnie Scott's is *the* place to go for jazz in London. Shows regularly sell out in advance—check at the box office when you pass by or reserve in advance (see page 455 for details).

Frith Street hits **Old Compton Street** at the center of the neighborhood. This street is the center of London's gay scene. Stroll a block to the right on Old Compton Street to take in the eclectic

variety of people going by. You're surrounded by the buzz of Soho.

At the corner of Dean Street, look left for the pagoda-style arch down the street. South of here, on the other side of Shaftesbury Avenue, is London's underwhelming **Chinatown.** With Gerrard Street as its spine, it occupies what was once just more of Soho, with the same Soho artsy vibe. In the 1960s, the Chinese community gathered here, eventually dominated this zone, and non-Asian businesses moved out. The Chinese population swelled when the former British colony of Hong Kong was returned to China in 1997, but the neighborhood's identity is now threatened by developers eyeing this high-rent real estate.

• *Continue along Old Compton Street to where it hits Wardour Street (with a string of enticing restaurants just to the right). Crossing Wardour, Old Compton squeezes down into a narrow alley (Tisbury Court). Penetrate this sleazy passage of sex shows and blue-video shops, tolerate the barkers' raunchy come-ons, then jog a half-block right and turn on Brewer Street.*

❼ Brewer Street: Sleaze, Porn Shops, and Prostitutes

Soho was a bordello zone in the 19th century. A bit of that survives today in this area. Sex shops, video arcades, and prostitution

mingle with upscale restaurants here in west Soho. While it's illegal in Britain to sell sex on the street, well-advertised "models" entertain (profitably) in their tiny apartments. And these days massage parlors that promise memorable endings are harder for the police to bust.

One block north of Brewer Street— up Walker's Court—Berwick Street hosts a produce market (Mon-Sat).

• *Our walk is nearly finished. Continue a few short blocks along Brewer Street, observing the fascinating metamorphosis of a neighborhood from sleaze to gentrification. When you reach The Crown tavern, at the intersection of Brewer Street and Sherwood Street (also called Lower James Street), turn left onto Sherwood Street and walk one block down, emerging into the bustling intersection known as...*

❽ Piccadilly Circus

London's most touristy square got its name from the fancy ruffled shirts—*picadils*—made in the neighborhood long ago. In the late 20th century, the square veered toward the gimmicky and tacky—look no further than the gargantuan Ripley's Believe-It-or-Not Museum.

The square's center features a statue-on-a-pillar of a tipsy-but-perfectly balanced Eros. (Actually, scholars say it's Anteros, the love god's brother, but Londoners call it Eros.) Until just a couple of years ago, Piccadilly was a famously busy traffic circle, with cars and big red buses spinning around the statue. Now—though still busy with cars—it's also a packed people zone. At night it's as bright as day—with neon pulsing and the 20-foot-high video ads painting the classic Georgian facades in a rainbow of colors. Black cabs honk, tourists crowd the attractions, and Piccadilly shows off big-city London at its glitziest.

• *Our walk is done. If you're up for more sightseeing, it's easy to connect from here to my "Regent Street Shopping Walk" (page 439). Several of my recommended restaurants are nearby (see map on page 400). If you're ready to move on, the Piccadilly Tube stop is here, and handy buses #23, #38, and #159 stop near here (see page 28). It's all ready for you— you're at the center of London.*

BRITISH MUSEUM TOUR

In the 19th century, the British flag flew over one-fourth of the world. London was the empire's capital, where women in saris walked the streets with men in top hats. And England collected art as fast as it collected colonies.

The British Museum is *the* chronicle of Western civilization. History is a modern invention. Three hundred years ago, people didn't care about crumbling statues and dusty columns. Nowadays, we value a look at past civilizations, knowing that "those who don't learn from history are condemned to repeat it."

The British Museum is the only place I can think of where you can follow the rise and fall of three great civilizations—Egypt, Assyria (ancient Iraq), and Greece—in a few hours, with a coffee break in the middle. And while the sun never set on the British Empire, it will on you, so on this tour we'll see just the most exciting two hours.

Orientation

Cost: Free, £5 suggested donation (unload your spare change). Interesting temporary exhibits usually require a separate admission (and a timed ticket).

Hours: The museum is open daily 10:00-17:30, Fri until 20:30 (not all galleries are open Fri night, but most of our tour is). The **Great Court**—the grand entrance with eateries, gift shops, and an exhibit gallery—is open daily 9:00-18:00, Fri until 20:30.

Information: Ticket desk tel. 020/7323-8181, www.britishmuseum.org.

When to Go: Rainy days and Sundays are the most crowded times;

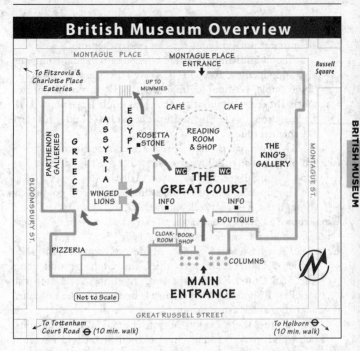

British Museum Overview

MONTAGUE PLACE

MONTAGUE PLACE ENTRANCE

Russell Square

← To Fitzrovia & Charlotte Place Eateries

UP TO MUMMIES

CAFÉ   CAFÉ

E G Y P T

A S S Y R I A

PARTHENON GALLERIES

G R E E C E

ROSETTA STONE

READING ROOM & SHOP

THE KING'S GALLERY

WINGED LIONS

WC   WC

THE GREAT COURT

INFO   INFO

BOUTIQUE

CLOAK-ROOM   BOOK-SHOP

PIZZERIA

COLUMNS

MAIN ENTRANCE

BLOOMSBURY ST.

MONTAGUE ST.

Not to Scale

GREAT RUSSELL STREET

To Tottenham Court Road ⊖ (10 min. walk)

To Holborn ⊖ (10 min. walk)

BRITISH MUSEUM

the same goes for school holidays. The museum is least crowded late on weekday afternoons, especially on Fridays.

Getting There: The main entrance is on Great Russell Street. From the Tottenham Court Road Tube stop, take exit #2, walk straight ahead, and take the first right on Great Russell Street. If exit #2 is closed, take exit #3, then, with the tall Centrepoint building on your right, walk to Museum Street and hang a left. The Holborn and Russell Square Tube stops are also nearby. Buses #38 and #24 are among the many that stop here (see page 28).

Visitor Information: Information desks are just inside the Great Court. You can pick up the basic map (£2 donation), but it's not essential for this tour. The *Visitor's Guide* (£5) offers 15 different tours and skimpy text.

Tours: Free 30- to 40-minute **EyeOpener tours** are led by volunteers, who focus on select rooms (daily 11:00-15:45, generally every 15 minutes). Free 45-minute **gallery**

talks on specific subjects are offered Tue-Sat at 13:15; a free 20-minute **spotlight** tour runs on Friday evenings.

The £6 **multimedia guide** offers dial-up audio commentary and video on 200 objects, as well as several theme tours (for example, 1.5-hour highlights tour or Parthenon sculptures tour). They're substantial and cerebral (must leave photo ID). There's also a fun family multimedia guide (£5) offering various themed routes.

🎧 Download my free British Museum **audio tour.**

Length of This Tour: Allow at least two hours. If you have less time, be sure to see the Parthenon Galleries (㉗); you can skip the long upstairs detour to the mummies (❻) and go quickly through the Assyrian collection (⓭-⓴).

Cloakroom: £1.50 per item. You can carry a daypack in the galleries, but big backpacks must be checked.

Eateries: You have three choices inside the complex. The self-service **$ Court Café** is on the Great Court ground floor. The **$$$ Court Restaurant** is on the upper level atop the Reading Room. The **$$ Pizzeria** is deeper into the museum, near the Greek art in Room 12.

Nearby, there are lots of fast, cheap, and colorful cafés, pubs, and markets along Great Russell Street and Museum Street. For other recommendations and some handy sit-down chains, see page 406. The sumptuous **$$ Princess Louise** pub is nearby (see page 408). Karl Marx picnicked on the benches near the museum entrance and in nearby Russell Square.

Starring: Rosetta Stone, Egyptian mummies, Assyrian lions, and the Parthenon sculptures.

The Tour Begins

The main entrance on Great Russell Street spills you into the Great Court, a glass-domed space with the round Reading Room in the center. From the Great Court, doorways lead to all wings. To the left are the exhibits on Egypt, Assyria, and Greece—our tour. You'll notice that this tour does not follow the museum's numbered sequence of rooms. Instead, we'll try to hit the highlights as we work chronologically.

Enjoy the Great Court, Europe's largest covered square, which is bigger than a football field. This people-friendly court—delightfully spared from the London rain—was for 150 years one of London's great lost spaces...closed off and gathering dust. Since the year 2000, it's been the 140-foot-wide hub of a two-acre cultural complex.

The Ancient World

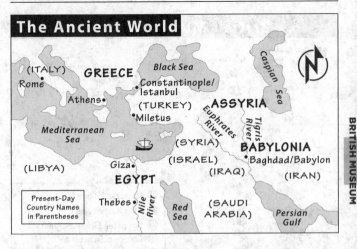

BRITISH MUSEUM

The stately Reading Room now hosts special exhibitions, but in years past, it was a study hall for Oscar Wilde, Arthur Conan Doyle, Rudyard Kipling, T. S. Eliot, Virginia Woolf, W. B. Yeats, Mark Twain, and V. I. Lenin. Karl Marx formulated his ideas on communism and wrote *Das Kapital* here.

• *The Egyptian Gallery is in the West Wing, to the left of the round Reading Room. Enter the Egyptian Gallery. The Rosetta Stone is directly in front of you.*

ANCIENT EGYPT

Egypt was one of the world's first "civilizations"—a group of people with a government, religion, art, free time, and a written language. The Egypt we think of—pyramids, mummies, pharaohs, and guys who walk funny—lasted from 3000 to 1000 B.C. with hardly any change in the government, religion, or arts. Imagine two millennia of Nixon.

❶ The Rosetta Stone

When this rock was unearthed in the Egyptian desert in 1799, it was a sensation in Europe. This black slab, dating from 196 B.C.,

caused a quantum leap in the study of ancient history. Finally, Egyptian writing could be decoded.

The hieroglyphic writing in the upper part of the stone was indecipherable for a thousand years. Did a picture of a bird mean "bird"? Or was it a sound, forming part of a larger word, like "burden"? As it

British Museum—Egypt

To ⑤ ⑥ & ⑦

Not to Scale

④ ③ ②

GREAT COURT & READING ROOM

①

⑨

A S S Y R I A

⑧

⑩

⑪

⑫

WINGED LIONS

CLOAKROOM

① Rosetta Stone
② King Ramesses II
③ Egyptian Gods as Animals
④ Colossal Scarab
⑤ Up to Nebamun Hunting in the Marshes
⑥ Up to Egyptian Funeral Objects
⑦ Up to Gebelein Man
⑧ Head & Arm of Amenhotep III
⑨ Four Figures of Sekhmet
⑩ Beard Piece of Great Sphinx
⑪ False Door & Architrave of Ptahshepses
⑫ Statue of Nenkheftka

BRITISH MUSEUM

turned out, hieroglyphics are a complex combination of the two, surprisingly more phonetic than symbolic. (For example, the hieroglyph that looks like a mouth or an eye is the letter "R.")

The Rosetta Stone allowed linguists to break the code. It contains a single inscription repeated in three languages. The bottom third is plain old Greek (find your favorite frat or sorority), while the middle is medieval Egyptian. By comparing the two known languages with the one they didn't know, translators figured out the hieroglyphics.

The breakthrough came when they discovered that the large ovals (such as in the sixth line from the top) represented the name of the ruler, Ptolemy. Simple.

• *In the gallery to the right of the Stone, find the huge head of Ramesses.*

❷ King Ramesses II

When Moses told the king of Egypt, "Let my people go!" this was the stony-faced look he got. Ramesses II ruled for 66 years (c. 1290-1223 B.C.) and may have been in power when Moses cursed Egypt with plagues, freed the Israeli slaves, and led them out of

Egypt to their homeland in Israel (according to the Bible, but not exactly corroborated by Egyptian chronicles).

This seven-ton statue (c. 1250 B.C.), made from two different colors of granite, is a fragment from a temple in Thebes. It shows Ramesses with the traditional features of a pharaoh—goatee, cloth headdress, and cobra diadem on his forehead. Ramesses was a great builder of temples, palaces, tombs, and statues of himself. There are probably more statues of him in the world than there are cheesy fake *David*s. He was so concerned about achieving immortality that he even chiseled his own name on other people's statues. Very cheeky.

Picture what the archaeologists saw when they came upon this: a colossal head and torso separated from the enormous legs and toppled into the sand—all that remained of the works of a once-great pharaoh. Kings, megalomaniacs, and workaholics, take note.

• *Say, "Ooh, heavy," and climb the ramp behind Ramesses, looking for animals.*

❸ Egyptian Gods as Animals

Before technology made humans the alpha animal on earth, it was easier to appreciate our fellow creatures. Animals were stronger, swifter, and fiercer than feeble *Homo sapiens*. The Egyptians worshipped animals as incarnations of the gods.

Though the displays here change, you may see the powerful ram—the god Amun (king of the gods)—protecting a puny pharaoh under his powerful chin. The falcon is Horus, the god of the living. The speckled, standing hippo (with lion head) is Taweret, protectress of childbirth. Her stylized breasts and pregnant belly are supported by ankhs, symbols of life. (Is Taweret grinning or grimacing in labor?) Finally, the cat (with ear- and nose-rings) served Bastet, the popular goddess of stress relief.

Scattered around the floor are huge stone boxes. The famous mummies of ancient Egypt were wrapped in linen and then encased in finely decorated wooden coffins, which were then placed in these massive stone outer coffins.

• *At the end of the Egyptian Gallery is a big stone beetle.*

❹ Colossal Scarab

This species of beetle would burrow into the ground, then reappear—it's a symbol of resurrection, like the sun rising and setting, or death and rebirth. Scarab amulets were placed on mummies' chests to protect the spirit's heart from acting impulsively. Pharaohs wore the symbol of the beetle, and tombs and temples were decorated with them (this one, from c. 332 B.C., probably once sat in a temple). The hieroglyph for scarab meant "to come into being."

Like the scarab, Egyptian culture was buried—first by Greece, then by Rome. Knowledge of the ancient writing died, condemning the culture to obscurity. But since the discovery of the Rosetta Stone, Egyptology has boomed, and Egypt has come back to life.

• *You can't call Egypt a wrap until you visit the mummies upstairs. Continue to the end of the gallery and up the West Stairs (four flights or elevator) to floor 3. At the top, turn left into Room 61 (a.k.a. the Michael Cohen Gallery), with objects and wall paintings from the tomb of Nebamun. As you enter the room, veer slightly left and head to the far wall to find a...*

❺ Painting of Nebamun Hunting in the Marshes

Nebamun stands in a reed boat, gliding through the marshes. He raises his arm, ready to bean a bird with a snakelike hunting

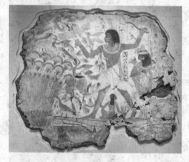

stick. On the right, his wife looks on, while his daughter crouches between his legs, a symbol of fatherly protection.

This nobleman walks like Egyptian statues look—stiff and flat, like he was just run over by a pyramid. We see the torso from the front and everything else—arms, legs, face—in profile, creating the funny walk that has become an Egyptian cliché. (As in an early version of Cubism, we see various perspectives at once.)

But the stiffness is softened by a human touch. It's a family snapshot of loved ones from a happy time. The birds, fish, and plants are painted realistically, like encyclopedia entries. (The first "paper" came from papyrus plants like the bush on the left.) The only unrealistic element is the house cat (thigh-high, in front of the man) acting as a retriever—possibly the only cat in history that ever did anything useful.

When Nebamun passed into the afterlife, his awakening soul could look at this painting (c. 1350 B.C.) on the tomb wall and think of his wife and daughter—doing what they loved for all eternity.

• *Browse through Rooms 62–63, filled with displays in glass cases. There are several corpses on display. Find yourself a mummy. In other glass cases you'll find coffins, tomb paintings, canopic jars, statuettes, even animal mummies. These objects all have something to do with...*

❻ The Egyptian Funeral

Mummifying a body is much like following a recipe. First, disembowel it (but leave the heart inside), then pack the cavities with

pitch, and dry it with natron, a natural form of sodium carbonate (and, I believe, the active ingredient in Twinkies). Then carefully bandage it head to toe with hundreds of yards of linen strips. Let it sit 2,000 years, and...*voilà!* Or just dump the corpse in the desert and let the hot, dry, bacteria-killing Egyptian sand do the work—you'll get the same results.

The mummy was placed in a wooden coffin, which was put in a stone coffin, which was placed in a tomb. (The pyramids were supersized tombs for the rich and famous.) The result is that we now have Egyptian bodies that are as well preserved as Larry King.

The internal organs were preserved alongside the mummy in canopic jars, and small-scale statuettes of the deceased *(shabtis)* were scattered around. Written in hieroglyphs on the coffins and the tomb walls were burial rites from the Book of the Dead. These were magical spells to protect the body and crib notes for the waking soul, who needed to know these passwords to get past the guardians of eternity.

Many of the mummies here are from the time of the Roman occupation, when fine memorial portraits painted in wax became popular. X-ray photos in the display cases tell us more about these people.

Don't miss the animal mummies. Cats (Room 62) were popular pets. They were also considered incarnations of the cat-headed goddess Bastet. Worshipped in life as the sun god's allies, preserved in death, and memorialized with statues, cats were given the adulation they've come to expect ever since.

• *Linger in Rooms 62 and 63, but remember that eternity is about the amount of time it takes to see this entire museum. In Room 64, in a glass case, you'll find what's left of a visitor who tried to see it all...*

❼ Gebelein Man, Known as "Ginger"

This man died 5,400 years ago, a thousand years before the pyramids. His people buried him in the fetal position, where he could "sleep" for eternity. The hot sand naturally dehydrated and protected the body. With him are a few of his possessions: bowls, beads, and the flint blade next to his arm. His grave was covered with stones. Named "Ginger" by scientists for his wisps of red hair, this man from a distant time seems very human.

• *Backtrack to Room 61 and head back down the stairs to the Egyptian Gallery and the Rosetta Stone. Just past the Rosetta Stone, find a huge head (facing away from you) with a hat like a bowling pin.*

❽ Head and Arm of a Statue of Amenhotep III

Art served as propaganda for the pharaohs, kings who called themselves gods on earth. Put this red-granite head (c. 1370 B.C.) on

top of an enormous body (which still stands in Egypt), and you have the intimidating image of an omnipotent ruler who demands servile obedience. Next to the head is, appropriately, the pharaoh's powerful fist—the long arm of the law.

Amenhotep's crown is actually two crowns in one. The pointed upper half is the royal cap of Upper Egypt. This rests on the flat, fez-like crown symbolizing Lower Egypt. A pharaoh wearing both crowns together is bragging that he rules a combined Egypt. As both "Lord of the Two Lands" and "High Priest of Every Temple," the pharaoh united church and state.

• *Along the wall to the left of the red-granite head (as you're facing it) are four black lion-headed statues.*

❾ Four Figures of the Goddess Sekhmet

The lion-headed goddess Sekhmet looks pretty sedate here (in these sculptures dating to c. 1360 B.C.), but she could spring into a

fierce crouch when crossed. She was the pharaoh's personal bodyguard, who could burn his enemies to a crisp with flaming arrows.

The gods ruled the Egyptian cosmos like dictators in a big banana republic (or the US Congress). Egyptians bribed their gods for favors, offering food, animals, or money, or erecting statues like these.

Sekhmet holds an ankh. This key-shaped cross was the hieroglyph meaning "life" and was a symbol of eternal life. Later, it was adopted as a Christian symbol because of its cross shape and religious overtones.

• *Continuing down the Egyptian Gallery, a few paces directly in front of you and to the left, find a glass case containing a...*

❿ Beard Piece of the Great Sphinx

The Great Sphinx—a statue of a pharaoh-headed lion—crouches in the shadow of the Great Pyramids in Cairo. Time shaved off the sphinx's soft, goatee-like limestone beard, and a piece is now preserved here in a glass case. This hunk of stone is only a whisker—about three percent of the massive beard—giving an idea of the scale of the six-story-tall, 250-foot-long statue.

The Sphinx is as old as the pyramids (c. 2500 B.C.), built during the time known to historians as the Old Kingdom (2686-2181 B.C.), but this beard may have been added later, during a restoration (c. 1420 B.C., or perhaps even later under Ramesses II).

• *Ten steps past the Sphinx's soul patch is a 10-foot-tall, red-tinted "building" covered in hieroglyphics.*

⓫ False Door and Architrave of Ptahshepses

This limestone "false door" (c. 2400 B.C.) was a ceremonial entrance (never meant to open) for a sealed building, called a *mastaba*, that marked the grave of a man named Ptahshepses. The hieroglyphs of eyes, birds, and rabbits serve as his epitaph, telling his life story, how he went to school with the pharaoh's kids, became an honored vizier, and married the pharaoh's daughter.

The deceased was mummified, placed in a wooden coffin that was encased in a stone coffin, then in a stone sarcophagus (like

BRITISH MUSEUM

the **red-granite sarcophagus** in front of Ptahshepses' door), and buried 50 feet beneath the *mastaba* in an underground chamber.

Mastabas like Ptahshepses' were decorated inside and out with statues, steles, and frescoes like those displayed nearby. These pictured things that the soul would find useful in the next life—magical spells, lists of the deceased's accomplishments, snapshots of the deceased and his family while alive, and secret passwords from the Egyptian Book of the Dead. False doors like this allowed the soul (but not grave robbers) to come and go.

• *Just past Ptahshepses' false door is a glass case with a red-tinted statue.*

⑫ Statue of Nenkheftka

Painted statues such as this one (c. 2400 B.C.) represented the soul of the deceased. Meant to keep alive the memory and personality

of the departed, this image would have greeted Nenkheftka's loved ones when they brought food offerings to place at his feet to nourish his soul. (In the mummification rites, the mouth was ritually opened, to prepare it to eat soul food.)

In ancient Egypt, you *could* take it with you. The Egyptians believed that after death, your soul lived on, enjoying its earthly possessions—sometimes including servants, who might be walled up alive with their dead master. (Remember that even the great pyramids were just big tombs for Egypt's most powerful.)

Statues functioned as a refuge for the soul on its journey after death. The rich scattered statues of themselves everywhere, just in case. Statues needed to be simple and easy to recognize, mug shots for eternity: stiff, arms down, chin up, nothing fancy. This one has all the essential features, like the simplified human figures on international traffic signs. To a soul caught in the fast lane of astral travel, this symbolic statue would be easier to spot than a more detailed one.

With their fervent hope for life after death, Egyptians created calm, dignified art that seems built for eternity.

• *Relax. One civilization down, two to go. Near the end of the gallery, on the right, are two huge, winged Assyrian lions (with bearded human heads) standing guard over the Assyrian exhibit halls.*

BRITISH MUSEUM

ANCIENT ASSYRIA

Long before Saddam Hussein, Iraq was home to other palace-building, iron-fisted rulers—the Assyrians.

Assyria was the lion, the king of beasts of early Middle Eastern civilizations. These Semitic people from the agriculturally challenged hills of northern Iraq became traders and conquerors, not farmers. They conquered their southern neighbors and dominated the Middle East for 300 years (c. 900-600 B.C.).

Their strength came from a superb army (chariots, mounted cavalry, and siege engines), a policy of terrorism against enemies ("I tied their heads to tree trunks all around the city," reads a royal inscription), ethnic cleansing and mass deportations of the vanquished, and efficient administration (roads and express postal service). They have been called the "Romans of the East."

The British Museum's valuable collection of Assyrian artifacts has become even more priceless since the recent destruction of ancient sites in the Middle East by ISIS terrorists.

⓭ Two Human-Headed Winged Lions

These stone lions guarded an Assyrian palace (11th-8th century B.C.). With the strength of a lion, the wings of an eagle, the brain of a man, and the beard of ZZ Top, they protected the king from evil spirits and scared the heck out of foreign ambassadors and left-wing newspaper reporters. (What has five legs and flies? Take a close look. These winged quintupeds, which appear complete from both the front and the side, could guard both directions at once.)

Carved into the stone between the bearded lions' loins, you can see one of civilization's most impressive achievements—writing. This wedge-shaped (**cuneiform**) script is the world's first writ-

ten language, invented 5,000 years ago by the Sumerians (of southern Iraq) and passed down to their less-civilized descendants, the Assyrians.

• *Walk between the lions, glance at the large reconstructed wooden gates from an Assyrian palace, and turn right into the long, narrow red gallery (Room 7) lined with stone relief panels.*

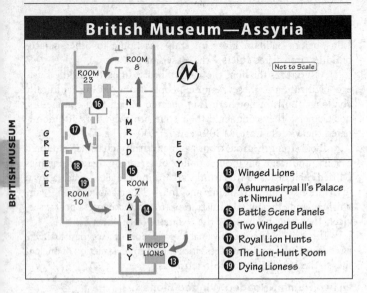

British Museum—Assyria

ROOM 8

ROOM 23

⑯

N
I
M
R
U
D

⑰

G
R
E
E
C
E

⑱

⑮

⑲

ROOM 10

ROOM 7

G
A
L
L
E
R
Y

E
G
Y
P
T

⑭

WINGED
LIONS

⑬

Not to Scale

⑬ Winged Lions
⑭ Ashurnasirpal II's Palace at Nimrud
⑮ Battle Scene Panels
⑯ Two Winged Bulls
⑰ Royal Lion Hunts
⑱ The Lion-Hunt Room
⑲ Dying Lioness

⑭ Ashurnasirpal II's Palace at Nimrud

This gallery is a mini version of the throne room and royal apartments of King Ashurnasirpal II's Northwest Palace at Nimrud (9th century B.C.). The 30,000-square-foot palace was built atop a 50-acre artificial mound. The new palace was inaugurated with a 10-day banquet (according to an inscription), where the king picked up the tab for 69,574 of his closest friends. Entering, you would have seen the king on his throne at the far end, surrounded by these pleasant, sand-colored, gypsum relief panels (which were, however, originally painted and varnished).

That's Ashurnasirpal himself in the **first panel on your right,** with braided beard, earring, and fez-like crown, flanked by his supernatural hawk-headed henchmen, who sprinkle incense on him with pinecones. The bulging forearms tell us that Ashurnasirpal II (r. 883-859 B.C.) was a conqueror's conqueror who enjoyed his reputation as a merciless warrior, using torture and humiliation as part of his distinctive management style. The room's panels chronicle his bloody career.

Under Ashurnasirpal's reign, the Assyrians dominated the Mideast from their capital at Nineveh (near modern Mosul). Ashurnasirpal II proved his power by building a brand-new palace in nearby Nimrud (called "Calah" in the Bible).

The cuneiform inscription running through the center of the panel is Ashurnasirpal's résumé: "The king who has enslaved all mankind, the mighty warrior who steps on the necks of his enemies, tramples all foes and shatters the enemy; the weapon of the gods, the mighty king, the King of Assyria, the king of the world, B.A., M.B.A., Ph.D., etc....."

• *A dozen paces farther down, on the left wall, are several relief panels (among many in this room that are worth focusing on.*

⓯ Panels with Battle Scenes

These relief panels show Assyria at war. Find the panel in which the Assyrians lay siege with a crude "tank" that shields them as they advance to the city walls to smash down the gate with a battering ram. The king stands a safe distance away behind the juggernaut and bravely shoots arrows.

In another panel nearby (called *Enemy Escape*), enemy soldiers flee the slings and arrows of outrageous Assyrians by swimming

across the Euphrates, using inflated animal bladders as life preservers. Their friends in the castle downstream applaud their ingenuity.

Next (in *Review of Prisoners*), prisoners are paraded before the Assyrian king, who is shaded by a parasol. Ashurnasirpal II sneers and tells the captured chief, "Drop and give me 50." Above the prisoners' heads, we see the rich spoils of war—elephant tusks, metal pots, and so on. The Assyrians, whose economy depended on booty, depopulated conquered lands with slavery and ethnic cleansing, then moved in Assyrian settlers. Despite their ruthless reputation, the Assyrians left a legacy as builders, rather than destroyers.

• *Exit the gallery at the far end, then hang a U-turn left. Pause at the entrance of Room 10c to see the impressive...*

⓰ Two Winged Bulls from the Palace of Sargon

These marble bulls (c. 710-705 B.C.) guarded the entrance to the city of Dur-Sharrukin ("Sargonsburg"), a new capital (near Nineveh/Mosul) with vast palaces built by Sargon II (r. 721-705 B.C.). The 30-ton bulls were cut from a single block, tipped on their sides, then dragged to their place by POWs. (In modern times, when the British transported them here, they had to cut them in half; you can see the horizontal cracks through the bulls' chests.)

Sargon II gained his reputation as a general by subduing the Israelites after a three-year siege of Jerusalem (2 Kings 17:1-6). He solidified his conquest by ethnically cleansing the area and deporting many Israelites (inspiring legends of the "Lost" Ten Tribes).

In 710 B.C., while these bulls were being carved for his palace, Sargon II marched victoriously through the streets of Babylon (near present-day Baghdad), having put down a revolt there against him. His descendants would also have to deal with the troublesome Babylonians.

• *Sneak between these bulls and veer right (into Room 10), where horses are being readied for the big hunt.*

⑰ Royal Lion Hunts from the North Palace of Ashurbanipal

Lion hunting was Assyria's sport of kings. On the right wall are horses; on the left are the hunting dogs. And next to them, lions,

resting peacefully in a garden, unaware that they will shortly be roused, stampeded, and slaughtered.

Lions lived in Mesopotamia up until modern times, and it was the king's duty to keep the lion population down to protect farmers and herdsmen. This duty soon became sport, with staged hunts and zoo-bred lions, as the kings of men proved their power by taking on the king of beasts.

• *Continue ahead into the larger lion-hunt room. Reading the panels like a comic strip, start on the right and gallop counterclockwise.*

⑱ The Lion-Hunt Room

In these panels (c. 650 B.C.), the king's men release lions from their cages, then riders on horseback herd them into an enclosed arena. The king has them cornered. Let the slaughter begin. The chariot carries King Ashurbanipal, the great-grand-

son of Sargon II (not to be confused with Ashurnasirpal II, who ruled 200 years earlier, mentioned previously).

The last of Assyria's great kings, Ashurbanipal has reigned now for 50 years. Having left a half-dozen corpses in his wake, he moves on, while spearmen hold off lions attacking from the rear.

• *At about the middle of the long wall...*

The fleeing lions, cornered by hounds, shot through with arrows, and weighed down by fatigue, begin to fall. The lead lion carries on even while vomiting blood.

This low point of Assyrian cruelty is, perhaps, the high point of their artistic achievement. It's a curious coincidence that civilizations often produce their greatest art in their declining years. Hmm.

• *On the wall opposite the vomiting lion is the...*

⑲ Dying Lioness

A lion roars in pain and frustration. She tries to run, but her body is too heavy. Her muscular hind legs, once a source of power, are now paralyzed.

Like these brave, fierce lions, Assyria's once-great warrior nation was slain. Shortly after Ashurbanipal's death, Assyria was conquered, and its capital at Nineveh was sacked and looted by an ascendant Babylon (612 B.C.). The mood of tragedy, dignity, and proud struggle in a hopeless cause makes this dying lioness one of the most beautiful of human creations.

• *Exit the lion-hunt room at the far end. Make your way back to the huge, winged lions who welcomed you to Assyria. Exit between them and make a U-turn to the right to head for the Greek section. Pass through Rooms 11-12 and turn right (if you're hungry, you can go straight to the Pizzeria) into Room 13, filled with Greek vases in glass cases.*

ANCIENT GREECE

In this room, you'll see lots of pottery—from the earliest, with geometric patterns (8th century B.C.), to painted black silhouettes on the natural orange clay, and then a few crudely done red human figures on black backgrounds. As you

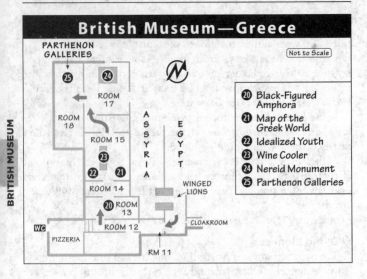

marvel at these beautiful creations, think of the people who made them.

The history of ancient Greece (600 B.C.-A.D. 1) could be subtitled "making order out of chaos." While Assyria was dominating the Middle East, "Greece"—a gaggle of warring tribes roaming the Greek peninsula—was floundering in darkness. But by about 700 B.C., these tribes began settling down, experimenting with democracy, forming self-governing city-states, and making ties with other city-states. Scarcely two centuries later, they would be a relatively united community and the center of the civilized world.

During its Golden Age (500-430 B.C.), Greece set the tone for all of Western civilization to follow. Democracy, theater, literature, mathematics, philosophy, science, gyros, art, and architecture as we know them, were virtually all invented by a single generation of Greeks in a small town of maybe 80,000 citizens.

• *Roughly in the middle of Room 13 is a Z-shaped glass case marked #8. On the lower shelf, the item marked #231 is a...*

⓴ Black-Figured Amphora with Achilles Killing Penthesilea

Greeks poured wine from jars like this one, which is painted with a legend from the Trojan War. The Trojan War (c. 1200 B.C.)—part fact but mostly legend—symbolized Greece's long struggle to rise above war and chaos.

On the vessel (540-530 B.C.), Achilles of Greece faces off against the Queen of the Amazons, Penthesilea, who was fighting for Troy. (The Amazons were a legendary race of warrior women who cut off one breast to facilitate their archery skills.) Achilles bears down, plunging a spear through her neck, as blood spurts. In her dying moment, Penthesilea looks up, her gaze locking on Achilles. His eyes bulge wide, and he falls instantly in love with her. She dies, and Achilles is smitten.

Greek pottery was a popular export product for the sea-trading Greeks. On this jar, see the names of the two enemies/lovers ("AXILEV" and "PENOESIIEA") as well as the signature of the craftsman, Exekias.

• *Continue to Room 15, then relax on a bench and read, surrounded by statues and vases in glass cases. On the entrance wall, find a...*

㉑ Map of the Greek World, 520-430 B.C.

After Greece drove out Persian invaders in 480 B.C., the city of Athens became the most powerful of the city-states and the center of the Greek world. Golden Age Greece was never really a full-fledged empire, but more a common feeling of unity among Greek-speaking people.

A century after the Golden Age, Greek culture was spread still farther by Alexander the Great, who conquered the Mediterranean world and beyond (including Persia). By 300 B.C., the "Greek" world stretched from Italy and Egypt to India (including most of what used to be the Assyrian Empire). Two hundred years later, this Greek-speaking Hellenistic Empire was conquered by the Romans.

• *There's a nude male statue (missing his arms and legs) on the left side of the room.*

㉒ Torso of an Idealized Youth (Kouros)

The Greeks saw their gods in human form...and human beings were godlike. They invented a statue type—the kouros (literally, "youth")—to showcase idealized bodies. In this example (c. 520-510 B.C.), the youth would have exemplified the divine orderliness of the universe with his once perfectly round head (it's now missing), symmetrical pecs, and navel in the center. The ideal man was geometrically perfect, a balance of opposites, the Golden Mean. In a statue, that meant finding the right balance between movement and stillness, between realistic human anatomy (with human flaws) and the perfection of a Greek god. Our youth is still a bit uptight, stiff as the rock from which he's carved. But—as we'll see—in

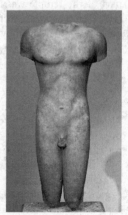

just a few short decades, the Greeks would cut loose and create realistic statues that seemed to move like real humans.

• *Two-thirds of the way down Room 15 (on the left) is a glass case containing a vase. (Circle the glass case to take in both sides.)*

㉓ Red-Figured Wine Cooler Signed by Douris as Painter

This clay vessel (490 B.C.), called a *psykter*, would have been topped off with wine and floated in a bowl of cooling water. Its red-fig-

ure drawings show satyrs at a *symposium*, or drinking party. These half-man/half-animal creatures (notice their tails) had a reputation for lewd behavior, reminding the balanced and moderate Greeks of their rude roots.

The reveling figures painted on this jar are realistic and three-dimensional; their movements are more naturalistic than the literally three-dimensional but quite stiff kouros. The Greeks are beginning to conquer the natural world in art. The art, like life, is more in bal-

ance. And speaking of "balance," if that's a Greek sobriety test, revel on.

• *Carry on into Room 17 and sit facing the Greek temple at the far end.*

㉔ Nereid Monument

Greek temples (like this reconstruction of a temple-shaped tomb from Xanthos, c. 390-380 B.C.) housed a statue of a god or god-

dess. Unlike Christian churches, which serve as meeting places, Greek temples were the gods' homes. Worshippers gathered outside, so the most impressive part of the temple was its exterior. Temples were rectangular buildings surrounded by rows of columns and topped by slanted roofs.

The triangle-shaped space above the columns—the pediment—is filled with sculpture. Supporting the pediment are decorative relief panels, called metopes. Now look through the columns to the building itself. Above the doorway, another set of relief panels—the frieze—runs around the building (under the eaves).

The statues between the columns are Nereids—friendly sea nymphs with dramatic wavelike poses and windblown clothes; some appear to be borne aloft by sea animals. Notice the sculptor's delight in capturing the body in motion, and the way the wet clothes cling to the figures' anatomy.

BRITISH MUSEUM

Next, we'll see pediment, frieze, and metope decorations from Greece's greatest temple.

• *Enter through the glass doors labeled* Parthenon Galleries. *(The rooms branching off the entryway usually have helpful exhibits that reconstruct the Parthenon and its once-colorful sculptures.)*

㉕ Parthenon Galleries

If you were to leave the British Museum, take the Tube to Heathrow, and fly to Athens, there, in the center of the old city, on top of

the high, flat hill known as the Acropolis, you'd find the Parthenon—the temple dedicated to Athena, goddess of wisdom and the patroness of Athens. It was the crowning glory of an enormous urban-renewal plan during Greece's Golden Age. After Athens was ruined in a war with Persia, the city—under the bold leadership of Pericles—constructed the greatest building of its day (447-432 B.C.). The Parthenon was a model of balance, simplicity, and harmonious elegance, the symbol of the Golden Age. Phidias, the greatest Greek sculptor, decorated the exterior with statues and relief panels.

While the building itself remains in Athens, many of the Parthenon's best sculptures are right here in the British Museum—the so-called Elgin Marbles, named for the shrewd British ambassador who had his men hammer, chisel, and saw them off the Parthenon in the early 1800s. Though the Greek government complains about losing its marbles, the Brits feel they rescued and preserved the sculptures. The often-bitter controversy continues.

The marble panels you see lining the walls of this large hall are part of the frieze that originally ran around the exterior of the

Parthenon, under the eaves. The statues at either end of the hall once filled the Parthenon's triangular-shaped pediments. Near the pediment sculptures, we'll also find the relief panels known as metopes.

The Frieze: These 56 relief panels show Athens' "Fourth of July" parade, celebrating the birth of the city. On this day, citizens marched up the Acropolis to symbolically present a new robe to the 40-foot-tall, gold-and-ivory statue of Athena housed in the Par-

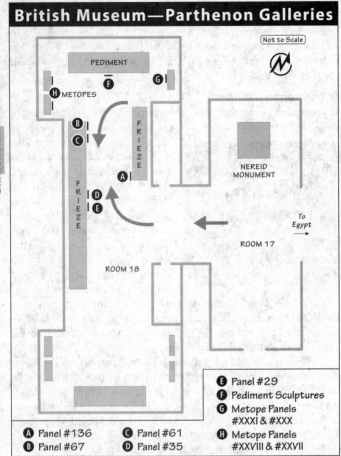

British Museum—Parthenon Galleries

Not to Scale

PEDIMENT

H METOPES

F

G

B
C

FRIEZE

A

FRIEZE

D
E

NEREID
MONUMENT

ROOM 17

To
Egypt →

ROOM 18

A Panel #136
B Panel #67
C Panel #61
D Panel #35
E Panel #29
F Pediment Sculptures
G Metope Panels
#XXXI & #XXX
H Metope Panels
#XXVIII & #XXVII

thenon. The grand parade featured chariots, musicians, children, animals for sacrifice, and young maidens with offerings.

• *Start at the panels by the entrance (#136), and work counterclockwise.*

Men on horseback lead the parade, all heading in the same direction—uphill. Prance on.

Notice the muscles and veins in the horses' legs and the intricate folds in the cloaks and dresses. Some panels have holes drilled in them, where gleaming bronze reins were fitted to heighten the festive look. All of these panels were originally painted in realistic colors. As you move

BRITISH MUSEUM

along, notice that, despite the bustle of figures posed every which way, the frieze has one unifying element—all the people's heads are at the same level, creating a single ribbon around the Parthenon.

• *Cross to the opposite wall.*

A two-horse chariot **(#67),** cut from only a few inches of marble, is more lifelike and three-dimensional than anything the Egyptians achieved in a freestanding statue.

Enter the girls (five yards to the left, **#61**), the heart of the procession. Dressed in pleated robes, they shuffle past the parade

marshals, carrying incense burners and jugs of wine and bowls to pour out an offering to the thirsty gods.

The procession culminates **(#35)** in the presentation of the robe to Athena. A man and a child fold the robe for the goddess while the rest of the gods look on. There are Zeus and Hera **(#29),** the king and queen of the gods, seated, enjoying the fashion show and wondering what length hemlines will be this year.

• *Head for the set of pediment sculptures at the far right end of the hall.*

The Pediment Sculptures: These statues were originally nestled nicely in the triangular pediment above the columns at the Parthenon's main (east) entrance. The missing statues at the peak of the triangle once showed the birth of Athena. Zeus had his head split open, allowing Athena, the goddess of wisdom, to rise from his brain fully grown and fully armed, inaugurating the Golden Age of Athens.

The other gods at this Olympian banquet slowly become aware of the amazing event. The first to notice is the one closest to them, Hebe, the cupbearer of the gods (tallest surviving fragment). Frightened, she runs to tell the others, her dress whipping behind her. A startled Demeter (just left of Hebe) turns toward Hebe.

The only one who hasn't lost his head is laid-back Dionysus (the cool guy farther left). He just raises another glass of wine to his lips. Over on the right, Aphrodite, goddess of love, leans back into her mother's lap, too busy admiring her own bare shoulder to even notice the hubbub. A chess-set horse's head screams, "These people are nuts—let me out of here!"

The scene had a message. Just as wise Athena rose above the lesser gods, who were scared, drunk, or vain, so would her city, Athens, rise above her lesser rivals.

This is amazing workmanship. Compare Dionysus, with his natural, relaxed, reclining pose, to all those stiff Egyptian statues standing eternally at attention.

Appreciate the folds of the clothes on the female figures (on the right half), especially Aphrodite's clinging, rumpled robe. Some sculptors would first build a nude model of their figure, put real clothes on it, and study how the cloth hung down before actually sculpting in marble. Others found inspiration at the *taverna* on wet T-shirt night.

Even without their heads, these statues, with their detailed anatomy and expressive poses, speak volumes.

Wander behind. The statues originally sat 40 feet above the ground. The backs of the statues, which were never intended to be seen, are almost as detailed as the fronts.

• *The metopes are the panels on the walls to either side. Start with the three South Metope panels on the right wall.*

The Metopes: The metopes once decorated the gaps between the crossbeams above the Parthenon's columns. Here's the scene: The humans have invited some centaurs—barbarian half-man/half-horse creatures—to a wedding feast. All goes well until the brutish centaurs, the original party animals, get too drunk and try to carry off the women. A brawl breaks out.

In the central panel of the three (**#XXXI**), a centaur grabs a man by the throat while the man pulls his hair. Meanwhile, the man tries fending off the centaur with his knee, while the cen-

Centaurs Slain Around the World

Dateline 500 B.C.—Greece, China, India: Man no longer considers himself an animal. Bold new ideas are exploding simultaneously around the world. Socrates, Confucius, Buddha, and others are independently discovering a nonmaterial, unseen order in nature and in man. They say man has a rational mind or soul. He's separate from nature and different from the other animals.

taur wraps his forelegs around the man's leg. The two stand eye to eye, and, at this point, the battle seems pretty evenly matched. But in **#XXX,** the centaur does the hair-pulling, and begins to drive the man to his knees.

The story continues on the opposite wall. In the central panel (**#XXVIII**), the centaurs take control of the party, as one rears back and prepares to trample the helpless man. The leopard skin draped over the centaur's arm roars a taunt.

But the humans rally. To the left (**#XXVII**), the humans rise up and drive off the brutish centaurs. A centaur tries to run, but the man grabs him by the neck and raises his (missing) right hand to prepare to finish him off. Notice how graceful the man is, with his smooth skin offset by the rough folded cloak.

These metopes tell the story of the struggle between the forces of human civilization and animal-like barbarism. The Greeks had always prided themselves on creating order out of chaos. Within just a few generations, they went from nomadic barbarism to the

pinnacle of early Western civilization. Now, the centaurs have been
defeated. Civilization has triumphed
over barbarism, order over chaos, and
rational man over his half-animal
alter ego.

Why are the Parthenon sculptures so treasured? The British of the
19th century saw themselves as the
new "civilized" race, subduing "barbarians" in their far-flung empire.
Maybe these carved stones made them stop and wonder—will our
great civilization also turn to rubble?

THE REST OF THE MUSEUM

You've toured only the foundations of Western civilization on the
ground floor of the West Wing. Upstairs you'll find still more artifacts from these ancient lands, plus Rome and the medieval civilization that sprang from it. Locate the rooms with themes you find
interesting (Etruscan, Persian, Roman Britain, Dark Age Europe,
and so on) and explore. Some highlights:

Lindow Man (a.k.a. the Bog Man): This victim of a Druid
human-sacrifice ritual, with wounds still visible, was preserved for
2,000 years in a peat bog (Room 50, upper floor, via East Stairs).

Sutton Hoo Ship-Burial: Finds from a seventh-century
Anglo-Saxon burial site (Room 41, upper floor, via East Stairs).

Treasures of the Persian Civilization: The collection here is
far better than what remains to be seen in Iran (Room 52, upper
floor).

Michelangelo's Drawings: The museum owns a complete
cartoon (a full-scale preliminary drawing for another work of art)
by Michelangelo—it's one of only two that survive (Room 90, level
4, accessed via the North Stairs or from the top of the Reading
Room).

Enlightenment Gallery: Formerly known as the King's Library, this room held the British Library's treasures when it was
founded in 1753. Today it displays objects that reveal the learning
and wonder of the Age of Discovery (Room 1; the long hall to the
right of the main entry).

And, of course, history doesn't begin and end in Europe. Look
for remnants of the sophisticated, exotic cultures of Asia and the
Americas (in North Wing, ground floor) and Africa (lower floor)—
all part of the totem pole of the human family.

BRITISH LIBRARY TOUR

The British Empire built its greatest monuments out of paper. It's through literature that England has made her lasting contribution to history and the arts. These national archives of Britain include more than 150 million items. A copy of every publication in the UK and Ireland is sent here. It's all housed on 380 miles of shelving in the deepest basement in London.

But everything that matters for your visit is in a single room dubbed "The Treasures." We'll concentrate on a handful of documents—literary and historical—that changed the course of history. Start with these top stops, then stray according to your interests.

Orientation

Cost: Free (£5 suggested donation); admission charged for special exhibits.

Hours: Mon-Fri 9:30-18:00, Tue-Thu until 20:00, Sat 9:30-17:00, Sun 11:00-17:00.

Information: Tel. 019/3754-6060; general info tel. 020/7412-7676, www.bl.uk.

Getting There: From the King's Cross St. Pancras Tube station, follow signs to British Library, exit on Euston Road. You'll hit a big noisy road. Turn right and go uphill (past a towering brick hotel) one block to 96 Euston Road. Euston Tube station is also nearby. Buses #10, #30, #59, #63, #73, and #91 (among others) also stop nearby.

Rotating Exhibits: Exhibits change often, and many of the museum's old, fragile manuscripts need to "rest" periodically in order to stay well-preserved. Even some of the major items I describe here could be out of view.

Tours: There are no guided tours or audioguides for the permanent collection. There are, however, guided tours of the building itself—the archives and reading rooms (for details, call 020/7412-7639 or see the website). Touch-screen computers in the permanent collection let you page virtually through some of the rare books.

🎧 Download my free British Library audio tour.

Length of This Tour: Allow one hour.

Services: The library has a free coat check and pay lockers (no large bags). There's free Wi-Fi throughout the building.

Eating: The **$$$** upper-level restaurant has good hot meals. The **$$** ground-floor café (sandwiches and drinks) is next to the vast and fun pull-out stamp collection.

Starring: Bibles, Shakespeare, English Lit 101, Magna Carta, and—ladies and gentlemen—the Beatles.

The Tour Begins

Entering the library courtyard, you'll see a big statue of a naked Isaac Newton bending forward with a compass to measure the uni-

verse. The statue symbolizes the library's purpose: to gather all knowledge and promote humanity's endless search for truth.

Stepping inside, you'll find the information desk and shop (the cloakroom and WC are down a short staircase to the right). A 50-foot-tall wall of 65,000 books teasingly exposes its shelves in the middle of the building. In 1823 King George IV gifted the collection to the people under the condition the books remain on display for all to see. The high-tech bookshelf—with moveable lifts to reach the highest titles—sits behind glass, inaccessible to commoners but ever-visible. Likewise, the reading rooms upstairs are not open to the public. The PACCAR Gallery houses temporary exhibits (requiring an admission charge).

Our tour is of the tiny but exciting area variously called "The Sir John Ritblat Gallery," "Treasures of the British Library," or just "The Treasures." This priceless literary and historical collection is held in one large, carefully designed, dimly lit room.

• *The entrance to the Treasures room is directly ahead, up the stairs to the left. The room has display cases grouped according to theme: maps, sacred*

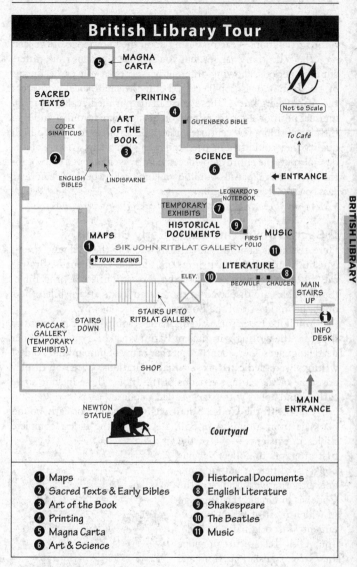

British Library Tour

MAGNA CARTA ➎

SACRED TEXTS

PRINTING

➍

ART OF THE BOOK ➌

CODEX SINAITICUS

➋

ENGLISH BIBLES

LINDISFARNE

GUTENBERG BIBLE

To Café

Not to Scale

SCIENCE ➏

◄ ENTRANCE

LEONARDO'S NOTEBOOK

TEMPORARY EXHIBITS ➐

HISTORICAL DOCUMENTS

➒

FIRST FOLIO

MUSIC

➓

MAPS ➊

SIR JOHN RITBLAT GALLERY

🎧 TOUR BEGINS

LITERATURE ➑

ELEV. ➓

BEOWULF CHAUCER

MAIN STAIRS UP

STAIRS UP TO RITBLAT GALLERY

STAIRS DOWN

INFO DESK

PACCAR GALLERY (TEMPORARY EXHIBITS)

SHOP

NEWTON STATUE

Courtyard

MAIN ENTRANCE

BRITISH LIBRARY

➊ Maps
➋ Sacred Texts & Early Bibles
➌ Art of the Book
➍ Printing
➎ Magna Carta
➏ Art & Science

➐ Historical Documents
➑ English Literature
➒ Shakespeare
➓ The Beatles
⓫ Music

texts, music, and so on. The key to my self-guided tour is the title above the various cases. Focus on the big picture, and don't be too worried about locating every specific exhibit.

Start at the far side of the room with the display case of...

➊ Maps

These historic maps show how humans' perspective of the world has expanded over the centuries. These pieces of paper, encoded with information gleaned from travelers, could be passed along to future generations—each building upon the knowledge of the last.

The collection changes, but you'll likely see maps from different time periods, showing different perspectives. The earliest maps of, say, Britain or Europe featured only the small, local world that the mapmakers knew. These early maps put medieval man in an unusual position—looking down on his homeland from 50 miles in the air. Within a few centuries, maps of Europe were of such high quality they could still be used today to plan a trip. After Columbus' journey, the entire globe became fairly well mapped, except for the mysterious expanse of unknown land that lay beyond America's east coast—"Terra Incognita."

· *Move into the area dedicated to sacred texts from several cultures.*

❼ Sacred Texts (Including Early Bibles)

Here the cases contain sacred texts such as the Hebrew Torah, Muslim Quran, Buddhist sutras, and Hindu Upanishads. Browse the different versions of the sacred text of Christians, the Bible. (Some Bibles are displayed in the Sacred Texts area, while others might be in the Art of the Book display cases nearby.)

You'll likely see some old decaying fragments of parchment or papyrus. The writing is in ancient Latin, Greek, Egyptian, or other dead languages. Consider the fact that many of humankind's oldest writings were dedicated to spiritual aspirations. Often on display are some of the earliest versions of the Bible. These include some early bound books with pages, called a codex.

Start with the **Codex Sinaiticus.** This codex, or early bound book, is from around A.D. 350. It's one of the oldest complete Bibles in existence—one of the first attempts to collect various books by different authors into one authoritative anthology. The Codex is in Greek, the language in which most of the New Testament was originally written. The Old Testament portions are Greek translations from the original Hebrew.

Jesus didn't speak English, of course—nor did Moses or Isaiah or Paul or any other Bible authors or characters. Jesus spoke Aramaic, a form of Hebrew. His words were written down in Greek, decades after Jesus' death. Various Greek manuscripts were compiled into anthologies like the Codex Sinaiticus. These were then translated into Latin, the language of medieval monks and scholars. Greek and Latin manuscripts were later translated into English. So our present-day English Bible didn't come directly from the mouths and pens of these religious figures; rather, it's the fitful product of centuries of oral tradition, evolution, and translation. Today, Bible scholars pore diligently over every word from these earliest known versions of the Bible, trying to separate Jesus' authentic words from those that seem to have been added later.

Nearby, you may find another early Bible: the **Codex Alexandrinus** (from A.D. 425). These two early Bibles contain some writings not included in most modern Bibles. (Even today, Catholic Bibles contain books not found in Protestant Bibles.) So, there are several things that editors must do to compile the most "accurate" Bible: decide which books actually belong, find the oldest and most accurate version of each book, and translate it correctly.

• *Nearby, you'll find more early Bibles (along with other texts) in the display cases called...*

❸ Art of the Book

Here you'll see various medieval-era books, some beautifully illustrated. The lettering is immaculate, but all are penned by hand.

Some are labeled "Bibles," meaning collections of sacred writings. Others are "Gospels," which specifically cover the history of Jesus. There are "Psalters," or songs from the Bible, and "Books of Hours," filled with prayers and inspiring Bible quotes. What they all have in common is their beauty, in both the calligraphy and the illustrations.

After the fall of Rome, the Christian message was preserved by monks, who reproduced ancient Bibles by hand. This was a painstaking process, usually done for a rich patron. The Bibles were often beautifully illustrated, or "illuminated."

The most magnificent of these medieval British "monk-uscripts" is the **Lindisfarne Gospels,** from A.D. 698. The text is in Latin, the language of scholars ever since the Roman Empire. The illustrations—with elaborate tracery and interwoven decoration—mix Irish, classical, and even Byzantine forms. (You can read an electronic copy of these manuscripts by using one of the touch-screen computers scattered around the room.)

These Gospels are a reminder that Christianity almost didn't make it in Europe. After the fall of Rome (which had established Christianity as the empire's official religion), much of Europe reverted to its pagan ways. People worshipped woodland spirits and terrible Teutonic gods. Lindisfarne was an obscure monastery of

BRITISH LIBRARY

Irish monks on a remote island off the east coast of England. But during that chaotic time, it was one of the few beacons of light, tending the embers of civilization through the long night of the Dark Ages. It took 500 years before Christianity was fully re-established in Europe.

Elsewhere in the Art of the Book (or possibly in Sacred Texts), you'll likely see some **Early English Bibles**—the King James version, the Wycliffe Bible, or others. These date from the 15th, 16th, and 17th centuries. As recently as 1400, there was no English version of the Bible, though only a small percentage of the population understood Latin. A few brave reformers risked death to translate these sacred books into English and print them using Gutenberg's invention, the printing press. Within two centuries, English translations were both legal and popular. These Bibles were written in the same language you speak, but try reading them. The lettering is strange; the words are out of date and unintelligible. It clearly shows how quickly languages evolve.

The King James version (so-called because it was done during his reign) has been the most widely used English translation. Fifty scholars worked for four years, borrowing heavily from previous translations, to produce this Bible. Its impact on the English language was enormous, making Elizabethan English something of the standard, even after people stopped saying "thee" and "thou" and "verily verily."

Recent translations are more readable, using modern English speech patterns, and aim to be more accurate, based on better scholarship and translations of the earliest manuscripts. But there are still problems trying to translate old phrases to fit contemporary viewpoints. Case in point? Our generation's debate over whether the God of the Bible should be a he or a she.

• *Move on to the wall of glass cases featuring early...*

❹ Printing

Printing was invented by the Chinese (what wasn't?). Centuries before the printing press in Europe, pictures of Buddha surrounded by prayers in Chinese characters were mass-produced. The faithful gained a blessing by saying the prayer, and so did the printer by reproducing it. The prints were made using wooden blocks carved with Chinese characters, dipped into paint or ink, and pressed by hand onto the page.

The **Gutenberg Bible**—though it may look like just another monk-made Latin manuscript—was so revolutionary because it was the first book printed in Europe using movable type (c. 1455).

Johann Gutenberg (c. 1397-1468), a German silversmith, devised a convenient way to reproduce written materials quickly, neatly, and cheaply—by printing with movable type. You scratch each letter onto a separate metal block, then arrange them into words, ink them up, and press them onto paper. When one job was done you could reuse the same letters for a new one.

This simple idea had immediate and revolutionary consequences. Suddenly, the Bible was available for anyone to read, fueling the Protestant Reformation. Knowledge became cheap and accessible to a wide audience, not just the rich. Books became the mass medium of Europe, linking people by a common set of ideas.

• *Through a doorway near the Printing and Art of the Book displays is a small room with the...*

❺ Magna Carta

How did Britain, a tiny island with a few million people, come to rule a quarter of the world? Not by force, but by law. The 1215 Magna Carta was the basis for England's constitutional system of government. Though historians talk about *the* Magna Carta, several different versions of the document exist, some of which are kept in this room.

The Articles of the Barons (labeled *King John*): In 1215, England's barons rose in revolt against the slimy King John. (The same King John appears as a villain in the legends of Robin Hood.) After losing London, John was forced to negotiate. The barons presented him with this list of demands. John, whose rule was worthless without the barons' support, had no choice but to acquiesce and affix his seal to it.

Magna Carta: A few days after John agreed to this original document, it was rewritten in legal form, and some 35 copies of the final version of the "Great Charter" were distributed around the kingdom.

This was a turning point in the history of government. Until then, kings

BRITISH LIBRARY

had ruled by God-given authority, above the laws of men. Now, for the first time, there were limits—in writing—on how a king could treat his subjects. More generally, it established the idea of "due process"—the notion that a government can't infringe on citizens' freedom without a legitimate legal reason. This small step became the basis for all constitutional governments, including yours.

So what did this radical piece of paper actually say? Not much, by today's standards. The specific demands had to do with things such as inheritance taxes, the king's duties to widows and orphans, and so on. It wasn't the specific articles that were important, but the simple fact that the king had to abide by them as law.

• *If you'd like to actually read the document, turn around: the writing's on the wall. Now return to the main room to find display cases featuring...*

❻ Art and Science

The printed word helped disseminate ideas across Europe, both religious and secular. During the Renaissance, men began turning their attention away from heaven and toward the nuts and bolts of the material world around them. Among the documents here, you might find some by trailblazing early scientists such as Galileo, Isaac Newton, and many more.

Pages from **Leonardo da Vinci's notebook** show his powerful curiosity, his genius for invention, and his famous backward and inside-out handwriting, which makes sense only if you know Italian and have a mirror. Leonardo's restless mind pondered diverse subjects, from how birds fly, to the flow of the Arno River, to military fortifications, to an early helicopter, to the "earthshine" reflecting onto the moon.

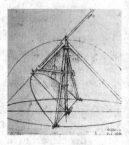

One person's research inspired another's, and books allowed knowledge to accumulate. Galileo championed the counter-common-sense notion that the Earth spun around the sun, and Isaac Newton later explained the mathematics of those moving celestial bodies.

❼ Historical Documents

Nearby are many more historical documents. You may see letters by Henry VIII, Queen Elizabeth I, Darwin, Freud, Gandhi, and others. It's clear you could spend days in here browsing the collection. But for now, let's trace the evolution of...

❽ English Literature

As you peruse the various manuscripts, from many different time periods, think of how much the English language has changed.

Four out of every five English words have been borrowed from other languages. The English language, like English culture (and London today), is a mix derived from foreign invaders. Some of the historic ingredients that make this cultural stew:

- First, there was the language of the original Celtic tribesmen from Bronze Age times.
- Next came the Latin-speaking Romans (A.D. 1-500), who conquered and colonized the isle of Britain.
- After the fall of Rome, Germanic tribes called Angles and Saxons moved in. English is a Germanic language, and the invaders named the island "Angle-land"—England.
- Next came the Vikings from Denmark (A.D. 800).
- Finally, there's the French-speaking Normans under William the Conqueror who arrived in the year 1066.

The English Literature exhibit is kept small and changes radically from month to month. In other words, not every treasure described below is likely to be on display.

Beowulf is the first English literary masterpiece. The Anglo-Saxon epic
poem, written in Old English (the earliest version of our language), almost
makes the hieroglyphics on the Rosetta
Stone look easy. The manuscript is from
A.D. 1000, although the story itself dates
to about 750. In this epic story, the young
hero Beowulf defeats two half-human
monsters threatening the kingdom. Beowulf symbolizes England's emergence
from the chaos and barbarism of the
Dark Ages.

Look for **The Canterbury Tales.** Six hundred years later, England was Christian, but it was hardly the pious, predictable, Sun-
day-school world we might imagine. Geoffrey Chaucer's bawdy
collection of stories (c. 1410), told by pilgrims on their way to Canterbury, gives us the full range of life's experiences—happy, sad,
silly, sexy, and devout. (Late in life, Chaucer wrote an apology for
those works of his "that tend toward sin.")

While most serious literature of the time was written in scholarly Latin, the stories in *The Canterbury Tales* were written in Middle English, the language that developed after the French invasion
of 1066 added a Norman twist to Old English.

This display is often a greatest-hits sampling of literature in
English, from Brontë to Kipling to Woolf to Joyce to Dickens,
whose novels were as popular in his time as blockbuster movies are
today. Jane Austen's novels of upper-class young women seeking
suitable husbands, though set in the 19th century, have become

BRITISH LIBRARY

William Shakespeare (1564-1616)

William Shakespeare is the greatest author in any language, period. He expanded and helped define modern English. In one fell swoop, he made the language of everyday people as important as Latin. In the process, he gave us phrases like "one fell swoop," which we quote without knowing they're Shakespeare. (Without him, no one would ever "vanish into thin air," "play fast and loose," "have seen better days," do anything "without rhyme or reason," become a "laughingstock," or wish anything "good riddance.")

Shakespeare was born in Stratford-upon-Avon in 1564 to John Shakespeare and Mary Arden. Though his parents were probably illiterate, Shakespeare is thought to have attended Stratford's grammar school, finishing his education at 14. When he was 18, he married a 26-year-old local girl, Anne Hathaway, who was three months pregnant at the time with their daughter Susanna.

The next few years are a blank—following his marriage, Shakespeare disappeared from any historical record, not turning up again until seven years later. By this point, he was a budding poet and playwright in London. He soon hit the big time, writing and performing for royalty, founding (along with his troupe) the Globe Theatre (a replica of which now sits along the Thames' South Bank—see page 89), and raking in enough dough to buy New Place, a swanky mansion back in his hometown. Around 1611, the rich-and-famous playwright retired from the theater, moving back to Stratford, where he died at the age of 52.

With plots that entertained both the highest and the lowest minds, Shakespeare taught the theater-going public about human nature. His tool was an unrivaled mastery of the English language. Using borrowed plots, outrageous puns, and poetic language,

enormously popular in the 21st. The original *Alice's Adventures in Wonderland* by Lewis Carroll created a fantasy world, where grown-up rules and logic were turned upside down. Also on display are superb works by contemporary writers, making it clear that Britain continues to be a powerful force in the world of ideas and imagination.

• *The most famous of England's writers generally gets his own display case.*

Shakespeare wrote comedies (c. 1590—*Taming of the Shrew, As You Like It*), tragedies (c. 1600—*Hamlet, Othello, Macbeth, King Lear*), and fanciful combinations (c. 1610—*The Tempest*), exploring the full range of human emotions and reinventing the English language.

Perhaps as important was his insight into humanity. His father was a glovemaker and wool merchant, and his mother was the daughter of a landowner from a Catholic family. Some scholars speculate that Shakespeare's parents were closet Catholics, practicing their faith during the rise of Protestantism. It is this tug-of-war between two worlds, some think, that helped enlighten Shakespeare's humanism. Think of his stock of great characters and great lines: Hamlet ("To be or not to be, that is the question"), Othello and his jealousy ("It is the green-eyed monster"), ambitious Mark Antony ("Friends, Romans, countrymen, lend me your ears"), rowdy Falstaff ("The better part of valor is discretion"), and the star-crossed lovers Romeo and Juliet ("But soft, what light through yonder window breaks"). Shakespeare probed the psychology of human beings 300 years before Freud. Even today, his characters strike a familiar chord.

The scope of his brilliant work, his humble beginnings, and the fact that no original Shakespeare manuscripts survive raise a few scholarly eyebrows. Some have wondered if maybe Shakespeare had help on several of his plays. After all, they reasoned, how could a journeyman actor with little education have written so many masterpieces? And he was surrounded by other great writers, such as his friend and fellow poet, Ben Jonson. Most modern scholars, though, agree that Shakespeare did indeed write the plays and sonnets attributed to him.

His contemporaries had no doubts about Shakespeare—or his legacy. As Jonson wrote in the preface to the First Folio, "He was not of an age, but for all time!"

❾ Shakespeare

Shakespeare wrote his plays to be performed, not read. He published a few, but as his reputation grew, unauthorized "bootleg" versions began to circulate. Some of these were written by actors who were trying (with faulty memories) to re-create plays they had appeared in years before. Publishers also put out different versions of his plays.

It wasn't until seven years after his death, in 1623, that a nearly complete collection of Shakespeare's plays was published, commonly

known as the **First Folio.** Of the 750 printed, about 230 survive (most are in the US). Western literature owes much to this folio, which collects 36 of the 37 known Shakespeare plays (*Pericles* missed out). If the First Folio is not out for viewing, the library should have other Shakespeare items on display.

The engraving of Shakespeare on the title page is reportedly one of only two portraits done during his lifetime. Is this what he really looked like? No one knows. The best answer probably comes from Ben Jonson, in the introduction on the facing page. Jonson concludes, "Reader, look not on his picture, but his book."

⓾ The Beatles

Bach, Beethoven, Brahms, Bizet...Beatles. Future generations will have to judge whether this musical quartet ranks with such artists, but no one can deny their historical significance. Look for photos of John Lennon, Paul McCartney, George Harrison, and Ringo Starr, who all hailed from Liverpool. The

Beatles burst onto the scene in the early 1960s to unheard-of popularity. With their long hair and loud music, they brought counterculture and revolutionary ideas to the middle class, affecting the values of a whole generation. Touring the globe, they served as a link between young people everywhere.

Among the displays, you may find manuscripts of song lyrics written by Lennon and McCartney, the two guiding lights of the group. "I Want to Hold Your Hand" was the song that launched them to superstardom in America. "A Hard Day's Night" and "Help" were title songs of two films capturing the excitement and chaos of their hectic touring schedule. Some call "Ticket to Ride" the first heavy-metal song. "Michelle," with a line in French, seemed oh-so-sophisticated. "Yesterday," by Paul, was recorded with guitar and voice backed by a string quartet—a touch of class from producer George Martin. Also, glance at the rambling, depressed, and cynical but humorous "untitled verse" by a young John Lennon. Is that a self-portrait at the bottom?

⓫ Music

Kind of an anticlimax after the Fab Four, I know, but there are manuscripts by Mozart, Beethoven, Schubert, and others. George Frideric Handel's famous oratorio, the *Messiah* (1741), is often on display. Handel, a German, became the toast of London in the early 1700s, where musical theater was all the rage. Increasingly, he left Italian-language operas behind in favor of productions in

English. The *Messiah* was written in a flash of inspiration—three hours of music in 24 days. When it got its London premiere in Covent Garden, King George II reportedly stood in respect during its most famous tune, the  "Hallelujah" chorus. Here are the final bars. Hallelujah.

HISTORIC LONDON: THE CITY WALK

From Charing Cross Station to London Bridge

In Shakespeare's day, London consisted of a one-square-mile area surrounding St. Paul's. Well before then, back in Roman times, that square mile was a walled town called Londinium. Today, this neighborhood—known as both "The City" and the "Square Mile"—is the financial heart of London, densely packed with history and bustling with business.

This two-mile walk from Charing Cross Station to London Bridge parallels the Thames, on the same main road that's been used for centuries. Along the way, you'll see sights from The City's storied past, such as St. Paul's Cathedral, the steeples of other Wren churches, historic taverns, a Crusader church, and narrow alleyways with faint remnants of the London of Shakespeare and Dickens.

But you'll also catch The City in action today, especially if you visit on a weekday at lunchtime, when workers spill out onto the streets and The City is at its liveliest. See lawyers and judges in robes and wigs taking cigarette breaks, brokers in pin-striped power suits buying newspapers from Cockneys, and the last of a dying breed—elderly gentlemen with bowler hats and brollies (umbrellas) browsing for tailored shirts and Cuban cigars. Sip a pint in the same pub where Dickens did, and eavesdrop on a power lunch. Use this walk to help resurrect the London that was, then let The City of today surprise you with what is.

Orientation

Length of This Walk: Allow three or more hours, depending on what you visit. With less time, you can skip a mile's worth of the Strand by taking the Tube directly to Temple, picking up the walk at St. Clement Danes, then ending at St. Paul's. Less-important stops along the way include the Temple Church, Inns of Court, and Dr. Johnson's House.

Getting There: Start near Trafalgar Square at Charing Cross Station (Tube: Charing Cross or Embankment). You'll head east on the Strand and end at London Bridge (where the Bankside Walk begins). Handy buses #15 and #11 (see page 28) travel along the Strand and Fleet Street from Trafalgar Square.

Tourist Information: The City of London TI is located next to St. Paul's; open Mon-Sat 9:30-17:30, Sun 10:00-16:00.

Courtauld Gallery: £7 (price can change with exhibit), generally daily 10:00-18:00 but set to close in mid-2018 for a multiyear renovation.

St. Clement Danes: Free, Mon-Fri 9:00-16:00, Sat-Sun 9:30-15:00, closed to sightseers during worship (generally Sun at 11:00, Wed and Fri at 12:30); tel. 020/7242-2382, www.raf. mod.uk/stclementdanes.

Royal Courts of Justice: Free, Mon-Fri 10:00-16:30, closed Sat-Sun, on the Strand; tel. 020/7947-6000, www.justice.gov.uk/courts/rcj.

Twinings Tea Shop: Mon-Fri 9:30-19:00, Sat 10:00-17:00, Sun 11:00-18:00.

Temple Church: £5, irregular visiting hours, often 10:00-16:00, not open every day, closed Sun to visitors, confirm schedule at www.templechurch.com.

St. Dunstan-in-the-West: Mon-Fri 10:00-16:00, usually hosts free 45-minute lunchtime concerts Wed at 13:15; you're welcome to bring a bag lunch; confirm schedule at www. stdunstaninthewest.org.

Dr. Johnson's House: £6 (cash only), Mon-Sat 11:00-17:30, until 17:00 Oct-April, closed Sun year-round, audioguide-£2, tel. 020/7353-3745, www.drjohnsonshouse.org.

St. Bride's Church: Free, Mon-Fri 8:00-18:00, Sat generally 10:00-15:00, Sun 10:00-18:30; free lunch concerts usually Tue and Fri at 13:15; Sun choral Eucharist at 11:00 and evensong at 17:30; tel. 020/7427-0133, www.stbrides.com.

Old Bailey: Free, public galleries only; opening hours depend on court schedule, but generally Mon-Fri 10:00-13:00 & 14:00-17:00, last entry at 12:40 and 15:40 but often closes an hour or so earlier, closed Sat-Sun, reduced hours in Aug, no kids under 14, on Old Bailey Street. No bags, mobile phones, cameras, iPods, or food, but small purses OK; you can check bags at many nearby businesses, including the Capable Travel agency just down the street at 4 Old Bailey (£5/bag, £1/phone or camera).

St. Paul's Cathedral: £18, includes church entry, dome climb, crypt, tour, and audioguide; Mon-Sat 8:30-16:30, dome opens at 9:30, closed Sun except for worship.

St. Mary-le-Bow: Free, Mon-Thu 7:30-18:00, Fri until 16:00, closed Sat-Sun.

The Guildhall: Free, Mon-Sat 10:00-17:00, Sun 12:00-16:00; tel. 020/7332-3404.

Bank Museum: Free, Mon-Fri 10:00-17:00, closed Sat-Sun; tel. 020/7601-5545, www.bankofengland.co.uk/museum.

The Monument: £4.50 (cash only) to climb the steps for the view, daily 9:30-18:00, Oct-March until 17:30.

Tours: ∩ Download my free Historic London: The City audio tour.

Services: You'll find pay WCs toward the back of the terrace café at Somerset House, in front of the Royal Courts of Justice (in a traffic island), and free WCs in the basement of St. Paul's (around the left side) and in the One New Change shopping mall (behind St. Paul's).

OVERVIEW

The City stretches from Temple Church (near Blackfriars Bridge) to the Tower of London. This was the London of the ancient Romans, William the Conqueror, Henry VIII, Shakespeare, and Elizabeth I.

But The City has been stripped of its history by the Great Fire (1666), the WWII Blitz (1940-1941), and modern economic realities. Today, it's a neighborhood of modern bank buildings and retail stores. Only about 10,000 people actually live here, but The City is a hive of business activity on workdays—packed with almost half a million commuting bankers, legal assistants, and coffee-shop baristas.

The route is simple—a two-mile walk east along a single street that changes names as you go. The Strand becomes Fleet Street, which becomes Cannon Street.

The Walk Begins

• *Make your way to the front (Strand) entrance of Charing Cross Station (Tube: Charing Cross or Embankment; also just a short walk along the Strand from Trafalgar Square).*

If you're coming via the Embankment stop, consider first climbing up to the Golden Jubilee pedestrian bridge (follow signs for the Embankment Pier exit) for good views of the London Eye and skyscrapers before starting this walk. (If you miss this photo op, there's another good one early in the walk, on Waterloo Bridge.)

Remember, you can skip a mile's worth of the Strand by taking the Tube directly to Temple and starting the walk at St. Clement Danes.

The Strand

This busy boulevard, home to theaters and retail stores, was formerly a high-class riverside promenade, back before the Thames was tamed with retaining walls in the 19th century.

The venerable **Charing Cross Station** still has a terminus hotel (a standard part of station design in the early days of rail travel) and remains a busy transportation hub.

The station is named for the **Charing Cross monument,** which stands quietly out of place amid all the commotion in front of the station. This monument is a Victorian Age replacement of the original, medieval "Eleanor Cross." When Queen Eleanor died in 1290, her body was carried from Nottingham to Westminster Abbey. King Edward I had a memorial "Eleanor Cross" built at each of the 12 places his wife's funeral procession spent the night during that long, sad trek. Charing Cross marks the final overnight stop.

A few blocks up the Strand on the left is Southampton Street, which leads to **Covent Garden** (described on page 53).

Ahead on the right is the drive-up entrance to the ❶ **Savoy Hotel** and **Savoy Theatre.** The hotel sparkles after a recent £250 million renovation. Its shiny gold knight represents the Earl of Savoy, who built the original riverside palace here in 1245. This is one of London's ritziest locales, with Rolls-Royces, fancy shops, Simpson's Restaurant, and the doorman in top hat and tails. Everyone has stayed here. Monet painted the Thames at the Savoy; Oscar Wilde romanced Lord Douglas; Chaplin, Sinatra, and Burton-and-Taylor made the scene; as did the Beatles, The Who, and Bob Dylan, who filmed his cue-card-flipping film for *Subterranean Homesick Blues* in an alley around back—one of the earliest examples of a music video. Step inside to see the spiffy foyer under the pretext of asking about their (overpriced) afternoon tea under the glass cupola or visiting the tea shop.

At the next major intersection, a side-trip out onto **Waterloo Bridge** affords you the other good photo op promised earlier: an unobstructed bridge-level view of the city in both directions.

A half-block farther down the Strand is **Gibraltar House** (at

THE CITY

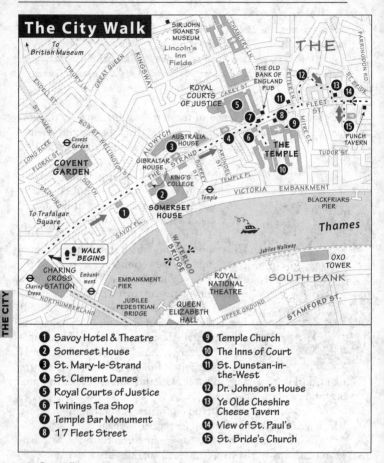

The City Walk

To British Museum

SIR JOHN SOANE'S MUSEUM

Lincoln's Inn Fields

THE OLD BANK OF ENGLAND PUB

ROYAL COURTS OF JUSTICE

THE TEMPLE

PUNCH TAVERN

Dr. Johnson's House

Ye Olde Cheshire Cheese Tavern

COVENT GARDEN

Covent Garden

AUSTRALIA HOUSE

GIBRALTAR HOUSE

KING'S COLLEGE

SOMERSET HOUSE

To Trafalgar Square

WALK BEGINS

CHARING CROSS

Charing Cross STATION

EMBANKMENT PIER

JUBILEE PEDESTRIAN BRIDGE

QUEEN ELIZABETH HALL

ROYAL NATIONAL THEATRE

Jubilee Walkway

SOUTH BANK

OXO TOWER

Thames

BLACKFRIARS PIER

VICTORIA EMBANKMENT

Temple

1. Savoy Hotel & Theatre
2. Somerset House
3. St. Mary-le-Strand
4. St. Clement Danes
5. Royal Courts of Justice
6. Twinings Tea Shop
7. Temple Bar Monument
8. 17 Fleet Street
9. Temple Church
10. The Inns of Court
11. St. Dunstan-in-the-West
12. Dr. Johnson's House
13. Ye Olde Cheshire Cheese Tavern
14. View of St. Paul's
15. St. Bride's Church

THE CITY

150 Strand), a quasi-embassy and visitors center for one of Britain's last little "colonies," located on the southern tip of Spain.

Next up is ❷ **Somerset House,** the last of the many great riverside mansions that once lined the Strand. Today, it houses the Courtauld Gallery (likely closed for restoration) and has a people-friendly courtyard with playful fountains, a riverside terrace, and a choice of cafés (with WCs). The courtyard is a busy public space all year long, with ice skating in the winter and concerts in the summer.

You'll encounter two different churches left Strand-ed in the middle of traffic when the road was widened around them. The first, ❸ **St. Mary-le-Strand,** with its clean, white interior lit by blue-and-green stained glass, is an oasis of quiet (see photo). Charles Dickens'

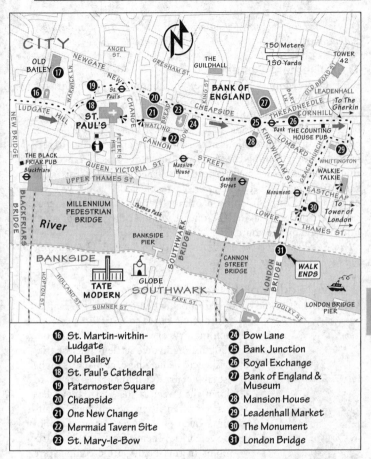

⑯	St. Martin-within-Ludgate	㉔	Bow Lane
⑰	Old Bailey	㉕	Bank Junction
⑱	St. Paul's Cathedral	㉖	Royal Exchange
⑲	Paternoster Square	㉗	Bank of England & Museum
⑳	Cheapside	㉘	Mansion House
㉑	One New Change	㉙	Leadenhall Market
㉒	Mermaid Tavern Site	㉚	The Monument
㉓	St. Mary-le-Bow	㉛	London Bridge

parents were married here. To the right of the church (in the ugly concrete building) is **King's College,** one of the world's top universities, with 20,000 current students and a distinguished list of former students that includes John Keats, Florence Nightingale, and Desmond Tutu.

Straight ahead and across the street is **Bush House,** former home of the BBC's World Service. And just beyond is **Australia House,** a kind of embassy for that member of the British Commonwealth. It's most famous for its role as the goblin-run Gringotts Wizarding Bank in the Harry Potter movies. Though it's not open to visiting Muggles, you can step into the lobby—enter at the far side—and gaze through glass doors at the chandeliered room they filmed in. The building sits on a multibranched intersection where the flow of traffic is a marvel to watch.

• *Also in the intersection, behind the statue of William Gladstone—*

Queen Victoria's longest-serving prime minister—is the second traffic-island church of...

❹ St. Clement Danes

Built by Christopher Wren (1682), the church was blitzed heavily in World War II. Today, it's a busy Royal Air Force chapel and a memorial to the 125,000 RAF servicemen who gave their lives in both world wars. Outside stand statues of brave airmen. Inside, hundreds of gray medallions in the stone floor are dedicated to various squadrons. Lining the walls are Books of Remembrance—10 thick volumes (with a page respectfully turned each day). This is the first of several Wren-built churches (steeple added later) we'll see on the walk. Of the 50-some he originally built, 23 Wren churches still dot London. Pick up the tourist guide at the entry for more information on the church.

• *Past St. Clement Danes, on the left side of street are the Gothic arches, pinnacles, and turrets of the...*

❺ Royal Courts of Justice

When celebrities sue tabloids for libel, when media mogul Rupert

Murdoch is called to testify in a corruption inquiry, or when ex-Beatles pay out $50 million divorce settlements, the trial is likely to be held here, at Britain's highest civil court. (Criminal cases are heard down the street at the Old Bailey.) Paparazzi often litter the entrance, awaiting a celeb or a lawyer (many of whom are celebrities themselves). The 76 courtrooms in this Neo-Gothic complex are open to the public. At least step into the lobby to see the vast Gothic entry hall (submit to a security check to go farther in). This is just one of several legal buildings in the neighborhood.

• *Across the street is...*

❻ Twinings Tea Shop (216 Strand)

When this slender store first opened its doors ("established 1706"), tea was an exotic concoction from newly explored lands. (The Chinese statues at the entrance remind us that tea came first from China, then India.) This store has been in the Twining family for nearly 300 years. The Twinings

shop is narrow, but explore its depths. In the back, there are a few display cases of historic tea-related knickknacks, and a tea-tasting area (help yourself to a sample of whichever tea you like, whether bagged or loose, and enjoy the tea tips of the chatty hostess).

In the 1700s, London was in the grip of a coffee craze, and "coffee houses" were everywhere. These were rather seedy places, where "gentlemen" went for coffee, tobacco, and female companionship. Tea offered a refreshing change of pace, and the late-in-the-day "cuppa" (as well as "afternoon tea") soon became a national institution. These days—as you'll see on this walk—coffee has made a comeback in London in the form of modern Starbucks-style coffee shops.

• *Pass a Thai restaurant at #229, which used to be a pub called The Wig and Pen. A small plaque on the front of the wood-and-stained-glass facade commemorates the old pub building as a rare survivor of the Great Fire of 1666. Up ahead, in the middle of the street, is a small statue of a winged creature.*

❼ Temple Bar Monument

A statue of a griffin, a mythological beast with an eagle's wings and a lion's body, marks the official border between the City of West-

minster and The City of London. The Queen, who presides over Westminster, does not pass this point without ceremonial permission of The City's Lord Mayor. The relief at its base shows Queen Victoria submitting to this ritual in 1837.

• *Cross the border, leaving Westminster and entering The City. Ahead on the left (194 Fleet Street) is The Old Bank of England pub—a former bank with a lavish late-Victorian interior that serves lunches to the 9-to-5 crowd. (To imagine a fancy 19th-century bank, pop inside.) Up a few store-fronts, on the right side of the street, look above the street-level shops*
to find an old building with black-framed, stained-glass bay windows.

❽ 17 Fleet Street

This half-timbered, three-story, Tudor-style building (1610) is one of the few to survive the Great Fire. In Shakespeare's day, the entire City was packed, rooftop to rooftop, with wood and plaster build-ings like this. Many were five and six stories high, with narrow frontage. Little

THE CITY

wonder that a small fire could spread so quickly and become the Great Fire of 1666.

The building may be flying the red-and-yellow flag of Spain's Catalan region, as it now houses the Catalan tourist board.

• *Pass underneath the house, through the passageway called Inner Temple Lane. This leads a half-block to the exotic...*

❾ Temple Church

Exterior: The church's round shape and crenellated, castle-turret roofline mark this as a Crusader church (1185) from the days of King Richard the Lionheart. In the courtyard, a tiny statue of a Crusader knight on horseback stands atop a pillar. This church was the headquarters of the Knights Templar, a band of heavily armed, highly trained monks who dressed in long white robes (decorated with red crosses) beneath heavy armor. In their secret rituals, the knights were sworn to chastity and to the protection of pilgrims on their way to the Muslim-held Holy Land.

Interior: If the church is open (it has erratic hours), step inside. Some honored knights lie face-up on the floor under the rotunda of the circular "nave," patterned after the Church of the Holy Sepulchre in Jerusalem. A knight's crossed legs indicate that he probably died peacefully at home. Surrounding the serene knights are grotesque faces, perhaps the twisted expressions seen in distant wars. Fans of *The Da Vinci Code* (book and movie) will recognize the Temple Church as a place

the protagonist comes to find clues leading to a special tomb.

By 1300, the Knights Templars' mission of protecting pilgrims had become a corrupt "protection" racket, and they'd grown rich loaning money to kings and popes. Those same kings and popes condemned the monks as heretics and sodomites and confiscated their lands (1312). The Temple Church was rented to lawyers, who built the Inns of Court around it.

• *Abutting, surrounding, and extending from the Temple Church is a vast complex of buildings covering a full city block between the Strand/Fleet Street and the Thames, known collectively as...*

THE CITY

⓾ The Inns of Court

Wander through the peaceful maze of buildings, courtyards, narrow lanes, nooks, gardens, fountains, and century-old gas lamps, where lawyers take a break from the Royal Courts. The complex is a self-contained city of lawyers, with offices, lodgings, courtrooms, chapels, and dining halls. Law students must live here (and are even required to eat a number of meals on the premises) to complete their legal internship.

You'll see barristers in modern business suits and ties, plus a few in traditional wigs and robes, as they prepare to do legal battle. The wigs are a remnant of French manners of the 1700s, when every self-respecting European gentleman wore one.

• *Get lost. Don't worry—when you go uphill, you'll eventually spill back out onto the busy street. Return to 17 Fleet Street, which marks the spot where the Strand becomes...*

Fleet Street

"The Street" was the notorious haunt of a powerful combination—lawyers and the media. In 1500, Wynkyn de Worde moved here with a newfangled invention, a printing press, making this area the center of an early Information Age. In 1702, the first daily news-

paper appeared. Soon you had the *Tatler,* the *Spectator,* and many others pumping out both hard news and paparazzi gossip for the hungry masses. Just past St. Dunstan church (described next), you'll see a building decorated with mosaiced names of some bygone newspapers: the *Dundee Evening Telegraph,* the *People's Journal,* and so on.

London became the nerve center of a global, colonial empire, and Fleet Street was where every twitch found expression. Hard-drinking, ink-stained reporters gathered in taverns and coffeehouses, pumping lawyers for juicy pretrial information, scrambling for that choice bit of must-read gossip that would make their paper number one. They built an industry that still endures. Even in this digital age, Britain supports about a dozen national newspapers, selling more than 9 million papers a day.

Today, busy Fleet Street bustles with almost every business *except* newspapers. The industry made a mass exodus in the 1980s for offices elsewhere, replaced by financial institutions. As you walk along, you'll see the former offices of the *Daily Telegraph* (135 Fleet Street) and the *Daily Express* (#121—peek into the lobby to see its classic 1930s Art Deco interior). The last major institution to leave (in the summer of 2005) was the Reuters news agency (#85, opposite the *Daily Express*).

• *Heading 50 yards east past 17 Fleet Street, you'll find...*

⓫ St. Dunstan-in-the-West

This church stands where the Great Fire of September 1666 finally ended. The fire started near London Bridge. For three days it swept westward, fanned by hot and blustery weather, leveling everything in its path. As it approached St. Dunstan, 40 theology students battled the blaze, holding it off until the wind shifted, and the fire slowly burned itself out.

From this survivor to the end of our walk (1.5 miles), we'll be passing through the fire's path of destruction. It left London a Sodom-and-Gomorrah wasteland so hot it couldn't be walked on for weeks. (For more on the fire, 📖 see the end of the Bankside Walk chapter.)

Today, St. Dunstan is one of the few churches with a thriving congregation (of Orthodox Romanians) in this now depopulated and secularized district. An unbroken line of vicars dating back to 1237 is listed in the vestibule. The clock on the bell tower outside (1670) features London's first minute hand and has two slaves gonging two bells four times an hour.

Alongside the church is a rare contemporary statue of Queen Elizabeth I. Surviving from her reign, this 1586 depiction of Elizabeth is as accurate as anything we have. The scepter and orb symbolize her religious and secular authority.

• *Continue east on Fleet Street. A half-block past Fetter Lane, turn left through a covered alleyway at #167. (Don't take the alleyway called Red Lion Court; you want the alleyway 20 paces farther, immediately across from #54.) Follow signs through the narrow lanes directing you to* Dr. Johnson's House.

Narrow Lanes—1700s London

"Sir, if you wish to have a just notion of the magnitude of this city, you must...survey the innumerable little lanes and courts," said the writer Samuel Johnson in 1763 to his young friend and biographer, James Boswell. These twisting alleyways and cramped buildings that house urban hobbits give a faint glimpse of rebuilt 1700s London, a crowded city of half a million

London's Great Plague of 1665

The Grim Reaper—in the form of the bacteria *Yersinia pestis* (bubonic plague)—rode through London on fleas atop a black rat. It killed one in six people, while leaving the buildings standing. (The next year, the Great Fire consumed the buildings.) It started in the spring as "the Poore's Plague," neglected until it spread to richer neighborhoods. During the especially hot summer, 5,000 died each week. By December, the congregation at St. Bride's (you'll see the church later) was 2,111 souls fewer.

Victims passed through several days of agony: headaches, vomiting, fever, shivering, swollen tongue, and swollen buboes (lumps) on the groin glands. After their skin turned blotchy black (the "Black Death"), they died. "Searchers of the Dead" carted bodies off to mass graves, including one near St. Bride's. Both the victims and their families were quarantined under house arrest, with a red cross painted on the door and a guard posted nearby, and denied access to food, water, or medical attention for 40 days—a virtual death sentence even for the uninfected.

The disease was blamed on dogs and cats, and paid dog-killers destroyed tens of thousands of pets—which brought even more rats. People who didn't die tried to leave. The Lord Mayor quarantined the whole city within the walls, so the only way out was to produce (or purchase) a "certificate of health."

By fall, London was a ghost town, and throughout England, people avoided Londoners like the Plague. It took the Great Fire of 1666 to fully cleanse London of the disease. Some scholars have suggested that a popular nursery rhyme refers to the dreaded disease (while others brush this off as bunk):

> *Ring around the rosie* (flower garlands
>   to keep the Plague away)
> *A pocket full of posies* (buboes on the groin)
> *Ashes, ashes* (your skin turns black)
> *We all fall down* (dead).

people. After the Great Fire, London was resurrected in brick and stone instead of wood, but they stuck to the same medieval street plan, resulting in narrow lanes of brick buildings like these.

• *The narrow lanes eventually spill out onto Gough Square, about a block north of Fleet Street, where you'll find...*

⓬ Dr. Johnson's House (17 Gough Square)

"When a man is tired of London, he is tired of life," wrote Samuel Johnson, "for there is in London all that life can afford." Johnson (1709-1784) loved to wander these twisting lanes, looking for pungent slices of London street life that he could pass along in his weekly columns called "The Rambler" and "The Idler."

At age 28, Johnson arrived in London with one of his former students, David Garrick, who went on to revolutionize London theater. Dr. Johnson prowled the pubs, brothels, coffeehouses, and illicit gaming pits where terriers battled cornered rats while men bet on the outcome. Johnson—described as "tall, stout," and "slovenly in his dress"—became a well-known eccentric and man-about-town, though he always seemed to live on the fringes of poverty. At the far end of Gough Square is a statue of Johnson's beloved black cat Hodge, who dined on oysters. The pedestal quotes Johnson himself: "Hodge—a very good cat indeed."

Johnson inhabited this house from 1748 to 1759. He prayed at St. Clement Danes, drank in Fleet Street pubs, and, in the attic of the house, produced his most famous work, *A Dictionary of the English Language*. Published in 1755, it was the first great English-language dictionary, starring Johnson's 42,773 favorite words culled from all the books he'd read. It took Johnson and six assistants more than six years to sift through all the alternate spellings and Cockney dialects of the world's most complex language. He standardized spelling and pronunciation, explained each word's etymology, and occasionally put his own droll spin on words. ("Oats: a grain, which is generally given to horses, but in Scotland supports the people.")

Today, the house is a museum. While the exhibits are fascinating for hard-core Johnson fans (I met one once), the old house is interesting in itself, even for the casual visitor. See a video and climb four stories through period furniture, passing a first edition of Johnson's dictionary and pictures of Johnson, Garrick (in the role of Richard III), and Boswell. Nothing is roped off or behind glass, and you can browse at will. See objects Johnson once owned: his walking stick, a chair, a letter carrier, and a brick from something that fascinated him—the Great Wall of China. Portraits bring to life his urbane circle of friends (which included actress Sarah Siddons, painter Sir Joshua Reynolds, and writer Oliver Goldsmith), many of whom socialized at the home of the sophisticated Elizabeth Montagu. Finally, you arrive in the top-floor garret where literary history was made—the birthplace of the dictionary that standardized our English language.

• *At the other end of Gough Square, turn right at the statue of Hodge and head back toward Fleet Street, noticing the lists of barristers (trial*

The Great Fire

The stones of St. Paul's flew from the building, the lead melting down the streets in a stream... God grant mine eyes may never

behold the like... Above 10,000 homes all in one flame, the noise and crackling and thunder of the impetuous flames, the shrieking of women and children, the hurry of the people, the fall of the towers, houses, and churches was like a hideous storm.

—John Evelyn, eyewitness

lawyers) on the doorways (e.g., next to the door at 9 Gough Square). They work not as part of a firm, but as freelancers sharing offices and clerks. Stay to the left as you wind downhill through the alleys, and look near Fleet Street for the entrance of...

🔞 Ye Olde Cheshire Cheese Tavern

Johnson often—and I do mean often—popped 'round here for a quick one, sometimes with David Garrick and his sleazy actor friends.

"The Cheese" dates from 1667, when it was rebuilt after the Great Fire, but it's been a tavern since 1538. It's a four-story warren of small, smoky, wood-lined rooms, each offering different menus, from pub grub to white-tablecloth meals. A traditional "chop house," it serves hearty portions of meats to power-lunching businessmen. Even if you don't go in, check out the menu posted outside, and the list of monarchs who have reigned during the Cheese's existence—right up to Queen Elizabeth II.

Inside, you can sit in Charles Dickens' favorite seat, next to a coal fireplace (in the "Chop Room," main floor) and order a steak-and-kidney pie and some spotted dick (sponge pudding with currants, served in winter). Sip a pint of Samuel Smith (the house beer of the current owners) and think of Samuel Johnson, who drank here pondering various spellings: "pint" or "pynte," "color" or "colour," "theater" or "theatre." Immerse yourself in a world largely unchanged for centuries—a world of reporters scribbling the news over lunch, of

Alfred, Lord Tennyson inventing rhymes and Arthur Conan Doyle solving crimes, of W. B. Yeats, Teddy Roosevelt, and Mark Twain.

• *Back out on Fleet Street, you're met with a cracking...*

ⓔ View of St. Paul's

If you were standing here on December 30, 1940, the morning after a German Luftwaffe firebomb raid, you'd see nothing but a flat, smoldering landscape of rubble, with St. Paul's rising above it almost miraculously intact. (For more on the Blitz, see the sidebar on page 270.)

Standing here in September of 1666, you'd see nothing but smoke and ruins. The Great Fire razed everything, including the original St. Paul's Cathedral. And standing here a year earlier, in September of 1665, you'd hear "Bring out yer dead!" as they carted away 70,000 victims of the bubonic plague. After the double-whammy of plague and fire, the architect Christopher Wren was hired to rebuild St. Paul's and The City.

Even today, we see the view that Wren intended—a majestic dome hovering above the hazy rooftops, surrounded by the thin spires of his lesser churches. In the foreground below St. Paul's (between you and the dome) is the slender, lead-covered steeple of St. Martin-within-Ludgate, perfectly offsetting St. Paul's more massive dome. Wren's 23 surviving churches are more than plenty for today's secular ghost town of a city.

• *Go a block downhill from Ye Olde Cheshire Cheese, cross the street, and walk a half-block down tiny St. Bride's Avenue to see the stacked-tier steeple of...*

ⓔ St. Bride's Church

The 226-foot steeple, Wren's tallest, is stacked in layers as it tapers to a point. It's said to have inspired the wedding cake. Supposedly, a Fleet Street baker named Mr. Rich gazed out his shop window at St. Bride's as he made the first multitiered cake. (By the way, the word "Bride" in St. Bride's is only coincidental. The church

Christopher Wren (1632-1723)

After London burned, King Charles II turned to his childhood friend Christopher Wren to rebuild it. The 33-year-old Wren was not an architect, but he'd proven his ability in every field he'd touched: astronomy (mapping the moon and building a model of Saturn), medicine (using opium as a general anes-

thetic, making successful blood transfusions between animals), mathematics (a treatise on spherical trigonometry), and physics (his study of the laws of motion influenced Newton's "discovery" of gravity). Wren also invented a language for the deaf, studied refraction and optics, and built weather-watching instruments.

Though domed St. Paul's is Wren's most famous church, the smaller churches around it better illustrate his distinctive style: a steeple over the west entrance; an uncluttered, well-lit interior; Neoclassical (Greek-style) columns; a curved or domed plaster ceiling; geometrical shapes (e.g., round rosettes inside square frames); and fine carved woodwork, often by his favorite whittler, Grinling Gibbons.

THE CITY

was dedicated to St. Brigid—or Bride—of Kildare long before the steeple or any wedding cakes.)

St. Bride's, built between 1671 and 1675, was one of the first of Wren's churches to open its doors after the Fire. St. Bride's is nicknamed both "The Cathedral of Fleet Street" and "The Printer's Church." Notice that the pews bear the names of departed journalists. It has been home to newspaper reporters, scholars, and literati ever since 1500, when Wynkyn de Worde set up his printing press here on church property. De Worde's press first served the literate clergy of St. Bride's, but was soon adopted by secular scholars, bookmakers, and newspapers, as Fleet Street became a global center for printed information.

During World War II, St. Bride's suffered terribly in the Blitz. (Today's structure was largely rebuilt after the war.) But thanks to Hitler's bombs, St. Bride's was instantly excavated down to its sixth-century Saxon foundations. Layers of previously unknown history were revealed from six previous churches that stood on this spot, including items such as Roman coins, medieval stained glass, and 17th-century tobacco pipes.

Also in the crypt is a wedding dress—worn by the wife of the Fleet Street baker whose wedding cake was inspired by St. Bride's steeple.

• Just past St. Bride's Church on Fleet Street is **$$$ The Punch Tavern**, draped with memories of the venerable London political magazine famous for its satirical cartoons. Peek in to see Punch and his twin wife Judy looking down on a perfectly Victorian scene. These characters from a

popular puppet show came onto the London scene 350 years ago. The characters gave the magazine its name, and the pub became the magazine staff's hangout. In the back room hang huge, colorful Victorian-era pastels of Punch and Judy. Don't be shy—the tavern is proud of their history and welcomes curious visitors popping in for a quick look. It's also a friendly place to order a drink or a meal (respected for their gins and pies, 99 Fleet Street). The valley between St. Bride's and St. Paul's is the...

Fleet River and Ludgate

The Fleet River—now covered over by Farringdon Road—still flows southward, crossing underneath Fleet Street on its way to the Thames at Blackfriars Bridge. In medieval times, the river formed the western boundary of the walled city. As you cross the "river"

and continue toward St. Paul's, you're hiking up Ludgate Hill. This was one of the three hills in the area, and was where some of London's first inhabitants built. The ancient Romans of Londinium may have built a temple to their goddess of hunting where St. Paul's stands today. You're getting closer and closer to the city's medieval origins—the city Shakespeare would have known.

Up ahead, you'll spy the lead-covered steeple that graces another of Wren's churches—⓰ **St. Martin-within-Ludgate.** The church stands on the site of what was once the city wall. In medieval and Elizabethan times, this was one of the gated entrances to the city, known as Ludgate.

• Just before St.-Martin-within-Ludgate, pause and look left down Old Bailey Street to see a dome crowned by a golden statue of justice, which marks the...

⓱ Old Bailey—Central Criminal Court

England's most infamous criminals—from the king-killers of

the Civil War to the radically religious William Penn, from the

"criminally homosexual" Oscar Wilde to the Yorkshire Ripper—were tried here, in Britain's highest criminal court. On top of the copper dome stands the famous golden Lady who weighs and executes Justice with scale and sword. The Old Bailey is built on the former site of Newgate Prison, with its notorious execution-by-hanging site. Inside, you can visit courtrooms and watch justice doled out the old-fashioned way to modern-day offenders (see page 71). Bewigged barristers argue before stern judges while the accused sit in the dock.

• *Continue up Ludgate Hill to...*

⑱ St. Paul's Cathedral

The greatest of Wren's creations is the rebuilt St. Paul's—England's national church and the heart of The City. Wren labored for more than 40 years on the church, both designing and overseeing construction of what was then the second-largest dome in the world. Unlike many church architects, Wren lived long enough to see his masterpiece completed.

(For details on St. Paul's, 📖 see the St. Paul's Cathedral Tour chapter or 🎧 download my free audio tour.)

If you're not paying to enter the great church, you can pop into the basement (entry to left of front) for a café, fine WCs, a shop, and a peek at the memorials in the crypt. Belly up to the iron Churchill Gates. Standing on a plaque honoring Churchill, you can see the tomb of Admiral Lord Nelson directly below the dome.

• *A right turn at St. Paul's would take you to the Millennium Bridge, leading across the Thames to the Tate Modern and Bankside area. Instead, look for the Temple Bar gate—a white stone archway—directly to the left of the church. The gate was once the west entrance to the City of London. Relocated here, it now welcomes you to...*

⑲ Paternoster Square

This gate originally stood a half-mile west of here. It marked "Temple Bar," the boundary between the City of London and Westminster, where the griffin monument now stands (see page 243). The original Temple Bar gate was built of stone by St. Paul's architect,

Christopher Wren, in 1672. But given the increase in traffic and new construction around it, the gate didn't "fit" at Temple Bar anymore. It was disassembled in 1878 and carted off to ornament the rural estate of a brewery owner. Finally, in 2004, the 2,700 stones were brought back to The City and painstakingly rebuilt here in Paternoster Square.

Go through the arch into the fine square and enjoy a view of the dome from behind the church's red-brick Chapter House (a

good example of Wren's Neoclassicism). This square was designed in the early 21st century to save views of the church, while allowing maximum modern development here in the city center.

• *Stride right past the* Shepherd and Sheep *statue and head up the pedestrian street, then bear right onto the busy, noisy street called...*

⓴ Cheapside—Shakespeare's London

This was the main east-west street of Shakespeare's London, which had a population of about 200,000 back then. The wide street hosted The City's marketplace ("cheap" meant market), seen today in the names of the streets that branch off from it: Bread, Milk, Honey.

Rebuilt cheaply after the war, more recently it has been upgraded with brand-new glassy facades—leaving Cheapside anything but.

A half-block past New Change Street (at around 40 Cheapside, on the right), you could enter the ⓴ **One New Change** shopping mall and find the (free) glass elevator up to the rooftop terrace for a view of St. Paul's Cathedral and the London cityscape.

Continue along Cheapside Street. If you were to detour two blocks south on Bread Street, you would not see even a trace of the ⓴ **Mermaid Tavern,** Shakespeare's favorite haunt—but that's where it stood, near the modern junction with Cannon Street. In the early 1600s, "Sweet Will" would meet Ben Jonson, Sir Walter Raleigh, and John Donne at the Mermaid for food, ale, and literary conversation. Francis Beaumont, one of the group, wrote: "What things have we seen / Done at the Mermaid! heard words that have been / So nimble, and so full of subtle flame..."

• *Otherwise, head straight toward the pointy steeple just past One New Change on the right. This marks...*

㉓ St. Mary-le-Bow

From London's earliest Christian times, a church has stood here. The steeple of St. Mary-le-Bow, rebuilt after the Fire, is one of Wren's most impressive. He incorporated the ribbed-arch design of the former church (a "bow" is an arch) in the steeple's midsection. In the courtyard is a statue of a smiling figure from American history—Captain John Smith. In 1607, Smith established an English colony in Jamestown, Virginia, USA before retiring here near the church. Inside the church, see not one but two pulpits, used today for point-counterpoint debates of moral issues. The church was rebuilt after being hit by WWII bombs. The crucifix hanging from the ceiling is a gift of atonement from the people of Bavaria.

This is the very center of old London, where, in medieval times, the church's bells rang each evening, calling Londoners safely back in to the walled town before the gates were locked. To be born "within the sound of Bow bells" long defined a true local, or "Cockney."

This is also the "Cockney" neighborhood of plucky streetwise urchins, where a distinctive Eliza Doolittle dialect is sometimes still spoken. Today's Cockney is the hard accent of rough-and-tumble, working-class Londoners. A famous example of Cockney today would be the GEICO gecko on American TV ads. There are no H's. "Are you 'appy, 'arry?" "Where's your 'orse? ...'urry up now." (Another fun element of the Cockney dialect—its creative rhyming slang—is described in the sidebar.) Nineteenth-century social climbers added extra H's in order not to sound Cockney. "I hunderstand you are hinterested in renting my hattic."

These days, few people actually live within the sound of Bow bells. The City's population, while over 400,000 during working hours, falls to about 10,000 at night.

• *Just around and behind St. Mary-le-Bow is...*

㉔ Bow Lane

Today, pedestrian-only Bow Lane features smart clothing shops, sandwich bars, and pubs. The entire City once had narrow lanes like Bow, Watling, and Bread Streets. Explore this area between Cheapside and Cannon Street.

When Shakespeare bought his tights and pointy shoes in Bow Lane, the shops were wooden, the streets were dirt, and the toilet was a ditch down the middle of the road. (The garbage brought rats, and rats brought plagues, like the one in 1665.) You bought your water in buckets carted up from the Thames. And at night, the bellman walked the streets, ringing the hour.

THE CITY

Cockney Rhyming Slang

The East End (specifically, the area around the Church of St. Mary-le-Bow) is known as the traditional home of the Cockneys. This colorful, working-class group spoke in a quirky pastiche that was the opposite of the Queen's English...think Audrey Hepburn as Eliza Doolittle in *My Fair Lady,* Dick van Dyke as the chimneysweep in *Mary Poppins,* or Don Cheadle in *Ocean's Eleven.*

One colorful Cockney invention that survives from the mid-19th century is the neighborhood's unique rhyming slang. According to urban legend, the Cockneys devised this secret way of talking to confuse policemen who might be listening. Another theory suggests that it was used between market vendors in order to rip off customers. Either way, Cockney rhyming slang helped create a sort of neighborhood pride for this downtrodden community.

Here's how it works: Simply replace an everyday word with a nonsensical phrase that rhymes with it. Instead of stairs, it's "apples and pears"—often shortened to simply "apples," as in, "I'm walking up the apples." For teeth, it's "Hampstead Heath" (or just "hampstead": "The dentist took a bloody good whack at me hampsteads").

Some Cockney rhyming slang words have become integrated into everyday American speech. For example, "blow a raspberry" comes from the slang "raspberry tart" for fart. And did you ever notice that "getting down to brass tacks" rhymes with "facts"? Many others—including several on the list on the next page—remain widely used as slang throughout the UK (if not in the US).

The tradition has continued into the 21st century—though these days it's done as a fun bit of irony, rather than as an actual secret language. For curry, they might say "Ruby Murray"—also

(For more Shakespearean ambience, it's a three-block walk south from St. Paul's to the river, where the Millennium Bridge crosses the Thames to Shakespeare's Globe, a reconstruction of the theater where many of Shakespeare's plays premiered. See page 89.)

• *Turn left on Bow Lane and then right on Cheapside. After a block, you can side-trip left on King Street to the fanciful facade of The Guildhall, a free art gallery and a fine medieval meeting hall, described on page 71. Continue east on Cheapside a few blocks to the long, wide intersection where nine streets meet, called Bank Junction (Tube: Bank). In the middle of all the traffic is a tiny park with a Wellington statue. Walk there and find the pyramid-shaped metal info post showing "The Heart of the City." From here, survey...*

㉕ Bank Junction

You're at the center of financial London, which helped invent the

the name of an Irish pop singer from the 1950s. Someone might suggest, "After work, let's head to the pub for some Britneys" (Britney Spears = beers), or "Go wash yer Chevy" (Chevy Chase = face).

Cockney Rhyming Slang	Translation
a la mode	code
Adam and Eve	believe
Barnet Fair (barnet)	hair (hairstyle)
bubble and squeak (bubble)	Greek
butcher's hook (butcher's)	look
china plate (china)	mate (friend)
deep sea diver	fiver (£5 note)
loaf of bread (loaf)	head
Mutt and Jeff (mutton)	deaf
plates of meat (plates)	feet
porkpies (porkies)	lies
rabbit and pork (rabbit)	talk
Scapa Flow (scarper)	go
septic tank (septic, seppo)	Yank (American)
tea leaf	thief
trouble and strife	wife
whistle and flute	suit

So the next time you find yourself 'avin' a rabbit with a Cockney, slip the bartender a deep sea diver to buy him a Britney and ask him about his trouble and strife's new barnet. Or take a butcher's at his fancy whistle and flute, and try out the local a la mode. Maybe he'll tap his loaf and say, "Not bad fer a seppo."

capitalist economy centuries ago. The skyscrapers surrounding you house the multinational companies that continue to make London one of the globe's financial capitals. The "Square Mile" hosts 500 foreign and British banks. London, centrally located amid the globe's time zones, can find someone around the world to trade with 24 hours a day. Bank Junction is also the place where crowds of angry demonstrators often gather to protest greedy bankers and governments that seem to enable them.

• Look across the square at the eight-columned entrance to the...

❷⑥ Royal Exchange: When London's original stock exchange opened, "stock" meant whatever could be loaded and unloaded onto a boat in the Thames. Remember, London got its start as a river-trading town. Soon, Londoners were gathering here, trading slips of paper and "futures" in place of live goats and chickens. Traders needed money changers, who needed bankers...and London's financial district boomed. Today, you can step inside to a skylight-

covered courtyard lined with traders of retail goods and cappuccinos.

• *To the left of the Royal Exchange is the city-block-sized Bank of England (main entrance just across Threadneedle Street from the Royal Exchange entrance).*

㉗ Bank of England: This 3.5-acre, two-story complex houses the country's national bank. In 1694, it loaned £1.2 million to King William III at 8 percent interest to finance a war with France; it's managed the national debt ever since. It's an investment bank (a banker's bank), loaning money to other financial institutions. Working in tandem with the government (nationalized 1946, independent 1997), "The Old Lady of Threadneedle Street" sets interest rates, prints pound notes, and serves as the country's Fort Knox, housing stacks of gold bars.

The complex has a good **Bank Museum** inside (enter from far side, on Bartholomew Lane). See banknotes from 1699, an old safe, and account books. Also see current pound notes—with a foil hologram and numbers visible under UV light (to stay one step ahead of counterfeiters). The museum's highlight is under the rotunda, displaying a real gold bar that's worth more than $500,000 (check today's rates at the entrance) and weighs 28 pounds. Try lifting it.

• *Opposite the Royal Exchange is Mansion House, marked by its six (not eight) columns.*

㉘ Mansion House: This is the official residence of The City's Lord Mayor. The Lord Mayor governs not all of London but just this neighborhood. In the year 2000, a new post was created—"Mayor of London"—overseeing all of London. But the "Lord Mayor of the City" still carries out the old traditions, presiding from this palatial building. Once a year, he rides the streets in the Lord Mayor's Coach, a gilded carriage pulled by six white horses that looks like something out of *Cinderella*.

• *Walk a block down Cornhill, with the Royal Exchange on your left, and a monument to James Henry Greathead (the 19th-century engineer who made constructing the Tube possible by inventing the "traveling shield"). On the right, at Cornhill #50, pop into The Counting House pub, built as a bank in 1893 (and my favorite lunch stop in this area).*

Cross over Gracechurch Street to nearby Leadenhall Street. At the first corner, look right at the ornate entry to the Leadenhall Market (with the giant "Walkie-Talkie" skyscraper towering above it). We'll turn here after a quick side-trip—zip ahead to the next corner to see towering modern forest of skyscrapers, the new face of The City. Also called "One Square Mile," this is the richest square mile on earth. When there's bad economic news, TV reporters declare, "The Square Mile won't like this." Backtrack half a block, turn left on Whittington Avenue and enter...

㉙ Leadenhall Market

Site of Londinium's Roman Forum, this spot has hosted 2,000 years of commerce. It was named for the new-fangled lead roof of the medieval market hall. Today's hall—a classic 19th-century Victorian structure, still sporting its evocative iron meat hooks—is a getaway for office workers. Given the value of land in this 21st-century environment of skyscrapers, this survives only because it's protected by the government.

· *At the center of the market, turn right and head out to big and busy Gracechurch Street, then turn left and go three blocks to...*

㉚ The Monument to the Great Fire of 1666

The monument, called "The Monument," recalls two themes that have dominated this walk—the Great Fire and Christopher Wren. This 202-foot column is Wren's tribute to the Great Fire that gave him a blank canvas upon which to create modern London. At 2:00 in the morning of September 2, 1666, a small fire broke out in a

baker's oven in nearby Pudding Lane. Supposedly, if you tipped the Monument over (to the east), its top would fall on the exact spot. Fanned by hot, blustery weather, the fire swept westward, leaping from house to house until The City was a square mile of flame.

Wren's memorial is a classic—a Doric column made of Portland stone that was quarried in Dorset in southwestern England and London's new favorite building material. The column's bristly top is made of gilded bronze and meant to depict a Greek urn sprouting flames, symbolizing the 1666 Fire. Inside the hollow column is a spiral staircase you can pay to climb—after 311 steps, the view is still pretty good, despite modern buildings.

· *From here, go uphill a short block on Monument Street, then turn left to hike out over the river on...*

㉛ London Bridge

We'll end our walk at The City's beginning. (For the history of London Bridge, see page 292.)

The City was born as a river-trading town. The Thames flows west to east, from the interior of England to the open sea. It's a tidal river from here to the sea, so ancient and medieval boats could hitch rides on the tide in both directions. London Bridge, first built by the ancient Romans, established a north-south axis through the city. Soon, goods from every corner of the world were pouring into this, one of the modern world's first great urban centers. Today, the bridge is overshadowed by the mammoth skyscraper known as The Shard, which rockets dramatically up over a thousand feet—a symbol of a still-growing city. With its worldwide financial network and cultural heritage, The City—a proud survivor of plagues, fires, blitzes, and economic changes (even great recessions)—is thriving. Today's London still straddles the Thames as you look downstream to the rest of the world.

• From here, the **Tower of London** (□ see the Tower of London Tour chapter) is a 10-minute walk east, down the parklike riverside path. The **Bankside Walk** (□ see the Bankside Walk chapter) begins right here on London Bridge. The start of the **East End Walk** (see page 78 in the Sights in London chapter) is a 20-minute walk (up Gracechurch/Bishopsgate) or one Tube stop to the north, at Liverpool Street Station. Or you can return to **Charing Cross** and **Trafalgar Square** on the Tube (Monument stop nearby) or bus #15 (from Cannon Street).

ST. PAUL'S CATHEDRAL TOUR

No sooner was Sir Christopher Wren selected to refurbish Old St. Paul's Cathedral than the Great Fire of 1666 incinerated it. Within a week, Wren had a plan for a whole new building...and for the city around it, complete with some 50 new churches. For the next four decades he worked to achieve his vision—a spacious church, topped by a dome, surrounded by a flock of Wrens.

St. Paul's is England's national church. There's been a church on this spot since 604. It was the symbol of London's rise from the Great Fire of 1666 and of the city's survival of the Blitz of 1940. It's been the site of important weddings (Prince Charles and Lady Diana) and state funerals (Prime Ministers Churchill and Thatcher). It's the masterpiece of England's greatest Neoclassical architect. Today, it's the center of the Anglican faith. Military buffs will find memorials to many great wars and their war heroes. Dome climbers will be rewarded with expansive views over London's skyline.

Orientation

Cost: £18, £16 in advance online. Admission includes church entry, dome climb, crypt, tour, and audio/videoguide. Free on Sun but officially open only to worshippers. You can use the entrance on the north side of the cathedral to go directly to the café and WC in the crypt (which grants a free, decent glimpse of Nelson's tomb).

Hours: Mon-Sat 8:30-16:30 (dome opens at 9:30), closed Sun except for worship. Sometimes closed for special events—check online. The church is also open Mon-Sat 16:15-18:00 for evening worship (must enter before 17:00). It's always free to enter the church to worship, but your visit is restricted to the back of the nave.

Information: Recorded info tel. 020/7246-8348, reception tel. 020/7246-8350, www.stpauls.co.uk.

Avoiding Lines: Purchasing online tickets in advance saves a little time (and a little money); otherwise the wait can be 15-30 minutes in summer and on weekends. To avoid the crowds in general, arrive first thing in the morning or late in the afternoon.

Getting There: Located in The City; Tube: St. Paul's (other nearby Tube stops include Mansion House, Cannon Street, and Blackfriars). You can take handy buses #15 and #11 (see page 28), as well as #4, #23, or #26. Careful: Don't head for tiny St. Paul's Church near Covent Garden; your destination is St. Paul's Cathedral, in The City.

Music and Church Services: Worship times are available on the church's website. Communion is generally Mon-Sat at 8:00 and 12:30. On Sunday, services are held at 8:00, 10:15 (Matins), 11:30 (sung Eucharist), 15:15 (evensong), and 18:00. The rest of the week, evensong is at 17:00 (Mon is spoken—not sung). If you come 20 minutes early for evensong worship (under the dome), you may be able to grab a big wooden stall in the choir, next to the singers. On some Sundays, there's a free organ recital at 16:45.

Tours: Guided 1.5-hour **tours** are offered Mon-Sat at 10:00, 11:00, 13:00, and 14:00 (call to confirm or ask at church). Free 20-minute **introductory talks** are offered throughout the day. The **audio/videoguide** (included with admission) contains video clips that show the church in action.

🎧 Download my free St. Paul's Cathedral **audio tour.**

Climbing the Dome: It's 528 steps to the top and a mere 257 to the first viewing level. (While there's an elevator for people with disabilities, it does not go up into the dome's galleries—only down to the crypt.) Allow an hour to go up and down. The tower has three levels, called galleries. The climb gets steeper, narrower, and more claustrophobic as you go higher. It's a one-way system, so you can't come back down until you reach the next level.

Length of This Tour: Allow one hour, two if you climb the dome. If you're in a rush, skip the crypt and the dome.

Eating: There's a good **$ café** with soups, sandwiches, and main dishes in the crypt; free access from north side of church. Several places to get a quick bite are on Paternoster Square; for another choice, see page 408.

Nearby: A helpful TI is located to the right of the church. Just behind the church, to the east, is the One New Change modern shopping mall topped by a terrace with great views of the church—not a bad substitute for the dome climb for those disinclined to pay the entry fee and/or climb so many steps (free elevator to top floor). Millennium Bridge is a five-minute walk south, leading to the South Bank (Tate Modern and Shakespeare's Globe).

Starring: Sir Christopher Wren, his dome, and World War II.

The Tour Begins

Even now, as skyscrapers encroach, the 365-foot-high dome of St. Paul's rises majestically above the rooftops of the neighborhood. The tall dome is set on classical columns, capped with a lantern, topped by a six-foot ball, and iced with a cross. As the first Anglican cathedral built in London after the Reformation, it is Baroque: St. Peter's in Rome filtered through clear-eyed English reason.

Viewing St. Paul's facade from in front of the church, you can see the story of Paul's conversion told in the stone pediment. A blinding flash of light leaves Saul sightless on the road to Damascus (see cityscape, lower left). When his sight is restored he becomes Paul, the Christian. This was the pivotal moment in the life of the man who established Christianity as a world religion through his travels, writing, and evangelizing.

While Paul stands on the top, Peter (with the annoying cock that crowed three times, symbolizing his betrayal of Jesus) is to the left, and James is on the right. The four evangelists at the towers' bases each carry the gospel they wrote. As Queen Anne was on the

throne when the church was finished in 1710, the statue in front portrays her.

• *Enter, buy your ticket, and stand at the far back of the nave, behind the font.*

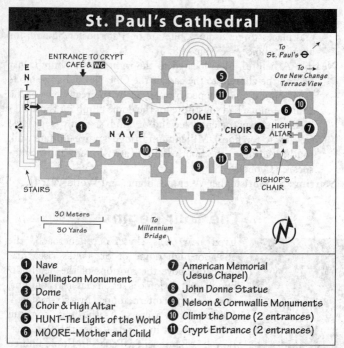

St. Paul's Cathedral

ENTRANCE TO CRYPT
CAFÉ & WC

ENTER

STAIRS

DOME

NAVE

CHOIR

HIGH
ALTAR

BISHOP'S
CHAIR

To
St. Paul's ⊖

To
One New Change
Terrace View

To
Millennium
Bridge

30 Meters

30 Yards

N

1. Nave
2. Wellington Monument
3. Dome
4. Choir & High Altar
5. HUNT–The Light of the World
6. MOORE–Mother and Child
7. American Memorial (Jesus Chapel)
8. John Donne Statue
9. Nelson & Cornwallis Monuments
10. Climb the Dome (2 entrances)
11. Crypt Entrance (2 entrances)

ST. PAUL'S CATHEDRAL

❶ Nave

Look down the nave through the choir stalls to the stained glass at the far end. This big church feels big. At 515 feet long and 250 feet wide, it's Europe's fourth largest, after those in Rome (St. Peter's), Sevilla, and Milan. The spaciousness is accentuated by the relative lack of decoration. The simple, cream-colored ceiling and the clear glass in the windows light everything evenly. Wren wanted this: a simple, open church with nothing to hide. Unfortunately, only this entrance area keeps his original vision—the rest was encrusted with 19th-century Victorian ornamentation.

A diamond-shaped plaque on the floor honors the guards ("Men and Women of St. Paul's Watch") who worked so valiantly from 1939 until 1945 to save the church from WWII destruction. On the wall next to the door, a dirty panel of stone remains, reminding visitors how dark the entire church was before undergoing a huge cleaning in preparation for the 300th anniversary of the first service held here. Remarkably, this is the first great church completed in the lifetime of its architect (built 1675-1710).

• *Glance up and behind. The organ trumpets say, "Come to the evensong and hear us play." Ahead and on the left is the towering, black-and-white...*

❷ Wellington Monument

It's so tall that even Wellington's horse has to duck to avoid bumping its head. Wren would have been appalled, but his church has become so central to England's soul that many national heroes are buried here (in the basement crypt). General Wellington, Napoleon's conqueror at Waterloo (1815) and the embodiment of British stiff-upper-lippedness, was honored here in a funeral packed with 13,000 fans. The church is littered with memorials. While all the monuments are upstairs, all the tombs are downstairs.

• *Stroll up the same nave Prince Charles and Lady Diana walked on their 1981 wedding day. Imagine how they felt making the hike to the altar with the world watching. Grab a chair underneath the impressive...*

❸ Dome

The dome you see from here, painted with scenes from the life of St. Paul, is only the innermost of three. From the painted interior

of the first dome, look up through the opening to see the light-filled lantern of the second dome. Finally, the whole thing is covered on the outside by the third and final dome, the shell of lead-covered wood that you see from the street. Wren's ingenious three-in-one design was psychological as well as functional—he wanted a low, shallow inner dome so worshippers wouldn't feel diminished.

You'll see tourists walking around the base of the dome in the Whispering Gallery. The dome is constructed with such acoustic precision that secrets whispered from one side of it are heard on the opposite side, 170 feet away.

Christopher Wren (1632-1723) was the right man at the right time. Though the 31-year-old astronomy professor had never built a major building in his life when he got the commission for St. Paul's, his reputation for brilliance and his unique ability to work with others carried him through. The church has the clean lines and geometric simplicity of the age of Newton, when reason was holy and God set the planets spinning in perfect geometrical motion.

For more than 40 years, Wren worked on this site, overseeing every detail of St. Paul's and the 65,000-ton dome. It's estimated that the dome cost $850 million (in today's dollars). At age 75, Wren got to look up and see his son place the cross on top of the dome, completing the masterpiece.

On the floor directly beneath the dome is a brass grate—part of a 19th-century attempt to heat the church. Encircling it is Christopher Wren's name and epitaph, written in Latin: *Lector, si monumentum requiris circumspice (Reader, if you seek his monument, look around you)*.

Now review the ceiling: Behind is Wren simplicity and ahead is Victorian ornateness.

• *The choir area blocks your way, but you can see the altar at the far end under a golden canopy.*

❹ Choir and High Altar

English churches, unlike most in Europe, often have a central choir area (a.k.a. a "quire" or "chancel"), where church officials and the singers sit. (You can see St. Paul's well-known choir of 30 boys and 12 men in action, singing psalms, at the evensong service, held daily except Monday, when it is spoken rather than sung.) St. Paul's—a cathedral since 604—is home to the local Anglican bishop. He presides in the chair at the far end, on the right, which may have a carved bishop's hat hanging overhead.

The ceiling above the choir is a riot of glass mosaics, representing God (above the altar) and his creation. The mosaics are very Victorian. In fact, Queen Victoria complained that the earlier ceiling was "dreary and undevotional." The Dean and chapter wisely took note and had it spiffed up with this brilliant mosaic work... textbook late Victorian. In separate spheres, eight "Angels of the Morning" hold up creatures of the earth, sea, and sky.

The high altar (the marble slab with crucifix and candlesticks—you'll get a close look later) sits under a huge canopy with corkscrew columns. The canopy looks ancient, but it only dates from 1958, when it was rebuilt after being heavily damaged in October 1940 by the bombs of Hitler's Luftwaffe. For regular services, the priest stands beneath the dome on the low wooden platform.

• *In the north transept (to your left as you face the altar), find the big painting of Christ, in a golden wood altarpiece. Glare? Try walking side to side to find the best viewing angle.*

❺ *The Light of the World,* 1904

In the dark of night, Jesus—with a lantern, halo, jeweled cape, and crown of thorns—approaches an out-of-the-way home in the woods, knocks on the door, and listens for an invitation to come in. A Bible passage on the picture frame says: "Behold, I stand at the door and knock..." (Revelation 3:20).

The Anglican Communion

St. Paul's Cathedral is the symbolic (but not official) nucleus of the earth's 70 million Anglicans. The Anglican Communion is a loose association of churches—including the Church of England and the Episcopal Church in the US—with common beliefs. The rallying point is *The Book of Common Prayer,* their handbook for worship services.

Forged in the fires of Europe's Reformation, Anglicans see themselves as a "middle way" between Catholics and Protestants. They retain much of the pomp and ceremony of traditional Catholic worship but with Protestant elements such as married priests (and, recently, female priests); attention to Scripture; and a less hierarchical, more consensus-oriented approach to decision making. Among Anglicans there are divisions, from Low Church congregations (more evangelical and "Protestant") to High Church (more traditional and "Catholic").

The Church of England, the largest single body, is still the official religion of the state, headed by the Archbishop of Canterbury (who presides in Canterbury but lives in London). In 1982, Pope John Paul II and the then-Archbishop of Canterbury met face-to-face. In 2010, Pope Benedict XVI visited London and joined the Archbishop in prayer. Pope Francis has indicated that he wants to continue bridging the gap that has existed since the Reformation. These symbolic gestures signal a new ecumenical spirit.

In his early twenties, William Holman Hunt (1827-1910) was in the dark night of a spiritual crisis when he heard this verse knocking in his head. He opened his soul to Christ, his life changed forever, and he tried to capture the experience in paint. As one of the Pre-Raphaelites who adored medieval art (see page 339), he used symbolism, but only images the average Brit-on-the-street could understand. The door is the closed mind, the weeds the neglected soul, the darkness is malaise, while Christ carries the lantern of spiritual enlightenment.

In 1854, Hunt debuted *The Light of the World* (not this version, but a smaller one now at Oxford). The critics savaged it—"syrupy," "too Catholic," "simple"—but the masses lapped it up. It became the most famous painting in Victorian England—in fact, in the whole world. It was taken on tour through the vast British Empire, and was reproduced in countless engravings. It became a pop icon that inspired sermons, poems, hymns, and countless Christ-at-the-door paintings in churches and homes. Hunt's humble-hippie image of Christ was stamped forever on the minds of generations of schoolkids. It was so popular that late in life Hunt was asked to do this larger version specifically for St. Paul's. Nearly blind, he needed an assistant. (*The Guardian* newspaper once published a list of "Britain's Ten Worst Paintings." They honored *The Light of the World* as number seven, comparing it to a plastic crucifix.)

• *Return to the area underneath the dome and walk toward the altar, along the left side of the choir. We're headed for a couple of sights that remember World War II, when London—and St. Paul's—were heavily bombed by the Germans. Londoners took refuge underground, in Tube stations called into use as ad-hoc bomb shelters. Pause at the modern statue—an egg-shaped mother cradling a blob-shaped baby.*

❻ Mother and Child, 1983

Britain's (and perhaps the world's?) greatest modern sculptor, Henry Moore, rendered a traditional subject in marble in an abstract, minimalist way. This Mary-and-Baby-Jesus was inspired by the sight of British moms nursing babies in WWII bomb shelters. Moore intended the viewer to touch and interact with the art. It's OK.

• *Continue up the four steps to the altar at the far end of the church.*

❼ American Memorial Chapel (Jesus Chapel)

St. Paul's is a place of remembrance for many victims of Britain's wars. The church took on special significance in World War II.

The neighborhood around St. Paul's was largely destroyed during the Blitz and the Battle of Britain, but the church itself—thanks to good fortune and a heroic effort by Londoners—survived.

In 1940, however, one bomb did pierce the dome and obliterate the high altar. As you admire today's beautiful altar—the canopy with its corkscrew columns, the carved wood of the choir stalls, the mosaics overhead, the stained-glass windows—remember that this whole space had to be rebuilt.

There's no better place to appreciate the sacrifices of World

War II than the area behind the main altar with three stained-glass windows, dubbed the American Memorial Chapel. This special spot in St. Paul's honors the Americans who sacrificed their lives to save Britain in World War II. An inscription on the floor reads: "To the American Dead of the Second World War, From the People of Britain."

Each of the three windows has a central core of religious scenes, but the brightly colored panes that arch around them have some unusual iconography: American. Spot the American eagle (center window, to the left of Christ), George Washington (right window, upper-right corner), and symbols of all 50 states (find your state seal). In the carved wood beneath the windows, you'll see birds and foliage native to the US. And at the very far right of the paneling, check out the tiny tree "trunk" (amid foliage, below the bird)—it's a US rocket ship circa 1958, shooting up to the stars.

Britain is very grateful to its WWII saviors, the Yanks, and remembers them religiously with the Roll of Honor (immediately behind the altar). This 500-page book under glass lists the names of 28,000 US servicemen and women based in Britain who gave their lives during the war.

• *Take a close look at the high altar and the view back to the entrance from here. Look up and enjoy the Victorian mosaic ceiling above the choir. Then continue around the altar and head back toward the entrance. On the left wall of the aisle, standing white in a black niche, is a statue of...*

❽ John Donne

John Donne (1573-1631), shown here wrapped in a burial shroud, was not only a great poet, but also a passionate preacher. He spent

the last decade of his life working in old St. Paul's. Donne personally chose to be portrayed here in a shroud to capture the melancholy he felt after his wife's death. The statue is one of the few treasures to survive the Great Fire of 1666. You can still see the dark scorch marks on the urn beneath Donne's feet.

Imagine hearing Donne deliver a funeral sermon here, with the huge church bell tolling in the background: "No man is an island...Any man's death diminishes me, because I am involved in Mankind. Therefore, never wonder for whom the bell tolls—it tolls for thee."

• *And also for dozens of people who lie buried beneath your feet, in the crypt where you'll end your tour. But first, in the south transept, find the...*

St. Paul's, the Blitz, and the Battle of Britain

Nazi planes mercilessly firebombed London in 1940. Even though The City around it burned to the ground, St. Paul's survived, giving hope to the citizens. The church took two direct hits, crumbling the altar and collapsing the north transept. On December 29, 1940, some 28 bombs fell on the church. The surrounding neighborhood was absolutely flattened, while the church rose above it, nearly intact. Some swear that many bombs bounced miraculously off Wren's dome,

while others credit the heroic work of local firefighters. (There's a memorial chapel to the firefighters who kept watch over St. Paul's with hoses cocked.) Still, it's clear from the damage that St. Paul's was not fully Blitz-proof.

Often used synonymously, the Blitz and the Battle of Britain are actually two different phases of the Nazi air raids of 1940-1941. The Battle of Britain (June-Sept 1940) pitted Britain's Royal Air Force against German planes trying to soften up Britain for a land-and-sea invasion. The Blitz (Sept 1940-May 1941) was Hitler's punitive terror campaign against civilian London.

In the early days of World War II, the powerful, technologically superior Nazi army quickly overran Poland, Belgium, and France. The British army hightailed it out of France, crossing the English Channel from Dunkirk, and Britain hunkered down, waiting to be invaded. Hitler bombed R.A.F. airfields while his

⑨ Horatio Nelson Monument and Charles Cornwallis Monument

Admiral Horatio Nelson (1758-1805) leans on an anchor, his coat draped discreetly over the arm he lost in battle.

In October 1805, England trembled in fear as Napoleon—bent on world conquest—prepared to invade from across the Channel. Meanwhile, hundreds of miles away, off the coast of Spain, the daring Lord Nelson sailed the HMS *Victory* into battle against the French and Spanish navies. His motto: England expects that every man shall do his duty.

Nelson's fleet smashed the enemy at Trafalgar, and Napoleon's hopes for a naval invasion of Britain sank. Unfortunately, Nelson

ground troops massed along the Channel. Britain was hopelessly outmatched, but Prime Minister Winston Churchill vowed, "We shall fight on the beaches...We shall fight in the fields and in the streets...We shall never surrender."

Britain fought back. Though greatly outgunned, they had a new and secret weapon—radar—that allowed them to get the jump on puzzled Nazi pilots. Speedy Spitfires flown by a new breed of young pilots shot down 1,700 German planes. By September 1940, the German land invasion was called off, Britain counterattacked with a daring raid on Berlin...and the Battle of Britain was won.

A frustrated Hitler retaliated with a series of punishing air raids on London itself, known as the Blitz. All through the fall, winter, and spring of 1940-1941, including 57 consecutive nights, Hermann Göring's Luftwaffe pummeled a defenseless London, killing 20,000 and leveling half the city (mostly from St. Paul's eastward). Residents took refuge deep in the Tube stations. From his Whitehall bunker, Churchill made radio broadcasts exhorting his people to give their all, their "blood, toil, sweat, and tears."

Late in the war (1944-1945), Hitler ordered another round of terror-inducing attacks on London (sometimes called the "second Blitz") using car-sized V-1 and V-2 bombs, an early type of cruise missile. But Britain's resolve had returned, the United States had entered the fight, and the pendulum shifted. Churchill could say that even if the empire lasted a thousand years, Britons would look back and say, "This was their finest hour."

Churchill's state funeral was held in 1965 at St. Paul's in a bittersweet remembrance of Britain's victory.

ST. PAUL'S CATHEDRAL

took a sniper's bullet in the spine and died. The lion at Nelson's feet groans sadly, and two little boys gaze up—one at Nelson, one at Wren's dome. You'll find Nelson's tomb directly beneath the dome, downstairs in the crypt.

Opposite Nelson is a monument to another great military man, Charles Cornwallis (1738-1805), honored here for his service as Governor General of Bengal (India). Yanks know him better as the general who lost the American Revolutionary War (or "American War," as it's known here) when George Washington—aided by French ships—forced his surrender at Yorktown in 1780.

• *There are several entrances to the dome and its galleries, but only one is open to the public at any given time—look for signboards or ask one of the church volunteers.*

⑩ Climb the Dome

The 528-step climb is worthwhile, and each level (or gallery) offers something different.

First you get to the Whispering Gallery (257 steps, with views of the church interior). Whisper sweet nothings into the wall, and your partner (and anyone else) standing far away can hear you. Exactly how it works is debated (some even question *if* it works). Most likely, the sound does not travel up and over the dome to the diametrically opposite side (as it would in a perfect sphere). Rather, it goes around the curved wall horizontally, so you don't have to stand in any particular spot. For best effects, try whispering (not talking) with your mouth close to the wall, while your partner stands a few dozen yards away with his or her ear to the wall.

After another set of stairs, you're at the Stone Gallery, with views of London. If you're exhausted, claustrophobic, or wary of heights, this middle level might be high enough. (The top level has very little standing room for tourists.)

Finally, a long, tight metal staircase takes you to the very top of the cupola, the Golden Gallery. (Just before the final dozen stairs to the top, there's a tiny window at your feet that allows you to peek directly down—350 feet—to the church floor.) Once at the top, you emerge to stunning, unobstructed views of the city. Looking west, you'll see the London Eye and Big Ben. To the south, across

the Thames, is the rectangular smokestack of the Tate Modern, with Shakespeare's Globe nestled nearby. To the east sprouts a glassy garden of skyscrapers, including the 600-foot-tall, black-topped Tower 42, the bullet-shaped 30 St. Mary Axe building (nicknamed "The Gherkin"), and two more buildings easily ID'd by their nicknames—"The Cheese Grater" and "The Walkie-Talkie." Farther in the distance, the cluster of skyscrapers marks Canary Wharf. Just north of that was the site of the 2012 Olympic Games, now a pleasant park. Demographers speculate that the rapidly growing East End and Docklands may eventually replace the West End and The City as the center of London. So as you look to the east, you're gazing into London's future.

• Descend the dome to church level, then follow signs directing you downstairs to the...

⓫ Crypt

Many famous people are buried here. Start by locating the central tomb of **Horatio Nelson,** who wore down Napoleon. It's a big coffin-on-a-pedestal in a round alcove at the center of the crypt, directly beneath the dome. Nearby (toward the altar) is the black granite tomb of the Duke of Wellington (who finished Napoleon off). The flags near the tomb were carried at his funeral procession.

Continuing up the central axis of the crypt, you enter a chapel. At the chapel's altar, turn right to reach **Christopher Wren**'s tomb—a simple black slab with no statue. Next to it is a hunk of rough Portland stone quarried but unused by Wren while building St. Paul's; see his triangle brand on the left end. These few stones are not much of an honor for the man who built this great church. "If you seek his monument..." you'll be disappointed.

Use your visitor's map to find other **tombs and memorials:** of painters Turner and Reynolds (located near Wren); of Florence Nightingale (near Wellington); and a memorial to George Washington, who lies buried back in old Virginny.

Back near Nelson's tomb you'll find **temporary exhibits** (they change frequently) that chronicle important events in the church's long history, and models of previous churches that stood on this spot.

The crypt contains a fine gift shop, a WC, and the grim-sounding **Crypt Café,** which nevertheless serves tasty food.

ST. PAUL'S CATHEDRAL

TOWER OF LONDON TOUR

William I, still getting used to his new title of "the Conqueror," built the stone "White Tower" (1077-1097) to keep the Londoners in line. The Tower also served as an effective lookout for seeing invaders coming up the Thames. His successors enlarged it to its present 18-acre size. Because of the security it provided, the Tower served over the centuries as a royal residence, the Royal Mint, the Royal Jewel House, and, most famously, as the prison and execution site of those who dared oppose the Crown.

The Tower's hard stone and glittering jewels represent the ultimate power of the monarch. So does the executioner's block. You'll find more bloody history per square inch in this original tower of power than anywhere else in Britain. Today, though its military purpose is history, it's still home to the Yeoman Warders, a.k.a. the "Beefeaters," who host three million visitors a year.

Your visit has four parts: the lively Beefeater tour (included in admission price, 1 hour), the White Tower (a serious museum and armory, which many rush through and underappreciate), the crown jewels (best in Europe, generally with a bit of a wait), and the grounds and walls (a simple and enjoyable stroll).

Orientation

Cost: £28, family-£70 (for 2 adults plus up to 3 kids ages 5-15), includes "voluntary donation."

Hours: March-Oct Tue-Sat 9:00-17:30, Sun-Mon 10:00-17:30; Nov-Feb closes one hour earlier.

Information: Switchboard tel. 0844-482-7788, www.hrp.org.uk.

Advance Tickets: To avoid the long ticket-buying lines, and save a few pounds off the gate price, buy a **voucher** in advance. You can purchase vouchers at the Trader's Gate gift shop, located down the steps from the Tower Hill Tube stop (pick it up on your way to the Tower; vouchers here can be used any day), or on the Tower website (£24, family-£59, vouchers purchased online are valid any day up to 7 days after the date you select). All vouchers, regardless of where you purchase, must be exchanged for tickets at the Tower's group ticket office (see map).

You can also try buying tickets, with credit card only, at the Tower Welcome Centre to the left of the normal ticket lines—though on busy days they may turn you away. Tickets are also sold by phone (tel. 0844-482-7788 within UK or tel. 011-44-20-3166-6000 from the US; £2 fee, pick up your tickets at the Tower's group ticket office).

More Crowd-Beating Tips: It's most crowded in summer, on weekends (especially Sundays), and during school holidays. Any time of year, the line for the crown jewels—the best on earth—can be just as long as the line for tickets. For fewer crowds, arrive before 10:00 and go straight for the jewels. Alternatively, arrive in the afternoon, tour the rest of the Tower first, and see the jewels an hour before closing time, when crowds die down.

Getting There: The Tower is located in East London (Tube: Tower Hill). For speed, take the Tube there (about 10-12 minutes from central London); for romance, take the boat. Thames Clippers boats make the trip between the Tower of London and Westminster Pier near Big Ben in 30-45 minutes; the boat continues on to Greenwich from the Tower Pier. For details about these cruises, see page 39. Buses #15 and #RV1 make the trip from Trafalgar Square and Covent Garden, respectively (see map on page 28).

Visitor Information: Upon arrival, pick up the free map/guide and printed schedule of the day's events and special demonstrations (such as knights in armor explaining medieval fighting techniques; these are most common on particularly busy days such as school holidays). Everything inside is well described—skip the £4 audioguide and £5 Tower guidebook.

Sunday Worship: On Sunday morning, visitors are welcome on the grounds for free to worship in the Chapel Royal of St. Peter ad Vincula. You get in without the lines, but you can only see the chapel—no sightseeing (9:15 Communion or 11:00 service with fine choral music, meet at west gate 30 minutes early, dress for church, may be closed for ceremonies—call ahead; phone number listed above).

Yeoman Warder (Beefeater) Tours: Free, worthwhile, one-hour Beefeater tours leave every 30 minutes from just inside the entrance gate (first tour Tue-Sat at 10:00, Sun-Mon at 10:30, last one at 15:30—or 14:30 in Nov-Feb). The boisterous Beefeaters are great entertainers, whose historical talks include lots of bloody anecdotes and corny jokes. Check the clock inside the entrance gate. If you just miss the start of a tour, you can join it in progress (just catch up to the group a bit ahead).

Length of This Tour: Allow two hours (or three if you add a Beefeater tour). If you have less time, see the crown jewels, and try to squeeze in a Beefeater tour to get an overview. If time allows, also tour the White Tower Museum.

Eating: The **$$ New Armouries Café,** inside the Tower, is a big, efficient, inviting cafeteria (large, splittable meals). Outside the Tower, there's a row of familiar fast-food joints along the river and behind the Welcome Centre, and various **$ takeout stands** all around. Picnicking is allowed on Tower grounds but not inside the buildings.

Nearby: Adjacent to the Tower is **Tower Hill,** with two memorials (WWI and WWII) and part of the old **Roman Wall.**

The Tower is also close to three of my self-guided walks: You could walk from Trafalgar Square to the Tower following 📖 Historic London: The City Walk (also a 🎧 free Rick Steves audio tour). Across the river is the start of the 📖 Bankside Walk (begins at London Bridge, upstream). And just to the north, near Liverpool Street Station, is the start of the "East End Walk" (see page 78). Also, the Tower is a short Thames cruise away from Greenwich (see page 36).

Starring: The crown jewels, Beefeaters, William the Conqueror, and Henry VIII.

The Tour Begins

❶ Entrance Gate

Even an army the size of the ticket line couldn't storm this castle. After the drawbridge was pulled up and the iron portcullis slammed down, you'd have to swim a 120-foot moat; cross an island prowled by wild animals; then toss a grappling hook onto a wall and climb up while the enemy poured boiling oil on you. If you made it this far, you'd only

be halfway there. You'd still have to swim a second moat (eventually drained to make the grassy parade ground we see today), then, finally, scale a second, higher wall. In all, the central keep (tower) was surrounded by two concentric rings of complete defenses. Yes, it was difficult to get into the Tower (if you were a foreign enemy)...

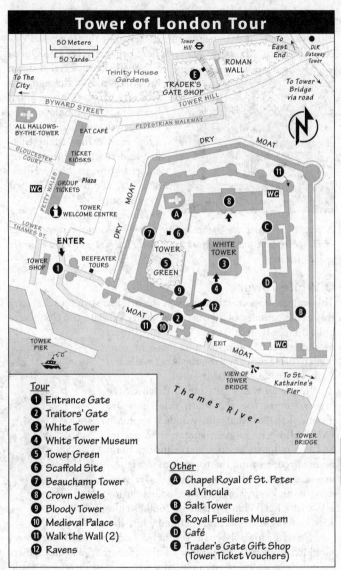

Tower of London Tour

Tour
1. Entrance Gate
2. Traitors' Gate
3. White Tower
4. White Tower Museum
5. Tower Green
6. Scaffold Site
7. Beauchamp Tower
8. Crown Jewels
9. Bloody Tower
10. Medieval Palace
11. Walk the Wall (2)
12. Ravens

Other
A. Chapel Royal of St. Peter ad Vincula
B. Salt Tower
C. Royal Fusiliers Museum
D. Café
E. Trader's Gate Gift Shop (Tower Ticket Vouchers)

but it was almost as impossible to get out (if you were an enemy of the state).

• Show your ticket, enter, consult the daily event schedule, and consider catching a one-hour Beefeater tour. If you didn't get a free map on the way in, pick one up at the bookstore up ahead (you may have to ask for it). WCs are 100 yards ahead.

When you're all set, go 50 yards straight ahead to the...

❷ Traitors' Gate

This was the boat entrance to the Tower from the Thames. Princess Elizabeth, who was a prisoner here before she became Queen

Elizabeth I, was carried down the Thames and through this gate on a barge, thinking about her mom, Anne Boleyn, who had been decapitated inside just a few years earlier. Many English leaders who fell from grace entered through here—Elizabeth was one of the lucky few to walk out.

• *Continue straight and turn left to pass underneath the archway just before the cannons (opposite the exit), which leads into the inner courtyard. The big, white tower in the middle is the...*

❸ White Tower

This square, 90-foot-tall tower was the original structure that gave this castle complex of 20 towers its name. William the Conqueror

built it more than 900 years ago to put 15 feet of stone between himself and those he conquered. Over the centuries, the other walls and towers were built around it.

The keep was a last line of defense. The original entry (on the south side) is above ground level so that the wooden approach (you'll climb its modern successor to get in, and lots more stairs once you're inside) could be removed, turning the tower into a safe refuge. Originally, there were even fewer windows—the lower windows were added during a Christopher Wren-ovation in 1660. In the 13th century, the tower was painted white (hence the name).

Standing high above the rest of old London, the White Tower provided a gleaming reminder of the monarchs' absolute power over their subjects. If you made the wrong move here, you could be feasting on roast boar in the Banqueting Hall one night and chained to the walls of the prison the next. Torture ranged from stretching on the rack to the full monty: hanging by the neck until nearly dead, then "drawing" (cut open to be gutted), and finally quartering, with your giblets displayed on the walls as a warning. (Guy Fawkes, who tried to blow up Parliament with 36 barrels of gunpowder, received this treatment after being tortured here.) Any cries for help were muffled by the thick stone walls—15 feet at the base, a mere 11 feet at the top.

• *Either now or later, find time to go inside the White Tower for its excellent museum.*

❹ White Tower Museum

Inside the White Tower, a one-way route winds through exhibits re-creating medieval life and the Tower's bloody history of torture and executions.

The **Line of Kings,** greeting you and spread throughout this level, includes an array of painted wooden horses, some carved in the 17th century by revered sculptor Grinling Gibbons, the "King's Carver." For centuries, these horses held the royal suits of armor in the Tower's original exhibits.

In the **Royal Armory,** you'll see some suits of armor of Henry VIII—on a horse, slender in his youth (c. 1515), then more heavy-set by 1540 (with his bigger-is-better codpiece). Next to Henry is the child-size armor once thought to be for his long-awaited male heir, Edward VI, who died young. But the armor actually belonged to Henry, Prince of Wales (1594-1612), the popular son of James I. Get up close to see the incredibly detailed battle scenes. Continuing along, other suits of armor, including those of a 6'8" giant and a 3'1" midget (more likely a child), and swords are identified by king.

Upstairs, pass through the long hall to reach the rare and lovely **St. John's Chapel** (1080). This is where Lady Jane Grey (described later) offered up a last unanswered prayer. The oldest surviving part of the original Tower—and the oldest church in London—the chapel's round Norman (Romanesque) arches and column capitals decorated with the T-shaped Tau cross evoke the age of William the Conqueror.

Moving on, the **Arsenal** displays the heaviest suit of armor in the world (130 pounds!), as well as various weapons used through the ages, including machine guns and the jeweled "Tiffany Revolver."

On the top floor, ogle the giant dragon made out of old weapons. In the case at the end of this hall, see the Tower's actual **execution ax** and chopping block. In 1747, this seven-pound ax sliced through the neck of Lord Lovat, a

The Beefeaters

The original duty of the Yeoman Warders (called "Beefeaters") was to guard the Tower, its prisoners, and the jewels. Their nickname may come from an original perk of the job—large rations of the king's beef. The Beefeaters dress in blue knee-length coats with red trim and a top hat. The "ER" on the chest stands for the monarch they serve—Queen Elizabeth II (Elizabetha Regina in Latin). On special occasions, they wear red. All are retired noncommissioned officers from the armed forces with distinguished service records.

These days, the Yeoman Warders are no longer expected to protect the Tower. Instead, they've evolved into great entertainers, leading groups of tourists through the Tower. At night, they ritually lock up the Tower in the Ceremony of the Keys (possible to watch if you book upwards of four months in advance). There are 35 Yeoman Warders, including one woman. They and their families make for a Beefeating community of 120 that live inside the Tower.

Scottish supporter of Bonnie Prince Charlie's claim to the throne. With his death, the ax was retired.

In the next room, kid-oriented, hands-on exhibits bring the history engagingly to life. I learned how hard it is to nock an arrow (to properly align the arrow on the bow prior to release).

• *Back outside, find the courtyard to the left of the White Tower, called...*

❺ Tower Green

In medieval times, this spacious courtyard within the walls was the "town square" for those who lived in the castle. Knights exercised and jousted here, and it was the last place of refuge in troubled times. The Tower is still officially a royal residence, and the Queen's lodgings are on the south side of the green, in the white half-timbered buildings where a bearskin-hatted soldier stands guard.

The north side of the Green is bordered by the stone **Chapel Royal of St. Peter ad Vincula** ("in Chains"). The current structure was built by Henry VIII, and his most famous victims are buried here (among them his wives Anne Boleyn and Catherine Howard). The chapel's interior is open only on the Beefeater tour, except during the last hour of the day, when anyone can go inside to see it. If you aren't on a tour, wait for one to come around, discreetly squeeze into the group while the Beefeater is talking outside the chapel, and go in with the group.

• *Near the middle of Tower Green is a granite-paved square marked* Site of Scaffold.

❻ Scaffold Site

The actual execution site looks pleasant enough today; the chopping block has been moved to inside the White Tower, and a modern sculpture encourages visitors to ponder those who died.

It was here that enemies of the Crown would kneel before the king for the final time. With their hands tied behind their backs, they would say a final prayer, then lay their heads on a block, and—*shlit*—the blade would slice through their necks, their heads tumbling to the ground. The headless corpses were buried in unmarked graves in Tower Green or under the floor of the Chapel Royal of St. Peter ad Vincula. The heads were stuck on a stick and displayed at London Bridge. Passersby did not really see the heads—they saw spheres of insects and parasites.

Tower Green was the most prestigious execution site at the Tower. Common criminals were hanged outside the Tower. More prominent evil-doers were decapitated before jeering crowds atop Tower Hill (near today's Tube station). Inside the Tower walls was reserved for the most heinous traitors.

Henry VIII axed a couple of his ex-wives here (divorced readers can insert their own cynical joke). Anne Boleyn was the appealing young woman Henry had fallen so hard for that he broke with the Catholic Church in order to divorce his first wife and marry her. But when Anne failed to produce a male heir, the court turned against her. She was locked up in the Tower, tried in a kangaroo court, branded an adulteress and traitor, and decapitated.

Henry's fifth wife, teenage Catherine Howard, was beheaded and her body laid near Anne's in the church. Jane Boleyn (Anne's sister-in-law) was also executed here for arranging Catherine's adulterous affair behind Henry's back. Next.

Henry even beheaded his friend Thomas More (a Catholic) because he refused to recognize (Protestant) Henry as head of the Church of England. (Thomas died at the less-prestigious Tower Hill site near the Tube stop.)

The most tragic victim was 17-year-old Lady Jane Grey, who was manipulated into claiming the Crown for nine days during the scramble for power after Henry's death and the six-year reign and death of his sickly young son, Edward VI. When Bloody Mary (Mary I, Henry's daughter) took control, she forced her Protestant cousin Jane to kneel before the executioner. Young Jane bravely blindfolded herself, but then couldn't find the block. She crawled around the scaffolding pleading, "Where is it?!"

Years ago, a Beefeater, tired of what he called "Hollywood coverage" of the Tower, grabbed my manuscript, read it, and told me that in more than 900 years as a fortress, palace, and prison, the place held 8,500 prisoners. But only 120 were executed, and, of those, only six were executed inside it. Stressing the hospitality of the Tower, he added, "Torture was actually quite rare here."

• *Overlooking the scaffold site is the...*

❼ Beauchamp Tower—Prisoners

The Beauchamp Tower (pronounced "BEECH-um") was one of several places in the complex that housed Very Important Prisoners. Climb upstairs to a room where the walls are covered with dozens of final messages—graffiti carved into the stone by bored and despondent inmates.

Picture Philip Howard, the Earl of Arundel (c. 1555-1595), warming himself by this fireplace and glancing out at the execution site during his 10-year incarcer-

ation. Having lived a devil-may-care life of pleasure in the court of Queen Elizabeth, the pro-Catholic Arundel was charged with treason by the Protestant government. He pleaded with the queen—his former friend—to at least let him see his wife and young children. She refused, unless he would renounce his faith. On June 22, 1587, he carved his family name "Arundell" into the chimney (graffiti #13) and wrote in Latin: *"Quanto plus afflictionis..."* ("The more we suffer for Christ in this world, the more glory with Christ in the next.") Arundel suffered faithfully another eight years here before he wasted away and died at age 40.

Graffiti #85 belongs to Lady Jane Grey's young husband, Lord Guilford Dudley. Locked in the Beauchamp Tower and executed the same day as his wife, Dudley vented his despair by scratching "IANE" into the stone. Cynics claim he was actually whining for his mommy, who was also named Jane.

Read other pitiful graffiti, like the musings of James Typping (#18). Imprisoned for three years "in great disgrace," he wonders what will happen to him: "I cannot tell but be death." Consider the stoic cry of Thomas Miagh (#29), an Irish rebel, who writes: "By torture straynge my truth was tried," having suffered some form of the rack. Thomas Clarke (#28), a Catholic priest who later converted to Protestantism, wrote pathetic poetry: "Unhappy is that man whose acts doth procure / the misery of this house in prison to endure." Many held on to their sense of identity by carving their family's coats of arms.

The last enemy of the state imprisoned in the Tower complex was one of its most infamous: the renegade Nazi Rudolf Hess. In 1941, Hitler's henchman secretly flew to Britain with a peace proposal (Hitler denied any such plan). He parachuted into a field, was arrested and held for four days in the Tower, and was later given a life sentence.

• *Join the looooong line leading to the crown jewels. Pass time in line reading ahead—it's too dark inside to read.*

❽ Crown Jewels

When you finally enter the building, you'll pass through a series of rooms with instructive warm-up videos. Don't let the crowd rush you—just step aside if you want to keep watching. The videos touch on the many kings and queens who have worn the crown jewels, from William I the Conqueror (1066), to Henry VIII, to his daughter Elizabeth I, to the current Queen Elizabeth II. Film clips show you close-up highlights of coronation regalia, as well as the most recent coronation—Elizabeth II's, in 1953.

After the videos, you enter the exhibits, seeing each of the actual coronation items in the order that they're used whenever a new king or queen is crowned. First, you walk down a hallway displaying the ceremonial maces, swords, and trumpets that lead the actual coronation procession into Westminster Abbey.

Next comes a room with the royal regalia. The monarch-to-be is anointed with holy oil poured from the eagle-beak flask; handed the jeweled Sword of Offering; and dressed in the 20-pound gold robe and other gear. (Other items in the first case are simply standing by. The 12th-century coronation spoon, last used in 1953 to anoint the head of Queen Elizabeth, is the most ancient object here.) Most of the original crown jewels from medieval times were lost during Cromwell's 1648 revolution.

After being dressed and anointed, the new monarch prepares for the "crowning" moment.

• *Five glass cases display the various crowns, orbs, and scepters used in royal ceremonies. Ride the moving sidewalk that takes you past them. You're welcome to circle back and glide by again (I did, several times). Or, to get away from the crowds, hang out on the elevated viewing area with the guard. Chat with the guards—they're actually here to provide*

TOWER OF LONDON

information (and to keep you from taking photos, which aren't allowed). As you glide by on the walkway, you'll see the following items. (The collection rotates, so you may not see all of the crowns described here.)

Scepter and Orb: After being crowned, the new monarch is handed these items. The **Sovereign's Scepter** is encrusted with the world's largest cut diamond—the 530-carat Star of Africa, beefy as a quarter-pounder. This was one of nine stones cut from the original 3,106-carat (1.37-pound) Cullinan diamond. The **orb** symbolizes how Christianity rules over the earth, a reminder that even a "divine monarch" is not above God's law. The coronation is a kind of marriage between the church and the state in Britain, since the king or queen is head of both, and the ceremony celebrates the monarch's power to do good for the whole of the nation.

St. Edward's Crown: This coronation crown is the one placed by the archbishop upon the head of each new monarch on coronation day in Westminster Abbey. It's worn for 20 minutes, then locked away until the next coronation. The original crown, destroyed by Cromwell, was older than the Tower itself and dated back to 1061, the time of King Edward the Confessor, "the last English king" before William the Conqueror invaded from France (1066). This 1661 remake is said to contain some of the original's gold amid its 443 precious and semiprecious stones. Because the crown weighs nearly five pounds, weak or frail monarchs have opted not to wear it.

Other Crowns: Various other crowns illustrate a bit of regalia symbolism. Kings and queens get four arches on their crowns, emperors get eight arches (e.g., the Imperial Crown of India in the next case), and princes get only two (for example, see the crowns of Prince George—before he became King George V—and Prince Frederick; today's Prince Charles keeps his two-arch crown in Wales).

The Crown of the Queen Mother: This crown, last worn by Elizabeth II's famous mum (who died in 2002), has the 106-carat Koh-I-Noor diamond glittering on the front. The Koh-I-Noor diamond is considered unlucky for male rulers and, therefore, only adorns the crown of the king's wife. If Charles becomes king, Camilla might wear it, but most Brits prefer to imagine it atop Kate's regal dome. This crown was remade in 1937 and given an innovative platinum frame.

• *Continuing on from the moving walkway, but in the same room (toward the exit), you'll find...*

Queen Victoria Small Diamond Crown: It's tiny. Victoria had a normal-sized head, but this was designed to sit atop the widow's veil she insisted on wearing for decades after the death of her husband, Prince Albert. This four-ounce job was made in 1870 for £50,000—personally paid for by the queen.

• *Moving on, you'll see gilded platters and bowls used in the post-cor-onation banquet before you reach one final room, with one last crown.*

The **Imperial State Crown** is what the Queen wears for official functions such as the State Opening of Parliament. When

Victoria was queen, she insisted on wearing her small crown, but by law, this State Crown had to be carried next to her on a pillow, as it represents the sovereign. Among its 3,733 jewels are Queen Elizabeth I's former earrings (the hanging pearls, top center), a stunning 13th-century ruby look-alike in the center, and Edward the Confessor's ring (the blue sapphire on top, in the center of the Maltese cross of diamonds). When Edward's tomb was exhumed—a hundred years after he was buried—his body was "incorrupted." The ring on his saintly finger featured this sapphire and ended up on the crown of all future monarchs. This is the stylized crown you see representing the royalty on Britain's coins and stamps. It's depicted on the Beefeater uniforms and on the pavement at the end of the sliding walk.

• *The final room is the epilogue of the jewels collection, with videos show-ing attendants putting all of these precious items back into their cases after the last coronation—emphasizing that these aren't just pretty mu-seum pieces, but a vital part of an ongoing tradition.*

Leave the jewels by exiting through the thick vault doors and head back toward the Scaffold Site. Find the entrance to the Bloody Tower, at the far end of Tower Green.

❾ Bloody Tower

Not all prisoners died at the block. The 13-year-old King Edward V and his kid brother were kidnapped in 1483 during the Wars of the Roses by their uncle Richard III ("Now is the winter of our dis-content...") and locked in the Bloody Tower, never to be seen again. End of story? Two centuries later, the skeletons of two unidentified children were found here. The 2013 discovery of the remains of Richard III (in Leicester, in central England) may allow modern forensics to solve this centuries-old mystery.

Sir Walter Raleigh—poet, explorer, and political radical—was imprisoned here for 13 years. In 1603, the English writer and ad-venturer was accused of plotting against King James and sentenced to death. The king commuted the sentence to life imprisonment in the Bloody Tower. While in prison, Raleigh wrote the first volume of his *History of the World*. Check out his rather cushy bedroom, study, and walkway (courtesy of the powerful tobacco lobby?). Raleigh promised the king a wealth of gold if he would release him to search for El Dorado. The expedition was a failure. Upon Raleigh's return, the displeased king had him beheaded in 1618.

• *Next door to the Bloody Tower, inside the base of the Lower Wakefield Tower, is a cellar filled with some replica torture equipment. To reach the next sight, walk under the Bloody Tower, cross the cobbled road, and bear right a few steps to find the stairs up onto the wall.*

⑩ Medieval Palace

The Tower was a royal residence as well as a fortress. These rooms were built around 1240 by Henry III, the king most responsible for the expansive Tower of London complex we see today. The well-described rooms are furnished as they might have been during the reign of his son, Edward I ("Longshanks"). You'll see his re-created bedroom, then—up a flight of stairs—his throne room, both with massive fireplaces to keep this cold stone palace cozy. After Cromwell temporarily deposed the monarchy (in the 17th century), the Tower ceased to be a royal residence except in name.

• *From the throne room, continue up the stairs to...*

⑪ Walk the Wall

The Tower was defended by state-of-the-art walls and fortifications in the 13th century. This walk offers a good look. From the walls, you also get a fine view of the famous bridge straddling the Thames, with the twin towers and blue spans. It's not London Bridge (which is the nondescript bridge  just upstream), but **Tower Bridge.** Although it looks somewhat medieval, this drawbridge was built in 1894, of steel and concrete. Sophisticated steam engines raise and lower the bridge, allowing tall-masted ships to squeeze through.

Gaze out at the bridge, the river, City Hall (the egg-shaped glass building across the river—see page 95), the Shard (London's bold exclamation point—see page 94), and life-filled London.

• *Between the White Tower and the Thames are cages housing the...*

⑫ Ravens

According to goofy tradition, the Tower and the British throne are only safe as long as ravens are present here. These eight impressive birds—the traditionally required six, plus two spares—have clipped wings to keep them close. World War II bombing raids reduced the population to one. Some years ago, with their clipped wings, the birds had trouble mating, so a slide was built to help them get a bit of lift to facilitate the process. Happily, that worked, and a baby raven was born. A children's TV show sponsored a nationwide contest to come up with a name. The winner: "Ronald

Raven." Today, they mimic and answer tourists like Edgar Allan Poe's Magic 8 Ball (though I've only heard them answer German *Fraus* with something akin to "Google it") and are as much a part of the Tower as the jewels. As you leave through the riverside exit, look into the moat on the right for the tiny raven graveyard. There lie Cedric (2003), Gundolf (2005), Hardey (2006), and Jubilee and Grip (2013). RIP.

Other Sights

Get out your Tower-issued map to check out other areas you can visit. The **Salt Tower** has graffiti by Henry Walpole, a staunch Catholic who was imprisoned here by Queen Elizabeth I, tortured on the rack, and had a finger torn off. At the **Royal Fusiliers Regimental Museum** you can see the uniforms, swords, and fusils (flintlock rifles) of the army of Redcoats who fought Napoleon, the American War of Independence, two World Wars ("Monty"— Field Marshal Bernard Montgomery of D-Day fame—was a Fusilier), and wars in the Persian Gulf.

Take one final look at the stern stone walls of the Tower. Be glad you can leave.

BANKSIDE WALK

Along the South Bank of the Thames

Bankside—the neighborhood between London Bridge and Blackfriars Bridge—is the historic heart of the revamped southern bank of the Thames. In ancient times "greater London" consisted of two Roman settlements straddling the easiest place to ford the river: One settlement was here, and the other was across the river—in the financial district known today as "The City."

From the Roman era until recently, the south side of the river was the wrong side of the tracks. For centuries, it was London's red light district. In the 20th century, it became an industrial wasteland of empty warehouses and street crime. Today, the prostitutes and pickpockets are gone, replaced by a riverside promenade dotted with trendy pubs, cutesy shops, and historic tourist sights.

This half-mile Bankside Walk gives you plenty of history and sights to choose from—you can see it all, design your own plan, or just enjoy the view of London's skyline across the river.

Orientation

Length of This Walk: One hour (or up to a half-day if you tour Shakespeare's Globe and the Tate Modern).

Getting There: Take the Tube to the London Bridge stop to begin the walk. (The Monument stop, on the Circle Line, is also nearby.)

Old Operating Theatre Museum and Herb Garret: £6.50, daily 10:30-17:00, closed Dec 15-Jan 5.

Southwark Cathedral: Free, £1 map acts as photo permit, Mon-Fri 8:00-18:00, Sat-Sun 8:30-18:00 (but partially closed during frequent services—schedule posted out front).

Borough Market: London's oldest fruit-and-vegetable market is open Wed-Sat 10:00-17:00, Fri until 18:00, closed Sun-Tue; surrounding eatery stalls open daily 10:00-17:00.

Golden Hinde Replica: £6, daily 10:00-17:30, may be closed during your visit but still viewable.

The Clink Prison Museum: Overpriced at £7.50 for adults, £5.50 for kids 15 and under, family ticket available; July-Sept daily 10:00-21:00; Oct-June Mon-Fri 10:00-18:00, Sat-Sun until 19:30.

Shakespeare's Globe: £16 for adults, £9 for kids 5-15, free for kids 5 and under, family ticket available; includes museum, audioguide, and 40-minute guided tour; open daily 9:00-17:30, late April-mid-Oct last tour Mon at 17:00, Tue-Sat at 12:30, Sun at 11:30 (see page 89 or the Entertainment in London chapter for how to buy tickets to a performance).

Tate Modern: Free, but £4 donation appreciated (fee for special exhibits), daily 10:00-18:00, Fri-Sat until 22:00, last entry to temporary exhibits 45 minutes before closing, view restaurants.

Starring: Shakespeare's world, London Bridge, historic pubs, and views of the London skyline.

The Walk Begins

• *Start at the south end of London Bridge (across from where my Historic London: The City Walk ends; see page 260). From the London Bridge Tube stop, take the "Borough High Street east" exit and turn right (north), pass the One London Bridge complex, and walk out on the bridge about 100 yards.*

❶ London Bridge

The City (across the river) is to the north, Tower Bridge is east, and the Thames flows from west to east (left to right). Looking to the east (downstream) and turning counterclockwise, you'll see the following:

Downstream
- Tower Bridge, the Neo-Gothic towered drawbridge that many Americans mistakenly call London Bridge.
- The HMS *Belfast* (in the foreground, docked on the southern bank), a WWII cruiser that's open to tourists.
- Canary Wharf Tower (the distant 800-foot skyscraper with pyramid top and blinking light), built in 1990 on the Isle

BANKSIDE

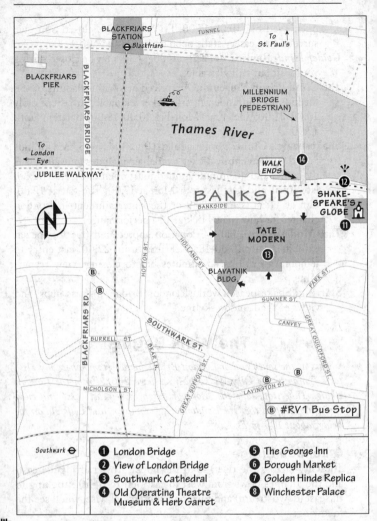

1 London Bridge
2 View of London Bridge
3 Southwark Cathedral
4 Old Operating Theatre Museum & Herb Garret
5 The George Inn
6 Borough Market
7 Golden Hinde Replica
8 Winchester Palace

of Dogs. It recently lost its standing as the UK's tallest building to The Shard. This marks the Docklands, London's "new Manhattan" and a thriving business district. This was once the biggest port in the world, serving the empire upon which "the sun never set," but today the wharves have moved farther out to accommodate bigger ships.

• The "Pool of London." This is the stretch of river between Tower Bridge (a drawbridge) and London Bridge, which marks the farthest point seagoing vessels can sail inland. In the 18th century this was the busiest port in the world.

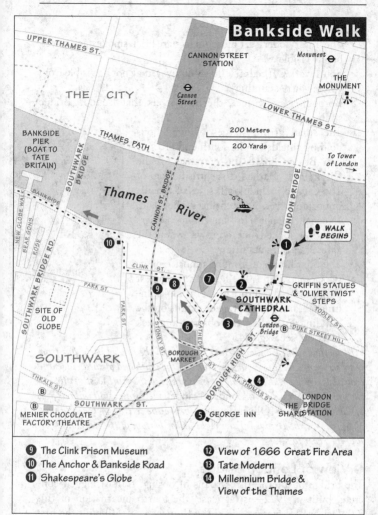

Bankside Walk

UPPER THAMES ST.

THE CITY

CANNON STREET STATION

Cannon Street

Monument

THE MONUMENT

LOWER THAMES ST.

BANKSIDE PIER (BOAT TO TATE BRITAIN)

THAMES PATH

SOUTHWARK BRIDGE

200 Meters

200 Yards

To Tower of London

NEW GLOBE WALK

BEAR GDNS.

ROSE

BANKSIDE

Thames River

CANNON ST. BRIDGE

LONDON BRIDGE

⑩

WALK BEGINS

①

SOUTHWARK BRIDGE RD.

PARK ST.

CLINK ST.

⑨ ⑧

⑦

②

GRIFFIN STATUES & "OLIVER TWIST" STEPS

SITE OF OLD GLOBE

PARK ST.

STONEY ST.

⑥

CATHEDRAL ST.

③

SOUTHWARK CATHEDRAL

London Bridge Ⓑ

DUKE STREET HILL

TOOLEY ST.

SOUTHWARK

THRALE ST.

Ⓑ

BOROUGH MARKET

BOROUGH HIGH ST.

ST. THOMAS ST.

④

LONDON BRIDGE STATION

Ⓑ

MENIER CHOCOLATE FACTORY THEATRE

SOUTHWARK ST.

⑤ GEORGE INN

THE SHARD

⑨ The Clink Prison Museum
⑩ The Anchor & Bankside Road
⑪ Shakespeare's Globe

⑫ View of 1666 Great Fire Area
⑬ Tate Modern
⑭ Millennium Bridge & View of the Thames

North Bank

- The Tower of London (four domed spires and a flag rising above the trees).
- The 20 Fenchurch Street skyscraper (a.k.a. "The Walkie-Talkie") and, behind it, the Leadenhall Building (a.k.a. "The Cheese Grater").
- St. Paul's Cathedral (to the northwest, with a dome like a state capitol and twin spires).
- St. Bride's Church, the pointed, stacked steeple (nestled among office buildings) that supposedly inspired the wedding cake.
- BT Tower, a communications tower.

BANKSIDE

South Bank

- The Tate Modern art museum (square brick smokestack tower, barely visible).
- Southwark Cathedral (100 yards away, may not be visible from where you're standing).
- Borough High Street, the busy street that London Bridge spills onto.
- The small griffin statues (winged lions holding shields) at the south end of London Bridge guard the entrance to The City. They marked the jurisdiction of The City to include both sides of the all-important river. For centuries, they said, "Neener neener" to late-night partiers who got locked out of town when the gates shut tight at curfew.
- The Shard, one of London's most famous skyscrapers. At 1,020 feet, it's the tallest building in Western Europe. It looks unfinished, but that's art. (For details on the building, including the observation deck at its tip, see page 94.)

- *The best view of London Bridge is not from the bridge itself, but from the riverbank. Retrace your steps back to the south end of the bridge and cross the street. Find the small staircase next to the southwest griffin, by the building marked Two London Bridge. These stairs will impress fans of Charles Dickens' Oliver Twist—they're the setting of the infamous "Meeting on the Bridge." Turn right at the bottom of the stairs and follow the river to a...*

❷ View of London Bridge

The bridge of today—three spans of boring, traffic-clogged concrete, built in 1972—is (at least) the fourth incarnation of this 2,000-year-old river crossing. The Romans (A.D. 50) built the first

wooden footbridge to Londinium (rebuilt many times), which was pulled down by boatmen in 1014 to retake London from Danish invaders. (They celebrated with a song passed down to us as "London Bridge is falling down, my fair lady.")

The most famous version—crossed by everyone from Richard the Lionheart, to Henry VIII, to Shakespeare, to Newton, to Darwin—was built around 1200 and stood for more than six cen-

BANKSIDE

turies, the only crossing point into this major city. Built of stone on many thick pilings, stacked with houses and shops that arched over the roadway and bulged out over the river, with its own chapel and a fortified gate at each end, it was a neighborhood unto itself (pop. 300). Picture Mel Gibson's head boiled in tar and stuck on a spike along the bridge (like the Scots rebel William Wallace in 1305, depicted in Gibson's movie *Braveheart*), and you'll capture the local color of that time.

In 1823, the famous bridge was replaced with a more modern (but less impressive) brick one. In 1967, that brick bridge was sold to an American, dismantled, shipped to Arizona, and reassembled (all 10,000 bricks) in Lake Havasu City. (Humor today's Brits, who'd like to believe the Yank thought he was buying Tower Bridge.) It was only then that today's bridge was built.

· *Circle the cathedral and find the entrance just around the corner.*

❸ Southwark Cathedral

This neighborhood parish church is where Shakespeare prayed while his brother Edmund rang the bells. The Southwark (SUTH-uck) church dates back to 1207, though the site has had a church for at least a thousand years, and inhabitants for 2,000. The church is simply filled with history (pick up the info flier).

❹ **View down the Nave:** Clean and sparse, with warm golden stone, the church is a symbol of the urban renewal of the whole Bankside/Southwark area. Its WWII damage has been repaired, with replacement windows of unstained glass on the right side. The nave bends slightly to the left (the chandelier, ceiling arches, and altar don't line up until you take two baby steps left) as a medieval tribute to Christ's bent body on the cross.

· *Work your way counterclockwise around the church.*

❺ **Shakespeare Monument:** William reclines in front of a backdrop of the 16th-century Bankside skyline (view looking

north). Find (left to right) the original Globe Theatre, Winchester Palace, Southwark Cathedral, and the old London Bridge with its arched gate—complete with heads on pikes, ISIS-style. Shakespeare seems to be dreaming about the many characters of his plays, depicted

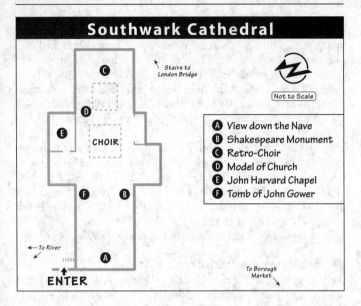

Southwark Cathedral

Stairs to
London Bridge

Not to Scale

CHOIR

Ⓐ View down the Nave
Ⓑ Shakespeare Monument
Ⓒ Retro-Choir
Ⓓ Model of Church
Ⓔ John Harvard Chapel
Ⓕ Tomb of John Gower

← To River

Ⓐ

ENTER

To Borough
Market ↘

in the stained-glass window above (see Hamlet addressing a skull, right window). To the right is a plaque to the American actor Sam Wanamaker, who spearheaded the building of a replica of Shakespeare's Globe Theatre (explained later in this chapter). Shakespeare's brother Edmund is buried in the church, possibly under a marked slab on the floor of the choir area, near the very center of the church. (The Bard lies buried in his hometown of Stratford-upon-Avon.)

Ⓒ **Retro-Choir:** The 800-year-old crisscross arches and stone tracery in the windows are some of the oldest parts of this historic church. Located in the heart of the industrial district, the church was heavily bombed during World War II and then rebuilt.

Ⓓ **Model of Church:** Tucked in behind the choir, find a model (marked *Church and Priory of St. Mary Overy*) of the church and old Winchester Palace complex—a helpful reconstruction before we visit the paltry Winchester Palace ruins.

Ⓔ **John Harvard Chapel:** The Southwark-born son of an innkeeper (see the record of baptism at the bottom of the window) inherited money from the sale of The Queen's Head tavern, got married, and sailed to Boston (1637), where he soon died. The money and his 400-book library funded the start of Harvard University.

Ⓕ **Tomb of John Gower:** The poet and friend of Chaucer (c. 1400) rests his head on his three books, one written in Middle English, one in French, and one in Latin—the three languages from which modern English soon emerged.

• *This walk is a pick-and-choose collection of sights. If you're interested in visiting the Old Operating Theatre Museum and Borough High Street inns, described next, see them first before heading west (use the map to locate these nearby sights).*

❹ Old Operating Theatre Museum and Herb Garret

Back when the common cold was treated with a refreshing blood-letting, the Old Operating Theatre—a surgical operating room from the 1800s—was a shining example of "modern" medicine. Today a museum, this is a quirky, sometimes gross look at that painful transition from folk remedy to clinical health care. Originally part of a larger hospital complex, the Old Operating Theatre was boarded up when the hospital relocated, lying untouched for 100 years until its chance discovery in 1956. The location alone—in a long-forgotten attic above a church, reached by a steep spiral staircase—makes this odd place worth a visit.

After buying your ticket, climb a few more stairs into a big room under heavy timbers—the Herb Garret, which was used to dry herbs for the former hospital. Today, it displays healing plants used for millennia—different ones for each of the traditional four ailments (melancholic, choleric, sanguine, phlegmatic), supposedly caused by an imbalance in the body's traditional four substances, or "humours" (black bile, yellow bile, blood, and phlegm), corresponding to the earth's traditional four elements (earth, wind, fire, and Ringo). Florence Nightingale, the nurse famed for saving so many Crimean War soldiers wounded in Russia, worked here to improve sanitation and to turn nurses from low-paid domestics into trained doctors' assistants.

The small hallway leading to the theater displays crude anesthetics (ether, chloroform, three pints of ale), surgical instruments by Black & Decker (knives, saws, drills), and a glaring lack of antiseptics—that is, until young Dr. Joseph Lister discovered carbolic acid, which reduced the high rates of mortality (and halitosis).

Up the stairs, the Old Operating Theatre is the highlight—a semicircular room surrounded by railings for 150 spectators (truly a "theater"), where doctors operated on patients while med students observed.

The patients were often poor women, blindfolded for their own modesty. The doctors donated their time to help, practice, and teach (see the motto *Miseratione non Mercede:* "Out of compassion, not for profit"). The surgeries, usually amputations, were performed under very crude working conditions—under the skylight or by gaslight, with no sink, and only sawdust to sop up blood. (A false floor held another layer of sawdust to stop the blood before it dripped through to the ceiling of the church below.) The wood still bears bloodstains. Nearly one in three patients died. There was a fine line between Victorian-era surgeons and Jack the Ripper.

• *Farther down Borough High Street (past the King's Head, on the left-hand side), you'll find...*

❺ The George Inn and (Faint Echoes of) Other Historic Taverns

The George is the last of many "coaching inns" that lined the main highway from London to all points south. Like Greyhound bus stations, each inn was a terminal for far-flung journeys, since coaches were forbidden inside The City. They offered food, drink, beds, and entertainment for travelers—Shakespeare, as a young actor, likely performed in The George's courtyard. On a sunny day, the courtyard is a fine place for a break from the Borough High Street bustle (food served all day long, five ales on tap—including their own brew).

• *Walk back to Southwark Cathedral. On your way, you'll find the...*

❻ Borough Market

Historically, the first trading started at 2:00 in the morning at this open-air wholesale produce market. Workers could knock off by sunrise for a pint at the specially licensed Market Porter tavern (on Park Street—and still popular). From Wednesday through Saturday, the colorful market opens for retail sales to Londoners seek-

ing trendy specialty and organic foods, and the surrounding lunch market sizzles all week long. It's great for gathering a picnic on a sunny day. Of the many market stalls, the Ginger Pig is *the* place

for serious English sausage and bacon (west end of market, across from Park Street), while Maria's Market Café is a colorful eatery popular with market workers (the red stall in the middle of the market).

First started a thousand years ago on London Bridge, where country farmers brought fresh goods to the city gates, the market now sits here under a Victorian arcade. The railroad rumbling overhead, knifing right through dingy apartment houses (and the Globe Tavern), only adds to the color of London's oldest vegetable market and public gathering spot.

A detour westward through the market leads to Park Street, with an old 19th-century ambience that makes it popular as a filming location. Check out the colorful pub and the fragrant cheese shop at Neal's Yard Dairy.

If you're hungry, food stalls are plentiful here (and open daily), but seating is scarce. A new glassed-in section by High Street has lots of benches for munching.

• *Walk to the river along Cathedral Street, veering left at the Y. (Alternatively, from the far end of the market, turn right down Stoney Street, then right again on Clink Street.)*

❼ *Golden Hinde* Replica

As we all learned in school, "Sir Francis Drake circumcised the globe with a hundred-foot clipper." Or something like that...

Imagine a hundred men on a boat this size (yes, this replica is full-size) circling the globe on a three-year voyage, sleeping on the wave-swept decks, suffering bad food, floggings, doldrums, B.O., and attacks from foreigners. They explored unknown waters and were paid only from whatever riches they could find or steal along the way. (I took a bus tour like that once.)

The *Golden Hinde* (see the female deer, or hind, on the prow and stern) was Sir Francis Drake's flagship as he circumnavigated the globe (1577-1580). Drake, a farmer's son who followed the lure of the sea, hated Spaniards. So did Queen Elizabeth I, who hired him to plunder rich

Spanish vessels and New World colonies in England's name.

With 164 men on five small ships (the *Hinde* was the largest, at 100 tons and 18 cannons), he sailed southwest, dipping around South America, raiding Spanish ships and towns in Chile, and inching up the coast perhaps as far as Canada. By the time it continued across the Pacific to Asia and beyond, the *Hinde* was so full of booty that its crew replaced the rock ballast with gold ingots and silver coins. Three years later, Drake—with only one remaining ship and 56 men—sailed the *Hinde* up the Thames, unloading a fabulously valuable hoard of gold, silver, emeralds, diamonds, pearls, silks, cloves, and spices before the queen. A grateful Elizabeth knighted Drake on the main deck and kissed him on his *Golden Hinde*.

The *Hinde* was retired gloriously, but rotted away from neglect. Drake received a large share of the wealth, became enormously famous, and later gained more glory defeating the Spanish Armada (aided by "the winds of God") in the decisive battle in the English Channel, off Plymouth (1588), making England ruler of the waves.

The galleon replica, a working ship that has itself circled the globe, is berthed at St. Mary Overie Dock ("St. Mary's over the river"), a public dock available for free to all Southwark residents. A victim of WWII bombing and container ships that require big berths and deep water, the Thames river trade that used to thrive even this far upstream is now concentrated east of Tower Bridge. Only a few brick warehouses remain (just west of here), waiting to be leveled or yuppified. Although you can pay to enter the ship, it's not worth the cost of admission.

• *There's a fine view (with a handy chart to identify things) from the riverside. The beach below is fun for beachcombing—old red roof tiles and little chunks of disposable clay tobacco pipes litter the rocks at low tide. From here, the Monument is visible across London Bridge, poking its bristly bronze head above the ugly postwar buildings. Londoners have fun nicknaming their new skyscrapers. See if you can pick out The Gherkin, The Cheese Grater, and The Walkie-Talkie. Now go up the street across from the* Golden Hinde's *gangplank (Pickfords Wharf) and head west. About 25 yards ahead on the left are the excavated ruins of...*

❽ Winchester Palace

All that remains today is a wall with a medieval rose window, but this was once a lavish 80-acre estate stretching along 200 feet of waterfront. It had a palace, gardens, fountains, stables, tennis courts, a working farm, and a fish-stocked lake. The wall marks the west end of the Great Hall (134 feet by 29 feet), the banquet room for receptions held by the palace's owner, the Bishop of Winchester.

Bishops from 1106 to 1626 lived here as wealthy, worldly rulers of the Bankside area, outside the jurisdiction of The City. They profited from activities that were illegal across the river, such as prostitution and gambling. They were a law unto themselves, with their own courts and prisons. One famous prison—the

Clink—built by the bishops remained even after its creators were ousted by a Puritan Parliament.
• *Fifty yards farther west (along what is now called Clink Street) is...*

❾ The Clink Prison Museum

Now an overpriced and disappointing museum that feels like a Disney ride with a few historic artifacts tossed in, this prison  gave us our expression "thrown in the Clink," from the sound of prisoners' chains. It burned down in 1780, but the underground cells remain, featuring historical information on wall plaques, many torture devices, and a generally creepy, claustrophobic atmosphere.

Originally part of Winchester Palace, it housed troublemakers who upset the smooth running of the bishop's 22 licensed brothels (called "the stews"), gambling dens, and taverns. Bouncers delivered drunks who were out of control, johns who couldn't pay, and prostitutes ("women living by their bodies") who tried to go freelance or cheated loyal customers. Offending prostitutes had their heads shaved and breasts bared, and were carted through the streets and whipped while people jeered. They might share cells side by side with "heretics"—namely, priests who'd crossed their bishops.

In 1352, debtors (who'd maxed out their MasterCards) became criminals, housed here among harder criminals in harsh conditions. Prisoners were not fed. They had to bribe guards to get food, to avoid torture, or even to gain their release. (The idea was that you'd brought this on yourself.) Prisoners relied on their families for money, prostituted themselves to guards and other inmates, or reached through the bars at street level, begging from passersby. Murderers, debtors, Protestants, priests, and many innocent people experienced this strange brand of justice...all part of the rough crowd that gave Bankside such a seedy reputation.
• *Continuing west and crossing under the Cannon Street Bridge, just ahead and across the street is...*

❿ The Anchor and Bankside Road

The Anchor is the last of the original 22 licensed "inns" (tavern/brothel/restaurant/nightclub/casino) of Bankside's red light district heyday in the 1600s. A tavern has stood here for 800 years. The big brick buildings behind the inn were once part of the mass-producing Anchor brewery, with the inn as its brewpub. (Even back in the

BANKSIDE

1300s, Chaucer wrote, "If the words get muddled in my tale / Just put it down to too much Southwark ale.")

In the cozy, mazelike interior are memories of greats who've drunk here (I have) or indulged in a new drug that hit London in the 1560s—tobacco. Shakespeare, who may have lived along Clink Street, may have tippled here, especially because the original Globe Theatre was right behind The Anchor (see map on page 291). Dr. Samuel Johnson also worked here while writing the famous dictionary that helped codify the English language and spelling (for more on Dr. Johnson, see page 247).

ANCHOR TAP

The Anchor marks the start of the once-notorious Bankside Road that runs along a river retaining wall. In Elizabethan times (16th century), the street was lined with "inns" offering one-stop shopping for addictive personalities. The streets were jammed with sword-carrying punks in tights looking for a fight, prostitutes, gaping tourists from the Borough High Street coaching inns, pickpockets, river pirates, highwaymen, navy recruiters kidnapping drunks, and many proper ladies and gentlemen who ferried across from The City for an evening's entertainment. And then there were the really seedy people—yes, actors.

• *Crossing under the green-and-yellow Southwark Bridge, notice the metal reliefs depicting London's "Frost Fair" of 1564. Because the old London Bridge was such a wall of stone, the swift-flowing Thames would back up and even freeze over during cold winters. Emerging from under the bridge, head farther west on Bankside to...*

⓫ Shakespeare's Globe

> *All the world's a stage,*
> *And all the men and women merely players.*
> *They have their exits and their entrances,*
> *And one man, in his time, plays many parts.*
> —As You Like It

By 1599, 35-year-old William Shakespeare was a well-known actor, playwright, and businessman in the booming theater trade (see sidebar on page 232). His acting company, the Lord Chamberlain's Men, built the 3,000-seat Globe Theatre, by far the largest of its day (200 yards from today's replica, where only a plaque

stands now). The Globe premiered Shakespeare's greatest works—*Hamlet, Othello, King Lear, Macbeth*—in open-air summer afternoon performances, though occasionally at night by the light of torches and buckets of tar-soaked ropes.

In 1612, it featured Shakespeare's *All Is True (Henry VIII)*. During Scene 4, a stage cannon boomed, announcing the arrival of King Henry, who started flirting with Anne Boleyn. As the two actors generated sparks onstage, play-watchers smelled fire. Some stray cannon wadding had sparked a real fire offstage. Within an hour, the wood-and-thatch building had burned completely to the ground, but with only one injury: A man's pants caught fire and were quickly doused with a tankard of ale.

Built in 1997, the new Globe—round, half-timbered, thatched, with wooden pegs for nails—is a quite realistic replica, though slightly smaller (seating 1,500 spectators), located near the original site, and constructed with fire-repellent materials. Performances are staged almost nightly in summer—check at the box office (at the east end of the complex). For more on touring the Globe, see page 89.

Bankside's theater scene vanished in the 1640s, closed by a Parliament dominated by hard-line Puritans. Drama seemed to portray and promote immoral behavior, and actors—men who also played women's roles—parodied and besmirched fair womanhood. Bearbaiting was also outlawed by the outraged moralists (to paraphrase the historian Thomas Macaulay)—not because it caused bears pain, but because it gave people pleasure.

• *From the Globe, belly up to the railing overlooking the Thames and imagine the view on September 2, 1666.*

⓬ View of 1666 Great Fire Area

On Sunday, September 2, 1666, stunned Londoners quietly sipped beers in Bankside pubs and watched The City across the river go up in flames. ("When we could endure no more upon the water," wrote Samuel Pepys in his diary, "we went to a little alehouse on the Bankside.") Started in a bakery shop near the Monument (north end of London Bridge) and fanned by strong winds, the fire swept westward, engulfing the mostly wooden city, devouring Old St. Paul's, and moving past what is now Blackfriars Bridge and St. Bride's to Temple Church (near the pointy, black, gold-tipped steeple of the Royal Courts of Justice).

In four days, 80 percent of The City was incinerated, including 13,000 houses and 89 churches. The good news? Incredibly, only nine people died, the fire cleansed a plague-infested city, and Christopher Wren was around to rebuild London's skyline.

The fire also marked the end of Bankside's era as London's naughty playground. Having recently been cleaned up by the Puritans, it now served as a temporary refugee camp for those displaced by the fire. And, with the coming Industrial Age, businessmen demolished the inns and replaced them with brick warehouses, docks, and factories to fuel the economy of a world power.

• *At the pedestrian bridge is a towering former power plant, now turned into a huge modern art museum.*

⓭ Tate Modern

London's large, impressive modern art collection is housed mostly in a former power station—typical of the move to renovate empty, ugly Industrial Age hulks on the South

Bank. Even if you don't tour the collection, pop inside the north entrance (free) to view the spacious interior, decorated each year with a new industrial-sized installation by one of the world's top contemporary artists. The Tate recently expanded into the Blavatnik Building (Switch House) annex, opening up even more galleries and public spaces to celebrate the vibrant city's progressive scene.

📖 See the Tate Modern Tour chapter.

• *End this walk on the Millennium Bridge, enjoying a view of the Thames.*

⓮ Millennium Bridge and View of the Thames

This pedestrian bridge was built in 2000 to connect the Tate Modern with St. Paul's Cathedral and The City. For its first two glori-

ous days, Londoners made the pleasant seven-minute walk across...before the $25 million "bridge to the next millennium" started wobbling dangerously (insert your own ironic joke here) and was closed for rethinking. After much work, 20 months, and $8 million in retrofits, the bridge reopened. Nicknamed the "blade of light," it was designed (partly by Lord Norman Foster, who also did The Gherkin and City Hall downstream) to allow a wide-open view of St. Paul's. Now stabilized, it links two revitalized sections of London.

From the Cotswolds to the North Sea, the Thames winds eastward a total of 210 miles. London is close enough to the estuary to be affected by the North Sea's tides, so the river level does indeed rise and fall twice a day. In fact, one of the reasons Romans found this a practical location—even though it was about 40 miles inland—was that their boats could hitch a free ride with the tides between the sea and the town twice a day. But tides also mean floods. After centuries of periodic flooding (spring rains plus high tides), barriers to regulate the tides were built in 1982, east of Tower Bridge. The barriers also slow down the once fast-moving river.

The Thames is still a major commercial artery (east of Tower Bridge). In the previous two centuries, it ran brown with Industrial Revolution pollution. Today it's brown because of estuary silt—the Thames is now one of the cleanest rivers in the industrialized world.

• *Your tour is over. From here you can enjoy the Tate Modern or continue strolling the South Bank (follow the Jubilee Walkway 20 minutes or so to the London Eye and Big Ben—particularly enjoyable in the evening). Or cross the Thames on the Millennium Bridge to a pedestrian mall that leads past the glassy Salvation Army headquarters (good café and small, free Salvation Army history display in daylight basement) to St. Paul's Cathedral and Tube station.*

TATE MODERN TOUR

Remember the 20th century? Accelerated by technology and fragmented by war, it was an exciting and chaotic time, with art as turbulent as the world that created it. The Tate Modern lets you walk through the explosive last century with a glimpse at its brave new art.

This Is Not a "Tour": The Tate Modern displays change frequently, making a painting-by-painting tour impossible. In addition, its collection is (controversially) organized by concept—"Artist and Society," for example—rather than by artist and chronology. Unlike the museum, this chapter is neatly chronological. It's not intended as a painting-by-painting tour, but to give context to the various cultural periods that produced the art of the Tate Modern.

Read through this chapter for a general introduction, use it as a reference, then take advantage of the Tate's excellent multimedia guide to focus on specific works. With this background in 20th-century art, you'll appreciate the Tate's even greater strength: art of the 21st century. After you see the Old Masters of Modernism (Matisse, Picasso, Kandinsky, and so on), push your mental envelope with works by Pollock, Miró, Bacon, Picabia, Beuys, Twombly, and beyond. Look past the painted canvases to appreciate the museum's many installations: entire rooms given over to a single artist to create a multimedia display.

When the Tate Modern opened in 2000, they anticipated two million visitors a year. More than twice that visited. In response, they've opened a new wing, doubling its exhibition space. The goal of the expansion—to foster interaction between art and community in the 21st century—is as modern as the collection itself.

Orientation

Cost: Free, £4 suggested donation; fee for special exhibits.

Hours: Daily 10:00-18:00, Fri-Sat until 22:00, last entry to special exhibits 45 minutes before closing.

Information: Tel. 020/7887-8888, www.tate.org.uk.

When to Go: This popular place is especially crowded on weekends. Crowds thin out on Friday and Saturday evenings and midday during the week.

Getting There: Located on the South Bank of the Thames, across from St. Paul's and near the Globe Theatre. You can get here by Tube, ferry, or foot:

> **By Tube:** Take the Tube to Southwark, London Bridge, St. Paul's, Mansion House, or Blackfriars, then follow signs to the museum (10- to 15-minute walk).

> **By Ferry:** Catch Thames Clippers' Tate Boat ferry from the Tate Britain (Millbank Pier) for a 15-minute crossing (£8 one-way, departs every 40 minutes Mon-Fri 10:00-16:00, Sat-Sun 9:15-18:40, www.tate.org.uk/visit/tate-boat).

> **On Foot:** Walk across the Millennium Bridge from St. Paul's Cathedral.

Visitor Information: The two lowest floors (levels 0 and 1) have info desks, bookstores, multimedia guide rentals, and tickets for temporary exhibits.

The helpful staff at the info desk (level 1) can give you the location of specific works. The floor plan (£1 suggested donation) is also useful. In addition, a few touch-screen computers are scattered throughout the museum.

Tours: The £4.75 **multimedia guide** covers the entire permanent collection, and includes a tour geared for kids ages 8-12. Free 45-minute **guided tours** are offered at 11:00, 12:00, 14:00, and 15:00. Free 10-minute **gallery talks** take place Friday and Saturday (see info desk for details).

Length of This Tour: Allow at least an hour. Read this chapter ahead of time, then browse according to your tastes.

Services: You can check bags at the cloakroom on Level 0 (free, £2 suggested donation). WCs are located near the escalator or elevator on most levels.

Cuisine Art: View coffee shops are on levels 1 and 3. On level 6, there's a **$$$ table-service restaurant** and **$$ casual bar**

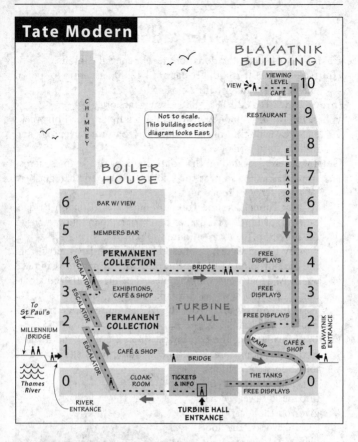

Tate Modern

offering better views and lower prices (drinks and snacks). This perch provides stunning panoramas of St. Paul's and The City. The **$$$$ restaurant** in the museum's Blavatnik Building promises another fine dining experience with views. Some trendy restaurants are several blocks southwest of the Tate, along the street named "the Cut" (near Southwark Tube stop).

Starring: Picasso, Matisse, Dalí, and all the "classic" modern artists, plus the Tate Modern's specialty—British and American artists of the last half of the 20th century.

Know Your Tates: Don't confuse the Tate Modern with the Tate Britain (south of Big Ben), which features British art (📖 see the Tate Britain Tour chapter). But there is some crossover: Both Tates include some 20th- and 21st-century British artists.

Getting Started

The best place to start any visit to this sprawling museum is at the main entrance: With the Thames at your back, walk to the right, to the west (upstream) end of the building.

The main entrance puts you in the vast Turbine Hall. At the info desk, pick up a map and get orien-tate-d. Note that the museum is made up of two buildings connected by skybridges: the Boiler House (where you're standing) and the Blavatnik House (a.k.a. the Switch House). You're in the Boiler House, on underground level 0.

The permanent collection (with the art described in this chapter) is generally on Levels 2 and 4 of the Boiler House (elevators are near the ground floor cloakroom). Remember, paintings are arranged according to theme, not artist. Paintings by Picasso, for example, might be scattered in different rooms on different levels. Adding to the confusion, there may also be temporary exhibits (some requiring admission fees) in some rooms on these levels. To help you get started, the museum may have a room labeled *Start Display*, highlighting a range of artworks.

Besides the permanent collection, there's art all over the two buildings—some free, some requiring a special admission.

Use the museum's map to figure out what you'd like to see, and use this chapter's overview of 20th-century art to augment your sightseeing. Or—if you'd rather just browse—consider the sidebar on the next page, which gives a quick once-over of the buildings.

Overview of Modern Art

• *The following is not a painting-by-painting tour but rather a chronological overview of some of the modern artists and trends you will encounter at the Tate.*

1900—VICTORIA'S LEGACY

Anno Domini 1900, a new century dawns. Europe is at peace, Britannia rules the world. Technology is about to usher in a golden age.

Claude Monet

Monet (1840-1926) captures the relaxed, civilized spirit of belle époque France and Victorian England with Impressionist snapshots of peaceful landscapes and middle-class family picnics. But the true subject is the shimmering effect of reflected light, rendered with rough brushstrokes and bright paints that look messy up close but blend at a distance. The newfangled camera made camera-eye realism obsolete. Artists began placing more importance on *how* something was painted rather than on *what* was painted.

The Building as "Art"

Besides the art it houses, the Tate Modern's display space is a sight in and of itself. Here's a quick, round-trip route through the buildings that hits the highlights. You'll enjoy the modern architecture, get a sense of the wide variety of art on display, and be treated to a great view of London. As you go, linger wherever you'd like, seeing unexpected art that catches your eye.

Boiler House

The Turbine Hall—Level 0: Start at the main entrance, strolling majestically down the sloping ramp and into the massive empty space of this former electricity-generating powerhouse. The power station (with its 325-foot brick chimney) closed in 1981. It was refurbished with a glass roof, and reopened as a museum in the year 2000. Today, the Turbine Hall displays major art installations by contemporary artists—always one of the highlights of the art world. More exhibits are displayed in "The Tanks," to the right of the main hall.

• *Head upstairs (via the escalator near the ground-floor cloakroom) to level 2.*

The Permanent Collection—Levels 2-4: These levels house the

1905—COLONIAL EUROPE

Europe ruled a global empire, tapping its dark-skinned colonies for raw materials, cheap labor, and bold new ways to look at the world. The cozy Victorian world was shattering. Nietzsche murdered God. Darwin stripped off Man's robe of culture and found a naked ape. Primitivism was modern. Ooga-booga.

Henri Matisse

Matisse (1869-1954) was one of the Fauves, or "wild beasts," who tried to inject a bit of the jungle into civilized European society. Inspired by "primitive" African and Oceanic masks and voodoo dolls, the Fauves made modern art that looked primitive: long, masklike faces with almond eyes; bright, clashing colors; simple figures; and "flat," two-dimensional scenes.

Matisse simplifies. A man is a few black lines and blocks of paint. A snail is a spiral of colored paper. A woman's back is an outline. Matisse's colors are unnaturally bright. The "distant" land-

core of the permanent collection—that is, the artwork described in this chapter. There are also major temporary exhibitions (some free, some requiring special admission).

• *Sightsee your way up through levels 2, 3, and 4. On level 4, walk across the "bridge" (with great views down into the Turbine Hall) and into the new annex—the Blavatnik Building (Switch House).*

Blavatnik Building (Switch House)

Level 4: The twisted-pyramid, 10-story Blavatnik Building was constructed on the site of the power station's old switch house, and was designed by the same architectural firm that refurbished the Boiler House. It gave the Tate an extra quarter-million square feet of display space. Besides showing off more of the Tate's impressive collection, the space hosts changing themed exhibitions, performance art, experimental film, and interactive sculpture incorporating light and sound. Higher floors offer social and educational activities, including a children's gallery and several cafés. Some of this building's rooms are free to enter, while others require special admission fees.

• *After exploring level 4, take the (often-crowded) elevator up to...*

The Viewing Level—Level 10: This wraparound terrace (with a small café) offers stunning views of London.

• *Take the elevator down to level 2, where there are more rooms of free art. Then make your way down (past more art and the misty fountain) to level 0. You're back at the Turbine Hall.*

scape is as crisp and clear as close objects, and the slanted lines meant to suggest depth are crudely done.

Traditionally, the canvas was like a window that you looked "through" to see a slice of the real world stretching off into the horizon. With Matisse, you look "at" the canvas like you do wallpaper—to appreciate the decorative pattern of colors and shapes.

Though his style is modern, Matisse builds on 19th-century art—the bright colors of Van Gogh, the primitive figures of Gauguin, the colorful designs of Japanese wood-block prints, and the Impressionist patches of paint that blend together only at a distance.

Paul Cézanne

Cézanne (1839-1906) brings Impressionism into the 20th century. Whereas Monet uses separate dabs of different-colored paint to "build" a figure, Cézanne "builds" a man with somewhat larger slabs of paint, giving him a kind of 3-D chunkiness. It's not hard to see the progression from Monet's dabs to Cézanne's slabs to Picasso's cubes—Cubism.

1910—THE MODERNS

The modern world was moving fast, with automobiles, factories, and mass communication. Motion pictures captured the fast-moving world, while Einstein explored the fourth dimension: time.

Cubism and Pablo Picasso

Born in Spain, Picasso (1881-1973) moved to Paris as a young man. He worked with painter and sculptor Georges Braque in poverty so dire they often didn't know where their next bottle of wine was coming from.

Picasso's Cubist works show the old European world shattering to bits. He pieces the fragments back together in a whole new way, showing several perspectives at once (for example, looking up the left side of a woman's body and, at the same time, down at her right).

Whereas newfangled motion pictures capture several perspectives in succession, Picasso achieves it on a canvas with overlapping images. A single "cube" might contain an arm (in the foreground) and the window behind (in the background), both painted the same color. The foreground and background are woven together so that the subject dissolves into a pattern.

Picasso, the most famous and—OK, I'll say it—the greatest artist of the 20th century, constantly explored and adapted his style to new trends. He made collages, tried his hand at "statues" of wood, wire, or whatever, and even made art out of everyday household objects. These multimedia works, so revolutionary at the time, have become stock-in-trade today. Scattered throughout the museum are works from the many periods of Picasso's life.

Futurism

The Machine Age is approaching, and the whole world gleams with promise in cylindrical shapes ("Tubism"), like an internal-combustion engine. Or is it the gleaming barrel of a cannon?

1914—WORLD WAR I

A soldier—shivering in a trench, ankle-deep in mud, waiting to be ordered "over the top," to run through barbed wire, over fallen comrades, and into a hail of machine-gun fire, only to capture a few hundred yards of meaningless territory that would be lost the next day. This soldier was not thinking about art.

World War I left nine million dead. (At times, England lost more men per month than America lost during the entire Vietnam War.) The war also killed the optimism and faith in humankind that had guided Europe since the Renaissance.

Expressionism

Cynicism and decadence settled over postwar Europe. Artists such as Grosz, Beckmann, and Kokoschka "expressed" their disgust by showing a distorted reality that emphasized the ugly. Using the lurid colors and simplified figures of the Fauves, they slapped paint on in thick brushstrokes, depicting a hypocritical, hard-edged, dog-eat-dog world—a civilization watching its Victorian moral foundations collapse.

Dada

When they could grieve no longer, artists turned to grief's giddy twin, laughter. The war made all old values a joke, including artistic ones. The Dada movement, choosing a purposely childish name, made art that was intentionally outrageous: a moustache on the *Mona Lisa*, a shovel hung on the wall, or a modern version of a Renaissance "fountain"—a urinal (by Marcel Duchamp...or was it I. P. Freeley?).

Dada was a dig at all the pompous prewar artistic theories based on the noble intellect of Rational Women and Men. While the experts ranted on, Dadaists sat in the back of the class and made cultural fart noises.

Hey, I love this stuff. My mind says it's sophomoric, but my heart belongs to Dada.

1920s—ANYTHING GOES

In the Jazz Age, the world turned upside down. Genteel ladies smoked cigarettes. Gangsters laid down the law. You could make a fortune in the stock market one day and lose it the next. You could dance the Charleston with the opposite sex, and even say the word "sex" while talking about Freud over cocktails. It was almost...surreal.

Surrealism

Artists caught the jumble of images on a canvas. A telephone made from a lobster, an elephant with a heating-duct trunk, Venus sleepwalking among skeletons. Take one mixed bag of reality, jumble it in a blender, and serve on a canvas—Surrealism.

The artist scatters seemingly unrelated—yet easily recognizable—objects on the canvas, leaving us to trace the connections in a kind of connect-the-dots without numbers.

Abstract Art

Abstract art simplifies. A man becomes a stick figure. A squiggle is a wave. A streak of red expresses anger. Arches make you want a cheeseburger. These are universal symbols that everyone from a caveman to a banker understands. Abstract artists capture the essence of reality in a few lines and colors, boldly capturing objects and ideas that even a camera can't—emotions, abstract concepts, musical rhythms, and spiritual states of mind.

With abstract art, you don't look "through" the canvas to see the visual world, but "at" it to read the symbolism of lines, shapes, and colors. Most 20th-century paintings are a mix of the real world (representation) and colorful patterns (abstraction).

Further complicating the modern world was Freud's discovery of the "unconscious" mind, which thinks dirty thoughts while we sleep. Surrealists let the id speak. The canvas is an uncensored, stream-of-consciousness "landscape" of these deep urges, revealed in the bizarre images of dreams. Salvador Dalí, the most famous Surrealist, combined an extraordinarily realistic technique with an extraordinarily twisted mind. He painted "unreal" scenes with photographic realism, making us believe they could really happen. Dalí's images—crucifixes, political and religious figures, and naked bodies—pack an emotional punch.

1930s—DEPRESSION

As capitalism failed around the world, governments propped up their economies with vast building projects. The architecture style was modern, stripped-down (i.e., cheap), and functional. Propagandist campaigns championed noble workers in the heroic Social Realist style.

Piet Mondrian

Like blueprints for modernism, Mondrian's T-square style boils painting down to its basic building blocks: a white canvas, black lines, and the three primary colors—red, yellow, and blue—arranged in orderly patterns. (When you come right down to it, that's all painting ever has been. A schematic drawing of, say, the *Mona Lisa* shows that it's less about a woman than about the triangles and rectangles she's composed of.)

Mondrian (1872-1944) started out painting realistic landscapes of the orderly fields in his native homeland of Holland. Increasingly, he simplified his style into horizontal and vertical patterns. For Mondrian, who was heavily into Eastern mysticism, "up versus down" and "left versus right" were the perfect metaphors for life's dualities: good versus evil, body versus spirit, fascism versus communism, man versus woman. The canvas is a bird's-eye view of Mondrian's personal landscape.

1940s—WORLD WAR II

World War II was a global war (involving Europe, the Americas, Australia, Africa, and Asia) and a total war (saturation bombing of civilians and ethnic cleansing). It left Europe in ruins.

Alberto Giacometti's skinny statues have the emaciated, haunted, and faceless look of concentration-camp survivors. In the sweep of world war and overpowering technology, man is frail and fragile. All he can do is stand at attention and take it like a man.

Meanwhile, Francis Bacon's caged creatures speak for all of war-torn Europe when they scream, "Enough!" (For more on Bacon, see page 342.)

1950s—AMERICA, THE GLOBAL SUPERPOWER

As converted war factories turned swords into kitchen appliances, America helped rebuild Europe while pumping out consumer goods for its own booming population. Prosperity, a stable government, national television broadcasts, and a common fear of Soviet communism threatened to turn America into a completely homogeneous society.

Some artists, centered in New York, rebelled against conformity and superficial consumerism. (They'd served under Eisenhower in war and now had to in peace, as well.) They created art that was the very opposite of the functional, mass-produced goods of the American marketplace.

Art was a way of asserting your individuality by creating a completely original and personal vision. The trend was toward bigger canvases, abstract designs, and experimentation with new materials and techniques. It was called "Abstract Expressionism"—expressing emotions and ideas using color and form alone.

Jackson Pollock

"Jack the Dripper" attacks convention with a can of paint, dripping and splashing a dense web onto the canvas. Picture Pollock (1912-1956) in his studio, jiving to the hi-fi, bouncing off the walls, throwing paint in a moment of enlightenment. Of course, the artist loses some control this way—over the paint flying in midair and over himself in an ecstatic trance. Painting becomes a whole-body activity, a "dance" between the artist and his materials.

The intuitive act of creating is what's important, not the final product. The canvas is only a record of that moment of ecstasy.

Big, Empty Canvases

With all the postwar prosperity, artists could afford bigger canvases. But what reality are they trying to show?

In the modern world, we find ourselves insignificant specks in a vast and indifferent universe. Every morning, each of us must confront that big, blank, existential canvas, and decide how we're going to make our mark on it.

Another influence was the simplicity of Japanese landscape painting. A Zen master studies and meditates for years to achieve the state of mind in which he can draw one pure line. These canvases, again, are only a record of that state of enlightenment. (What is the sound of one brush painting?)

On more familiar ground, postwar painters were following in the footsteps of artists such as Mondrian. The geometrical forms here reflect the same search for order, but these artists painted to the musical 5/4 asymmetry of the Dave Brubeck Quartet's jazzy *Take Five*.

Patterns and Textures

Enjoy the lines and colors, but also a new element: texture. Some works have very thick paint piled on, where you can see the brushstrokes clearly. Some have substances besides paint applied to the canvas, or the canvas is punctured so the fabric itself (and the hole) becomes the subject. Artists show their skill by mastering new materials. The canvas is a tray, serving up a delightful buffet of different substances with interesting colors, patterns, shapes, and textures.

Mark Rothko

Rothko (1903-1970) made two-toned rectangles, laid on their sides, that seem to float in a big, vertical canvas. The edges are blurred, so if you get close enough to let the canvas fill your field of vision (as Rothko intended), the rectangles appear to rise and sink from the cloudy depths like answers in a Magic 8 Ball.

Serious students appreciate the subtle differences in color between the rectangles. Rothko experimented with different bases for the same color and used a single undercoat (a "wash") to unify them. His early works are warmer, with brighter reds, yellows, and oranges; his later works are maroon and brown, approaching black.

Still, these are not intended to be formal studies in color and form. Rothko was trying to express the most basic human emotions in a pure language. (A "realistic" painting of a person is inher-

---

20th-Century British Artists

Since 1960, London has rivaled New York as a center for the visual arts. You'll find British artists displayed in both the Tate Modern and the Tate Britain. Check out the Tate Britain Tour chapter for more on the following artists: David Hockney, Jacob Epstein, Gilbert and George, Henry Moore, Francis Bacon, and Barbara Hepworth.

---

ently fake because it's only an illusion of the person.) Staring into these windows onto the soul, you can laugh, cry, or ponder, just as Rothko did when he painted them.

Rothko, the previous century's "last serious artist," believed in the power of art to express the human spirit. When he found out that his nine large Seagram canvases were to be hung in a corporate restaurant, he refused to sell them, and they ended up in the Tate. (A 2010 Tony Award-winning play called *Red* dealt with Rothko's anguished decision.)

In his last years, Rothko's canvases—always rectangles—got bigger, simpler, and darker. When Rothko finally slashed his wrists in his studio, one nasty critic joked that what killed him was the repetition. Minimalism was painting itself into a blank corner.

1960s—POP AND POLITICS

The decade began united in idealism—young John F. Kennedy pledged to put a man on the moon, newly launched satellites signaled a united world, the Beatles sang exuberantly, peaceful race demonstrations championed equality, and the Vatican II Council preached liberation. By decade's end, there were race riots, assassinations, student protests, and America's floundering war in distant Vietnam. In households around the world, parents screamed, "Turn that down...and get a haircut!"

Culturally, every postwar value was questioned by a rising, wealthy, and populous baby-boom generation. London—producer of rock-and-roll music, film actors, mod fashions, and Austin Powers joie de vivre—once again became a world cultural center.

Though government-sponsored public art was dominated by big, abstract canvases and sculptures, other artists pooh-poohed the highbrow seriousness of abstract art. Instead, they mocked lowbrow popular culture by embracing it in a tongue-in-cheek way (Pop Art), or they attacked authority with absurd performances to make a political statement (conceptual art).

Pop Art

America's postwar wealth made the consumer king. Pop Art is created from the popular objects of that throwaway society—soup cans, car fenders, tacky plastic statues, movie icons. Take a Sears product, hang it in a museum, and you have to ask: Is this art? Are mass-produced objects beautiful, or crap? Why do we work so hard to acquire them? Pop Art, like Dadaism before it, questions our society's values.

Andy Warhol (who coined "15 minutes of fame") concentrated on another mass-produced phenomenon: celebrities. He took publicity photos of famous people and reproduced them. The repetition—like the constant bombardment we get from recurring images on TV—cheapens even the most beautiful things.

Roy Lichtenstein took a comic strip, blew it up, hung it on a wall, and charged a million bucks—whaam, Pop Art. Lichtenstein supposedly was inspired by his young son, who challenged him to do something as good as Mickey Mouse. The huge newsprint dots never let us forget that the painting—like all commercial art—is an illusionistic fake. The work's humor comes from portraying a lowbrow subject (comics and ads) on the epic scale of a masterpiece.

Op Art
Optical illusions play tricks with your eyes, the way a spiral starts to spin when you stare at it. These obscure scientific experiments in color, line, and optics suddenly became trendy in the psychedelic '60s.

1970s—THE "ME DECADE"
All forms of authority—"The Establishment"—seemed bankrupt. America's president resigned in the Watergate scandal, corporations were polluting the earth, and capitalism nearly ground to a halt when Arabs withheld oil.

Artists attacked authority and institutions, trying to free individuals to discover their full human potential. Even the concept of "modernism"—that art wasn't good unless it was totally original and progressive—was questioned. No single style could dictate in this postmodern period.

Earth Art
Fearing for the health of the earth's ecology, artists rediscovered the beauty of rocks, dirt, trees, even the sound of the wind, using them to create natural art. A rock placed in a museum or urban square is certainly a strange sight.

TATE MODERN

Performance Art

The Tate Modern's collection of "sculptures" by Joseph Beuys—assemblages of steel, junk, wood, and, especially, felt and animal fat—only hint at his greatest artwork: Beuys himself.

Imagine Beuys walking through the museum, carrying a dead rabbit, while he explains the paintings to it. Or taking off his clothes, shaving his head, and smearing his body with fat.

This charismatic, ex-Luftwaffe art shaman did ridiculous things to inspire others to break with convention and be free. He choreographed "Happenings"—spectacles where people did absurd things while others watched—and pioneered performance art, in which the artist presents himself as the work of art. Beuys inspired a whole generation of artists to walk on stage, cluck like a chicken, and stick a yam up themselves. Beuys will be Beuys.

New Media

Minimalist painting and abstract sculpture were old hat, and there was an explosion of new art forms. Performance art was the most controversial, combining music, theater, dance, poetry, and the visual arts. New technologies brought video, assemblages, installations, artists' books (paintings in book form), and even (gasp!) realistic painting.

Conceptual Art

Increasingly, artists are not creating an original work (painting a canvas or sculpting a stone) but assembling one from premade objects. The *concept* of which object to pair with another to produce maximum effect ("Let's stick a crucifix in a jar of urine," to cite one notorious example) is the key.

1980s—MATERIAL GIRL

Ronald Reagan in America, Margaret Thatcher in Britain, and corporate executives around the world ruled over a conservative and materialistic society. On the other side were starving Ethiopians, gay men with the new disease AIDS, people of color, and women—all demanding power. Intelligent, peaceful, straight white males assumed a low profile.

The art world became big business, with a Van Gogh painting fetching $54 million. Corporations paid big bucks for large, colorful, semi-abstract canvases. Marketing became an art form. Gender and sexual orientation were popular themes. Many women picked up paintbrushes, creating bright-colored abstract forms hinting at vulva and penis shapes. Visual art fused with popular music, bringing us installations in dance clubs and fast-edit music videos. The crude style of graffiti art demanded to be included in corporate society.

TATE MODERN

1990s—MULTICULTURAL DIVERSITY

The communist-built Berlin Wall was torn down, ending four decades of a global Cold War between capitalism and communism. The new battleground was the "Culture Wars," the struggle to include all races, genders, and lifestyles within an increasingly corporate-dominated, global society.

Artists looked to Third World countries for inspiration and championed society's outsiders against government censorship and economic exclusion. A new medium, the Internet, arose, allowing instantaneous multimedia communication around the world through electronic signals carried by satellites and telephone lines.

2000—?

A new millennium dawned. Thanks to the Internet, art has taken on a new sense of connectivity. A work of art can mean strangers meeting for intricate Flashmob street performances; graffiti artists like Banksy reaching the masses by tagging public spaces; and people everywhere sharing moments through social networking sites. Instagram selfies have become the modern Gainsborough portrait, presenting an idealized image to the world of how we wish to be seen. Technology has empowered everyone to make art.

VICTORIA & ALBERT MUSEUM TOUR

With one of the biggest, most eclectic collections of objects any-where, the Victoria and Albert (V&A) has something for everyone. It bills itself as a museum for the decorative arts, and Martha Stewart types will be in hog heaven. You'll see furniture, glassware, clothing, jewelry, and carpets from every corner of the world. Throw in historical artifacts, and a few fine-arts masterpieces (painting and sculpture), and you have a museum built for browsing.

The V&A grew out of the Great Exhibition of 1851, that ultimate celebration of the Industrial Revolution. Now "art" could be brought to the masses through modern technology and mass production. The museum was founded on the idealistic Victorian notion that anyone can be continually improved by education and example. After much support from Queen Victoria and Prince Albert, the museum was renamed for the royal couple, and its present building was opened in 1909.

You could spend days in this place. The museum is large and gangly, with over 150 rooms and more than 12 miles of corridors. My quick tour gives you a sample of the V&A's range, covering fine art, historical objects, interior design, fashion, and beautiful objects from around the globe. Use this tour to get your bearings, then use the museum's map to wander at will.

The V&A is a purpose-built museum designed to face its sister, the Natural History Museum, set across from each other on Exhibition Road. But up until 2017, there was no Exhibition Road entrance: People entered the V&A via Cromwell Road, and the museum evolved around this Grand Entrance. A new Exhibition Road entrance is now open—but it really doesn't matter to visitors. My coverage starts at the Cromwell Road entry. (If entering from Exhibition Road, simply head for the Cromwell Road entrance and its landmark Dale Chihuly glass chandelier.)

Orientation

Cost: Free, £5 suggested donation; fee for some special exhibits.

Hours: Daily 10:00-17:45. Some galleries—including most on this tour—stay open Fri until 22:00.

Information: Tel. 020/7942-2000, www.vam.ac.uk.

Getting There: The museum is in the South Kensington neighborhood (Tube: South Kensington). The Grand Entrance—where our tour begins—is on Cromwell Road. A new entrance along Exhibition Road takes visitors through the Sackler Courtyard, entering via Blavatnik Hall (see map on page 323).

You can also reach the museum via a tunnel that leads directly from the South Kensington Tube station: Once inside the museum (on level 1), continue straight down the long sculpture gallery. After about 100 yards, turn right through the gift shop, which takes you to the Grand Entrance lobby.

Visitor Information: Check the V&A's helpful website in advance for a list of current exhibits. Once at the museum, pick up the much-needed museum map (£1 suggested donation). Strategically located computer terminals tell you more about the collection.

Tours: Free one-hour tours (general orientation and other more specific topics) leave from the Grand Entrance lobby daily from 10:30 to 15:30 (1-2/hour). Additional tours and lectures are offered sporadically; check the website for details.

Length of This Tour: Allow 1.5 hours (not counting the British Galleries). With limited time, don't miss the Cast Courts, the Fashion Galleries, and Raphael's Tapestry Cartoons.

Cloakroom: £1 per item, mandatory for large bags.

Cuisine Art: The **$$ V&A Café** offers self-service lunch and a £30 Queen Victoria afternoon tea in the elegant Morris, Gamble, and Poynter rooms. These three rooms formed the world's first museum restaurant. There's also a **$ self-service café** in the Madejski Garden—grab a bite there or bring a picnic—and another **$ café** in the Sackler Courtyard. A food circus of fun eateries is two blocks away, where Exhibition Road approaches the South Kensington Tube station (see page 411).

Starring: A little of everything—and all of it beautiful.

The Tour Begins

• *Start at the Grand Entrance lobby, on level 1. Look up into the rotunda.*

❶ Dale Chihuly Chandelier

This modern chandelier/sculpture by the American glass artist epitomizes the spirit of the V&A's collection—beautiful manufactured objects that demonstrate technical skill and innovation, wedding the old with the new, and blurring the line between arts and crafts.

Each blue-and-yellow strand of the chandelier is tied with a wire to a central spine. When the chandelier first went up in 2001, Chihuly said, "Too small," had it disassembled, and fired up still more glass bubbles.

Dale Chihuly (b. 1941)—face-famous for the eye patch he's worn since a car accident—studied glassmaking in Venice, then set up his own studio/factory in Seattle, making art as the director of a creative team. He makes an old medium seem fresh and modern...and the V&A keeps his chandelier looking fresh with a long feather duster.

• *From the lobby, look up to the balcony (above the shop) and see the pointed arches of the...*

❷ Hereford Screen, 1862

In the 1800s, just as Britain was steaming into the future on the cutting edge of the Industrial Revolution, the public's taste went

retro. This 35-by-35-foot, eight-ton rood screen (built for the Hereford Cathedral's sacred altar area) looks medieval, but it was created with the most modern materials the Industrial Revolution could produce. The metal parts were not hammered and hand-worked as in olden days, but are made of electroformed copper. The parts were first cast in plaster, then bathed in molten copper with an electric current running through it, leaving a metal skin around the plaster. The entire project—which might have taken years in medieval times—was completed in five months.

George Gilbert Scott (1811-1878), who built the screen, re-

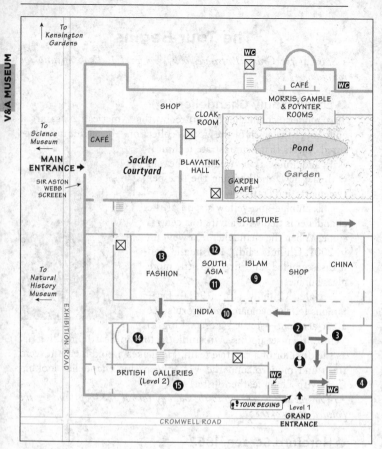

designed much of London in the Neo-Gothic style, restoring old churches such as Westminster Abbey, renovating the Houses of Parliament, and building new structures like St. Pancras Station and the Albert Memorial—some 700 buildings in all.

The world turns, and a century later (1960s), the Gothic style was "out" again, modernism was in, and this screen was neglected and ridiculed. Considering that the V&A was originally called the Museum of Manufactures (1857), it's appropriate that the screen was brought here, where it shows off the technical advances of the Industrial Revolution.

• To the right of the Grand Entrance lobby, look into a large hall of statues (Room 50a), including a spiraling statue of two battling men.

❸ Giambologna, *Samson Slaying a Philistine*, c. 1562

Carved from a single block of marble, the statue shows the testy Israelite warrior rearing back, brandishing the jawbone of an ass,

V&A MUSEUM

Victoria & Albert Museum Tour

TEMPORARY
EXHIBITS

1 Dale Chihuly Chandelier
2 Hereford Screen (above lobby)
3 GIAMBOLOGNA – Samson Slaying
   a Philistine
4 Medieval & Renaissance Galleries
5 Becket Casket
6 Boar & Bear Hunt Tapestry
7 Stairs to Leonardo Notebook
8 Michelangelo Casts
9 Islamic Art
10 Shiva Nataraja Statue
11 Possessions of Emperor Shah Jahan
12 Tipu's Tiger
13 Fashion Galleries
14 RAPHAEL – Tapestry Cartoons
15 British Galleries
16 Stairs up to Jewelry, Theater
   & British Silver

WC

To
16

JAPAN

CAST
COURT

ROOM
46

CAST
COURT

8

STAIRS
TO CAST
COURTS
VIEW

KOREA

7

5

6

⊠ ELEVATOR/LIFT

N

Not to Scale

To Harrods &
Hyde Park Corner →

BROMPTON ROAD

preparing to decapitate a man who'd insulted him. Samson pauses to make sure the Philistine looks him in the eye so he can see what's coming. Circle the statue and watch it spiral around its axis. Giambologna was clearly influenced by Michelangelo, who pioneered both the theme of the fallen enemy and the spiral-shaped pose that many artists imitated. Originally destined for a fountain in Florence, *Samson* instead found its way to London—the only major work of Giambologna's to leave Italy—in 1623. The V&A has (arguably) the best collection of Italian Renaissance sculpture outside Italy. We'll see more fine examples later.

• *From the Cromwell Road entry (near the revolving glass doors), find*

the entrance to the rooms labeled Medieval & Renaissance, 300-1500. *It's down a few steps, on level 0 (Rooms 8-10).*

❹ Medieval and Renaissance Galleries, A.D. 300-1500

Walk through 1,200 years of decorative arts, seeing how the mix of pagan-Roman and medieval-Christian elements created modern Europe.

It's A.D. 300, and Rome's Europe-wide empire is beginning to unravel. Within two centuries, its political dominance would be over, but Rome's culture lived on in the Christian faith. Rooms 8-10 show how traditional Roman media (mosaics, carved ivory, column-and-arch building techniques) were adapted to make Christian-themed art and churches.

• *About three-fourths of the way down the long Room 8 is a glass case displaying the shoebox-sized...*

❺ Becket Casket, c. 1180

The blue-and-gold box contains the mortal remains (or relics) of St. Thomas Becket, who was brutally murdered. Look at the scene depicted along the side—the Arch-bishop of Canterbury is about to grab a chalice from the altar, when knights tiptoe up, draw their swords, and slice off his head. Two shocked priests throw up their hands.

Becket's soul (upper right) is borne aloft on a sling by two angels. His body is laid to rest (upper left) and blessed by the new bishop. Mourners kneel at the tomb, just as the man behind Becket's murder— King Henry II—is said to have done, out of remorse.

Henry II had handpicked his good friend Thomas Becket (1118-1170) for the job of archbishop, assuming he'd follow the king's orders. In two days, Thomas was made a priest, a bishop, then archbishop—the head of all England's Christians. But when Becket proved loyal to the Church and opposed Henry's policies, the king, in a rash fit of anger, said he wanted Becket dead. Remorseful after his knights murdered the archbishop, Henry had 80 monks whip him, and then he spent all night at the foot of the tomb.

Just three years after his death, Becket was made a saint. Pieces of Becket's DNA—valuable relics—were conserved in this enamel-and-metal work box, a specialty of Limoges, France.

• *Continue straight to the far end of this long set of rooms. In Room 10a, you'll run right into...*

❻ Boar and Bear Hunt Tapestry, c. 1425-1430

Though most medieval art depicted the Madonna and saints, this colorful wool tapestry—woven in Belgium—provides a secular slice of life.

"Read" it from right to left: The nobles want to go hunting, so they hire some professional guides. One pro (in red) enters with his dogs and hunting horn, leading two nobles. His colleague (above) rousts bear cubs from their den, so the mama and papa bears can be flushed out into the open. Men and dogs (in the center) surround a bear, while another is lanced by a nobleman on horseback. Below, well-dressed ladies look on.

Continuing to the left, the hunt turns to wild boar, as two dogs flush one out of hiding. Finally (far left, bottom corner), the boar has been caught, and they begin to skin him for dinner.

In the nearby Room 10c, you'll find a **world map** (c. 1300) showing Christ sitting at the center of the known universe: Jerusalem. Try a little **brass rubbing** at the hands-on station.

• *Backtrack 50 yards and find the nearby staircase (or use the elevator). Head upstairs two floors to level 2 to see how the foundation of civilization laid in medieval times would launch the Renaissance. You'll spill out into Rooms 62-64b, labeled* Medieval & Renaissance, 1400-1600. *Enter through Room 64b, where you'll find (hiding behind a partition on the left) the tiny, pocket-size...*

❼ Notebook by Leonardo da Vinci, *Codex Forster III,* 1490-1493

Leonardo da Vinci—painter, sculptor, engineer, musician, and scientist—epitomized the merging of art, knowledge, and science

we call the Renaissance. He recorded his observations and inventions in tiny notebooks like this. This particular codex (or bound manuscript) dates from years when he was living in Milan, shortly before undertaking his famous *Last Supper* fresco. He was always busy, but completed little from this time.

The book's contents are all over the map: meticulous sketches of the human head, diagrams illustrating nature's geometrical perfection, a horse's leg for a huge equestrian statue, and even draw-ings of the latest ballroom fashions. The adjacent computer lets you scroll through three of his notebooks and even flip his backwards handwriting to make it readable.

In Room 64a (off to the left), an exhibit shows works by the sculptor Donatello, who blazed the artistic path followed by his fellow Florentine Michelangelo. This all leads (in Room 63, at the opposite end of Room 64) to works showing the new wealth of Europe as it enters the modern age.

• *Return to the top of the stairs and look across at the* Korea *and* Cast Courts *signs opposite. To go there, descend to level 1. Cross the big sculpture hall (Room 50b), and find two huge courts, Rooms 46a and 46b, labeled* The Cast Courts—*filled with replicas of famous statues. (Room 46a is closed for a few years, so we'll focus on 46b.)*

These two rooms recently took turns being renovated. Because these plaster casts are gigantic and hard to move, they were rehabbed right here where they stand. (For an overhead view of both galleries, go up the stairs at the Cast Courts entryway, and then come back down.) Enter Room 46b, and find...

❽ Michelangelo Casts and Other Replica Statues

These plaster-cast versions of famous Renaissance statues by Mi-chelangelo and others allowed 19th-century art students who

couldn't afford a rail pass to study the classics.

The statues were made by coating the original with a nonstick substance, then laying wet plaster strips over it that dried to form a mold, from which a plaster cast was made. They look solid but are very fragile. In a single glance, you can follow Michelangelo's career, from youthful optimism *(David)*, to his never-finished masterpiece (statues from the tomb of Julius II, including *Moses* and two *Slaves*), to full-blown midlife crisis (while sculpting the brooding Medici Tomb statues of Lorenzo and Giuliano). Compare Michelangelo's mon-umental *David* with Donatello's girlish *David* (nearby), and see Ghiberti's bronze Baptistery doors, which inspired the Florentine Renais-sance.

David was a gift from Tuscany to Queen Victoria, who immediately donated it to the museum. *David*'s giant clip-on fig leaf is usually hanging around somewhere nearby (ask a guard). This is the actual fig leaf that was hung on him when modest aristocrats visited (it was "the Victorian Age," after all). On the wall above David's right shoulder, you might recognize a copy of Raphael's *School of Athens* painting, pairing the biggest players of the Renaissance with the stars of antiquity (the original is in Rome's Vatican Museums). With Michelangelo front and center, it hangs appropriately over his most famous statue.

• *From the Cast Courts entryway, head down the long hallway, past Asian art and the shop, then turn right into Room 42, which contains art of the Islamic Middle East.*

❾ Islamic Art

While owing much to Islam as a religion, Islamic art also reflected a sophisticated secular culture. Many Islamic artists expressed themselves with beautiful but functional objects.

In the center of the room is the 630-square-foot Ardabil Carpet (1539-1540). Its silk-thread underpinnings are topped by a dense wool pile made of 304 knots per square inch. (Carpet connoisseurs will nod approvingly at this impressively high KPI number.) Woven on a huge standing loom, it likely took a dozen workers years to make. In the center of the design is a yellow medallion ringed with ovals, supporting two hanging lamps. If you sat on the carpet near the smaller of the two lamps, you'd have the illusion of a symmetrical pattern. The carpet is illuminated on the hour and half-hour.

Also in the room are more carpets, ceramics (mostly blue-and-white or red-and-white), and glazed tile—all covered top to bottom in similarly complex patterns. The intricate interweaving, repetition, and unending lines suggest the complex, infinite nature of God (Allah).

You'll likely see only a few pictures of humans or animals—the Islamic religion reserves the creation of living beings to God alone. However, secular art for homes and palaces was not bound by this, and you may see realistic depictions of men and women enjoying a garden paradise, a symbol of the Muslim heaven.

Notice floral patterns (twining vines, flowers, arabesques) and geometric designs (stars, diamonds). But the most common pattern is calligraphy—elaborate lettering of an inscription in Arabic, the language of the Quran (and the lettering used even in non-Arabic languages). A quote from the Quran on a vase or lamp combines the power of the message with the beauty of the calligraphy.

• *Return to the hall and continue on. In the hallway (technically "Room" 47b) is a glass case with a statue of...*

❿ Shiva Nataraja, 12th Century

The Hindu god Shiva—one of the hundreds, if not thousands, of godlike incarnations of Hinduism's eternal being, Brahma—steps lively and creates the world by dancing. His four arms are busy creating, and he treads on the sleepy dwarf of ignorance.

This bronze statue, one of Hinduism's most popular, is loaded with symbolism, summing up where humans came from and where we're going. Surrounded by a ring of fire, Shiva crosses a leg in time to the music. Smiling serenely, he blesses with one hand, while another beats out the rhythm of life with a hand drum. The cobra draped over his arm symbolizes the *Kundalini Sakti*, the cosmic energy inside each of us that can, with the right training, uncoil and bring us to enlightenment.

As long as Shiva keeps dancing, the universe will continue. But Shiva also holds a flame, a reminder that, at the end of time, he will transform into his female alter ego, Kali, and destroy the world by fire, clearing the slate for another round of existence.

• *Head through the doorway into the adjoining Room 41, labeled* South Asia. *You'll run right into a glass case in the center of the room containing small items that were the...*

⓫ Possessions of Emperor Shah Jahan, r. 1628-1658

Look at the cameo portrait, thumb ring, and wine cup (made of white nephrite jade, 1657) that belonged to one of the world's most powerful men.

Shah Jahan—or "King of the World"—ruled the largest empire of the day, covering northern India, Pakistan, and Afghanistan. His Mughal Empire was descended from Genghis Khan and the Mongol horde, who conquered and then settled in central Asia and converted to Islam. Shah Jahan was known for his building projects, especially the Taj Mahal (see a picture of it nearby), built as a mausoleum for his favorite wife, Mumtaz, who bore him 14 children before dying in childbirth.

The British in India

December 31, 1600: The British East India Company—a multinational trading company owned by stockholders—is founded with a charter from Queen Elizabeth I. They're given a virtual monopoly on trade with India.

1600s: The British trade peacefully with Indian locals on the coast, competing with France, Holland, and Portugal for access to spices, cotton, tea, indigo, and jute (for ropemaking).

1700s: As the Mughal (Islamic) Empire breaks down, Britain and France vie for trade ports and inland territory. By the 1750s, Britain is winning. Britain establishes itself in Bombay, Madras, and Calcutta. First they rule through puppet Mughal leaders, then dump local leaders altogether.

1800s: By midcentury, two-thirds of the subcontinent is under British rule, exporting opium and tea (transplanted from its native China) and importing British-made cloth. Britain tries to reform Indian social customs (such as outlawing widow suicides) with little long-lasting effect. They build railways, roads, and irrigation systems.

1857-1858: The "Indian Mutiny"—sparked by high taxes, British monopoly of trade, and a chafing against foreign rule—is the first of many uprisings that slowly erode British power.

1900s: Two world wars drain and distract Britain while Indians lobby for self-rule.

August 15, 1947: After a decade of peaceful protests led by Mahatma Gandhi, India gains its independence.

His unsuccessful attempts to expand the empire drained the treasury. In his old age, his sons quarreled over the inheritance. Imprisoned by his sons in the Agra fort, Shah Jahan died gazing across the river at the Taj Mahal, where he, too, would be buried. India's glory days were ending. And then came the British.

• *At the far end of Room 41 (in a case facing the rear door) is the huge wood-carved...*

⑫ Tipu's Tiger, 1790s

This life-size robotic toy, once owned by an oppressed Indian sultan (see Tipu's portrait and belongings nearby), is perhaps better called "India's revenge." The  Bengal tiger has a British redcoat down, sinking its teeth into his neck. When you turned the crank, the Brit's left arm would flail, and both he and the tiger would roar through organ pipes. (The mechanism still works.)

Tipu, the Sultan of Mysore (1750-1799), called himself the "Tiger of Mysore." He was well-educated in several languages and collected a library of 2,000 books. An enlightened ruler, he built roads and dams and promoted new technology. Tipu could see that India was being swallowed up by the all-powerful British East India Company. He allied himself with France and fought several successful wars against the British, but he was eventually defeated and forced to give up half his kingdom to them. Tipu was later killed by the Brits in battle (1799), his palace ransacked, and his possessions—including this toy—were taken, like much of India, by the British East India Company.

• *Backtrack out of Room 41 and turn right, then right again into Room 40. Here you'll find the...*

⓭ Fashion Galleries

Centuries of English fashion are corseted chronologically into 40 display cases along a runway. You'll see the evolution of fashion from ladies' underwear, hoop skirts, and rain gear to high-society evening wear, men's suits, and more. The mantua dress, on the far right, is an example of court couture from the mid-18th century. Temporary exhibits here usually enliven the displays. Circle the room and reminisce about old trends—and how some are becoming new again. For more on English fashion, visit the British Galleries (described later).

• *Directly across the hall from Room 40 is the cavernous Room 48a, filled with...*

⓮ Raphael's Tapestry Cartoons

For Christmas in 1519, Pope Leo X unveiled 10 new tapestries in the Sistine Chapel, designed by the famous artist Raphael. The project was one of the largest ever undertaken by a painter—it cost far more than Michelangelo's Sistine ceiling—and when it was done, the tapestries were a hit, inspiring princes across Europe to decorate their palaces in masterpieces of cloth.

The V&A owns seven of the full-size designs by Raphael that were used to produce the tapestries (approximately 13 by 17 feet, done in tempera on paper, now mounted on canvas). The cartoons were sent to factories in Brussels, cut into strips (see the lines), and placed on the looms. The scenes are the reverse of the final product—lots of left-handed saints.

Raphael (1483-1520) chose scenes from the Acts of the Apostles—particularly of Peter and Paul, the two early saints most associated with Rome, the seat of the popes. Knowing where the tapes-

tries were to be hung, Raphael was determined to top Michelangelo's famous Sistine ceiling, with its huge, dramatic figures and subtle color effects. He matched Michelangelo's body-builder muscles (for example, the fishermen in *The Miraculous Draught of Fishes*), dramatic gestures, and reaction shots (as in the busy crowd scenes in *St. Paul Preaching in Athens*), and he exceeded Michelangelo in the subtleties of color.

Unfortunately, it was difficult to reproduce Raphael's painted nuances in the tapestry workshop. Traditional tapestries were simple, depicting either set patterns or block figures on a neutral background. Raphael challenged the Flemish weavers. Each brushstroke had to be reproduced by a colored thread woven horizontally. The finished tapestries (which are still in the Vatican) were glorious, but these cartoons capture Raphael's original vision.

• *From the Raphael room (48a), go up the staircase. At the top of the stairs (on level 2), turn left into Room 57. This is the heart of the British Galleries, featuring the Great Bed of Ware and Elizabethan miniatures.*

⓯ British Galleries

Room 57 covers the era of Queen Elizabeth I. Find rare miniature portraits—a popular item of the day—including Hilliard's oft-reproduced *Young Man Among Roses* miniature, capturing the romance of a Shakespeare sonnet. Also in the room are musical instruments and suits of armor—a love-and-war combination appropriate to the Elizabethan Age. Finally, there's the Great Bed of Ware. Built as a tourist-attracting gimmick by an English inn around 1600, this four-

poster bed still wows. Look closely to see where couples notched their initials into the headboard and bedposts. You and six of your favorite friends could bed down here, taking a well-earned rest after this eclectic tour.

Continue into the next room (Room 58), dedicated to *Birth, Marriage, and Death*, and displaying swaddling clothes, a wedding portrait, and a casket pall. Continuing on, you'll pass through a couple of alcoves with Tudor-era tapestries. The far end of Room 58, devoted to Henry VIII, has a portrait of him; his writing box (with quill pens, ink, and sealing wax); and a whole roomful of the fancy furniture, tapestries, jewelry, and dinnerware that may have decorated his palaces.

If you're interested, there's much more to the British Galleries, which sweep chronologically through 400 years of British high-class living (1500-1900)—all laid out over two floors and beautifully described.

• For now, pop out the doorway of Room 58. You'll notice we've come full circle: You're overlooking the Grand Entrance lobby. This tour is officially over. But if you'd like more suggestions, there's great stuff upstairs.

⑯ Jewelry, Theater, Silver, and More

• From the Grand Entrance lobby, pass through the shop, turn right into Room 24, and climb the staircase to level 3.

Jewelry (Rooms 91-93): This collection is understandably popular. In one long, glittering gallery, you can trace the evolution of jewelry from ancient Egyptian, Greek, and Roman to the 20th century. The Art Nouveau style of Parisian jeweler Rene Lalique is hard not to love.

• Exit the jewelry rooms at the far end and turn right to find...

Theater and Performance (Rooms 103-106): With artifacts from Hamlet skulls to rock-and-roll tour posters, this exhibit records the history of live performance in the UK. Kids will enjoy the costumes from *The Lion King* and the dress-up costume box. Nearby, aging boomers will see Mick Jagger's jumpsuit...and marvel that he used to fit into it.

• Exit the collection where you entered, turn right (into "Prints & Drawings"), then left to find...

British Silver (Rooms 65-69): The displays in these galleries are bursting with flamboyant silver treasures dating from the 1600s to modern times, including teething rattles, gambling counters, punch bowls, and pitchers.

• I'll leave you here (find exit stairs at the far-right end of Room 74), but there's plenty left to see. If you have stamina, use your V&A map to plot the rest of your Grand Tour of this museum.

TATE BRITAIN TOUR

The National Gallery of British Art, otherwise known as the Tate Britain, features the world's best collection of British art—sweeping you from 1500 until today. This is people's art, with realistic paintings rooted in the individuals, landscape, and stories of the British Isles. The Tate shows off Hogarth's stage sets, Gainsborough's ladies, Blake's angels, Constable's clouds, Turner's tempests, the naturalistic realism of the Pre-Raphaelites, and the camera-eye portraits of Hockney and Freud. Even if these names are new to you, don't worry. You'll likely see a few "famous" works you didn't know were British and exit the Tate Britain with at least one new favorite artist.

Orientation

Cost: Free, £4 suggested donation; fee for special exhibits.

Hours: Daily 10:00-18:00, last entry 45 minutes before closing.

Information: Tel. 020/7887-8888, www.tate.org.uk.

Getting There: It's on the Thames River, south of Big Ben and north of Vauxhall Bridge. You can reach the museum by Tube, ferry, bus, or on foot:

>**By Tube:** Tube: Pimlico plus seven-minute walk.

>**By Ferry:** Hop on Thames Clippers' Tate Boat ferry from the Tate Modern (Bankside Pier) for a 15-minute crossing (£8 one-way, departs every 40 minutes Mon-Fri 10:15-15:45, Sat-Sun 9:40-18:15).

>**By Bus:** Bus #87 leaves from the National Gallery, and drops off in front of the Tate. Bus #88 leaves from Oxford Circus, and drops off behind the museum. Both connect the museum to Westminster.

On Foot: From Big Ben, walk 15 minutes south along the Thames.

Visitor Information: Pick up a map (£1 suggested donation) at the information desk. The museum's shops are great for books, magazines, and trinkets.

Tours: Free **guided tours** are generally offered daily at 11:00, 12:00, 14:00, and 15:00. Or download the Tate's handy **app** for a room-by-room guide.

Length of This Tour: Allow one hour.

Services: Bag and coat check are free.

Cuisine Art: Your options are a **$ café** with an affordable gourmet buffet line (daily 10:00-17:30) or a pricey **$$$$ restaurant** serving two- or three-course fixed-price meals (daily 12:00-15:00).

Starring: Hogarth, Gainsborough, Reynolds, Blake, Constable, Pre-Raphaelites, and Turner.

Know Your Tates: Don't confuse the Tate Britain (British art) with the Tate Modern (on the South Bank of the Thames across from St. Paul's Cathedral), which features modern art.

ORIEN-TATE: GALLERY IN MOTION

This tour covers, in roughly chronological order, British paintings from 1500 to today. Works from the early centuries are located in the west half of the building, 20th-century art is in the east half, the works of J. M. W. Turner and John Constable are in an adjacent wing (the Clore Gallery), and William Blake's work is upstairs. There are also temporary exhibits (some free, some requiring an entrance fee).

The Tate rotates its vast collection of paintings, so it's difficult to predict exactly which works will be on display. Pick up the latest map as you enter or download the museum's helpful app. Consider reading this chapter ahead of time as an overview of British art, then let the Tate surprise you with its current array of masterpieces.

The Tour Begins

British artists painted people, countrysides, and scenes from daily life, realistically and without the artist passing judgment (substance over style). What you won't see here are the fleshy goddesses, naked baby angels, and Madonna-and-child altarpieces so popular elsewhere in Europe. The largely Protestant English abhorred the "graven images" of the wealthy Catholic world; many such images were destroyed during the 16th-century Reformation. They preferred portraits of flesh-and-blood English folk.

• *Services are nearly all downstairs. From the main Millbank entrance,*

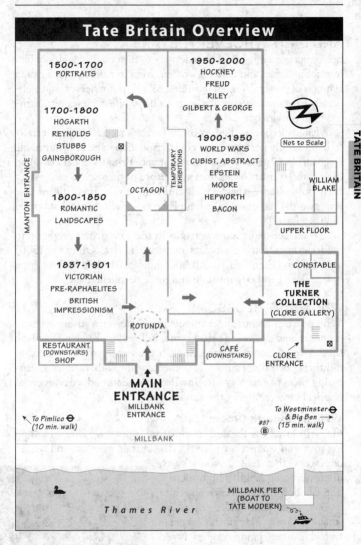

Tate Britain Overview

1500-1700
PORTRAITS

1700-1800
HOGARTH
REYNOLDS
STUBBS
GAINSBOROUGH

1800-1850
ROMANTIC
LANDSCAPES

1837-1901
VICTORIAN
PRE-RAPHAELITES
BRITISH
IMPRESSIONISM

1950-2000
HOCKNEY
FREUD
RILEY
GILBERT & GEORGE

1900-1950
WORLD WARS
CUBIST, ABSTRACT
EPSTEIN
MOORE
HEPWORTH
BACON

MANTON ENTRANCE

OCTAGON

TEMPORARY EXHIBITIONS

ROTUNDA

RESTAURANT
(DOWNSTAIRS)
SHOP

CAFÉ
(DOWNSTAIRS)

Not to Scale

WILLIAM
BLAKE

UPPER FLOOR

CONSTABLE

**THE
TURNER
COLLECTION**
(CLORE GALLERY)

CLORE
ENTRANCE

**MAIN
ENTRANCE**
MILLBANK
ENTRANCE

← To Pimlico ⊖
(10 min. walk)

To Westminster ⊖
& Big Ben →
(15 min. walk)

#87
Ⓑ

MILLBANK

MILLBANK PIER
(BOAT TO
TATE MODERN)

Thames River

TATE BRITAIN

you can walk directly under the bright white rotunda and down the long central hall, usually adorned with sculpture or temporary installations.

Near the far end, look for the **Walk Through British Art** sign and, on the wall, a small brass representation of the museum labeled 500 Years of British Art *(with dates ringing the building like a map)*. You'll see these same dates inset in brass as you enter each room. Throughout this tour, I'll refer to these numbers (in parentheses) to make following along easier.

From here, step into the beginnings of British painting. *(Look on the floor and find the inset 1540.)*

1500-1700—PORTRAITS OF LORD AND LADY WHOEVERTHEYARE

Stuffy portraits of a beef-fed society try to turn crude country nobles into refined men and delicate women. Men in ruffled collars clutch symbols of power. Women in ruffled collars, puffy sleeves, and elaborately patterned dresses display their lily-white complexions, turning their pinkies out.

English country houses often had a long hall built specially to hang family portraits. You could stroll along and see your noble forebears looking down their noses at you. Britain's upper crust had little interest in art other than as a record of themselves along with their possessions—their wives, children, jewels, furs, ruffled collars, swords, and guns. (With no Facebook back then, what option did they have?)

You'll see many more portraits in the Tate Britain, right up to modern times. Each era had its own style. Portraits from the 1500s are stern and dignified. The 1600s (room marked *1650*) brought a more relaxed and elegant style and more décolletage.

1700s—ART BLOSSOMS

With peace at home (under three King Georges), a strong overseas economy, and a growing urban center in London, England's artistic life began to bloom. As the English grew more sophisticated, so did their portraits. Painters branched out into other subjects, capturing slices of everyday life. The Royal Academy added a veneer of classical Greece to even the simplest subjects.

William Hogarth (Room 1730)

Hogarth loved the theater. "My picture is my stage," he said, "and my men and women my players." The curtain goes up, and we see one scene that tells a whole story, often satirizing English high society. The London theater scene came into its own (after post-Shakespeare censorship) during Hogarth's generation. He often painted series based on popular plays of the time.

A born Londoner, Hogarth loved every gritty aspect of the big city. You'd find him in seedy pubs and brothels, at the half-price ticket booth in Leicester Square, at prizefights, cockfights, duels, and public executions—all with sketchbook in hand. An 18th-century Charles Dickens, he exposed the hypocrisy of fat-bellied squires, vain ladies, and gluttonous priests. He also gave the upper classes a glimpse into the hidden poverty of "merry olde England"—poor soldiers with holes in their stockings, overworked servants, and unwed mothers.

Hogarth's portraits (and self-portraits) are unflinchingly honest, quite different from the powdered-wig fantasies of his contemporaries. Hogarth was an accomplished engraver; his works were mass-produced, giving Londoners a sense of their city and themselves.

Sir Joshua Reynolds and the "Grand Manner" (Room 1760)

Real life wasn't worthy of a painting. So said Sir Joshua Reynolds, the pillar of Britain's Royal Academy. Instead, people, places, and

things had to be gussied up with Greek columns, symbolism, and great historic moments, ideally from classical Greece.

In his portraits, he'd pose Lady Bagbody like the Medici Venus, or Lord Milquetoast like Apollo Belvedere. In landscapes you get Versailles-type settings of classical monuments amid perfectly manicured greenery. Inspired by Rembrandt, Reynolds sometimes used dense, clotted paint to capture the look of the Old Masters.

This art was meant to elevate the viewer, to appeal to his rational nature and fill him with noble sentiment. Sir Joshua Reynolds stood for all that was upright, tasteful, rational, brave, clean, reverent, and...zzzzzzz....

George Stubbs (Room 1760)

Stubbs was the Michelangelo of horse painters. He understood these creatures from the inside out, having dissected them in his studio. He even used machinery to prop the corpses up into lifelike poses. He painted the horses first on a blank canvas, then filled in the background landscape around them (notice the heavy outlines that make them stand out clearly from

the countryside). The result is both incredibly natural—from the veins in their noses to their freshly brushed coats—and geometrically posed.

Thomas Gainsborough (Room 1780)

Gainsborough showcased the elegant, educated women of his generation. He portrayed them as they wished to see themselves: a feminine ideal, patterned after fashion magazines. The cheeks are rosy, the poses relaxed and S-shaped, the colors brighter and more pastel, showing the influence of the refined French culture of the court at Versailles. His ladies tiptoe gracefully toward us, with clear, Ivory-soap complexions that stand out from the swirling greenery of English gardens. (Though he painted portraits, he longed to do landscapes.) Gainsborough worked hard to prettify his subjects, but the results were always natural and never stuffy.

1800-1850—THE INDUSTRIAL REVOLUTION

Newfangled inventions were everywhere. Railroads laced the land. You could fall asleep in Edinburgh and wake up in London, a trip that used to take days or weeks. But along with technology came factories coating towns with soot, urban poverty, regimentation, and clock-punching. Machines replaced honest laborers, and once-noble Man was viewed as a naked ape.

Strangely, you'll see little of the modern world in paintings of the time—except in reaction to it. Many artists rebelled against "progress" and the modern world. They escaped the dirty cities to commune with nature (John Constable and the Romantics). Or they found a new spirituality in intense human emotions (dramatic scenes from history or literature). Or they left the modern world altogether.

• *Step into the grand Harry and Carol Djanogly Gallery.*

"Romantic" Landscapes—Art and the Sublime (Room 1810)

Artists in the Romantic style saw the most intense human emotions reflected in the drama and mystery of nature. Some of them mixed landscapes with intense human emotion to produce huge, colorful canvases depicting storms, burning sunsets, towering clouds, and crashing waves, all dwarfing puny humans.

History paintings reflected great moments from the past, from ancient Greece to medieval knights, Napoleon to Britain's battles abroad. These were seen as the classiest form of art, combining the high drama of heroic acts with refined technique.

Other artists made supernatural, religious fantasy-scapes. God is found within nature, and nature is charged with the grandeur and power of God. (You'll see this in the extreme with Blake at the end of this tour.)

1837-1901—THE VICTORIAN ERA

In the world's wealthiest nation, the prosperous middle class dictated taste in art. They admired paintings that were realistic

(showcasing the artist's talent and work ethic), depicting Norman Rockwell-style slices of everyday life.

We see families and ordinary people eating, working, and relaxing. Some paintings tug at the heartstrings, with scenes of parting couples, the grief of death, or the joy of families reuniting. Dramatic scenes from classical (Chaucer and Shakespeare) and popular literature get the heart beating. There's the occasional touching look at the plight of the honest poor, reminiscent of Dickens. Many paintings warn us to be good little boys and girls by showing the consequences of a life of sin. And then there are the puppy dogs with sad eyes.

TATE BRITAIN

The Pre-Raphaelites (Room 1840)

You'll see medieval damsels in dresses and knights in tights, legendary lovers from poetry, and even a very human Virgin Mary as a delicate young woman. The women wear flowing dresses and have long, wavy hair and delicate, elongated, curving bodies. Beautiful.

Overdosed with the gushy sentimentality of their day, a band of 20-year-old artists—including Sir John Everett Millais, Dante Gabriel Rossetti, and William Holman Hunt—said "Enough!" and dedicated themselves to creating less saccharine art. Their "Pre-Raphaelite Brotherhood" (you may see the initials P. R. B. by the artist's signature) returned to a style "pre-Raphael"—that is, "medieval" in its simple style, in its melancholy mood, and often in its subject matter.

"Truth to Nature" was their slogan. Like the Impressionists who followed them, they donned their scarves, barged out of the stuffy studio, and set up outdoors, painting trees, streams, and people, like scientists on a field trip. Still, they often captured nature

with such a close-up clarity that it's downright unnatural. And despite the Pre-Raphaelite claim to paint life just as it is, this is so beautiful it hurts.

This is art from the cult of femininity, worshipping Woman's haunting beauty, compassion,

and depth of soul (proto-feminism or nouveau-chauvinism?). The artists' wives and lovers were their models and muses, and the art echoed their love lives. The people are surrounded by nature at its most beautiful, with every detail painted crystal clear. Even without the people, there is a mood of melancholy.

The Pre-Raphaelites hated overacting. Their subjects—even in the face of great tragedy, high passions, and moral dilemmas—barely raise an eyebrow. Outwardly, they're reflective, accepting their fate. But sinuous postures—with lovers swooning into each other, and parting lovers swooning apart—speak volumes. These volumes are footnoted by the small objects with symbolic importance placed around them: red flowers denoting passion, lilies for purity, pets for fidelity, and so on.

The colors—greens, blues, and reds—are bright and clear, with everything evenly lit, so that we see every detail. To get the luminous color, some painted a

thin layer of bright paint over a pure white, still-wet undercoat, which subtly "shines" through. These canvases radiate a pure spirituality, like stained-glass windows.

Stand for a while and enjoy the exquisite realism and human emotions of these Victorian-era works...flesh-and-blood people painted realistically. Get your fill, because beloved Queen Victoria is about to check out, the modern world is coming, and, with it, new art to express modern attitudes.

BRITISH IMPRESSIONISM

Realistic British art stood apart from the modernist trends in France, but some influences drifted across the Channel (Rooms 1890 and 1900). John Singer Sargent (American-born) studied with Parisian Impressionists, learning the thick, messy brushwork and play of light at twilight. James Tissot used Degas' snapshot technique to capture a crowded scene from an odd angle. And James McNeill Whistler (born in America, trained in Paris, lived in London) composed his paintings like music—see some of his paintings' titles. These collages of shapes and colors please the eye like a song tickles the ear.

Whistler signed his paintings with his initials in the shape of a butterfly. You may also see sophisticated works by London's own

"Bloomsbury Group," who put a British spin on French Post-Impressionism.

1900-1950—WORLD WARS

As two world wars whittled down the powerful British Empire, it still remained a major cultural force.

British art mirrored many of the trends and "-isms" pioneered in Paris (room marked *1930*). You'll see Cubism like Picasso's, abstract art like Mondrian's, and so on. But British artists also continued the British tradition of realistic paintings of people and landscapes. (Note: You'll find 20th-century artists' work both here in the Tate Britain and in the Tate Modern—☐ see also the Tate Modern Tour chapter.)

World War I, in which Britain lost a million men, cast a long shadow over the land. Artists expressed the horror of war, particularly of dehumanizing battles pitting powerful machines against puny human pawns. **Jacob Epstein**'s gleaming, abstract statues (room marked *1940*) suggest mangled half-human/half-machine forms.

Henry Moore

Twice a week, young Henry Moore went to the British Museum to sketch ancient statues, especially reclining ones (as in the Parthenon pediment or the Mayan god, Chac Mool, which he saw in a photo). His statues—mostly female, mostly reclining—catch the primitive power of carved stone. Moore almost always carved with his own hands (unlike, say, Rodin, who modeled a small clay figure and let assistants chisel the real thing), capturing the human body in a few simple curves, with minimal changes to the rock itself.

The statues do look vaguely like what their titles say, but it's the stones themselves that are really interesting. Notice the texture and graininess of these mini Stonehenges; feel the weight, the space they take up, and how the rock forms intermingle.

During World War II, Moore passed time in the bomb shelters sketching mothers with babes in arms, a theme found in later works.

Moore carves the human body with the epic scale and restless poses of Michelangelo but with the crude rocks and simple lines of the primitives.

Barbara Hepworth (Room 1930)

Hepworth's small-scale carvings in stone and wood—like "mini Moores"—make even holes look interesting. Though they're not exactly realistic, it isn't hard to imagine them being inspired by, say, a man embracing a woman (she called it "sex harmony"), or the shoreline encircling a bay near her Cornwall-coast home, or a cliff penetrated by a cave—that is, two forms intermingling.

Francis Bacon (Room 1940)

With a stiff upper lip, Britain survived the Blitz, World War II, and the loss of hundreds of thousands of men—but at war's end, the bottled-up horror came rushing out. Bacon's 1945 exhibition, opening just after Holocaust details began surfacing, stunned London with its unmitigated ugliness.

His deformed half-humans/half-animals—caged in a claustrophobic room, with twisted hunk-of-meat bodies and quadriplegic, smudged-mouth helplessness—can do nothing but scream in anguish and frustration. The scream becomes a blur, as though it goes on forever.

Bacon, largely self-taught, uses "traditional" figurativism, painting somewhat recognizable people and things. His subjects express the existential human predicament of being caught in a world not of your making, isolated and helpless to change it.

• *From here (the room marked 1940), you could venture into the Turner Collection in the Clore Gallery. But first, finish this walk through 500 years of British art.*

1950-2000—MODERN WORLD

No longer a world power, Britain in the Swinging '60s became a major exporter of pop culture. British art's traditional strengths—realism, portraits, landscapes, and slice-of-life scenes—were redone in the modern style (Room 1950 and on). Be aware that of all the Tate's changing displays, the modern collection changes the most. These particular artists may not all be on display, but other equally-deserving artists will be.

David Hockney

The "British Andy Warhol"—who is bleach-blond, horn-rimmed, gay, and famous—paints "pop"-ular culture with photographic realism. Large, airy canvases of L.A. swimming pools, double portraits of his friends in their stylish homes, or mundane scenes from the artist's own life capture the superficial materialism of the 1970s and 1980s. (Is he satirizing or glorifying it by painting it on a monumental scale with painstaking detail?)

Hockney saturates the canvas with bright (acrylic) paint, eliminating any haze, making distant objects as clear and bright as close ones. This technique, combined with his slightly simplified "cutout" figures, gives the painting the flat look of a billboard.

Lucian Freud

Sigmund's grandson (who emigrated from Nazi Germany as a boy) puts every detail on the couch for analysis, then reassembles them

into works that are still surprisingly realistic. His subjects look you right in the eye, slightly on edge. Even the plants create an ominous mood. Everything is in sharp focus (unlike in real life, where you concentrate on one thing while your peripheral vision is blurred). Thick brushwork is especially good at capturing the pallor of British flesh.

In the great tradition of British portrait painting, Freud completed an unflinching (and controversial) portrait of Queen Elizabeth in 2001.

Bridget Riley

The pioneer of Op Art paints patterns of lines and alternating colors that make the eye vibrate (the way a spiral will "spin") when you stare at them. These obscure, scientific experiments in human optics suddenly became trendy in the psychedelic, cannabis-fueled 1960s. Like, wow.

Gilbert and George

The Siegfried and Roy of art satirize the "Me Generation" and its shameless self-marketing by portraying their nerdy, three-piece-suited selves on the monumental scale normally dedicated to kings, popes, and saints.

• *You've finished your walk through 500 years of British art. Now, return to the room marked* 1940 *and head into the Clore Gallery, where you'll find several rooms dedicated to Turner, a single room for Constable, and across from that room a staircase leading you up into the otherworldly domain of William Blake.*

THE TURNER COLLECTION

The Tate Britain has the world's best collection of works by J. M. W. Turner (1775-1851). Walking through his life's work, you can trace his progression from a painter of realistic historical scenes, through his wandering years, to Impressionist paintings of color-and-light patterns.

• *As you explore the collection, you'll watch Turner's style evolve from clear-eyed realism to hazy proto-Impressionism. You'll also see how Turner dabbled in different subjects: landscapes, seascapes, Roman ruins, snapshots of Venice, and so on. (While some of the specific paintings I refer to may not be on display, similar ones will be in their place.)*

TATE BRITAIN

Self-Portrait as a Young Man

At 24, Turner has just been elected the youngest Associate of the Royal Academy. The son of a Covent Garden barber now dresses like a gentleman. His clear, realistic painting style caught the public's fancy. The full-frontal pose and intense gaze of this portrait show a young man ready to take on the world.

The Royal Academy Years

Trained in the Reynolds school of grandiose epics, Turner painted the obligatory big canvases of great moments in history—*The Destruction of Sodom, Hannibal and His Army Crossing the Alps, The Lost ATM Card, Jason and the Argonauts,* and various shipwrecks. Not content to crank them out in the traditional staid manner, he sets them in expansive landscapes. Nature's stormy mood mirrors the human events, but is so grandiose it dwarfs them.

This is a theme we'll see throughout his works: The forces of nature—the burning sun, swirling clouds, churning waves, gathering storms, and the weathering of time—overwhelm men and wear down the civilizations they build.

Travels with Turner

Turner's true love was nature—he was a born hobo. Oblivious to the wealth and fame that his early paintings gave him, he set out traveling—mostly on foot—throughout England and the Continent, with a rucksack full of sketch pads and painting gear. He sketched the English countryside—not green, leafy, and placid as so many others had done, but churning in motion, hazed over by a burning sunset.

He found the "sublime" not in the studio or in church, but in the overwhelming power of nature. The landscapes throb with life and motion. He sets Constable's clouds on fire.

Italy's Landscape and Ruins

With a Rick Steves guidebook in hand, Turner visited the great museums of Italy, drawing inspiration from the Renaissance masters. He painted the classical monuments and Renaissance architecture. He copied masterpieces, admired the works of the French classicist Claude Lorrain, and fused a great variety of styles—a true pan-European vision. Turner's Roman ruins are not grand; they're dwarfed by the landscape around them and eroded by swirling, misty, luminous clouds.

Stand close to a big canvas of Roman ruins, close enough so that it fills your whole field of vision. Notice how the buildings seem to wrap around you. Turner was a master of using multiple perspectives to draw the viewer in. On the one hand, you're right in the thick of things, looking "up" at the tall buildings. Then again, you're looking "down" on the distant horizon, as though standing on a mountaintop.

Venice

I know what color the palazzo is. But what color is it at sunset? Or through the filter of the watery haze that hangs over Venice? Can

I paint the glowing haze itself? Maybe if I combine two different colors and smudge the paint on....

Venice stoked Turner's lust for reflected, golden sunlight. You'll see both finished works and unfinished sketches...uh, which is which?

Seascapes

The ever-changing sea was his specialty, with waves, clouds, mist, and sky churning and mixing together, all driven by the same forces.

Turner used oils like many painters use watercolors. First, he'd lay down a background (a "wash") of large patches of color, then he'd add a few dabs of paint to suggest a figure. (Some artists might use pencil lines to sketch out their figures, but Turner avoided that.) The final product lacked photographic clarity but showed the power and constant change in the forces of nature. He was perhaps the most prolific painter ever, with some 2,000 finished paintings and 20,000 sketches and watercolors.

Late Works

The older Turner got, the messier both he and his paintings became. He was wealthy, but he died in a run-down dive, where

he'd set up house with a prostitute. Yet the colors are brighter and the subjects less pessimistic than in the dark and brooding early canvases. His last works—whether landscape, religious, or classical scenes—are a blur and swirl of colors in motion, lit by the sun or a lamp burning through the mist. Even Turner's own creations were finally dissolved by the swirling forces of nature.

These paintings are "modern" in that the subject is less important than the style. You'll have to read the title to "get" it. You could argue that an Englishman helped invent Impressionism a generation before Monet and his ilk boxed the artistic ears of Paris in the 1880s. Turner's messy use of paint to portray reflected light "Chunneled" its way to France to inspire the Impressionists.

• *Now, head for the corner room of the Clore Gallery that's dedicated to Turner's great rival and contemporary...*

JOHN CONSTABLE

Constable (1776-1837) brought painting back into the real world. Although the Royal Academy thought Nature needed makeup, Constable thought she was just fine. He painted the English landscape as it was—realistically, without idealizing it. With simple earth tones he caught leafy green trees, gathering gray skies, brown country lanes, and rivers the color of the clouds reflected in them. Many details came from actual landscapes and villages from his childhood roots in Suffolk.

Clouds are Constable's trademark. Appreciate the effort involved in sketching ever-changing cloud patterns for hours on end—the mix of dark clouds and white clouds, cumulus and stratus, the colors of sunset. A generation before the Impressionists, he actually set up his easel outdoors and painted on the spot, a painstaking process before the invention of ready-made paints-in-a-tube (about 1850).

It's rare to find a Constable (or any British) landscape that doesn't have the mark of man in it—a cottage, hay cart, field hand, or a country road running through the scene. For him, the English countryside and its people were one.

In his later years, Constable's canvases became bigger, the style more "Impressionistic" (messier brushwork), and he worked more from memory than observation.

Constable's commitment to unvarnished nature wasn't fully recognized in his lifetime, and he was forced to paint portraits for his keep. The neglect caused him to ask a friend, "Can it therefore be wondered at that I paint continual storms?"

• *Across the last Turner room from here (about 30 yards away) is a nondescript stairway leading upstairs to the William Blake collection. Good luck...*

WILLIAM BLAKE

At the age of four, Blake (1757-1827) saw the face of God. A few years later, he ran across a flock of angels swinging in a tree. Twenty years later, he was living in a run-down London flat with an illiterate wife, scratching out a thin existence as an engraver. But even in this squalor, ignored by all but a few fellow artists, he still had his heavenly visions, and he described them in poems, paintings, drawings, and prints.

One of the original space cowboys, Blake also was a unique artist, often classed with the Romantics because he painted in a fit of ecstatic inspiration rather than by studied technique. He painted angels, not the dull material world. While Britain was conquering the world with guns and nature with machines, and while his fellow Londoners were growing rich, fat, and self-important, Blake turned his gaze inward, illustrating the glorious visions of the soul.

Blake's work hangs in a darkened room to protect his watercolors from deterioration. Enter his mysterious world and let your pupils dilate opium-wide.

His pen and watercolor sketches glow with an unearthly aura. In visions of the Christian heaven or Dante's hell, his figures have superhero musculature. The colors are almost translucent.

Blake saw the material world as bad, trapping the divine spark inside each of our bodies and keeping us from true communion with God. Blake's prints illustrate his views on the ultimate weakness of material, scientific man. Despite their Greek-god anatomy, his men look noble but tragically lost.

A famous poet as well as painter, Blake summed up his distrust of the material world in a poem addressed to "The God of this World"—that is, Satan:

Tho' thou art Worship'd by the Names Divine
Of Jesus and Jehovah, thou art still
The Son of Morn in weary Night's decline,
The lost Traveller's Dream under the Hill.

THE REST OF THE MUSEUM

We've covered 500 years, with social satire from Hogarth to Hockney, from Constable's placid landscapes to Turner's churning scenes, from Blake's inner visions to Pre-Raphaelite fantasies, from realistic portraits to...realistic portraits.

But the Tate's great strength is championing contemporary British art in special exhibitions. There are generally two exhibition spaces: one in the east half of the main floor (often free), and another downstairs (usually requiring separate admission). Explore the cutting-edge art from one of the world's thriving cultural capitals: London.

Or, enough Tate? Great. It's late.

GREENWICH TOUR

Still well within the city limits of London, the Royal Borough of Greenwich (GREN-ich)—England's maritime capital—feels like a small town all its own. Visitors come here for all things salty. The area's premier attraction is the *Cutty Sark* clipper. Next on the list is the Royal Observatory Greenwich, where you can literally straddle the planet's prime meridian and learn how the invention of Greenwich Mean Time advanced the art of seafaring.

Beyond these, choose your favorites. The fine National Maritime Museum traces the days when Britannia ruled the waves. The former Naval College—a campus of stately Baroque buildings dotting sweeping lawns—features the glorious Sistine-Chapel-like Painted Chapel. Then there's the town of Greenwich itself, with its appealing markets, Georgian architecture, fleet of nautical shops, plentiful parks, historic taverns, and hordes of tourists.

Greenwich's sights appeal to both serious students of the maritime sciences as well as kids and families. It makes for an easy day trip by boat or the Docklands Light Railway (DLR). And where else can you set your watch with such accuracy? Note that Greenwich pairs perfectly with a quick visit to the neighboring Docklands, London's glittering skyscraper zone (covered in the next chapter).

GETTING TO GREENWICH

It's a joy by boat or a snap by the DLR. I take the boat there for the scenery and commentary, and take the DLR back to avoid late-afternoon boat crowds—and in case I want to stop at the Docklands on the way home.

By Boat: From central London, various tour boats—with commentary and open-deck seating—leave for Greenwich from the piers at Westminster, the London Eye, and the Tower of London (2/hour, 30-75 minutes).

Thames Clippers offers faster trips, with no commentary and only a small deck at the stern (departs every 20-30 minutes from several piers in central London, 20-45 minutes). Thames Clippers also connects Greenwich to the Docklands' Canary Wharf Pier (2-3/hour, 10 minutes).

For cruising details, see page 36.

By Docklands Light Railway (DLR): From the Bank-Monument Station in central London, take the DLR to Cutty Sark Station in central Greenwich; it's one stop before the main—but less central—Greenwich Station (departs at least every 10 minutes, 20 minutes, all in Zone 2). The DLR works like the Tube; be sure to touch your card to the reader on the platform before and after your journey, or risk being fined.

Many DLR trains terminate at Canary Wharf, so make sure you get on one that continues to Lewisham or Greenwich. (If you do end up at Canary Wharf, you can catch a train to Greenwich's Cutty Sark Station within a few minutes). Some DLR trains terminate at Island Gardens, where you can disembark and enjoy the unique experience of walking under the Thames into Greenwich: To reach the pedestrian tunnel, exit the station, cross the street, and follow signs to *Island Gardens* for a good photo op. Then enter the red-brick Greenwich Foot Tunnel (opened in 1902), descend 86 spiral stairs (or ride the lift), hold your breath, and re-emerge on dry land at the bow of the *Cutty Sark*.

By Bus: Catch bus #188 from Russell Square near the British Museum (about 45 minutes to Greenwich).

Orientation to Greenwich

When to Go: To allow enough time to see everything—and to fit in a Docklands visit on your way back—head to Greenwich in the morning. Some sights can get crowded with families and school groups, especially in summer and on weekends. You can save a little time by reserving your *Cutty Sark* visit in advance (see page 352).

Opening Times: Greenwich's main sights are open daily from 10:00 to 17:00; some stay open later (complete hours listed later for each individual sight).

Information: The TI is within the **Discover Greenwich visitors center,** inside the Old Royal Naval College gates (daily 10:00-17:00, Pepys House, 2 Cutty Sark Gardens, tel. 0870-608-2000, www.visitgreenwich.org.uk). For more on Discover Greenwich, see the listing later in this chapter.

Tours: Guided city walks, which depart from the TI within Discover Greenwich, offer an overview and go past most of the big sights (£8, daily at 12:15 and 14:15, 1.5 hours; the 12:15 tour leaves you at the door of the Royal Observatory; the 14:15 tour enters the Painted Hall and Chapel of Sts. Peter and Paul).

Services: Free WCs are located inside the Discover Greenwich visitors center. For eating recommendations, see the sidebar on page 355.

Markets: Thanks to its markets, Greenwich throbs with browsing Londoners on weekends. The **Greenwich Market** is an entertaining mini Covent Garden, located in the middle of the block between the Cutty Sark DLR station and the Old Royal Naval College—right on your way to the sights (farmers market, arts and crafts, and food stands; daily 10:00-17:30; antiques Mon, Tue, Thu, and Fri, www.greenwichmarketlondon.com).

The **Clocktower Market** sells overpriced old odds and ends on Greenwich High Road, near the post office (Sat-Sun and bank holidays 10:00-17:00, www.clocktowermarket.co.uk).

Exploring Back Streets: Allow time to browse Greenwich. The town has two sides: prim and proper (east of Church Street) and lived-in local (west of Church Street). Wander beyond touristy Church Street and Greenwich High Road to where flower stands spill onto the side streets, antique shops sell brass nautical knickknacks, and salty pubs tempt passersby. King William Walk, College Approach, and Nelson Road (all in the vicinity of Greenwich Market) are worth a look.

Length of This Tour: Allow about two hours simply to stroll about and enjoy the parks. Add several hours more to enter the sights (figure about an hour for the *Cutty Sark,* 30 minutes each for the Royal Naval College and the Queen's House, and an hour or two apiece for the National Maritime Museum and the Royal Observatory).

Starring: The *Cutty Sark,* the Royal Observatory with its prime meridian, the National Maritime Museum, the Painted Chapel, and expansive great views.

BACKGROUND

Greenwich—with its safe, deep harbor not far from the mouth of the Thames—helped put Britain on the map as a seafaring nation. For a thousand years, oceangoing ships docked and embarked from here (and from the Docklands, directly across the river). England's kings built palaces here. In the 1500s, Henry VIII (who was born here) made Greenwich the principal residence of his early reign. Elizabeth I was born here, and later queens would make Greenwich their London getaway.

In the 1600s, various monarchs commissioned architects Inigo Jones and Christopher Wren to beautify the town and palace. A Royal Observatory was built atop the bluff for charting the heavens to aid in seafaring. Other grand structures were built nearby to house retired seamen, and as a college for training naval officers. In modern times, as Britain's maritime focus shifted elsewhere, Greenwich's buildings were transformed into a pincushion of sights that connect today's Brits with their illustrious maritime past.

The Tour Begins

I've linked Greenwich's major sights with handy walking directions. Each attraction is described in full and rated; you can pick and choose which ones to enter. If you're in a rush, make a beeline to the sights that interest you. We'll start with the must-see *Cutty Sark*, meander through various other sights, and finish atop the hill at the Royal Observatory.

• *Our first stop is the* Cutty Sark. *If you arrive by boat, it's right in front of you. If you come by DLR, get off at the Cutty Sark stop, exit the station to the left, pass under the brick archway, and turn left. The* Cutty Sark *is just ahead on the right.*

▲▲Cutty Sark

When first launched in 1869, the Scottish-built *Cutty Sark* was the last of the great China tea clippers and the queen of the seas. She was among the fastest clippers ever built, the culmination of centuries of ship design. With 32,000 square feet of sail—and favorable winds—she could travel 300 miles in a day. But as a new century dawned, steamers began to outmatch sailing ships for speed, and by the mid-1920s the *Cutty Sark* was the world's last operating clip-

per ship. After a stint as a training ship, she was retired and turned into a museum in the 1950s.

In 2012, the ship was restored and reopened with a spectacular new glass-walled display space (though one critic groused that the ship now "looks like it has run aground in a giant greenhouse").

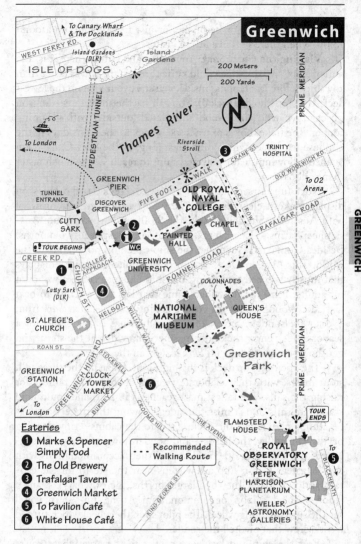

Displays explore the *Cutty Sark*'s 140-year history and the cargo she carried—everything from tea to wool to gunpowder—as she raced between London and ports all around the world.

Cost and Hours: £13.50, kids ages 5-15-£7, free for kids under age 5, family tickets available, combo-ticket with Royal Observatory-£18.50—saves money if you plan to visit both sights, kids combo-ticket-£8.50; daily 10:00-17:00; unnecessary £5 guidebook, reservation tel. 020/8312-6608, www.rmg.co.uk.

Crowd-Beating Tips: The ship can get busy on school holidays and on weekends. To skip the ticket-purchasing line, you can reserve ahead online or by phone, or just try showing up around 13:00, when there's often a lull in visitors.

Visiting the *Cutty Sark:* You enter, and bam—there it is: the hull of a massive ship that could knife through the waves faster than any ship before it. Stepping inside, you start your visit on the lowest deck, the ship's hold (**Deck 0**). You can see the ship's guts—an iron rib cage, covered with wood and plated (outside) with gleaming copper. The (fake) boxes of tea harken back to the ship's days in the Chinese tea trade...which didn't last long, as the Suez Canal soon opened, allowing steam-powered ships to reach China much faster than sailboats.

Next (upstairs on the low-ceilinged **Deck 1**), the bales on display make it clear that the *Cutty Sark* turned to trading wool with Australia. She could make the 8,000-mile voyage from Aussie sheep farms to English textile factories in just over two months. Besides China and Australia, the ship called on ports all over the world. This "Tween Deck" is full of not-quite-gimmicky displays that mostly succeed in making the ship's history come alive, even for adults. Find the fun video game that lets you attempt to beat Captain Woodget's record voyage sailing a wool-laden *Sark* from Sydney to London. Sit on the tilting benches of tea crates for a seaborne feel, enjoy the oddly mesmerizing video at the stern, and get the figurehead's take on *Sark* history in the bow.

The open-air **top deck** is the highlight. Gaze up the three tall, stout masts, with their elaborate rigging of ropes and pulleys for raising the sails. The tallest mast reaches 150 feet, and could hold six square sails. Don't miss the video showing the rigger's view as he climbs high above the deck. Explore the cabins—tiny sleeping berths, the galley, the heads—and ponder how little space was allotted to the crew of 30-35. Compare their accommodations with the "Master's Cabin" (up a few steps near the stern) for the captain and first mate. They had larger berths, their own WCs, and a wood-paneled "saloon" or common room. At the ship's stern, you'll see the ship's steering wheel. The pilot spun the wheel which turned a corkscrew that pivoted the rudder.

Exit the ship and head downstairs to the area where you're literally **Under the Ship.** Relax and enjoy the various exhibits while the 400,000-pound ship dangles overhead. Videos describe how the mighty vessel was designed and then preserved. Beneath the bow, note the compass rose that shows how many days at sea it'd take to reach major ports from here.

Finally, admire the colorful collection of figurehead statues that once adorned the prows of ships (most are from other ships). In the center of the group is the Cutty Sark's own figurehead: a white statue of a beautiful-but-fierce bare-breasted witch, holding the horse's tail she grabbed while chasing off a suitor. This mytho-

Eating in Greenwich

Picnicking: Greenwich's parks are picnic-perfect. Gather picnic supplies before heading up the hill to the National Maritime Museum and Royal Observatory. **$ Marks & Spencer Simply Food** sells ready-made lunches (between the DLR station and the *Cutty Sark* at 55 Greenwich Church Street).

Pub Grub: Greenwich has almost 100 pubs, with some boasting that they're mere milliseconds from the prime meridian. **$$$ The Old Brewery,** in the Discover Greenwich center, is a gastropub decorated with all things beer. A brewery on this site once provided the daily ration of four pints of beer for pensioners at the hospital. Today it offers a selection of craft beers, wines, and cocktails along with classic British cuisine (daily 10:00-23:00, tel. 020/3327-1280). **The Trafalgar Tavern,** with a casual **$$** pub and elegant ground-floor **$$$$** dining room, is a historical place for an overpriced meal (food served Mon-Sat 12:00-22:00, Sun until 19:00, Park Row, tel. 020/8858-2909).

Greenwich Market: From Yorkshire pudding to paella to Thai cuisine, food stalls at the Greenwich Market offer an international variety of tasty options.

Tea and Coffee: The elegant 1906 **$ Pavilion Café**—behind the planetarium in Greenwich Park—offers tea, coffee, and counter-service food in a stylish, updated interior (daily 9:00-18:00, until 16:00 in winter). At the bottom of Greenwich Park, near Croom's Hill, its affiliated **$$ White House Café** offers an assortment of baked goodies and sandwiches. It has a small seating area inside and relaxing garden tables outside (daily 9:00-17:30).

logical figure gave the ship its name, and the ship, in turn, inspired a famous whisky. The other figureheads range from the usual goddesses and maidens to Indian chiefs, Cleopatra, the goateed Prime Minister Benjamin Disraeli, and even Abraham Lincoln.

• *Leaving the museum, head left, and find the visitors center called...*

Discover Greenwich

As well as having a helpful information desk, the visitors center contains a few exhibits introducing you to Greenwich over the centuries, as it served as a harbor, royal residence, seaman's hospital, scientific center, and nautical college. Models show how the various buildings evolved, and you'll see artifacts of the many people—kings, sailors, architects, and scientists—who left their mark on the town. Tours of the Royal Naval College leave from the reception desk. Adjoining Discover Greenwich are the TI, free WCs, and, of course, a pub.

Cost and Hours: Free, daily 10:00-17:00, tel. 020/8269-4747, www.ornc.org.

• *Leave through the far exit (away from the* Cutty Sark*), turn right, then left, and make your way between the buildings to the open quad, where dramatic identical-twin buildings make up the heart of the Old Royal Naval College. The twin buildings (to your right) house the Painted Hall (under the dome on the right) and the Chapel of Sts. Peter and Paul (left). Between the twin buildings is the Queen's House. Beyond that is the hill with the Royal Observatory.*

▲Old Royal Naval College—The Painted Hall and the Chapel

Despite the name, these grand structures were built (1692) as a veterans' hospital to house disabled and retired sailors who'd served their country. King William III and Queen Mary II spared no expense. They donated land from the former royal palace and hired the great Christopher Wren to design the complex (though other architects completed it). Wren created a virtual temple to seamen. It was perfectly symmetrical, with classical double-columned arcades topped by soaring domes. The honored pensioners ate in the Painted Hall and prayed in the Chapel of Sts. Peter and Paul.

In 1873, the hospital was transformed into one of the world's most prestigious universities for training naval officers. Here they studied math, physics, and engineering for use at sea. During World War II, the college was a hive of activity, as Britain churned out officers to face the Nazis. In 1998, the Royal Navy moved out. Today, the buildings host university students, music students, business conventions, concerts, and film crews drawn to the awe-inspiring space. And the public is invited to view the elaborate Painted Hall and the (less interesting) Chapel.

Cost and Hours: Both the Painted Hall and Chapel are free (£3 suggested donation), daily 10:00-17:00, sometimes closed for private events, service Sun at 11:00 in chapel—all are welcome, www.ornc.org. The Painted Hall interior may be covered with scaffolding during 2018. During these renovations, you can see the painted ceiling up close on a £10 guided tour (book online in advance).

Visitor Information: Each building sells a descriptive guide (£1), or you can buy the fun *Nasty Naval College* brochure (made for children, but with entertaining offbeat facts about the place; £1). Volunteers are often standing by to answer questions.

Painted Hall: Originally intended as a dining hall for pensioners, this sumptuously painted room was deemed too glorious (and, in the winter, too cold) for that purpose. So almost as soon as it was completed, it became simply a place to impress visitors.

Enter the hall, climb the stairs, and gape up at one of the largest painted ceilings in Europe—112 feet long. It's a big propaganda scene, glorifying the building's founders, William and Mary (William, as a Protestant monarch, had recently trounced the Catholic French King Louis XIV in a pivotal battle). Crane your neck—or use the clever wheeled mirrors—to examine the scene. In the center are William and Mary. Under his foot, William is crushing a dark figure with a broken sword...

Louis XIV. William is handing a red cap (representing liberty) to the woman on the right, who holds the reins of a white horse (symbolizing Europe). On the left, a white-robed woman hands him an olive branch, a sign of peace. The message: William has granted Europe liberty by saving it from the tyranny of Louis XIV. Below the royal couple, the Spirit of Architecture shows them the plans for this very building (commemorating the sad fact that Mary died before its completion). Ringing the central image are the four seasons (represented by Zodiac signs), the four virtues, and—at the

top and bottom—a captured Spanish galleon and a British man-of-war battleship.

Up the steps at the end of the room, along the wall of the upper hall, is a portrait of the family of King George I. On the right is the artist who spent 19 years of his life painting this hall, James Thornhill (he finally finished it in 1727). He's holding out his hand—reportedly, he didn't feel he was paid enough for this Sistine-sized undertaking.

• *Exit the hall, and cross the field to enter the...*

Chapel of Sts. Peter and Paul: Not surprisingly, you'll sense a nautical air in this fine chapel. Notice the rope motif in the floor tiles down the aisle. The

enormous painting above the altar is by American Benjamin West. It depicts Paul (standing in red, near the luminous center) being bit by a poisonous viper. The crowd around him ripples in horror, but Paul casually drops the viper in the fire, miracu-

lously without being harmed. Soon after the chapel was completed, it was gutted by a fire and had to be redecorated all over again. The plans were too ambitious, so the designers cut corners. The six Ionic columns framing the entrance are expensive stone, but many others are painted wood. And the "sculptures" lining the nave high above are actually trompe l'oeil—3-D paintings meant to look real. But some items, such as the marble frame around the main door, are finely crafted from expensive materials.

• *Leave the chapel, and walk straight down to the water—enjoying the sweeping views across to the Docklands. When you hit the river, turn right for a quick...*

Riverside Stroll

Start by looking back toward the Old Royal Naval College for a great photo-op. Notice how it's split into two parts; reportedly, Queen Mary, who lived in the Queen's House, didn't want her view blocked.

Wander east along the Thames on Five Foot Walk (named for the width of the path). The tallest of the Docklands skyscrapers is the 50-story, pyramid-shaped Canary Wharf Tower. The Dock-

lands sits atop the Isle of Dogs, a formerly marshy patch in the Thames, where the river takes a hairpin turn. That slowed the river's flow, and made Greenwich a natural harbor from earliest times. From here you can also see the big, white, spiky **O2** dome a mile downstream. This stadium languished for nearly a decade after its controversial construction and brief life as the Millennium Dome. Intended to be a world's fair-type site and the center of London's year 2000 celebration, it ended up as the topic of heated debates about cost overruns and its controversial looks. The site was finally bought by a developer a few years ago and rechristened "The O2" (a telecommunications company paid for the naming rights). Today it hosts sporting events and concerts. Next to the O2 are the towers of the Emirates Air Line cable car, which ferries passengers from the O2 across the Thames to, essentially, nowhere.

Continuing downstream, just outside the fenced college grounds, you'll find the recommended **Trafalgar Tavern.** Dickens knew the pub well, and used it as the setting for the wedding breakfast in *Our Mutual Friend*. Built in 1837 in the Regency style to attract Londoners downriver, the upstairs Nelson Room is still used for weddings. Its formal moldings and elegant windows with balconies over the Thames are a step back in time and worth a peek.

• *From the Trafalgar Tavern, walk two long blocks up Park Row. After crossing busy Romney Road, turn right (through the gate near the corner) into the park. Walk past a row of huge anchors, toward the palatial buildings in the middle of the park. There's the Queen's House (closest to you), the National Maritime Museum (a little farther), and the Royal Observatory on the hilltop. This trio, paired with the* Cutty Sark, *form the Royal Museums of Greenwich.*

Queen's House

This perfectly proportioned building is the best surviving reminder of the days when Greenwich was the palatial home to Britain's kings and queens. From earliest times, monarchs had a manor on these grounds, culminating in Henry VIII's grand Palace of Placentia. In 1616 the great architect Inigo Jones was hired by James I to build a house for his wife, Queen Anne of Denmark. James's act of devotion to his wife became a tradition, and the House was subsequently passed down from queen to queen, as a pleasant retreat.

Cost and Hours: Free, daily 10:00-17:00; tel. 020/8858-4422, www.rmg.co.uk.

Exterior: Jones created a cubical building with geometric proportions and simple unadorned lines. It was surrounded by gardens, becoming the first Italian-style Palladian villa in Britain. Along with Jones's more-famous Banqueting House (see page 48), the Queen's House helped set the tone for the Neoclassical architecture that has become London's signature "look."

Interior: Inside, enjoy the Great Hall—a perfect 40-foot cube, ringed with a balcony. Here queens entertained their guests with grand views of the Thames between Wren's magnificent Old Royal Naval College. Exploring the house's many rooms, you'll see different quarters reserved for the queen, the king, and various servants. On the walls hang many paintings—most of them forgettable, and most of nautical themes: ships, famous sea battles, and portraits of admirals.

Upstairs, the Queen's Presence Chamber gives the best feel for the place as a luxurious residence. There's a portrait (the largest) of steely-eyed Anne of Denmark, who first owned the place, and of Mary II, who later chose Greenwich as the site of a hospital for seamen. In the King's Presence Chamber, don't miss the "curiosities": a 2,000-year-old coin, a miniature portrait of Robert (boyfriend of Queen Elizabeth?) Devereux, a fossilized mammoth's tooth, and the serrated nose of a sawfish.

• *The National Maritime Museum is to the right, connected to the*

Queen's House by a colonnade. To reach the museum entrance, walk toward the hill, pass through the colonnade, and turn right. You'll soon see a giant ship in a bottle, marking the...

▲National Maritime Museum

Great for anyone interested in the sea, this museum holds everything from a giant working paddlewheel to the uniform Admiral Horatio Nelson wore when he was killed at Trafalgar. A big glass roof tops three levels of slick, modern, kid-friendly exhibits about all things seafaring.

Cost and Hours: Free, daily 10:00-17:00, tel. 020/8858-4422, www.rmg.co.uk. The museum hosts frequent family-oriented events—singing, treasure hunts, and storytelling—particularly on weekends; ask at the desk. Inside, listen for announcements alerting visitors to free tours on various topics.

Visiting the Museum: For a quick once-over, start on the top floor and work your way down. (Entering the museum, turn right, pass through the shop, and go upstairs.)

Floor 2: In "Nelson, Navy, Nation," you'll see models of ships, uniforms, weapons, and whips used to keep sailors in line—all attesting to the vital importance of sea trade in making Britain great. Focus on the watershed Battle of Trafalgar (1805), when the Royal Navy defeated Napoleon's fleet, confirming that Britannia ruled the waves. See the Union Jack that flew from one of the 27 ships in Britain's convoy and the French cannonball that lodged itself into the bow of the British flagship, the HMS *Victory*. Finally, see holy relics of the great hero Admiral Horatio Nelson who led the British to victory. There's the uniform he was wearing on that fateful day. Notice how the jacket's right arm is pinned to the stomach—the way Nelson wore it after losing an arm in a previous battle. You can still make out traces of blood on the left sleeve. And in the left shoulder, you can see the bullet hole from a French musket. Just when victory was at hand, Nelson was mortally wounded, but he died knowing he'd secured Britain's future.

Also on Floor 2, you'll see "Forgotten Fighters" (WWI ships and weapons), the kid-friendly "All Hands" (where you can send a Morse code message), and the "Ship Simulator" (where you can pilot a virtual ship down the Thames).

Floor 1: The floor's central courtyard is a big people-friendly space with a great map of the world on the floor, where kids play and adults sip lattes. In the "Traders" exhibit, you'll learn how this small island nation grew rich by trading all across the globe. Queen Elizabeth I sent forth explorers (1600s), and soon the East India Company (1700s) was importing silks, tea, and opium from China and India.

Meanwhile (in the "Atlantic Worlds" exhibit), Britain was colonizing the New World and fighting the Seven Years War (1756-63) with France for superiority over North America. The American colonies provided Britain with cotton, coffee, sugar, tobacco, fish, and metals. This productivity was largely thanks to slaves—and you'll see some chilling reminders of this. Continue downstairs (dipping into the peaceful stained glass of the Baltic Exchange, honoring the dead of WWI), to the...

Ground Floor: These large-scale exhibits are easy to enjoy. There are big ships, colorful figureheads, a long 1700s barge that once cruised the Thames, lighthouse technology, a detailed exhibit on the Battle of Trafalgar, the *Miss Britain III* that could travel at speeds up to 100 miles per hour, and many more salty odds and ends.

• *To reach the final sight in town—the Royal Observatory Greenwich— exit the Maritime Museum and follow signs and the crowds as you huff up the steep hill (allow 10-15 minutes).*

Just below the observatory entrance, note the unassuming iron gate where cheapskates could see a free, more simplistic (and significantly less crowded) display of the prime meridian. A few steps further uphill, pause at the display of public standards of length and see how your foot measures up to the official "foot." Buy your ticket and enter the courtyard of the...

▲▲Royal Observatory Greenwich

Located on the prime meridian (0° longitude), this observatory is famous as the point from which all time and distances on earth are measured. It was here that astronomers studied the heavens in order to help seafarers navigate. In the process, they used the constancy of the stars to establish standards of measurement for time and distance used by the whole world.

The observatory's various sights walk you through these heady concepts. First, you can snap a selfie straddling the famous prime meridian line in the pavement. There's the original 1600s-era observatory and several early telescopes. You'll see the famous clocks from the 1700s that first set the standard of global time, as well as ingenious more-recent timekeeping devices. Other science-oriented sights (requiring separate admission) are nearby, including a planetarium and a kid-friendly astronomy museum. Topping your visit off are great views over Greenwich and the distant London skyline.

A visit here gives you a taste of the sciences of astronomy, timekeeping, and seafaring—and how they all meld together.

Cost and Hours: Observatory-£9.50, includes audioguide, combo-ticket with *Cutty Sark*-£18.50, combo-ticket with planetarium-£12.50, daily 10:00-17:00, until later in summer; **Weller Astronomy Galleries**-Free, daily 10:00-17:00; **Peter Harrison Planetarium**-£7.50, combo-ticket with observatory-£12.50; 30-minute shows generally run every hour (usually Mon-Fri 13:00-16:00, Sat-Sun 11:00-16:00, fewer in winter). Confirm times in advance by phone or online, or by picking up a flier at the observatory. As these shows can sell out, consider calling ahead or ordering online for tickets. Most shows are family-oriented, with early shows intended for young children.

Information: Tel. 020/8858-4422, reservations tel. 020/8312-6608, www.rmg.co.uk.

◐ Self-Guided Tour: After purchasing your ticket, enter the courtyard.

Prime Meridian: Running through the middle of the small courtyard is "The Line"—the prime meridian. Visitors wait pa-

tiently to have their photographs taken as they straddle the line in front of the monument, with one foot in each hemisphere. This line divides the globe into 360 imaginary lines of longitude about 69 miles apart—180 lines to the east of here and 180 west. So, New York City (as the line markings say) is 73 degrees west of here. The prime meridian is set by lining it up with a huge telescope pointed at the constant heavens. (You can glimpse today's telescope, located at the end of The Line, inside the low brick building.)

While watching all this fuss over a little line, consider that—unlike the equator—the placement of the prime meridian is totally arbitrary. It could just as well have been at my house, in Timbuktu, or even a few feet over—as, for a time, it was (the trough along the building's roofline shows where one astronomer had placed it).

The prime meridian established a fixed point from which to measure how fast the earth rotates on its axis, from 0° longitude back to 0° again. This allowed Greenwich's scientists to set a standard for time. This standard was soon adopted throughout the world as Greenwich Mean Time (GMT). Find the red Time Ball (on the tower atop the observatory's roof), which—since 1833—

The Longitude Problem

Around 1700, as the ships of seafaring nations began to venture farther from their home bases, the alarming increase in the number of shipwrecks made it clear that navigational tools had to be improved. Determining latitude—the relative position between the equator and the North or South Pole—was straightforward; sailors needed only to measure the angle of the sun at noon. But figuring out longitude, or their east-west position, was not as easy without a fixed point (such as the equator) from which to measure.

In 1714, the British government offered the £20,000 Longitude Prize. Two successful solutions emerged, and both are tied to Greenwich.

The first approach was to observe the position of the moon, which moves in relation to the stars. Sailors would compare the night sky they saw with the sky over Greenwich by consulting a book of tables prepared by Greenwich astronomers. This told them how far they were from Greenwich—their longitude. Visitors to the Royal Observatory can still see the giant telescopes—under retractable roofs—that were used to carefully chart the heavens to create these meticulous tables.

The second approach was to create a clock that would remain completely accurate on voyages—no easy feat back then, when turbulence and changes in weather and humidity made timepieces notoriously unreliable at sea. John Harrison spent 45 years working on this problem, finally succeeding in 1760 with his fourth effort, the H4 (which won him the Longitude Prize). All four of his attempts are on display at the Royal Observatory.

So, how can a clock determine longitude? Every 15° of longitude equals an hour when comparing the difference in sunrise or sunset times between two places. For example, the time gap between Greenwich and New York City is five hours, which translates into a longitudinal difference of 75°. Equipped with an accurate timepiece set to Greenwich Mean Time, sailors could figure out their longitude by comparing sunset time at their current position with sunset time back in Greenwich.

Notice that both approaches use Greenwich as a baseline—either on an astral map or on a clock. That's why, to this day, the prime meridian and official world time are both centered in this unassuming London suburb.

has dropped down the mast daily at exactly 13:00, helping all who see it to set their clocks.

• *Turn your attention to the cube-shaped building that holds the ball, the...*

Flamsteed House: This building was the original observatory—a simple tower atop a hill, away from city lights, where astronomers could set up telescopes to observe the heavens. It was built in 1675, a time when British ships were exploring and colonizing the globe. Astronomers here were tasked with finding more accurate navigating techniques than the old astrolabes and quadrants.

Inside, you first pass through the **apartments** of the head astronomer, now decorated with their portraits. You'll see John (first Astronomer Royal) Flamsteed, his successor Edmond (comet-discovering) Halley, and William Herschel, whose telescopes were so accurate that astronomers could set earth time according to the stars (not the sun).

Upstairs is the impressive, high-ceilinged **Octagon Room,** designed by Christopher Wren. The tall windows accommodated telescopes (as you can see from the replica on display). There's a portrait of (black-haired) Charles II, who started the observatory. Peruse the various Tompion-designed clocks that astronomers used here, and the 10-foot-tall grandfather clock powered by a swinging pendulum. These clocks were state-of-the-art in the 1600s, but so fragile and unwieldy that they could never be taken on board a ship to aid in navigation. For that part of the puzzle, head downstairs to the museum exhibits.

One level down you'll find a fascinating series of displays on **the "Longitude Problem"** and how it was solved (see the sidebar for an overview). First, see how the globe of the earth is divided into its 360-degree lines of longitude. Scientists knew it takes the earth 24 hours to spin all 360 degrees (or four minutes to spin one degree). Now, if you only had a clock accurate enough, you could figure out exactly what degree you were at anywhere on the earth. So, in the 1700s, Britain offered a £20,000 prize to anyone who could invent a clock that accurate.

The museum displays the **four original clocks** invented by one of the contestants, John Harrison. First up is so-called "H1." It took Harrison five years to build this clock. It was powered not by a pendulum but by two springs, which slowly uncoiled to constantly keep the cogwheels turning. (Springs would be much more reliable than a swinging pendulum aboard a rocking ship at sea.) Harrison had created the best clock ever—but not good enough to win the prize. So he spent the next five years building and testing H2, and another seventeen years working on H3. After six more years of work he'd produced the winning design—H4. It was not a huge sea clock but a tiny pocket watch. See the portrait at the end of the room of curly-haired Harrison holding the watch that won him 20,000 quid. On the scale of human achievement, this little timepiece is right up there with the printing press, the cotton gin, the telegraph, and the money belt.

Downstairs another floor, you'll find a roomful of **time-keeping devices,** from ancient sundials to a church-tower clock to an incredibly accurate atomic clock which measures the ultra-stable rate of decay of cesium atoms. Today, the Greenwich time signal is linked with the BBC, which broadcasts the famous "pips" world-wide at the top of the hour, so listeners can set their clocks.

• *Back outside in the courtyard, take in the prime meridian once again, and consider that you're standing at the what could be considered the nexus of space and time on Planet Earth.*

Then check out a few final sights around the courtyard.

Meridian Observatory Building: This has a wide assortment of historical telescopes. The humongous one in the final room, de-signed by George Airy, is used today to define the prime meridian. (A video nearby shows the telescope in action.) The telescope, fixed firmly to the spinning earth, tracks the stars as they pass overhead, marking when they cross the start/finish line of the prime meridi-an. Glancing outside, notice that The Line is perfectly aligned with the shaft of the telescope.

Camera Obscura: Hiding in a corner of the courtyard is a thrillingly low-tech device. It's simply a dark room (or *camera ob-scura* in Latin) that lets in light through a pinhole-size prick in the roof. The light is reflected downward by a mirror and projected onto a flat disc. The effect is like watching a live feed of the scene outside. For thousands of years, humans have mastered this tech-nology, for science and entertainment, done without electricity or machinery—Caveman TV.

View: Enjoy a great view of the symmetri-cal royal buildings, the Thames, and the Dock-lands and its busy cranes (including the prominent Canary Wharf Tower, with its pyramid cap). A chart helps you find various landmarks: Canary Wharf, the huge O2 dome, and the towers of the Emirates Air Line cable car. To the left lies the square-mile City of London with its sky-scrapers, the dome of St. Paul's Cathedral, and the Shard (farther to the left). At night (17:00-24:00), look for the green laser beam that

the observatory projects into the sky. It extends along the prime meridian for 15 miles—a godsend for orbiting space aliens trying to get their bearings.

• *Our tour through Greenwich is finished. If you have more time or interest, near the Royal Observatory are a couple of sights requiring a separate ticket.*

GREENWICH

Nearby: The **Weller Astronomy Galleries** has interactive, kid-pleasing displays allowing you to guide a space mission and touch a 4.5-billion-year-old meteorite. And the state-of-the-art, 120-seat **Peter Harrison Planetarium** offers entertaining and informative shows several times a day where they project a view of the heavens onto the interior of the dome.

• *To get back to town, head back down the hill along The Avenue. The road becomes King William Walk and ends at the* Cutty Sark *and* Greenwich Pier, *where you can catch a boat or DLR train back to downtown London. If you have time, you could hop off the DLR for a quick visit to the Docklands; for details, see the next chapter.*

THE DOCKLANDS WALK

Survey London's skyline (or a Tube map), and it becomes clear that London is shifting east. The thundering heart of this new London is the Docklands. Nestled around a hairpin bend in the Thames, this area was London's harbor and warehouse district back in the 19th century, when Britannia ruled the waves. Today it's been gentrified into a futuristic skyscraper-filled landscape rising from the canals and docks.

The heart of the Docklands is the Isle of Dogs, a marshy peninsula in the river's curve. From the Isle rises the 800-foot-tall Canary Wharf Tower (officially the "One Canada Square" building), which is surrounded by a cluster of other office buildings.

Don't expect Jolly Olde England here. The Docklands is more about businessmen in suits, creatively planned parks, art-filled plazas, and trendy cafés and restaurants. But there are also traces of its rugged dockworker past. You'll see canals, former docks, brick warehouses, and a fine history museum. Most impressive of all, there's not a tourist in sight.

If your London visit is brief and focused on the big, famous sights, the Docklands is not worth a special trip. But if you're visiting nearby Greenwich, it's very easy to add on a quick peek at the Docklands (which you'll pass by—or under—as you travel to Greenwich anyway). You can also combine the Docklands with a quick look at London's newest park, Queen Elizabeth Olympic Park, to the north.

If you want to say you've seen today's London, visit the Docklands.

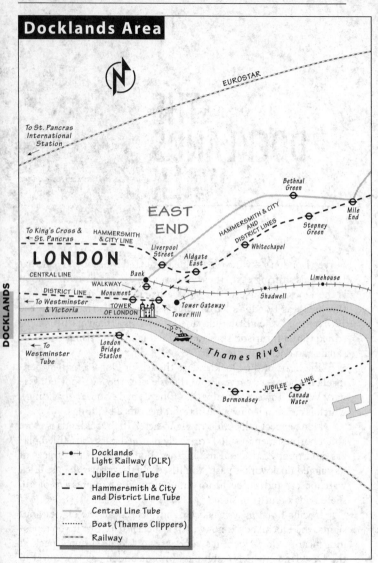

Orientation

Length of This Walk: 1.5 hours, including museum visit.

When to Go: As it's now a financial district, the Docklands bustles only on weekdays. (On weekends, it can be laid-back and festive if it's sunny...or empty and dead if rainy.)

Ideally, time your visit here for late afternoon on a weekday, when the area is enlivened by business workers headed for

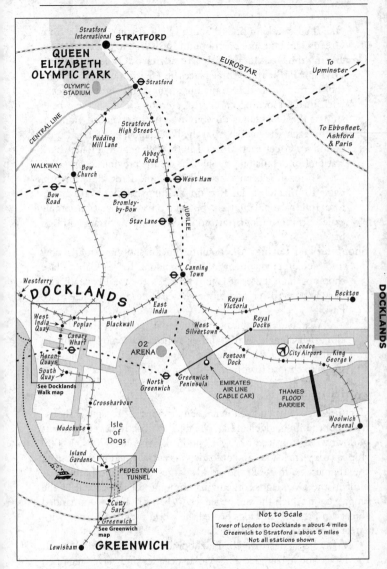

happy hour. But don't wait too long—the museum at the end of this walk closes at 18:00, with last entry at 17:00. To catch the *après*-work bustle and still make it to the museum, I'd aim to begin this walk by 16:00.

Getting There: This walk starts at the South Quay canal footbridge near the South Quay Docklands Light Railway (DLR) stop. If you're coming from central London, take the Tube to a DLR stop (the Bank/Monument stops are the most central), then take the Lewisham line to South Quay. If you're coming from Greenwich, take any northbound DLR line to South Quay.

Combining the Docklands with Greenwich or Queen Elizabeth Olympic Park: These three places lie a few minutes apart along the north-south DLR train line. You could sightsee Greenwich in the morning and early afternoon, then make a brief stop at the Docklands on your way back to central London. Or, to reach Greenwich from the Docklands, hop a DLR train bound for Greenwich or Lewisham, then get off at Cutty Sark station (for details on Greenwich, see the previous chapter).

To reach Queen Elizabeth Olympic Park (described on page 104), catch a DLR train heading north toward Stratford International Station, but get off at the station simply called Stratford (not Stratford International or Stratford High Street).

Shopping and Eating: Three subterranean shopping malls flow into each other via underground corridors. There's Cabot Place shopping mall (enter at Cabot Square), the mall beneath Canary Wharf Tower, and Jubilee Place (enter from Jubilee Place Park).

Waterside restaurants abound—at the West India Dock, along Mackenzie Walk, and elsewhere. Or enjoy a picnic in Jubilee Place Park (there are plenty of delis and sandwich shops to choose from).

OVERVIEW

Centuries ago, this end of town was notorious for its smelly industries (bone boiling, gluemaking, chemical works). It was conveniently downwind from the rest of London. By the late 1700s, 13,000 ships a year were loaded and unloaded in central London, congesting the Thames. So in 1802, the world's largest-of-its-kind harbor was built in the Docklands, organizing shipping for the capital of the empire upon which the sun never set. When Britannia commanded the oceans, the Isle of Dogs hosted the world's leading harbor, with direct connections to the North Sea.

After being destroyed by Nazi bombers during World War II, the Docklands struggled for several decades and never regained its status as a port. With the advent of container shipping in the 1960s, London's shipping industry moved farther east, to deepwater docks. The old Docklands became a derelict and dangerous wasteland. Until a generation ago, local surveys ranked it as one of the least desirable places to call home. It was said that for every Tube stop you lived east of central London, your life expectancy dropped one year.

But all of this misfortune paid off in the 1980s, when investors realized that the Docklands was ripe for redevelopment...the per-

DOCKLANDS

fect place to host a new and vibrant economic center. Over the past few decades, Britain's new Information Age industries—banking, finance, publishing, and media—have vacated downtown London and set up shop here. You'll still see remnants of the

past—those 1802 West India warehouses survive, but rather than trading sugar and rum, today they house the excellent Museum of London Docklands and a row of happening restaurants.

Our walk takes us from the heart of the modern Docklands, through some pleasant squares, and ends at the Museum of London Docklands.

The Walk Begins

• *Start at the South Quay DLR stop. Descend from the platform, cross busy Marsh Wall Street, and turn left in front of South Quay Square. Follow signs to* Canary Wharf, *turning right after the Hilton hotel, and when you reach water (the South Dock canal), turn left. Continue on to the curvy, modernistic footbridge, pausing before you cross to take in the full skyline.*

❶ South Quay, with View of the O2

Across the water, in the distance, you see Greenwich. The prickly white dome pierced with crane-like projections is the O2 (a.k.a.

"the Dome," described on page 358), a costly and long-unpopular edifice that's now primarily the locus of sports matches, arena concerts, and Londoners' habitual disdain.

In front of you, a bouquet of skyscrapers blossoms from London's former wasteland. Of the many buildings, the tallest, in the center, is

One Canada Square (a.k.a. Canary Wharf Tower, and—for Doctor Who fans—the scene of the pivotal Battle of Canary Wharf). The 800-foot, 50-story building is known throughout London for its distinctive pyramid cap. Once the tallest building in the UK, and, for a time, in Europe, it was surpassed by The Shard in 2012.

• *Cross the bridge, walk through the office building, and continue straight into...*

DOCKLANDS

Docklands Walk

MUSEUM OF LONDON DOCKLANDS

To Central London

To Stratford (Olympic Park) & London City Airport

Poplar

MARRIOTT

BILLINGSGATE FISH MARKET

West India Quay

7

6 WEST INDIA DOCK

CANARY WHARF TOWER

Cabot Square

Westferry Cross

WEST INDIA AVE.

Canary Wharf DLR

5

THAMES CLIPPERS BOAT DOCK

To London

To Greenwich

STAIRS

MIDDLE DOCK

4

2

Canary Wharf Tube (Jubilee Line)

3 Jubilee Place Park

WESTFERRY RD.

MARSHWALL

Heron Quays

Thames River

SOUTH DOCK

1

HILTON

South Quay Square

WALK BEGINS

South Quay

To Greenwich

1 South Quay, with View of the O2
2 Canada Square
3 Jubilee Place Park
4 Mackenzie Walk
5 Cabot Square
6 West India Quay
7 Museum of London Docklands

Docklands Light Railway (DLR)

❷ Canada Square

Stand in the square and take it all in. You're surrounded by soaring skyscrapers, three glitzy shopping malls, lively cafés, and hurried businesspeople.

Standing in this busy square, it can seem like continual rush hour—with the young high-tech workforce coursing through the battery of turnstiles. Flash back 200 years to this area's heyday as a shipping harbor. "Canary Wharf"—the name for the whole neighborhood—is a reminder of the trading connection London had with distant ports such as the Canary Islands, off the western coast of Africa. Where sailors once drank grog while stevedores unloaded cargo, today thousands of office workers (the stevedores of the Information Age) populate a forest of skyscrapers, towering high above the remnants of the Industrial Age.

Canary Wharf Tower is filled with big banks and financial and media companies. The plaza under it has a playful display of clocks on lampposts. If you like modern art, enter the lobby from street level and poke around to see what's on display.

• *Behind the Canary Wharf Tube station is a grassy park. You can reach it by a path to the right of the Tube entrance.*

❸ Jubilee Place Park

Opened in 2002 on the 50th anniversary ("Golden Jubilee") of Queen Elizabeth's rule, this delightful little park is an example

of how the new Canary Wharf was de- signed with a futuristic people-friendli- ness. Workers and residents enjoy plenty of green spaces, waterways, public art, and good public-transit service. The entire ensemble sits upon one of three underground shopping malls—the en- trance is in the middle of the park. Stroll through the park past meandering foun- tains and outdoor art.

• *Return to Canada Square. Head north (directly toward Canary Wharf Tower), turning left along the canalside promenade called...*

❹ Mackenzie Walk

Stroll along the canal, called Middle Dock, past All Bar One and other inviting eateries, and under the train bridge. The canal is

a surviving remnant of the many artificial har- bors and canals from the Docklands' 19th-century shipping heyday. The land here on the Isle of Dogs was marshy, flooded by the Thames, and unsuit- able for farming or habi- tation. But it was perfect for accommodating large seagoing vessels. Beginning around 1800, industrious Londoners channeled the water into canals and lined them with docks. Picture the lively scene: burly men off-loading goods from ships at anchor, while an army of poor laborers bustled between storage warehous- es, dry docks for ship repair, and various ship-building enterprises. Each dock specialized in a particular product—spices, coal, what- ever. By the mid-1800s, the Docklands had siphoned away shipping from London's traditional port (near London Bridge) and was the world's busiest harbor.

• *Cross under the DLR bridge and keep going. When you reach the arched footbridge, turn right, passing a sculpture of two figures sitting on a bench, and hike up Cubitt Steps into...*

❺ Cabot Square

Enjoy the square's big fountain and views of domineering skyscrapers. From the west (left) end of the square, you have the iconic photo-op of Canary Wharf Tower with the fountain in the foreground. Many newlyweds come here for their wedding photos.

• *Exit the square at the north side (near another sculpture couple), where steps lead down to a footbridge that crosses another canal to the...*

❻ West India Quay

This row of 19th-century brown-brick warehouses typifies today's Docklands. Standing side by side are elements of the old Docklands (the warehouses, canal, a few barges) and

the new (the esplanade of umbrella-shaded restaurants, the futuristic Marriott skyscraper). Back in the 19th century, the water originally lapped up right against those buildings. You can still see the rustic gates to the lofts. Imagine heavily laden cargo boats off-loading there.

The Docklands thrived as a shipping port until the mid-20th century; two big gray cranes-on-tracks are reminders of the two events that eventually doomed the area. First, the Blitz of World War II obliterated the Docklands—it was hit by more than 2,000 bombs. Hitler's aim was to wipe out this vital industrial area.

The Docklands couldn't survive the next hit—when the shipping industry converted to containers. The large container ships couldn't make it this far up the shallow Thames, and almost overnight, the industry rapidly shifted to seaports. In the 1970s, the Docklands became London's poorest area.

• *In the left part of the row of warehouses you'll find the...*

❼ Museum of London Docklands

This modern and interesting museum, which fills an old sugar warehouse, gives the Docklands historic context. In telling the story of the world's leading 19th-century port, it also conveys the story of London. It has a nice café, a hip bar, and a great kids' play area. Ride the elevator up to the third floor, then work your way down, going on a 2,000-year walk through the story of commerce on the Thames.

Cost and Hours: Free, £2.50 suggested donation, daily 10:00-18:00, last entry one hour before closing, tel. 020/7001-9844, www.museumoflondon.org.uk/docklands.

Visiting the Museum: Start on the **third floor.** In old London, back when London's port was at London Bridge, the Docklands was a barely inhabited swamp far to the east. Exhibits show how the Docklands rapidly developed in the 1800s, including a history of the building itself, the tools and techniques used for weighing and storing goods, and even a mummified Tom and Jerry. Next, a thought-provoking section traces the ramifications of transatlantic trade, sugar, and slavery.

The **second floor** explores London's growth after 1800—its population was more than one million by 1810. Kids enjoy strolling through a gritty reconstruction of "Sailortown," listening to the salty voices of those who lived and worked in quarters like this. A painted *Stevedores* banner from the 1889 Dock Strike is a reminder that while the Industrial Revolution first exploited workers, it later empowered them to rise up. During World War II, the Docklands was a prime target for Nazi bombers bent on crippling British shipping. Find the claustrophobic, dome-shaped "consul shelter," where dockworkers could take cover in case of attack. There's also a re-creation of the top-secret fuel pipeline that was laid under the English Channel after D-Day to supply the Allies on the Continent. The final section, "New Port, New City," traces the Docklands' post-WWII rebuilding.

When you're finished, step out into today's Docklands and take in this combination of old and new.

• *Our walk is over. You have several options from here:*

Return to Central London: The Tube is your fastest way back into the city—retrace your steps to the Canary Wharf Tube station and catch the Jubilee line. Depending on where you're going in London, it may be more convenient to head to the other end of the West India Quay to catch the DLR (stop: West India Quay) toward Bank, where you can transfer to the Tube's Central line, or toward Tower Gateway,

where you can transfer to the Circle and District lines.

DOCKLANDS

To catch a boat (slower but very scenic), return to Cabot Square, turn right, and walk five minutes along West India Avenue to the round Westferry Circus park; the Thames Clippers dock is just beyond (£8 one-way, boats leave every 20-30 minutes, 10- to 30-minute trip to major London docks).

Visit Greenwich or Queen Elizabeth Olympic Park: It's easy to catch a DLR train from West India Quay or Canary Wharf to Greenwich (south) or to the Olympic Park (north). For details, see "Orientation" earlier in this chapter.

Ride the Emirates Air Line Cable Car: The much-hyped aerial gondola makes a pointless trip across the Thames between the O2 dome and what has to be London's least-interesting district. There's not much to see there, but the ride is a thrill, reasonably priced, and easily tacked on to a day of Docklands sightseeing.

To reach the gondola, take the Jubilee Line from Canary Wharf one stop to North Greenwich Pier. Above ground, follow signs to Air Emirates (about 5 minutes away). The ride costs £3.50 with an Oyster card (otherwise £4.50); you can head right to the turnstiles if you have enough credit on your Oyster card. The gondola ride itself is a 10-minute dangle 300 feet above the Thames that lands you at the Royal Docks station.

From there it's a two-minute walk to the Royal Victoria DLR station; ride one stop (on either line) to Canning Town. From Canning Town, you can hop a DLR train bound for Bank or Tower Gateway back to central London.

SLEEPING IN LONDON

Choosing the right neighborhood in London is as important as choosing the right hotel. I've focused on several favorite neighborhoods (Victoria Station, South Kensington, Bayswater, Notting Hill, and Paddington Station, among others) and recommend the best accommodations values for each, from £20 bunks to deluxe £300 doubles with all the comforts. I've also listed big, good-value, modern chain hotels scattered throughout London, along with hostels, dorms, and apartment rental information. For accommodations in Windsor and Cambridge, see the Day Trips from London chapter.

London is an expensive city for lodging. Cheaper rooms are relatively dumpy. Don't expect £160 cheeriness in an £80 room. For £80, you'll get a double with breakfast in a safe, cramped, and dreary place with minimal service and the bathroom down the hall. For £100, you'll get a basic, reasonably cheery double with worn carpet and a private bath in a usually cramped, somewhat outdated, cracked-plaster building, or a soulless but comfortable room without breakfast in a huge Motel 6-type place. My London splurges, at £160-300, are spacious, thoughtfully appointed places good for entertaining or romancing.

Given London's high hotel prices, it's worth searching for a deal. For some travelers, short-term, Airbnb-type rentals can be a good alternative; search for places in my recommended hotel neighborhoods. Various websites list rooms in London in high-

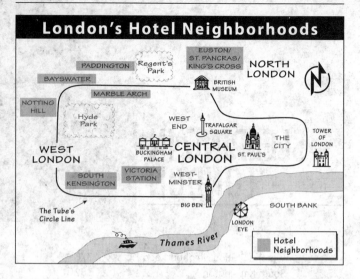

London's Hotel Neighborhoods

rise, three- and four-star business hotels. You'll give up the charm and warmth of a family-run establishment, and breakfast probably won't be included, but you might find that the price is right. Start by browsing the websites of several chains to get a sense of typical rates and online deals (I've described some budget chains on page 391). Pricier London hotel chains include Millennium/Copthorne, Grange, Firmdale, Thistle, InterContinental/Holiday Inn, Radisson, Hilton, and Red Carnation. Auction-type sites (such as Priceline and Hotwire) match flexible travelers with empty hotel rooms, often at prices well below the hotel's normal rates. You can also browse these accommodation discount sites: www.londontown.com (an informative site with a discount booking service), athomeinlondon.co.uk and www.londonbb.com (both list central B&Bs), www.lastminute.com, www.visitlondon.com, and www.eurocheapo.com.

I rank accommodations from $ budget to $$$$ splurge. To get the best deal, contact my family-run hotels directly by phone or email. By going direct, the owner avoids a roughly 20 percent commission and may be able to offer you a discount. Book your accommodations well in advance if you'll be traveling during peak season or if your trip coincides with a major holiday or festival (see page 581). For information and tips on hotel rates and deals, making reservations, finding a short-term rental, and more, see page 551.

VICTORIA STATION NEIGHBORHOOD

The streets behind Victoria Station teem with little, moderately-priced-for-London B&Bs. It's a safe, surprisingly tidy, and decent area without a hint of the trashy, touristy glitz of the streets in front of the station. I've divided these accommodations into two broad categories: Belgravia, west of the station, feels particularly posh, while Pimlico, to the east, is still upscale and dotted with colorful eateries. While I wouldn't go out of my way just to dine here, each area has plenty of good restaurants (see the Eating in London chapter). All of my recommended hotels are within a five-minute walk of the Victoria Tube, bus, and train stations. On hot summer nights, request

a quiet back room; most of these B&Bs lack air-conditioning and may front busy streets.

Laundry: The nearest laundry option is **Pimlico Launderette,** on the east—Pimlico—side about five blocks southwest of Warwick Square. Low prices and friendly George brighten your chore (self-service and same-day full service, daily 8:00-19:00, last wash at 17:30; 3 Westmoreland Terrace—go down Clarendon Street, turn right on Sutherland, and look for the launderette on the left at the end of the street; tel. 020/7821-8692).

Parking: The 400-space Semley Place **NCP parking garage** is near the hotels on the west/Belgravia side (£42/day, possible discounts with hotel voucher, just west of Victoria Coach Station at Buckingham Palace Road and Semley Place, tel. 0845-050-7080, www.ncp.co.uk). **Victoria Station car park** is cheaper but a quarter of the size; check here first, but don't hold your breath (£30/day on weekdays, £15/day on weekends, entrance on Eccleston Bridge between Buckingham Palace Road and Bridge Place, tel. 0345-222-4224, www.apcoa.co.uk).

West of Victoria Station (Belgravia)

In Belgravia, the prices are a bit higher and your neighbors include some of the world's wealthiest people. These two places sit on tranquil Ebury Street, two blocks over from Victoria Station (or a slightly shorter walk from the Sloane Square Tube stop). You can cut the walk from Victoria Station to nearly nothing by taking a short ride on frequent bus #C1 (leaves from Buckingham Palace Road side of Victoria Station and drops you off on corner of Ebury and Elizabeth streets).

$$$$ Lime Tree Hotel, enthusiastically run by Charlotte and Matt, is a gem, with 28 spacious, stylish, comfortable, thoughtfully decorated rooms, a helpful staff, and a fun-loving breakfast room (small lounge opens onto quiet garden, 135 Ebury Street, tel. 020/7730-8191, www.limetreehotel.co.uk, info@limetreehotel.co.uk, Laura manages the office).

SLEEPING

Victoria Station Neighborhood

Hotels
1. Lime Tree Hotel
2. B&B Belgravia
3. Luna Simone Hotel
4. Bakers Hotel
5. New England Hotel
6. Best Western Victoria Palace
7. Jubilee Hotel
8. Cherry Court Hotel
9. EasyHotel Victoria

Eateries
10. Ebury Wine Bar
11. La Bottega Deli
12. The Thomas Cubitt
13. To The Duke of Wellington
14. The Orange
15. Daylesford Deli
16. La Poule au Pot
17. Grumbles
18. Pimlico Fresh
19. Seafresh Fish Restaurant
20. The Jugged Hare
21. St. George's Tavern
22. Boisdale Restaurant

Services
23. Grocery Stores (3)
24. To Launderette
25. Hop-On Bus Tours (3)
26. Tube, Taxis, City Buses
27. Green Line Coach Terminal
28. Buses to Luton & Stansted Airports

SLEEPING

$$$ B&B Belgravia comes with bright rooms, high ceilings, and spring-loaded slamming doors. It's a little worn around the edges and feels less than homey, but still offers good value for the location. Most of its 26 rooms come with closets and larger-than-average space. If you're a light sleeper, ask for a room in the back (family rooms, 64 Ebury Street, tel. 020/7259-8570, www.bb-belgravia.com, info@bb-belgravia.com).

East of Victoria Station (Pimlico)

This area feels a bit less genteel than Belgravia, but it's still plenty inviting, with eateries and grocery stores. Most of these hotels are

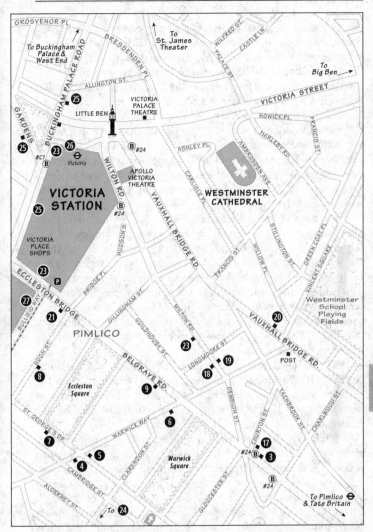

on or near Warwick Way, the main drag through this area. Generally the best Tube stop for this neighborhood is Victoria (though the Pimlico stop works equally well for the Luna Simone). Bus #24 runs right through the middle of Pimlico, connecting the Tate Britain to the south with Victoria Station, the Houses of Parliament, Trafalgar Square, the British Museum, and much more to the north.

$$$ Luna Simone Hotel rents 36 fresh, spacious, remodeled rooms with modern bathrooms. It's a smartly managed place, run for more than 40 years by twins Peter and Bernard—and Bernard's son Mark—and they still seem to enjoy their work (RS%, family rooms, 47 Belgrave Road near the corner of Charlwood Street, handy bus #24 stops out front, tel. 020/7834-5897, www. lunasimonehotel.com, stay@lunasimonehotel.com).

$$ Bakers Hotel shoehorns 12 brightly painted rooms into a seedy building, but it's conveniently located and offers modest prices and a small breakfast (RS%, cheaper rooms with shared bath, family rooms, 126 Warwick Way, tel. 020/7834-0729, www. bakershotel.co.uk, reservations@bakershotel.co.uk, Amin Jamani).

$$ New England Hotel, run by Jay and the Patel family, has very worn public spaces but well-priced rooms in a tight, old corner building (family rooms, breakfast is very basic, 20 Saint George's Drive, tel. 020/7834-8351, www.newenglandhotel.com, mystay@ newenglandhotel.com).

$$ Best Western Victoria Palace offers modern business-class comfort compared with some of the other creaky old hotels listed here. Choose from the 43 rooms in the main building (elevator, at 60 Warwick Way), or pay about 20 percent less by booking a nearly identical room in one of the annexes, each a half-block away—an excellent value for this neighborhood if you skip breakfast (breakfast extra, air-con, no elevator, 17 Belgrave Road and 1 Warwick Way, reception at main building, tel. 020/7821-7113, www.bestwesternvictoriapalace.co.uk, info@ bestwesternvictoriapalace.co.uk).

$$ Jubilee Hotel is a well-run but slightly shabby slumbermill with 26 simple rooms, high ceilings, and neat beds. The cheapest rooms, which share bathrooms, are just below street level (family rooms, 31 Eccleston Square, tel. 020/7834-0845, www. jubileehotel.co.uk, stay@jubileehotel.co.uk, Bob Patel).

$ Cherry Court Hotel, run by the friendly and industrious Patel family, rents 12 very small but bright and well-designed rooms with firm mattresses in a central location. Considering London's sky-high prices, this is a fine budget choice (family rooms, fruit-basket breakfast in room, air-con, laundry, 23 Hugh Street, tel. 020/7828-2840, www.cherrycourthotel.co.uk, info@ cherrycourthotel.co.uk, daughter Neha answers emails and offers informed restaurant advice).

$ EasyHotel Victoria, at 34 Belgrave Road, is part of the budget chain described on page 391.

"SOUTH KENSINGTON," SHE SAID, LOOSENING HIS CUMMERBUND

To stay on a quiet street so classy it doesn't allow hotel signs, make "South Ken" your London home. The area has plenty of colorful restaurants, and shoppers like being a short walk from Harrods and the designer shops of King's Road and Chelsea. When I splurge, I splurge here. Sumner Place (where my first two listings are located)

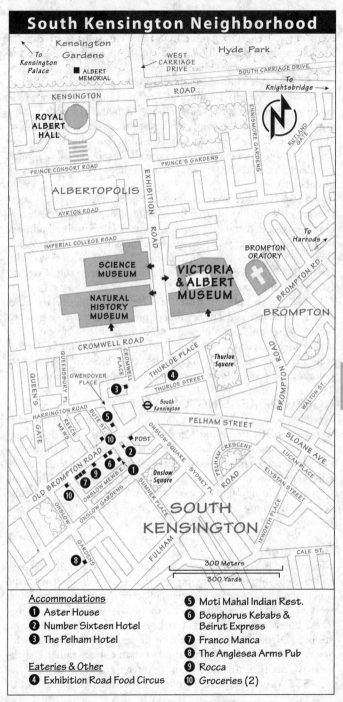

South Kensington Neighborhood

Kensington Gardens
To Kensington Palace
ALBERT MEMORIAL
Hyde Park
WEST CARRIAGE DRIVE
SOUTH CARRIAGE DRIVE
To Knightsbridge →
KENSINGTON ROAD
ROYAL ALBERT HALL
N
RUTLAND GATE
ENNISMORE GARDENS
PRINCE CONSORT ROAD
PRINCE'S GARDENS
ALBERTOPOLIS
EXHIBITION ROAD
AYRTON ROAD
IMPERIAL COLLEGE ROAD
To Harrods →
BROMPTON ORATORY
BROMPTON RD.
SCIENCE MUSEUM
VICTORIA & ALBERT MUSEUM
NATURAL HISTORY MUSEUM
BROMPTON
CROMWELL ROAD
QUEEN'S GATE
QUEENSBURY PL.
GWENDOVER PLACE
CROMWELL PLACE
THURLOE PLACE
THURLOE STREET
Thurloe Square
BROMPTON ROAD
❸
❹
HARRINGTON ROAD
REECE MEWS
BUTE ST.
South Kensington
WALTON ST.
❺
PELHAM STREET
SLOANE AVE.
❿
POST
❷
PELHAM CRESCENT
LUCAN PLACE
OLD BROMPTON ROAD
❻
❾
❶
ONSLOW SQUARE
SYDNEY PL.
ROAD
ELYSTAN STREET
❼
ONSLOW MEWS E.
Onslow Square
SUMNER PLACE
INWORTH PLACE
❿
ONSLOW GARDENS
SOUTH KENSINGTON
ONSLOW GARDENS
FULHAM
CALE ST.
❽
300 Meters
300 Yards

SLEEPING

Accommodations
❶ Aster House
❷ Number Sixteen Hotel
❸ The Pelham Hotel

Eateries & Other
❹ Exhibition Road Food Circus

❺ Moti Mahal Indian Rest.
❻ Bosphorus Kebabs & Beirut Express
❼ Franco Manca
❽ The Anglesea Arms Pub
❾ Rocca
❿ Groceries (2)

is just off Old Brompton Road, 200 yards from the handy South Kensington Tube station (on Circle Line, two stops from Victoria Station; and on Piccadilly Line, direct from Heathrow). See the map on page 383 for locations.

$$$$ Aster House, in a lovely Victorian town house, is run with care by friendly Simon and Leonie Tan, who've been welcoming my readers for years (I call it "my home in London"). It's a great value, with 13 comfy and quiet rooms, a cheerful lobby, and lounge. Enjoy breakfast or just kicking back in the whisper-elegant Orangery, a glassy greenhouse (RS%, air-con, TV, 3 Sumner Place, tel. 020/7581-5888, www.asterhouse.com, asterhouse@gmail.com).

$$$$ Number Sixteen, for well-heeled travelers, packs over-the-top class into its 41 artfully imagined rooms, plush designer-chic lounges, and tranquil garden. It's in a labyrinthine building, with boldly modern decor—perfect for an urban honeymoon (breakfast extra, elevator, 16 Sumner Place, tel. 020/7589-5232, US tel. 1-888-559-5508, www.numbersixteenhotel.co.uk, sixteen@firmdale.com).

$$$$ The Pelham Hotel, a 52-room business-class hotel with crisp service and a pricey mix of pretense and style, is genteel, with low lighting and a pleasant drawing room among the many perks (breakfast extra, air-con, elevator, fitness room, 15 Cromwell Place, tel. 020/7589-8288, US tel. 1-888-757-5587, www.pelhamhotel.co.uk, reservations.thepelham@starhotels.com).

NORTH OF KENSINGTON GARDENS

From the core of the tourist's London, the vast Hyde Park spreads west, eventually becoming Kensington Gardens. Three good accommodations neighborhoods line up side by side along the northern edge of the park: Bayswater (with the highest concentration of good hotels) anchors the area; it's bordered by Notting Hill to the west and Paddington to the east. This area has quick bus and Tube access to downtown and, for London, is very "homely" (Brit-speak for cozy).

Bayswater

Most of my Bayswater accommodations flank a tranquil, tidy park called Kensington Gardens Square (not to be confused with the much bigger Kensington Gardens adjacent to Hyde Park), a block west of bustling Queensway, north of Bayswater Tube station. These hotels are quiet for central London, but the area feels a bit sterile, and the hotels here tend to be impersonal. Popular with young international travelers, the Bayswater street called Queensway is a multicultural festival of commerce and eateries.

$$$ Vancouver Studios offers one of the best values in this neighborhood. Its 45 modern, tastefully furnished rooms come with fully equipped kitchenettes (utensils, stove, microwave, and fridge) rather than breakfast. It's nestled between Kensington Gardens Square and Prince's Square and has its own tranquil garden patio out back (30 Prince's Square, tel. 020/7243-1270, www. vancouverstudios.co.uk, info@vancouverstudios.co.uk).

$$$ Garden Court Hotel is understated, with 40 simple, homey-but-tasteful rooms (family rooms, includes continental breakfast, elevator, 30 Kensington Gardens Square, tel. 020/7229-2553, www. gardencourthotel.co.uk, info@gardencourthotel.co.uk).

$$$ Phoenix Hotel offers spacious public spaces and 125 modern-feeling rooms. Its prices—which range from fine-value to rip-off—are determined by a greedy computer program (elevator, 1 Kensington Gardens Square, tel. 020/7229-2494, www. phoenixhotel.co.uk, reservations@phoenixhotel.co.uk).

$$$ Princes Square Guest Accommodation is a crisp (if impersonal) place renting 50 businesslike rooms with pleasant, modern decor. It's well located, practical, and a very good value, especially if you can score a good rate (elevator, 23 Prince's Square, tel. 020/7229-9876, www.princessquarehotel.co.uk, info@ princessquarehotel.co.uk).

$$ London House Hotel has 103 spiffy, modern, cookie-cutter rooms on Kensington Gardens Square. Its rates are great considering the quality and fine location (family rooms, breakfast extra, elevator, 81 Kensington Gardens Square, tel. 020/7243-1810, www. londonhousehotels.com, reservations@londonhousehotels.com).

$$ Kensington Gardens Hotel, with the same owners as the Phoenix Hotel, laces 17 rooms together in a tall, skinny building (breakfast extra—served at Phoenix Hotel, 9 Kensington Gardens Square, tel. 020/7243-7600, www.kensingtongardenshotel.co.uk, info@kensingtongardenshotel.co.uk).

$$ Bayswater Inn Hotel's 140 tidy, perfectly adequate rooms come with dated style, an impersonal feel, and outrageously high official rack rates. But rooms commonly go for much lower prices, making this a decent—sometimes great—budget option (family rooms, elevator, 8 Prince's Square, tel. 020/7727-8621, www. bayswaterinnhotel.com, reservations@bayswaterinnhotel.com).

Notting Hill and Nearby

The Notting Hill neighborhood, just west of Bayswater (spreading out from the northwest tip of Kensington Gardens) is famous for two things: It's the site of the colorful Portobello Road Market (see page 435) and the setting of the 1999 Hugh Grant/Julia Roberts film of the same name. While the neighborhood is now a bit more upscale and less funky than the one shown in that film, it's still a pleasant place to stay.

North of Kensington Gardens

SLEEPING

SLEEPING

Accommodations
1. Vancouver Studios
2. Garden Court Hotel
3. Phoenix & Kensington Gardens Hotels
4. Princes Square Guest Accommodation
5. London House Hotel
6. Bayswater Inn Hotel
7. Portobello Hotel
8. To Norwegian YWCA
9. To Earl's Court Hotels
10. Tudor Court Hotel
11. St. David's Hotels
12. Falcon Hotel
13. EasyHotel
14. Stylotel
15. Olympic House Hotel

Eateries
16. Maggie Jones's
17. Geales
18. The Churchill Arms Pub & Thai Kitchen
19. Hereford Road
20. The Prince Edward
21. Café Diana
22. Royal China Restaurant
23. Groceries (4)
24. The Orangery (Afternoon Tea)

$$$$ Portobello Hotel is on a quiet residential street in the heart of Notting Hill. Its 21 rooms are funky yet elegant—both the style and location give it an urban-fresh feeling (elevator, 22 Stanley Gardens, tel. 020/7727-2777, www.portobellohotel.com, stay@portobellohotel.com).

Near Holland Park: English is definitely a second language at ¢ **Norwegian YWCA (Norsk K.F.U.K.)**—which is open to any Norwegian woman and to non-Norwegian women under 30. (Men must be under 30 with a Norwegian passport.) Located on a quiet, stately street, it offers a study, TV room, piano lounge, and an open-face Norwegian ambience (goat cheese on Sundays!). They have mostly quads, so those willing to share with strangers are most likely to get a bed (private rooms available, 52 Holland Park, Tube: Holland Park, tel. 020/7727-9346, www.kfukhjemmet.org.uk, kontor@kfukhjemmet.org.uk). With each visit, I wonder which is easier to get—a sex change or a Norwegian passport?

Near Earl's Court

These accommodations are south of Holland Park, near the Earl's Court Tube station.

$$$$ K+K Hotel George occupies a grand Georgian building on a quiet street near the Earl's Court Tube station. With spacious public areas, a wellness center, and standard amenities in each of its 154 rooms, it has all the makings for predictable comfort (air-con, elevator, 1 Templeton Place, tel. 020/7598-8700, www.kkhotels.com, hotel.george@kkhotels.co.uk).

$$$ NH London Kensington, part of a Spanish hotel chain, has 121 business-style rooms offering reliable comfort and class. Bonuses include a pleasant garden patio, a fitness center, and an extensive, tempting optional breakfast buffet (air-con, elevator, 202 Cromwell Road, tel. 020/7244-1441, www.nh-hotels.com/hotel/nh-london-kensington, nhkensington@nh-hotels.com).

$$$ The Nadler Kensington, situated on a residential block five minutes' walk from Earl's Court tube station, offers 65 self-catering rooms. High ceilings help the smallish rooms feel a bit larger, and in-room kitchenettes are great for preparing cheap meals (breakfast vouchers available, air-con, elevator, 25 Courtfield Gardens, tel. 020/7244-2255, www.thenadler.com, kensington.info@thenadler.com). The chain also has locations in Soho (between Tottenham Court and Oxford Circus) and near Victoria Station (between the station and St. James's Park—two blocks from the palace).

Paddington Station Neighborhood

Just to the east of Bayswater, the neighborhood around Paddington Station—while much less charming than the other areas I've recommended—is pleasant enough and very convenient to the Heathrow Express airport train. The area is flanked by the Paddington and Lancaster Gate Tube stops. Most of my recommendations circle Norfolk Square, just two blocks in front of Paddington Station, but are still relatively quiet and comfortable. The main drag, London Street, is lined with handy eateries—pubs, Indian, Italian, Moroccan, Greek, Lebanese—plus convenience stores and more. (Better restaurants are a short stroll to the west, near Bayswater and Notting Hill—see page 412.)

To reach this area, exit the station toward Praed Street (with your back to the tracks, it's to the left). Once outside, continue straight across Praed Street and down London Street; Norfolk Square is a block ahead on the left.

On Norfolk Square

These places (and many more on the same street) all offer small rooms at a reasonable-for-London price in tall buildings with lots of stairs and no elevator. I've chosen the ones that offer the most reasonable prices and the warmest welcome.

$$$ Tudor Court Hotel has 38 tired, tight rooms with prefab plastic bathrooms and creaky plumbing. It's run by Connan and the Gupta family (family rooms, 10 Norfolk Square, tel. 020/7723-5157, www.tudorcourtpaddington.co.uk, reservations@tudorcourtpaddington.co.uk).

$$ St. David's Hotels, run by the Neokleous family, has 60 basic but comfortable rooms in several interconnected buildings. The friendly staff members treat you like a member of the family and are happy to share their native London knowledge. Their rooms with shared bath are a workable budget option (Wi-Fi in lobby, 14 Norfolk Square, tel. 020/7723-3856, www.stdavidshotels.com, info@stdavidshotels.com).

$$ Falcon Hotel, a lesser value, has less personality and 19 simple, old-school, slightly dingy rooms (family rooms, 11 Norfolk Square, tel. 020/7723-8603, www.falcon-hotel.com, info@falcon-hotel.com).

$ EasyHotel, the budget chain described on page 393, has a branch at 10 Norfolk Place.

On Sussex Gardens

To reach these hotels, follow the directions to Norfolk Square (earlier), but continue away from the station past the square to the big intersection with Sussex Gardens; you'll find them immediately to the left.

$$ Stylotel feels like the stylish, super-modern, aluminumclad big sister of the EasyHotel chain. Their tidy 39 rooms come with hard surfaces—hardwood floors, prefab plastic bathrooms, and metallic walls. While rooms can be cramped, the beds have

SLEEPING

space for luggage underneath. You may feel like an astronaut in a retro science-fiction film, but if you don't need ye olde doilies, this place offers a good value (family rooms, elevator, 160 Sussex Gardens, tel. 020/7723-1026, www.stylotel.com, info@stylotel.com, well-run by Andreas). They have eight fancier, pricier, air-conditioned suites across the street with kitchenettes and no breakfast.

$$ Olympic House Hotel has clean public spaces and a no-nonsense welcome, but its 38 business-class rooms offer predictable comfort and fewer old-timey quirks than many hotels in this price range (air-con extra, elevator, pay Wi-Fi, 138 Sussex Gardens, tel. 020/7723-5935, www.olympichousehotel.co.uk, olympichousehotel@btinternet.com).

NORTH LONDON

$$$$ The Sumner Hotel rents 19 rooms in a 19th-century Georgian townhouse sporting large contemporary rooms and a lounge with fancy modern Italian furniture. This swanky place packs in all the amenities and is conveniently located north of Hyde Park and near Oxford Street, a busy shopping destination—close to Selfridges and a Marks & Spencer (RS%, air-con, elevator, 54 Upper Berkeley Street, a block and a half off Edgware Road, Tube: Marble Arch, tel. 020/7723-2244, www.thesumner.com, reservations@thesumner.com).

$$$$ Charlotte Street Hotel has 52 rooms with a bright countryside English garden motif, and inviting public spaces in the up-and-coming Fitzrovia neighborhood close to the British Museum. Their rooms start at twice the cost of my favorite London B&Bs—but are worth considering if you want to splurge (connecting family rooms, air-con, elevator, 15 Charlotte Street, Tube: Tottenham Court Road, tel. 020/7806-2000, www.charlottestreethotel.com, reservations@charlottestreethotel.com).

$$$$ The Mandeville Hotel, at the center of the action just one block from Bond Street Tube station, has a genteel British vibe, with high ceilings, tasteful art, and just-vibrant-enough colors. It's a worthy splurge for its amenities and location, especially if you score a good deal (breakfast extra, air-con, elevator, Mandeville Place, tel. 020/7935-5599, www.mandeville.co.uk, info@mandeville.co.uk).

$$$$ The Fielding Hotel is a simple and slightly more affordable place lodged in the center of all the action—just steps from Covent Garden—on a quiet lane. They rent 25 basic rooms, serve no breakfast, and have almost no public spaces. Grace, the manager, sticks with straight pricing (family rooms, air-con, 4 Broad Court off Bow Street, Tube: Covent Garden—for location see map on page 400, tel. 020/7836-8305, www.thefieldinghotel.co.uk, reservations@thefieldinghotel.co.uk).

$$$ The 22 York Street B&B offers a casual alternative in the city center, with an inviting lounge and 10 traditional, hardwood, comfortable rooms, each named for a notable London landmark (near Marylebone/Baker Street: From Baker Street Tube station, walk 2 blocks down Baker Street and take a right to 22 York Street—no sign, just look for #22; tel. 020/7224-2990, www.22yorkstreet.co.uk, mc@22yorkstreet.co.uk, energetically run by Liz and Michael Callis).

$$ Seven Dials Hotel's 18 no-nonsense rooms are plain and fairly tight, but they're also clean, reasonably priced, and incredibly well located. Since doubles here all cost the same, request a larger room when you book (family rooms, 7 Monmouth Street, Tube: Leicester Square or Covent Garden—for location see map on page 400, tel. 020/240-0823, www.sevendialshotel.co.uk, info@sevendialshotel.co.uk, run by friendly and hardworking Hanna).

OTHER SLEEPING OPTIONS
Big, Good-Value, Modern Hotels

These chain hotels—popular with budget tour groups—offer all the modern comforts in a no-frills, practical package. If you can score a double for £90-100 (or less—often possible with promotional rates) and don't mind a modern, impersonal, American-style hotel, one of these can be a decent value in pricey London. This option is especially worth considering for families, as kids often stay for free. While most of these hotels have 24-hour reception and elevators, breakfast and Wi-Fi generally cost extra, and the service lacks a personal touch (at some, you'll check in at a self-service kiosk). When comparing your options, keep in mind that for about the same price, you can get a basic room at a budget hotel or B&B that has less predictable comfort but more funkiness and friendliness in a more enjoyable neighborhood.

Midweek prices are generally higher than weekend rates, and Sunday nights can be cheap. The best deals generally must be prepaid a few weeks ahead and may not be refundable—read the fine print carefully.

I've listed a few of the dominant chains, along with a quick rundown on their more convenient London locations (see the map on page 386 to find chain hotels in North London). Some of these branches sit on busy streets in dreary train-station neighborhoods, so use common sense after dark and wear a money belt.

$$ Motel One, the German chain that specializes in affordable style, has a branch at Tower Hill, a 10-minute walk north of

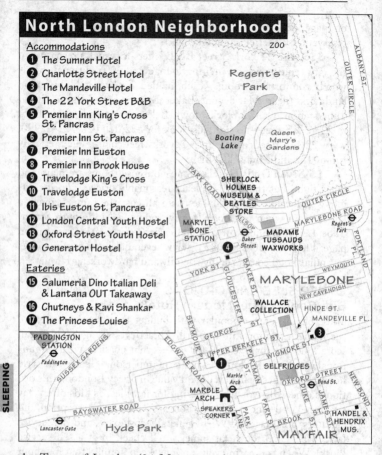

North London Neighborhood

Accommodations
1. The Sumner Hotel
2. Charlotte Street Hotel
3. The Mandeville Hotel
4. The 22 York Street B&B
5. Premier Inn King's Cross St. Pancras
6. Premier Inn St. Pancras
7. Premier Inn Euston
8. Premier Inn Brook House
9. Travelodge King's Cross
10. Travelodge Euston
11. Ibis Euston St. Pancras
12. London Central Youth Hostel
13. Oxford Street Youth Hostel
14. Generator Hostel

Eateries
15. Salumeria Dino Italian Deli & Lantana OUT Takeaway
16. Chutneys & Ravi Shankar
17. The Princess Louise

the Tower of London (24 Minories, tel. 020/7481-6427, www. motel-one.com, london-towerhill@motel-one.com).

$$ Premier Inn has more than 70 hotels in greater London. Convenient locations include a branch inside **London County Hall** (next to the London Eye), at **Southwark/Borough Market** (near Shakespeare's Globe, 34 Park Street), **Southwark/Tate Modern** (Great Suffolk Street), **Kensington/Earl's Court** (11 Knaresborough Place), **Victoria** (82 Eccleston Square), and **Leicester Square** (1 Leicester Place). In North London, the following branches cluster between King's Cross St. Pancras and the British Museum: **King's Cross St. Pancras, St. Pancras, Euston,** and **Brook House.** Avoid the **Tower Bridge** location, south of the bridge and a long walk from the Tube—but **London City Tower Hill,** north of the bridge on Prescot Street, works fine (www.premierinn.com, tel. 0871-527-9222; from North America dial 011-44-1582-567-890).

$$ Travelodge has close to 70 locations in London, including

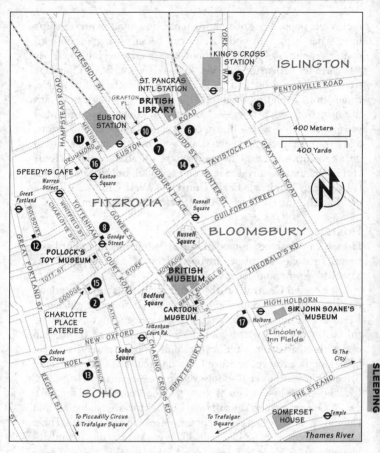

at **King's Cross** (200 yards in front of King's Cross Station, Gray's Inn Road) and **Euston** (1 Grafton Place). Other handy locations include **King's Cross Royal Scot, Marylebone, Covent Garden, Liverpool Street, Southwark,** and **Farringdon;** www.travelodge. co.uk.

$$ Ibis, the budget branch of the AccorHotels group, has a few dozen options across the city, with a handful of locations convenient to London's center, including **Euston St. Pancras** (on a quiet street a block west of Euston Station, 3 Cardington Street), **London City Shoreditch** (5 Commercial Street), and the more design-focused **Ibis Styles** branches at **Kensington** (15 Hogarth Road) and **Southwark,** with a theater theme (43 Southwark Bridge Road); www.ibishotel.com.

$ EasyHotel, with several branches in good neighborhoods, has a unique business model inspired by its parent company, the easyJet budget airline. The generally tiny, super-efficient, no-frills rooms feel popped out of a plastic mold, down to the prefab ship's head-type "bathroom pod." Rates can be surprisingly low (with doubles as cheap as £30 if you book early enough)—but you'll pay à la carte for expensive add-ons, such as TV use, Wi-Fi, luggage storage, fresh towels, and daily cleaning (breakfast, if available, comes from a vending machine). If you go with the base rate, it's like hosteling with privacy—a hard-to-beat value. But you get what you pay for (thin walls, flimsy construction, noisy fellow guests, and so on). They're only a good deal if you book far enough ahead to get a good price and skip the many extras. Locations include **Victoria** (34 Belgrave Road—see map on page 380), **South Kensington** (14 Lexham Gardens), **Earl's Court** (44 West Cromwell Road), and **Paddington** (10 Norfolk Place); www.easyhotel.com.

Hostels

Hostels can slash accommodation costs while meeting your basic needs. The following places are open 24 hours, have private rooms as well as dorms, and come with Wi-Fi.

¢ **London Central Youth Hostel** is the flagship of London's hostels, with all the latest in security and comfortable efficiency. Families and travelers of any age will feel welcome in this wonderful facility. You'll pay the same price for any bed—so try to grab one with a bathroom (families welcome to book an entire room, book long in advance, between Oxford Circus and Great Portland Street Tube stations at 104 Bolsover Street—see map on page 392, tel. 0845-371-9154, www.yha.org.uk, londoncentral@yha.org.uk).

¢ **Oxford Street Youth Hostel** is right in the shopping and clubbing zone in Soho (14 Noel Street—see map on page 392, Tube: Oxford Street, tel. 0845-371-9133, www.yha.org.uk, oxfordst@yha.org.uk).

¢ **St. Paul's Youth Hostel,** near St. Paul's Cathedral, is modern, friendly, well-run, and a bit scruffy (36 Carter Lane, Tube: St. Paul's, tel. 020/7236-4965 or 0845-371-9012, www.yha.org.uk, stpauls@yha.org.uk).

¢ **Generator Hostel** is a brightly colored, hip hostel with a café and a DJ spinning the hits. It's in a renovated building tucked behind a busy street halfway between King's Cross and the British Museum (37 Tavistock Place—see map on page 392, Tube: Russell Square, tel. 020/7388-7666, www.generatorhostels.com, london@generatorhostels.com).

¢ A cluster of three **St. Christopher's Inn** hostels, south of the Thames near London Bridge, have cheap dorm beds; one branch (the Oasis) is for women only. All have loud and friendly bars attached (must be over 18 years old, 161 Borough High Street, Tube: Borough or London Bridge, reservations tel. 020/8600-7500, www.st-christophers.co.uk, bookings@st-christophers.co.uk).

Dorms

$ The University of Westminster makes some high-rise dorm rooms in central London available to travelers during summer break (mid-June through mid-September). They all come with access to well-equipped kitchens and big lounges (cheaper rooms with shared bath, tel. 020/7911-5181, www.westminster.ac.uk/summeraccommodation, summeraccommodation@westminster.ac.uk).

$ The London School of Economics has openings in its dorms from July through September (cheaper rooms with shared bath, tel. 020/7955-7676, www.lsevacations.co.uk, vacations@lse.ac.uk).

$ University College London has rooms for travelers from late June until mid-September (cheaper rooms with shared bath, tel. 020/7387-4537, www.ucl.ac.uk/residences, accommodation@ucl.ac.uk).

Apartment Rentals

Consider this option if you're traveling as a family, in a group, or staying five days or longer. Websites such as Airbnb and VRBO let you correspond directly with European property owners or managers, or consider one of the sites listed below. Some specialize in London, while others also cover areas outside of London. For more information on short-term rentals, see page 556 in the Practicalities chapter.

LondonConnection.com is a Utah-based company that owns and rents several properties around London. The owner, Thomas, prides himself on providing personal service.

OneFineStay.com focuses on finding stylish, contemporary flats (most of them part-time residences) in desirable London neighborhoods. While pricey, it can be a good choice if you're seeking a hip, nicely decorated home away from home.

SuperCityUk.com gives travelers a taste of what local London life is like, renting chic, comfortable aparthotels and serviced apartments in three buildings.

Other options include **Cross-Pollinate.com**, **Coach House Rentals** (www.chsrentals.com), **GoWithIt.co.uk**, **HomeFromHome.co.uk**, **APlaceLikeHome.co.uk**, and **London-House.com**.

Staying near the Airports

It's so easy to get to Heathrow and Gatwick from central London, I see no reason to sleep at either one. But if you do, here are some options.

Heathrow: A **Yotel** is inside the airport (Terminal 4), while **EasyHotel** and **Hotel Ibis London Heathrow** are a short bus or taxi ride away.

Gatwick: The South Terminal has a **Yotel,** while **Gatwick Airport Central Premier Inn** rents cheap rooms 350 yards away, and **Gatwick Airport Travelodge** has budget rooms about two miles from the airport.

EATING IN LONDON

Whether it's dining well with the upper crust, sharing hearty pub fare with the blokes, or joining young professionals at the sushi bar, eating out has become an essential part of the London experience. You could try a different cuisine for each meal and never eat "local" English food, even on a lengthy stay in London. The sheer variety of foods—from every corner of Britain's former empire and beyond—is astonishing.

But the thought of a £50 meal in Britain generally ruins my appetite, so my London dining is limited mostly to easygoing, fun, moderately priced alternatives. I've listed places by neighborhood—handy to your sightseeing or hotel. Considering how expensive London can be, if there's any good place to cut corners to stretch your budget, it's by eating cheaply here.

EATING TIPS

I rank restaurants from **$** budget to **$$$$** splurge. For even more advice on eating in London, including information on pubs, beer, and ethnic eats, plus details on restaurant pricing, tipping, eating on a budget, English breakfasts, and afternoon tea, see page 559.

Finding Restaurants: London's food scene is constantly changing. If you want the latest on dining (as opposed to eating), drop by a newsstand to get a weekly entertainment guide or an annual restaurant guide (both have extensive restaurant listings). Or visit www.london-eating.co.uk, www.squaremeal.co.uk, www.

timeout.com, or the food section of www.theguardian.com for restaurant reviews and can't-miss meals.

Pubs: Many of London's 7,000 pubs serve traditional British classics at moderate prices (around £8-12). You can get beer almost any time of day (about 11:00-23:00, and later on Fridays and Saturdays). You can usually get food around 12:00-14:00 and 18:00-20:00. For more on pubs and pub grub, see page 563. For tips on ordering beer, see page 568. I list several historic pubs in London on page 408.

Chain Restaurants: Budget eating in London often means a modern, super-efficient chain restaurant—available in countless varieties, from burgers (Byron) and sushi (Yo!, Wasabi, and Itsu) to Indian (Masala Zone), Thai (Thai Square, Busaba Eathai), and more (Côte Brasserie, Ask, Pizza Express, Wagamama, Eat, and Loch Fyne)—offering essentially the same menu items at each location. For a description of some of my favorite chains, see page 564.

Street Markets: London thrives with street markets, many featuring the latest and trendiest food stalls. As some of these are close to major sights (for instance, Borough Market, Southbank Centre Food Market, and Ropewalk), consider a meal here instead of settling for another fast-food, bland-and-boring McLunch (for a list of markets, see page 435).

Picnicking: London has an array of carryout options, from Pret and Eat—selling fresh salads and sandwiches—to Marks & Spencer department stores (with a good deli) and their offshoot M&S Simply Food. I've listed several well-located supermarkets in this chapter.

CENTRAL LONDON

I've arranged these options by neighborhood, but they're all within about a 15-minute walk of each other. Survey your options before settling on a place. A large number of trendy chain restaurants permeate Central London. There's no need to clutter up my listings and maps with these—like Starbucks or McDonald's, you can count on seeing them wherever you go without worrying about an address. They're generally fast, good, and reasonably priced, and they range from glorified fast food to impressively classy dining experiences. The main sense you get wandering these streets: Trendy people fill trendy places and millennials with money rule the world. Weekends and later in the evenings, bars overflow as the sidewalks and even the streets become congested with people out clubbing. If you're looking for peace and quiet and a calm meal, avoid Friday and Saturday evenings here and come early on other nights.

Soho and Nearby

London has a trendy scene that many Beefeater seekers miss. Foodies who want to eat well head to Soho. Make it a point to dine in Soho at least once to feel the pulse of London's eclectic urban melting pot of international flavors. These restaurants are scattered throughout a chic, creative, and borderline-seedy zone that teems with hipsters, theatergoers, and London's gay community. Even if you plan to have dinner elsewhere, it's a treat just to wander around Soho in the evening, when it's seething with young Londoners out and about (see my 📖 West End Walk, which takes you through Soho).

On and near Wardour Street

$$ Princi is a vast, bright, efficient, wildly popular Italian deli/bakery with Milanese flair. Along one wall is a long counter with display cases offering a tempting array of *pizza rustica*, *panini* sandwiches, focaccia, pasta dishes, and desserts. Order your food at the counter, then find a space to share at a long table; or get it to go. They also have a classy restaurant section with reasonable prices if you'd rather have table service (daily 8:00-24:00, 135 Wardour Street, tel. 020/7478-8888).

$$$ The Gay Hussar, dressy and tight, squeezes several elegant tables into what the owners say is the only Hungarian restaurant in England. It's traditional Hungarian fare: cabbage, sauerkraut, sausage, paprika, and pork, as well as duck and chicken and, of course, Hungarian wine (Mon-Sat 12:15-14:30 & 17:30-22:45, closed Sun, 2 Greek Street, tel. 020/7437-0973).

$$$ Bocca di Lupo, a stylish and popular option, serves half and full portions of classic regional Italian food. Dressy but with a fun energy, it's a place where you'll be glad you made a reservation. The counter seating, on cushy stools with a view into the lively open kitchen, is particularly memorable, or you can take a table in the snug, casual back end (daily 12:30-15:00 & 17:15-23:00, 12 Archer Street, tel. 020/7734-2223, www.boccadilupo.com).

$$ Yalla Yalla is a bohemian-chic hole-in-the-wall serving up high-quality Beirut street food—hummus, baba ghanoush, tabbouleh, and *shawarmas*. It's tucked down a seedy alley across from a sex shop. Eat in the cramped and cozy interior or at one of the few outdoor tables (£4 sandwiches and *meze*, £8 *meze* platter available until 17:00, daily 10:00-24:00, 1 Green's Court—just north of Brewer Street, tel. 020/7287-7663).

Gelato: Across the street from Bocca di Lupo (listed earlier) is its sister *gelateria*, **Gelupo,** with a wide array of ever-changing but always creative and delicious dessert favorites. Take away or enjoy their homey interior (daily 11:00-23:00, 7 Archer Street, tel. 020/7287-5555).

EATING

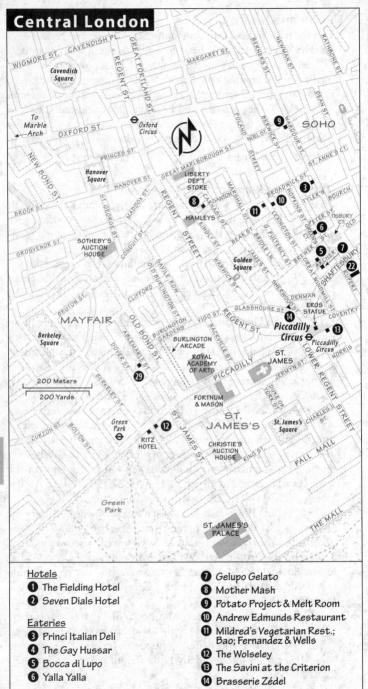

Central London

Hotels
1. The Fielding Hotel
2. Seven Dials Hotel

Eateries
3. Princi Italian Deli
4. The Gay Hussar
5. Bocca di Lupo
6. Yalla Yalla
7. Gelupo Gelato
8. Mother Mash
9. Potato Project & Melt Room
10. Andrew Edmunds Restaurant
11. Mildred's Vegetarian Rest.; Bao; Fernandez & Wells
12. The Wolseley
13. The Savini at the Criterion
14. Brasserie Zédel

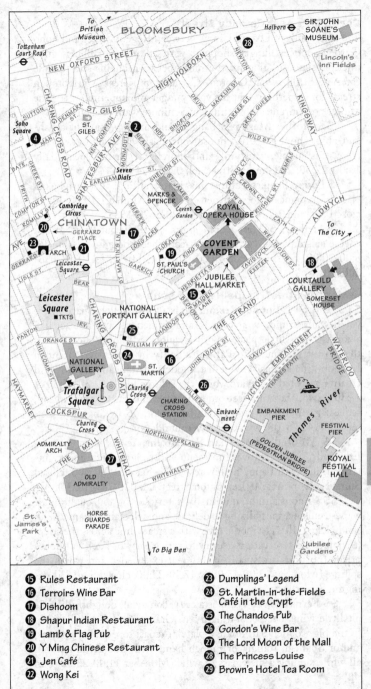

15 Rules Restaurant

16 Terroirs Wine Bar

17 Dishoom

18 Shapur Indian Restaurant

19 Lamb & Flag Pub

20 Y Ming Chinese Restaurant

21 Jen Café

22 Wong Kei

23 Dumplings' Legend

24 St. Martin-in-the-Fields Café in the Crypt

25 The Chandos Pub

26 Gordon's Wine Bar

27 The Lord Moon of the Mall

28 The Princess Louise

29 Brown's Hotel Tea Room

Cheap Eats near Carnaby Street

The area south of Oxford Circus between Regent Street and Soho Gardens entices hungry shoppers with attention-grabbing, gimmicky restaurants that fill the niche between chains and upscale eateries. Stroll along Ganton, Carnaby, or Great Marlborough streets for something that fits your budget and appetite, or try one of these restaurants, all within a five-minute walk of each other.

$$ Mother Mash is a bangers-and-mash version of a fish-and-chips shop. For £10, choose your mash, meat, and gravy and enjoy this simple, satisfying, and thoroughly British meal (daily 10:00-22:00, 26 Ganton Street, tel. 020/7494-9644).

$ Potato Project features imaginative fillings that turn baked "jacket" potatoes into gourmet creations (Mon-Fri 10:00-18:00, closed Sat-Sun, 27 Noel Street, tel. 020/3620-1585).

Next door, **$ Melt Room** crafts anything-but-Kraft grilled cheese masterpieces—including a bacon-cheese doughnut (Mon-Fri 8:00-20:00, Sat-Sun 11:00-18:00, 26 Noel Street, tel. 020/7096-2002).

Lexington Street, in the Heart of Soho

$$$ Andrew Edmunds Restaurant is a tiny candlelit space where you'll want to hide your camera and guidebook and not act like a tourist. This little place—with a jealous and loyal clientele—is the closest I've found to Parisian quality in a cozy restaurant in London. The extensive wine list, modern European cooking, and creative seasonal menu are worth the splurge (daily 12:30-15:30 & 17:30-22:45, these are last-order times, come early or call ahead, request ground floor rather than basement, 46 Lexington Street, tel. 020/7437-5708, www.andrewedmunds.com).

$$ Mildred's Vegetarian Restaurant, across from Andrew Edmunds, has a creative, fun menu and a tight, high-energy interior filled with happy herbivores (Mon-Sat 12:00-23:00, closed Sun, vegan options, 45 Lexington Street, tel. 020/7494-1634).

$$$ Bao is a tight, minimalist eatery selling top-quality Taiwanese cuisine, specializing in delicate and delectable steamed-bun sandwiches. This is a foodie fave with a steady line across the street (they take no reservations, so try to arrive early or late). While it's pricey (portions are small), it's a great experience and worth the splurge (Mon-Sat 12:00-15:00 & 17:30-22:00, closed Sun, 53 Lexington Street).

$$ Fernandez & Wells is a cozy, convivial, delightfully simple little wine, cheese, and ham bar. Grab a stool as you belly up to the big wooden bar. Share a plate of tapas, top-quality cheeses, and/or Spanish, Italian, or French hams with fine bread and oil, all while sipping a nice glass of wine (Mon-Sat 11:00-23:00, Sun until 18:00, quality sandwiches at lunch, 43 Lexington Street, tel. 020/7734-1546).

Swanky Splurges

$$$$ The Wolseley is the grand 1920s showroom of a long-defunct British car. The last Wolseley drove out with the Great Depression, but today this old-time bistro bustles with formal waiters serving traditional Austrian and French dishes in an elegant black-marble-and-chandeliers setting fit for its location next to the Ritz. Although the food can be unexceptional, prices are reasonable considering the grand presentation and setting. Reservations are a must (cheaper soup, salad, and sandwich "café menu" available in all areas of restaurant, daily 7:00-24:00, 160 Piccadilly, tel. 020/7499-6996, www.thewolseley.com). They're popular for their fancy cream tea or afternoon tea (for details, see page 418).

$$$$ The Savini at the Criterion is a palatial dining hall offering an Italian menu in a dreamy neo-Byzantine setting from the 1870s. It's right on Piccadilly Circus but a world away from the punk junk, with fairly normal food served in an unforgettable Great Gatsby space. It's a deal for the visual experience during lunch or early (before 19:00) or late (after 22:00)—and if you order the £29-36 fixed-price meal or £16 cream tea (daily 12:00-23:30, 224 Piccadilly, tel. 020/7930-1459, www.saviniatcriterion.co.uk).

$$$ Brasserie Zédel is the former dining hall of the old Regent Palace Hotel, the biggest hotel in the world when built in 1915. Climbing down the stairs from street level, you're surprised by a gilded grand hall that feels like a circa 1920 cruise ship, filled with a boisterous crowd enjoying big, rich French food—old-fashioned brasserie dishes. With vested waiters, fast service, and paper tablecloths, it's great for a group of friends. After 21:30 the lights dim, the candles are lit, and it gets more romantic with live jazz (nightly inexpensive *plats du jour,* daily 11:30-23:00, 20 Sherwood Street, tel. 020/7734-4888). Across the hall is the hotel's original Bar Américain (which feels like the 1930s) and the Crazy Coqs venue—busy with "Live at Zédel" music, theater, comedy, and literary events (see www.brasseriezedel.com for schedule).

$$$$ Rules Restaurant, established in 1798, is as traditional as can be—extremely British, classy yet comfortable. It's a big, borderline-stuffy place, where you'll eat in a plush Edwardian atmosphere with formal service and plenty of game on the menu. (A warning reads, "Game birds may contain lead shot.") This is the place to dress up and splurge for classic English dishes (daily 12:00-23:00, between the Strand and Covent Garden at 34 Maiden Lane, tel. 020/7836-5314, www.rules.co.uk).

Near Covent Garden

Covent Garden bustles with people and touristy eateries. The area feels overrun, but if you must eat around here, you have some good choices.

$$$ Terroirs Wine Bar is an enticing place with a casual but classy ambience that exudes happiness. It's a few steps below street level, with a long zinc bar that has a kitchen view and two levels of tables. The fun menu is mostly Mediterranean and designed to share. The meat and cheese plates complement the fine wines available by the glass (Mon-Sat 12:00-15:00 & 17:30-23:00, closed Sun, reservations smart, just two blocks from Trafalgar Square but tucked away from the tourist crowds at 5 William IV Street, tel. 020/7036-0660, www.terroirswinebar.com).

$$$ Dishoom is London's hotspot for upscale Indian cuisine, with top-quality ingredients and carefully executed recipes. The dishes seem familiar, but the flavors are a revelation. People line up early (starting around 17:30) for a seat, either on the bright, rollicking, brasserie-like ground floor or in the less appealing basement. Reservations are possible only until 17:45 (daily 8:00-23:00, 12 Upper St. Martin's Lane, tel. 020/7420-9320). They also have locations near King's Cross Station, Carnaby Street, and in Shoreditch.

$$$ Shapur Indian Restaurant is a well-respected place serving classic Indian dishes from many regions, fine fish, and a tasty £19 vegetarian *thali* (combo platter). It's small, low energy, and dressy with good service (Mon-Fri 12:00-14:30 & 17:30-23:30, Sat 15:00-23:30, closed Sun, next to Somerset House at 149 Strand, tel. 020/7836-3730, Syed Khan).

$$ Lamb and Flag Pub is a survivor—a spit-and-sawdust pub serving traditional grub (like meat pies) two blocks off Covent Garden, yet seemingly a world away. Here since 1772, this pub was a favorite of Charles Dickens and is now a hit with local workers. At lunch, it's all food. In the evening, the ground floor is for drinking and the food service is upstairs (long hours daily, 33 Rose Street, across from Stanfords bookstore entrance on Floral Street, tel. 020/7497-9504).

Chinatown and Good Chinese Nearby

The main drag of Chinatown (Gerrard Street, with the ornamental archways) is lined with touristy, interchangeable Chinese joints— but these places seem to have an edge.

$$ Y Ming Chinese Restaurant—across Shaftesbury Avenue from the ornate gates, clatter, and dim sum of Chinatown—has dressy, porcelain-blue European decor, serious but helpful service, and authentic Northern Chinese cooking. London's food critics consider this well worth the short walk from the heart of Chinatown for food that's a notch above (good £15 meal deal offered

12:00-18:00, open Mon-Sat 12:00-23:30, closed Sun, 35 Greek Street, tel. 020/7734-2721, run for 22 years by William).

$ Jen Café, across the little square called Newport Place, is a humble Chinese corner eatery much loved for its homemade dumplings. It's just stools and simple seating, with fast service, a fun and inexpensive menu, and a devoted following (Mon-Wed 11:00-20:30, Thu-Sun until 21:30, cash only, 4 Newport Place, tel. 020/7287-9708).

$$ Wong Kei Chinese restaurant, at the Wardour Street (west) end of the Chinatown drag, offers a bewildering variety of dishes served by notoriously brusque waiters in a setting that feels like a hospital cafeteria. Londoners put up with the abuse and lack of ambience to enjoy one of the satisfying BBQ rice dishes or hot pots. Individuals and couples are usually seated at communal tables, while larger parties are briskly shuffled up or down stairs (£10-15 chef special combos, daily 11:30-23:30, cash only, 41 Wardour Street, tel. 020/7437-8408).

$$$ Dumplings' Legend is a cut above Wong Kei if you'd like to spend a bit more. They serve a standard Chinese menu with full dim sum only until 18:00 (open daily for lunch and dinner, no reservations, on pedestrian main drag, 15 Gerrard Street, tel. 020/7494-1200).

Pubs and Crypts near Trafalgar Square

These places, all of which provide a more "jolly olde" experience than high cuisine, are within about 100 yards of Trafalgar Square.

$$ St. Martin-in-the-Fields Café in the Crypt is just right for a tasty meal on a monk's budget—maybe even on a monk's tomb. You'll dine sitting on somebody's gravestone in an ancient crypt. Their enticing buffet line is kept stocked all day, serving breakfast, lunch, and dinner (hearty traditional desserts, free jugs of water). They also serve a restful £10 afternoon tea (daily 12:00-18:00). You'll find the café directly under St. Martin-in-the-Fields, facing Trafalgar Square—enter through the glass pavilion next to the church (generally about 8:00-20:00 daily, profits go to the church, Tube: Charing Cross, tel. 020/7766-1158). On Wednesday evenings you can dine to the music of a live jazz band at 20:00 (£8-15 tickets). While here, check out the concert schedule for the busy church upstairs (or visit www.stmartin-in-the-fields.org).

$$ The Chandos Pub's Opera Room floats amazingly apart from the tacky crush of tourism around Trafalgar Square. Look for it opposite the National Portrait Gallery (corner of William IV Street and St. Martin's Lane) and climb the stairs—to the left or right of the pub entrance—to the Opera Room. This is a fine Trafalgar rendezvous point and wonderfully local pub. They serve £7 sandwiches and a better-than-average range of traditional pub

EATING

meals for £10—meat pies and fish-and-chips are their specialty. The ground-floor pub is stuffed with regulars and offers snugs (private booths) and more serious beer drinking. To eat on that level, you have to order upstairs and carry it down (kitchen open daily 11:30-21:00, Fri until 18:00, order and pay at the bar, 29 St. Martin's Lane, Tube: Leicester Square, tel. 020/7836-1401).

$$ Gordon's Wine Bar is a candlelit 15th-century wine cellar filled with dusty old bottles, faded British memorabilia, and nine-to-fivers. At the "English rustic" buffet, choose a hot meal or cold meat dish with a salad (figure around £11/dish); the £12 cheese plate comes with two big hunks of cheese (from your choice of 20), bread, and a pickle. Then step up to the wine bar and consider the many varieties of wine and port available by the glass (this place is passionate about port—even the house port is excellent). The low carbon-crusted vaulting deeper in the back seems to intensify the Hogarth-painting atmosphere. Although it's crowded—often downright packed with people sitting at shared tables—you can normally corral two chairs and grab the corner of one. When sunny, the crowd spills out onto the tight parkside patio, where a chef often cooks at a BBQ grill for a long line of happy customers (daily 11:00-23:00, 2 blocks from Trafalgar Square, bottom of Villiers Street at #47—the door is locked but it's just around the corner to the right, Tube: Embankment, tel. 020/7930-1408, manager Gerard Menan).

$ The Lord Moon of the Mall Pub is a sloppy old eating pub, actually filling a former bank, right at the top of Whitehall. While nothing extraordinary, it's a very handy location and cranks out cheap, simple pub grub and fish-and-chips all day (long hours daily, 16 Whitehall, Tube: Charing Cross, tel. 020/7839-7701).

Near the British Museum

To avoid the touristy crush right around the museum, head a few blocks west to the Fitzrovia area. Here, tiny Charlotte Place is lined with small eateries (including the first two listed next); nearby, the much bigger Charlotte Street has several more good options. The higher street signs you'll notice on Charlotte Street are a holdover from a time when they needed to be visible to carriage drivers. This area is a short walk from the Goodge Street Tube station—convenient to the British Museum, and just two blocks from Pollock's Toy Museum. See the map on page 392 for locations.

$ Salumeria Dino serves up hearty £5 sandwiches, pasta, and Italian coffee. Dino, a native of Naples, has run his little shop for more than 30 years and has managed to create a classic-feeling Italian deli (cheap takeaway cappuccinos, Mon-Fri 9:00-18:00, closed Sat-Sun, 15 Charlotte Place, tel. 020/7580-3938).

$ Lantana OUT, next door to Salumeria Dino, is an Australian coffee shop that sells modern soups, sandwiches, and salads at their takeaway window (£8 daily hot dish). **Lantana IN** is an adjacent sit-down café that serves pricier meals (both open long hours daily, 13 Charlotte Place, tel. 020/7637-3347).

$$ Indian Food near the British Library: Drummond Street (running just west of Euston Station) is famous for cheap and good Indian vegetarian food. For a good, moderately priced *thali* (combo platter) consider **Chutneys** (124 Drummond, tel. 020/7388-0604) and **Ravi Shankar** (135 Drummond, tel. 020/7388-6458, both open long hours daily).

WEST LONDON
Near Victoria Station Accommodations

These restaurants are within a few blocks of Victoria Station—and all are places where I've enjoyed eating. As with the accommodations in this area, I've grouped them by location: east or west of the station (see the map on page 380).

Cheap Eats: For groceries, try the following places (all open long hours daily). Inside Victoria Station you'll find an **M&S Simply Food** (near the front, by the bus terminus) and a **Sainsbury's Local** (at rear entrance, on Eccleston Street). A larger Sainsbury's is on Wilton Road near Warwick Way, a couple of blocks southeast of the station (closes early on Sun). A string of good ethnic restaurants lines Wilton Road. For affordable if forgettable meals, try the row of cheap little eateries on Elizabeth Street.

West of Victoria Station (Belgravia)

$$$$ Ebury Wine Bar, filled with young professionals, provides a cut-above atmosphere. In the delightful **back room,** the fancy menu features modern European cuisine with a French accent, including delicious main dishes and a £25 two-course or £30 three-course special (available Mon-Fri at lunch and daily 18:00-19:30 and again after 21:15; three-course meal includes a glass of Prosecco that you're welcome to swap for house wine). At the less expensive **wine bar,** find a cheaper bar menu that's better than your average pub grub. This is emphatically a "traditional wine bar," with no beers on tap (open daily 12:00-15:00 & 18:00-22:30, reservations smart, at intersection of Ebury and Elizabeth Streets, 139 Ebury Street, tel. 020/7730-5447, www.eburyrestaurant.co.uk).

$ La Bottega is an Italian delicatessen that fits its upscale Belgravia neighborhood. It offers tasty, freshly cooked pastas, lasagnas, and salads, great sandwiches, and a good coffee bar with Italian pastries. It's fast (order at the counter). Grab your meal to go, or enjoy the Belgravia good life with locals, either sitting inside or at a sidewalk table (Mon-Fri 8:00-19:00, Sat-Sun 9:00-18:00, on corner of Ebury and Eccleston Streets, tel. 020/7730-2730).

EATING

Pub Appreciation

The pub is the heart of the people's England, where all manner of folks have, for generations, found their respite from work and a home away from home. England's classic pubs are national treasures, with great cultural value and rich history, not to mention good beer and grub (you'll find details on beer and pub food on pages 568 and 563). Their odd names can go back hundreds of years. Because so many medieval pub-goers were illiterate, pubs were simply named for the picture hung outside (e.g., The Crooked Stick, The Queen's Arms—meaning her coat of arms).

The Golden Age for pub-building was in the late Victorian era (c. 1880-1905), when pubs were independently owned and land prices were high enough to make it worthwhile to invest in fixing them up. The politics were pro-pub as well: Conservatives, backed by Big Beer, were in, and temperance-minded Liberals were out.

Especially in class-conscious Victorian times, traditional pubs were divided into sections by elaborate screens (now mostly gone), allowing the wealthy to drink in a more refined setting, while commoners congregated on the pub's rougher side. These were really "public houses," featuring nooks (snugs) for groups and clubs to meet, friends and lovers to rendezvous, and families to get out of the house at night.

Historic pubs still dot the London cityscape. The only place to see the very oldest-style tavern in the "domestic tradition" is at **$$ Ye Olde Cheshire Cheese,** which was rebuilt in 1667 (after the Great Fire) from a 16th-century tavern (see description on page 249; pub grub, pricier meals in the **restaurant,** open daily, 145 Fleet Street, Tube: Blackfriars, tel. 020/7353-6170). Imagine this mazelike place, with three separate bars, in the pre-Victorian era: With no bar, drinkers gathered around the fireplaces, while tap boys shuttled tankards up from the cellar. (This was long before barroom taps were connected to casks in the cellar. Oh, and don't say "keg"—that's a gassy modern thing.)

Late-Victorian pubs are more common, such as the lovingly restored **$$ Princess Louise,** dating from 1897 (daily midday until 23:00, lunch and dinner served Mon-Sat 12:00-21:00 in less atmospheric upstairs lounge, no food Sun, 208 High Holborn, see map on page 400, Tube: Holborn, tel. 020/7405-8816). These places are fancy, often with heavily embossed wallpaper ceilings, decorative tile work, fine-etched glass, ornate carved stillions (the big central hutch for storing bottles and glass), and even urinals equipped with a place to set your glass.

London's best Art Nouveau pub is **$$ The Black Friar** (c. 1900-1915), with fine carved capitals, lamp holders, and quirky phrases worked into the decor (Mon-Sat 10:00-23:00, Sun 12:00-22:30, food daily until 22:00, outdoor seating, 174 Queen Victoria Street, Tube: Blackfriars, tel. 020/7236-5474).

EATING

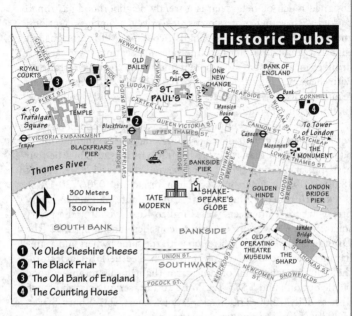

Historic Pubs

THE CITY

NEWGATE

OLD BAILEY

ROYAL COURTS

FETTER LN.

CHANCERY LANE

ST. BRIDE

FLEET ST.

To Trafalgar Square

THE TEMPLE

Temple

VICTORIA EMBANKMENT

St. Paul's

ST. PAUL'S

LUDGATE

CARTER LN.

WARWICK

NEW CHANGE

ONE NEW CHANGE

CHEAPSIDE

BANK OF ENGLAND

Bank

KING WILLIAM ST.

CORNHILL

Mansion House

QUEEN VICTORIA ST.

UPPER THAMES ST.

CANNON ST.

Cannon St.

EASTCHEAP

LOWER THAMES ST.

To Tower of London

Monument

THE MONUMENT

Blackfriars

BLACKFRIARS BRIDGE

BLACKFRIARS PIER

Thames River

300 Meters

300 Yards

N

SOUTH BANK

MILLENNIUM BRIDGE

BANKSIDE PIER

TATE MODERN

SHAKE-SPEARE'S GLOBE

BANKSIDE

SOUTHWARK

SOUTHWARK BRIDGE

GOLDEN HINDE

LONDON BRIDGE

LONDON BRIDGE PIER

UNION ST.

REDCROSS WAY

OLD OPERATING THEATRE MUSEUM

THE SHARD

London Bridge Station

ST. THOMAS ST.

POCOCK ST.

NEWCOMEN ST.

SNOWFIELDS

❶ Ye Olde Cheshire Cheese
❷ The Black Friar
❸ The Old Bank of England
❹ The Counting House

The "former-bank pubs" represent a more modern trend. As banks move out of lavish, high-rent old buildings, many are being

refitted as pubs with elegant bars and freestanding stillions, which provide a fine centerpiece.

Three such pubs are **$$$ The Old Bank of England** (Mon-Fri 11:00-23:00, food served until 21:00, Sat 12:00-18:00, closed Sun, 194 Fleet Street, Tube: Temple, tel. 020/7430-2255), **$$ The Jugged Hare** (open daily, 172 Vauxhall Bridge Road—see map on page 380, Tube: Victoria, tel. 020/7614-0134, also see listing on page 411), and **$$ The Counting House,** with great sandwiches, homemade meat pies, fish, and fresh vegetables (open Mon-Fri 11:00-23:00, food served until 22:00, closed Sat-Sun; gets really busy with the buttoned-down 9-to-5 crowd after 12:15, especially Thu-Fri; 50 Cornhill, Tube: Bank, tel. 020/7283-7123).

Go pubbing in the evening for a lively time, or drop by during the quiet late morning (from 11:00), when the pub is empty and filled with memories.

EATING

$$$ The Thomas Cubitt, named for the urban planner who designed much of Belgravia, is a trendy neighborhood gastropub packed with young professionals. It's pricey, a pinch pretentious, and popular for its modern English cooking. With a bright but slightly cramped interior and fine sidewalk seating, it's great for a drink or meal. Upstairs is a more refined and expensive **restaurant** with the same kitchen (food served daily 12:00-22:00, reservations recommended, 44 Elizabeth Street, tel. 020/7730-6060, www.thethomascubitt.co.uk).

$$ The Duke of Wellington pub is a classic neighborhood place with forgettable grub, sidewalk seating, and an inviting interior. A bit more lowbrow than my other Belgravia listings, this may be your best shot at meeting a local (food served Mon-Sat 12:00-15:00 & 18:00-21:00, Sun lunch only, 63 Eaton Terrace, tel. 020/7730-1782).

South End of Ebury Street: A five-minute walk down Ebury Street, where it intersects with Pimlico Road, you'll find a pretty square with a few more eateries to consider—including **$$$ The Orange,** a high-priced gastropub with the same owners and a similar menu to The Thomas Cubitt (described earlier); **$ Daylesford,** the deli and café of an organic farm (light meals to go—a good picnic option); and **$$$$ La Poule au Pot,** serving classic French dishes (daily 12:00-23:00, reservations smart, 231 Ebury Street, tel. 020/7730-7763, www.pouleaupot.co.uk).

East of Victoria Station (Pimlico)

$$$ Grumbles brags it's been serving "good food and wine at non-scary prices since 1964." Offering a delicious mix of "modern eclectic French and traditional English," this unpretentious little place with cozy booths inside (on two levels) and a few nice sidewalk tables is the best spot to eat well in this otherwise workaday neighborhood. Their traditional dishes are their forte (early-bird specials, open daily 12:00-14:30 & 18:00-23:00, reservations wise, half a block north of Belgrave Road at 35 Churton Street, tel. 020/7834-0149, www.grumblesrestaurant.co.uk).

$$ Pimlico Fresh's breakfasts and lunches feature fresh, organic ingredients, served up with good coffee and/or fresh-squeezed juices. Choose from the dishes listed on the wall-sized chalkboard that lines the small eating area, then order at the counter. This place is heaven if you need a break from your hotel's bacon-eggs-beans routine (takeout lunches, plenty of vegetarian options; Mon-Fri 7:30-18:30, breakfast served until 15:00; Sat-Sun 9:00-18:00; 86 Wilton Road, tel. 020/7932-0030).

$$ Seafresh Fish Restaurant is the neighborhood place for plaice—and classic and creative fish-and-chips cuisine. You can either take out on the cheap or eat in, enjoying a white-fish ambience. Though Mario's father started this place in 1965, it feels like the chippy of the 21st century (Mon-Sat 12:00-15:00 & 17:00-22:30, closed Sun, 80 Wilton Road, tel. 020/7828-0747).

$$ The Jugged Hare, a 10-minute walk from Victoria Station, fills a lavish old bank building, with vaults replaced by kegs of beer and a kitchen. They have a traditional menu and a plush, vivid pub scene good for a meal or just a drink (food served Mon-Fri 11:00-21:00, Sat-Sun until 20:00, 172 Vauxhall Bridge Road, tel. 020/7828-1543).

$$ St. George's Tavern is the neighborhood's best pub for a full meal. They serve dinner from the same menu in three zones: on the sidewalk to catch the sun and enjoy some people-watching, in the ground-floor pub, and in a classier downstairs dining room with full table service. The scene is inviting for just a beer, too (food served daily 12:00-22:00, corner of Hugh Street and Belgrave Road, tel. 020/7630-1116).

South Kensington

These places are close to several recommended hotels and just a couple of blocks from the Victoria and Albert Museum and Natural History Museum (Tube: South Kensington; for locations see map on page 383).

$$ Exhibition Road Food Circus, a one-block-long road (on the Victoria and Albert Museum side of the South Kensington Tube station), is a traffic-free pedestrian zone lined with enticing little eateries, including **Fernandez and Wells** (if you want wine, fine meats, and cheese), **Thai Square** (for good Thai), **Comptoir Libanais** (a Lebanese canteen), **Casa Brindisa** (for tapas and shared Mediterranean-style dishes), **Le Pain Quotidien** (hearty soups and sandwiches on homemade rustic bread), **Daquise** (a venerable Polish restaurant much loved by the local Polish community—and the only non-chain mentioned here; at 20 Thurloe Street), and much more.

$$$ Moti Mahal Indian Restaurant, with minimalist-yet-upscale ambience and attentive service, serves delicious, mostly Bangladeshi cuisine. Consider chicken *jalfrezi* if you like spicy food, and buttery chicken if you don't (daily 12:00-14:30 & 17:30-23:30, 3 Glendower Place, tel. 020/7584-8428).

$ Bosphorus Kebabs is the student favorite for a quick, fast, and hearty Turkish dinner served with a friendly smile. While mostly for takeaway, they have a few tight tables indoors and on the sidewalk (daily 10:30-24:00, 59 Old Brompton Road, tel. 020/7584-4048).

$ Beirut Express has fresh, well-prepared Lebanese cuisine. In the front, you'll find takeaway service as well as barstools for a quick bite. In the back is a pricier sit-down **restaurant** (daily 12:00-24:00, 65 Old Brompton Road, tel. 020/7591-0123).

EATING

$ Franco Manca, a taverna-inspired pizzeria, is part of a chain serving Neapolitan-style pies using organic ingredients and boasting typical Italian charm. If you skip the pricey drinks you can feast very cheaply here (daily 11:30-23:00, 91 Old Brompton Road, tel. 020/7584-9713).

$$$ The Anglesea Arms, with a great terrace buried in a classy South Kensington residential area, is a destination pub that feels like the classic neighborhood favorite. It's a thriving and happy place, with a woody ambience. While the food is the main draw, this is also a fine place to just have a beer. Don't let the crowds here put you off. Behind all the drinkers, in back, is an elegant, mellow step-down dining room a world away from any tourism (meals served daily 12:00-15:00 & 18:00-22:00; heading west from Old Brompton Road, turn left at Onslow Gardens and go down a few blocks to 15 Selwood Terrace; tel. 020/7373-7960).

$$ Rocca is a bright and dressy Italian place with a heated terrace (daily 11:30-23:30, 73 Old Brompton Road, tel. 020/7225-3413).

Supermarkets: Tesco Express (50 Old Brompton Road) and **Little Waitrose** (99 Old Brompton Road) are both open long hours daily.

Near Bayswater and Notting Hill Accommodations

For locations, see the map on page 386.

$$$$ Maggie Jones's has been feeding locals for over 50 years. Its countryside antique decor and candlelight make a visit a step back in time. It's a longer walk than most of my recommendations, but you'll get solid English cuisine. The portions are huge (especially the meat-and-fish pies, their specialty), and prices are a bargain at lunch. You're welcome to split your main course. The candlelit upstairs is the most romantic, while the basement is kept lively with the kitchen, tight seating, and lots of action. The staff is young and slightly aloof (daily 12:00-14:00 & 18:00-22:30, reservations recommended, 6 Old Court Place, east of Kensington Church Street, near High Street Kensington Tube stop, tel. 020/7937-6462, www.maggie-jones.co.uk).

$$$ Geales, which opened its doors in 1939 as a fish-and-chips shop, has been serving Notting Hill ever since. Today, while the menu is more varied, the emphasis is still on fish. The interior is casual, but the food is upscale. The crispy battered cod that put them on the map is still the best around (£10 two-course express lunch menu; Tue-Sun 12:00-15:00 & 18:00-22:00, closed Mon, reservations smart, 2 Farmer Street, just south of Notting Hill Gate Tube stop, tel. 020/7727-7528, www.geales.com).

$$ The Churchill Arms Pub and Thai Kitchen is a combo establishment that's a hit in the neighborhood. It offers good beer

and a thriving old-English ambience in fron
plates in an enclosed patio in the back. You c
in the tropical hideaway (table service) or in th
section (order at the counter). The place is festoor
memorabilia and chamber pots (including one wi
it—hanging from the ceiling farthest from Thai ....—sure to
cure the constipation of any Brit during World War II). Arrive by
18:00 or after 21:00 to avoid a line (food served daily 12:00-22:00,
119 Kensington Church Street, tel. 020/7727-4242 for the pub
or 020/7792-1246 for restaurant, www.churchillarmskensington.
co.uk).

$$$ Hereford Road is a cozy, mod eatery tucked away on
Leinster Square. It's stylish but not pretentious, serving heavy,
meaty English cuisine made with modern panache. Cozy two-
person booths face the open kitchen up top; the main dining room
is down below. There are also a few sidewalk tables (daily 12:00-
15:00 & 18:00-22:00, reservations smart, 3 Hereford Road, tel.
020/7727-1144, www.herefordroad.org).

$$ The Prince Edward serves good grub in a comfy, family-
friendly, upscale-pub setting and at its sidewalk tables (daily 10:30-
22:30, 2 blocks north of Bayswater Road at the corner of Dawson
Place and Hereford Road, 73 Prince's Square, tel. 020/7727-2221).

$ Café Diana is a healthy little eatery serving sandwiches,
salads, and Middle Eastern food. It's decorated—almost shrine-
like—with photos of Princess Diana, who used to drop by for pita
sandwiches. You can dine in the simple interior, or order to-go
(daily 8:00-23:00, cash only, 5 Wellington Terrace, on Bayswater
Road, opposite Kensington Palace Garden gates, where Di once
lived, tel. 020/7792-9606, Abdul).

On Queensway: The road called Queensway is a multiethnic
food circus, lined with lively and inexpensive eateries—browse the
options along here and choose your favorite. For a cut above, head
for **$$$ Royal China Restaurant**—filled with London's Chinese,
who consider this one of the city's best eateries. It's dressed up in
black, white, and gold, with candles and brisk waiters. While it's
pricier than most neighborhood Chinese restaurants, the food is
noticeably better (£9-10 dim sum menu served until 17:00, £25-40
special dishes, daily 12:00-23:00, 13 Queensway, tel. 020/7221-
2535).

Supermarkets: Tesco is a half-block from the Notting Hill
Gate Tube stop (near intersection with Pembridge Road at 114
Notting Hill Gate). Queensway is home to several supermarkets,
including **Sainsbury's Local** and **Tesco Express** (both next to Bay-
swater Tube stop; a larger **Tesco** is near the post office farther along
Queensway), and **Marks & Spencer** (inside Whiteleys Shopping
Centre). All of these open early and close late (except on Sundays).

LONDON

With its heritage of welcoming immigrants, it's no surprise that London's East End is its up-and-coming foodie mecca. Lively restaurants, food trucks, and "pop-ups" come here to get a toehold in an ever-evolving culinary scene. When in-the-know young locals eat out, they head for East London—especially trendy Shoreditch. In many ways, this area is what Soho was 40 years ago (before tourism and gentrification): a bit raw, unapologetically edgy, and simmering with vibrant sights, sounds, and flavors. I've focused on three areas: around Liverpool Street Station and Spitalfields Market; along Brick Lane; and near the Shoreditch High Street Tube station. For tips on street markets in this area, see page 435.

Near Liverpool Street Station and Spitalfields Market

Outside the station and around the market, you'll find the predictable chains. For something more interesting, check out Spitalfields Market and the surrounding streets.

In Spitalfields Market: This cavernous market hall is a festival of tempting eateries—some chains, others well-established favorites, and still others that sign a "pop-up" lease of just a few months. The lineup changes constantly, but look for these options: At the north end of the old market are **$$ Androuet** (takeaway toasted cheese baguettes, sit-down cheese pastas and raclette; attached shop sells even more cheese) and **$$$ Wright Brothers** (£1 oysters and other sea-to-plate specialties). Also inside the market—and just outside, along Lamb Street—look for food trucks, including **$ Sud Italia**'s mobile oven (piping-hot pizzas) and **Crosstown Donuts** (gourmet sourdough doughnuts). Nearby is a wall of **$** cheap eats: **Poppies** (fish-and-chips), **Indi Go Go** (Indian street food), **Pilpel** (falafel), and other Italian, Turkish, Mexican, and Indian counters.

$$$$ Boisdale Restaurant, down narrow Swedeland Court, is part of a small local chain of brasserie/piano bars specializing in Scottish fare. It offers tartan touches, a meat-heavy menu, and live jazz, blues, and soul music nearly nightly (steaks and seafood; downstairs restaurant Mon-Fri 12:00-15:00 & 18:00-late, closed Sat-Sun; reservations recommended, live music Tue-Fri 19:30-21:30, tel. 020/7283-1763, www.boisdale.co.uk). Other locations include Belgravia (see map on page 380), Canary Wharf, and Mayfair.

$$ Honest Burger, another small local chain, is a good place to try Britain's version of an American staple (daily 11:30-22:00, 12 Widegate Street, tel. 020/3693-3423).

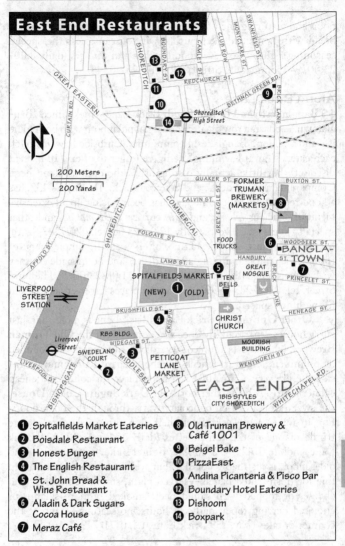

East End Restaurants

1. Spitalfields Market Eateries
2. Boisdale Restaurant
3. Honest Burger
4. The English Restaurant
5. St. John Bread & Wine Restaurant
6. Aladin & Dark Sugars Cocoa House
7. Meraz Café
8. Old Truman Brewery & Café 1001
9. Beigel Bake
10. PizzaEast
11. Andina Picanteria & Pisco Bar
12. Boundary Hotel Eateries
13. Dishoom
14. Boxpark

EATING

    $$$$ The English Restaurant, across from the south end of Spitalfields Market, started out as a Jewish bakery in the 17th century. Today it serves up traditional British cuisine with a Belgian flair—like updated bread-and-butter pudding—in a snug dining room or a bistro-style bar area (Mon-Fri 8:00-23:00, Sat-Sun 9:30-18:00, 52 Brushfield Street, tel. 020/7247-4110).

    $$$ St. John Bread and Wine Restaurant, with a "nose to tail" philosophy, is especially popular at breakfast—served until noon and featuring their award-winning bacon sandwich on thick bread with homemade ketchup (see if you can guess the special seasoning). They also have good lunches and dinners (daily 8:00-23:00, 94 Commercial Street, tel. 020/7251-0848).

Along Brick Lane

$$ Bangladeshi and Indian Food: Brick Lane—nicknamed "Banglatown"—boasts a row of curry houses popular both with both tourists and London's Bangladeshi community. Curbside hawkers pitch each eatery's "award-winning" pedigree (eager to offer a 10 percent discount), but little actually distinguishes the options along here. Compare menus and deals, and take your pick. **Aladin,** at #132, has a good reputation—the same chef has been spicing up an extensive menu of delicious *madras* and *balti* curries, *tikka masala,* and other specialty items for 30 years (daily 12:00-23:00, tel. 020/7247-8210). **Meraz Café,** just off Brick Lane, offers a small, simple menu of Indian, Pakistani, and Bangladeshi dishes and homemade chutney with a focus on quality over variety (daily 11:00-23:00, 56 Hanbury Street, tel. 020/7247-6999). And many places have very cheap and filling lunch specials.

Other Options on Brick Lane: Brick Lane is more than just curry houses—particularly once you get north of the **Old Truman Brewery,** which hosts a fun courtyard of **$ food trucks** surrounded by prominent street art (check out the Shepard Fairey mural). Inside the brewery, **Café 1001** is a good place for coffee and cheap cafeteria fare. A bit farther north, at **Dark Sugars Cocoa House,** the sweet aroma of rich chocolate wafts through the open doors. Pop in for a taste—ask about their signature cardamom orange truffle or one of the fun pipettes (daily 10:00-22:00, 124 Brick Lane, mobile 07429-472-606). **$ Beigel Bake,** unpretentious and old-school, is justifiably popular, but well worth the short wait in line for fresh-baked bagels—served plain, smothered with cream cheese, or topped with salted beef, smoked salmon, salami, or chopped herring (open daily 24 hours, no seating—stand at the counter or take away, 159 Brick Lane, tel. 0171/729-0616).

Near Shoreditch High Street Tube Station

For upmarket, trendy, sit-down restaurants, head for the epicenter of East London's foodie scene: Shoreditch High Street. These choices are within a short walk of the area's Tube stop. Just north of here, Kingsland Road is nicknamed "Pho Mile" for its many Vietnamese eateries.

$$$ PizzaEast delivers modern Italian pizzas and main dishes (crispy pork belly), all baked in their wood oven. Happy crowds perch on stools at communal tables under concrete rafters in this subway-tiled industrial space. For dessert, their salted caramel tart is a favorite. It can get noisy at dinnertime and on Sundays with the market crowd; for a quieter ambience, come at lunch (daily 12:00-24:00, 56 Shoreditch High Street, tel. 020/7729-1888).

$$ Andina Picanteria & Pisco Bar is a colorful, contemporary Peruvian place known for its ceviche (Mon-Fri 12:00-23:00, Sat-Sun from 16:00, 1 Redchurch Street at the corner of Shoreditch High Street, tel. 020/7920-6499).

$$$$ Boundary Restaurant is a trendy splurge where local foodies go for special occasions. In the cellars of Boundary Hotel, you'll dine on sophisticated French haute cuisine under vaulted ceilings and soft lighting (Mon-Sat 18:30-22:30, closed Sun, reservations smart, 2 Boundary Street, tel. 020/7729-1051, www. theboundary.co.uk). The hotel also houses the **$$$ Albion shop and café** (British favorites and homemade bread/pastries, daily 8:00-23:00) and a **$$$ rooftop bar and restaurant** with good views and pricey cocktails (daily 10:00-23:00).

$$$ Dishoom's original Shoreditch location offers a similar upmarket Indian menu (and the same wild popularity) as its Covent Garden outpost (see page 404), with seating in the British Imperialist dining room or outdoor enclosed veranda. Try their creative cocktails while you wait for a table (long hours daily, 7 Boundary Street, entrance tucked around the corner from busy Shoreditch High Street, tel. 020/7420-9324).

Boxpark Food Court: Just outside the Shoreditch High Street Tube station, you'll find this elevated food court housed in repurposed train boxcars. Entrepreneurs rent time-limited "pop-up" space—an approach that allows them more stability than traveling to food markets, without the financial risk of opening a full restaurant. Wander through and see what's available—usually a sampling of ethnic food with a modern twist (like Korean BBQ burritos). Their website lists the current lineup and each vendor's story (Mon-Sat 8:00-23:00, Sun 12:00-22:00, 2 Bethnal Green, tel. 020/7033-2899, www.boxpark.co.uk).

TAKING TEA IN LONDON

While visiting London, consider partaking in this most British of traditions. While some tearooms—such as the wallet-draining £50-a-head tea service at Claridges and the finicky Fortnum & Mason—still require a jacket and tie, most others happily welcome tourists in jeans and sneakers. Most tearooms are usually open for lunch and close about 17:00. At all the places listed below, it's perfectly acceptable for two people to order one afternoon tea and one cream tea and share the afternoon tea's goodies. For details on afternoon tea, see page 566.

EATING

Traditional Tea Experiences

$$$ The Wolseley serves a good afternoon tea between their meal service. Split one with your companion and enjoy two light meals at a great price in classic elegance (£13 cream tea, £30 afternoon tea, £40 champagne tea, generally served 15:00-18:30 daily, see full listing on page 403).

$$$$ The Orangery at Kensington Palace serves a £28 "Orangery tea" and a £35 champagne tea in its bright white hall near William and Kate's residence. You can also order treats à la carte. The portions aren't huge, but who can argue with eating at a royal orangery or on the terrace? (Tea served 12:00-18:00; a 10-minute walk through Kensington Gardens from either Queensway or High Street Kensington Tube stations to the orange brick building, about 100 yards from Kensington Palace—see map on page 386; tel. 020/3166-6113, www.hrp.org.uk.)

$$$$ The Capital Hotel, a luxury hotel a half-block from Harrods, caters to weary shoppers with its intimate five-table, linen-tablecloth tearoom. It's where the ladies-who-lunch meet to decide whether to buy that Versace gown they've had their eye on. Even so, casual clothes, kids, and sharing plates are all OK (£30 afternoon tea, daily 14:00-17:30, call to book ahead—especially on weekends, 22 Basil Street—see color map on page V, Tube: Knightsbridge, tel. 020/7591-1202, www.capitalhotel.co.uk).

$$$$ Fortnum & Mason department store offers tea at several different restaurants within its walls. You can "Take Tea in the Parlour" for £22 (including ice cream and scones; Mon-Sat 10:00-19:30, Sun 11:30-17:00). The pièce de résistance is their Diamond Jubilee Tea Salon, named in honor of the Queen's 60th year on the throne (and, no doubt, to remind visitors of Her Majesty's visit for tea here in 2012 with Camilla and Kate). At these royal prices, consider it dinner (£48, Mon-Sat 12:00-19:00, Sun until 18:00, dress up a bit—no shorts, "children must be behaved," 181 Piccadilly— see map on page 432, smart to reserve at least a week in advance, tel. 020/7734-8040, www.fortnumandmason.com).

$$$$ Brown's Hotel in Mayfair serves a fancy £55 afternoon tea (you're welcome to ask for second helpings of your favorite scones and sandwiches) in its English tea room. Said to be the inspiration for Agatha Christie's *At Bertram's Hotel,* the wood-paneled walls and inviting fire set a scene that's more contemporary-cozy than pinky-raising classy (daily 12:00-18:00, reservations smart, no casual clothing, 33 Albemarle Street—see map on page 400, Tube: Green Park, tel. 020/7518-4155, www.roccofortehotels.com).

Other Places to Sip Tea

Taking tea is not just for tourists and the wealthy—it's a true English tradition. If you want the teatime experience but are put off by the price, consider these options.

$$$ Browns Restaurant at Butler's Wharf serves a £14 afternoon tea with brioche sandwiches, traditional scones, and sophisticated desserts (daily 14:30-17:00, 26 Shad Thames facing Tower Bridge, tel. 020/7378-1700).

$$ The Café at Sotheby's, on the ground floor of the auction giant's headquarters, gives shoppers a break from fashionable New Bond Street (£9-26, tea served Mon-Fri 15:00-16:45, reservations smart, 34 New Bond Street—see map on page 54, Tube: Bond Street or Oxford Circus, tel. 020/7293-5077, www.sothebys. com/cafe).

At **$ Waterstones** bookstore you can put together a spread for less than £10 in their fifth-floor view café (203 Piccadilly).

Museum Cafés: Many museum restaurants offer a fine inexpensive tea service. The **$$$ National Dining Rooms,** within the Sainsbury Wing of the National Gallery on Trafalgar Square, serves a £7 cream tea and £18 afternoon tea with a great view from 14:30 to 16:30 (tea also served in National Café at the museum's Getty entrance, from 14:30 to 17:30; Tube: Charing Cross or Leicester Square, tel. 020/7747-2525). The **$$ Victoria and Albert Museum** café serves a classic cream tea in an elegant setting that won't break your budget and the **$$$ Wallace Collection** serves reasonably priced afternoon tea in its atrium (see page 63).

Shop Cafés: You'll find good-value teas at various cafés in shops and bookstores across London. Most department stores on Oxford Street (including those between Oxford Circus and Bond Street Tube stations) offer an afternoon tea.

EATING

LONDON WITH CHILDREN

London is a great city for kids. Big parks, colorful pageantry, engaging museums, and evocative historical sights make for happy little travelers. Add to that the buses, boats, trains, and Ferris wheels ready for riding, and your newly minted Londoners might never want to go home. The key to a successful family trip to this big city is making everyone happy, including the parents. My family-tested recommendations are designed to do just that.

Trip Tips

PLAN AHEAD

Involve your kids in trip planning. Have them read about the places that you may include in your itinerary (even the hotels you're considering), and let them help with your decisions.

Where to Stay

- Choose hotels in a kid-friendly area near a park. Bayswater and Notting Hill neighborhoods put you close to Kensington Gardens, with its imaginative playground (see Hyde Park listing later). Some of my recommended spots in North London are a stone's throw from Regent's Park.
- If you're staying more than a few days, think about renting an apartment (for more info on short-term rentals, see page 556).
- Consider hotels with restaurants, so older kids can go back to the room while you finish a pleasant dinner.
- London's big, budget chain hotels generally allow kids to sleep for free (see page 391).

What to Bring

- Bring your own drawing supplies and books, as these supplies are pricey in Britain.

- For a touch of home at the hotel, bring some favorite movies.

EATING (AND DRINKING)

Try these tips to keep your kids content throughout the day.

- Eat dinner early (around 18:00) to miss the romantic crowd.
- Skip the famous places. Look instead for relaxed cafés, pubs (kids are welcome, though sometimes restricted to the restaurant section or courtyard area), or fast-food restaurants where kids can move around without bothering others.
- Quality chain restaurants pop up at many of the places you're likely to visit, providing some good go-to options that should please young palates. Look for Byron Hamburgers, Wagamama Noodle Bar, and Pizza Express.
- Picnics work well; stop by a grab-and-go shop—such as Pret or Eat—or a supermarket with good takeout food, such as Sainsbury's Local or M&S Simply Food. Fun places to picnic are Hyde Park's rose garden, the grounds of the Tower of London, Greenwich Park, Jubilee Place Park in the Docklands area, or on the move—aboard a boat cruising the Thames or on an open-top sightseeing bus.
- Some of London's sights offer atmospheric eating options and good deals for families. Kids under age 12 eat free at the British Museum's cafeteria-style Gallery Café. St. Martin-in-the-Fields' Café in the Crypt, underneath the church, is more cozy than creepy. Would-be knights love The Medieval Banquet near the Tower of London, where costumed servers, minstrels, jesters, and contortionists accompany the four-course meal (described later). Aspiring royals will enjoy having high tea in the Orangery at Kensington Palace.
- For older kids, be aware that the drinking age is 18 in Britain, but 16-year-olds can have beer, wine, and cider if accompanied by a meal and an adult. It's best to decide on a family policy beforehand.

SIGHTSEEING

The key to a successful London family vacation is to slow down. Tackle one or two key sights each day, mix in a healthy dose of pure fun at a park or square, and take extended breaks when needed.

Planning Your Time

- Involve your children in the trip. Let them help choose daily activities, lead you through the Tube, pick lunch spots, and so on.
- Older kids and teens can help plan the details of a museum visit, such as what to see, how to get there, and ticketing details.
- Take advantage of Time Out London's frequently updated

website, which includes handy kids' calendars listing activities, shows, and museum events, all searchable by date and location (www.timeout.com/london/kids). Their annually updated guidebook, *London for Children* (available in bookstores and many newsstands), is chockablock with ideas for the serious parent tour-guide in London.

Successful Sightseeing

- Follow this book's crowd-beating tips. Kids despise long lines even more than you do.
- Museum audioguides are great for older children. For younger children, hit the gift shop first so they can buy postcards and have a scavenger hunt to find the pictured artwork. When boredom sets in, try "I spy" games or have them count how many babies or dogs they can spot in all the paintings in the room. At each sight, ask about a kids' guide or flier.
- Bring a sketchbook to a museum and encourage kids to select a painting or statue to draw. It's a great way for them to slow down and observe.
- Most of the big museums—such as the Tate Modern, Tate Britain, and National Gallery—schedule children's activities on weekends. Some museums also offer "backpacks" with activities to make the visit more interesting. Ask at museum information desks.
- Many museums—such as the Science Museum, National Army Museum, and Museum of London Docklands—have play areas for children under age seven.
- Public WCs can be hard to find. Try department stores, museums, and restaurants, particularly fast-food places.

Making or Finding Quality Souvenirs

- Buy your child a trip journal, and encourage him or her to write down observations, thoughts, and favorite sights and memories. This journal could end up being your child's treasured souvenir.
- For a group project, keep a family journal. Pack a small diary and a glue stick. While relaxing over tea and scones, take turns writing or drawing about the day's events and include mementos such as ticket stubs from museums and postcards.
- Teens might love shopping (or even window-shopping). See the Shopping in London chapter for fun areas.

MONEY, SAFETY, AND STAYING CONNECTED

Before your trip gets underway, talk to your kids about safety and money.

- Give your child a money belt and an expanded allowance; you are on vacation, after all. Let your children budget their funds by comparing and contrasting the dollar and pound.

- If you allow kids to explore a museum or neighborhood on their own, be sure to establish a clear meeting time and place.
- It's good to have a "what if" procedure in place in case something goes wrong. Give your kids your hotel's business card and emergency taxi fare. Let them know to ask to use the phone at a hotel if they are lost. Make sure they have your phone number (if you brought a mobile phone).
- If your kids have mobile phones, show them how to make calls in Britain. If traveling with older kids, you can help them keep in touch with friends at home with cheap texting plans and by email.
- Hotel guest computers and Wi-Fi hotspots are a godsend. Readily available Wi-Fi (at hotels, some cafés, and all Starbucks and McDonald's) makes bringing a mobile device worthwhile.
- Most parents find it worth the peace of mind to buy a supplemental messaging plan for the whole family: Adults can stay connected to teenagers while allowing them maximum independence (see page 569).

Top Kids' Activities and Sights

CENTRAL LONDON
Covent Garden
This is a great area for people-watching and candy-licking. Kids like the **London Transport Museum,** with its interactive zone (see page 54).

Trafalgar Square and Nearby
This grand square, complete with huggable lion statues, is fun for kids (Tube: Charing Cross). At the **National Gallery** on Trafalgar Square, ask about their children's printed guides, audioguide programs, and events (Sunday mornings are especially kid-friendly), and look for the "Family Fun" brochure at the information desk. 📖 See the National Gallery Tour chapter.

Also on Trafalgar Square is **St. Martin-in-the-Fields** church (see page 52). Next to the church is a glass pavilion, with a brass-rubbing center below that's fun for kids who'd like a souvenir to show for their efforts (£4.50 and up, Mon-Wed 10:00-18:00, Thu-Sat until 20:00, Sun 11:30-18:00, tel. 020/7766-1122). For a

CHILDREN

meal, try the affordable Café in the Crypt, which has just the right spooky tables-on-gravestones ambience (see page 405).

Changing of the Guard and Horse Guards

Kids enjoy the bands and pageantry of the Buckingham Palace Changing of the Guard, but little ones get a better view at the inspection at St. James's Palace or Wellington Barracks (see page 58).

Most kids also like to watch the Horse Guards change daily (on Whitehall, between Trafalgar Square and #10 Downing Street, Tube: Westminster, see page 47).

Piccadilly Circus

This titillating district has lots of schlocky amusements, such as the pricey Ripley's Believe It or Not. Be careful of fast-fingered riff-raff. Hamleys toy store is just two blocks up Regent Street (listed below), and Cool Britannia (across from Ripley's) has cheap Union Jack souvenirs kids love.

Shopping

If your teenager wants to bring home a few chic and cheap London fashions, **Oxford Street** (at the intersection of Regent Street) is a good place to start. Take the Tube to the Oxford Circus stop, and you'll be surrounded by lots of shops selling inexpensive, trendy clothes for teens. Stores include Topshop, Miss Selfridge, Zara, H&M, and music stores like HMV. Sandwich shops and coffeehouses (including a half-dozen Starbucks) offer easy rest stops. Also see the "Regent Street Shopping Walk" (on page 439).

Hamleys is the biggest toy store in Britain, with seven floors of toys (daily, 188 Regent Street, Tube: Oxford Circus, www.hamleys.com).

Harrods in Knightsbridge, with its over-the-top toy and food departments, can be fun for kids of all ages (see page 431).

Markets, particularly the Camden Lock Market, will hit the spot for finicky teenagers in need of loud music, cool clothes, and plenty of food choices (see page 435).

NORTH LONDON

Madame Tussauds Waxworks

Despite the lines outside and the crowds inside, the waxworks are popular with kids for gory stuff, pop and movie stars, everyone's favorite royals, and more (see page 65).

London Zoo and Regent's Park

This venerable animal habitat features more than 17,000 creatures and a fine petting zoo. Call for feeding and event times (£18 for kids 3-15, free for kids 2 and under, £24.30 for adults, discount for families; daily 10:00-18:00, last entry one hour before closing;

Books and Films for Kids

Get your kids into the spirit of London with these books and movies:

101 Dalmatians (1961). In this Disney animation set in London, two Dalmatian dogs and their owners must save a group of puppies before the evil Cruella de Vil turns their fur into a coat.

A Bear Called Paddington (Michael Bond, 1958). A bear from Peru winds up in a London train station, where he's found and adopted by a human family.

The Chronicles of Narnia (C. S. Lewis, 1949-1954). The story of four siblings and their escape from WWII London into the magical world of Narnia unfolds in this classic of children's literature (also a BBC miniseries and three feature-length films).

Harry Potter books (J. K. Rowling, 1997-2007) and films (2001-2011). After discovering he's a wizard, a young boy in England gets whisked off to a magical world of witchcraft and wizardry. There, he finds great friendships as well as grave evils.

A Little Princess (1939). In this film adaptation of the classic novel, Shirley Temple plays a girl whose fortunes fall and rise again in a Victorian London boarding school.

The London Eye Mystery (Siobhan Dowd, 2007). Ted and Kat try to solve the mystery of their missing cousin, who disappeared after boarding the London Eye.

London Through Time (Angela McAllister, 2015). A boy and girl journey through time as they walk down one London street that folds out of this book to reveal the past.

Mary Poppins (1964). Though filmed on a set in California, this beloved musical starring Julie Andrews and Dick Van Dyke is set in Edwardian London.

Mission London: A Scavenger Hunt Adventure (Catherine Aragon, 2014). Young explorers will have hands-on fun tackling spy-themed tasks while discovering the city.

This Is London (Miroslav Sasek, 1959, updated 2004). Vivid illustrations bring the English capital to life in this classic picture book.

A Walk in London (Salvatore Rubbino, 2011). A mother and daughter experience the city—from the changing of the guard to St. Paul's Cathedral—in this charming picture book.

Wallace & Gromit TV series and films (1990-2012). Absent-minded inventor Wallace and his dog Gromit may live in northwest England, but these uniquely British characters are beloved by children around the country and the world.

Young Sherlock Holmes (1985). In this film, young Sherlock and his sidekick, Watson, work to solve the mystery of a series of nonsensical suicides (some scenes may be frightening for younger children).

CHILDREN

in Regent's Park, tel. 0344/225-1826, www.zsl.org). Regent's Park also has rental rowboats.

While you can take the subway/bus to the zoo (Tube: Camden Town, then bus #274), a more scenic approach is to ride the London Waterbus down Regent's Canal. They drop you off right at the entry (ticket includes one-way trip and admission to the zoo; board at Camden Lock Market, Tube: Camden Town, or at Little Venice, Tube: Warwick Avenue; www.londonwaterbus.com).

Pollock's Toy Museum

Kids will wonder how their grandparents ever survived without Xbox as they wander through this rickety old house filled with toys that predate batteries and microchips. Be aware, though, that you must exit through a neat toy shop (see page 67).

EAST LONDON
Tower of London

The crown jewels are awesome, the Beefeater tour plays off kids in a memorable and fun way, and the welcome center offers quizzes, badges, and activities. Avoid the long ticket lines by buying a voucher in advance. 📖 See the Tower of London Tour chapter.

Medieval Meal near the Tower: In **$$$$** **The Medieval Banquet**'s underground brick-arched room, costumed wenches bring you a four-course medieval-themed meal as minstrels, knights, jesters, and contortionists perform. If you enjoy an act, pound on the table. Reserve online or by phone (£30 for kids, £50 for adults, £130 family deal for 2 adults and 2 kids—Wed, Thu, and Sun only, ask for Rick Steves discount—can't combine with family deal, doors open Wed-Sat at 19:15, Sun at 17:15, show starts about 30 minutes later, closed Mon-Tue, veggie option—request in advance, rentable medieval garb, St. Katharine Docks, enter docks off East Smithfield Street, Tube: Tower Hill, tel. 020/7480-5353, www.medievalbanquet.com).

Museum of London

The museum has a very kid-friendly presentation that takes you from prehistoric times to the present. The events guide at the entrance details current kids' activities (see page 73).

THE SOUTH BANK

The Bankside Walk (see page 288) links several sights children might enjoy: The *Golden Hinde* ship, Shakespeare's Globe Theatre, Clink Prison Museum, and Old Operating Theatre.

London Eye and Nearby

The London Eye, a giant Ferris wheel, is a delight for the whole family (see page 84 for more information and crowd-avoidance tips). The same company runs the other two sights in the same complex (listed later), Madame Tussauds Waxworks, and the skippable London Dungeon—if you think you'll visit more than one of them, consider buying a combo-ticket to save some money (available at the website or ticket counter of any of these attractions).

In the London Eye complex (Tube: Waterloo or Westminster), the small, pricey, but entertaining **Sea Life aquarium** resembles an overpriced theme park. Although there are far better aquariums elsewhere, this place packs in school groups and families looking for a break from museums (daily, www.visitsealife.com).

Next door, **Shrek's Adventure** is part walk, part 4-D ride. The crowded journey through Shrek's swamp re-creates scenes from the movie series (timed entry daily every 15 minutes, www.shreksadventure.com).

The free **playground** in Jubilee Gardens, next to the London Eye complex, has an adventurous jungle gym of nets and logs for climbing and balancing, and the little **carousel** in the London Wonderground carnival area nearby delights for a small fee.

HMS *Belfast*

Older kids might like scrambling across the decks of this WWII warship (see page 94).

WEST LONDON
Hyde Park

London's backyard is the perfect place for museum'd-out kids to play and run free. For older kids, the park has a tennis court, a putting green, and trails for running or biking. Young children will enjoy the Diana, Princess of Wales Memorial Playground in adjacent Kensington Gardens, with its Peter Pan-themed climbing equipment, including a huge wooden pirate ship (Tube: Queensway). Events such as music, plays, and clown acts are scheduled throughout the summer. The Serpentine Lake offers paddleboat rentals and a swimming area with a playground and a shallow kiddie pool (Easter-Oct daily 10:00-dusk, closed off-season; Tube: Knightsbridge, South Kensington, and more). The park is open daily from 5:00 in the morning until midnight (www.royalparks.org.uk).

Science Museums

The **Natural History Museum** features a wonderful world of dinosaurs, volcanoes, meteors, and creepy-crawlies, along with creative interactive displays (see page 100).

Next door to the Natural History Museum, the **Science Mu-**

CHILDREN

seum offers lots of hands-on fun and IMAX movies (see page 102). The Garden play area on Floor B (basement level) entertains younger children (3-6) with water, textures, sounds, and climbing areas. This free museum also offers a variety of activities—like the Wonderlab—for a small fee.

Both the Natural History and Science museums are kid-friendly and can be clogged with school groups during the school year. Check for special events and exhibits (noted at each museum's entry and on their websites).

OUTSIDE THE CENTER
Cutty Sark
This beautifully restored sailing ship, now on dry land in Greenwich, is full of kid-friendly, hands-on displays (see page 352).

Queen Elizabeth Olympic Park
London's biggest park, complete with play areas, waterways, Olympic sights, and the world's longest, tallest tunnel slide is sure to please kids and teens alike (see page 104).

The Making of Harry Potter: Warner Bros. Studio Tour
A nirvana for Potterphiles, this attraction (in Leavesden, a 20-minute train ride from London) lets fans young and old see the actual sets and props that were used to create the Harry Potter films. Shuttle buses run to the studio from the Leavesden train station; for details, see page 109.

For a rundown of places in London where scenes from the movies were filmed, see the sidebar on page 110.

Kew Gardens
These famous 300-acre gardens include the Rhizotron and Xstrata Treetop Walkway, which lets kids explore the canopy 60 feet above the ground on a 200-yard-long scenic steel walkway. Younger children will love the Climbers and Creepers indoor play area and kid-size zip line (see page 105).

London Museum of Water and Steam
This impressive collection of steam-powered pumping engines that once powered waterworks across the UK is mesmerizing for children. The engines operate only on weekends—search the website for "What's On" to make sure they're "in steam." An outdoor water-play area is fun in nice weather (£5 for kids, £12.50 for adults, daily 11:00-16:00, Green Dragon Lane, tel. 020/8568-4757, www.waterandsteam.org.uk).

Day Trip to Windsor
If your kids are loopy over Legos, they'll love a day trip to Legoland Windsor. While older kids will probably enjoy it, the park is really

aimed at the 11-and-under crowd (see page 486 for cost, hours, and other details).

OTHER ACTIVITIES
Fun Transportation
A **Thames cruise** is a pleasant and easy way to see the city. Westminster Pier (near Big Ben) offers a lot of action, with round-trip cruises and boats to the Tower of London, Greenwich, and Kew Gardens. For details, see page 36.

Double-decker **hop-on, hop-off buses** drive by all the biggies in a two-hour loop and are fun for kids and stress-free for parents. You can stay on the bus the entire time, or hop on and hop off at any of the nearly 30 stops (see page 31). The Original London Sightseeing Tour's "City Sightseeing Tour" bus (marked with a yellow triangle) has a kids' soundtrack on the earphones. Bus-top picnics are allowed.

Theater
Long-running shows (such as *Wicked, Aladdin,* and *The Lion King*) are kid- and parent-pleasers (see the Entertainment in London chapter). Or check out what's playing at the **Unicorn Theatre.** This modern complex presents professional theater for children on two stages (ask about family discounts, on the South Bank just behind City Hall, 147 Tooley Street, Tube: London Bridge; tel. 020/7645-0560, www.unicorntheatre.com).

WHAT TO AVOID
The **London Dungeon**'s popularity with teenagers makes it one of London's most-visited sights. I enjoy gore and torture as much as the next boy, but this is lousy gore and torture, and I would not waste the time or money on it with my child. **The London Bridge Experience** (not to be confused with the Tower Bridge Exhibition) and **The London Tombs** are also to be avoided. They're copycat rip-offs of the London Dungeon.

CHILDREN

SHOPPING IN LONDON

London is great for shoppers—and, thanks to the high prices, perhaps even better for window-shoppers. This chapter will tell you where to get essentials, where to get souvenirs, where to browse through colorful street markets, and where to gawk at some high-end stores in this major fashion capital.

Most stores are open Monday through Saturday from roughly 9:00 or 10:00 until 17:00 or 18:00, with a late night on Wednesday or Thursday (usually until 19:00 or 20:00). Many close on Sundays. Large department stores stay open later during the week (until about 21:00 Mon-Sat) with shorter hours on Sundays.

Consider these tips for shopping in London:

- If all you need are souvenirs, a surgical strike at any souvenir shop will do.
- London's museums have extraordinarily good shops. The Transport Museum's is one of the best, and stays open at least a half-hour later than the museum itself (listed on page 54). Other sights with great shops include the British Museum (page 61), the National Gallery (page 49), the Victoria and Albert Museum (page 100), the Museum of London (page 73), the National Portrait Gallery (page 49), the Tate Modern (page 88), and the wacky selections at Pollock's Toy Museum (page 67) and the Old Operating Theatre (page 93).
- Large department stores offer relatively painless one-stop shopping. Consider the down-to-earth Marks & Spencer (Mon-Sat 9:00-21:00, Sun 12:00-18:00, 173 Oxford Street, Tube: Oxford Circus; another at 458 Oxford Street, Tube: Bond Street or Marble Arch; see www.marksandspencer.com for more locations). Fancier department stores are listed later.
- For flea-market fun and bargains, try one of the many street markets.

- Gawkers as well as serious bidders can attend high-end auctions.

For information on **VAT refunds** and **customs regulations,** see page 546. Refuse any offers to charge your credit card in dollars. This is called **dynamic currency conversion** (DCC), and it's offered by some stores (including Harrods) as a "convenience." The very bad exchange rate they use is convenient only for increasing the store's profits.

Where to Shop

SHOPPING STREETS

London is famous for its shopping. The best and most convenient shopping streets are in the West End and West London (roughly between Soho and Hyde Park). You'll find mid-range shops along **Oxford Street** (running east from Tube: Marble Arch), and fancier shops along **Regent Street** (stretching south from Tube: Oxford Circus to Piccadilly Circus) and **Knightsbridge** (where you'll find Harrods and Harvey Nichols;  Tube: Knightsbridge). Other streets are more specialized, such as **Jermyn Street** for old-fashioned men's clothing (just south of Piccadilly Street) and **Charing Cross Road** for books. **Floral Street,** connecting Leicester Square to Covent Garden, is lined with fashion boutiques. My **"Regent Street Shopping Walk,"** at the end of this chapter, connects several shopping areas, including Oxford, Regent, Carnaby, and Jermyn streets.

FANCY DEPARTMENT STORES IN WEST LONDON
Harrods

Harrods is London's most famous and touristy department store. With more than four acres of retail space covering seven floors, it's a place where some shoppers could spend all day. (To me, it's still just a department store.) Big yet classy, Harrods has everything from elephants to toothbrushes (Mon-Sat 10:00-21:00, Sun 11:30-18:00; baggage check outside on Basil Street—follow *left luggage* signs at back of the

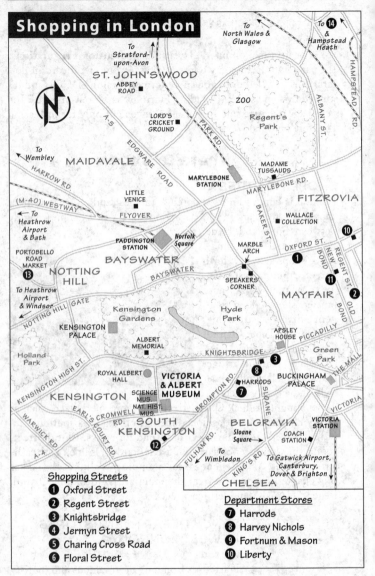

Shopping in London

To North Wales & Glasgow

To 14 & Hampstead Heath

To Stratford-upon-Avon

ST. JOHN'S WOOD

ABBEY ROAD

LORD'S CRICKET GROUND

ZOO

Regent's Park

HAMPSTEAD RD.

ALBANY ST.

PARK RD.

To Wembley

MAIDAVALE

HARROW RD.

EDGWARE ROAD

MARYLEBONE STATION

MADAME TUSSAUDS

MARYLEBONE RD.

FITZROVIA

(M-40) WESTWAY

LITTLE VENICE

FLYOVER

BAKER ST.

WALLACE COLLECTION

To Heathrow Airport & Bath

PADDINGTON STATION

Norfolk Square

MARBLE ARCH

OXFORD ST.

10

REGENT ST.

NEW BOND

PORTOBELLO ROAD MARKET

13

NOTTING HILL

BAYSWATER

BAYSWATER

SPEAKERS CORNER

MAYFAIR

11

2

OLD BOND

To Heathrow Airport & Windsor

NOTTING HILL GATE

Kensington Gardens

Hyde Park

1

KENSINGTON PALACE

ALBERT MEMORIAL

APSLEY HOUSE

PICCADILLY

Green Park

Holland Park

KNIGHTSBRIDGE

3

KENSINGTON HIGH ST.

ROYAL ALBERT HALL

VICTORIA & ALBERT MUSEUM

8

HARRODS

BUCKINGHAM PALACE

THE MALL

KENSINGTON

SCIENCE MUS.

NAT. HIST. MUS.

BROMPTON RD.

7

SLOANE

VICTORIA

EARL'S COURT RD.

CROMWELL RD.

BELGRAVIA

VICTORIA STATION

WARWICK RD.

A-4

SOUTH KENSINGTON

12

FULHAM RD.

Sloane Square

COACH STATION

To Wimbledon

KING'S RD.

To Gatwick Airport, Canterbury, Dover & Brighton

CHELSEA

Shopping Streets
1 Oxford Street
2 Regent Street
3 Knightsbridge
4 Jermyn Street
5 Charing Cross Road
6 Floral Street

Department Stores
7 Harrods
8 Harvey Nichols
9 Fortnum & Mason
10 Liberty

SHOPPING

store, a hefty £25/bag; Brompton Road, Tube: Knightsbridge, tel. 020/7730-1234, www.harrods.com).

Sightseers should pick up the free *Store Guide* at any info post. Here's what I enjoy: On the ground floor, find the Food Halls, with their Edwardian tiled walls, creative and exuberant displays, and staff in period costumes—not quite like your local supermarket back home.

Descend to the lower ground floor (fewer crowds) and follow

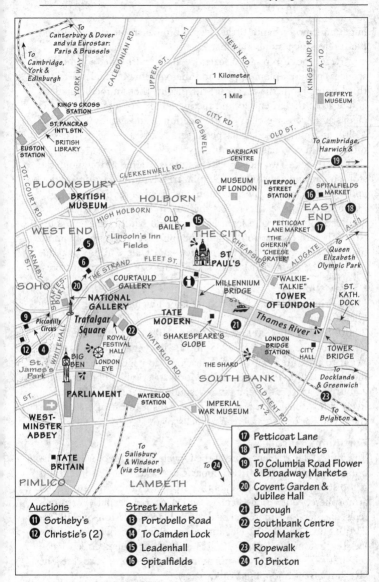

To Canterbury & Dover
and via Eurostar:
Paris & Brussels

To Cambridge,
York &
Edinburgh

KING'S CROSS
STATION

ST. PANCRAS
INT'L STN.

BRITISH
LIBRARY

EUSTON
STATION

1 Kilometer

1 Mile

GEFFRYE
MUSEUM

To Cambridge,
Harwich &

19

BLOOMSBURY

**BRITISH
MUSEUM**

HOLBORN

BARBICAN
CENTRE

MUSEUM
OF LONDON

LIVERPOOL
STREET
STATION

SPITALFIELDS
MARKET

16

18

EAST
END

WEST END

High Holborn

OLD
BAILEY

15

THE CITY

Cheapside

PETTICOAT
LANE MARKET

17

"THE
GHERKIN"

"CHEESE
GRATER"

To
Queen
Elizabeth
Olympic Park

Lincoln's Inn
Fields

5

6

THE STRAND

FLEET ST.

**ST.
PAUL'S**

SOHO

20

COURTAULD
GALLERY

**NATIONAL
GALLERY**

MILLENNIUM
BRIDGE

"WALKIE-
TALKIE"

**TOWER
OF LONDON**

ST.
KATH.
DOCK

9

Piccadilly
Circus

12

4

Trafalgar
Square

22

**TATE
MODERN**

21

Thames River

ROYAL
FESTIVAL
HALL

SHAKESPEARE'S
GLOBE

LONDON
BRIDGE
STATION

CITY
HALL

TOWER
BRIDGE

St.
James's
Park

BIG
BEN

LONDON
EYE

THE SHARD

SOUTH BANK

To
Docklands
& Greenwich

PARLIAMENT

WATERLOO
STATION

IMPERIAL
WAR MUSEUM

To
Brighton

23

**WEST-
MINSTER
ABBEY**

To
Salisbury
& Windsor
(via Staines)

To **24**

**TATE
BRITAIN**

PIMLICO

LAMBETH

Auctions	Street Markets		
11 Sotheby's	**13** Portobello Road	**17** Petticoat Lane	
12 Christie's (2)	**14** To Camden Lock	**18** Truman Markets	
	15 Leadenhall	**19** To Columbia Road Flower & Broadway Markets	
	16 Spitalfields	**20** Covent Garden & Jubilee Hall	
		21 Borough	
		22 Southbank Centre Food Market	
		23 Ropewalk	
		24 To Brixton	

signs to the Egyptian Escalator (in the center of the store). Here you'll find a memorial to Princess Diana and her boyfriend, Dodi Fayed, who both died in a car crash in Paris in 1997 (Dodi's father, Mohamed Al Fayed, was the store's former owner). Photos and flowers honor the late princess and her lover. Inside a small, clear pyramid, you can see a wine glass still dirty from their last dinner and the engagement ring that Dodi purchased the day before they died. True Di-hards can even sign the official condolence book. A huge (and more than a little creepy) bronze statue shows Di and Dodi releasing a symbolic albatross.

Ride the Egyptian Escalator—lined with pharaoh-headed sconces, papyrus-plant lamps, and hieroglyphic balconies—to the third floor. From the escalator, turn right, then immediately left, and head to the far end to find the incredible Toy Land, which includes an impressive Harry Potter section (wands go for upwards of £100), and child-size luxury pedal cars (£7,000)—the perfect gift for the child who has everything.

More than two dozen eateries are scattered throughout the store, including a sushi bar, deli, pizzeria, Ladurée *macaron* parlor, and—for the truly homesick—an American burger bar.

Many of my readers report that Harrods is overpriced, snooty, and teeming with American, Japanese, and Middle Eastern tourists with zero concept of bargain shopping. It's the only shopping mall I've seen with its own gift store—and Dale Chihuly chandelier (near the door 3 exit). Still, it's the palace of department stores.

Harvey Nichols

Once Princess Diana's favorite and later Duchess Kate's, "Harvey Nick's" remains the department store *du jour* (Mon-Sat 10:00-20:00, Sun 11:30-18:00, near Harrods, 109 Knightsbridge, Tube: Knightsbridge, tel. 020/7235-5000, www.harveynichols.com). Want to pick up a £20 scarf? You won't do it here, where they're more like £200. The store's fifth floor is a veritable food fest, with a gourmet grocery store, a fancy restaurant, a Yo! Sushi bar, and a lively café. Consider a takeaway tray of sushi to eat on a bench in the Hyde Park rose garden two blocks away.

Fortnum & Mason

The official department store of the Queen, Fortnum & Mason embodies old-fashioned, British upper-class taste. While some feel it is too stuffy, you won't find another store with the same storybook atmosphere. With rich displays and deep red carpet, Fortnum's feels classier and more relaxed than Harrods (Mon-Sat 10:00-21:00, Sun 11:30-18:00, elegant tea served in their Diamond Jubilee Tea Salon—see page 418, 181 Piccadilly, Tube: Green Park, tel. 020/7734-8040, www.fortnumandmason.com; also see the "Regent Street Shopping Walk," later).

Liberty

Designed to make well-heeled shoppers feel at home, this half-timbered, mock-Tudor emporium is a 19th-century institution that thrives today. Known for its gorgeous "Liberty Print" floral fabrics, well-stocked crafts department, and castle-like interior, this iconic shop was a favorite of writer Oscar Wilde, who called it "the chosen resort of the artistic shopper" (Mon-Sat 10:00-20:00, Sun

12:00-18:00, Great Marlborough Street, Tube: Oxford Circus, tel. 020/7734-1234, www.liberty.co.uk, also see the "Regent Street Shopping Walk," later).

STREET MARKETS

Antique buffs, foodies, people-watchers, and folks who brake for garage sales love London's street markets. There's good early-morning market activity somewhere any day of the week. The best markets—which combine lively stalls and a colorful neighborhood with cute and characteristic shops of their own—are Portobello Road and Camden Lock Market. Hagglers will enjoy the no-holds-barred bargaining encouraged in London's street markets. **Greenwich** (a quick DLR ride from central London) also has its share of great markets, especially lively on weekends (see page 350).

Warning: Markets attract two kinds of people—tourists and pickpockets.

Portobello Road Market (Notting Hill)

Arguably London's best street market, Portobello Road stretches for several blocks through the delightful, colorful, funky-yet-quaint Notting Hill neighborhood. Already-charming streets lined with pastel-painted houses and offbeat antique shops are enlivened on Fridays and Saturdays with 2,000 additional stalls (9:00-19:00), plus food, live music, and more. (The best strategy is to come on Friday; most stalls are open, with half the crowds of Saturday.) If you start at Notting Hill Gate and work your way north, you'll find these general sections: antiques, new goods, produce, vintage clothing, more new goods, a flea market, and more food. While Portobello Road is best on Fridays and Saturdays, it's enjoyable to stroll this street on most other days as well, since the quirky shops are fun to explore (Tube: Notting Hill Gate, near recommended accommodations, tel. 020/7727-7684, www.portobelloroad.co.uk).

Camden Lock Market (Camden Town)

This huge, trendy arts-and-crafts festival is divided into three areas, each with its own vibe (but all of them fresh and funky). The whole complex sprawls around an old-fashioned, still-functioning lock (used mostly for leisure boats) and its retro-chic, yellow-brick industrial buildings. The main market, set alongside the picturesque canal, features a mix of shops and stalls selling boutique crafts and artisanal foods. The market on the opposite side of Chalk Farm Road is edgier, with cheap ethnic food stalls, lots of canalside seating, and punk crafts. The Stables, a sprawling, incense-scented complex, is decorated with fun statues of horses and squeezed into tunnels under the old rail bridge just behind the main market. It's a little lowbrow and wildly creative, with cheap clothes, junk jew-

SHOPPING

elry, and loud music (daily 10:00-19:00, busiest on weekends, tel. 020/3763-9999, www.camdenmarket.com).

To escape the crowds, stroll for a while in either direction along the tranquil canal; it's possible to walk east from here all the way to Queen Elizabeth Olympic Park in Stratford (about six miles away).

Arriving by Tube, avoid the tacky, crowded area between the market and the Camden Town Tube station (which bills itself as "The Camden Market," but lacks the real one's canalside charm) by getting off at the Chalk Farm stop. Better yet, arrive via a scenic waterbus ride from Little Venice: Consider London Waterbus Company (tel. 020/7482-2660, www.londonwaterbus.com), Jason's Trip (www.jasons.co.uk), or the *Jenny Wren* (tel. 020/7485-4433, www.walkersquay.com). Bus #24 heads from Pimlico to Victoria Station to Trafalgar Square and then straight up to Camden, before continuing on to Hampstead Heath.

Leadenhall Market (The City)
One of London's oldest, Leadenhall Market stands on the original Roman center of town. Today, cheese and flower shops nestle between pubs, restaurants, and fashion boutiques, all beneath a beautiful Victorian arcade (Harry Potter fans may recognize it as Diagon Alley). This is not a "street market" in the true sense, but more a hidden gem in the midst of London's financial grind (Mon-Fri 10:00-18:00, tel. 020/7332-1523, Tube: Monument or Liverpool; off Gracechurch Street near Leadenhall Street and Fenchurch).

East End Markets
Most of these East End markets are busiest and most interesting on Sundays; the Broadway Market is best on Saturdays. For a walk tying together several of these markets—and a lot more in this neighborhood, which combines Cockney memories with London's biggest Bangladeshi community—see page 78.

Spitalfields Market: This huge, mod-feeling market hall combines a shopping mall with old brick buildings and sleek modern ones, all covered by a giant glass roof. The shops, stalls, and a rainbow of restaurant options are open every day, tempting you with ethnic eateries, crafts, trendy clothes, bags, and an antiques-and-junk market (Mon-Fri 10:00-17:00, Sat from 11:00, Sun from 9:00, Tube: Liverpool Street; from the Tube stop, take Bishopsgate East exit, turn left, walk to Brushfield Street, and turn right; www.spitalfields.co.uk).

Petticoat Lane Market: Just a block from Spitalfields Market, this line of stalls sits on the otherwise dull, glass-skyscraper-filled Middlesex Street; adjoining Wentworth Street is grungier and more characteristic. Expect budget clothing, leather, shoes, watches, jewelry, and crowds (Sun 9:00-14:00, sometimes later; smaller market Mon-Fri on Wentworth Street only; Middlesex Street and Wentworth Street, Tube: Liverpool Street).

Truman Markets: Housed in the former Truman Brewery on Brick Lane, this cluster of markets is in the heart of the "Banglatown" Bangladeshi community. Of the East End market areas, these are the grittiest and most avant-garde, selling handmade clothes and home decor as well as ethnic street food. The markets are in full swing on Sundays (roughly 10:00-17:00), though you'll see some action on Saturdays (11:00-18:00). The Boiler House Food Hall and the Backyard Market (hipster arts and crafts) go all weekend—and the Vintage Market (clothes) even operates on Thursdays and Fridays (11:00-16:00). Surrounding shops and eateries, including a fun courtyard of food trucks tucked off Brick Lane, are open all week (Tube: Liverpool Street or Aldgate East, tel. 020/7770-6028, www.bricklanemarket.com).

Columbia Road Flower Market: From the Truman Brewery complex, Brick Lane is lined with Sunday market stalls all the way up to Bethnal Green Road, about a 10-minute walk. Continuing straight (north) about five more minutes takes you to Columbia Road, where you can turn right (east) to find a colorful shopping street made even more so by the Sunday-morning commotion of shouting flower vendors. The prices are good (why not brighten up your hotel room with a bouquet?), and the sales pitches are entertaining (Sun 8:00-15:00, http://columbiaroad.info). Halfway up Columbia Road, be sure to loop left up little Ezra Street, with characteristic eateries, boutiques, and antique vendors.

Broadway Market: While the other listed East End markets are best on Sundays, Saturdays are best for the festive market sprawling through this aptly named neighborhood—ground zero for London's hipsters. A bit farther out, this market can be tricky to reach; it's easiest to take the Overground from Liverpool Street Station three stops to London Fields, then walk through that park to the market. Several blocks are filled with foodie delights, along with a few arts and crafts. The Broadway Schoolyard section is home to popular food trucks—many of them satellites of brick-and-mortar restaurants spread across London—selling trendy, affordable bites. The lineup changes constantly, but if you happen to see Le Swine, Dumpling Shack, Shrimpy, or The Frenchie, you know you came on a good day (Sat 9:00-17:00, www.broadwaymarket.co.uk). On sunny days, the London Fields park just north of the market is filled with thousands of picnicking and sunbathing locals enjoying their little slice of the city.

West End Markets

Covent Garden Market: Originally the convent garden for Westminster Abbey, the iron-and-glass market hall hosted a produce market until the 1970s (earning it the name "Apple Market"). Now it's a mix of fun shops, eateries, markets, and a more modern-day Apple store on the corner. Mondays are for antiques, while arts and crafts dominate the rest of the week. Yesteryear's produce stalls are open daily 10:30-18:00, and on Thursdays, a food market brightens up the square (Tube: Covent Garden, tel. 020/7395-1350, www.coventgardenlondonuk.com, also see 📖 West End Walk).

Jubilee Hall Market: This market features antiques on Mondays (5:00-17:00); a general market Tuesday through Friday (10:30-19:00); and arts and crafts on Saturdays and Sundays (10:00-18:00). It's located on the south side of Covent Garden (tel. 020/7379-4242, www.jubileemarket.co.uk).

South London Markets

Borough Market: London's oldest fruit-and-vegetable market has been serving the Southwark community for over 800 years. These days there are as many people taking photos as buying fruit, cheese, and beautiful breads, but it's still a fun carnival atmosphere with fantastic stall food. For maximum market and minimum crowds, join the locals on Thursdays (full market open Wed-Sat 10:00-17:00, Fri until 18:00, surrounding food stalls open daily; south of London Bridge, where Southwark Street meets Borough High Street; Tube: London Bridge, tel. 020/7407-1002, www.boroughmarket.org.uk, also see 📖 Bankside Walk).

Southbank Centre Food Market: You'll find some of the city's most popular vendors in this paradise of street food near the London Eye (Fri-Sat 12:00-20:00, Sun-Mon until 18:00, closed midweek; between the Royal Festival Hall and BFI Southbank at Hayward Gallery, Tube: Waterloo, or Embankment and cross the Jubilee Bridge; tel. 020/3879-9555, www.southbankcentre.co.uk). The market also hosts various festivals throughout the year (German Christmas, coffee, and chocolate are among the favorites).

Ropewalk (Maltby Street Market): This short-but-sweet, completely untouristy food bazaar bustles on weekends under a nondescript rail bridge in the shadow of the Shard. Two dozen vendors fill the narrow passage with a festival of hipster/artisan food carts, offering everything from gourmet burgers to waffles to scotch eggs to ice-cream sandwiches. Come as hungry as possible and graze your way to a satisfying lunch (Sat 9:00-16:00, Sun from 11:00, www.maltby.st). This area of South London—called Bermondsey—is a lowbrow but emerging neighborhood that's fun to explore for a slice of youthful, untrampled city. A short walk south-east of Tower Bridge, it has several rustic microbreweries tucked between self-storage shops and auto-repair garages.

Brixton Market: This seedy neighborhood south of the Thames features yet another thriving market. Here the food, clothing, records, and hair-braiding throb with an Afro-Caribbean beat (shops and stalls open Mon-Sat 8:00-18:00, Wed until 15:00, farmers market Sun 10:00-14:00 but otherwise dead on Sun; Tube: Brixton, www.brixtonmarket.net).

FAMOUS AUCTIONS

London's famous auctioneers welcome the curious public for viewing and bidding. You can preview estate catalogs or browse auction calendars online. To ask questions or set up an appointment, contact **Sotheby's** (opening times vary, tel. 020/7293-5000, www.sothebys.com; recommended café on site, 34 New Bond Street, Tube: Oxford Circus) or **Christie's** (Mon-Fri 9:00-17:00; 85 Old Brompton Road, Tube: South Kensington, tel. 020/7930-6074; second location at 8 King Street, Tube: Green Park, tel. 020/7839-9060; www.christies.com).

Regent Street Shopping Walk

This mile-long walk—along Regent Street to Piccadilly Circus, then up the street called Piccadilly and down Jermyn Street—takes you by the most typically London stores and shops. While useful for true shoppers, this walk is also a lot of fun for window-shoppers. Only you know how much time—and money—to allow for this walk.

• *Start your walk at the Oxford Circus Tube stop.*

❶ Oxford Street

Today, Oxford Street is a midrange shopping area, lined by less-distinguished chains and department stores, and a bit scruffy. But it was once one of London's great shopping streets, and is still one of the most decorative at Christmastime. The original Selfridges (250 yards west of Oxford Circus), opened in 1910, helped pioneer the modern concept of the department store.

• *From the Oxford Circus Tube stop, head south on Regent Street (heading slightly downhill, away from the steeple in the road). Stay along the left (east) side of Regent Street. Two blocks down, where Regent crosses Great Marlborough Street, look left to spot...*

❷ Liberty Department Store

The venerable Liberty is a big, stately, local-favorite department store established in 1875. Its distinctive faux-Tudor building was

Regent Street Shopping Walk

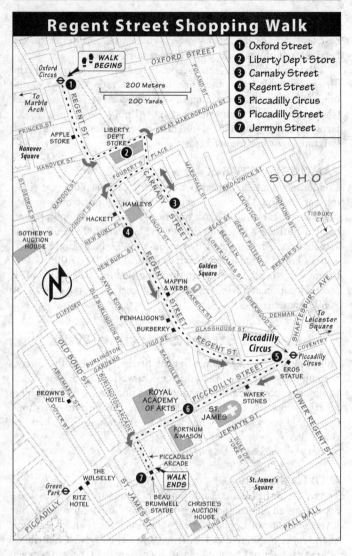

1. Oxford Street
2. Liberty Dep't Store
3. Carnaby Street
4. Regent Street
5. Piccadilly Circus
6. Piccadilly Street
7. Jermyn Street

WALK BEGINS

OXFORD STREET

Oxford Circus

To Marble Arch

200 Meters
200 Yards

PRINCES ST.

APPLE STORE

REGENT ST.

LIBERTY DEP'T STORE

GREAT MARLBOROUGH ST.

POLAND ST.

Hanover Square

HANOVER ST.

FOUBERT'S PLACE

MARSHALL ST.

BROADWICK ST.

S O H O

MADDOX ST.

ST. GEORGE'S

CONDUIT ST.

HAMLEYS

HACKETT

NEW BURL. ST.

KINGLY ST.

CARNABY STREET

BEAK ST.

LEXINGTON ST.

GREAT PULTENEY ST.

HOPKINS ST.

TISBURY CT.

SOTHEBY'S AUCTION HOUSE

N

NEW BURL. ST.

SAVILE ROW

OLD BURLINGTON ST.

REGENT STREET

Golden Square

LOWER JAMES ST.

BRIDLE LN.

BREWER ST.

SHAFTESBURY AVE.

CLIFFORD ST.

MAPPIN & WEBB

WARWICK ST.

To Leicester Square

PENHALIGON'S

BURBERRY

GLASSHOUSE ST.

REGENT ST.

DENMAN ST.

SHERWOOD ST.

COVENTRY

BURLINGTON GARDENS

VIGO ST.

SACKVILLE ST.

Piccadilly Circus

Piccadilly Circus

OLD BOND ST.

ALBEMARLE ST.

BROWN'S HOTEL

DOVER ST.

BURLINGTON ARCADE

ROYAL ACADEMY OF ARTS

ST. JAMES

PICCADILLY STREET

WATER-STONES

EROS STATUE

LOWER REGENT ST.

FORTNUM & MASON

JERMYN ST.

DUKE OF YORK ST.

PICCADILLY ARCADE

WALK ENDS

The Wolseley

Green Park

RITZ HOTEL

BEAU BRUMMELL STATUE

ST. JAMES'S ST.

CHRISTIE'S AUCTION HOUSE

St. James's Square

PICCADILLY

KING ST.

PALL MALL

SHOPPING

constructed from the timbers of two decommissioned Royal Navy battleships; for more information, see page 434.

Before moving on, note the nearby Apple Store—it's behind you, a half-block up from Liberty at #235 Regent Street. The building looks more like a palace. It's popular with tourists who appreciate its free Wi-Fi...and Londoners who are astounded by its customer service. The English are capable of good service too, but, as a Londoner put it to me, "not the obsequious butt-kissing some Americans expect, because that makes you feel like a servant."

• *Turn left on Great Marlborough Street, go past Liberty, and turn right onto...*

❸ Carnaby Street

In the Swinging '60s, when Pete Townshend needed a paisley shirt, John Lennon a Nehru jacket, or Twiggy a miniskirt, they came here—where those mod fashions were invented. If you

were a "Dedicated Follower of Fashion" (as a Kinks' song put it), you were one of the trendy "Carnaby-tian army." Today, there's not a hint of hippie. For the most part, Carnaby Street looks like everything else from the '60s does now—sanitized and co-opted by upscale franchises. At least the upper end of the street retains a whiff of funkiness.

• *After exploring Carnaby Street, walk back toward Great Marlborough Street, heading left (west) on Foubert's Place (near the Shakespeare's Head Pub). Then turn left again to continue strolling downhill along...*

❹ Regent Street

You're in the heart of London's shopping neighborhood. By now, you may have noticed a sort of class divide among London shoppers.

Where the area near Oxford Circus was a bit low-rent, you've now entered London's high-class, top-dollar boulevard. This street has wide sidewalks, fine architecture, and royal-family connections. Most of its shops call the Queen their landlord, as she owns much of the land here.

Once on Regent Street, follow the giddy kids to **Hamleys** (just downhill from Foubert's Place, on the left at #188), Britain's biggest toy store. In 2010 it marked its 250th anniversary of delighting children. Seven floors buzz with 50,000 toys, managed by a staff of 200. Employees, some dressed in playful costumes, give demos of the latest gadgets. It was here at Hamleys that the world first got to know London's genteel Paddington Bear, and the less-genteel Build-a-Bear Workshop (now a fixture at malls everywhere).

On this stretch of Regent Street, fine bits of old English class dominate. **Hackett** (across from Hamleys at #193) is the place to go for preppy young English menswear. Farther down, **Mappin**

and Webb (on the left, at #132) is the Queen's jeweler. **Penhaligon's** (on the right, at #125) is the quintessential English perfumery, where royals shop (note the coat of arms at the door) for classic English scents like lavender and rose (fine sampler gift packs and free sniff samples). Once dowdy—it's a clothier of the royal family—**Burberry** (on the corner past Penhaligon's, at #121) is now hip.

• *Regent Street arcs seductively into the ever-vibrant...*

❺ Piccadilly Circus

Piccadilly Circus is where common tastes steamroll the elegance of Regent Street. **Lillywhites** (at the bottom of the square, near the Eros fountain) is a sports store popular as a place to buy the jersey of your favorite football (soccer) team. Farther left (at the start of Coventry Street) is **Cool Britannia,** a tacky palace of English kitsch and a Union Jack fantasy for anyone needing to buy a Brit-themed gift.

• *From Piccadilly Circus, take a sharp right and wander down the busy...*

❻ Piccadilly Street

After a block on your left (at #203), escape from the frenzy of Piccadilly into the quiet of **Waterstones,** Europe's largest bookshop and the flagship store of its widespread chain. Page through seven orderly floors. The fifth floor offers a hip bar with minimalist furniture and great views (see sidebar on page 90).

Next you'll pass Christopher Wren's **St. James's Church** (with free lunchtime concerts several days a week at 13:10—the current schedule is posted on its iron fence out front; for more details, see page 453) and a tiny all-day flea market (food Mon-Tue 10:00-18:30, arts and crafts Wed-Sat 11:00-18:00, closed Sun). One block farther (on the left, at #181) is the **Fortnum & Mason** department store, which eschews the glitz of bigger stores and revels in understated old-school elegance. At the top of the hour, the fancy clock on the facade is the scene of a low-key spectacle, as the venerable store's founders—Fortnum and Mason—come out and bow to each other (best viewed from across the street). This reminds shoppers of the store's humble beginnings 300 years ago, when it was started by these two footmen of Queen Anne; for more information, see page 434.

An elegant way to cap your shopping stroll (we'll finish just a block from here) is with a tradi-

SHOPPING

tional **afternoon tea.** While it's a pricey ritual, many consider it an essential part of any London visit. My two favorite places in town for a traditional afternoon tea are within a block of here: Fortnum & Mason (with several restaurants and price ranges), and a block farther down Piccadilly Street, **The Wolseley,** the grand 1920s former showroom of a now-defunct car manufacturer (where couples are allowed to split a £29.75 tea in sumptuous surroundings; on the left at #160). Nearby **Brown's Hotel** serves a fancy £55 afternoon tea in its wood-paneled English Tea Room (33 Albemarle Street). For more details on these and other options, see "Taking Tea in London" on page 417. Another fancy spot for tea nearby is the original **Ritz Hotel.**

• *But before we part ways, we'll stroll a block south of big and busy Piccadilly Street. The Piccadilly Arcade leads to quiet...*

❼ Jermyn Street

A statue of **Beau Brummell,** the ultimate dandy, meets you as if to say, "Within a block in either direction are numerous fine gentlemen's shirtmakers and many other delightful small shops." It was Brummell (1778-1840) who popularized the understated jacket-trousers-and-tie ensemble that men still wear today. As the quote on his statue reads, "To be truly elegant, one should not be noticed."

Face the statue and survey the landscape of man-scaping options: To the right, **Bates Hats** (#73, inside Hilditch & Key) still sells bowlers and top hats, as it has for a century. **Turnbull & Asser** (#71) has dressed Winston Churchill, Prince Charles, and James Bond with its "bespoke" (custom-made) shirts and suits. **Tricker's** (#67) has been making shoes for the gentleman since the days of Beau Brummell. To the left, **John Lobb** (#88) has sold boots to Princes William and Harry. Straight ahead, **Taylor of Old Bond Street** (#74), established in the mid-19th century, specializes in gentleman's shaving and botanical products. After sauntering these few blocks, even the weariest traveler will leave Jermyn Street feeling (if not looking) more refined.

• *Our walk is finished. From here, you have several nearby options. If you're ready for **teatime,** cut back through the block to Piccadilly Street and the places I mentioned earlier.*

*Or, to head back to **Piccadilly Circus** (and its handy Tube stop), walk east down Jermyn Street, pausing at the classic perfume shop*

SHOPPING

Floris (at #89) and at Paxton & Whitfield (#93), which has served exceptional cheese since 1797, with generous tastings. On the little Duke of York Street (behind St. James's Church) is an old-fashioned barbershop called Geo. F. Trumper (selling top-quality shaving gear) and the classic Red Lion Pub. If all of this is just too elegant, dip into Piccadilly Circus' Cool Britannia and buy some Union Jack undies.

ENTERTAINMENT IN LONDON

London bubbles with top-notch entertainment seven days a week: plays, movies, concerts, exhibitions, walking tours, shopping, and children's activities. For the best list of what's happening and a look at the latest London scene, check www.timeout.com/london. The free monthly *London Planner* covers sights, events, and plays, though generally not as well as the Time Out website.

Choose from classical, jazz, rock, and far-out music, Gilbert and Sullivan, tango lessons, comedy, Baha'i meetings, poetry readings, spectator sports, theater, and the cinema. In Leicester Square, you might be able to catch a film that has yet to be released in the States—if Colin Firth (or any other A-list celebrity) is attending an opening-night premiere in London, it will likely be at one of the big movie houses here.

There are plenty of free performances, such as lunch concerts at St. Martin-in-the-Fields (at Trafalgar Square) and summertime events at The Scoop amphitheater near City Hall (see "Summer Evenings Along the South Bank," later).

Theater (a.k.a. "Theatre")

London's theater scene rivals Broadway's in quality and sometimes beats it in price. Choose from 200 offerings—Shakespeare, musicals, comedies, thrillers, sex farces, cutting-edge fringe, revivals starring movie celebs, and more. London does it all well.

Seating Terminology: Just like at home, London's theaters sell seats in a range of levels—but the Brits use different terms: stalls (ground floor), dress circle (first balcony), upper circle (second balcony), balcony (sky-high third balcony), and slips (cheap seats on the fringes). Discounted tickets are called "concessions" (abbrevi-

ENTERTAINMENT

ated as "conc" or "s"). For floor plans of the various theaters, see www.theatremonkey.com.

BIG WEST END SHOWS

Nearly all big-name shows are hosted in the theaters of the West End, clustering around Soho (especially along Shaftesbury Avenue) between Piccadilly and Covent Garden. With a centuries-old tradition of pleasing the masses, they present London theater at its grandest.

I prefer big, glitzy—even bombastic—musicals over serious chamber dramas, simply because London can deliver the lights, booming voices, dancers, and multimedia spectacle I rarely get back home. If that's not to your taste—or you already have access to similar spectacles at home—you might prefer some of London's more low-key offerings.

Well-known musicals may draw the biggest crowds, but the West End offers plenty of other crowd-pleasers, from revivals of classics to cutting-edge works by the hottest young playwrights. These productions tend to have shorter runs than famous musicals. Many productions star huge-name celebrities—London is a magnet for movie stars who want to stretch their acting chops.

You'll see the latest offerings advertised all over the Tube and elsewhere. The free *Official London Theatre Guide*, updated weekly, is a handy tool (find it at hotels, box offices, the City of London TI, and online at www.officiallondontheatre.co.uk). You can check reviews at www.timeout.com/london.

Most performances are nightly except Sunday, usually with two or three matinees a week. The few shows that run on Sundays are mostly family fare (such as *The Lion King*). Tickets range from about £25 to £120 for the best seats at big shows. Matinees are generally cheaper and rarely sell out.

Buying Tickets for West End Shows

For most visitors, it makes sense to simply buy tickets in London. Most shows have tickets available on short notice—likely at a discount. But if your time in London is limited—and you have your heart set on a particular show that's likely to sell out (usually the newest shows, and especially on weekends)—you can buy peace of mind by booking your tickets from home.

Advance Tickets: It's generally cheapest to buy your tickets directly from the theater, either through its website or by calling the theater box office. Often, a theater will reroute you to a third-party ticket vendor such as Ticketmaster. You'll pay with a credit card, and generally be charged a per-ticket booking fee (around £3). You can have your tickets emailed to you or pick them up before show time at the theater's Will Call window. Note that many third-party websites sell all kinds of London theater tickets, but these generally charge higher prices and fees. It's best to try the theater's website or box office first.

Discount Tickets from the TKTS Booth: This famous outlet at Leicester Square sells discounted tickets (25-50 percent off) for many shows (£3/ticket service charge included, open Mon-Sat 10:00-19:00, Sun 11:00-16:30). TKTS offers a wide variety of shows on any given day, though they may not have the hottest shows in town. You must buy in person at the kiosk, and the best deals are same-day only.

The list of shows and prices is posted outside the booth and updated throughout the day. The same info is available on their constantly refreshed website (www.tkts.co.uk), which is worth checking before you head to Leicester Square. For the best choice and prices, come early in the day—the line starts forming even before the booth opens (it moves quickly). Have a second-choice show in mind, in case your first choice is sold out by the time you reach the ticket window. If you're less picky, come later in the day, when lines (and choices) diminish.

TKTS also sells advance tickets for some shows (but not as cheaply) and some regular-price tickets to extremely popular shows—convenient, but no savings. If  TKTS runs out of its ticket allotment for a certain show, it doesn't necessarily mean the show is sold out—you can still try the theater's box office.

If you're not committed to a particular show and just want a decent deal, TKTS is a great option. You might snag a top-price seat for a popular-but-not-too-popular show (say, *Wicked*) for about half-price through TKTS. But if you're committed to a particular show—especially a popular one—or if you want the absolutely cheapest seats, it's better to book directly at the theater—read on.

Take note: The real TKTS booth (with its prominent sign) is a freestanding kiosk at the south edge of Leicester Square. Several dishonest outfits nearby advertise "official half-price tickets"—avoid these, where you'll rarely pay anything close to half-price.

Tickets at the Theater Box Office: Even if a show is "sold out," there's usually a way to get a seat. Many theaters offer various discounts or "concessions": same-day tickets, cheap returned tick-

ENTERTAINMENT

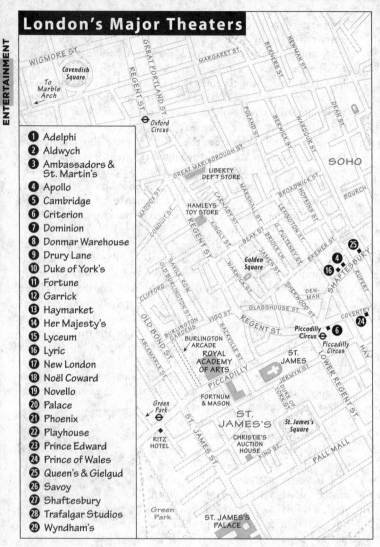

London's Major Theaters

1. Adelphi
2. Aldwych
3. Ambassadors & St. Martin's
4. Apollo
5. Cambridge
6. Criterion
7. Dominion
8. Donmar Warehouse
9. Drury Lane
10. Duke of York's
11. Fortune
12. Garrick
13. Haymarket
14. Her Majesty's
15. Lyceum
16. Lyric
17. New London
18. Noël Coward
19. Novello
20. Palace
21. Phoenix
22. Playhouse
23. Prince Edward
24. Prince of Wales
25. Queen's & Gielgud
26. Savoy
27. Shaftesbury
28. Trafalgar Studios
29. Wyndham's

ets, standing-room, matinee, senior or student standby deals, and more. Start by checking the show's website, call the box office, or simply drop by (many theaters are right in the tourist zone).

Same-day tickets (called "day seats") are generally available only in person at the box office starting at 10:00 (people start lining up well before then). These tickets (£20 or less) tend to be either in the nosebleed rows or have a restricted view (behind a pillar or extremely far to one side).

Another strategy is to show up at the box office shortly before show time (best on weekdays) and—before paying full price—ask

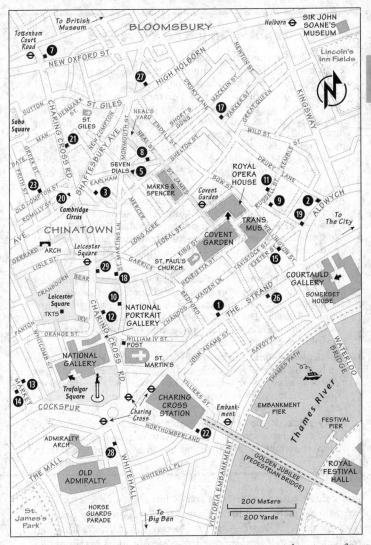

about any cheaper options. Last-minute return tickets are often sold at great prices as curtain time approaches.

For a helpful guide to "day seats," consult www.theatremonkey. com/dayseatfinder.htm; for tips on getting cheap and last-minute tickets, visit www.londontheatretickets.org and www.timeout. com/london/theatre.

Booking Through Other Agencies: Although booking through a middleman such as your hotel or a ticket agency is quick and easy (and may be your last resort for a sold-out show), prices are greatly inflated. Ticket agencies and third-party websites are often

What's On in the West End

You're likely to find these perennial favorites among the West End's evening offerings. If spending the time and money for a London play, I like a full-fledged, high-energy musical (which all of these are). Of course you could go for this year's hit, but you'll need to book long in advance and pay top price. These long-running shows are fun, and you're likely to find some of them on the discount list at the TKTS booth (see page 447). Generally, ticket prices range from £25-120. Shows typically run Monday through Saturday at 19:30, with two or three matinees a week—confirm specifics on show websites. See the map on page 448 for locations.

Aladdin: A flying carpet, crystal-encrusted costumes, and songs from the Disney film enrich the Arabia-set tale of a street urchin, a wise-cracking genie, and a princess (Prince Edward Theatre, Old Compton Street, Tube: Leicester Square or Tottenham Court Road, box office tel. 0844-482-5151, https://aladdinthemusical.co.uk).

The Book of Mormon: Who else but the writers of *South Park* could create a snappy, irreverent, and sometimes crude musical about two Mormon missionaries and the nature of faith? (Prince of Wales Theatre, Coventry Street, Tube: Piccadilly Circus or Charing Cross, box office tel. 0844-482-5110, www.bookofmormonlondon.com).

Hamilton: An American Musical: There's a frenzy for tickets to this tour de force of lyrics and hip-hop/R&B that contemporizes early American history—book well in advance (Victoria Palace Theatre, Victoria Street, Tube: Victoria or St. James's Park, www.hamiltonthemusical.co.uk).

Kinky Boots: Cyndi Lauper wrote the score for this musical, based on the true story of a man striving to save his family's old-school shoe factory, and the drag queen who helps him shift to

just scalpers with an address. If you do buy from an agency, choose one who is a member of the Society of Ticket Agents and Retailers (look for the STAR logo—short for "secure tickets from authorized retailers"). These legitimate resellers normally add a maximum 25 percent booking fee to tickets.

Scalpers (or "Touts"): As at any event, you'll find scalpers hawking tickets outside theaters. And, just like at home, those people may either be honest folk whose date just happened to cancel at the last minute...or they may be unscrupulous thieves selling forgeries. London has many of the latter.

manufacturing the titular footwear (Adelphi Theatre, 409 Strand, Tube: Covent Garden, Charing Cross, or Embankment, box office tel. 020/3725-7068, www.kinkybootsthemusical.co.uk).

Les Misérables: This musical adaptation of Victor Hugo's epic follows the life of Jean Valjean as he struggles with the social and political realities of 19th-century France (Queen's Theatre, Shaftesbury Avenue, Tube: Piccadilly Circus, box office tel. 0844-482-5160, www.lesmis.com).

The Lion King: In this Disney extravaganza, Simba the lion learns about the delicately balanced circle of life on the savanna (Lyceum Theatre, Wellington Street, Tube: Charing Cross or Covent Garden, theater info tel. 020/7420-8100, box office tel. 0844-871-3000, www.thelionking.co.uk).

Mamma Mia!: This energetic, spandex-and-platform-boots musical weaves together a slew of ABBA hits to tell the story of a bride in search of her real dad as her promiscuous mom plans her Greek Isle wedding. The production has the audience dancing in their seats (Novello Theatre, Aldwych, Tube: Covent Garden or Charing Cross, box office tel. 0844-482-5115, www.mamma-mia.com).

Phantom of the Opera: A mysterious masked man falls in love with a singer in this haunting Andrew Lloyd Webber musical about life beneath the stage of the Paris Opera (Her Majesty's Theatre, Haymarket, Tube: Piccadilly Circus or Leicester Square, US toll-free tel. 800-334-8457, box office tel. 0844-412-2707, www.thephantomoftheopera.com).

Wicked: This lively prequel to *The Wizard of Oz* examines how the Witch of the West met Glinda the Good Witch, and later became so, you know... (Apollo Victoria Theatre, Wilton Road just east of Victoria Station, Tube: Victoria, AGT Tickets tel. 0844-871-3001, www.wickedthemusical.co.uk).

THEATER BEYOND THE WEST END

Tickets for lesser-known shows tend to be cheaper (figure £15-30), in part because most of the smaller theaters are government-subsidized. Remember that plays don't need a familiar title or famous actor to be a worthwhile experience—read up on the latest offerings online; Time Out's website is a great place to start.

Major Noncommercial Theaters

One particularly good venue is the **National Theatre,** which has a range of impressive options, often starring recognizable names. While the building is ugly on the outside, the acts that play out upon its stage are beautiful—as are the deeply discounted tickets it commonly offers (looming on the South Bank by Waterloo Bridge, Tube: Waterloo, www.nationaltheatre.org.uk).

The **Barbican Centre** puts on high-quality, often experimental work (right by the Museum of London, just north of The City, Tube: Barbican, www.barbican.org.uk), as does the **Royal Court Theatre,** which has £12 tickets for its Monday shows (west of the West End in Sloane Square, Tube: Sloane Square, www.royalcourttheatre.com).

Menier Chocolate Factory is a small theater in Southwark popular for its impressive productions and intimate setting. Check their website to see what's on—they tend to have a mix of plays, musicals, and even an occasional comedian (behind the Tate Modern at 53 Southwark Street, Tube: Southwark, www.menierchocolatefactory.com).

Royal Shakespeare Company: If you'll ever enjoy Shakespeare, it'll be in Britain. The RSC performs at various theaters around London and in Stratford-upon-Avon year-round. To get a schedule, contact the RSC (Royal Shakespeare Theatre, Stratford-upon-Avon, tel. 0844-800-1110, box office tel. 01789/403-493, www.rsc.org.uk).

Shakespeare's Globe

To see Shakespeare in a replica of the theater for which he wrote his plays, attend a play at the Globe. In this round, thatch-roofed, open-air theater, the plays are performed much as Shakespeare intended—under the sky, with no amplification.

The play's the thing from late April through early October (usually Tue-Sat 14:00 and 19:30, Sun either 13:00 and/or 18:30, tickets can be sold out months in advance). You'll pay £5 to stand and £20-45 to sit, usually on a backless bench. Because only a few rows and the pricier Gentlemen's Rooms have seats with backs, £1 cushions and £3 add-on backrests are considered a good investment by many. Dress for the weather.

The £5 "groundling" tickets—which are open to rain—are most fun. Scurry in early to stake out a spot on the stage's edge, where the most interaction with the actors occurs. You're a crude peasant. You can lean your elbows on the stage, munch a picnic dinner (yes, you can bring in food), or walk around. I've never enjoyed Shakespeare as much as here, performed as it was meant to be in the "wooden O." If you can't get a ticket, consider waiting around. Plays can be long, and many groundlings leave before the end. Hang around outside and beg or buy a ticket from someone leaving early (groundlings are allowed to come and go). A few non-Shakespeare plays are also presented each year. If you can't attend a show, you can take a guided tour of the theater and museum by day (see page 89).

The indoor Sam Wanamaker Playhouse allows Shakespearean-era plays and early-music concerts to be performed through the winter. Many of the productions in this intimate venue are one-offs and can be quite pricey.

To reserve tickets for plays at the Globe or Sam Wanamaker, call or drop by the box office (Mon-Sat 10:00-18:00, Sun until 17:00, open one hour later on performance days, New Globe Walk entrance, no extra charge to book by phone, tel. 020/7401-9919). You can also reserve online (www.shakespearesglobe.com, £2.50 booking fee). If the tickets are sold out, don't despair; a few often free up at the last minute. Try calling around noon the day of the performance to see if the box office expects any returned tickets. If so, they'll advise you to show up a little more than an hour before the show, when these tickets are sold (first-come, first-served).

The theater is on the South Bank, directly across the Thames over the Millennium Bridge from St. Paul's Cathedral (Tube: Mansion House or London Bridge). The Globe is inconvenient for public transport, but during theater season, a regular supply of black cabs wait nearby.

Outdoor and Fringe Theater

In summer, enjoy Shakespearean drama and other plays under the stars at the **Open Air Theatre,** in leafy Regent's Park in north London. You can bring your own picnic, order à la carte from the theater menu, or preorder a picnic supper from the theater at least 24 hours in advance (tickets from £25, available beginning in mid-Jan, season runs late May-mid-Sept; book at www.openairtheatre. org or—for an extra booking fee—by calling 0844-826-4242; grounds open 1.5 hours before evening performances, one hour before matinees; 10-minute walk north of Baker Street Tube, near Queen Mary's Gardens within Regent's Park; detailed directions and more info at www.openairtheatre.org).

London's rougher evening-entertainment scene is thriving. Choose from a wide range of **fringe theater** and comedy acts (find posters in many Tube stations, or search for "fringe theater" on www.timeout.com; tickets can start as cheap as £14).

Music, Opera, and Dance

CONCERTS AT CHURCHES

For easy, cheap, or free concerts in historic churches, attend a **lunch concert,** especially:
- St. Bride's Church, with free half-hour lunch concerts twice a week at 13:15 (usually Tue and Fri—confirm in advance, church tel. 020/7427-0133, www.stbrides.com).
- St. James's at Piccadilly, with 50-minute concerts on Mon,

Evensong

One of my favorite experiences in Britain is to attend evensong at a great church. Evensong is an evening worship service that is typically sung rather than said (though some parts—including scripture readings, a few prayers, and a homily—are spoken). It follows the traditional Anglican service in the Book of Common Prayer, including prayers, scripture readings, canticles (sung responses), and hymns that are appropriate for the early evening—traditionally the end of the working day and before the evening meal. In major churches with resident choirs, this service is filled with quality, professional musical elements. A singing or chanting priest leads the service, and a choir—usually made up of both men's and boys' voices (to sing the lower and higher parts, respectively)—sings the responses. The choir usually sings a cappella, or is accompanied by an organ. While regular attendees follow the service from memory, visitors—who are welcome—are given an order of service or a prayer book to help them follow along. (If you're not familiar with the order of service, watch the congregation to know when to stand, sit, and kneel.)

You can attend services in many of England's grandest churches—but be aware that evensong typically takes place in the small choir area—which is far more intimate than the main nave. (To see the full church in action, a concert is a better choice.) Evensong generally occurs daily between 17:00 and 18:00 (often two hours earlier on Sun)—check with individual churches for specifics. At smaller churches, evensong is sometimes spoken, not sung.

Note that evensong is not a performance—it's a somewhat somber worship service. If you enjoy worshipping in different churches, attending evensong can be a trip-capping highlight. But if regimented church services aren't your thing, consider getting a different music fix. Most major churches also offer organ or choral concerts—look for posted schedules or ask at the information desk or gift shop.

Wed, and Fri at 13:10 (suggested £3.50 donation, info tel. 020/7734-4511, www.sjp.org.uk).

- St. Martin-in-the-Fields, offering concerts on Mon, Tue, and Fri at 13:00 (suggested £3.50 donation, church tel. 020/7766-1100, www.stmartin-in-the-fields.org).

St. Martin-in-the-Fields also hosts fine **evening concerts** by candlelight (£9-28, several nights a week at 19:30) and live jazz in its underground Café in the Crypt (£8-15, Wed at 20:00).

Evensong services are held at several churches, including St. Paul's Cathedral (see details on page 261), Westminster Abbey (see page 131), Southwark Cathedral (see page 93), and St. Bride's Church (Sun at 17:30, tel. 020/7427-0133, www.stbrides.com).

Free **organ recitals** are usually held on Sunday at 17:45 in Westminster Abbey (30 minutes, tel. 020/7222-5152). Many other churches have free concerts; ask for the *London Organ Concerts Guide* at the TI.

OTHER PERFORMANCES

Prom Concerts: For a fun classical event (mid-July–mid-Sept), attend a Prom Concert (shortened from "Promenade Concert") during the annual festival at the Royal Albert Hall. Nightly concerts are offered at give-a-peasant-some-culture prices (cheap standing-room "Promming" spots sold at the door, nearly-as-cheap restricted-view seats and pricier good ones sold in advance, Tube: South Kensington, www.bbc.co.uk/proms).

Jazz: Ronnie Scott's is London's oldest, and by far most famous, jazz venue, hosting performances daily. As shows tend to sell out, it's best to book your tickets in advance online (47 Frith Street, Tube: Tottenham Court Road or Leicester Square, tel. 020/7439-0747, www.ronniescotts.co.uk). Boisdale also features live jazz, blues, and soul music at their restaurants (no cover charge at their Bishopsgate location; see page 414 for more details).

Opera: Some of the world's best opera is belted out at the prestigious Royal Opera House, near Covent Garden (www.roh.org.uk), and at the London Coliseum (English National Opera, St. Martin's Lane, Tube: Leicester Square, www.eno.org). Or consider taking in an unusual opera at the King's Head pub in Islington, home of London's Little Opera House (115 Upper Street, Tube: Angel, www.kingsheadtheatre.com). In the summer, Holland Park hosts open-air opera performances (Tube: Holland Park, www.operahollandpark.com).

Dance: The critically acclaimed Royal Ballet—where Margot Fonteyn and Rudolf Nureyev forged their famous partnership—is based at the Royal Opera House (www.roh.org.uk). Sadler's Wells Theatre features both international and UK-based dance troupes (Rosebery Avenue, Islington, Tube: Angel, www.sadlerswells.com).

More Entertainment Options

EVENING SIGHTSEEING

Museum Visits: Many museums are open an evening or two during the week, offering fewer crowds. See the sidebar on the next page.

Tours: Guided **walks** are offered several times a day and vary by theme: ancient London, museums, legal London, Dickens, Beatles, Jewish quarter, Christopher Wren, and so on. In the evening, expect a more limited choice: ghosts, Jack the Ripper, pubs, or literature. See a list of walking-tour companies on page 33.

Sights that Stay Open Late

Most sightseeing in London winds up by 18:00, but there are several exceptions. Keep in mind that many of these sights stop admitting visitors well before their posted closing times.

Madame Tussauds: July-Aug daily until 18:00 (last entry time; stays open about 2 hours later)

Westminster Abbey (main church only): Wed until 19:00

British Library: Tue-Thu until 20:00

London Eye: Last ascent daily 20:30 or later in summer, until 18:00 Sept-May

British Museum (some galleries): Fri until 20:30

Clink Prison Museum: July-Sept daily until 21:00, Oct-June Sat-Sun until 19:30

National Gallery: Fri until 21:00

National Portrait Gallery: Thu-Fri until 21:00

Houses of Parliament: House of Commons—Oct-late July Mon until 22:30, Tue-Wed until 19:30; House of Lords—Oct-late July Mon-Wed until 22:00, Thu until 19:30

Tate Modern: Fri-Sat until 22:00

Victoria and Albert Museum (some galleries): Fri until 22:00

To see the city illuminated at night, consider a **bus tour.** A 1.5-hour London by Night Sightseeing Tour leaves from Victoria Station and Green Park (see page 32).

Cruises: In summer, boats sail as late as 19:00 between Westminster Pier (near Big Ben) and the Tower of London. (For details, see page 36.)

A handful of outfits run expensive Thames River evening cruises with four-course meals and dancing. **London Showboat** offers the best value (nightly at 19:45, 3 hours, departs from Westminster Pier, reservations required, tel. 020/7740-0400, www.citycruises.com). Dinner cruises are also offered by **Bateaux London** (www.bateauxlondon.com).

SUMMER EVENINGS ALONG THE SOUTH BANK

If you're visiting London in summer, consider hitting the South Bank neighborhood after hours.

Take a trip around the **London Eye** while the sun sets over the city (the wheel spins until late—last ascent at 20:30 or later in summer). Then cap your night with an evening walk along the pedestrian-only **Jubilee Walkway,** which runs east-west along the river. It's where Londoners go to escape the heat. This pleasant stretch of the walkway—lined with pubs and casual eateries—goes from the

London Eye past Shakespeare's Globe to Tower Bridge (you can walk in either direction).

If you're in the mood for a movie, take in a flick at the **BFI Southbank,** located just across the river, alongside Waterloo Bridge. Run by the British Film Institute, the state-of-the-art theater shows mostly classic films, as well as art cinema (Tube: Waterloo or Embankment, check www.bfi.org.uk for schedules and prices).

Farther east along the South Bank is **The Scoop**—an outdoor amphitheater next to City Hall. It's a good spot for movies, concerts, dance, and theater productions throughout the summer—with Tower Bridge as a scenic backdrop. These events are free, nearly nightly, and family-friendly. For the latest event schedule, see www.morelondon.com and click on "Events" (next to City Hall, Riverside, The Queen's Walkway, Tube: London Bridge).

SPORTING EVENTS

Tennis, cricket, rugby, football (soccer), and horse races all take place within an hour of the city. In summer Wimbledon draws a half-million spectators (www.wimbledon.com), while big-name English Premier League soccer clubs—including Chelsea, Arsenal, Tottenham Hotspur, and West Ham United—take the pitch in London to sell-out crowds (www.premierleague.com). The two biggest horse races of the year take place in June: the Royal Ascot Races (www.ascot.co.uk) near Windsor and the Epsom Derby (www.epsomderby.co.uk) in Surrey are both once-in-a-lifetime experiences.

Securing tickets to anything sporting-related in London can be difficult—and expensive. Check the official team or event website several months in advance; tickets can sell out within minutes of going on sale to the general public. Third-party booking companies such as SportsEvents 365 (www.sportsevents365.com) and Ticketmaster (www.ticketmaster.co.uk) often have tickets to popular events at a premium price—a godsend for die-hard fans. Many teams also offer affordable, well-run stadium tours—check your favorite side's official website for details. Even if you can't attend a sports event in person, consider cheering on the action in a London pub.

Winter Diversions

London dazzles year-round, so consider visiting in winter, when airfares and hotel rates are generally cheaper and there are fewer tourists. Despite drearier weather and shorter days, London's museums, theaters, concert halls, and pubs offer a warm, cozy welcome.

London at Christmas is especially appealing, with its buildings dressed in their holiday best. Many holiday traditions have their roots in 19th-century Victorian Britain. Beginning in the 1840s, Queen Victoria's German husband, Prince Albert, popularized the decorating of Christmas trees and the sending of Christmas cards. And what could be more traditional than seeing the setting of Charles Dickens' *A Christmas Carol* come to life? God bless us, every one.

NOVEMBER TO JANUARY

Pantomimes, or "pantos," are a British holiday tradition. Though they have nothing to do with silent mimes—and they don't mention Christmas—these campy fairy-tale plays entertain with outrageous costumes, sets, and dance numbers. The audience is invited to chime in, and it doesn't take long to learn the lines. Adults will laugh at the more risqué jokes; kids will giggle at the slapstick. Two London theaters that usually stage pantos are the Hackney Empire (291 Mare Street, northeast London, Tube: Bethnal Green, then 10 minutes on bus #106 or #254, tel. 020/8985-2424, www.hackneyempire.co.uk) or the Old Vic (corner of Waterloo Road and The Cut, southeast of Waterloo Station, Tube: Waterloo, tel. 0844-871-7628, www.oldvictheatre.com). For more about the panto tradition, see www.its-behind-you.com.

Get some exercise at the **outdoor ice rinks** at the London Eye, Somerset House, Tower of London, Natural History Museum, and Hampton Court Palace, among other locations (rental skates, generally mid-Nov-mid-Jan, reservations smart).

The **Hyde Park Winter Wonderland** offers kitschy carnival fun with a Ferris wheel, carousel, and other rides, as well as an ice rink and vendors selling silly hats and plenty of food and drink (late Nov-early Jan, southeast corner of park, Tube: Hyde Park Corner, www.hydeparkwinterwonderland.com).

Stroll around and enjoy the elaborate **light displays** and store windows on major shopping streets from mid-November to early January, especially on Oxford Street, Bond Street, Regent Street, and Brompton Road. Postholiday sales start December 26 for many stores, including the famous Harrods January sale.

The Trafalgar Square **Christmas tree** is given to London every year from the people of Oslo, Norway in appreciation for British help during World

War II (lighting ceremony first Thu in Dec, stays up until Jan 6, www.london.gov.uk). Free carol concerts are held beneath the tree in December.

The **Geffrye Museum**'s 11 historic rooms are decorated for Christmas every year, highlighting holiday customs from the 17th century to today (free, see page 83).

The grand, red-velvet-draped **Royal Albert Hall** hosts seasonal concerts; ask about "carols by candlelight" events (Tube: South Kensington, box office tel. 020/7589-8212, www.royalalberthall.com).

Instead of visiting Santa Claus at the North Pole, British children see **Father Christmas** in his grotto. In London, the poshest Santa is at Harrods, and it may be worth reserving in advance to avoid long lines (early Nov-Christmas Eve, reservations available online as early as Sept, fees for reservations and photos; Tube: Knightsbridge, tel. 020/7730-1234). Father Christmas has also been known to visit the Hyde Park Winter Wonderland (described earlier), where you can see him for free.

Nibble your way through **Borough Market,** where you'll find lots of seasonal and gourmet treats (open daily the week before Christmas, closed Dec 25-26; see listing on page 438). While at the market, be sure to sample traditional favorites such as mulled wine, mince pie, Christmas cake, and Christmas pudding (see page 296).

Another popular holiday food event is the German **Christmas Market,** on the South Bank between the London Eye and the Royal Festival Hall (daily late Nov-Christmas Eve, Tube: Waterloo, www.southbankcentre.co.uk).

Don't forget to pick up some **Christmas crackers** to give your holiday meals some extra bang. Not to be confused with something you eat, these fun, popping party favors contain a paper crown, a teeny gift, and a corny joke. Buy them at grocery or department stores, find a friend, and pull hard.

CHRISTMAS DAY

Spending December 25 in London? While almost everything is closed, and there is no public transit (not even the Tube), you still have a few options for getting out.

Popular **church services** are held both Christmas Eve and Christmas Day at Westminster Abbey, Westminster Cathedral, St. Paul's, and St. Martin-in-the-Fields, among other places. Warning: These draw large crowds, so ask in advance about when to arrive. (For example, you may need to reserve free tickets in advance—available in Nov—and wait in line several hours for the Abbey's 16:00 service on Christmas Eve; 23:30 service is less crowded; tel. 020/7222-5152, www.westminster-abbey.org.)

Christmas Travel Strategies

- There is no public transit in London (Tube, train, or bus) at all on Christmas Day, and reduced services on Christmas Eve and Boxing Day (Dec 26). For specifics, see www.tfl. gov.uk. Taxis are scarce, so be prepared for a long wait (£4 holiday surcharge, tel. 0871-871-8710). Better yet, bundle up and walk.
- If arriving at Heathrow Airport on Christmas Day, research transport from the airport to your hotel in advance. There is no Tube or train service, but buses may run between Heathrow and Paddington Station, and between Gatwick Airport and Victoria Station (likely every 15-30 minutes; confirm in advance at www.heathrowexpress.com and www.nationalrail.co.uk, holiday schedules available in Nov). Or you could try Just Airports private car (book in advance, tel. 020/8900-1666, www.justairports.com).
- Pick a central location if staying over December 25, both to save money and avoid transportation difficulties. Stay somewhere with a kitchen (such as an apartment, hostel, or hotel room with kitchenette) so you can prepare some of your own meals. Don't forget to buy groceries before stores close on Christmas Eve. For tips on finding short-term rentals, see the Practicalities chapter.
- If you plan to eat out December 24-26 without reservations, go ethnic: Indian, Chinese, and Middle Eastern restaurants are usually open in Soho, Chinatown, along Edgware Road, or near the East End's Brick Lane.
- Expect closures. Museums are generally closed December 24-26, and smaller shops are usually closed December 26.

The Peter Pan Cup **swim race,** held in Hyde Park every Christmas morning since 1864, is named in honor of *Peter Pan* playwright J. M. Barrie, who presented the first cup. Only members of the local swimming club may compete, but spectators are welcome (9:00, south side of The Serpentine—a lake in the center of the park, www.serpentineswimmingclub.com). Break the ice by asking a local where to find the nearby Peter Pan statue.

London Walks offers two guided **walking tours** on December 25, with appropriate themes such as "Christmas Morning 1660" and "Charles Dickens' *A Christmas Carol*" (meet at Trafalgar Square Christmas tree, tel. 020/7624-3978 or recorded info tel. 020/7624-9255, www.walks.com).

Watch the Queen's annual **Christmas message** on the BBC at 15:00. If you miss it, you can watch it online on Her Majesty's Royal YouTube channel (www.youtube.com/TheRoyalChannel).

If your visit extends through the **New Year,** here are two events to be aware of: New Year's Eve **fireworks** from the London

Eye attract at least 500,000 revelers to the banks of the Thames, with required £10 tickets for good viewing spots sold months in advance (www.london.gov.uk/nye). Public transport is free after the festivities (generally 23:45-04:30). The next day, a **parade** featuring 10,000 performers snakes two miles from the Ritz Hotel, past Piccadilly Circus and Trafalgar Square, to Big Ben (free to stand, or pay for grandstand seats, 11:45-15:00, tel. 020/3275-0190, www.lnydp.com).

LONDON CONNECTIONS

London is well-connected with the rest of the planet: by train, plane, bus, and cruise ship. This chapter addresses your arrival and departure from the city.

By Plane

London has six airports; I've focused my coverage on the two most widely used—Heathrow and Gatwick—with a few tips for using the others (Stansted, Luton, London City, and Southend).

For accommodations at or near the major airports, see page 391. For more on flights within Europe, see page 577.

HEATHROW AIRPORT

Heathrow Airport is one of the world's busiest airports. Think about it: 75 million passengers a year on 500,000 flights from 185 destinations traveling on 80 airlines, like some kind of global maypole dance. For Heathrow's airport, flight, and transfer information, call the switchboard at 0844-335-1801, or visit the helpful website www.heathrow. com (airport code: LHR).

Heathrow's terminals are numbered T-1 through T-5. Though T-1 is now closed for arrivals and departures, it still supports other terminals with baggage, and the newly renovated T-2 ("Queen's Terminal") will likely expand into the old T-1 digs eventually. Each terminal is served by different airlines and alliances; for example, T-5 is exclusively for British Air and Iberia Air flights,

London's Airports

Luton

Luton

Stansted

N

Not to Scale

#75 & A1

ST. PANCRAS

Southend

PADDINGTON

LIVERPOOL STREET

Southend

Reading

Windsor
#71 & 77

Tube

VICTORIA

D.L.R.

London City

To Bath

Rail Air Link

VICTORIA COACH STN.

Heathrow

London

EUROSTAR

Thames

Guildford

Gatwick

Ashford

Rail ----
Eurostar Rail ====
Tube & D.L.R. ——
Bus - - -

ALL BUSES ARE NATIONAL EXPRESS
UNLESS NOTED

To Brighton

To Paris

English Channel

while T-2 serves mostly Star Alliance flights, such as United and Lufthansa. Screens posted throughout the airport identify which terminal each airline uses; this information should also be printed on your ticket or boarding pass.

You can walk between T-2 and T-3. From this central hub (called "Heathrow Central"), T-4 and T-5 split off in opposite directions (and are not walkable). The easiest way to travel between the T-2/T-3 cluster and either T-4 or T-5 is by Heathrow Express train (free to transfer between terminals, departs every 15-20 minutes). You can also take a shuttle bus (free, serves all terminals), or the Tube (requires a ticket, serves all terminals).

If you're flying out of Heathrow, it's critical to confirm which terminal your flight will use (look at your ticket/boarding pass, check online, or call your airline in advance)—if it's T-4 or T-5, allow extra time. Taxi drivers generally know which terminal you'll need based on the airline, but bus drivers may not.

Services: Each terminal has an airport information desk (open long hours daily), car-rental agencies, exchange bureaus, ATMs, a pharmacy, a VAT refund desk (tel. 0845-872-7627, you must present the VAT claim form from the retailer here to get your tax rebate on purchased items—see page 546 for details), and baggage storage (£6/item up to 2 hours, £11/item for 2-24 hours, long hours daily, www.left-baggage.co.uk). Heathrow offers both free Wi-Fi and pay Internet access points (in each terminal, check map for locations). You'll find a post office on the first floor of T-3 (departures area). Each terminal also has cheap eateries.

Heathrow's small "TI" (tourist info shop), even though it's a for-profit business, is worth a visit if you're nearby and want to pick up free information, including the *London Planner* visitors guide (long hours daily, 5-minute walk from T-3 in Tube station, follow signs to Underground; bypass queue for transit info to reach window for London questions).

Getting Between Heathrow and Downtown London

You have several options for traveling the 14 miles between Heathrow Airport and downtown London: Tube (about £6/person), bus (£8-10/person), express train with connecting Tube or taxi (about £10/person for slower train, £22-25/person for faster train, price does not include connecting Tube fare), car service (from £32/car), or taxi (about £75/group). The one that works best for you will depend on your arrival terminal, your destination in central London, and your budget.

By Tube (Subway): The Tube takes you from any Heathrow terminal to downtown London in 50-60 minutes on the Piccadilly Line (6/hour, buy ticket at Tube station ticket window or self-service machine). Depending on your destination in London, you may need to transfer (for example, if headed to the Victoria Station neighborhood, transfer at Hammersmith to the District line and ride six more stops). If you plan to use the Tube for transport in London, it makes

sense to buy a pay-as-you-go Oyster card (possibly adding a 7-Day Travelcard) at the airport's Tube station ticket window. (For details on these passes, see page 23.) If you add a Travelcard that covers only Zones 1-2, you'll need to pay a small supplement for the initial trip from Heathrow (Zone 6) to downtown.

If you're taking the Tube from downtown London *to* the airport, note that Piccadilly Line trains don't stop at every terminal. Trains either stop at T-4, then T-2/T-3 (also called Heathrow Central), in that order; or T-2/T-3, then T-5. When leaving central London on the Tube, allow extra time if going to T-4 or T-5, and check the reader board in the station to make sure that the train goes to the right terminal before you board.

By Bus: Most buses depart from the outdoor common area called the Central Bus Station, a five-minute walk from the T-2/T-3 complex. To connect between T-4 or T-5 and the Central Bus Station, ride the free Heathrow Express train or the shuttle buses.

National Express has regular service from Heathrow's Central Bus Station to Victoria Coach Station in downtown London, near several of my recommended hotels. While slow, the bus is affordable and convenient for those staying near Victoria Station (£8-10, 1-2/hour, less frequent from Victoria Station to Heathrow, 45-75 minutes depending on time of day, tel. 0871-781-8181, www.nationalexpress.com). A less-frequent National Express bus goes from T-5 directly to Victoria Coach Station.

By Train: Two different trains run between Heathrow Airport and London's Paddington Station. At Paddington Station, you're in the thick of the Tube system, with easy access to any of my recommended neighborhoods—my Paddington hotels are just outside the front door, and Notting Hill Gate is just two Tube stops away. The **Heathrow Connect** train is the slightly slower, much cheaper option, serving T-2/T-3 at a single station called Heathrow Central; use free transfers to get from either T-4 or T-5 to Heathrow Central (£10.30 one-way, £20.70 round-trip, 2/hour Mon-Sat, 1-2/hour Sun, 40 minutes, tel. 0345-604-1515, www.heathrowconnect.com). By the time you visit, the new **Crossrail Elizabeth line** may be operational, connecting Heathrow Central and T-4 to Paddington (and most likely replacing the Heathrow Connect train service).

The **Heathrow Express** train is fast and runs more frequently, but it's pricey (£22-25 one-way, price depends on time of day, £37 round-trip, £5 more if you buy your ticket on board, covered by BritRail pass; 4/hour, daily 5:00-24:00, 15 minutes to downtown from Heathrow Central Station serving T-2/T-3, 21 minutes from T-5; for T-4 take free transfer to Heathrow Central, tel. 0345-600-1515, www.heathrowexpress.co.uk). At the airport, you can use the Heathrow Express as a free transfer between terminals.

By Car Service: Just Airports offers a private car service between five London airports and the city center (see website for price quote, tel. 020/8900-1666, www.justairports.com).

By Taxi or Uber: Taxis from the airport cost £45-75 to west and central London (one hour). For four people traveling together, this can be a reasonable option. Hotels can often line up a cab back to the airport for about £50. If running, Uber also offers London airport pickup and drop-off.

GATWICK AIRPORT

More and more flights land at Gatwick Airport, which is halfway between London and the south coast (airport code: LGW, tel. 0844-892-0322, www.gatwickairport.com). Gatwick has two terminals, North and South, which are easily connected by a free monorail (two-minute trip, runs 24 hours daily). Note that boarding passes say "Gatwick N" or "Gatwick S" to indicate your terminal. British Airways flights generally use Gatwick South. The Gatwick Express trains (described next) stop only at Gatwick South. Schedules in each terminal show only arrivals and departures from that terminal.

Getting Between Gatwick and Downtown London: Gatwick Express trains are the best way into London from this airport. They shuttle conveniently between Gatwick South and London's **Victoria Station,** with many of my recommended hotels close by (£20 one-way, £35 round-trip, at least 10 percent cheaper if purchased online, Oyster cards accepted but no discount offered, 4/hour, 30 minutes, runs 5:00-24:00 daily, a few trains as early as 3:30, tel. 0845-850-1530, www.gatwickexpress.com). If you buy your tickets at the station before boarding, ask about possible group deals. (If you see others in the ticket line, suggest buying your tickets together.) When going *to* the airport, at Victoria Station note that Gatwick Express has its own ticket windows right by the platform (tracks 13 and 14). You'll also find easy-to-use ticket machines nearby.

A train also runs between Gatwick South and **St. Pancras International Station** (£10.40, 3-5/hour, 45-60 minutes, www.thetrainline.com)—useful for travelers taking the Eurostar train (to Paris or Brussels) or staying in the St. Pancras/King's Cross neighborhood.

While even slower, the **bus** is a cheap and handy option to the Victoria Station neighborhood. National Express runs a bus from Gatwick directly to Victoria Station (£9, at least hourly, 1.5 hours, tel. 0871-781-8181, www.nationalexpress.com); easyBus has one going to near the Earls Court Tube stop (£2-10 depending on how far ahead you book, 2-3/hour, www.easybus.co.uk).

LONDON'S OTHER AIRPORTS

Stansted Airport: From Stansted (airport code: STN, tel. 0844-335-1803, www.stanstedairport.com), you have several options for getting into or out of London. Two different **buses** connect the airport and London's Victoria Station neighborhood: National Express (£9-12, every 15 minutes, 2 hours, runs 24 hours a day, picks up and stops throughout London, ends at Victoria Coach Station or Liverpool Street Station, tel. 0871-781-8181, www.nationalexpress.com) and Terravision (£4-10, 2/hour, 1.5-2 hours, ends at Green Line Coach Station just south of Victoria Station). Or you can take the faster, pricier Stansted Express **train** (£19, cheaper if booked online, connects to London's Tube system at

Tottenham Hale or Liverpool Street, 4/hour, 45 minutes, 4:30-23:00, www.stanstedexpress.com). Stansted is expensive by **cab**; figure £100-120 one-way from central London.

Luton Airport: For Luton (airport code: LTN, airport tel. 01582/405-100, www.london-luton.co.uk), the fastest way to go into London is by **train** to St. Pancras International Station (£10-14 one-way, 1-5/hour, 35-45 minutes—check schedule to avoid slower trains, tel. 0345-712-5678, www.eastmidlandstrains.co.uk); catch the 10-minute shuttle bus (every 10 minutes) from outside the terminal to the Luton Airport Parkway Station. You can purchase a shuttle bus and train combo-ticket from kiosks or ticket machines inside the airport. When buying your train ticket *to* Luton, make sure you select "Luton Airport" as your destination rather than "Parkway Station" to ensure the shuttle fare is included.

The National Express **bus** A1 runs from Luton to Victoria Coach Station (£7-11 one-way, 2/hour, 1-1.5 hours, runs 24 hours, tel. 0871-781-8181, www.nationalexpress.com). The Green Line express **bus** #757 runs to Buckingham Palace Road, just south of Victoria Station, and stops en route near the Baker Street Tube station—best if you're staying near Paddington Station or in North London (£10 one-way, 2-4/hour, 1-1.5 hours, runs 24 hours, tel. 0344-800-4411, www.greenline.co.uk). If you're sleeping at Luton, consider EasyHotel (see listing on page 393).

London City and Southend Airports: To get into the city center from London City Airport (airport code: LCY, tel. 020/7646-0088, www.londoncityairport.com), take the Docklands Light Railway (DLR) to the Bank Tube station, which is one stop east of St. Paul's on the Central Line (less than £6 one-way, covered by Travelcard, a bit cheaper with an Oyster card, 20 minutes, www.tfl.gov.uk/dlr). Some easyJet flights land farther out, at Southend Airport (airport code: SEN, tel. 01702/538-500, www.southendairport.com). Trains connect this airport to London's Liverpool Street Station (£16.20 one-way, 3-8/hour, 55 minutes, www.abelliogreateranglia.co.uk).

CONNECTING LONDON'S AIRPORTS BY BUS

A handy **National Express bus** runs between Heathrow, Gatwick, Stansted, and Luton airports—easier than having to cut through the center of London—although traffic can be bad and can increase travel times (tel. 0871-781-8181, www.nationalexpress.com).

From Heathrow Airport to: Gatwick Airport (£25, 1-6/hour, about 1.5 hours—but allow at least three hours between flights), **Stansted Airport** (£27, 1-2/hour direct, 1.5 hours), **Luton Airport** (£27, roughly hourly, 1 hour).

By Train

London, the country's major transportation hub, has a different train station for each region. There are nine main stations (see the map):

Euston: Serves northwest England, North Wales, and Scotland.

St. Pancras International: Serves north and south England, plus the Eurostar to Paris or Brussels (see "Crossing the Channel," later).

King's Cross: Serves northeast England and Scotland, including York and Edinburgh.

Liverpool Street: Serves east England, including Essex and Harwich.

London Bridge: Serves south England, including Brighton.

Waterloo: Serves south England, including Salisbury and Southampton.

Victoria: Serves Gatwick Airport, Canterbury, Dover, and Brighton.

Paddington: Serves south and southwest England, including Heathrow Airport, Windsor, Bath, Oxford, South Wales, and the Cotswolds.

Marylebone: Serves southwest and central England, including Stratford-upon-Avon.

In addition, London has several smaller train stations that you're less likely to use, such as **Charing Cross** (serves southeast England, including Dover) and **Blackfriars** (serves Brighton).

Any train station has schedule information, can make reservations, and can sell tickets for any destination. Most stations offer a baggage-storage service (£12.50/bag for 24 hours, look for *left luggage* signs); because of long security lines, it can take a while to check or pick up your bag (www.left-baggage.co.uk). For more details on the services available at each station, see www.nationalrail.co.uk/stations. UK train and bus info is available at www.traveline.org.uk. For information on tickets and rail passes, see page 574 of the Practicalities chapter.

TRAIN CONNECTIONS FROM LONDON
To Points West

From Paddington Station to: Windsor (Windsor & Eton Central Station, 2/hour, 35 minutes, easy change at Slough), **Bath** (2/hour, 1.5 hours), **Oxford** (4/hour direct, 1 hour, more with transfer), **Moreton-in-Marsh** (hourly, 1.5 hours), **Penzance** (every 2 hours, 5 hours, more with change in Plymouth), **Cardiff** (2/hour, 2 hours).

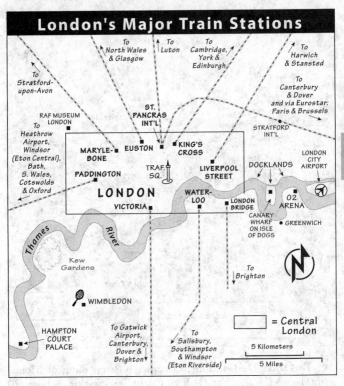

London's Major Train Stations

To Points North

From King's Cross Station: Trains run at least hourly, stopping in **York** (2 hours), **Durham** (3 hours), and **Edinburgh** (4.5 hours). Trains to **Cambridge** also leave from here (4/hour, 1 hour).

From Euston Station to: Conwy (nearly hourly, 3.5 hours, transfer in Chester), **Liverpool** (at least hourly, 3 hours, more with transfer), **Blackpool** (hourly, 3 hours, transfer at Preston), **Keswick** (hourly, 4 hours, transfer to bus at Penrith), **Glasgow** (1-2/hour, 4.5 hours).

From London's Other Stations

Trains run between London and **Canterbury**: St. Pancras International Station to Canterbury West (hourly, 1 hour, more with transfer); Victoria Station to Canterbury East (hourly, 2 hours); Charing Cross Station—with stops at Waterloo East and London Bridge—to Canterbury West (hourly, 1.5 hours, more with transfer).

Trains leave for **Stratford-upon-Avon** from Marylebone Station, located near the southwest corner of Regent's Park (2/day direct, 2.5 hours; also 1-2/hour, 2 hours, transfer in Leamington Spa, Dorridge, or Birmingham Moor).

Public Transportation near London

To North England & Scotland

To York & Scotland

King's Lynn

Norwich

Coventry

ENGLAND

Stratford-upon-Avon

Warwick

Long Buckby

Bedford

Hunt.

Ely

Cambridge

Worcester

Leam. Spa

Moreton

Banbury

Luton

To Hoek van Holland

Cheltenham

Stow

COTSWOLDS

Oxford

Stansted

Harwich

Bristol

Blenheim

Swindon

Didcot

London City

Southend

Bath

Avebury

Reading

Slough

London

Greenwich

Ramsgate

Wells

Bedwyn

Windsor

Heathrow

EUROSTAR

Canterbury

Dover

Glastonbury

Stonehenge

Gatwick

To Cornwall

Salisbury

Southampton

Ashford

Rye

(CHUNNEL)

Calais

Poole

Brighton

Eastbourne

Hastings

Calais-Fréthun

Weymouth

Bournemouth

Isle of Wight

Portsmouth

English Channel

To Paris

FRANCE

Rail — — — Bus ······· Boat

Area covered by London Plus Pass

30 Kilometers

30 Miles (approx. scale)

Note: Bus Lines Follow Most Rail Lines

To Other Destinations: Greenwich (from Bank or Monument Tube stop take the DLR to Cutty Sark Station, 6/hour, 20 minutes), **Windsor** (to Windsor & Eton Riverside Station, 2/hour, 1 hour, from Waterloo Station), **Dover** (hourly, 1 hour, direct from St. Pancras International Station; also 1-2/hour, 2 hours, direct from Victoria Station; or hourly, 2 hours, direct from Charing Cross Station), **Brighton** (2/hour, 1 hour, direct from Victoria Station; 2/hour, 1.5 hours, direct from Blackfriars Station), **Portsmouth** (3/hour, 2 hours, direct from Waterloo Station, a few with change in Clapham Junction from Victoria Station), **Salisbury** (2/hour, 1.5 hours, from Waterloo Station). For more information on trains to **Windsor, Cambridge,** or **Salisbury** (connecting to Stonehenge), check the Day Trips chapter.

By Bus

Buses are slower but considerably cheaper than trains for reaching destinations around Britain and beyond. Most depart from **Victoria Coach Station,** which is one long block south of Victoria Station (near many recommended accommodations, Tube: Victoria). Inside the station, you'll find basic eateries, kiosks, and a helpful information desk stocked with schedules and staff ready to point you to your bus or answer any questions. Watch your bags carefully—luggage thieves thrive at the station.

Ideally you'll buy your tickets online (for tips on buying tickets and taking buses, see page 574 of the Practicalities chapter). But if you must buy one at the station, try to arrive an hour before the bus departs, or drop by the day before. Ticketing machines are scattered around the station (separate machines for National Express/Eurolines and Megabus; you can buy either for today or for tomorrow); there's also a ticket counter near gate 21. For UK train and bus info, check www.traveline.org.uk.

National Express buses go to: **Bath** (nearly hourly, 3 hours), **Oxford** (2/hour, 2.5 hours), **Cambridge** (every 60-90 minutes, 2 hours), **Canterbury** (about hourly, 2 hours), **Dover** (every 2 hours, 2.5 hours), **Brighton** (hourly, 2.5 hours), **Penzance** (5/day, 9 hours, overnight available), **Cardiff** (hourly, 3.5 hours), **Stratford-upon-Avon** (3/day, 3.5 hours), **Liverpool** (8/day direct, 5.5 hours, overnight available), **Blackpool** (4/day direct, 7 hours, overnight available), **York** (4/day direct, 5 hours), **Durham** (3/day direct, 7 hours, train is better), **Glasgow** (2-4/day direct, 9 hours, train is much better), **Edinburgh** (2/day direct, 10 hours, go by train instead).

To Dublin, Ireland: This bus/boat journey, operated by Eurolines, takes 10-12 hours (£40, 1/day, departs Victoria Coach Station at 18:00, check in with passport one hour before). Consider a cheap 1-hour Ryanair flight instead.

To the Continent: Especially in summer, buses run to destinations all over Europe, including Paris, Amsterdam, Brussels, and Germany (sometimes crossing the Channel by ferry, other times through the Chunnel). For any international connection, you need to check in with your passport one hour before departure. For details, call 0871-781-8181 or visit www.eurolines.co.uk. For information on crossing the Channel by bus, see page 473.

Crossing the Channel

BY EUROSTAR TRAIN

The Eurostar zips you (and up to 800 others in 18 sleek cars) from downtown London to downtown Paris or Brussels at 190 mph in 2.5 hours (1-2/hour). The tunnel crossing is a 20-minute, silent, 100 mph nonevent. Your ears won't even pop.

Eurostar also runs direct service to Lyon, Avignon, and Marseille (5/week in summer, less frequent off-season), and by the time you visit, they may offer service to Amsterdam (with stops in Antwerp and at Amsterdam's Schiphol Airport). Germany's national railroad is also looking to run bullet trains between Frankfurt, Amsterdam, and London.

Eurostar Tickets and Fares: A one-way ticket between London and Paris or Brussels can vary widely in price; for instance, $45-200 (Standard class), $160-310 (Standard Premier), and $400 (Business Premier). Fares depend on how far ahead you reserve and whether you're eligible for any discounts—available for children (under age 12), youths (under 26), and adults booking months ahead or purchasing round-trip. You can book tickets 4-9 months in advance. Tickets can be exchanged before the scheduled departure for a fee (about $45 plus the cost of any price increase), but only Business Premier class allows any refund.

You can buy tickets online using the print-at-home eticket option (see www.ricksteves.com/eurostar or www.eurostar.com). You can also order by phone through Rail Europe (US tel. 800-387-6782) for home delivery before you go, or through Eurostar (tel. 0843-218-6186, priced in euros) to pick up at the station. In Britain, tickets are issued only at the Eurostar office in St. Pancras International Station. In continental Europe, you can buy Eurostar tickets at any major train station in any country or at any travel agency that handles train tickets (expect a booking fee). Seat reservations for travelers with a Eurail Pass covering France or Belgium are available at Eurostar departure stations, through US agents, or by phone with Eurostar, but they may be harder to get at other train stations and travel agencies ($34 in Standard, $44 in Standard Premier, can sell out, no benefit with BritRail Pass).

Taking the Eurostar: Eurostar trains depart from and arrive at London's St. Pancras International Station. Check in at least 30 minutes in advance (remember that times listed on tickets are local times; Britain's time zone is one hour earlier than France and Belgium's). Pass through airport-like security, show your passport to customs officials, and locate your departure gate (shown on a TV monitor). The waiting area has shops, newsstands, horrible snack bars, and cafés (bring food for the trip from elsewhere), free Wi-Fi, and a currency-exchange booth.

Building the Chunnel

The toughest obstacle to building a tunnel under the English Channel was overcome in 1986, when longtime rivals Britain and France reached an agreement to build it together. Britain began in Folkestone, France in Calais, planning a rendezvous in the middle.

By 1988, specially made machines three football fields long were boring 26-foot-wide holes under the ground. The dirt they hauled out became landfill in Britain and a hill in France. Crews crept forward 100 feet a day until June of 1991, when French and English workers broke through and shook hands midway across the Channel—the tunnel was complete. Rail service began in 1994.

The Chunnel is 31 miles long (24 miles of it underwater) and 26 feet wide. It sits 130 feet below the seabed in a chalky layer of sediment. It's segmented into three separate tunnels—two for trains (one in each direction) and one for service and ventilation. The walls are concrete panels and rebar fixed to the rock around it. Sixteen-thousand-horsepower engines pull 850 tons of railcars and passengers at speeds up to 100 mph through the tunnel.

The ambitious project—the world's longest undersea tunnel—helped to show the European community that cooperation between nations could benefit everyone.

CROSSING THE CHANNEL WITHOUT EUROSTAR

For speed and affordability, look into **cheap flights** (see page 577). Or consider the following old-fashioned ways of crossing the Channel (cheaper but more complicated and time-consuming than the Eurostar).

By Train and Boat: To reach **Paris,** take a train from London's St. Pancras International Station, Charing Cross Station, or Victoria Station to Dover's Priory Station (hourly, 1-2 hours), then catch a P&O ferry to Calais, France (hourly, 1.5 hours, www. poferries.com). From Calais, take the TGV train to Paris.

For **Amsterdam,** consider Stena Line's Dutchflyer service, which combines train and ferry tickets. Trains go from London's Liverpool Street Station to the port of Harwich (hourly, 1.5 hours, most transfer in Manningtree). From Harwich, Stena Line ferries sail to Hoek van Holland (8 hours), where you can catch a train to Amsterdam (book ahead for best price, 13 hours total, www. stenaline.co.uk, Dutch train info at www.ns.nl). For additional European ferry info, visit www.aferry.to.

By Bus and Boat: The bus from London's Victoria Coach Station goes directly to **Paris** (£40-45, 4-5/day, 8-10 hours), **Brussels** (£32-40, 4/day, 9 hours), or **Amsterdam** (4/day, 12 hours) via ferry or Chunnel (day or overnight; £36-70 one-way, cheaper in advance, tel. 0870-514-3219, www.eurolines.co.uk).

By Cruise Ship

Many cruises begin, end, or call at one of several English ports offering easy access to London. Cruise lines favor two ports: Southampton, 80 miles southwest of London; and Dover, 80 miles southeast of London. If you don't want to bother with public transportation, most cruise lines offer transit-only excursion packages into London. For more details, see my *Rick Steves Northern European Cruise Ports* guidebook.

SOUTHAMPTON CRUISE PORT

Within Southampton's sprawling port (www.cruisesouthampton. com), cruises use two separate dock areas, each with two terminals.

To reach London, it's about a 1.5-hour train ride. To get to Southampton Central Station from the cruise port, you can take a taxi or walk 10-15 minutes to the public ferry dock (Town Quay), where you can ride the QuayConnect bus to the train station. From there, trains depart at least every 30 minutes for London's Waterloo Station.

If you have time to kill in port, consider taking the train to Portsmouth (50-60 minutes), best known for its Historic Dockyard and many nautical sights, or stick around Southampton and visit the excellent SeaCity Museum, with a beautifully presented exhibit about the *Titanic*, which set sail from here on April 10, 1912.

DOVER CRUISE PORT

Little Dover has a huge port. Cruises put in at the Western Docks, with two terminals.

Trains go hourly from Dover Priory Station to London. From either cruise terminal, the best way into town (or to the train station) is by taxi or shuttle bus (take it to Market Square, then walk 15 minutes to the train station). From Dover's station, a fast train leaves for London's St. Pancras International Station (hourly, 1 hour); slower, direct trains go to Victoria Station (1-2/hour, 2 hours) and Charing Cross Station (hourly, 2 hours).

If you have extra time in port, Dover Castle, perched upon chalk cliffs, is well worth a visit for its WWII-era Secret Wartime Tunnels. Or take the train to Canterbury (2/hour, less than 30 minutes), notable for its important cathedral and fine historic core.

DAY TRIPS

Windsor • Cambridge • Stonehenge

Windsor, Cambridge, and Stonehenge are three great day-trip possibilities near London. Any one of these very different but equally enjoyable destinations makes for an entertaining visit from London.

The primary residence of Her Majesty the Queen, **Windsor** hosts a castle that's regally lived-in, yet open to the public. This is simply a charming town to relax in—and its proximity to Heathrow Airport (60 minutes by train west of London) makes Windsor easy to combine with a flight into or out of London. Nearby is an oddball collection of intriguing sights, including Legoland Windsor, Eton College (Britain's most elite high school), Ascot

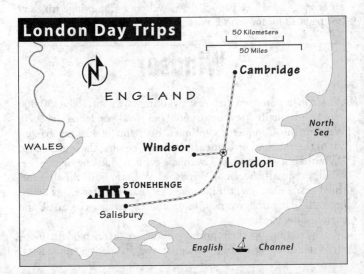

Racecourse (for horse racing), and Highclere Castle, where the TV series *Downton Abbey* was filmed.

Britain's venerable University of Cambridge is mixed into the delightful town of **Cambridge,** offering a mellow, fun-to-explore townscape with a big-league university.

Stonehenge, the world's most famous rock group, sits lonesome yet adored in a mysterious field 90 miles southwest of London.

Although I only cover these three destinations in this book, London's convenient public transit can easily whisk you to a wealth of other day-trip destinations: Bath (Roman ruins and Georgian townhouses), Canterbury (cathedral), Dover (castle-crowned chalk cliffs), Portsmouth (treasure trove of maritime history), Stratford-upon-Avon (all things Shakespeare), Warwick (fine medieval castle), Oxford (another classic university town), and Brighton (beach and pier). For details, see *Rick Steves England*.

GETTING AROUND

By Train: Take advantage of British Rail's discounts for day-trippers from London. The "off-peak day return" ticket is a round-trip fare that costs virtually the same as one-way, provided you depart London outside rush hour (usually after 9:30 on weekdays and anytime Sat-Sun). Be sure to specifically ask for the "day return" ticket (round-trip within a single day) rather than the more expensive standard "return." You can also save a little money if you purchase tickets before 18:00 the day before your trip.

By Train Tour: London Walks offers a variety of "Daytrips from London" tours year-round by train, including a Salisbury and Stonehenge tour (see page 510), as well as a Cambridge itinerary (see page 33 for more on London Walks).

Windsor

Windsor, a compact and easy walking town of about 30,000 people, originally grew up around the royal residence. In 1070, William the Conqueror continued his habit of kicking Saxons out of their various settlements, taking over what the locals called "Windlesora" (meaning "riverbank with a hoisting winch")—which eventually became "Windsor." William built the first fortified castle on a chalk hill above the Thames; later kings added on to his early designs, rebuilding and expanding the castle and surrounding gardens.

By setting up their primary residence here, modern monarchs increased Windsor's popularity and prosperity—most notably, Queen Victoria, whose stern statue glares at you as you approach the castle. After her death, Victoria rejoined her beloved husband, Albert, in the Royal Mausoleum at Frogmore House, a mile south of the castle in a private section of the Home Park (house and mausoleum rarely open). The current Queen considers Windsor her primary residence, and the one where she feels most at home. She generally hangs her crown here on weekends, using it as an escape from her workaday grind at Buckingham Palace

in the city. You can tell if Her Majesty is in residence by checking to see which flag is flying above the round tower: If it's the royal standard (a red, yellow, and blue flag) instead of the Union Jack, the Queen is at home.

While 99 percent of visitors just come to tour the castle and go, some enjoy spending the night. Daytime crowds trample Windsor's charm, which is most evident when the tourists are gone. Consider overnighting here—parking and access to Heathrow Airport are easy, and an evening at the horse races (on Mondays) is hoof-pounding, heart-thumping fun.

GETTING TO WINDSOR

By Train: Windsor has two train stations—Windsor & Eton Central and Windsor & Eton Riverside. London's Paddington Station connects with Windsor & Eton Central (2-3/hour, 35 minutes, easy change at Slough; £10 one-way standard class, £10-14 same-day return, www.gwr.com). London's Waterloo Station connects with Windsor & Eton Riverside (2/hour, no changes but slower—55 minutes; £10-13 one-way standard class, £12-20 same-day return, info tel. 0345-748-4950, www.nationalrail.co.uk).

If you're day-tripping into London *from* Windsor, ask at the train station about combining a same-day return train ticket with a Travelcard (£15-22, lower price for travel after 9:30, includes some London sightseeing discounts—ask or look for brochure at station, www.daysoutguide.co.uk).

By Bus: Green Line buses #701 and #702 run from London's Victoria Colonnades (between the Victoria train and coach stations) to the Parish Church stop on Windsor's High Street, before continuing on to Legoland (1-2/hour, 1.5 hours to Windsor, £6-10 one-way, £9-16 round-trip, prices vary depending on time of day, tel. 0871-200-2233, www.firstgroup.com).

By Car: Windsor is about 20 miles from London and just off Heathrow Airport's landing path. The town (and then the castle and Legoland) is well-signposted from the M-4 motorway. It's a convenient first stop if you're arriving at Heathrow and renting a car there and saving London until the end of your trip.

From Heathrow Airport: Traveling by train is the most efficient, though it requires two changes. Take the Heathrow Connect to Hayes & Harlington station, transfer to a train to Slough, then transfer again to Windsor (50 minutes total, £11.50, www. gwr.com). Alternatively, First Bus Company's bus #8 runs between Terminal 5 and Windsor, dropping you in the center of town at the Parish Church stop on High Street (£8-11, 2/hour, one hour, tel. 01753/524-144, www.firstgroup.com). London black cabs can (and do) charge whatever they like from Heathrow to Windsor; avoid them by calling a local cab company, such as Windsor Cars (includes 40 minutes waiting time—handy if you checked your luggage, tel. 01753/677-677, www.windsorcars.com).

Orientation to Windsor

Windsor's pleasant pedestrian shopping zone litters the approach to its famous palace with fun temptations. You'll find most shops and restaurants around the castle on High and Thames streets, and down the pedestrian Peascod Street (PESS-cot), which runs perpendicular to High Street.

TOURIST INFORMATION

The TI is in the Windsor Royal Shopping Centre's Old Booking Hall, which is immediately adjacent to Windsor & Eton Central Station (Mon-Sat 9:30-17:00, Sun 10:00-16:00; Nov-March Sun-Fri 10:00-16:00, Sat 10:00-17:00; tel. 01753/743-900, www. windsor.gov.uk). The TI sells discount tickets to Legoland and is extremely enthusiastic about their Royal Windsor Historical Tour.

ARRIVAL IN WINDSOR

By Train: Whichever train station you arrive at, you're only a five-minute walk to the castle. From Windsor & Eton Central, walk through the Windsor Royal Shopping Centre (which houses the TI), and up the hill to the castle. From Windsor & Eton Riverside, you'll see the castle as you exit—just follow the wall to the ticket office.

By Car: Follow signs from the M-4 motorway for pay-and-display parking in the center. River Street Car Park is closest to the castle, but it's pricey and often full. The cheaper, bigger Alexandra

Car Park (near the riverside Alexandra Gardens) is farther west. To walk to the town center from the Alexandra Car Park, head east through the tour-bus parking lot toward the castle. At the souvenir shop, walk up the stairs (or take the elevator) and cross the overpass to Windsor & Eton Central Station. Just beyond the station, you'll find the TI in the Windsor Royal Shopping Centre.

The cheapest parking option is the King Edward VII Avenue car-park-and-ride, northeast of the castle on B-470 (up to 5 hours-£5, includes shuttle bus into town).

HELPFUL HINTS

Supermarkets: Pick up picnic supplies at **Marks & Spencer** (Mon-Sat 8:00-19:00, Sun 11:00-17:00, 130 Peascod Street, tel. 01753/852-266) or at **Waitrose** (Mon-Fri 8:00-21:00, Sat until 20:00, Sun 11:00-17:00, King Edward Court Shopping Centre, just south of Windsor & Eton Central Station, tel. 01753/860-565). Just outside the castle, you'll find long benches near the statue of Queen Victoria—great for people-watching while you munch.

Bike Rental: Extreme Motion, near the river in Alexandra Gardens, rents 21-speed mountain bikes (£12.50/4 hours, £18/day, includes helmet, £150 credit-card deposit required, bring passport as ID, summer daily 10:00-18:00, Sat-Sun only off-season, tel. 01753/830-220).

Sights in Windsor

▲▲WINDSOR CASTLE

Windsor Castle, the official home of England's royal family for 900 years, claims to be the largest and oldest occupied castle in

the world. Thankfully, touring it is simple. You'll see sprawling grounds, lavish staterooms, a crowd-pleasing dollhouse, a gallery of Michelangelo and Leonardo da Vinci drawings, and an exquisite Perpendicular Gothic chapel.

Cost: £20.50, includes entry to castle grounds and all exhibits inside. Tickets are valid for one year of reentry (get it stamped at the exit).

Hours: Grounds and most interiors open daily 9:30-17:15, Nov-Feb 9:45-16:15, except St. George's Chapel, which is closed Sun to tourists (but open to worshippers; wait at the exit gate to be escorted in). Last entry to grounds and St. George's Chapel is 75 minutes before closing. Last entry to State Apartments and Queen Mary's Dolls' House is 45 minutes before closing.

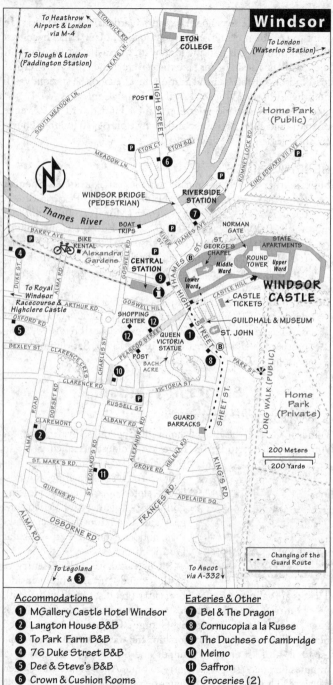

Windsor

To Heathrow Airport & London via M-4

To Slough & London (Paddington Station)

ETONWICK RD.

KEATS LN.

ETON COLLEGE

To London (Waterloo Station)

Home Park (Public)

SOUTH MEADOW LN.

HIGH STREET

POST

RAMSEY LOCK RD.

KING EDWARD VII AVE.

MEADOW LN.

ETON CT.

ETON SQ.

6

N

WINDSOR BRIDGE (PEDESTRIAN)

RIVERSIDE STATION

BARRY AVE.

Thames River

BOAT TRIPS

RIVER ST.

THAMES AVE.

NORMAN GATE

ST. GEORGE'S CHAPEL

STATE APARTMENTS

7

Middle Ward

ROUND TOWER

Upper Ward

BIKE RENTAL
Alexandra Gardens

GOSWELL RD.

CENTRAL STATION

9

THAMES ST.

HIGH STREET

B

Lower Ward

Castle Hill

WINDSOR CASTLE

DUKE ST.

ALMA RD.

To Royal Windsor Racecourse & Highclere Castle

ARTHUR RD.

GOSWELL HILL

CASTLE TICKETS

OXFORD RD.

SHOPPING CENTER

12

GUILDHALL & MUSEUM

ST. JOHN

1

BEXLEY ST.

CLARENCE CRES.

CHARLES ST.

PEASCOD STREET

QUEEN VICTORIA STATUE

POST

BACH ACRE

8

B

PARK ST.

LONG WALK (PUBLIC)

CLARENCE RD.

10

VICTORIA ST.

SHEET ST.

Home Park (Private)

ALMA ROAD

DORSET RD.

RUSSELL ST.

CLAREMONT

ALBANY RD.

2

ALEXANDRA RD.

GROVE RD.

GUARD BARRACKS

KING'S RD.

200 Meters

200 Yards

ST. MARK'S RD.

ST. LEONARD'S RD.

11

HELENA RD.

QUEENS RD.

OSBORNE RD.

FRANCES RD.

ADELAIDE SQ.

ALMA RD.

To Legoland & **3**

To Ascot via A-332

Changing of the Guard Route

Accommodations
1 MGallery Castle Hotel Windsor
2 Langton House B&B
3 To Park Farm B&B
4 76 Duke Street B&B
5 Dee & Steve's B&B
6 Crown & Cushion Rooms

Eateries & Other
7 Bel & The Dragon
8 Cornucopia a la Russe
9 The Duchess of Cambridge
10 Meimo
11 Saffron
12 Groceries (2)

Information: Tel. 020/7766-7324, www.royalcollection.org.uk.

Crowd Control: Ticket lines can be long in summer. You can expect the worst crowds between 11:00-13:00 any time of year. Avoid the wait by purchasing tickets in advance online at www. royalcollection.org.uk (collect them at the prepaid ticket window), or in person at the Buckingham Palace ticket office in London. There's nowhere in Windsor to buy advance tickets.

Possible Closures: On rare occasions when the Queen is entertaining guests, the State Apartments close (and tickets are reduced to £11.30). Sometimes the entire castle closes. It's smart to call ahead or check the website (especially in mid-June) to make sure everything is open when you want to go. While you're at it, confirm the Changing of the Guard schedule.

Tours: An included **audioguide** (dry, reverent, informative) covers both the grounds and interiors. For a good overview—and an opportunity to ask questions—consider the free 30-minute **guided walk** around the grounds (usually 2/hour, schedule posted next to audioguide desk). The official £5 guidebook is full of gorgeous images and makes a fine souvenir, but the information within is covered by the audioguide and tour.

Changing of the Guard: The Changing of the Guard takes place Monday through Saturday at 11:00 (April-July) and on alternating days the rest of the year (confirm schedule on website; get there by 10:30 or earlier if you expect a line for tickets). There is no Changing of the Guard on Sundays or in very wet weather. The fresh guards, led by a marching band, leave their barracks on Sheet Street and march up High Street, hanging a right at Victoria, then a left into the castle's Lower Ward, arriving at about 11:00. After about a half-hour, the tired guards march back the way the new ones came. To watch the actual ceremony inside the castle, you'll need to have already bought your ticket, entered the grounds, and staked out a spot. Alternatively, you could wait for them to march by on High Street or on the lower half of Castle Hill.

Evensong: An evensong takes place in the chapel nightly at 17:15 (free for worshippers, line up at exit gate to be admitted).

Best View: While you can get great views of the castle from any direction, the classic views are from the wooded avenue called the Long Walk, which stretches south of the palace and is open to the public.

The Order of the Garter

In addition to being the royal residence, Windsor is the home of the Most Noble Order of the Garter—Britain's most prestigious chivalrous order. The castle's history is inexorably tied to this order.

Founded in 1348 by King Edward III and his son (the "Black Prince"), the Order of the Garter was designed to honor returning Crusaders. This was a time when the legends of King Arthur and the Knights of the Round Table were sweeping England, and Edward III fantasized that Windsor could be a real-life Camelot. (He even built the Round Tower as an homage to the Round Table.)

The order's seal illustrates the story of the order's founding and unusual name: a cross of St. George encircled with a belt and a French motto loosely translated as "Shame be upon he who thinks evil of it." Supposedly while the king was dancing with a fair maiden, her garter slipped off onto the floor; in an act of great chivalry, he rescued her from embarrassment by picking it up and uttering those words.

The Order of the Garter continues to the present day as the single most prestigious honor in the United Kingdom. There can be only 24 knights at one time (perfect numbers for splitting into two 12-man jousting teams), plus the sitting monarch and the Prince of Wales. Aside from royals and the nobility, past Knights of the Garter have included Winston Churchill, Bernard "Monty" Montgomery, and Ethiopian Emperor Haile Selassie. In 2008, Prince William became only the 1,000th knight in the order's 669-year history. Other current members include various ex-military officers, former British Prime Minister John Major, and a member of the Colman's Mustard family.

The patron of the order is St. George—the namesake of the State Apartments' most sumptuous hall and of the castle's own chapel. Both of these spaces—the grandest in all of Windsor—are designed to celebrate and to honor the Order of the Garter.

Eating: There are no real eateries inside (other than shops selling gifty boxes of chocolates and bottled water), so consider bringing a snack with you.

◆ Self-Guided Tour

After buying your ticket and going through the security checkpoint, pick up your audioguide and start strolling along the path through...

The Grounds: Head up the hill, enjoying the first of many fine castle views you'll see today. The tower-topped conical hill on your left represents the historical core of the castle. William the Conqueror built this motte (artificial mound) and bailey (fortified stockade around it) in 1080—his first castle in England. Among the later monarchs who spiffed up Windsor were Edward III (flush with French war booty, he made it a palace fit for a 14th-century king), Charles II (determined to restore the monarchy properly in the 1660s), and George IV (Britain's "Bling King," who financed many such vanity projects in the 1820s). On your right, the circular bandstand platform has a seal of the Order of the Garter, which has important ties to Windsor (see sidebar).

Passing through the small gate, you approach the stately St. George's Gate. Peek through here to the Upper Ward's **Quadrangle,** which is surrounded by the State Apartments (across the field) and the Queen's private apartments (to the right).

Turn left and follow the wall. On your right-hand side, you enjoy great views of the **Round Tower** atop that original motte;

running around the base of this artificial hill is the delightful, peaceful garden of the castle governor. The unusual design of this castle has not one "bailey" (castle yard), but three, which today make up Windsor's Upper Ward (where the Queen lives, which you just saw), Middle Ward (the ecclesiastical heart of the complex, with St. George's Chapel, which you'll soon pass on the left), and Lower Ward (residences for castle workers).

Continue all the way around this mini moat to the **Norman Gate,** which once held a prison. Walking under the gate, look up to see the bottom of the portcullis that could be dropped to seal off the inner courtyard. Three big holes are strategically situated for dumping boiling goo or worse on whoever was outside the gate. Past the gate are even finer views of the Quadrangle.

Do a 180 and head back toward the Norman Gate, but before you reach it, go down the staircase on the right. You'll emerge onto a fine **terrace** overlooking the flat lands all around. It's easy to understand why this was a strategic place to build a castle. That's Eton College across the Thames. Imagine how handy it's been for royals to be able to ship off their teenagers to an elite prep school so close that they could easily keep an eye on them...literally. The power-plant cooling towers in the distance mark the workaday burg of Slough (rhymes with "plow," immortalized as the setting for Britain's original version of *The Office*).

• *Turn right and wander along the terrace. You'll likely see two lines. The long one leads to Queen Mary's Dolls' House, then to the State Apartments. The short line skips the dollhouse and heads directly to the*

DAY TRIPS

apartments. Read the following descriptions and decide if the dollhouse is worth the wait (or try again later in the day, when the line sometimes eases up). You can see the Drawings Gallery and the China Museum either way.

Queen Mary's Dolls' House: This palace in miniature (1:12 scale, from 1924) is "the most famous dollhouse in the world." It was a gift for the adult Queen Mary (the wife of King George V, and the current Queen's grandmother), who greatly enjoyed miniatures. It's basically one big, dimly lit room with the large dollhouse in the middle, executed with an astonishing level of detail. Each fork, knife, and spoon on the expertly set banquet table is perfect and made of real silver—and the tiny pipes of its plumbing system actually have running water. But you're kept a few feet away by a glass wall, and are constantly jostled by fellow sightseers in this crowded space, making it difficult to fully appreciate. Unless you're a dollhouse devotee, it's probably not worth waiting half an hour for a five-minute peek at this, but if the line is short it's definitely worth a look.

Drawings Gallery and China Museum: Positioned at the exit of Queen Mary's Dolls' House, this gallery displays a changing array of pieces from the Queen's collection—usually including some big names, such as Michelangelo and Leonardo. The China Museum features items from the Queen's many exquisite settings for royal shindigs.

State Apartments: Dripping with chandeliers, finely furnished, and strewn with history and the art of a long line of kings and queens, they're the best I've seen in Britain. This is where Henry VIII and Charles I once lived, and where the current Queen wows visiting dignitaries. Take advantage of the talkative docents in each room, who are happy to answer your questions.

You'll climb the Grand Staircase up to the **Grand Vestibule,** decorated with exotic items seized by British troops during their missions to colonize various corners of the world. Ask a docent to help you find which one of the many glass cases contains the bullet that killed Lord Nelson at Trafalgar. In the next room, the magnificent wood-ceilinged **Waterloo Chamber** is wallpapered with portraits of figures from the pan-European alliance that defeated Napoleon. Find General Wellington (high on the far wall, in red) who outmaneuvered him at Waterloo, and Pope Pius VII (right wall, in red and white) whom Napoleon befriended...then imprisoned. Next, you'll pass through a **series of living rooms**—bedchambers,

DAY TRIPS

DAY TRIPS

dressing rooms, and drawing rooms of the king and queen (who traditionally maintained separate quarters). Many rooms are decorated with canvases by Rubens, Van Dyck, and Holbein. Finally, you'll emerge into **St. George's Hall,** decorated with emblems representing the knights of the prestigious Order of the Garter (see sidebar). This is the site of some of the most elaborate royal banquets—imagine one long table stretching from one end of the hall to the other and seating 160 VIPs. From here, you'll proceed into the rooms that were restored after a fire in 1992, including the "Semi-State Apartments." The **Garter Throne Room** is where new members of the Order of the Garter are invested (ceremonially granted their titles).

• *Exiting the State Apartments, you have one more major sight to see. Get out your castle-issued map or follow signs to find...*

St. George's Chapel: This church is known for housing numerous royal tombs, and is an exquisite example of the Perpendicular Gothic style (dating from about 1500). Pick up a free map and circle the interior clockwise, finding these highlights:

Stand at the back and look down the **nave,** with its classic fan-vaulting spreading out from each slender pillar and nearly every joint capped with an elaborate and colorful roof boss. Most of these emblems are associated with the Knights of the Garter, who consider St. George's their "mother church." Under the upper stained-glass windows, notice the continuous frieze of 250 angels, lovingly carved with great detail, ringing the church.

In the corner (#4 on your church-issued map), take in the melodramatic monument to **Princess Charlotte of Wales,** the only child of King George IV. Heir to the throne, her death in 1817 (at 21, in childbirth) devastated the nation. Head up the left side of the nave and find the simple chapel (#6) containing the tombs of the current Queen's parents, **King George VI and "Queen Mum" Elizabeth;** the ashes of her younger sister, Princess Margaret, are also kept here (see the marble slab against the wall). It's speculated that the current Queen may choose this chapel for her final resting place. Farther up the aisle is the tomb of **Edward IV** (#8), who expanded St. George's Chapel.

Stepping into the **choir area** (#12), you're immediately aware that you are in the inner sanctum of the Order of the Garter. The banners lining the nave represent the knights, as do the fancy helmets and half-drawn swords at the top of each wood-carved seat.

These symbols honor only living knights; on the seats are some 800 golden panels memorializing departed knights. Under your feet lies the **Royal Vault** (#13), burial spot of Mad King George III (nemesis of American revolutionaries). Strolling farther up the aisle, notice the marker in the floor: You're walking over the burial site of **King Henry VIII** (#14) and Jane Seymour, Henry's favorite wife (perhaps because she was the only one who died before he could behead her). The body of King Charles I, who was beheaded by Oliver Cromwell's forces at the Banqueting House (see page 124), was also discovered here...with its head sewn back on.

On your way out, you can pause at the door of the sumptuous 13th-century **Albert Memorial Chapel** (#28), redecorated in 1861 after the death of Queen Victoria's husband, Prince Albert, and dedicated to his memory.

• *On exiting the chapel, you come into the castle's...*

Lower Ward: This area is a living town where some 160 people who work for the Queen reside; they include clergy, military, and castle administrators. Just below the chapel, you may be able to enter a tranquil little horseshoe-shaped courtyard ringed with residential doorways—all of them with a spectacular view of the chapel's grand entrance.

Back out in the yard, look for the guard posted at his pillbox. Like those at Buckingham Palace, he's been trained to be a ruthless killing machine...just so he can wind up as somebody's photo op. Click!

MORE SIGHTS IN WINDSOR
Legoland Windsor
Paradise for Legomaniacs under age 12, this huge, kid-pleasing park has dozens of tame but fun rides (often with very long lines) scattered throughout its 150 acres. The impressive Miniland has 40 million Lego pieces glued together to create 800 tiny buildings and a mini tour of Europe. Several of the more exciting rides involve getting wet, so dress accordingly or buy a cheap disposable poncho in the gift shop. While you may be tempted to hop on the Hill Train at  the entrance, it's faster and more convenient to walk down into the park. Food is available in the park, but you can save money by bringing a picnic.

Cost: £60 but varies by day, significant savings when booked online at least 7 days in advance, 10 percent discount at Windsor

TI, free for ages 3 and under, optional Q-Bot ride-reservation gadget allows you to bypass lines (£20-80 depending on when you go and how much time you want to save).

Hours: Generally late July-Aug daily 10:00-18:00; mid-March-late July and Sept-Oct Mon-Fri until 17:00, Sat-Sun until 18:00, often closed Tue-Wed; closed Nov-mid-March. Check website for exact schedule, tel. 0871-222-2001, www.legoland.co.uk.

Getting There: A £5 round-trip shuttle bus runs from opposite Windsor's Theatre Royal on Thames Street, and from the Parish Church stop on High Street (2/hour). If day-tripping from London, ask about rail/shuttle/park admission deals from Paddington or Waterloo train stations. For drivers, the park is on B-3022 Windsor/Ascot road, two miles southwest of Windsor and 25 miles west of London. Legoland is clearly signposted from the M-3, M-4, and M-25 motorways. Parking is easy (£6).

DAY TRIPS

Eton College

Across the bridge from Windsor Castle is the most famous "public" (the equivalent of our "private") high school in Britain. Eton was founded in 1440 by King Henry VI; today it educates about 1,300 boys (ages 13-18), who live on campus. Eton has molded the characters of 19 prime ministers as well as members of the royal family—most recently princes William and Harry. Sparse on actual sights, the college is closed to visitors except via guided tour, where you may get a glimpse of the schoolyard, chapel, cloisters, and the Museum of Eton Life. For more information visit www.etoncollege.com or call 01753/370-100.

Eton High Street

Even if you're not touring the college, it's worth the few minutes it takes to cross the pedestrian bridge and wander straight up Eton's High Street. A bit more cutesy and authentic-feeling than Windsor (which is given over to shopping malls and chain stores), Eton has a charm that's fun to sample.

Windsor and Royal Borough Museum

Tucked into a small space beneath the Guildhall (where Prince Charles remarried), this little museum does its best to give some insight into the history of Windsor and the surrounding area. They also have lots of special activities for kids. Ask at the desk whether tours are running to the Guildhall itself (visits only possible with a guide); if not, it's probably not worth the admission.

Cost and Hours: £2, includes audioguide, Tue-Sat 10:00-16:00, Sun from 12:00, closed Mon, located in the Guildhall on High Street, tel. 01628/685-686, www.rbwm.gov.uk.

Visiting Highclere Castle

If you're a fan of *Downton Abbey,* consider a day trip from London to Highclere Castle, the stately house where much of the show was filmed. Though the hugely popular TV series was set in Yorkshire, the actual house is located in Hampshire, about an hour's train ride west of London. Highclere has been home to the Earls of Carnarvon since 1679, but the present Jacobean-style house was rebuilt in the 1840s by Sir Charles Barry, who also designed London's Houses of Parliament. Noted landscape architect Capability Brown laid out the traditional gardens in the mid-18th century. The castle's Egyptian exhibit features artifacts collected by Highclere's fifth Earl, George Herbert, a keen amateur archaeologist. When Howard Carter discovered King Tut's tomb in 1922, he waited three weeks for his friend and patron Herbert to join him before looking inside. The Earl died unexpectedly a few months later, giving birth to the legend of a "mummy's curse."

Cost and Hours: £22 for castle, garden, and Egyptian exhibit; £15 for castle and garden only, or Egyptian exhibit and garden only; £7 for garden only.

Hours: Admission by timed entry only, mid-July–mid-Sept Sun-Thu castle open 10:30-17:00, grounds open 9:00-17:00, last entry one hour before closing, closed Fri-Sat; generally closed mid-Sept–mid-July except for special events; reserve well in advance online—tickets available several months ahead; 24-hour info tel. 01635/253-204, www.highclerecastle.co.uk.

Getting There: Highclere is six miles south of Newbury, about 70 miles west of London, off A-34.

By Train and Taxi: Great Western trains run from London's Paddington Station to Newbury (1-2/hour, 50-70 minutes, £25-56 same-day return, tel. 0345-700-125, www.gwr.com). From Newbury train station, you can take a taxi (£15-25 one-way, higher price is for Sun, taxis wait outside station) or reserve a car and driver (must arrange in advance, £12.50/person round-trip; £25 minimum, Webair, tel. 07818/430-095, mapeng@msn.com).

By Tour: Brit Movie Tours offers an all-day bus tour of *Downton Abbey* filming locations, including Highclere Castle and the fictional village of Downton (sells out early, £80, includes transport and castle/garden entry, £5 extra for Egyptian exhibit, 9 hours, depart London from outside Gloucester Road Tube Station, reservations required, tel. 0844-247-1007, from the US or Canada call 011-44-20-7118-1007, www.britmovietours.com).

Boat Trips

Cruise up and down the Thames River for classic views of the castle, the village of Eton, Eton College, and the Royal Windsor Racecourse. Choose from a 40-minute or two-hour tour, then relax onboard and nibble a picnic. Boats leave from the riverside promenade adjacent to Barry Avenue.

Cost and Hours: 40-minute tour-£8.50, family pass-about £23, mid-Feb-Oct 1-2/hour daily 10:00-17:00, fewer and Sat-Sun only in Nov; 2-hour tour-£14.50, family pass-about £40, late March-Oct only, 1-2/day; closed Dec-mid-Feb; online discounts, tel. 01753/851-900, www.frenchbrothers.co.uk.

Horse Racing

The horses race near Windsor every Monday at the Royal Windsor Racecourse (£25 entry, online discounts, under age 18 free with an adult, April-Aug and Oct, no races in Sept, sporadic in Aug, off A-308 between Windsor and Maidenhead, tel. 01753/498-400, www.windsor-racecourse.co.uk). The romantic way to get there from Windsor is by a 10-minute shuttle boat (£7 round-trip, www.frenchbrothers.co.uk). The famous Ascot Racecourse (described next) is also nearby.

NEAR WINDSOR
Ascot Racecourse

Located seven miles southwest of Windsor and just north of the town of Ascot, this royally owned track is one of the most famous horse-racing venues in the world. The horses first ran here in 1711, and the course is best known for June's five-day Royal Ascot race meeting, attended by the Queen and 299,999 of her loyal subjects. For many, the outlandish hats worn on Ladies Day (Thu) are more interesting than the horses. Royal Ascot is usually the third week in June (June 19-23 in 2018). The pricey tickets go on sale the preceding November; while the Friday and Saturday races tend to sell out far ahead, tickets for the other days are often available close to the date (check website). In addition to Royal Ascot, the racecourse runs the ponies year-round—funny hats strictly optional.

Cost: Regular tickets generally start from £18 and go as high as £80—may be available at a discount at TI, kids ages 17 and under sometimes free; parking from free to £20, depending on event; dress code enforced in some areas and on certain days, tel. 0844-346-3000, www.ascot.co.uk.

Sleeping in Windsor

Most visitors stay in London and do Windsor as a day trip. But here are a few suggestions for those staying the night.

$$$$ MGallery Castle Hotel Windsor, part of the boutique division of Accor Hotels, offers 108 rooms and elegant public spaces in a central location just down the street from Her Majesty's weekend retreat (breakfast extra, air-con, parking-£20/day, 18 High Street, tel. 01753/851-577, www.castlehotelwindsor.com, h6618@accor.com).

$$ Langton House B&B is a stately Victorian home with five spacious, well-appointed rooms lovingly maintained by Paul and Sonja Fogg (continental breakfast included but full English breakfast extra, family rooms, guest kitchen, 46 Alma Road, tel. 01753/858-299, www.langtonhouse.co.uk, bookings@langtonhouse.co.uk).

$$ Park Farm B&B, bright and cheery, is most convenient for drivers. But even if you're not driving, this beautiful place is such a good value, and the welcome is so warm, that you're unlikely to mind the bus ride into town (cash only—credit card solely for reservations, family room with bunk beds, shared fridge and microwave, free off-street parking, 1 mile from Legoland on St. Leonards Road near Imperial Road, 5-minute bus ride or 1-mile walk to castle, £5 taxi ride from station, tel. 01753/866-823, www.parkfarm.com, stay@parkfarm.com, Caroline and Drew Youds).

$$ 76 Duke Street has two nice rooms, but only hosts one set of guests at a time. While the bathroom is (just) outside your bedroom, you have it to yourself (15-minute walk from station at—you guessed it—76 Duke Street, tel. 01753/620-636 or 07884/222-225, www.76dukestreet.co.uk, bandb@76dukestreet.co.uk, Julia).

$ Dee and Steve's B&B is a friendly four-room place above a window shop on a quiet residential street about a 10-minute walk from the castle and station. The rooms are cozy, Dee and Steve are pleasant hosts, and breakfast is served in the contemporary kitchen/lounge (169 Oxford Road, tel. 01753/854-489, www.deeandsteve.com, dee@deeandsteve.com).

$ Crown and Cushion is a good option on Eton's High Street, just across the pedestrian bridge from Windsor's waterfront (a short uphill walk to the castle). While the pub it's situated over is worn and drab, you're right in the heart of charming Eton, and the eight creaky rooms—with uneven floors and old-beam ceilings—are nicely furnished (free parking, 84 High Street in Eton, tel. 01753/861-531, www.thecrownandcushioneton.co.uk, info@thecrownandcushioneton.com).

DAY TRIPS

Eating in Windsor

Elegant Spots with River Views: Several places flank Windsor Bridge, offering romantic dining after dark. The riverside promenade, with cheap takeaway stands scattered about, is a delightful place for a picnic lunch or dinner with the swans. If you don't see anything that appeals, continue up Eton's High Street, which is also lined with characteristic eateries.

In the Tourist Zone Around the Palace: Strolling the streets and lanes around the palace entrance—especially in the shopping zone near Windsor & Eton Station—you'll find countless trendy and inviting eateries. The central area also has a sampling of dependable British chains (including a Wagamama, Gourmet Burger Kitchen, and Thai Square). Residents enjoy a wide selection of unpretentious little eateries (including a fire station turned pub-and-cultural center) just past the end of pedestrian Peascod Street.

$$$ Bel & The Dragon is the place to splurge on high-quality classic British food in a charming half-timbered building with an upscale-rustic dining space (food served daily 12:00-15:00 & 18:00-22:00, afternoon tea served between lunch and dinner, bar open longer hours, on Thames Street near the bridge to Eton, tel. 01753/866-056).

$$$ Cornucopia a la Russe, with a cozy, woody atmosphere, serves tasty international dishes (two- and three-course lunch deals, open Mon-Sat 12:00-14:30 & 18:00-21:30, Fri-Sat until 22:00, closed Sun, 6 High Street, tel. 01753/833-009).

$$ The Duchess of Cambridge's friendly staff serves up the normal grub in a pub that's right across from the castle walls, and with an open fireplace to boot (daily 11:00-23:00 or later, 3 Thames Street, tel. 01753/864-405). While the pub predates Kate, it was named in her honor following a recent remodel, and has the photos to prove her endorsement.

$$ Meimo offers "Mediterranean/Moroccan" cuisine in a nicely subdued dining room at the quieter end of the pedestrian zone (several fixed-price meal options, daily 10:00-22:00, 69 Peascod Street, tel. 01753/862-222).

$$ Saffron restaurant, while a fairly long walk from the castle, is the local choice for South Indian cuisine, with a modern interior and attentive waiters who struggle with English but are fluent at bringing out tasty dishes. Their vegetarian *thali* is a treat (daily 12:00-14:30 & 17:30-23:30, 99 St. Leonards Road, tel. 01753/855-467).

DAY TRIPS

Cambridge

Cambridge, 60 miles north of London, is world-famous for its prestigious university. Wordsworth, Isaac Newton, Tennyson, Darwin, and Prince Charles are a few of its illustrious alumni. The university dominates—and owns—most of Cambridge, a historic town of about 125,000 people. Cambridge is the epitome of a university town, with busy bikers, stately residence halls, plenty of bookshops, and proud locals who can point out where DNA was originally modeled, the atom first split, and electrons discovered.

In medieval Europe, higher education was the domain of the Church and was limited to ecclesiastical schools. Scholars lived in "halls" on campus. This academic community of residential halls, chapels, and lecture halls connected by peaceful garden courtyards survives today in the colleges that make up the universities of Cambridge and Oxford. By 1350, Cambridge had eight colleges, each with a monastic-type courtyard, chapel, library, and lodgings. Today, Cambridge has 31 colleges, each with its own facilities, and about 12,000 undergrads. In the town center, these grand old halls date back centuries, with ornately decorated facades that try to one-up each other. While students' lives revolve around their independent colleges, the university organizes lectures, presents degrees, and promotes research.

The university schedule has three terms: Lent term from mid-January to mid-March, Easter term from mid-April to mid-June, and Michaelmas term from early October to early December. During exams (roughly the month of May), the colleges are closed to visitors, which can impede access to some of the town's picturesque little corners. But the main sights—King's College Chapel and the Wren Library at Trinity College—stay open, and Cambridge is never sleepy.

PLANNING YOUR TIME

Cambridge can easily be seen as a day trip from London. A good five-hour plan is to follow my self-guided walk, spend an hour on a punt ride, tour the Fitzwilliam Museum (closed Mon), and see the Wren Library at Trinity College (open Mon-Sat for only two hours a day, so plan ahead). For a little extra color, consider joining a walk through town with a local guide from the TI (2 hours, repeats much of my self-guided walk but splices in local flavor). The

TI's town walk includes King's College Chapel, so don't do that on your own.

If you're in town for the evening, the evensong service at King's College Chapel (Mon-Sat at 17:30, Sun at 15:30) is a must. If you like plays and music, events are always happening in this thriving cultural hub.

GETTING TO CAMBRIDGE

By Train: It's an easy trip from London and less than an hour away. Catch the train from London's King's Cross Station (2/hour, trains leave King's Cross at :15 and :44 past the hour, 45 minutes, £23.60 one-way standard class, £24.60 same-day return after 9:30, tel. 0845-748-4950, www.nationalrail.co.uk). Cheaper direct trains also run from London's Liverpool Street Station, but take longer (2/hour, 1.5 hours).

By Bus: National Express X90 coaches run from London's Victoria Coach Station to the Parkside stop in Cambridge (every 60-90 minutes, 2 hours, £12-22, discounted fares may be available in advance online, tel. 0871-781-8181, www.nationalexpress.co.uk).

Orientation to Cambridge

Cambridge is small. Everything is within a pleasant walk. The town has two main streets, separated from the River Cam by the most interesting colleges. The town center, brimming with tea-rooms, has a TI and a colorful open-air market square. The train station is about a mile to the southeast.

TOURIST INFORMATION

Cambridge's TI is well run and well signposted, just off Market Hill Square in the town center. They offer walking tours (see "Tours in Cambridge," later) and sell bus tickets and a £2.50 map/guide (Mon-Sat 10:00-17:00, Easter-Sept also Sun 11:00-15:00—otherwise closed Sun, phones answered from 9:00, Peas Hill, tel. 01223/791-500, www.visitcambridge.org). In the same building as the TI, you can duck into a former courtroom to catch a free video overview of the town and its history.

ARRIVAL IN CAMBRIDGE

By Train: Cambridge's train station doesn't have baggage storage or a TI. You can pick up a free map at the small info desk on the platform and other brochures on an interior wall to the left of the turnstiles.

To get from the station to downtown Cambridge, you can **walk** for about 25 minutes (exit straight ahead on Station Road, bear right at the war memorial onto Hills Road, and follow it into town); take public **bus** #1, #3, or #7 (referred to as "Citi 1," "Citi 3," and so on in schedules, but buses are marked only with the number; £1.70, pay driver, runs every 5-10 minutes, turn left when exiting station, cross the street, and walk half a block to find bus stands, get off when you see the Lion Yard shopping mall on the left); pay about £6 for a **taxi;** or take a City Sightseeing **bus tour** (described later).

By Car: To park in the middle of town, follow signs from the M-11 motorway to any of the central (but expensive) short-stay parking lots—including one at the Lion Yard shopping mall. Or leave your car at one of six park-and-ride lots outside the city, then take the shuttle into town (parking-£1/day; shuttle-£3 round-trip).

HELPFUL HINTS

Live Theater and Entertainment: With all the smart and talented students in town, there is always something going on. Make a point of enjoying a play or concert. The ADC **(Cambridge University Amateur Dramatic Club)** is Britain's oldest university playhouse, offering a steady stream of performances since 1855. It's lots of fun and casual, with easy-to-get and inexpensive tickets. This is your chance to see a future Emma Thompson or Ian McKellen—alumni who performed here as students—before they become stars (tel. 01223/300-085, www.adctheatre.com).

    Cambridge Live Tickets is a very helpful service, offering event info and ticket sales in person and online (Mon-Fri 12:00-18:00, Sat from 10:00, Sun from 18:00 until 30 minutes before showtime, 2 Wheeler Street, tel. 01223/357-851 answered Mon-Sat 10:00-18:00, www.cambridgelivetrust. co.uk). The TI also has lists of what's on.

Festivals: The **Cambridge Folk Festival** gets things humming and strumming in late July (tickets go on sale several months ahead and often sell out; www.cambridgefolkfestival.co.uk). From mid-July through August, the town's **Shakespeare Festival** attracts 25,000 visitors for outdoor performances in some of the college's gardens (£16, book tickets online, www. cambridgeshakespeare.com).

Bike Rental: Rutland Cycling, inside the Lion Yard shopping mall, offers pay luggage lockers and rents bikes (£7/4 hours, £10/day, helmets-£1, £60 deposit); Mon-Fri 8:00-18:00, Sat 9:00-18:00, Sun 10:00-17:00; tel. 01223/307-655, www. rutlandcycling.com.

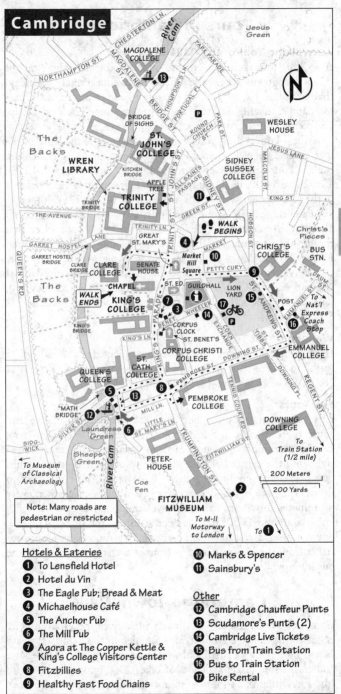

Cambridge

Jesus Green

River Cam

CHESTERTON LN.

MAGDALENE COLLEGE

NORTHAMPTON ST.

MAGDALENE ST.

BRIDGE ST.

THOMPSON'S LN.

PARK PARADE

PORTUGAL PL.

PARK ST.

Jesus Lane

WESLEY HOUSE

ROUND CHURCH ST.

MALCOLM ST.

The Backs

BRIDGE OF SIGHS

ST. JOHN'S COLLEGE

WREN LIBRARY

KITCHEN BRIDGE

ST. JOHN'S ST.

ALL SAINTS PASSAGE

SIDNEY ST.

SIDNEY SUSSEX COLLEGE

KING ST.

TRINITY BRIDGE

APPLE TREE

TRINITY COLLEGE

ST. JOHN'S ST.

GREEN ST.

THE AVENUE

GARRET HOSTEL LANE

TRINITY LN.

GREAT ST. MARY'S

TRINITY ST.

WALK BEGINS

Christ's Pieces

CHRIST'S COLLEGE

BUS STN.

DRUM ST.

GARRET HOSTEL BRIDGE

CLARE BRIDGE

CLARE COLLEGE

SENATE HOUSE

Market Hill Square

MARKET

PETTY CURY

HOBSON ST.

The Backs

QUEEN'S RD.

CHAPEL

WALK ENDS

KING'S COLLEGE

KING'S PARADE

ST. ED.

GUILDHALL

LION YARD

ST. ANDREW'S ST.

POST

To Nat'l Express Coach Stop

KING'S BRIDGE

BENE'T ST.

WHEELER

CORN EXCHANGE

EMMANUEL ST.

CORPUS CLOCK

ST. BENET'S

KING'S LN.

CORPUS CHRISTI COLLEGE

DOWNING ST.

EMMANUEL COLLEGE

SIDG-WICK

ST. CATH. COLLEGE

PEMBROKE ST.

TIBB'S

REGENT ST.

QUEEN'S COLLEGE

MILL LN.

PEMBROKE COLLEGE

TENNIS COURT RD.

DOWNING PL.

"MATH BRIDGE"

SILVER ST.

Laundress Green

LITTLE ST. MARY'S LN.

TRUMPINGTON ST.

DOWNING COLLEGE

To Train Station (1/2 mile)

Sheeps Green

PETER-HOUSE

FITZWILLIAM ST.

200 Meters

200 Yards

To Museum of Classical Archaeology

River Cam

Coe Fen

FITZWILLIAM MUSEUM

To M-11 Motorway to London ↓

To ① ↓

Note: Many roads are pedestrian or restricted

Hotels & Eateries

1. To Lensfield Hotel
2. Hotel du Vin
3. The Eagle Pub; Bread & Meat
4. Michaelhouse Café
5. The Anchor Pub
6. The Mill Pub
7. Agora at The Copper Kettle & King's College Visitors Center
8. Fitzbillies
9. Healthy Fast Food Chains
10. Marks & Spencer
11. Sainsbury's

Other

12. Cambridge Chauffeur Punts
13. Scudamore's Punts (2)
14. Cambridge Live Tickets
15. Bus from Train Station
16. Bus to Train Station
17. Bike Rental

Tours in Cambridge

▲▲Walking Tour of the Colleges

A walking tour is the best way to understand Cambridge's mix of "town and gown." The walks can be more educational (read: dry) than entertaining, but they do provide a good rundown of the historic and scenic highlights of the university, some fun local gossip, and plenty of university trivia.

The TI offers **daily walking tours** that include the King's College Chapel, as well as another college—usually Queen's College (£20, 2 hours, includes entry fees; July-Aug daily at 11:00, 12:00, 13:00, and 14:00, no 11:00 tour on Sun; generally fewer tours rest of the year—check website for schedule; tel. 01223/791-500, www.visitcambridge.org). Groups are limited to 20, so it's smart to call ahead or drop in at the TI in advance to reserve a spot. Note that the 12:00 tour overlaps with the limited opening times of the Wren Library, so you'll miss out on the library if you take the noon tour.

Private guides are available through the TI and affordable if you can assemble a group to share the cost (2-hour tour-£97.50; does not include individual college entrance fees, tel. 01223/791-500, tours@visitcambridge.org).

Walking Ghost Tour

If you're in Cambridge on the weekend, consider a £6.50 "ghost walk" to where spooky sightings have been reported (Fri-Sat at 18:00, organized by the TI, tel. 01223/791-500).

Bus Tours

City Sightseeing hop-on, hop-off bus tours are informative and cover the outskirts, including the American WWII Cemetery. But keep in mind that buses can't go where walking tours can—right into the center (£15.50, 80 minutes for full 19-stop circuit, buy ticket with credit card at the bus-stop kiosk or pay cash to driver when you board, departs every 20 minutes in summer, every 40 minutes in winter, first bus leaves train station around 10:00, last bus around 17:30, recorded commentary, tel. 01223/433-250, www.city-sightseeing.com). If arriving by train, you can buy your ticket from the kiosk directly in front of the station, then ride the bus into town.

Cambridge Town Walk

Cambridge is built along its dreamy little river and around its 31 colleges (the first, Peterhouse, was founded in the 1280s). It's easy to sort out. There's a small and youthful commercial center—quiet and traffic free (except for lots of bikes), one important museum (the Fitzwilliam), and lots of minor museums (all generally free).

Cambridge Colleges 101

Cambridge's 31 colleges, where students spend most of their time, are central to the life of the university. They house, feed, and parent the students, while the overall university offers formal teaching and lectures. Each college also has a "home professor" who coaches students as they navigate the higher education system.

Some colleges are free to visit and welcoming to the public, some are closed off and very private, and others are famous and make money by charging for visits. Most are open only in the afternoons, and all have a similar design and etiquette. At their historic front gates, you'll find a porter's lodge where the porter keeps an eye on things. He delivers mail, monitors who comes and goes, and keeps people off the grass. The exclusive putting-green quality of the courtyard lawns is a huge deal here: Only fellows (senior professors) can walk on the courts, which are the centerpiece of each college campus. Whether a college is open to visitors or private, you can usually at least pop in through the gate, chat with the porter, and enjoy the view of the grassy court.

The court is ringed by venerable buildings, always including a library, dormitories, a dining hall, and a chapel. The dining halls are easy to identify because they have big bay windows that mark the location of a "high table" where VIPs eat. A portrait of the college's founder usually hangs above the high table, and paintings of rectors and important alumni also decorate the walls. Students still eat in these halls, which is why they are rarely open to the public (but you can look in from the main door). A college's chapel is the building that most often allows visitors (including at evensong services, usually at 17:30 or 18:00). In the chapel, seating is usually arranged in several rows of pews that face each other to allow for antiphonal singing and chanting—where one side starts and the other responds. The chapels often contain memorials to students who died in World Wars I and II. Libraries are treasured and generally not open to the public. There's also a Senior Common Room (like a teachers' lounge but much fancier), where fellows share ideas in an exclusive social hall, creating a fertile intellectual garden. Students live on campus not along halls but in "staircases" (never open to the public). Their address includes their college, their staircase, and their room number.

The River Cam has boat tours, three public bridges, and a strip of six colleges whose gardens basically own the river through the center of town and make it feel like an exclusive park. The university includes two dominant colleges (Trinity with its famous Wren Library, and King's College with its famous chapel), but also plenty of minor ones, each with a grand front gate. The city is filled with students year-round—scholars throughout the regular terms and visiting students enjoying summer programs.

In the following self-guided walk, I cover the essential town sights (including two less-visited colleges), finishing at King's College Chapel. Trinity College and the Fitzwilliam Museum are covered in "Sights in Cambridge," later. To trace the route, see the map on page 495.

• *Start this self-guided walk on Market Hill Square (the TI is just half a block away). To find the square from the lively street called King's Parade—which feels like the center of town and is where this walk ends—go behind Great St. Mary's Church (with the tall tower).*

Market Hill Square

DAY TRIPS

This square has been a center of commerce for more than a thousand years. Think of the history this place has seen: Romans first built a bridge over the Cam in A.D. 43, Anglo-Saxons and Danes established a market here in the Dark Ages, and Normans built a castle here (now gone) in the 11th century.

But the big year was 1209, when scholars and students first arrived. After scuffles in Oxford between its townsfolk and university (which is roughly 100 years older than Cambridge), Oxford's students and professors fled here and settled. (The Oxford-Cambridge rivalry just seems natural.) Where's the university? Everywhere, mixed into the town, with the 31 individual colleges, university halls, and student dorms scattered about. Even on this square you can see dorms (the more modern, tasteless buildings around you). Cambridge suffered no bomb damage in World War II, so the older buildings you see are originals. As you walk, notice how peaceful the town is. Almost no cars, but bikes everywhere—be careful! They are silent and pack a punch.

The Guildhall facing this square (the seat of the city council today) overlooks market stalls. The big market is on Sunday (9:30-16:30) and features produce, arts, and crafts. On other days, you'll find mostly clothes and food (Mon-Sat generally 9:30-16:00).

• *Facing the Guildhall, exit the square to your left down Petty Cury Lane, a modern pedestrian shopping street. At its end (with three fast-food places: Eat, Pret, and Wasabi) you hit St. Andrews Street. On the left side of the street is the fine 16th-century gatehouse of Christ's College. Step inside to enjoy the classic court, next to a bust of Charles Darwin (a notable alum). The college is open to the public daily 9:00-16:00 if you want to poke around. Otherwise continue down St. Andrews Street a long block to Emmanuel College.*

Emmanuel College

This college welcomes the public and offers a classic peek at a typical Cambridge college (free, open 9:00-18:00). Emmanuel was founded in 1584 as a Protestant college on land that had once been a Dominican friary. (Like many monasteries and convents in the 16th century, the friary had been dissolved by the English king in an epic power struggle that left England with its own version of Christianity and the government with lots of land once owned by the Catholic Church.)

Facing the court, with the big clock, is one of two chapels in town designed by the famed architect Christopher Wren. Above the church is the Senior Common Room, a social hall for college fellows. On the left is the dining hall—marked by its big bay window.

At this point you could visit the church (find the portrait of John Harvard—the Emmanuel College student who went to America and founded another prestigious school—in the stained glass on the left), look through the doorway into the dining hall, enjoy the garden behind the chapel (typical of these colleges; the fish pond goes back to monastic days when the fish were part of the diet), or chat with the porter.

• *Leaving Emmanuel College, walk straight ahead along Downing Street. You'll pass several museums that are owned by the university to support various fields of study (generally free to enter). Downing Street ends at King's Parade, with Pembroke College on the left and the recommended Fitzbillies Café on the right (famous for its local cinnamon roll, the Chelsea Bun).*

Pembroke College

Founded in 1347, Pembroke is the third-oldest college in Cambridge. Step into the court, past the porter's lodge—it's polite to say hello and ask whether you can wander around. Survey the court. Two chapels face it. The original chapel (on the left) was replaced by the bigger one on the right. Ahead of you is the medieval dining hall. The fancy building with the pointed clock tower is the library (the statue in front is alumnus William Pitt the Younger—a great 18th-century prime minister), with a charming garden beyond.

The highlight here is the chapel on the right, which dates from about 1660 and is the first building Christopher Wren completed. Before stepping inside to enjoy the interior, pause for a moment at the somber WWI and WWII memorial.

• *From Pembroke College, cross King's Parade and follow Mill Lane directly down to the River Cam and its mill pond.*

River Cam, the Mill Pond, and Punting

From this perch you see the "harbor action" of Cambridge. The city was a sort of harbor in medieval times: Trading vessels from the North Sea could navigate to here. Today a weir divides the River Cam from the River Granta (on the left), which leads through idyllic countryside to the town of Grantchester. Filling the mill pond is a commotion of the iconic Cambridge boats called punts (note that punts cannot cross the weir). Students hustle to take visitors on a 45-minute trip along the park known as "the Backs," with views of the backs of colleges that line the river from here to the far side of town (about £20, see page 506). You can share a boat with others and enjoy a colorful narration as you're poled past fine college architecture. Skilled residents rent boats for themselves, as do not-so-skilled tourists—much to the amusement of locals who sip their beer while watching clumsy visitors fumble with the boats (which are tougher to maneuver than they look).

Walk along the harbor past the recommended Anchor Pub (with waterfront tables and fancier seating upstairs) to the Silver Street Bridge. From here you can watch more punt action and check out the famous "Mathematical Bridge," which links the old and new buildings of Queens' College. This wooden bridge, although curved, is made of straight boards. (It was not designed by Isaac Newton, as a popular fable would have it—Newton died before the bridge was constructed.)

Gazing upstream past the wooden bridge, you see the start of "the Backs" stretch of six colleges, most with bridges connecting campus grounds or buildings on both sides of the river.

• *Walk up Silver Street, back to King's Parade, and turn left toward this walk's finale—King's College. On the first corner, find the fancy gilded clock.*

The Corpus Clock, Benet Street, and Eagle Pub

Designed and commissioned by Corpus Christi College alum John Taylor, this clock was unveiled by Cambridge physicist Stephen Hawking in a 2008 ceremony. Perched on top is the Chronophage—the "time eater"—a grotesque giant grasshopper that keeps the clock moving and periodically winks at passersby. The message? Time is passing, so live every moment to the fullest.

The Eagle Pub, a venerable joint, is just down Benet Street on the left. This is Cambridge's oldest pub and a sight in itself. Poke into the courtyard and atmospheric rooms even if you don't eat or drink here.

From the courtyard outside, look up at the balcony of second-floor guest rooms that date back to when this was a coachmen's inn as well as a pub. (It's said that in Shakespeare's time, plays were performed from this perch to entertain guests below.) The faded *Bath* sign indicates that this was a posh place—you could even wash. Notice that the window on the right end is open; any local will love to tell you why.

Step past the "glancing stones" that protected the corner from careening coaches. During World War II, US Army Air Corps pilots famously hung out here before missions over Germany. The fun interior is plastered with stickers of air crews and WWII memorabilia. Next to the fireplace a photo and plaque remember two esteemed regulars—Francis Crick and James Watson—the scientists who first described the structure of DNA. They announced their finding here in 1953, and if you'd like to drink to that, there's a beer on tap for you—a bitter called DNA.

St. Benet's Church, across the street from the pub, is the oldest surviving building in Cambridgeshire. The Saxons who built the church in the 11th century included circular holes in its bell tower to encourage owls to roost there and keep the mouse population under control.

• *Return to the creepy grasshopper clock and turn right, continuing down King's Parade past the regal front facade of King's College Chapel (we'll return here shortly) to the...*

Senate House

This stately classical building with triangular pediments is the ceremonial and administrative heart of the University of Cambridge and the meeting place of the university's governing body. In June, you might notice green boxes lining the front of this house. Traditionally, at the end of the term, students came to these boxes to see whether they had earned their degree; those not listed knew they had flunked. Amazingly, until 2010 this was the only notification students received about their status. (Now they first get an email.)

Looming across the street from the Senate House is **Great St. Mary's Church** (a.k.a. the University Church), with a climbable

bell tower (£4, Mon-Sat 9:30-16:30, Sun 12:30-16:00, 123 stairs). On the corner nearby is **Ryder and Amies** (22 King's Parade), which has been the official university outfitter for 150 years. It's a great shop for college gear: sweaters, ties, and so on. Upstairs, if you ask, you can try on an undergraduate gown and mortar board.

• *Just after the Senate House, take the first left possible (on Senate House passage); at the end, bear left on Trinity Lane to reach the gate where you pay to enter...*

▲▲King's College Chapel

Built from 1446 to 1515 by Henrys VI through VIII, England's best example of Perpendicular Gothic architecture is the single most impressive building in Cambridge.

Cost and Hours: £9, erratic hours depending on school events; during academic term usually Mon-Fri 9:30-15:30, Sat until 15:15, Sun 13:15-14:30; during breaks (see page 492) usually daily 9:30-16:30; recorded info tel. 01223/331-1212. Buy tickets at the King's College visitors center at 13 Kings Parade, across the street from the main entrance gate.

Evensong: When school's in session, you're welcome to enjoy an evensong service in this glorious space, with a famous choir made up of men and boys (free, Mon-Sat at 17:30, Sun at 15:30; for more on evensong, see page 454). Line up at the front entrance (on King's Parade) by 17:00 if you want prime seats in the choir.

Visiting the Chapel: Stand inside, look up, and marvel, as Christopher Wren did, at what was then the largest single span of **vaulted roof** anywhere. Built between 1512 and 1515, its 2,000 tons of incredible fan vaulting—held in place by the force of gravity—are a careful balancing act resting delicately on the buttresses visible outside the building.

While Henry VI—who began work on the chapel—wanted it to be austere, his descendants decided it should glorify the House of Tudor (of which his distant relative, Henry VII, was the first king). Lining the walls are giant **Tudor coats-of-arms.** The shield is supported by symbolism for each branch of the family: the fleur-de-lis because an earlier ancestor, Edward III, woke up one day and somewhat arbitrarily declared himself king of France; a rose and the dragon of Wales represent the family of Henry VII's father; and the greyhound holding the

shield and the portcullis (the iron grate) symbolize the family of Henry VII's mother, Lady Margaret Beaufort.

The 26 **stained-glass windows** date from the 16th century. It's the most Renaissance stained glass anywhere in one spot. (Most of the stained glass in English churches dates from Victorian times, but this glass is three centuries older.) The lower panes show scenes from the New Testament, while the upper panes feature corresponding stories from the Old Testament. Considering England's turbulent history, it's miraculous that these windows have survived for nearly half a millennium in such a pristine state. After Henry VIII separated from the Catholic Church in 1534, many such windows and other Catholic features around England were destroyed. (Think of all those ruined abbeys dotting the English countryside.) However, since Henry had just paid for these windows, he couldn't bear to destroy them. A century later, in the days of Oliver Cromwell, another wave of iconoclasm destroyed more windows around England. Though these windows were slated for removal, they stayed put. (Historians speculate that Cromwell's troops, who were garrisoned in this building, didn't want the windows removed in the chilly wintertime.) Finally, during World War II, the windows were taken out and hidden away for safekeeping, then painstakingly replaced after the war ended. The only nonmedieval windows are on the west wall (opposite the altar). These are in the Romantic style from the 1880s; when Nazi bombs threatened the church, all agreed they should be left in place.

The **choir screen** that bisects the church was commissioned by King Henry VIII to commemorate his marriage to Anne Boleyn. By the time it was finished, so was she (beheaded). But it was too late to remove her initials, which were carved into the screen (look on the far left and right for *R.A.*, for *Regina Anna*—"Queen Anne"). Behind the screen is the **choir** area, where the King's College Choir performs a daily evensong (during school terms). On Christmas Eve, a special service is held here and broadcast around the world on the BBC—a tradition near and dear to British hearts.

Walk to the altar and admire Rubens' masterful ***Adoration of the Magi*** (1634). It's actually a family portrait: The admirer in the front (wearing red) is a self-portrait of Rubens, Mary looks an awful lot like his much-younger wife, and the Baby Jesus resembles their own newborn at the time. The chapel to the right of the altar is a moving memorial to those who died in the two world wars.

Finally, check out the long and fascinating series of rooms that run the length of the nave on the left. Dedicated to the history and art of the church, these are a great little King's College Chapel museum (including a model showing how the fan vaults were constructed).

• *Exit the church opposite where you entered, into the college court. From here you can stroll the rich grounds all the way to the River Cam and then back, passing through the grand entry gate and onto King's Parade.*

Sights in Cambridge

My self-guided walk takes you to most of the main sights in Cambridge, but not all. Your time is well spent visiting these places as well.

▲▲Trinity College and Wren Library

More than a third of Cambridge's 83 Nobel Prize winners have come from this richest and biggest of the town's colleges, founded in 1546 by Henry VIII. The college has three sights to see: the entrance gate, the grounds, and the magnificent Wren Library.

Cost and Hours: Grounds—£3, daily 10:00-17:00; library—free, Mon-Fri 12:00-14:00, during full term also Sat 10:30-12:30, closed Sun year-round; only 20 people allowed in at a time, tel. 01223/338-400, www.trin.cam.ac.uk.

Visiting the College: To see the Wren Library without paying for the grounds, access it from the riverside entrance (a long walk around the college via the Garret Hostel Bridge).

Trinity Gate: You'll notice gates like these adorning facades of colleges around town. Above the door is a statue of **King Henry VIII,** who founded Trinity because he feared that Cambridge's existing colleges were too cozy with the Church. Notice Henry's right hand holding a chair leg instead of the traditional scepter with the crown jewels. This is courtesy of Cambridge's Night Climbers, who first replaced the scepter a century ago, and continue to periodically switch it out for other items. According to campus legend, decades ago some of the world's most talented mountaineers enrolled at Cambridge...in one of the flattest parts of England. (Cambridge was actually a seaport until Dutch engineers drained the surrounding swamps.) Lacking

opportunities to practice their skill, they began scaling the frilly facades of Cambridge's college buildings under cover of darkness (if caught, they'd have been expelled). In the 1960s, climbers actually managed to haul an entire automobile onto the roof of the Senate House. The university had to bring in the army to cut it into pieces and remove it. Only 50 years later, at a class reunion, did the guilty parties finally fess up.

In the little park to the right, notice the lone **apple tree.** Supposedly, this tree is a descendant of the very one that once stood in the garden of Sir Isaac Newton (who spent 30 years at Trinity). According to legend, Newton was inspired to investigate gravity when an apple fell from the tree onto his head. This tree stopped bearing fruit long ago; if you do see apples, they've been tied on by mischievous students.

Beyond the gate are the Trinity grounds. Note that there's often a fine and free view of Trinity College courtyard—if the gate is open—from Trinity Lane (leading, under a uniform row of old chimneys, around the school to the Wren Library).

Trinity Grounds: The grounds are enjoyable to explore. Inside the **Great Court,** the clock (on the tower on the right) double-rings at the top of each hour.

It's a college tradition to take off running from the clock when the high noon bells begin (it takes 43 seconds to clang 24 times), race around the court-yard, touching each of the four corners without setting foot on the cobbles, and try to return to the same spot before the ringing ends. Supposedly only one student (a young lord) ever managed the feat—a scene featured in *Chariots of Fire* (but filmed elsewhere).

The **chapel** (entrance to the right of the clock tower)—which pales in comparison to the stunning King's College Chapel—feels like a shrine to thinking, with statues honoring great Trinity minds both familiar (Isaac Newton, Alfred, Lord Tennyson, Francis Bacon) and unfamiliar. Who's missing? The poet Lord Byron, who was such a hell-raiser during his time at Trinity that a statue of him was deemed unfit for Church property; his statue stands in the library instead.

Wren Library: Don't miss the 1695 Christopher Wren-designed library, with its wonderful carving and fascinating original manuscripts. Just outside the library entrance, Sir Isaac Newton clapped his hands and timed the echo to measure the speed of sound as it raced down the side of the cloister and back. In the library's 12 display cases (covered with cloth that you flip back), you'll see handwritten works by Sir Isaac Newton and John Milton, alongside A. A. Milne's original *Winnie the Pooh* (the real Christopher Robin attended Trinity College). Unlike the other libraries at Cambridge, Wren designed his to be used from the first floor up—instead of the damp, dark ground floor. As a result, Wren's library is flooded with light, rather than water (and it's also brimming with students during exam times).

▲▲Fitzwilliam Museum

Britain's best museum of antiquities and art outside London is the Fitzwilliam. Housed in a grand Neoclassical building, a 10-minute walk south of Market Square, it's a palatial celebration of beauty and humankind's ability to create it.

Cost and Hours: Free but £5 donation suggested, Tue-Sat 10:00-17:00, Sun 12:00-17:00, closed Mon, lockers, Trumpington Street, tel. 01223/332-900, www.fitzmuseum.cam.ac.uk.

Visiting the Museum: The Fitzwilliam's broad collection is like a mini-British Museum/National Gallery rolled into one; you're bound to find something you like. Helpful docents—many with degrees or doctorates in art history—are more than willing to answer questions about the collection. The ground floor features an extensive range of antiquities and applied arts—everything from Greek vases, Mesopotamian artifacts, and Egyptian sarcophagi to Roman statues, fine porcelain, and suits of armor.

Upstairs is the painting gallery, with works that span art history: Italian Venetian masters (such as Titian and Canaletto), a worthy English section (featuring Gainsborough, Reynolds, Hogarth, and others), and a notable array of French Impressionist art (including Monet, Renoir, Pissarro, Degas, and Sisley). Rounding out the collection are old manuscripts, including some musical compositions from Handel.

Museum of Classical Archaeology

Although this museum contains no originals, it offers a unique chance to study accurate copies (19th-century casts) of virtually every famous ancient Greek and Roman statue. More than 450 statues are on display. If you've seen the real things in Greece, Istanbul, Rome, and elsewhere, touring this collection is like a high school reunion..."Hey, I know you!" But since it takes some time to get here, this museum is best left to devotees of classical sculpture.

Cost and Hours: Free, Mon-Fri 10:00-17:00, Sat 10:00-13:00 during term, closed Sun year-round, Sidgwick Avenue, tel. 01223/330-402, www.classics.cam.ac.uk/museum.

Getting There: The museum is a five-minute walk west of Silver Street Bridge; after crossing the bridge, continue straight until you reach a sign reading *Sidgwick Site.*

▲Punting on the Cam

For a little levity and probably more exercise than you really want, try renting one of the traditional flat-bottom punts at the river and pole yourself up and down (or around and around, more likely) the lazy Cam. This is one of the best memories the town has to offer, and once

you get the hang of it, it's a fine way to enjoy the scenic side of Cambridge. It's less crowded in late afternoon (and less embarrassing).

Several companies rent punts and also offer punting tours with entertaining narration. Hawkers try to snare passengers in the thriving people zone in front of King's College. Prices are soft in slow times—try talking them down a bit before committing.

Scudamore's has two locations: on Mill Lane, just south of the central Silver Street Bridge, and at the less convenient Quayside at Magdalene Bridge, at the north end of town (£27.50/hour, credit-card deposit required; 45-minute tours-£19/person, ask for discount; open daily 9:00-dusk, tel. 01223/359-750, www.scudamores.com).

Cambridge Chauffeur Punts, just under the Silver Street Bridge, also rents punts. Take yourself and up to five friends for a spin, or they will chauffeur (£24/hour; passport, credit card, or £60 cash deposit required; 45-minute shared tours-£16/person; open daily March-Nov 9:00-dusk, tel. 01223/354-164, www.punting-in-cambridge.co.uk).

NEAR CAMBRIDGE
Imperial War Museum Duxford

This former airfield, nine miles south of Cambridge, is popular with aviation fans and WWII history buffs. Wander through seven exhibition halls housing 200 vintage aircraft (including Spitfires, B-17 Flying Fortresses, a Concorde, and a Blackbird, some of which you can enter) as well as military land vehicles and special displays on Normandy and the Battle of Britain. The American Air wing thoughtfully portrays the achievements and controversies of British/US wartime collaboration, including the stories of American airmen based at Duxford. On many weekends, the museum holds special events, such as air shows (extra fee)—check the website for details.

Cost and Hours: £18, show local bus ticket for discount, daily 10:00-18:00, off-season until 16:00, last entry one hour before closing; tel. 01223/835-000, www.iwm.org.uk/visits/iwm-duxford.

Getting There: The museum is located off the A-505 in Duxford. On Sundays, direct Myalls bus #132 runs to the museum from the train station (4/day, 45 minutes, www.travelineeastanglia.org.uk). The rest of the week, it's best to take a taxi from Cambridge: Catch one at the taxi stand on St. Andrews Street next to the Lion Yard shopping mall (about £25 one-way).

Sleeping in Cambridge

While Cambridge is an easy side-trip from London (and you can enjoy an evening here before catching a late train back), its subtle charms might convince you to spend a night or two. Cambridge has few accommodations in the city center, and none in the tight maze of colleges and shops where you'll spend most of your time. These recommendations (each just past the Fitzwilliam Museum) are about a 10-minute walk south of the town center, toward the train station. (Though weak in hotel offerings, Cambridge does have plenty of B&Bs, which you can research and book online.)

$$$ Lensfield Hotel, popular with visiting professors, has 40 comfortable rooms—some old-fashioned, some refurbished (spa and fitness room, 53 Lensfield Road, tel. 01223/355-017, www.lensfieldhotel.co.uk, enquiries@lensfieldhotel.co.uk).

$$$ Hotel du Vin is a pretentious place that rents 41 decent rooms at a high price. It has duck-your-head character and a good location (breakfast extra, Trumpington Street 15, tel. 01223/928 991, www.hotelduvin.com, reception.cambridge@hotelduvin.com).

Eating in Cambridge

$$$ The Eagle, near the TI and described earlier in my town walk, is the oldest pub in town. While the food is mediocre, the pub is a Cambridge institution with a history so rich that a visit here practically qualifies as sightseeing (food served daily 11:00-22:00, 8 Benet Street, tel. 01223/505-020).

$ Michaelhouse Café is a heavenly respite from the crowds, tucked into the repurposed St. Michael's Church, just north of Great St. Mary's Church. At lunch, choose from salads and sandwiches, as well as a few hot dishes and a variety of tasty baked goods (Mon-Sat 8:00-17:00, breakfast served until 11:30, lunch served 11:30-15:50, closed Sun, Trinity Street, tel. 01223/309-147). Between 15:00 and 17:00 whatever they have left from lunch is half-price.

$$$ The Anchor Pub's claim to fame is as the setting of Pink Floyd's first gig. Today it's known for the best people-watching—and some locals say best food—in Cambridge. Choose from its outdoor riverside terrace, inside bar, or more romantic upstairs restaurant (all seating areas serve the same menu, but the upstairs menu has a few added specials; daily 12:00-21:30, on the riverfront at Silver Street, tel. 01224/353-554).

$$ The Mill Pub is a livelier, less formal alternative to The

Anchor, but enjoys a similar location right on the river. The clientele is a mixture of students and tourists; the tipples are craft brews, local ales, and ciders; and the food is an eclectic mix ranging from updated pub standards to Indian and Asian options (daily 11:00-23:00, 14 Mill Lane, tel. 01223/311-829).

$ Bread & Meat serves simple soups and hearty sandwiches. Grab a signature *porchetta* sandwich to take away or snag a rustic table in the small dining room (Sun-Thu 11:00-19:30, Fri-Sat 10:00-21:00, 4 Benet Street, tel. 0791/808-3057).

$$ Agora at The Copper Kettle is a popular place for Greek and Turkish *meze*, beautifully situated facing King's College on King's Parade (also fish-and-chips at lunch, daily 8:00-20:30, later in summer, 4 King's Parade, tel. 01223/308-448).

$$ Fitzbillies, long a favorite for cakes (Chelsea buns) and coffee, offers inviting lunch and afternoon tea menus (daily, 51 Trumpington Street, tel. 01223/352-500).

$ Fast Food: For healthy fast-food chains, the corner of Petty Cury Lane and Sidney Street (a long block off Market Hill Square) has three good places: **Eat, Pret,** and **Wasabi.**

Supermarkets: There's a **Marks & Spencer Simply Food** at the train station (Mon-Sat 7:00-23:00, Sun from 9:00) and a larger Marks & Spencer department store on Market Hill Square (Mon-Tue 8:00-18:00, later Wed-Sat, Sun 11:00-17:00). **Sainsbury's** supermarket has longer hours (Mon-Sat 7:30-23:30, Sun 11:00-17:00, 44 Sidney Street, at the corner of Green Street).

A good picnic spot is Laundress Green, a grassy park on the river, at the end of Mill Lane near the Silver Street Bridge punts. There are no benches, so bring something to sit on. Remember, the college lawns are private property, so walking or picnicking on the grass is generally not allowed. When in doubt, ask at the college's entrance.

Cambridge Connections

From Cambridge by Train to: York (hourly, 2.5 hours, transfer in Peterborough), **Oxford** (2-3/hour, 2.5-3 hours, change in London involves Tube transfer between train stations), **London** (King's Cross Station: 2/hour, 45 minutes; Liverpool Street Station: 2/hour, 1.5 hours). Train info: Tel. 0345-748-4950, www.nationalrail.co.uk.

By Bus to: London (every 60-90 minutes, 2 hours), **Heathrow Airport** (1-2/hour, 2-3 hours), **Oxford** (2/hour, 3.5 hours). Bus info: Tel. 0871-781-8181, www.nationalexpress.com.

Stonehenge

As old as the pyramids, and far older than the Acropolis and the Colosseum, this iconic stone circle amazed medieval Europeans, who figured it was built by a race of giants. And it still impresses visitors today. As one of Europe's most famous sights, Stonehenge, worth ▲▲▲, does a valiant job of retaining an air of mystery and majesty (partly because cordons, which keep hordes of tourists from trampling all over it, foster the illusion that it stands alone in a field).

Although cynics manage to be underwhelmed by Stonehenge, most of its almost one million annual visitors agree that it's well worth the trip. At few sights in Europe will you overhear so many awe-filled comments.

GETTING TO STONEHENGE

Stonehenge is about 90 miles southwest of central London. To reach it from London, you can take a bus tour; go on a guided tour that uses public transportation; or do it on your own using public transit, connecting via Salisbury. It's not worth the hassle or expense to rent a car just for a Stonehenge day trip.

By Bus Tour from London: Several companies offer big-bus day trips to Stonehenge from London, often with stops in Bath, Windsor, Salisbury, and/or Avebury. These generally cost about £45-85 (including Stonehenge admission), last 8-12 hours, and pack a 45-seat bus. Some include hotel pickup, admission fees, and meals; understand what's included before you book. The more destinations listed for a tour, the less time you'll have at any one stop. Well-known companies are **Evan Evans** (their bare-bones Stonehenge Express gets you there and back for £48, tel. 020/7950-1777 or US tel. 866-382-6868, www.evanevanstours.co.uk) and **Golden Tours** (£48, tel. 020/7630-2028 or US toll-free tel. 800-509-2507, www.goldentours.com). **International Friends** runs pricier but smaller 16-person tours that include Windsor and Bath (£139, tel. 01223/244-555, www.internationalfriends.co.uk).

By Guided Tour on Public Transport: London Walks offers a guided "Stonehenge and Salisbury Tour" from London by train and bus on Tuesdays from May through October (£78, includes all transportation, Salisbury walking tour, entry fees, and guided tours of Stonehenge and Salisbury Cathedral; pay guide, cash only, Tue at 8:45, meet at Waterloo Station's main ticket office, opposite Platform 16, verify price and schedule online, advance booking not required, tel. 020/7624-3978, recorded info tel. 020/7624-9255, www.walks.com).

On Your Own on Public Transport via Salisbury: From London, you can catch a train to Salisbury, then go by bus or taxi to Stonehenge. **Trains** to Salisbury run from London's Waterloo Station (around £38 for same-day return leaving weekdays after 9:30, 2/hour, 1.5 hours, tel. 0871-200-4950 or 0345-748-4950, www.southwesttrains.co.uk or www.nationalrail.co.uk).

From Salisbury, take **The Stonehenge Tour bus** to the site. These distinctive double-decker buses leave from the Salisbury train station, stop in Salisbury's center, then make a circuit to Stonehenge and Old Sarum, with lovely scenery and a decent light commentary along the way (£15, £29 includes Stonehenge as well as Old Sarum—whether you want it or not; tickets good all day, pay driver; daily June-Aug 10:00-18:00, 2/hour; may not run June 21 because of solstice crowds, shorter hours and hourly departures off-season; 30 minutes from station to Stonehenge, tel. 01202/338-420, timetable at www.thestonehengetour.info).

A **taxi** from Salisbury to Stonehenge can make sense for groups (about £40-50). Try City Cabs (inexpensive, tel. 01722/505-055) or Value Cars Taxis (tel. 01722/505-050, www.salisbury-valuecars.co.uk), or a local cabbie named Brian (tel. 01722/339-781, briantwort@ntlworld.com).

ORIENTATION TO STONEHENGE

The visitors center, located 1.25 miles west of the circle, is a minimalist steel structure with a subtly curved roofline, evoking the landscape of Salisbury Plain.

Cost: £17.50, includes shuttle-bus ride to stone circle, best to buy in advance online, covered by English Heritage Pass (see page 550).

Hours: Daily June-Aug 9:00-20:00, April-May and Sept-mid-Oct 9:30-19:00, mid-Oct-March 9:30-17:00. Note that the last ticket is sold two hours before closing. Expect shorter hours and possible closures June 20-22 due to huge, raucous solstice crowds.

Advance Tickets and Crowd-Beating Tips: Up to 9,000 visitors are allowed to enter each day. While Stonehenge rarely sells out completely, you can avoid the long ticket-buying line by prebooking at least 24 hours in advance at www.english-heritage.org.uk/stonehenge. Either print out an e-ticket or bring the booking number from your confirmation email to the designated window at the entrance.

When prebooking, you'll be asked to select a 30-minute entry window, but don't stress about being on time: You can typically enter anytime on the day of your ticket.

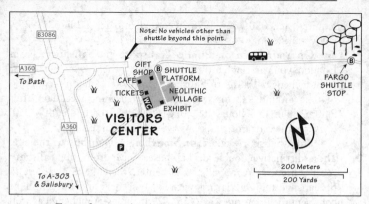

Even if you prebook, you may have to wait in line for the shuttle bus to and from the stones. For a less crowded, more mystical experience, come early or late. Things are pretty quiet before about 10:30 (head out to the stones first, then circle back to the exhibits); at the end of the day, aim to arrive just before the "last ticket" time (two hours before closing). Stonehenge is most crowded when school's out: summer weekends (especially holiday weekends) and anytime in August.

Information: Tel. 0870-333-1181, www.english-heritage.org.uk/stonehenge.

Tours: Worthwhile audioguides are available behind the ticket counter (included with Heritage Pass, otherwise £3). Or you can use the visitors center's free Wi-Fi to download the free "Stonehenge Audio Tour" app.

Visiting the Inner Stones: For the true Stonehenge fan, special one-hour access to the stones' inner circle is available early in the morning (times vary depending on sunrise; the earliest visit is at 5:00 in June and July) or after closing to the general public. Touching the stones is not allowed. Only 30 people are allowed at a time, so reserve well in advance (£35, allows you to revisit the site the same day at no extra charge, tel. 0370-333-0605). For details see the English Heritage website (select "Prices and Opening Times," then "Stone Circle Access").

Length of This Tour: Allow at least two hours to see everything.

Services: The visitors center has WCs, a large gift shop, and free Wi-Fi. Services at the circle itself are limited to emergency WCs. Even in summer, carry a jacket, as there are no trees to act as a wind-break and there's a reason Salisbury Plain is so green.

Eating: A large **$ café** within the visitors center serves hot drinks, soup, sandwiches, and salads.

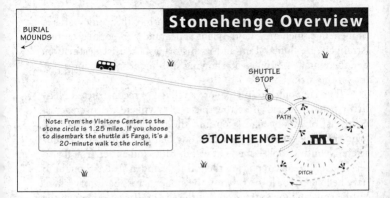

○ SELF-GUIDED TOUR

This commentary is designed to supplement the sight's audioguide. Start by touring the visitors center, then take a shuttle (or walk) to the stone circle. If you arrive early in the day, do the stones first—before they get crowded—then circle back to the visitors center.

• *As you enter the complex, on the right is the...*

Permanent Exhibit

This excellent, state-of-the-art exhibit uses an artful combination of multimedia displays and actual artifacts to provide context for the stones.

You'll begin by standing in the center of a virtual Stonehenge, watching its evolution through 5,000 years—including simulated solstice sunrises and sunsets.

Then you'll head into the exhibits, where prehistoric bones, tools, and pottery shards tell the story of the people who built Stonehenge, how they lived, and why they might have built the stone circle. Find the forensic reconstruction of a Neolithic man, based on a skeleton unearthed in 1863. Small models illustrate how Stonehenge developed from a simple circle of short, stubby stones to the stout ring we know today. And a large screen shows the entire archaeological area surrounding Stonehenge (which is just one of many mysterious prehistoric landmarks near here). In 2010, within sight of Stonehenge, archaeologists discovered another 5,000-year-old henge, which they believe once encircled a wooden "twin" of the famous circle. Recent excavations revealed that people had been living on the site since around 3,000 B.C.—about five centuries earlier than anyone had realized.

In the small side room, an exhibit examines the iconic status of Stonehenge, including its frequent appearances in popular culture (strangely, no Spinal Tap) and its history as a tourist destination. See the vintage Guinness ad showing smiling people having a picnic on the rocks.

Then step outside and explore a village of reconstructed **Neolithic huts** modeled after the traces of a village discovered just northeast of Stonehenge. Step into the thatched-roof huts to see primitive "wicker" furniture and straw blankets. Docents demonstrate Neolithic tools—made of wood, flint, and antler. You'll also see a huge, life-size replica of the rolling wooden sledge thought to have been used to slo-o-owly roll the stones across Salisbury Plain. While you can't touch the stones at the site itself, you can touch the one loaded onto this sledge.

• *Shuttle buses to the stone circle depart every 5-10 minutes from the platform behind the gift shop (there may be a wait). The trip takes six minutes. If you'd prefer, you can walk 1.25 miles through the fields to the site (use the map you receive with your ticket, or ask a staff member for directions).*

*Along the way, you have the option of stopping at **Fargo Plantation,** where you can see several burial mounds (tell the shuttle attendant if you want to disembark here). After wandering through the burial mounds, you'll need to walk the rest of the way to the stone circle (about 20 minutes).*

Stone Circle

As you approach the massive structure, walk right up to the knee-high cordon and let your fellow 21st-century tourists melt away. It's just you and the druids...

England has hundreds of stone circles, but Stonehenge—which literally means "hanging stones"—is unique. It's the only one that has horizontal cross-pieces (called lintels) spanning the

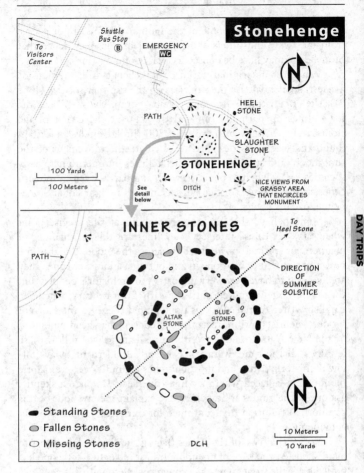

vertical monoliths, and the only one with stones that have been made smooth and uniform. What you see here is a bit more than half the original structure—the rest was quarried centuries ago for other buildings.

Now do a slow **clockwise spin** around the monument, and ponder the following points. As you walk, mentally flesh out the missing pieces and re-erect the rubble. Knowledgeable guides posted around the site are happy to answer your questions.

It's now believed that Stonehenge, which was built in phases between 3000 and 1500 B.C., was originally used as a cremation cemetery. But that's not the end of the story, as the monument was expanded over the millennia. This was a hugely significant location to prehistoric peoples. There are several hundred burial mounds within a three-mile radius of Stonehenge—some likely belonging to kings or chieftains. Some of the human remains are of people from far away, and others show signs of injuries—evidence that Stonehenge may have been used as a place of medicine or healing.

Whatever its original purpose, Stonehenge still functions as a celestial calendar. As the sun rises on the summer solstice (June 21), the "**heel stone**"—the one set apart from the rest, near the road—lines up with the sun and the altar at the center of the stone circle. A study of more than 300 similar circles in Britain found that each was designed to calculate the movement of the sun, moon, and stars, and to predict eclipses in order to help early societies know when to plant, harvest, and party. Even in modern times, as the summer solstice sun sets in just the right slot at Stonehenge, pagans boogie.

Some believe that Stonehenge is built at the precise point where six "**ley lines**" intersect. Ley lines are theoretical lines of magnetic or spiritual power that crisscross the globe. Belief in the power of these lines has gone in and out of fashion over time. They are believed to have been very important to prehistoric peoples, but then were largely ignored until the early 20th century, when the English writer Alfred Watkins popularized them (to the scorn of serious scientists). More recently, the concept has been embraced by the New Age movement. Without realizing it, you follow these ley lines all the time: Many of England's modern highways follow prehistoric paths, and most churches are built over prehistoric monuments—placed where ley lines intersect. If you're a skeptic, ask one of the guides at Stonehenge to explain the mystique of this paranormal tradition that continued for centuries; it's creepy...and convincing.

Notice that two of the stones (facing the shuttle bus stop) are blemished. At the base of one monolith, it looks like someone has pulled back the stone to reveal a concrete skeleton. This is a clumsy **repair job** to fix damage done long ago by souvenir seekers, who actually rented hammers and chisels to take home a piece of Stonehenge. Look to the right of the repaired stone: The back of another stone is missing the same thin layer of protective lichen that covers the others. The lichen—and some of the stone itself—was sandblasted off to remove graffiti. (No wonder they've got Stonehenge roped off now.) The repairs were intentionally done in a different color, so as not to appear like the original stone.

Stonehenge's builders used two different types of stone. The tall, stout monoliths and lintels are sandstone blocks called **sarsen stones.** Most of the monoliths weigh about 25 tons (the largest is 45 tons), and the lintels are about 7 tons apiece. These sarsen stones were brought from "only" 20 miles away. Scientists have chemically matched the shorter stones in the middle—called **bluestones**—to outcrops on the south coast of Wales...240 miles away (close if you're taking a train, but far if you're packing a megalith). Imagine the logistical puzzle of floating six-ton stones across Wales' Severn Estuary and up the River Avon, then rolling them on logs about 20 miles to this position...an impressive feat, even in our era of skyscrapers.

Why didn't the builders of Stonehenge use what seem like perfectly adequate stones nearby? This, like many other questions about Stonehenge, remains shrouded in mystery. Think again about the ley lines. Ponder the fact that many experts accept none of the explanations of how these giant stones were transported. Then imagine congregations gathering here 5,000 years ago, raising thought levels, creating a powerful life force transmitted along the ley lines. Maybe a particular kind of stone was essential for maximum energy transmission. Maybe the stones were levitated here. Maybe psychics really do create powerful vibes. Maybe not. It's as unbelievable as electricity used to be.

BRITAIN: PAST & PRESENT

To fully appreciate the many fascinating sights you'll encounter in your travels, learn the basics of the sweeping story of this land and its people. (Generally speaking, the fascinating stories you'll hear from tour guides are not true...and the boring ones are.)

Regardless of the revolution we had nearly 240 years ago, many American travelers feel that they "go home" to Britain. This most popular tourist destination has a strange influence and power over us. The more you know of Britain's roots, the better you'll get in touch with your own.

This chapter starts with a once-over of Britain's illustrious history. It's speckled throughout with more in-depth information about current issues and this great country's future.

British History

ORIGINS (2000 B.C.-A.D. 500)

When Julius Caesar landed on the misty and mysterious isle of Britain in 55 B.C., England entered the history books. He was met by primitive Celtic tribes whose druid priests made human sacrifices and worshipped trees. (Those Celts were themselves immigrants, who had earlier conquered the even more

mysterious people who built Stonehenge.) The Romans eventually settled in England (A.D. 43) and set about building towns and roads and establishing their capital at Londinium (today's London).

But the Celtic natives—consisting of Gaels, Picts, and Scots—were not easily subdued. Around A.D. 60, Boadicea, a queen of the

Isle's indigenous people, defied the Romans and burned Londinium before the revolt was squelched. Some decades later, the Romans built Hadrian's Wall near the Scottish border as protection against their troublesome northern neighbors. Even today, the Celtic language and influence are strongest in these far reaches of Britain.

Londinium became a bustling Roman river-and-sea trading port. The Romans built the original London Bridge and a city wall, encompassing one square mile, which set the city boundaries for 1,500 years. By A.D. 200, London was a thriving, Latin-speaking capital of Roman-dominated England.

Sights

- Boadicea statue near Westminster Bridge
- Roman Wall near the Tower of London or at the Museum of London

DARK AGES (500-1000)

As Rome fell, so fell Roman Britain—a victim of invaders and internal troubles. Barbarian tribes from Germany, Denmark, and northern Holland, called Angles, Saxons, and Jutes, swept through the southern part of the island, establishing Angle-land. These were the days of the real King Arthur, possibly a Christianized Roman general who fought valiantly—but in vain—against invading barbarians.

In 793, England was hit with the first of two centuries of savage invasions by barbarians from Norway, called the Vikings or Norsemen. King Alfred the Great (849-899) liberated London from Danish Vikings, reunited England, reestablished Christianity, and fostered learning. Nevertheless, for most of this 500-year period, the island was plunged into a dark age—wars, plagues, and poverty—lit only by the dim candle of a few learned Christian monks and missionaries trying to convert the barbarians. Today, visitors see little from this Anglo-Saxon period.

Sights

- Lindisfarne Gospels, *Beowulf* manuscript (British Library)

WARS WITH FRANCE, WARS OF THE ROSES (1000-1500)

Modern England began with yet another invasion. In 1066, William the Conqueror and his Norman troops crossed the English Channel from France. William crowned himself king in Westminster Abbey (where all subsequent coronations would take place). He began building the Tower of London, as well as Windsor Castle, which would become the residence of many monarchs to come.

Over the succeeding centuries, French-speaking kings would

rule England, and English-speaking kings invaded France as the
two budding nations defined their
modern borders. Richard the Lionheart (1157-1199) ruled as a
French-speaking king who spent
most of his energy on distant Cru-
sades. This was the time of the legendary (and possibly real) Robin
Hood, a bandit who robbed from

the rich and gave to the poor—a populace that felt neglected by its
francophone rulers. In 1215, King John (Richard's brother), under
pressure from England's barons, was forced to sign the Magna
Carta, establishing the principle that even kings must follow the
rule of law.

London asserted itself as England's trade center. London
Bridge—the famous stone version, topped with houses—was built
(1209), and Old St. Paul's Cathedral was finished (1314).

Then followed two centuries of wars, chiefly the Hundred
Years' War with France (1337-1443), in which France's Joan of Arc
rallied the French to drive English forces back across the Channel.
In 1348, the Black Death (bubonic plague) killed half of London's
population.

In the 1400s, noble families duked it out for the crown. The
York and Lancaster families fought the Wars of the Roses, so-
called because of the white and red flowers the combatants chose as
their symbols. Rife with battles and intrigues, and with kings, nobles, and ladies imprisoned and executed in the Tower, it's a wonder
the country survived its rulers.

Sights

- Tower of London
- Westminster Abbey
- Windsor Castle
- Magna Carta, *The Canterbury Tales* (British Library)
- Temple Church

THE TUDOR RENAISSANCE (1500s)

England was finally united by the "third-party" Tudor family.
Henry VIII, a Tudor, was England's Renaissance king. Powerful,
charismatic, handsome, athletic, highly sexed, a poet, a scholar,
and a musician, Henry VIII thrust England onto the world stage.
He was also arrogant, cruel, gluttonous, and paranoid. He went
through six wives in 40 years, divorcing, imprisoning, or executing
them when they no longer suited his needs. (To keep track of each

one's fate, British kids learn this rhyme: "Divorced, beheaded, died; divorced, beheaded, survived.")

When the Pope refused to grant Henry a divorce so he could marry his mistress Anne Boleyn, Henry "divorced" England from the Catholic Church. He established the Protestant Church of England (the Anglican Church), thus setting in motion a century of bitter Protestant/Catholic squabbles. Henry's own daughter, "Bloody" Mary, was a staunch Catholic who presided over the burning of hundreds of prominent Protestants. (For more on Henry VIII, see the sidebar on page 176.)

Henry was followed by another daughter (by Anne Boleyn)— Queen Elizabeth I. She reigned for 45 years, making England a

great trading and naval power (defeating the Spanish Armada) and treading diplomatically over the Protestant/Catholic divide. Elizabeth presided over a cultural renaissance known (not surprisingly) as the "Elizabethan Age." Playwright William Shakespeare moved from Stratford-upon-Avon to London, beginning a remarkable career as the earth's greatest playwright. Sir Francis Drake circumnavigated the globe. Sir Walter Raleigh explored the Americas, and Sir Francis Bacon pioneered the scientific method. London's population swelled.

But Elizabeth—the "Virgin Queen"— never married or produced an heir. So the English Parliament invited Scotland's King James (Elizabeth's first cousin twice removed) to inherit the English throne. The two nations have been tied together ever since, however fitfully.

Sights

- Shakespeare's Globe
- Shakespeare folios (British Library)
- Tower of London execution site
- Chapel of Henry VII and Elizabeth I's tomb in Westminster Abbey
- Kings College Chapel in Cambridge

KINGS VS. PARLIAMENT (1600s)

The enduring quarrel between England's kings and Parliament's nobles finally erupted into the Civil War (1642). The war pitted (roughly speaking) the Protestant Puritan Parliament against the Catholic aristocracy. Parliament forces under Oliver Cromwell defeated—and beheaded—King Charles I. After Cromwell died,

Parliament invited Charles' son to take the throne—the "restoration of the monarchy." To emphasize the point, Cromwell's corpse was subsequently exhumed and posthumously beheaded.

This turbulent era was followed by back-to-back disasters—the Great Plague of 1665 (which killed 100,000) and the Great Fire of 1666 (which incinerated London). London was completely rebuilt in stone, centered around New St. Paul's Cathedral, which was built by Christopher Wren. With a population over 200,000, London was now Europe's largest city. At home, Isaac Newton watched an apple fall from a tree, leading him to discover the mysterious force of gravity.

In the war between kings and Parliament, Parliament finally got the last word, when it deposed Catholic James II and imported the Dutch monarchs William and Mary in 1688, guaranteeing a Protestant succession.

Sights

- Banqueting House (site of Charles I's beheading)
- Crown jewels (Tower of London)
- City of London
- Fire Monument
- St. Paul's and other Wren churches
- Isaac Newton's apple tree (outside Trinity College Gate, Cambridge)
- Kensington Palace (residence of William, Mary, and Anne)

COLONIAL EXPANSION (1700s)

Britain grew as a naval superpower, colonizing and trading with all parts of the globe. Eventually, Britannia ruled the waves, exploiting the wealth of India, Africa, and Australia. (And America...at least until they lost its most important colony when those ungrateful Yanks revolted in 1776 in the "American War.") Throughout the century, the country was ruled by the German Hanover family, including four kings named George.

The "Georgian Era" was one of great wealth. London's population was now half a million, and one in seven Brits lived in London. The nation's first daily newspapers hit the streets. The cultural scene was refined: painters (like William Hogarth, Joshua Reynolds, and Thomas Gainsborough), theater (with

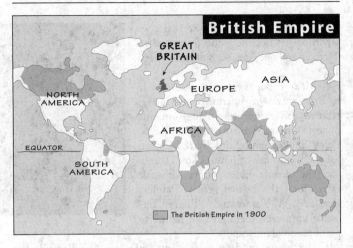

The British Empire in 1900

actors like David Garrick), music (Handel's *Messiah*), and literature (Samuel Johnson's dictionary). Scientist James Watt's steam engines laid the groundwork for a coming Industrial Revolution.

In 1789, the French Revolution erupted, sparking decades of war between France and Britain. Britain finally prevailed in the early 1800s, when Admiral Horatio Nelson defeated Napoleon's fleet at the Battle of Trafalgar and the Duke of Wellington stomped Napoleon at Waterloo. (Nelson and Wellington are memorialized by many arches, columns, and squares throughout England.)

By war's end, Britain had emerged as Europe's top power.

Sights
- Nelson's Column at Trafalgar Square
- Apsley House (Wellington Museum) and adjacent Wellington Arch
- Portraits by Reynolds and Gainsborough and slices of life by Hogarth (Tate Britain)
- Royal Observatory and National Maritime Museum, Greenwich
- Dr. Johnson's House in The City
- Handel's compositions (British Library)

VICTORIAN GENTILITY AND THE INDUSTRIAL REVOLUTION (1800s)

Britain reigned supreme, steaming into the Industrial Age with her mills, factories, coal mines, gas lights, and trains. By century's end, there was electricity, telephones, and the first Underground.

In 1837, eighteen-year-old Victoria became queen. She ruled for 64 years, presiding over an era of unprecedented wealth, peace, and middle-class ("Victorian") values. Britain was at its zenith of power, with a colonial empire that covered one-fifth of the world (for more on Victoria and her Age, see sidebar on page 102).

Meanwhile, there was another side to Britain's era of superiority and industrial might. A generation of Romantic poets (William Wordsworth, John Keats, Percy Shelley, and Lord Byron) longed for the innocence of nature. Jane Austen and the Brontë sisters wrote romantic tales about the landed gentry. Painters like J. M. W. Turner and William Constable immersed themselves in nature to paint moody landscapes.

The gritty modern world was emerging. Popular novelist Charles Dickens brought literature to the masses, educating them about Britain's harsh social and economic realities. Rudyard Kipling critiqued the colonial system. Charles Darwin questioned the very nature of humanity when he articulated the principles of natural selection and evolution. Jack the Ripper, a serial killer of prostitutes, terrorized east London and was never caught. Not even by Sherlock Holmes—a fictional detective living at 221B Baker Street who solved fictional crimes that the real Scotland Yard couldn't.

Sights

- Big Ben and Halls of Parliament
- Buckingham Palace, the Mall, and Hyde Park
- The Tube
- Paintings by Turner and Constable (Tate Britain)
- Writers' manuscripts in the British Library
- Poets' Corner in Westminster Abbey
- Victoria and Albert Museum
- Kensington Palace
- Sherlock Holmes Museum
- London's East End tenements (reminiscent of the Jack the Ripper days)

WORLD WARS AND RECOVERY (20th Century)

The 20th century was not kind to Britain. Two world wars and economic struggles whittled Britain down from a world empire to an island chain struggling to compete in a global economy.

In World War I, Britain joined France and other allies to battle Germany in trench warfare. A million British men died. Meanwhile, after decades of rebellion, Ireland finally gained its independence—except for the Protestant-leaning Northern Ireland, which remained tied to Britain. This division of the Emerald Isle would result in decades of bitter strife, protests, and terrorist attacks known as "The Troubles."

In the 1920s, London was home to a flourishing literary scene, including T. S. Eliot (American-turned-British), Virginia Woolf, and E. M. Forster. In 1936, the country was rocked and scandalized when King Edward VIII abdicated to marry a divorced American commoner, Wallis Simpson. He was succeeded by his brother, George VI—"Bertie" of *The King's Speech* fame, and father of Queen Elizabeth II.

In World War II, the Nazi Blitz (aerial bombing campaign) reduced much of London to rubble, sending residents into Tube stations for shelter and the government into a fortified bunker (now the Churchill War Rooms). Britain was rallied through its darkest hour by two leaders: Prime Minister Winston Churchill, a remarkable orator, and King George VI, who overcame a persistent stutter. Amid the chaos of war, the colonial empire began to dwindle to almost nothing, and Britain emerged from the war as a shell of its former superpower self.

The postwar recovery began, aided by the United States. Many cheap, concrete (ugly) buildings rose from the rubble.

Culturally, Britain remained world-class. Oxford professor J. R. R. Tolkien wrote *The Lord of the Rings* and his friend C. S. Lewis wrote *The Chronicles of Narnia*. In the 1960s, "Swinging London" became a center for rock music, film, theater, youth culture, and Austin Powers-style joie de vivre. America was conquered by a "British Invasion" of rock bands (The Beatles, The Rolling Stones, and The Who, followed later by Led Zeppelin, Elton John, David Bowie, and others), and James Bond ruled the box office.

The 1970s brought massive unemployment, labor strikes, and recession. A conservative reaction followed in the 1980s and 90s, led by Prime Minister Margaret Thatcher—the "Iron Lady." As proponents of traditional Victorian values—community, family, hard work, thrift, and trickle-down economics—the Conservatives took a Reaganesque approach to Britain's serious social and economic problems. They cut government subsidies to old-fashioned heavy industries (closing many factories, earning working-class ire), as they tried to nudge Britain toward a more modern economy.

In 1981, the world was captivated by the spectacle of Prince Charles marrying Lady Diana in St. Paul's Cathedral. Their children, Princes William and Harry, grew up in the media spotlight, and when Diana died in a car crash (1997), the nation—and the world—mourned.

The 1990s saw Britain finally emerging from decades of economic stagnation and social turmoil. An energized nation prepared for the new millennium.

Sights

- Cabinet War Rooms
- Cenotaph
- Imperial War Museum
- National Army Museum
- Blitz photos at St. Paul's
- Beatles memorabilia (British Library)
- Harrods

EARLY 2000s

London celebrated the millennium with a new Ferris wheel (the London Eye), the Millennium Bridge, and the Millennium Dome exhibition (now "The O2"). Britain was now ruled by a Labour (left-of-center) government under Prime Minister Tony Blair. But Blair's popularity was undermined when he joined the US invasion of Iraq. On "7/7" in 2005, London was rocked by a terrorist attack—a harbinger of others to come.

Britain suffered mightily in the global recession of the early 2000s. British voters turned for answers to the Conservative party under Prime Minister David Cameron. Cameron's austerity measures—cutting government spending and benefits while raising taxes—had mixed results and remains a topic of great debate.

Thankfully, one hot spot—Northern Ireland—was healed. In the spring of 2007, ultra-nationalists sat down with ultra-unionists and arrived at an agreement. After almost 40 years of the "Troubles," the British Army withdrew from Northern Ireland.

In 2011, Prince William married commoner Catherine "Kate" Middleton in a lavish ceremony that stirred renewed enthusiasm for the monarchy. The couple's two children, George (born in 2013) and Charlotte (2015), round out the picture-perfect royal family. (See the "Royal Families" sidebar.)

In 2012, in a one-two punch of festivity, the Brits hosted two huge events: the London Olympics and the Queen's Diamond Jubilee, celebrating 60 years on the throne. A flurry of renovation turned former urban wastelands and industrial waterfronts into hip, thriving people zones, and left the country looking better than ever.

Sights

- The London Eye

PAST & PRESENT

- Millennium Bridge
- Tate Modern contemporary art exhibits
- West End theaters
- The Docklands skyscraper zone
- Queen Elizabeth Olympic Park

Britain Today

The Britain you visit today is vibrant and alive. It's smaller, and no longer the superpower it once was, but it's still a cultural and economic powerhouse.

WHAT'S SO GREAT ABOUT BRITAIN?

Think of it. At its peak in the mid-1800s, Britain owned one-fifth of the world and accounted for more than half the planet's industrial output. Today, the Empire is down to the Isle of Britain itself and a few token scraps (the Falklands, Gibraltar, Northern Ireland) and a loose association of former colonies (Canada, Australia) called the "British Commonwealth."

Geographically, the Isle of Britain is small—smaller than the state of Oregon—and its highest mountain (Scafell Pike in the Lake District at 3,209 feet) is a foothill by US standards. The population is a fifth that of the United States.

It's small, but Britain is still Great.

Economically, Great Britain's industrial production is about 5 percent of the world's total. Ethnically, it's become quite diverse. It's a mix of Celtic (the natives of Scotland, Ireland, Wales, and Cornwall), Anglo-Saxon (the former "barbarians" from Dark Age times), the conquering Normans, and the many recent immigrants from around the world.

The Britain you visit today remains a global superpower of heritage, culture, and tradition. It's a major exporter of actors, movies, and theater; of rock and classical music; and of writers, painters, and sculptors. It's the perfect place for you to visit and make your own history.

CURRENT ISSUES AND POLITICAL LANDSCAPE

Britain is ruled by the House of Commons, with some guidance from the mostly figurehead Queen and House of Lords. Just as the United States Congress is dominated by Democrats and Republicans, Britain's Parliament has traditionally been dominated by two parties: left-leaning Labour and right-leaning Conservative ("Tories"). In recent elections, the Scottish National Party became the third-largest party in the House of Commons, securing 56 of Scotland's 59 seats—many of these taken from the Labour Party. Other parties also attract votes (e.g., the center-left Liberal Democrats),

Get It Right

Americans tend to use "England," "Britain," and the "United Kingdom" (or "UK") interchangeably, but they're not quite the same.

- **England** is the country occupying the center and southeast part of the island.
- **Britain** is the name of the island.
- **Great Britain** is the political union of the island's three countries: England, Scotland, and Wales.
- The **United Kingdom** (UK) adds a fourth country, Northern Ireland.
- The **British Isles** (not a political entity) also includes the independent Republic of Ireland.
- The **British Commonwealth** is a loose association of possessions and former colonies (including Canada, Australia, and India) that profess at least symbolic loyalty to the Crown.

You can call the modern nation either the United Kingdom ("the UK"), "Great Britain," or simply "Britain."

and whoever rules must occasionally form some kind of coalition to remain strong.

Strangely, Britain's "constitution" is not one single document; the government's structures and policies are based on centuries of tradition, statutes, and doctrine, and much of it is not actually in writing. While this might seem potentially troublesome—if not dangerous—the British body politic takes pride in its ethos of civility and mutual respect, which has long made this arrangement work.

The prime minister is the chief executive but is not elected directly by voters; rather, he or she assumes power as the head of the party that wins a majority in parliamentary elections. While historically the prime minister could dissolve Parliament at will to make way for new elections, a law passed in 2011 now requires parliamentary elections to be held every five years.

The single biggest issue facing Britain today is dealing with the repercussions of the "Brexit"—the 2016 referendum in which 52 percent of Brits voted to leave the European Union. As a result, Conservative Prime Minister David Cameron (who supported remaining in the EU) resigned and was replaced by the Conservative Party's Theresa May (also a "Remain" supporter), who became Britain's first female prime minister since Margaret Thatcher left office in 1990. The Brexit vote stunned Britain, throwing it into uncharted territory with no clear path forward.

The Brexit vote demands a split with the EU. But it remains to be seen exactly what that will mean. Many Brits want to main-

Being in Britain During Brexit

In 2016 Britain voted to leave the European Union, rocking Europe's political landscape as much as the election of Donald Trump rocked ours. While it means a lot to British citizens, who will have more control over trade and immigration—but will not be playing ball so freely with the rest of Europe—it means very little to travelers. Britain won't formally leave the EU until 2019, so for now the border between Northern Ireland and the Republic of Ireland remains totally open, and both sides want to keep it that way (even though the Republic is an EU member). The biggest change so far affects your pocketbook. Because of the economic uncertainty—and because Great Britain will likely become a more isolationist "Lesser Britain"—the British pound has dropped by about 15 percent. The entire UK is currently on sale for American visitors—everything from beer to B&Bs to bagpipes just got cheaper. And while American tourists are enjoying the bargains, the price the British people will pay for their hasty exit from the European Union remains to be seen.

tain trade deals and close relationships with their neighbors on the Continent. Young British people have grown up in a world where they can travel freely and live anywhere in Europe. The Brexit also upset the traditional political order. In the past, the Labour Party was always pro-EU while Conservatives were the Euro-skeptics. Now it's a brave new world for all involved.

No country has ever left the EU—the process could take years. Politicians will need to hammer out the details, trying to keep what has worked with the EU while steering the path to independence.

The Brexit also fueled new worries that pro-EU Scotland may demand independence after all. Although Scotland rejected an independence referendum in 2014, that was before the Brexit, in which Scottish voters came down overwhelmingly on the "Remain" side. Nationalists insist a free Scotland would be rich (on oil reserves) and free from the "shackles" of London-based problems.

All of this comes against a backdrop of a sluggish British economy and concerns about immigration and terrorism. The 2008 global downturn hurt Britain enormously, and it's been a long slog back. The Brexit vote only compounded things, sending the pound into a tailspin and raising economic uncertainty. The dividing lines are similar to those in the States: should government nurture the economy through spending on social programs (Labour's platform), or cut programs and taxes to allow businesses to thrive (as Conservatives say)?

Britain has a large immigrant population (nearly 4 million). While 9 out of 10 Brits are white, the country has large minor-

Royal Families: Past and Present

Royal Lineage

802-1066	Saxon and Danish kings
1066-1154	Norman invasion (William the Conqueror), Norman kings
1154-1399	Plantagenet (kings with French roots)
1399-1461	Lancaster
1462-1485	York
1485-1603	Tudor (Henry VIII, Elizabeth I)
1603-1649	Stuart (civil war and beheading of Charles I)
1649-1653	Commonwealth, no royal head of state
1653-1659	Protectorate, with Cromwell as Lord Protector
1660-1714	Restoration of Stuart dynasty
1714-1901	Hanover (four Georges, William IV, Victoria)
1901-1910	Saxe-Coburg (Edward VII)
1910-present	Windsor (George V, Edward VIII, George VI, Elizabeth II)

The Royal Family Today

It seems you can't pick up a British newspaper without some mention of the latest event, scandal, or oddity involving the royal family. Here is the cast of characters:

Queen Elizabeth II wears the traditional crown of her great-great grandmother Victoria, who ruled for 63 years, 7 months, and 2 days. In September 2015, Queen Elizabeth officially over-took Victoria as England's longest-reigning monarch, and in April 2016 she became the first UK sovereign to reach 90 years old. Elizabeth's husband is Prince Philip, who's not considered king.

Their son, Prince Charles (the Prince of Wales), is next in line to become king—and already holds the title as the longest "heir in waiting."

But it's Prince Charles' sons who generate the tabloid buzz. The older son, Prince William (b. 1982), is a graduate of Scotland's St. Andrews University and served as a search-and-rescue helicopter pilot with the Royal Air Force. In 2011, when William married Catherine "Kate" Middleton, the TV audience was estimated at one-quarter of the world's population—more than two billion people. Kate—a commoner William met at university—is now the Duchess of Cambridge and will eventually become Britain's queen.

Their son, Prince George Alexander Louis, born in 2013—and voted the most powerful and influential person in London by a poll in the *Evening Standard* two months later—will ultimately suc-ceed William as sovereign. (A conveniently timed change in the law ensured that William and Kate's firstborn would inherit the throne, regardless of gender.) In 2015, the royal couple welcomed the arrival of their second child, daughter Princess Charlotte Elizabeth Diana.

William's brother, redheaded Prince Harry (b. 1984), has mostly shaken his earlier reputation as a bad boy: He's proved his mettle as a career soldier, completing a tour in Afghanistan, doing charity work in Africa, and serving as an Apache aircraft commander pilot with the Army Air Corps. Nonetheless, Harry's romances and high-wire party antics are popular tabloid topics.

For years, their parents' love life was also fodder for the British press: Charles' 1981 marriage to Princess Di, their bitter divorce, Diana's dramatic death in 1997, and the ongoing drama with Charles' longtime girlfriend—and now wife—Camilla Parker Bowles. Camilla, trying to gain the respect of the Queen and the public, doesn't call herself a princess—she uses the title Duchess of Cornwall. (And even when Charles becomes king, she will not be Queen Camilla—instead she plans to call herself the "Princess Consort.")

Charles' siblings are occasionally in the news: Princess Anne, Prince Andrew (who married and divorced Sarah "Fergie" Ferguson), and Prince Edward (who married Di look-alike Sophie Rhys-Jones).

Royal Sightseeing

You can see the trappings of royalty at Buckingham Palace (the

Queen's London residence) with its Changing of the Guard; Kensington Palace—with a wing that's home to Will, Kate, and kids, and a cottage that serves as Harry's bachelor pad; Clarence House, the London home of Prince Charles and Camilla; Althorp Estate (80 miles from London), the childhood home and burial place of Princess Diana; Windsor Castle, a royal country home near London; and the crown jewels in the Tower of London.

Your best chances to actually see the Queen are on three public occasions: State Opening of Parliament (on the first day of a new parliamentary session), Remembrance Sunday (early November, at the Cenotaph), or Trooping the Colour (one Saturday in mid-June, parading down Whitehall and at Buckingham Palace).

Otherwise, check www.royal.gov.uk, where you can search for royal events.

ity groups, mainly from Britain's former colonies: India, Pakistan, Bangladesh, and parts of Africa and the Caribbean. For the most part Britain is relatively integrated, with minorities represented in most (if not all) walks of life. A large Muslim population is just one thread in the tapestry of today's Britain.

You'll also see many Eastern Europeans (mostly Poles, Slovaks, and Lithuanians) working in restaurants, cafés, and B&Bs. These transplants—who started arriving after their home countries joined the EU in 2004—can make a lot more money working here than back home. But the "Leave" Brexit campaign was fueled in part by complaints about the EU's open-border policy, and concerns that immigrants are taking British jobs, diluting British culture, and receiving overgenerous financial aid.

Like the US, Britain has suffered a number of terrorist threats and attacks. Brits are stunned that many terrorists (like the notorious "Jihadi John" of ISIS) speak the Queen's English and were born and raised in Britain. It raises the larger questions: Just how well is the nation assimilating its many immigrants? And how to balance security with privacy concerns? The British have surveillance cameras everywhere—you'll frequently see signs warning you that you're being recorded.

Among social issues, binge-drinking is a serious problem. Since 2003, pubs can stay open past the traditional 23:00 closing time. An unintended consequence is that (according to one study) one in three British men and one in five British women routinely drinks to excess, carousing at pubs and sometimes in the streets.

Wealth inequality is also a hot button. The global recession sharpened unemployment and slashed programs for the working class, resulting in protests and riots that pitted poor young men against the police.

Then there's the eternal question of the royals. Is having a monarch (who's politically irrelevant) and a royal family (who can fill the tabloids with their scandals and foibles) worth it? In decades past, many Brits wanted to toss the whole lot of them. But the recent marriage of the popular William and Kate and the birth of their two cute kids have boosted royal esteem. According to pollsters, four out of five Brits want to keep their Queen and let the tradition live on.

BRITISH TV

Although it has its share of lowbrow reality programming, much British television is still so good—and so British—that it deserves a mention as a sightseeing treat. After a hard day of castle climbing, watch the telly over tea in your B&B.

For many years there were only five free channels, but now nearly every British television can receive a couple dozen. BBC television is government-regulated and commercial-free. Broadcasting of its eight channels (and of the five BBC radio stations) is funded by a mandatory £145.50-per-year-per-household television and radio license (hmmm, 60 cents per day to escape commercials and public-broadcasting pledge drives...not bad). Channels 3, 4, and 5 are privately owned, are a little more lowbrow, and have commercials—but those "adverts" are often clever and sophisticated, providing a fun look at British life. About 60 percent of households pay for cable or satellite television.

Whereas California "accents" fill US airwaves 24 hours a day, homogenizing the way our country speaks, Britain protects and promotes its regional accents by its choice of TV and radio announcers. See if you can tell where each is from (or ask a local for help).

Commercial-free British TV, while looser than it used to be, is still careful about what it airs and when. But after the 21:00 "watershed" hour, when children are expected to be in bed, some nudity and profanity are allowed, and may cause you to spill your tea.

American programs (such as *Game of Thrones, CSI, Family Guy,* and trash-talk shows) are very popular. But the visiting viewer should be sure to tune the TV to more typically British shows, including a dose of British situation- and political-comedy fun, and the top-notch BBC evening news. British comedies have tickled the American funny bone for years, from sketch comedy *(Monty Python's Flying Circus)* to sitcoms (*Fawlty Towers, Blackadder, Red Dwarf, Absolutely Fabulous,* and *The Office*). Quiz shows and reality shows are taken very seriously here (*American Idol, America's Got Talent, Dancing with the Stars, Who Wants to Be a Millionaire?,* and *The X Factor* are all based on British shows). Jonathan Ross is the Jimmy Fallon of Britain for sometimes-edgy late-night talk. Other popular late-night "chat show" hosts include Graham Norton and Alan Carr. For a tear-filled, slice-of-life taste of British soaps dealing in all the controversial issues, see the popular and remarkably long-running *Emmerdale, Coronation Street,* or *EastEnders.* The costume drama *Downton Abbey,* the long-running sci-fi serial *Doctor Who,* the small-town dramedy *Doc Martin,* and the modern crime series *Sherlock* have all become hits on both sides of the Atlantic.

NOTABLE BRITS OF TODAY AND TOMORROW

Only history can judge which British names will stand the test of time, but these days big names in the UK include politicians (Theresa May, David Cameron, Boris Johnson, Jeremy Corbyn, Nicola Sturgeon), actors (Helen Mirren, Emma Thompson, Helena Bonham Carter, Jude Law, Stephen Fry, Ricky Gervais, James Corden, Daniel Radcliffe, Kate Winslet, Benedict Cumberbatch, Martin Freeman, Peter Capaldi, Colin Firth), musicians (Adele, Chris

Martin of Coldplay, James Arthur, Ellie Goulding, One Direction, Ed Sheeran, Sam Smith), writers (J. K. Rowling, E. L. James, Hilary Mantel, Tom Stoppard, Nick Hornby, Ian McEwan, Zadie Smith), artists (Damien Hirst, Rachel Whiteread, Tracey Emin, Anish Kapoor), athletes (David Beckham, Bradley Wiggins, Andy Murray), entrepreneurs (Sir Richard Branson, Lord Alan Sugar)... and, of course, William, Kate, and their children, George and Charlotte.

Architecture in Britain

From Stonehenge to Big Ben, travelers are storming castle walls, climbing spiral staircases, and snapping the pictures of 5,000 years of architecture. Let's sort it out.

The oldest ruins—mysterious and prehistoric—date from before Roman times back to 3000 B.C. The earliest sites, such as Stonehenge and Avebury, were built during the Stone and Bronze ages. The remains from these periods are made of huge stones or mounds of earth, even man-made hills, and were created as celestial calendars and for worship or burial. Britain is crisscrossed with imaginary lines said to connect these mysterious sights (ley lines). Iron Age people (600 B.C.-A.D. 50) left desolate stone forts. The Romans thrived in Britain from A.D. 50 to 400, building cities, walls, and roads. Evidence of Roman greatness can be seen in lavish villas with ornate mosaic floors, temples uncovered beneath great English churches, and Roman stones in medieval city walls. Roman roads sliced across the island in straight lines. Today, unusually straight rural roads are very likely laid directly on these ancient roads.

As Rome crumbled in the fifth century, so did Roman Britain. Little architecture survives from Dark Ages England, the Saxon period from 500 to 1000. Architecturally, the light was switched on with the Norman Conquest in 1066. As William earned his title "the Conqueror," his French architects built churches and castles in the European Romanesque style.

English Romanesque is called Norman (1066-1200). Norman churches had round arches, thick walls, and small windows; Durham Cathedral and the Chapel of St. John in the Tower of London are prime examples. The Tower of London, with its square keep, small windows, and spiral stone stairways, is a typical Norman castle. You can see plenty of Norman castles around England—all built to secure the conquest of these invaders from Normandy.

Gothic architecture (1200-1600) replaced the heavy Norman style with light, vertical buildings, pointed arches, soaring spires, and bigger windows. English Gothic is divided into three stages. Early English Gothic (1200-1300) features tall, simple spires; beautifully carved capitals; and elaborate chapter houses (such as the Wells Cathedral). Decorated Gothic (1300-1400) gets fancier, with more elaborate tracery, bigger windows, and ornately carved pinnacles, as you see at Westminster Abbey. Finally, the Perpendicular Gothic style (1400-1600, also called "rectilinear") returns to square towers and emphasizes straight, uninterrupted vertical lines from ceiling to floor, with vast windows and exuberant decoration, including fan-vaulted ceilings (King's College Chapel at Cambridge). Through this evolution, the structural ribs (arches meeting at the top of the ceilings) became more and more decorative and fanciful (the most fancy being the star vaulting and fan vaulting of the Perpendicular style).

As you tour the great medieval churches of Britain, remember that almost everything is symbolic. For instance, on the tombs of knights, if the figure has crossed legs, he was a Crusader. If his feet rest on a dog, he died at home; but if his legs rest on a lion, he died in battle. Local guides and books help us modern pilgrims understand at least a little of what we see.

Wales is particularly rich in English castles, which were needed to subdue the stubborn Welsh. Edward I built a ring of powerful castles in North Wales, including Conwy and Caernarfon.

Gothic houses were a simple mix of woven strips of thin wood, rubble, and plaster called wattle and daub. The famous black-and-white Tudor (or "half-timbered") look came simply from filling in heavy oak frames with wattle and daub.

The Tudor period (1485-1560) was a time of relative peace (the Wars of the Roses were finally over), prosperity, and renaissance. But when Henry VIII broke with the Catholic Church and disbanded its monasteries, scores of Britain's greatest churches were left as gutted shells. These hauntingly beautiful abbey ruins (Glastonbury, Tintern, Whitby, Rievaulx, Battle, St. Augustine's in Canterbury, St. Mary's in York, and lots more), surrounded by lush lawns, are now pleasant city parks.

Typical Church Architecture

History comes to life when you visit a centuries-old church. Even if you wouldn't know your apse from a hole in the ground, learning a few simple terms will enrich your experience. Note that not every church has every feature, and that a "cathedral" isn't a type of church architecture, but rather a designation for a church that's a governing center for a local bishop.

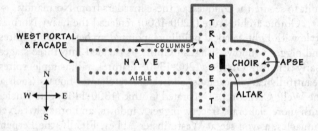

Aisles: The long, generally low-ceilinged arcades that flank the nave.

Altar: The raised area with a ceremonial table (often adorned with candles or a crucifix), where the priest prepares and serves the bread and wine for Communion.

Apse: The space beyond the altar, often bordered with small chapels.

Barrel Vault: A continuous round-arched ceiling that resembles an extended upside-down U.

Choir ("quire" in British English): A cozy area, often screened off, located within the church nave and near the high altar where services are sung in a more intimate setting.

Cloister: Covered hallways bordering a square or rectangular open-air courtyard, traditionally where monks and nuns got fresh air.

Facade: The exterior surface of the church's main (west) entrance, viewable from outside and usually highly decorated.

Groin Vault: An arched ceiling formed where two equal barrel vaults meet at right angles. Less common usage: term for a medieval jock strap.

Narthex: The area (portico or foyer) between the main entry and the nave.

Nave: The long, central section of the church (running west to east, from the entrance to the altar) where the congregation sits or stands through the service.

Transept: In a traditional cross-shaped floor plan, the transept is one of the two parts forming the "arms" of the cross. The transepts run north-south, perpendicularly crossing the east-west nave.

West Portal: The main entry to the church (on the west end, opposite the main altar).

Typical Castle Architecture

Castles were fortified residences for medieval nobles. Castles come in all shapes and sizes, but knowing a few general terms will help you understand them.

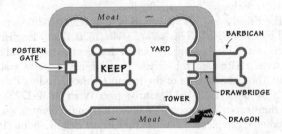

Barbican: A fortified gatehouse, sometimes a stand-alone building located outside the main walls.

Crenellation: A gap-toothed pattern of stones atop the parapet.

Drawbridge: A bridge that could be raised or lowered using counterweights or a chain and winch.

Great Hall: The largest room in the castle, serving as throne room, conference center, and dining hall.

Hoardings (or Gallery or Brattice): Wooden huts built onto the upper parts of the stone walls. They served as watch towers, living quarters, and fighting platforms.

The Keep (or Donjon): A high, strong stone tower in the center of the castle complex; the lord's home and refuge of last resort.

Loopholes (or Embrasures): Narrow wall slits through which soldiers could shoot arrows.

Machicolation: A stone ledge jutting out from the wall, with holes through which soldiers could drop rocks or boiling oil onto wall-scaling enemies below.

Moat: A ditch encircling the wall, often filled with water.

Motte-and-Bailey: A type of early English castle, with a hilltop fort (motte) and an enclosed, fortified yard (bailey).

Parapet: Outer railing of the wall walk.

Portcullis: A heavy iron grille that could be lowered across the entrance.

Postern Gate: A small, unfortified side or rear entrance from which to launch attacks or escape.

Towers: Tall structures with crenellated tops or conical roofs serving as lookouts, chapels, living quarters, or dungeons.

Turret: A small lookout tower rising up from the top of the wall.

Wall Walk (or Allure): A pathway atop the wall where guards could patrol and where soldiers stood to fire at the enemy.

The Yard (or Bailey): An open courtyard inside the castle walls.

Although few churches were built during the Tudor period, this was a time of house and mansion construction. Heating a home was becoming popular and affordable, and Tudor buildings featured small square windows and many chimneys. In towns, where land was scarce, many Tudor houses grew up and out, getting wider with each overhanging floor.

The Elizabethan and Jacobean periods (1560-1620) were followed by the English Renaissance style (1620-1720). English architects mixed Gothic and classical styles, then Baroque and classical styles. Although the ornate Baroque never really grabbed Britain, the classical style of the Italian architect Andrea Palladio did. Inigo Jones (1573-1652), Christopher Wren (1632-1723), and those they inspired plastered Britain with enough columns, domes, and symmetry to please a Caesar. The Great Fire of London (1666) cleared the way for an ambitious young Wren to put his mark on London forever with a grand rebuilding scheme, including the great St. Paul's Cathedral and more than 50 other churches.

The celebrants of the Boston Tea Party remember Britain's Georgian period (1720-1840) for its lousy German kings. But in architectural terms, "Georgian" is English for "Neoclassical." Its architecture was rich and showed off by being very classical. Grand ornamental doorways, fine cast-ironwork on balconies and railings, Chippendale furniture, and white-on-blue Wedgwood ceramics graced rich homes everywhere. John Wood Sr. and Jr. led the way, giving the trendsetting city of Bath its crescents and circles of aristocratic Georgian row houses.

The Industrial Revolution shaped the Victorian period (1840-1890) with glass, steel, and iron. Britain had a huge new erector set (so did France's Mr. Eiffel). This was also a Romantic period, reviving the "more Christian" Gothic style. London's Houses of Parliament are Neo-Gothic—they're just 140 years old but look 700, except for the telltale modern precision and craftsmanship. Whereas Gothic was stone or concrete, Neo-Gothic was often red brick. These were Britain's glory days, and there was more building in this period than in all previous ages combined.

The architecture of the mid-20th century obeyed the formula "form follows function"—it worried more about your needs than your eyes. But more recently, the dull "international style" has been nudged aside by a more playful style, thanks to cutting-edge architects such as Lord Norman Foster and Renzo Piano. In the last several years, London has added several creative buildings to its skyline: the City Hall (nicknamed "The Armadillo"), 30 St. Mary Axe ("The Gherkin"), 20 Fenchurch ("The Walkie-Talkie"), and the tallest building in Western Europe, the pointy Shard London Bridge (called simply, "The Shard").

Even as it sets trends for the 21st century, Britain treasures its heritage and takes great pains to build tastefully in historic districts and to preserve its many "listed" (government-protected) buildings. With a booming tourist trade, these quaint reminders of its past—and ours—are becoming a valuable part of the British economy.

For more about British history, consider Europe 101: History and Art for the Traveler *by Rick Steves and Gene Openshaw, available at www.ricksteves.com.*

PRACTICALITIES

This chapter covers the practical skills of European travel: how to get tourist information, pay for purchases, sightsee efficiently, find good-value accommodations, eat affordably but well, use technology wisely, and get between destinations smoothly. To round out your knowledge, check out "Resources from Rick Steves." For more information on these topics, see www.ricksteves.com/travel-tips.

Tourist Information

Before your trip, start with the TI's official website, (www.visitlondon.com). The Visit Britain website contains a wealth of knowledge on destinations, activities, accommodations, and transport in Great Britain. Families will especially appreciate the "Britain for Kids & Families" travel suggestions. Maps, airport transfers, sightseeing tours, and theater tickets can be purchased online (www.visitbritain.com, www.visitbritainshop.com/usa for purchases).

In London, a good first stop is generally the tourist information office (abbreviated **TI** in this book). London's fine TI, called the **City of London Information Centre,** is near St. Paul's Cathedral (see page 16).

TIs are in business to help you enjoy spending money in their town. While this corrupts much of their advice—and you can get plenty of information online—I still make a point to swing by the local TI to confirm sightseeing plans, pick up a city map, and get information on public transit (including bus and train schedules), walking tours, special events, and nightlife. Stop in with a list of questions and a proposed plan to double-check.

Other Helpful Websites: www.timeout.com/london, www.londontown.com.

Travel Tips

Emergency and Medical Help: In Britain, dial 999 for police help or a medical emergency. If you get sick, do as the locals do and go to a pharmacy and see a "chemist" (pharmacist) for advice. Or ask at your hotel for help—they'll know of the nearest medical and emergency services. St. Thomas' Hospital, across the river from Big Ben, has a fine reputation.

Theft or Loss: To replace a passport, you'll need to go in person to a US embassy (see page 581). If your credit and debit cards disappear, cancel and replace them (see "Damage Control for Lost Cards" on page 546). File a police report, either on the spot or within a day or two; you'll need it to submit an insurance claim for lost or stolen rail passes or travel gear, and it can help with replacing your passport or credit and debit cards. For more information, see www.ricksteves.com/help.

Time Zones: Britain, which is one hour earlier than most of continental Europe, is five/eight hours ahead of the East/West Coasts of the US. The exceptions are the beginning and end of Daylight Saving Time: Britain and Europe "spring forward" the last Sunday in March (two weeks after most of North America), and "fall back" the last Sunday in October (one week before North America). For a handy online time converter, see www.timeanddate.com/worldclock.

Business Hours: Most stores are open Monday through Saturday (roughly 9:00 or 10:00 until 17:00 or 18:00), with a late night on Wednesday or Thursday (until 19:00 or 20:00). Department stores are usually open later throughout the week (until about 21:00 Mon-Sat). On Sunday, when stores are closed or have shorter hours, many street markets are lively with shoppers.

Watt's Up? Britain's electrical system is 220 volts, instead of North America's 110 volts. Most newer electronics (such as laptops, battery chargers, and hair dryers) convert automatically, so you won't need a converter, but you will need an adapter plug with three square prongs, sold inexpensively at travel stores in the US. Avoid bringing older appliances that don't automatically convert voltage; instead, buy a cheap replacement in Britain. Low-cost hairdryers and other small appliances are sold at Superdrug and Boots (ask your hotelier for the closest branch). Or pop into a London department store (see the Shopping in London chapter).

Discounts: Discounts (called "concessions" or "concs" in Britain) for sights are generally not listed in this book. However, many sights, buses, and trains offer discounts to youths (up to age 18), students (with proper identification cards, www.isic.org), families, seniors (loosely defined as retirees or those willing to call themselves seniors), and groups of 10 or more. Always ask. Some discounts are available only for British citizens.

Money

Here's my basic strategy for using money in Europe:
- Upon arrival, head for a cash machine (ATM) at the airport and load up on local currency, using a debit card with low international transaction fees.
- Withdraw large amounts at each transaction (to limit fees) and keep your cash safe in a money belt.
- Pay for most items with cash.
- Pay for larger purchases with a credit card with low (or no) international fees.

PLASTIC VERSUS CASH

Although credit cards are widely accepted in Europe, day-to-day spending is generally more cash-based than in the US. I find cash is the easiest—and sometimes only—way to pay for cheap food, taxis, tips, and local guides. Some businesses (especially smaller ones, such as B&Bs and mom-and-pop cafés and shops) may charge you extra for using a credit card—or might not accept credit cards at all. Having cash on hand helps you out of a jam if your card randomly doesn't work.

I use my credit card to book and pay for hotel reservations, to buy advance tickets for events or sights, and to cover major expenses (such as car rentals or plane tickets). It can also be smart to use plastic near the end of your trip, to avoid another visit to the ATM.

WHAT TO BRING

I pack the following and keep it all safe in my money belt.

Debit Card: Use this at ATMs to withdraw local cash.

Credit Card: Use this to pay for larger items (at hotels, larger shops and restaurants, travel agencies, car-rental agencies, and so on).

PRACTICALITIES

Exchange Rate

1 British pound (£1) = about $1.30

While the euro (€) is now the currency of most of Europe, Britain is sticking with its pound sterling. The British pound (£), also called a "quid," is broken into 100 pence (p). Pence means "cents." You'll find coins ranging from 1p to £2 and bills from £5 to £50.

To convert prices from pounds to dollars, add about 30 percent: £20=about $26, £50=about $65. (Check www.oanda.com for the latest exchange rates.) London is so expensive that some travelers try to kid themselves that pounds are dollars. But when they get home, that £1,000-pound Visa bill isn't asking for $1,000...it wants around $1,300.

Backup Card: Some travelers carry a third card (debit or credit; ideally from a different bank), in case one gets lost, demagnetized, eaten by a temperamental machine, or simply doesn't work.

US Dollars: I carry $100-200 US dollars as a backup. While you won't use it for day-to-day purchases, American cash in your money belt comes in handy for emergencies, such as if your ATM card stops working.

What NOT to Bring: Resist the urge to buy pounds before your trip or you'll pay the price in bad stateside exchange rates. Wait until you arrive to withdraw money. I've yet to see a European airport that didn't have plenty of ATMs.

BEFORE YOU GO
Use this pretrip checklist.

Know your cards. Debit cards from any major US bank will work in any standard European bank's ATM (ideally, use a debit card with a Visa or MasterCard logo).

Newer credit and debit cards have chips that authenticate and secure transactions. In Europe, the cardholder inserts the chip card into the payment machine slot, then enters a PIN. (In the US, you provide a signature to verify your identity.)

Any American card, whether with a chip or an old-fashioned magnetic stripe, will work at Europe's hotels, restaurants, and shops. I've been inconvenienced a few times by self-service payment machines in Europe that wouldn't accept my card, but it's never caused me serious trouble.

If you're concerned, ask if your bank offers a true chip-and-PIN card. Cards with low fees and chip-and-PIN technology include those from Andrews Federal Credit Union (www.andrewsfcu.org) and the State Department Federal Credit Union (www.sdfcu.org).

Report your travel dates. Let your bank know that you'll be using your debit and credit cards in Europe, and when and where you're headed.

Know your PIN. Make sure you know the numeric, four-digit PIN for each of your cards, both debit and credit. Request it if you don't have one and allow time to receive the information by mail.

Adjust your ATM withdrawal limit. Find out how much you can take out daily and ask for a higher daily withdrawal limit if you want to get more cash at once. Note that European ATMs will withdraw funds only from checking accounts; you're unlikely to have access to your savings account.

Ask about fees. For any purchase or withdrawal made with a card, you may be charged a currency conversion fee (1-3 percent), a Visa or MasterCard international transaction fee (1 percent), and—for debit cards—a $2-5 transaction fee each time you use a foreign ATM (some US banks partner with European banks, allowing you to use those ATMs with no fees—ask).

If you're getting a bad deal, consider getting a new debit or credit card. Reputable no-fee cards include those from Capital One, as well as Charles Schwab debit cards. Most credit unions and some airline loyalty cards have low-to-no international transaction fees.

IN EUROPE
Using Cash Machines

European cash machines work just like they do at home—except they spit out local currency instead of dollars, calculated at the day's standard bank-to-bank rate.

In most places, ATMs are easy to locate—in England ask for a "cashpoint." When possible, withdraw cash from a bank-run ATM located just outside that bank. Ideally, use it during the bank's opening hours; if your card is munched by the machine, you can go inside for help.

If your debit card doesn't work, try a lower amount—your request may have exceeded your withdrawal limit or the ATM's limit. If you still have a problem, try a different ATM or come back later—your bank's network may be temporarily down.

Avoid "independent" ATMs, such as Travelex, Euronet, Moneybox, Cardpoint, and Cashzone. These have high fees, can be less secure than a bank ATM, and may try to trick users with "dynamic currency conversion" (see below).

Exchanging Cash

Avoid exchanging money in Europe; it's a big rip-off. In a pinch you can always find exchange desks at major train stations or airports—convenient but with crummy rates. Banks in some countries may not exchange money unless you have an account with them.

Using Credit Cards

European cards use chip-and-PIN technology, while most cards issued in the US use a chip-and-signature system. But most European card readers can automatically generate a receipt for you to sign, just as you would at home. If a cashier is present, you should have no problems. Some card readers will instead prompt you to enter your PIN (so it's important to know the code for each of your cards).

At self-service payment machines (transit-ticket kiosks, parking, etc.), results are mixed, as US chip-and-signature cards aren't configured for unattended transactions. If your card won't work, look for a cashier who can process your card manually—or pay in cash.

Drivers Beware: Be aware of potential problems using a credit card to fill up at an unattended gas station, enter a parking garage, or exit a toll road. Carry cash and be prepared to move on to the next gas station if necessary. When approaching a toll plaza, use the "cash" lane.

Dynamic Currency Conversion

Some European merchants and hoteliers cheerfully charge you for converting your purchase price into dollars. If it's offered, refuse this "service" (called dynamic currency conversion, or DCC). You'll pay extra for the expensive convenience of seeing your charge in dollars. Some ATM machines also offer DCC, often in confusing or misleading terms. If an ATM offers to "lock in" or "guarantee" your conversion rate, choose "proceed without conversion." Other prompts might state, "You can be charged in dollars: Press YES for dollars, NO for pounds." Always choose the local currency.

Security Tips

Even in Jolly Olde England, pickpockets target tourists. To safeguard your cash, wear a money belt—a pouch with a strap that you buckle around your waist like a belt and tuck under your clothes. Keep your cash, credit cards, and passport secure in your money belt, and carry only a day's spending money in your front pocket or wallet.

Before inserting your card into an ATM, inspect the front. If anything looks crooked, loose, or damaged, it could be a sign of a card-skimming device. When entering your PIN, carefully block other people's view of the keypad.

Don't use a debit card for purchases. Because a debit card pulls funds directly from your bank account, potential charges incurred by a thief will stay on your account while the fraudulent use is investigated by your bank.

To access your accounts online while traveling, be sure to use a secure connection (see page 573).

PRACTICALITIES

Damage Control for Lost Cards

If you lose your credit or debit card, report the loss immediately to the respective global customer-assistance centers. Call these 24-hour US numbers collect: Visa (tel. 303/967-1096), MasterCard (tel. 636/722-7111), and American Express (tel. 336/393-1111). In Britain, to make a collect call to the US, dial 0-800-89-0011. Press zero or stay on the line for an operator. European toll-free numbers (listed by country) can be found at the websites for Visa and MasterCard. Diner's Club has offices in Britain (tel. 0845-862-29357) and the US (tel. 514/877-1577; call collect).

You'll need to provide the primary cardholder's identification-verification details (such as birthdate, mother's maiden name, or Social Security number). You can generally receive a temporary card within two or three business days in Europe (see www.ricksteves.com/help for more).

If you report your loss within two days, you typically won't be responsible for unauthorized transactions on your account, although many banks charge a liability fee of $50.

TIPPING

Tipping in Britain isn't as automatic and generous as it is in the US. For special service, tips are appreciated, but not expected. As in the US, the proper amount depends on your resources, tipping philosophy, and the circumstances, but some general guidelines apply.

Restaurants: Many restaurants add a 12.5 percent tip to your bill, but this is optional and you should only tip what you think the service deserves (if good, generally 10-12.5 percent—see page 560).

Taxis: For a typical ride, round up your fare a bit, but not more than 10 percent (for instance, if the fare is £7.40, pay £8). If the cabbie hauls your bags and zips you to the airport to help you catch your flight, you might want to toss in a little more. But if you feel like you're being driven in circles or otherwise ripped off, skip the tip.

Services: In general, if someone in the tourism or service industry does a super job for you, a small tip of a pound or two is appropriate...but not required. If you're not sure whether (or how much) to tip, ask a local for advice.

GETTING A VAT REFUND

Wrapped into the purchase price of your British souvenirs is a Value-Added Tax (VAT) of about 20 percent. You're entitled to get most of that tax back if you purchase more than £30 (about $40) worth of goods at a store that participates in the VAT-refund scheme (although individual stores can require that you spend more—Harrods, for example, won't process a refund unless you spend £50). Typically, you must ring up the minimum at a single retailer—you can't add up your purchases from various shops to reach the required amount. (If the store ships the goods to your US home, VAT is not assessed on your purchase.)

Getting your refund is straightforward...and worthwhile if you spend a significant amount on souvenirs.

Get the paperwork. Have the merchant completely fill out the necessary refund document (either an official VAT customs form, or the shop or refund company's own version of it). You'll have to present your passport at the store. Get the paperwork done before you leave the shop to ensure you'll have everything you need (including your original sales receipt).

Get your stamp at the border or airport. Process your VAT document at your last stop in the European Union (such as at the airport) with the customs agent who deals with VAT refunds. Arrive an additional hour early before you need to check in to allow time to find the customs office—and to stand in line. Some customs desks are positioned before airport security; confirm the location before going through security.

It's best to keep your purchases in your carry-on. If they're too large or dangerous to carry on (such as knives), pack them in your checked bags and alert the check-in agent. You'll be sent (with your tagged bag) to a customs desk outside security; someone will examine your bag, stamp your paperwork, and put your bag on the belt. You're not supposed to use your purchased goods before you leave. If you show up at customs wearing your new Wellingtons, officials might look the other way—or deny you a refund.

Collect your refund. Many merchants work with a service that has offices at major airports, ports, or border crossings (at Heathrow, Travelex counters and customs desks are located before and after security in terminals 2-5). These services, which extract their own fee (usually around 4 percent), can refund your money immediately in cash or credit your card (within two billing cycles). Other refund services may require you to mail the documents from home, or more quickly, from your point of departure (using an envelope you've prepared in advance or one that's been provided by the merchant). You'll then have to wait—it can take months.

CUSTOMS FOR AMERICAN SHOPPERS

You can take home $800 worth of items per person duty-free, once every 31 days. Many processed and packaged foods are allowed, including vacuum-packed cheeses, dried herbs, jams, baked goods, candy, chocolate, oil, vinegar, mustard, and honey. Fresh fruits and vegetables and most meats are not allowed, with exceptions for some canned items. As for alcohol, you can bring in one liter duty-free (it can be packed securely in your checked luggage, along with any other liquid-containing items).

PRACTICALITIES

To bring alcohol (or liquid-packed foods) in your carry-on bag on your flight home, buy it at a duty-free shop at the airport. You'll increase your odds of getting it onto a connecting flight if it's packaged in a "STEB"—a secure, tamper-evident bag. But stay away from liquids in opaque, ceramic, or metallic containers, which usually cannot be successfully screened (STEB or no STEB).

For details on allowable goods, customs rules, and duty rates, visit http://help.cbp.gov.

Sightseeing

Sightseeing can be hard work. Use these tips to make your visits to London's finest sights meaningful, fun, efficient, and painless.

MAPS AND NAVIGATION TOOLS

A good map is essential for efficient navigation while sightseeing. The maps in this book are concise and simple, designed to help you locate recommended destinations, sights, and local TIs, where you can pick up more in-depth maps. Maps with even more detail are sold at newsstands and bookstores. *Bensons London Street Map,* sold at many newsstands and bookstores, is my favorite for efficient sightseeing and might be the best £4 you'll spend. I also like the *Handy London Map and Guide* version, which shows every little lane and all the sights, and comes with a transit map. The *Rough Guide* map to London is well-designed (£5, sold at London bookstores). The *Rick Steves Britain, Ireland & London City Map* has a good map of London ($9, www.ricksteves.com). Many Londoners, along with obsessive-compulsive tourists, rely on the highly detailed *London A-Z* map book (generally £5-7, called "A to Zed" by locals, available at newsstands). The color city maps and Tube map at the front of this book are also useful. Even the vending-machine maps sold in Tube stations are good.

You can also use a mapping app on your mobile device. Be aware that pulling up maps or looking up turn-by-turn walking directions on the fly requires an Internet connection: To use this feature, it's smart to get an international data plan (see page 569). With Google Maps or City Maps 2Go, it's possible to download a map while online, then go offline and navigate without incurring data-roaming charges, though you can't search for an address or get real-time walking directions. A handful of other apps—including Apple Maps, OffMaps, and Navfree—also allow you to use maps offline.

PLAN AHEAD

Set up an itinerary that allows you to fit in all your must-see sights. For a one-stop look at opening hours, see "London at a Glance" on page 50; also see the "Daily Reminder" on page 18. Most sights keep stable hours, but you can easily confirm the latest by checking with the TI or visiting museum websites.

Don't put off visiting a must-see sight—you never know when a place will close unexpectedly for a holiday, strike, or royal audience. Given how precious your vacation time is, I recommend getting reservations for any must-see sight that offers them (see page 7). Many museums are closed or have reduced hours at least a few days a year, especially on holidays such as Christmas, New Year's, and Bank Holiday Mondays in May and August. A list of holidays is on page 581; check online for possible museum closures during your trip. Off-season, many museums have shorter hours.

Going at the right time helps avoid crowds. This book offers tips on the best times to see specific sights. Try visiting popular sights very early or very late. Evening visits (when possible) are usually peaceful, with fewer crowds. In addition to the London Eye, at least one major London sight is open late every night (see the sidebar on page 74).

If you plan to hire a local guide, reserve ahead by email. Popular guides can get booked up.

Study up. To get the most out of the self-guided tours and sight descriptions in this book, read them before you visit. The British Museum rocks if you understand the significance of the Rosetta Stone.

AT SIGHTS

Here's what you can typically expect:

Entering: Be warned that you may not be allowed to enter if you arrive less than 30 to 60 minutes before closing time. And guards start ushering people out well before the actual closing time, so don't save the best for last.

Many sights have a security check, where you must open your bag or send it through a metal detector. Some sights require you to check daypacks and coats. (If you'd rather not check your daypack, try carrying it tucked under your arm like a purse as you enter.)

Photography: If the museum's photo policy isn't clearly posted, ask a guard. Generally, taking photos without a flash or tripod is allowed. Some sights ban selfie sticks; others ban photos altogether.

Temporary Exhibits: Museums may show special exhibits in addition to their permanent collection. An extra fee, which may not be optional, might be assessed for these shows.

Expect Changes: Artwork can be on tour, on loan, out sick, or shifted at the whim of the curator. Pick up a floor plan as you enter, and ask museum staff if you can't find a particular item.

Audioguides and Apps: Many sights rent audioguides, which

PRACTICALITIES

generally offer excellent recorded descriptions (about £5). If you bring your own earbuds, you can enjoy better sound. To save money, bring a Y-jack and share one audioguide with your travel partner. Museums and sights often offer free apps that you can download to your mobile device (check their websites). And, I've produced free, downloadable audio tours for my Westminster Walk, the British Museum, the British Library, St. Paul's Cathedral, and Historic London: The City Walk; look for the ⌂ symbol in this book. For more on my audio tours, see page 8.

Guided tours are most likely to occur during peak season (either for free or a small fee—figure £5-10—and widely ranging in quality). Some sights also run short introductory videos featuring their highlights and history. These are generally well worth your time and a great place to start your visit.

Services: Important sights and cathedrals may have a reasonably priced on-site café or cafeteria (usually a handy place to rejuvenate during a long visit—try a cheap "cream tea" to pick up your energy in midafternoon, like Brits do). The WCs at sights are free and generally clean.

Before Leaving: At the gift shop, scan the postcard rack or thumb through a guidebook to be sure that you haven't overlooked something that you'd like to see.

Every sight or museum offers more than what is covered in this book. Use the information in this book as an introduction—not the final word.

SIGHTSEEING PASSES

The following sightseeing passes are sold online and at the City of London Information Centre, near St. Paul's Cathedral; see page 16.

The **London Pass,** which covers many big sights and lets you skip some lines, is expensive but potentially worth the investment for extremely busy sightseers. Among the many sights it includes are the Tower of London, Westminster Abbey, Churchill War Rooms, and Windsor Castle, as well as many temporary exhibits and audioguides at otherwise "free" biggies. Think through your sightseeing plans, study their website to see what's covered, and do the math before you buy (£62/1 day, £85/2 days, £101/3 days, £139/6 days; days are calendar days rather than 24-hour periods; comes with 160-page guidebook, also sold at major train stations and airports, tel. 020/7293-0972, www.londonpass.com).

The **English Heritage** society sells passes and memberships that include free entry to its 400 sights (which are exclusive to England); they're worth it only if you'll be thoroughly exploring England, not just London. You can buy passes or memberships at any participating sight. For most travelers, the Overseas

Visitor Pass is a better choice than the pricier one-year membership (Visitor Pass: £31/9 days, £37/16 days, discounts for couples and families, www.english-heritage.org.uk/ovp; membership: £54 for one person, £96 for two, discounts for families, seniors, and students, children under 19 free, www.english-heritage.org.uk/membership; tel. 0370-333-1181).

Sleeping

I favor hotels and restaurants that are handy to your sightseeing activities. Rather than list accommodations scattered throughout a city, I choose places in my favorite neighborhoods. My recommendations run the gamut, from dorm beds to fancy rooms with all the comforts.

Extensive and opinionated listings of good-value rooms are a major feature of this book's Sleeping sections. I like places that are clean, central, relatively quiet at night, reasonably priced, friendly, small enough to have a hands-on owner and stable staff, and run with a respect for British traditions. I'm more impressed by a convenient location and a fun-loving philosophy than flat-screen TVs and a fancy gym. Most places I recommend fall short of perfection. But if I can find a place with most of these features, it's a keeper.

Britain has a rating system for hotels and B&Bs. Its stars are supposed to imply quality, but I find they mean only that the place is paying dues to the tourist board. Rating systems often have little to do with value.

Book your accommodations as soon as your itinerary is set, especially if you want to stay at one of my top listings or if you'll be traveling during busy times. See page 581 for a list of major holidays and festivals; for tips on making reservations, see page 556.

RATES AND DEALS

I've categorized my recommended accommodations based on price, indicated with a dollar-sign rating (see sidebar). The price ranges suggest an estimated cost for a one-night stay in a typical en suite double room with a private toilet and shower in high season, and assume you're booking directly with the hotel (not through a booking site, which extracts a commission). Room prices can fluctuate significantly with demand and amenities (size, views, room class, and so on), but relative price categories remain constant. City taxes are generally insignificant (a dollar or two per person, per night). For most places, the rates I list include the 20 percent VAT tax—but it's smart to ask when you book your room.

Room rates are especially volatile at larger hotels that use "dynamic pricing" to set rates. Prices can skyrocket during festivals

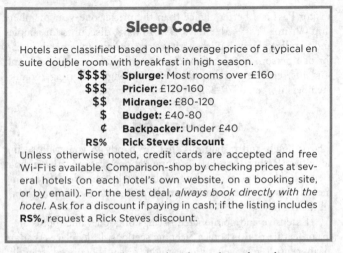

PRACTICALITIES

and conventions, while business hotels can have deep discounts on weekends when demand plummets. Of the many hotels I recommend, it's difficult to say which will be the best value on a given day—until you do your homework.

Once your dates are set, check the specific price for your preferred stay at several hotels. You can do this either by comparing prices on Hotels.com or Booking.com, or by checking the hotels' own websites. To get the best deal, contact my family-run hotels directly by phone or email. When you go direct, the owner avoids the 20 percent commission, giving them wiggle room to offer you a discount, a nicer room, or free breakfast if it's not already included (see sidebar). If you prefer to book online or are considering a hotel chain, it's in your advantage to use the hotel's website.

Some hotels offer a discount to those who pay cash or stay longer than three nights. To cut costs further, try asking for a cheaper room (for example, with a shared bathroom or no window) or offer to skip breakfast (if included).

Additionally, some accommodations offer a special discount for Rick Steves readers, indicated in the listing by the abbreviation "RS%." Discounts vary: Ask for details when you reserve. Generally, to qualify you must book directly (that is, not through a booking site), mention this book when you reserve, show this book upon arrival, and sometimes pay cash or stay a certain number of nights. In some cases, you may need to enter a discount code (which I've provided in the listing) in the booking form on the hotel's website. Rick Steves discounts apply to readers with ebooks as well as printed books. Understandably, discounts do not apply to promotional rates.

When establishing prices, confirm if the charge is per person or per room (if a price is too good to be true, it's probably per person). Because many places in England charge per person, small groups often pay the same for a single and a double as they would for a triple. In this book, I've categorized hotels based on the per room price, not per person.

TYPES OF ACCOMMODATIONS
Hotels

In London, you'll find big, Old World-elegant hotels with modern amenities, as well as familiar-feeling business-class and boutique hotels no different from what you might experience at home. But you'll also find hotels that are more uniquely European. You can expect to book a moderate (if not fancy) double for £100-120, including cooked breakfasts and tax. In pricey London, it's worth looking for deals at chain hotels (see page 391).

A "twin" room has two single beds; a "double" has one double bed. If you'll take either, let the hotel know, or you might be needlessly turned away. Some hotels can add an extra bed (for a small charge) to turn a double into a triple; some offer larger rooms for four or more people (I call these "family rooms" in the listings). If there's space for an extra cot, they'll cram it in for you. In general, a triple room is cheaper than the cost of a double and a single. Three or four people can economize by requesting one big room.

Note that to be called a "hotel," a place technically must have certain amenities, including a 24-hour reception (though this rule is loosely applied).

Arrival and Check-In: Many of my recommended hotels have three or more floors of rooms and steep stairs. Older properties often do not have elevators. If stairs are an issue, ask for a ground-floor room or choose a hotel with a lift (elevator). Air-conditioning isn't a given (I've noted which of my listings have it), but most places have fans. On hot summer nights, you'll want your window open—and in a big city, street noise is a fact of life. Bring earplugs or request a room on the back side. If you suspect night noise will be a problem (if, for instance, your room is over a noisy pub), ask for a quieter room on an upper floor.

If you're arriving in the morning, your room probably won't be ready. Check your bag safely at the hotel and dive right into sightseeing.

In Your Room: More pillows and blankets are usually in the closet or available on request. Towels and linens aren't always replaced every day. Hang your towel up to dry.

An "en suite" room has a bathroom (toilet and shower/tub) attached to the room; a room with a "private bathroom" can mean that the bathroom is all yours, but it's across the hall. If you want your own bathroom inside the room, request "en suite."

PRACTICALITIES

Hotels vs. Booking Websites vs. Consumers

In the last decade it's become almost impossible for independent-minded, family-run hotels to survive without playing the game as dictated by the big players in the online booking world. Priceline's Booking.com and Expedia's Hotels.com take roughly 80 percent of this business. Hoteliers note that without this online presence, "We become almost invisible." Online booking services demand about a 20 percent commission. And in order to be listed, a hotel must promise that its website does not undercut the price on the third-party's website. Without that restriction, hoteliers could say, "Sure, sell our rooms for whatever markup you like, and we'll continue to offer a fair rate to travelers who come to us directly"—but that's not allowed.

Here's the work-around: For independent and family-run hotels, book directly by email or phone, in which case hotel owners are free to give you whatever price they like. Research the price online, and then ask them for a room without the commission mark-up. You could ask them to split the difference—the hotel charges you 10 percent less but pockets 10 percent more. Or you can ask for a free breakfast (if not included) or upgrade.

If you do book online, be sure to use the hotel's website (you'll likely pay the same price as via a booking site, but your money goes to the hotel, not agency commissions).

As consumers, remember: Whenever you book with an online booking service, you're adding a needless middleman who takes roughly 20 percent. If you'd like to support small, family-run hotels whose world is more difficult than ever, book direct.

If money's tight, ask for a room with a shared bathroom. You'll almost always have a sink in your room, and as more rooms go en suite, the hallway bathroom is shared with fewer guests.

TVs are standard in rooms, but may come with limited channels (no cable). Note that all of Britain's accommodations are non-smoking. Most hotels have free Wi-Fi (although the Wi-Fi signal doesn't always make it to the rooms; sometimes it's only available in the lobby). There's often a guest computer with Internet access in the lobby.

Breakfast: Your room cost usually includes a traditional full English breakfast (fry-up) or a lighter, healthier continental breakfast.

Checking Out: While it's customary to pay for your room upon departure, it can be a good idea to settle your bill the day before, when you're not in a hurry and while the manager's in. That way you'll have time to discuss and address any points of contention.

Hotelier Help: Hoteliers can be a good source of advice. Most know their city well, and can assist you with everything from public transit and airport connections to finding a good restaurant, the nearest launderette, or a late-night pharmacy.

Hotel Hassles: Even at the best places, mechanical breakdowns occur: Sinks leak, hot water turns cold, toilets may gurgle or smell, the Wi-Fi goes out, or the air-conditioning dies when you need it most. Report your concerns clearly and calmly at the front desk. For more complicated problems, don't expect instant results. Above all, keep a positive attitude. Remember, you're on vacation. If your hotel is a disappointment, spend more time out enjoying the place you came to see.

To guard against theft in your room, keep valuables out of sight. Some rooms come with a safe, and other hotels have safes at the front desk. I've never bothered using one and in a lifetime of travel, I've never had anything stolen from my room.

B&Bs and Small Hotels

B&Bs and small hotels are generally family-run places with fewer amenities but more character than a conventional hotel. They range from large inns with 15 to 20 rooms to small homes renting out a spare bedroom. Places named "guesthouse" or "B&B" typically have eight or fewer rooms. The philosophy of the management determines the character of a place more than its size and facilities offered. I avoid places run as a business by absentee owners. My top listings are run by people who enjoy welcoming the world to their breakfast table.

Many B&Bs take credit cards, but may add the card service fee to your bill (about 3 percent). If you do need to pay cash for your room, plan ahead to have enough on hand when you check out.

B&Bs and small hotels come with their own etiquette and quirks. Keep in mind that owners are at the whim of their guests—if you're getting up early, so are they; and if you check in late, they'll wait up for you. Most B&Bs either have set check-in times (usually twice a day, in the morning and late afternoon), or will want to know when to expect you (call or email ahead to let them know).

In the Room: Every B&B offers "tea service" in the room—an electric kettle, cups, tea bags, coffee packets, and a pack of biscuits.

Your bedroom probably won't include a phone, but nearly every B&B has free Wi-Fi (if they don't, I'll generally note it in the listing). However, the signal may not reach all rooms; you may need to sit in the lounge to access it.

Making Hotel Reservations

Reserve your rooms as soon as you've pinned down your travel dates. For busy national holidays, it's wise to reserve far in advance (see page 581).

Requesting a Reservation: For family-run hotels, it's generally cheaper to book your room directly via email or a phone call. For business-class hotels, or if you'd rather book online, reserve directly through the hotel's official website (not a booking agency's site). For complicated requests, send an email.

Here's what the hotelier wants to know:
- type(s) of rooms you need and size of your party
- number of nights you'll stay
- your arrival and departure dates, written European-style as day/month/year (for example, 18/06/19 or 18 June 2019)
- special requests (such as en suite bathroom vs. down the hall, cheapest room, twin beds vs. double bed, quiet room)
- applicable discounts (such as a Rick Steves reader discount, cash discount, or promotional rate)

Confirming a Reservation: Most places will request a credit-card number to hold your room. If you're using an online reservation form, look for the *https* or a lock icon at the top of your browser. If you book direct, you can email, call, or fax this information.

Canceling a Reservation: If you must cancel, it's courteous—and smart—to do so with as much notice as possible, especially for smaller family-run places. Cancellation policies can be strict;

Short-Term Rentals

A short-term rental—whether an apartment, house, or room in a local's home—is an increasingly popular alternative, especially if you plan to settle in one location for several nights. For stays longer than a few days, you can usually find a rental that's comparable to—and even cheaper than—a hotel room with similar amenities. Plus, you'll get a behind-the-scenes peek into how locals live.

Many places require a minimum-night stay, and compared to hotels, rentals usually have less-flexible cancellation policies. Also, you're generally on your own: There's no hotel reception desk, breakfast, or daily cleaning service.

Finding Accommodations: Aggregator websites such as Airbnb, FlipKey, Roomorama, Booking.com, and the Home-Away family of sites (HomeAway, VRBO, and VacationRentals) let you browse properties and correspond directly with European property owners or managers. If you prefer to work from a curated list of accommodations, consider using a rental agency such as InterhomeUSA.com or RentaVilla.com. Agency-represented apartments typically cost more, but this method often offers more

From:	rick@ricksteves.com
Sent:	Today
To:	info@hotelcentral.com
Subject:	Reservation request for 19-22 July

Dear Hotel Central,

I would like to stay at your hotel. Please let me know if you have a room available and the price for:
• 2 people
• Double bed and en suite bathroom in a quiet room
• Arriving 19 July, departing 22 July (3 nights)

Thank you!
Rick Steves

read the fine print or ask about these before you book. Many discount deals require prepayment, with no cancellation refunds.

Reconfirming a Reservation: Always call or email to reconfirm your room reservation a few days in advance. For B&Bs or very small hotels, I call again on my day of arrival to tell my host what time to expect me (especially important if arriving late—after 17:00).

Phoning: For tips on calling hotels overseas, see page 570.

help and safeguards than booking direct. For a list of rental agencies for London, see page 395.

Before you commit, be clear on the details, location, and amenities. I like to virtually "explore" the neighborhood using the Street View feature on Google Maps. Also consider the proximity to public transportation, and how well-connected the property is with the rest of the city. Ask about amenities (elevator, air-conditioning, laundry, Wi-Fi, parking, etc.). Reviews from previous guests can help identify trouble spots.

Think about the kind of experience you want: Just a key and an affordable bed...or a chance to get to know a local? There are typically two kinds of hosts: those who want minimal interaction with their guests, and hosts who are friendly and may want to interact with you. Read the promotional text and online reviews to help shape your decision.

Apartments: If you're staying somewhere for four nights or longer, it's worth considering an apartment (shorter stays aren't worth the hassle of arranging key pickup, buying groceries, etc.). Apartments can be especially cost-effective for groups and families.

The Good and Bad of Online Reviews

User-generated review sites and apps such as Yelp, Booking. com, and TripAdvisor can give you a consensus of opinions about everything from hotels and restaurants to sights and nightlife. If you scan reviews of a hotel and see several complaints about noise or a rotten location, it tells you something important that you'd never learn from the hotel's own website.

But as a guidebook writer, my sense is that there is a big difference between the uncurated information on a review site and a guidebook. A user-generated review is based on the experience of one person, who likely stayed at one hotel in a given city and ate at a few restaurants there (and who doesn't have much of a basis for comparison). A guidebook is the work of a trained researcher who, year after year, visits many alternatives to assess their relative value. I recently checked out some top-rated user-reviewed hotel and restaurant listings in various towns; when stacked up against their competitors, some were gems, while just as many were duds.

Both types of information have their place, and in many ways, they're complementary. If something is well-reviewed in a guidebook, and also gets good ratings on one of these sites, it's likely a winner.

European apartments, like hotel rooms, tend to be small by US standards. But they often come with laundry machines and small, equipped kitchens, making it easier and cheaper to dine in. If you make good use of the kitchen (and Europe's great produce markets), you'll save on your meal budget. Also, determine how close the nearest Tube stop is, and factor transportation costs into the overall price.

Private and Shared Rooms: Renting a room in someone's home is a good option for those traveling alone, as you're more likely to find true single rooms—with just one single bed, and a price to match. Beds range from air-mattress-in-living-room basic to plush-B&B-suite posh. Some places allow you to book for a single night; if staying for several nights, you can buy groceries just as you would in a rental house. While you can't expect your host to also be your tour guide—or even to provide you with much info— some may be interested in getting to know the travelers who come through their home.

Other Options: Swapping homes with a local works for people with an appealing place to offer, and who can live with the idea of having strangers in their home (don't assume where you live is not interesting to Europeans). A good place to start is HomeExchange. To sleep for free, Couchsurfing.com is a vagabond's alternative to Airbnb. It lists millions of outgoing members, who host fellow "surfers" in their homes.

Confirming and Paying: Many places require you to pay the entire balance before your trip. It's easiest and safest to pay through the site where you found the listing. Be wary of owners who want to take your transaction offline to avoid fees; this gives you no recourse if things go awry. Never agree to wire money (a key indicator of a fraudulent transaction).

Hostels and Dorms

A hostel provides cheap beds in dorms where you sleep alongside strangers for about £20-30 per night. Travelers of any age are welcome if they don't mind dorm-style accommodations and meeting other travelers. Most hostels offer kitchen facilities, guest computers, Wi-Fi, and a self-service laundry. Hostels almost always provide bedding, but the towel's up to you (though you can usually rent one for a small fee). Family and private rooms are often available.

Independent hostels tend to be easygoing, colorful, and informal (no membership required; www.hostelworld.com). You may pay slightly less by booking directly with the hostel. **Official hostels** are part of Hostelling International (HI) and share an online booking site (www.hihostels.com). In Britain, these official hostels are run by the YHA (www.yha.org.uk). HI hostels typically require that you be a member or pay extra per night.

Many London **colleges** rent out their dorms during school holidays, mainly during July, August, and early September. Types of accommodations vary, but are usually somewhat spartan (no phones or TVs in the rooms) and come with single or twin beds. For listings, see "Dorms" on page 395.

Eating

These days, the stereotype of "bad food in Britain" is woefully dated. Britain has caught up with the foodie revolution, and I find it's easy to eat very well here.

British cooking has embraced international influences and good-quality ingredients, making "modern British" food quite delicious. While some dreary pub food still exists, you'll generally find the cuisine scene here innovative and delicious (but expensive). Basic pubs are more likely to dish up homemade, creative dishes than microwaved pies, soggy fries, and mushy peas. Even traditional pub grub has gone upmarket, with gastropubs that serve locally sourced meats and fresh vegetables.

All of Britain is smoke-free. Expect restaurants and pubs to be nonsmoking indoors, with smokers occupying patios and doorways

PRACTICALITIES

outside. You'll find the English eat at about the same time of day as Americans do.

When restaurant-hunting, choose a spot filled with locals, not tourists. Venturing even a block or two off the main drag leads to higher-quality food for a better price. Locals eat better at lower-rent locales. Rely on my recommendations in the Eating in London chapter.

Tipping: At pubs and places where you order at the counter, you don't have to tip. Regular customers ordering a round some-times say, "Add one for yourself," as a tip for drinks ordered at the bar—but this isn't expected.

At restaurants and fancy pubs with waitstaff, tip about 10-12.5 percent. Most restaurants in London now add a 12.5 percent "op-tional" tip onto the bill. Tip only what you think the service war-rants (if it isn't already added to your bill), and be careful not to tip double.

RESTAURANT PRICING

I've categorized my recommended eateries based on price, indicat-ed with a dollar-sign rating (see sidebar). The price ranges suggest the average price of a typical main course—but not necessarily a complete meal.

Obviously, expensive items (such as steak and seafood), fine wine, appetizers, and dessert can significantly increase your final bill.

The dollar-sign categories also indicate the overall personality and "feel" of a place:

$ Budget eateries include street food, takeaway, order-at-the-counter shops, basic cafeterias, bakeries selling sandwiches, and so on.

$$ Moderate eateries are typically nice (but not fancy) sit-down restaurants, ideal for a straightforward, fill-the-tank meal. Most of my listings fall in this category—great for getting a good taste of the local cuisine on a budget.

$$$ Pricier eateries are a notch up, with more attention paid to the setting, service, and cuisine. These are ideal for a memorable meal that's still relatively casual and doesn't break the bank. This category often includes affordable "destination" or "foodie" restau-rants.

$$$$ Splurge eateries are dress-up-for-a-special-occasion-swanky—Michelin star-type restaurants, typically with an elegant setting, polished service, pricey and intricate cuisine, and an ex-pansive (and expensive) wine list.

I haven't categorized places where you might assemble a pic-nic, snack, or graze: supermarkets, delis, ice-cream stands, cafés or bars specializing in drinks, chocolate shops, and so on.

Restaurant Price Code

I've assigned each eatery a price category, based on the average cost of a typical main course. Drinks, desserts, and splurge items (steak and seafood) can raise the price considerably.

$$$$	**Splurge:** Most main courses over £20
$$$	**Pricier:** £15-20
$$	**Moderate:** £10-15
$	**Budget:** Under £10

In Great Britain, carryout fish-and-chips and other takeout food is **$**; a basic pub or sit-down eatery is **$$**; a gastropub or casual but more upscale restaurant is **$$$**; and a swanky splurge is **$$$$**.

BREAKFAST (Fry-Up)

The traditional fry-up or full English breakfast—generally included in the cost of your room—is famous as a hearty way to start the day.

Also known as a "heart attack on a plate," your standard fry-up is a heated plate with eggs, Canadian-style bacon and/or sausage, a grilled tomato, sautéed mushrooms, baked beans, and sometimes potatoes, kippers (herring), or fried bread (sizzled in a greasy skillet). Toast comes in a rack (to cool quickly and crisply) with butter and marmalade.

The meal is typically topped off with tea or coffee. At a B&B or hotel, it may start with juice and cereal or porridge. Many progressive B&B owners offer vegetarian, organic, gluten-free, or other creative variations on the traditional breakfast.

Much as the full breakfast fry-up is a traditional way to start the morning, these days most hotels serve a healthier continental breakfast—with a buffet of everything you'd expect, such as yogurt, cereal, scrambled eggs, fruit, and veggies.

LUNCH AND DINNER ON A BUDGET

Even in pricey British cities, plenty of inexpensive choices are available: pub grub, daily lunch and early-bird dinner specials, ethnic restaurants, cafeterias, fast food, picnics, greasy-spoon cafés, cheap chain restaurants, and pizza.

I've found that portions are huge, and with locals feeling the economic pinch, **sharing plates** is generally just fine. Ordering two drinks, a soup or side salad, and splitting a £10 meat pie can make a good, filling meal. If you're on a limited budget, share a main course in a more expensive place for a nicer eating experience.

Pub grub is the most atmospheric budget option. You'll usually get hearty lunches and dinners priced reasonably at £8-12 under ancient timbers (see "Pubs," later). Gastropubs, with better food, are more expensive.

Classier restaurants have some affordable deals. Lunch is usually cheaper than dinner; a top-end, £25-for-dinner type restaurant often serves the same quality two-course lunch deals for about half the price.

Many restaurants have **early-bird** or **pre-theater specials** of two or three courses, often for a significant savings. Some places offer these on weekdays only; others have them every day. They are usually available only before 18:30 or 19:00. If you're bargain hunting and willing to eat a bit earlier, inquire or check websites for details.

Ethnic restaurants add spice to Britain's cuisine scene. Eating Indian, Bangladeshi, Chinese, or Thai is cheap (even cheaper if you do takeout). Middle East-ern stands sell gyro sandwiches, falafel, and *shwarmas* (grilled meat in pita bread). An Indian samosa (greasy, flaky meat-and-vegetable pie) costs about £2 and makes a very cheap, if small, meal. (For more, see "Indian Cuisine," later.) You'll find all-you-can-eat Chinese and Thai places serving £6 meals and offering even cheaper takeaway boxes. While you can't "split" a buffet, you can split a takeaway box. Stuff the box full, and you and your partner can eat in a park for under £3 each.

Fish-and-chips are a heavy, greasy, but tasty British classic. Every town has at least one "chippy" selling a takeaway box of fish-and-chips in a cardboard box or (more traditionally) wrapped in paper for about £4-7. You can dip your fries in ketchup, American-style, or "go English" and drizzle the whole thing with malt vinegar and fresh lemon.

Most large **museums** (and many historic **churches**) have handy, moderately priced cafeterias with forgettably decent food.

Picnicking saves time and money. Fine park benches and polite pigeons abound in most towns and city neighborhoods. You can easily get prepared food to go. The modern chain eateries on nearly every corner often have simple seating but are designed for takeout. Bakeries serve a wonderful array of fresh sandwiches and pasties (savory meat pies). Street markets, generally parked in pedestrian-friendly zones, are fun and colorful places to stock up for a picnic (see "Street Markets" in the Shopping chapter).

Open-air markets and supermarkets sell produce in small

quantities. The corner grocery store has fruit, drinks, fresh bread, tasty British cheese, meat, and local specialties. Supermarkets often have good deli sections, even offering Indian dishes, and sometimes salad bars. Decent packaged sandwiches (£3-4) are sold everywhere. Munch a relaxed "meal on wheels" picnic during your open-top bus tour or river cruise to save 30 precious minutes for sightseeing.

PUBS

Pubs are a fundamental part of the British social scene, and whether you're a teetotaler or a beer guzzler, they should be a part of your travel here. "Pub" is short for "public house." It's an extended common room where, if you don't mind the stickiness, you can feel the pulse of London. Smart travelers use pubs to eat, drink, get out of the rain, watch sporting events, and make new friends.

It's interesting to consider the role pubs filled for Britain's working class in more modest times: For workers with humble domestic quarters and no money for a vacation, a beer at the corner pub was the closest they'd get to a comfortable living room, a place to entertain, and a getaway. And locals could meet people from far away in a pub—today, that's you!

Though hours vary, pubs generally serve beer daily from 11:00 to 23:00, though many are open later, particularly on Friday and Saturday. (Children are served food and soft drinks in pubs, but you must be 18 to order a beer.) As it nears closing time, you'll hear shouts of "Last orders." Then comes the 10-minute warning bell. Finally, they'll call "Time!" to pick up your glass, finished or not, when the pub closes.

A cup of darts is free for the asking. People go to a public house to be social. They want to talk. Get vocal with a local. This is easiest at the bar, where people assume you're in the mood to talk (rather than at a table, where you're allowed a bit of privacy). The pub is the next best thing to having relatives in town. Cheers!

Pub Grub: For £8-12, you'll get a basic budget hot lunch or dinner in friendly surroundings. In high-priced London, this is your best indoor eating value. (For something more refined, try a **gastropub**, which serves higher-quality meals for £12-18.) The *Good Pub Guide* is an excellent resource (www.thegoodpubguide. co.uk). Pubs that are attached to restaurants, advertise their food, and are crowded with locals are more likely to have fresh food and a chef—and less likely to sell only lousy microwaved snacks.

Pubs generally serve traditional dishes, such as fish-and-chips, roast beef with Yorkshire pudding (batter-baked in the oven), and assorted meat pies, such as steak-and-kidney pie or shepherd's pie (stewed lamb topped with mashed potatoes) with cooked vegetables. Side dishes include salads, vegetables, and—invariably—

"chips" (French fries). "Crisps" are potato chips. A "jacket potato" (baked potato stuffed with fillings of your choice) can almost be a meal in itself. A "ploughman's lunch" is a "traditional English meal" of bread, cheese, and sweet pickles that nearly every tourist tries...once. These days, you'll likely find more pasta, curried dishes, and quiche on the menu than traditional fare.

Meals are usually served from 12:00 to 14:00 and again from 18:00 to 20:00—with a break in the middle (rather than serving straight through the day). Since they make more money selling beer, many pubs stop food service early in the evening—especially on weekends. There's generally no table service. Order at the bar, then take a seat. Either they'll bring the food when it's ready or you'll pick it up at the bar. Pay at the bar (sometimes when you order, sometimes after you eat). Don't tip unless it's a place with full table service. Servings are hearty, and service is quick. If you're on a tight budget, it's OK to share a meal. A beer, cider, or dram of whisky adds another couple of pounds. Free tap water is always available. For a list of recommended historic pubs in London, see page 408. For details on ordering beer and other drinks, see the "Beverages" section, later.

GOOD CHAIN RESTAURANTS

I know—you're going to Britain to enjoy characteristic little hole-in-the-wall pubs, so mass-produced food is the furthest thing from your mind. But several excellent chains with branches across the UK offer long hours, reasonable prices, reliable quality, and a nice break from pub grub. My favorites are Pret, Wasabi, and Eat. Expect to see these familiar names wherever you go:

Pret (a.k.a. Pret à Manger) is perhaps the most pervasive of these modern convenience eateries. Some are takeout only, and others have seating ranging from simple stools to restaurant-quality tables. The service is fast, the price is great, and the food is healthy and fresh. Their slogan: "Made today. Gone today. No 'sell-by' date, no nightlife."

Côte Brasserie is a contemporary French chain serving good-value French cuisine in reliably pleasant settings (early dinner specials).

Le Pain Quotidien is a Belgian chain serving fresh-baked bread and hearty meals in a thoughtfully designed modern-rustic atmosphere. Their satisfying sandwiches, salads, and main dishes prove that food can be simple without being boring or bland.

Byron Hamburgers, an upscale-hamburger chain with hip interiors, is worth seeking out if you need a burger fix. While British burgers tend to be a bit overcooked by American standards, Byron's burgers are your best bet.

Wagamama Noodle Bar, serving pan-Asian cuisine (udon

noodles, fried rice, and curry dishes), is a noisy, organic slurpathon. Portions are huge and splittable. There's one in almost every mid-size city in Britain, usually located in sprawling halls filled with long shared tables and busy servers who scrawl your order on the placemat.

Loch Fyne Fish Restaurant is a Scottish chain that raises its own oysters and mussels. Its branches offer an inviting, lively atmosphere with a fine fishy energy and no pretense (early-bird specials).

Marks & Spencer department stores have a new feature: inviting deli sections with cheery sit-down eating (along with their popular sandwiches-to-go section). M&S food halls are also handy if you're renting a flat in London and want to prepare your own meals.

Busaba Eathai is a hit with Londoners for its snappy (sometimes rushed) service, boisterous ambience, and good, inexpensive Thai cuisine. New locations pop up often.

Thai Square is a dependable Thai option with a nice atmosphere (salads, noodle dishes, curries, meat dishes, and daily lunch box specials).

Masala Zone is a London chain providing a good, predictable alternative to the many one-off, hole-in-the-wall Indian joints around town. Try a curry-and-rice dish, a *thali* (platter with several small dishes), or their street food specials. Each branch has its own personality.

Ask and **Pizza Express** serve quality pasta and pizza in a pleasant, sit-down atmosphere that's family-friendly. **Jamie's Italian** (from celebrity chef Jamie Oliver) is hipper and pricier.

Japanese: Three popular chains serve fresh and inexpensive Japanese food. **Itsu** and **Wasabi** are two bright and competitive chains that let you assemble your own plate in a fun and efficient way, while **Yo! Sushi** lets you pick your dish off a conveyor belt and pay according to the color of your plate. If you're in the mood for sushi, all are great.

Carry-Out Chains: While the following may have some seating, they're best as places to grab prepackaged food on the run.

Major supermarket chains have smaller, offshoot branches that specialize in sandwiches, salads, and other prepared foods to go. These can be a picnicker's dream come true. Some shops are stand-alone, while others are located inside a larger store. The most prevalent—and best—is **M&S Simply Food** (an offshoot of Marks & Spencer; there's one in every major train station). **Sainsbury's Local** grocery stores also offer decent prepared food; **Tesco Express** and **Tesco Metro** run a distant third.

Some "cheap and cheery" chains provide office workers with good, healthful sandwiches, salads, and pastries to go. These include **Apostróphe, Pod,** and **Eat** (with slightly higher-quality food and higher prices).

INDIAN CUISINE

Eating Indian food is "going local" in cosmopolitan, multiethnic Britain. You'll find Indian restaurants in most cities, and even in small towns. Take the opportunity to sample food from Britain's former colony. Indian cuisine is as varied as the country itself. In general, it uses more exotic spices than British or American cuisine—some hot, some sweet. Indian food is very vegetarian-friendly, offering many meatless dishes to choose from on any given menu.

For a simple meal that costs about £10-12, order one dish with rice and naan (Indian flatbread). Generally, one order is plenty for two people to share. Many Indian restaurants offer a fixed-price combination that offers more variety, and is simpler and cheaper than ordering à la carte. For about £20, you can make a mix-and-match platter out of several shareable dishes, including dal (simmered lentils) as a starter, one or two meat or vegetable dishes with sauce (for example, chicken curry, chicken *tikka masala* in a creamy tomato sauce, grilled fish tandoori, chickpea *chana masala,* or a spicy vindaloo dish), *raita* (a cooling yogurt that's added to spicy dishes), rice, naan, and an Indian beer (wine and Indian food don't really mix) or chai (cardamom/cinnamon-spiced tea, usually served with milk). An easy way to taste a variety of dishes is to order a thali—a sampler plate, generally served on a metal tray, with small servings of various specialties.

AFTERNOON TEA

Once the sole province of genteel ladies in fancy hats, afternoon tea has become more democratic in the 21st century. These days, people of leisure punctuate their day with an afternoon tea at a tearoom. Tearooms, which often serve appealing light meals, are usually open for lunch and close at about 17:00, just before dinner.

The cheapest "tea" on the menu is generally a "cream tea"; the most expensive is the "champagne tea." **Cream tea** is simply a pot of tea and a homemade scone or two with jam and thick clotted cream. (For maximum pinkie-waving taste per calorie, slice your scone thin like a miniature loaf of bread.) **Afternoon tea**—what many Americans would call "high tea"—is a pot of tea, small finger foods (such as sandwiches with the crusts cut off), scones, an assortment of small pastries, jam, and thick clotted cream. **Champagne tea** includes all of the goodies, plus a glass of bubbly. **High tea** to the English generally means a more substantial late afternoon or early evening meal, often served with meat or eggs.

> ## British Chocolate
>
> My chocoholic readers are enthusiastic about British chocolates. As with other dairy products, chocolate seems richer and creamier here than it does in the US, so even standbys such as Mars, Kit Kat, and Twix have a different taste. Some favorites include Cadbury Gold bars (filled with liquid caramel), Cadbury Crunchie bars, Nestlé's Lion bars (layered wafers covered in caramel and chocolate), Cadbury's Boost bars (a shortcake biscuit with caramel in milk chocolate), Cadbury Flake (crumbly folds of melt-in-your-mouth chocolate), Aero bars (with "aerated" chocolate filling), and Galaxy chocolate bars (especially the ones with hazelnuts). Thornton shops (in larger train stations) sell a box of sweets called the Continental Assortment, which comes with a tasting guide. (The highlight is the mocha white-chocolate truffle.) British M&Ms, called Smarties, are better than American ones. Many Brits feel that the ultimate treat is a box of either Nestlé Quality Street or Cadbury Roses—assortments of filled chocolates in colorful wrappers. (But don't mention the Kraft takeover of Cadbury in 2010—many Brits believe the American company changed the recipe for their beloved Dairy Milk bars, and they're not happy about it). At ice-cream vans, look for the beloved traditional "99p"—a vanilla soft-serve cone with a small Flake bar stuck right in the middle.

DESSERTS (SWEETS)

To the British, the traditional word for dessert is "pudding," although it's also referred to as "sweets" these days. Sponge cake, cream, fruitcake, and meringue are key players.

Trifle is the best-known British concoction, consisting of sponge cake soaked in brandy or sherry (or orange juice for children), then covered with jam and/or fruit and custard cream. Whipped cream can sometimes put the final touch on this "light" treat.

The English version of custard is a smooth, yellow liquid. Cream tops most everything that custard does not. There's single cream for coffee. Double cream is really thick. Whipped cream is familiar, and clotted cream is the consistency of whipped butter.

Fool is a dessert with sweetened pureed fruit (such as rhubarb, gooseberries, or black currants) mixed with cream or custard and chilled. Elderflower is a popular flavoring for sorbet.

Flapjacks here aren't pancakes, but are dense, sweet oatmeal cakes (a little like a cross between a granola bar and a brownie). They come with toppings such as toffee and chocolate.

Scones are tops, and many inns and restaurants have their secret recipes. Whether made with fruit or topped with clotted cream, scones take the cake.

BEVERAGES

Beer: The British take great pride in their beer. Many locals think that drinking beer cold and carbonated, as Americans do, ruins the taste. Most pubs will have **lagers** (cold, refreshing, American-style beer), **ales** (amber-colored, cellar-temperature beer), **bitters** (hop-flavored ale, perhaps the most typical British beer), and **stouts** (dark and somewhat bitter, like Guinness).

At pubs, long-handled pulls (or taps) are used to draw the traditional, rich-flavored "real ales" up from the cellar. These are the connoisseur's favorites and often come with fun names. Served straight from the brewer's cask at cellar temperature, real ales finish fermenting naturally and are not pasteurized or filtered, so they must be consumed within two or three days after the cask is tapped. Naturally carbonated, real ales have less gassiness and head; they vary from sweet to bitter, often with a hoppy or nutty flavor.

Short-handled pulls mean colder, fizzier, mass-produced, and less interesting keg beers. Mild beers are sweeter, with a creamy malt flavoring. Irish cream ale is a smooth, sweet experience. Try the draft cider (sweet or dry)...carefully.

Order your beer at the bar and pay as you go, with no need to tip. An average beer costs about £4. Part of the experience is standing before a line of hand pulls, and wondering which beer to choose.

As dictated by British law, draft beer and cider are served by the pint (20-ounce imperial size) or the half-pint (9.6 ounces). (It's almost feminine for a man to order just a half; I order mine with quiche.) In 2011, the government sanctioned an in-between serving size—the schooner, or two-thirds pint (it's become a popular size for higher alcohol-content craft beers). Proper English ladies like a **shandy** (half beer and half 7-Up).

Whisky: While bar-hopping tourists generally think in terms of beer, many pubs are just as enthusiastic about serving whisky. If you are unfamiliar with whisky (what Americans call "Scotch" and the Irish call "whiskey"), it's a great conversation starter. Many pubs have dozens of whiskies available. Lists describe their personalities (peaty, heavy iodine finish, and so on), which are much easier to discern than most wine flavors.

A glass of basic whisky generally costs around £2.50. Let a local teach you how to drink it "neat," then add a little water. Make a friend, buy a few drams, and learn by drinking. Keep experimenting until you discover the right taste for you.

Other Alcoholic Drinks: Many pubs also have a good selection of wines by the glass, a fully stocked bar for the gentleman's "G and T" (gin and tonic), and the increasingly popular bottles of alcohol-plus-sugar (such as Bacardi Breezers) for the younger working-class set. **Pimm's** is a refreshing and fruity summer liqueur, traditionally popular during Wimbledon. It's an upper-class drink—a rough bloke might insult a pub by claiming it sells more Pimm's than beer.

Non-Alcoholic Drinks: Teetotalers can order from a wide variety of soft drinks—both the predictable American sodas and other more interesting bottled drinks, such as ginger beer (similar to ginger ale but with more bite), root beers, or other flavors (Fentimans brews some unusual options that are stocked in many English pubs). Note that in Britain, "lemonade" is lemon-lime soda (like 7-Up).

Staying Connected

One of the most common questions I hear from travelers is, "How can I stay connected in Europe?" The short answer is: more easily and cheaply than you might think.

The simplest solution is to bring your own device—mobile phone, tablet, or laptop—and use it just as you would at home (following the tips below, such as connecting to free Wi-Fi whenever possible). Another option is to buy a European SIM card for your mobile phone—either your US phone or one you buy in Europe. Or you can use European landlines and computers to connect. Each of these options is described below, and more details are at www.ricksteves.com/phoning. For a very practical one-hour talk covering tech issues for travelers, see www.ricksteves.com/mobile-travel-skills.

USING A MOBILE PHONE IN EUROPE
Here are some budget tips and options.

Sign up for an international plan. Using your cellular network in Europe on a pay-as-you-go basis can add up (about $1.70/minute for voice calls, 50 cents to send text messages, 5 cents to receive them, and $10 to download one megabyte of data). To stay connected at a lower cost, sign up for an international service plan through your carrier. Most providers offer a simple bundle that includes calling, messaging, and data. Your normal plan may already include international coverage (T-Mobile's does).

Before your trip, call your provider or check online to confirm that your phone will work in Europe, and research your provider's international rates. Activate the plan a day or two before you leave, then remember to cancel it when your trip's over.

PRACTICALITIES

How to Dial

International Calls

Whether phoning from a US landline or mobile phone, or from a number in another European country, here's how to make an international call. I've used one of my recommended London hotels as an example (tel. 020/7730-8191).

Initial Zero: Drop the initial zero from international phone numbers—except when calling Italy.

Mobile Tip: If using a mobile phone, the "+" sign can replace the international access code (for a "+" sign, press and hold "0").

US/Canada to Europe

Dial 011 (US/Canada international access code), country code (44 for Britain), and phone number.

▶ To call the London hotel from home, dial 011-44-20/7730-8191.

Country to Country Within Europe

Dial 00 (Europe international access code), country code, and phone number.

▶ To call the London hotel from Spain, dial 00-44-20/7730-8191.

Europe to the US/Canada

Dial 00, country code (1 for US/Canada), and phone number.

▶ To call from Europe to my office in Edmonds, Washington, dial 00-1-425-771-8303.

Domestic Calls

To call within Britain (from one British landline or mobile phone to another), simply dial the phone number, including the initial 0 if there is one.

▶ To call the London hotel from Edinburgh, dial 020/7730-8191.

More Dialing Tips

British Phone Numbers: Numbers beginning with 071 through 079 are mobile numbers, which are more expensive to call than a landline. Avoid Britain's very expensive directory assistance (£0.50-4, plus a per-minute charge) by looking up numbers online instead. As a last resort, try 118-811

Use free Wi-Fi whenever possible. Unless you have an un-limited-data plan, you're best off saving most of your online tasks for Wi-Fi. You can access the Internet, send texts, and even make voice calls over Wi-Fi.

Most accommodations in Europe offer free Wi-Fi, but some—especially expensive hotels—charge a fee. Many cafés (including Starbucks and McDonald's) have free hotspots for customers; look for signs offering it and ask for the Wi-Fi password when you

(£0.50 flat rate from a landline; more from a mobile). To avoid further charges, dial the number yourself rather than being connected. Dial 155 for international operator assistance.

Toll and Toll-Free Calls: Numbers starting with 0800 and 0808 are toll-free. Those beginning with 084, 087, and 03 are generally inexpensive toll numbers (£0.15/minute from a landline, £0.20-40/minute from a mobile). Numbers beginning with 09 are pricey toll lines. If you have questions about a prefix, call 100 for free help. International rates apply to US toll-free numbers dialed from Britain—they're not free.

More Phoning Help: See www.howtocallabroad.com.

European Country Codes		Ireland & N. Ireland	353 / 44
Austria	43	Italy	39
Belgium	32	Latvia	371
Bosnia-Herzegovina	387	Montenegro	382
Croatia	385	Morocco	212
Czech Republic	420	Netherlands	31
Denmark	45	Norway	47
Estonia	372	Poland	48
Finland	358	Portugal	351
France	33	Russia	7
Germany	49	Slovakia	421
Gibraltar	350	Slovenia	386
Great Britain	44	Spain	34
Greece	30	Sweden	46
Hungary	36	Switzerland	41
Iceland	354	Turkey	90

PRACTICALITIES

buy something. You'll also often find Wi-Fi at TIs, city squares, major museums, public-transit hubs, airports, and aboard trains and buses. In Britain, another option is to sign up for Wi-Fi access through a company such as BT (one hour-£4, one day-£10, www.btwifi.co.uk) or The Cloud (free though sometimes slow, www.skywifi.cloud).

Minimize the use of your cellular network. Even with an international data plan, wait until you're on Wi-Fi to Skype, download apps, stream videos, or do other megabyte-greedy tasks. Using a navigation app such as Google Maps over a cellular network can take lots of data, so do this sparingly or use it offline.

Limit automatic updates. By default, your device constantly checks for a data connection and updates apps. It's smart to disable these features so your apps will only update when you're on Wi-Fi, and to change your device's email settings from "auto-retrieve" to "manual" (or from "push" to "fetch").

When you need to get online but can't find Wi-Fi, simply turn on your cellular network just long enough for the task at hand. When you're done, avoid further charges by manually turning off data roaming or cellular data (either works) in your device's Settings menu. Another way to make sure you're not accidentally using data roaming is to put your device in "airplane" mode (which also disables phone calls and texts), and then turn your Wi-Fi back on as needed.

It's also a good idea to keep track of your data usage. On your device's menu, look for "cellular data usage" or "mobile data" and reset the counter at the start of your trip.

Use Wi-Fi calling and messaging apps. Skype, Viber, Face-Time, and Google+ Hangouts are great for making free or low-cost voice and video calls over Wi-Fi. With an app installed on your phone, tablet, or laptop, you can log on to a Wi-Fi network and contact friends or family members who use the same service. If you buy credit in advance, with some of these services you can call any mobile phone or landline worldwide for just pennies per minute.

Many of these apps also allow you to send messages over Wi-Fi to any other person using that app. Be aware that some apps, such as Apple's iMessage, will use the cellular network if Wi-Fi isn't available: To avoid this possibility, turn off the "Send as SMS" feature.

USING A EUROPEAN SIM CARD

With a European SIM card, you get a European mobile number and access to cheaper rates than you'll get through your US carrier. This option works well for those who want to make a lot of voice calls or needing faster connection speeds than their US carrier provides. Fit the SIM card into a cheap phone you buy in Europe (about $40 from phone shops anywhere), or swap out the SIM card in an "unlocked" US phone (check with your carrier about unlocking it).

SIM cards are sold at mobile-phone shops, department-store electronics counters, some newsstands, and vending machines. Costing about $5-10, they usually include prepaid calling/messaging credit, with no contract and no commitment. Expect to pay $20-40 more for a SIM card with a gigabyte of data. If you travel

Tips on Internet Security

Make sure that your device is running the latest versions of its operating system, security software, and apps. Next, ensure that your device and key programs (like email) are password- or passcode-protected. On the road, use only secure, password-protected Wi-Fi hotspots. Ask the hotel or café staff for the specific name of their Wi-Fi network, and make sure you log on to that exact one.

If you must access your financial info online, use a banking app rather than accessing your account via a browser. A cellular connection is more secure than Wi-Fi. Avoid logging onto personal finance sites on a public computer.

Never share your credit-card number (or any other sensitive information) online unless you know that the site is secure. A secure site displays a little padlock icon, and the URL begins with *https* (instead of the usual *http*).

with this card to other countries in the European Union, there should be no extra roaming fees.

I like to buy SIM cards at a phone shop where there's a clerk to help explain the options. Certain brands—including Lebara and Lycamobile, both of which are available in multiple European countries—are reliable and especially economical. Ask the clerk to help you insert your SIM card, set it up, and show you how to use it. In some countries, you'll be required to register the SIM card with your passport as an antiterrorism measure (which may mean you can't use the phone for the first hour or two).

Find out how to check your credit balance. When you run out of credit, you can top it up at newsstands, tobacco shops, mobile-phone stores, or many other businesses (look for your SIM card's logo in the window), or online.

PUBLIC PHONES AND COMPUTERS

It's possible to travel in Europe without a mobile device. You can make calls from your hotel (or the increasingly rare public phone), and check email or browse websites using public computers.

Most **hotels** charge a fee for placing calls—ask for rates before you dial. You can use a prepaid international phone card (available at post offices, newsstands, street kiosks, tobacco shops, and train stations) to call out from your hotel. Dial the toll-free access number, enter the card's PIN code, then dial the number.

If there's no phone in your **B&B** room, and you have an important, brief call to make, politely ask your hosts if you can use their personal phone. Use a cheap international phone card with a toll-free access number, or offer to pay your host for the call.

Public pay phones are hard to find in Britain, and they're ex-

PRACTICALITIES

The English Accent

In the olden days, an English person's accent indicated his or her social standing. Eliza Doolittle had the right idea—elocution could make or break you. Wealthier families would send their kids to fancy private schools to learn proper pronunciation. But these days, in a sort of reverse snobbery that has gripped the nation, accents are back. Politicians, newscasters, and movie stars are favoring deep accents over the Queen's English. While it's hard for American ears to pick out the variations, most English people can determine where a person is from based on their accent...not just the region, but often the village, and even the part of town.

pensive. To use one, you'll pay with a major credit card (minimum charge-£1.20) or coins (minimum charge-£0.60).

Most hotels have **public computers** in their lobbies for guests to use; otherwise you may find them at Internet cafés or public libraries (ask your hotelier or the TI for the nearest location). On a European keyboard, use the "Alt Gr" key to the right of the space bar to insert the extra symbol that appears on some keys. If you can't locate a special character (such as @), simply copy it from a Web page and paste it into your email message.

MAIL

You can mail one package per day to yourself worth up to $200 duty-free from Europe to the US (mark it "personal purchases"). If you're sending a gift to someone, mark it "unsolicited gift." For details, visit www.cbp.gov, select "Travel," and search for "Know Before You Go."

The British postal service works fine, but for quick transatlantic delivery (in either direction), consider services such as DHL (www.dhl.com). For postcards, get stamps at the neighborhood post office, newsstands within fancy hotels, and some mini-marts and card shops.

Transportation

If your trip covers more of Britain than just London, you may need to take a long-distance train or bus, rent a car, or fly. Buses are an alternative to trains (and may be your only option for reaching some small British towns), but they are generally slower and less efficient. Renting a car is great for touring rural areas, such as the Cotswolds, northwest of London. I give some specifics on trains, buses, and flights here. For more detailed information on transportation throughout Europe, see www.ricksteves.com/transportation.

TRAINS

Regular tickets on Britain's great train system (15,000 departures from 2,400 stations daily) are the most expensive per mile in all of Europe. For the greatest savings, book online in advance and leave after rush hour (after 9:30).

Since Britain's railways have been privatized, it can be tricky to track down all your options; a single train route can be operated by multiple companies. However, one British website covers all train lines (www.nationalrail.co.uk), and another covers all bus and train routes (www.traveline.org.uk for information, not ticket sales). Another good resource, which also has schedules for trains throughout Europe, is German Rail's timetable (www.bahn.com).

As with airline tickets, British train tickets can come at many different prices for the same journey. A clerk at any station can figure out the cheapest fare for your trip.

Buying Train Tickets in Advance: To book ahead, go in person to any station, book online at www.nationalrail.co.uk, or call 0345-748-4950 (from the US, dial 011-44-20-7278-5240, phone answered 24 hours) to find out the schedule and best fare for your journey; you'll then be referred to the appropriate vendor—depending on the particular rail company—to book your ticket. If you order online, be sure you know what you want; it's tough to reach a person who can change your online reservation. You'll pick up your ticket at the station, or you may be able to print it at home. (BritRail pass holders, however, cannot use the Web to make reservations.)

A company called **Megabus** (through their subsidiary Mega-train) sells some discounted train tickets well in advance on a few specific routes, though their focus is mainly on selling bus tickets (info tel. 0871-266-3333, www.megatrain.com).

Buying Train Tickets as You Travel: If you'd rather have the flexibility of booking tickets as you go, you can save a few pounds by buying a round-trip ticket, called a "return ticket" (a same-day round-trip, called a "day return," is particularly cheap); buying before 18:00 the day before you depart; traveling after the morning rush hour (this usually means after 9:30 Mon-Fri); and going standard class instead of first class. Preview your options at www.nationalrail.co.uk.

Rail Passes: For train travel outside London, consider getting a BritRail pass. Choose between England-only BritRail passes and those that cover Scotland and Wales as well. More BritRail options include "London Plus" passes (good for travel in most of southeast England but not in London itself), and South West passes (good for the Cotswolds, Bath, Dorset, Devon, Cornwall, plus part of South Wales). These passes are sold outside of Europe only. For specifics, see www.ricksteves.com/rail.

Public Transportation Routes in Britain

Legend:
- — · — · Rail
- ——— Eurostar
- - - - Bus
- (8H) Ferry with crossing time

Orkney Islands

Lewis

Scrabster · Gill · John o' Groats
Thurso

Skye
Portree · Inverness · Elgin
· Culloden
Kyle · Loch · Aviemore
Mallaig · Ness · Aberdeen
Fort William

SCOTLAND
Pitlochry
Mull · Perth · Dundee
Iona · Oban · Leuchars
· Stirling · St. Andrews
Edinburgh

Berwick
Glasgow · Holy Island

To Amsterdam (15H)

Cairnryan · Hexham
Larne (2H) · Newcastle
(2-3H) Stranraer · Carlisle · Durham
Belfast · Keswick · Penrith · Danby · Whitby
NORTHERN · Windermere · North York · Scarborough
IRELAND · Isle · Moors
Irish · of Man · ENGLAND · York
Sea · Blackpool · Leeds · Hull
(7H) · Preston · To Zeebrugge (10H)
Dublin (2-3H) Holyhead · Conwy · Liverpool · Grimsby
· Bangor · Chester · Manchester
REPUBLIC · Caernarfon · Betws- · Stoke · Lincoln
OF · Bed · y-Coed · Derby · Peterborough
IRELAND · Pwllheli · Blaenau · Telford · King's Lynn
· Harlech · Ffest. · Wolv. · Birmingham · Ely · Norwich
· Aberystwyth · Ironbridge · Coventry · Cambridge
Rosslare (3.5H) · Gorge · Warwick · Harwich
· WALES · Stratford
Fishguard · Cheltenham · Moreton · To Hoek van Holland (6H)
· Carmarthen · Stow · Oxford · London · Ebbs- · Canterbury
· Swansea · Newport · Reading · fleet · Dover
Cardiff · Bath · STONE · Windsor · Woking · Ashford (1.5H)
· Bristol · HENGE · Salisbury · Brighton · Calais
· Wells · West- · EUROSTAR
Atlantic · Glastonbury · bury · Southampton · Newhaven (2.5H)
Ocean · Exeter · Portsmouth · To Dieppe (4H)
· Dartmoor · To Paris & Brussels
Truro · Plymouth · To Caen
St. Ives · English Channel · (Ouistreham) (6H)
Penzance · Falmouth · To Roscoff (6H) · To St-Malo (11H) · FRANCE

North Sea

50 Kilometers
50 Miles

N

BUSES

Most domestic buses are operated by **National Express** (tel. 0871-781-8181, www.nationalexpress.com); their international departures are called **Eurolines** (www.eurolines.co.uk).

A smaller company called **Megabus** undersells National Express with deeply discounted promotional fares—the further ahead you buy, the less you pay (some trips for just £1.50, toll tel. 0900-160-0900, www.megabus.com). While Megabus can be much cheaper than National Express, they tend to be slower than their competitor and their routes mainly connect cities, not smaller towns. They also sell discounted train tickets on selected routes.

Try to avoid bus travel on Friday and Sunday evenings, when weekend travelers are more likely to make buses sell out.

To ensure getting a ticket—and to save money with special promotions—book your ticket in advance online or over the phone. The cheapest pre-purchased tickets can usually be changed (for a £5 fee), but not refunded. Check if the ticket is only "amendable" or also "refundable" when you buy. If you have a mobile phone, you can order online and have a "text ticket" sent right to your phone for a small fee.

TAXIS AND UBER

Most British taxis are reliable and cheap. In many cities, couples can travel short distances by cab for little more than two bus or subway tickets. Taxis can be your best option for getting to the airport for an early morning flight or to connect two far-flung destinations. Ride-booking services like Uber usually work in Europe just like they do in the US: You request a car on your mobile device and the fare is automatically charged to your credit card. London's Uber is facing a legal challenge; check ahead to confirm it is operating.

FLIGHTS

The best comparison search engine for both international and intra-European flights is Kayak.com. An alternative is Google Flights, which has an easy-to-use system to track prices. For inexpensive flights within Europe, try Skyscanner.com.

Flying to Europe: Start looking for international flights about four to six months before your trip, especially for peak-season travel. Off-season tickets can usually be purchased a month or so in advance. Depending on your itinerary, it can be efficient to fly into one city and out of another. If your flight requires a connection in Europe, see my hints on navigating Europe's top hub airports at www.ricksteves.com/hub-airports.

Flying Within Europe: London is the hub for many cheap, no-frills airlines, which affordably connect the city with other destinations in the British Isles and throughout Europe. If you're considering a train ride that's more than five hours long, a flight may save you both time and money. When comparing your options, factor in the time it takes to get to the airport and how early you'll need to arrive to check in.

Well-known cheapo airlines include EasyJet and Ryanair. **EasyJet** flies from Gatwick, Luton, Stansted, and Southend while **Ryanair** flies mostly from Stansted Airport, as well as Gatwick and Luton. Other airlines to consider include **CityJet** (based at London City Airport, www.cityjet.com), **Monarch** (may cease operations in 2018, www.monarch.co.uk), **Thomson** (similar to Monarch, www.thomsonfly.com), **Flybe** (www.flybe.com), and **Brussels Airlines** (with frequent connections from Heathrow to its Brussels hub, www.brusselsairlines.com).

But be aware of the potential drawbacks of flying with a discount airline: nonrefundable and nonchangeable tickets, minimal or nonexistent customer service, pricey and time-consuming treks to secondary airports, and stingy baggage allowances with steep overage fees. If you're traveling with lots of luggage, a cheap flight can quickly become a bad deal. To avoid unpleasant surprises, read the small print before you book. These days you can also fly within Europe on major airlines affordably—and without all the aggressive restrictions—for around $100 a flight.

Flying to the US and Canada: Because security is extra tight for flights to the US, be sure to give yourself plenty of time at the airport. It's also important to charge your electronic devices before you board because security checks may require you to turn them on (see www.tsa.gov for the latest rules).

Resources from Rick Steves

Begin your trip at www.ricksteves.com: My mobile-friendly **website** is *the* place to explore Europe. You'll find thousands of fun articles, videos, photos, and radio interviews organized by country; a wealth of money-saving tips for planning your dream trip; monthly travel news dispatches; a practical video library of my travel talks; my travel blog; and my latest guidebook updates (www.ricksteves. com/update).

Our **Travel Forum** is an immense yet well-groomed collection of message boards where our travel-savvy community answers questions and shares their personal travel experiences—and our well-traveled staff chimes in when they can be helpful (www. ricksteves.com/forums).

Our **online Travel Store** offers travel bags and accessories that I've designed specifically to help you travel smarter and lighter. These include my popular carry-on bags (which I live out of four months a year), money belts, totes, toiletries kits, adapters, other accessories, and a wide selection of guidebooks and planning maps (www.ricksteves.com/shop).

Choosing the right **rail pass** for your trip—amid hundreds of options—can drive you nutty. Our website will help you find the perfect fit for your itinerary and your budget: We offer easy, one-stop shopping for rail passes, seat reservations, and point-to-point tickets (www.ricksteves.com/rail).

Small Group Tours: Want to travel with greater efficiency and less stress? We offer more than 40 itineraries and have over 900 departures annually reaching the best destinations in this book... and beyond. Three of our tours include London: our seven-day in-depth London city tour, our 14-day England tour, and our 13-day Family Europe: London to Florence tour. You'll enjoy great guides, a fun bunch of travel partners (with small groups of 24 to 28 travelers), and plenty of room to spread out in a big, comfy bus when touring between towns. You'll find European adventures to fit every vacation length. For all the details, and to get our Tour Catalog, visit www.ricksteves.com or call us at 425/608-4217.

Books: *Rick Steves London 2018* is one of many books in my series on European travel, which includes country and regional guidebooks (including Great Britain, Scotland, and England), city guidebooks, Snapshot guidebooks (excerpted chapters from my country guides), Pocket guidebooks (full-color little books on big cities, including London), "Best Of" guidebooks (condensed country guides in a full-color, easy-to-scan format), and my budget-travel skills handbook, *Rick Steves Europe Through the Back Door*. Most of my titles are available as ebooks.

My phrase books—for Italian, French, German, Spanish, and Portuguese—are practical and budget-oriented. My other books include *Europe 101* (a crash course on art and history designed for travelers); *Mediterranean Cruise Ports* and *Northern European Cruise Ports* (how to make the most of your time in port); and *Travel as a Political Act* (a travelogue sprinkled with tips for bringing home a global perspective). A more complete list of my titles appears near the end of this book.

TV Shows: My public television series, *Rick Steves' Europe*, covers Europe from top to bottom with over 100 half-hour episodes, and we're working on new shows every year. We have eight episodes on England—that's four hours of vivid video coverage of one of my favorite countries. To watch full episodes online for free, see www.ricksteves.com/tv.

Travel Talks on Video: You can raise your travel I.Q. with video versions of our popular classes (including talks on travel skills, packing smart, cruising, tech for travelers, European art for travelers, travel as a political act, and individual talks covering most European countries). See www.ricksteves.com/travel-talks.

Radio: My weekly public radio show, *Travel with Rick Steves*, features interviews with travel experts from around the world. It airs on 400 public radio stations across the US, and you can also listen to it as a podcast on iTunes, iHeartRadio, Stitcher, Tune In, and other platforms. A complete archive of programs (over 400 in all) is available at www.soundcloud.com/rick-steves.

Audio Tours on My Free App: I've also produced dozens of free, self-guided audio tours of the top sights in Europe, including sights in London. My audio tours and other audio content are available for free through my **Rick Steves Audio Europe app,** an extensive on-line library organized into handy geographic playlists. For more on my app, see page 8.

APPENDIX

Useful Contacts

Emergency Needs

Police, Fire, and Ambulance: 112 (Europe-wide in English)

Police and Ambulance: Tel. 999

US Consulate and Embassy: Tel. 020/7499-9000 (all services), no walk-in passport services; for emergency two-day passport service, schedule an appointment or fill out the online Emergency Passport Contact Form; 24 Grosvenor Square, Tube: Bond Street, https://uk.usembassy.gov/

Canadian High Commission: Tel. 020/7004-6000, passport services available Mon-Fri 9:30-12:30, Canada House, Trafalgar Square, Tube: Charing Cross, www.unitedkingdom.gc.ca

Holidays and Festivals

This list includes selected festivals in London, major events in Windsor and Cambridge, plus national holidays observed throughout Great Britain. Many sights and banks close on national holidays—keep this in mind when planning your itinerary. Before planning a trip around a festival, verify the dates with the festival website, London TI sites (www.visitlondon.com and www.

visitbritain.com), or my "Upcoming Holidays and Festivals in England" web page (www.ricksteves.com/europe/england/festivals).

In London, hotels get booked up on major holidays—New Year's Day, Easter weekend, Christmas, and Boxing Day—and on Fridays and Saturdays year-round. Some hotels require you to book the full three-day weekend around Bank Holiday Mondays.

Jan 1	New Year's Day
Feb 16-20	London Fashion Week (www.londonfashionweek.co.uk)
March 30	Good Friday
April 1-2	Easter Sunday and Monday
May 1	Early May Bank Holiday (first Monday in May)
May 28	Spring Bank Holiday (last Monday in May)
Late May	Chelsea Flower Show, London (book tickets ahead at www.rhs.org.uk/chelsea)
June 17	Trooping the Colour, London (military bands and pageantry, Queen's birthday parade; www.trooping-the-colour.co.uk)
Late June	Royal Ascot Horse Race, Ascot (near Windsor; www.ascot.co.uk)
Late June-early July	Wimbledon Tennis Championship, London (www.wimbledon.com)
Late July-early Aug	Cambridge Folk Festival, Cambridge (buy tickets early at www.cambridgefolkfestival.co.uk)
Late Aug	Notting Hill Carnival, London (costumes, Caribbean music, www.thelondonnottinghillcarnival.com)
Aug 27	Summer Bank Holiday (last Monday in Aug)
Sept 14-18	London Fashion Week (www.londonfashionweek.co.uk)
Nov 5	Bonfire Night (bonfires, fireworks, effigy burning of 1605 traitor Guy Fawkes)
Nov 12	Remembrance Sunday (second Sunday in November, royals lay wreaths at Cenotaph for WWI dead)
Mid-Nov	Lord Mayor's Show, London (second Saturday in November; huge parade in The City with fireworks, https://lordmayorsshow.london)
Dec 24-26	Christmas holidays (many sights close; limited or no public transport)

Books and Films

To learn more about London past and present, check out a few of these books and films. For kids' recommendations, see page 425.

Nonfiction

84, Charing Cross Road (Helene Hanff, 1970). Correspondence between a proper London bookseller and an outspoken New York writer turns into a trans-Atlantic friendship (also a 1987 movie with Anthony Hopkins and Anne Bancroft). In the sequel, *The Duchess of Bloomsbury Street*, the writer travels to London.

Elizabeth's London (Liza Picard, 2005). The author re-creates 16th-century life in the era of England's first great queen.

Fever Pitch (Nick Hornby, 1992). Hornby's memoir illuminates the British obsession with soccer.

A History of London (Stephen Inwood, 1998). Two thousand years of city history is laid out over 1,000 pages.

The Last Lion (William Manchester, final book completed by Paul Reid; 1983, 1988, and 2012). This superb three-volume biography recounts the amazing life of Winston Churchill from 1874 to 1965.

Letters from London (Julian Barnes, 1995). The *New Yorker*'s former London correspondent captures life in the city in the early 1990s.

London: The Biography (Peter Ackroyd, 2001). The author uses an imaginative biographical approach to tell London's story.

Longitude (Dava Sobel, 1995). A London clockmaker solves the problem of keeping time aboard a ship—a timely read for visitors to Greenwich.

Notes from a Small Island (Bill Bryson, 1995). In this irreverent and delightful memoir, US expat Bryson writes about his travels through Britain—his home for two decades.

St Pancras Station (Simon Bradley, 2007). Bradley presents a treasure trove of history about London's iconic gateway to Europe.

A Traveller's History of England (Christopher Daniell, revised 2005). A British archaeologist and historian provides a comprehensive yet succinct overview of English history.

With Wings Like Eagles (Michael Korda, 2009). An English-born writer gives a historical analysis of Britain's pivotal WWII air battles versus the German Luftwaffe.

Fiction

For the classics of British fiction, read anything—and everything—by Charles Dickens, Jane Austen, and the Brontës. Some favorites that feature London include *Persuasion,* the beloved Austen book partially set in Bath, and Charles Dickens' tale of a workhouse urchin, *Oliver Twist*. Here are some other good reads:

Brick Lane (Monica Ali, 2003). A Bangladeshi woman in an arranged marriage to an older man raises her family—and starts an affair with a young radical—in contemporary London (also a 2007 film).

Bridget Jones's Diary (Helen Fielding, 1996). A year in the life of a single 30-something woman in London is humorously chronicled in diary form (also a motion picture).

The Buddha of Suburbia (Hanif Kureishi, 1990). The son of a self-proclaimed suburban guru gets swept up in the fast lane of 1970s London.

Confessions of a Shopaholic (Sophie Kinsella, 2001). A London woman lives beyond her means in this funny tale of modern English life.

The Great Stink (Clare Clark, 2005). A Crimean War veteran seeks refuge working in the London sewer system, but is sucked into a murder mystery.

High Fidelity (Nick Hornby, 1995). This humorous novel traces the romantic misadventures and musical musings of a 30-something record-store owner. Another good read is Hornby's 1998 coming-of-age story, *About a Boy*. (Both books were also made into films.)

In the Presence of the Enemy (Elizabeth George, 1996). London's movers and shakers commit sins and scandals in this detective story.

The Jupiter Myth (Lindsey Davis, 2002). In A.D. 75, an investigator from Rome probes a murder in what was then known as Londinium.

London (Edward Rutherfurd, 1997). This big and sprawling historical novel begins in ancient times and continues through to the 20th century.

Mapp and Lucia (E. F. Benson, 1931). A rural village in the 1930s becomes a social battlefield. In *Lucia in London* (1927), the protagonist attempts social climbing in the big city.

The Paying Guests (Sarah Waters, 2014). This realistic and suspenseful tale of love, obsession, and murder plays out amid the shifting culture of post-WWII upper-class London.

Pygmalion (George Bernard Shaw, 1913). This stage play, on which the film *My Fair Lady* is based, tells the story of a young Cockney girl groomed for high society.

Rumpole of the Bailey (Sir John Mortimer, 1978). Mortimer's popular detective story about an aging London barrister spawned a series of books and TV shows.

Saturday (Ian McEwan, 2005). The protagonist endures a series of strange events in London during a day of protest over the invasion of Iraq.

SS-GB (Len Deighton, 1979). In Nazi-occupied Great Britain, a Scotland Yard detective finds there's more to a murder than meets the eye.

A Study in Scarlet (Sir Arthur Conan Doyle, 1888). This mystery novel introduced the world to detective Sherlock Holmes and his trusty sidekick, Dr. Watson.

Thank You, Jeeves (P. G. Wodehouse, 1934). The author's first full-length novel is about the competent valet to a wealthy and foolish Londoner (also many short stories and sequels).

White Teeth (Zadie Smith, 2000). The postwar lives of two army buddies, a native Englishman and a Bengali Muslim, are chronicled in this acclaimed novel.

Film and TV

Alfie (1966). In 1960s London, a womanizer (Michael Caine) eventually must face up to his boorish behavior (also a 2004 remake with Jude Law). Other "swinging London" films include *Blow-up* (1966) and *Georgy Girl* (1966).

Battle of Britain (1969). An all-star cast and marvelous aerial combat scenes tell the story of Britain's "finest hour" of World War II.

Blackadder (1983-1989). This wickedly funny BBC sitcom starring Rowan Atkinson skewers various periods of English history over the course of four series (also several TV specials).

Call the Midwife (2012-). London's poor East End comes to gritty, poignant life in this BBC drama tracing the lives of a team of nurse midwives in the late 1950s and early 1960s.

The Crown (2016-). Claire Foy stars as Elizabeth II in the Netflix biographical drama exploring the life of England's longest-reigning queen.

The Elephant Man (1980). A severely disfigured man reveals his sensitive soul in this stark portrayal of Victorian London.

GoldenEye (1995). This James Bond film features the first look at the iconic MI6 headquarters, located in the center of London.

A Hard Day's Night (1964). The Beatles star in their debut film, a comedy depicting several days in the life of the band.

Hope and Glory (1987). John Boorman directed this semi-autobiographical story of a boy growing up during World War II and the London Blitz.

The King's Speech (2010). Colin Firth stars as the stuttering King George VI on the eve of World War II.

My Beautiful Laundrette (1985). This gritty, compelling movie tells the story of two gay men in urban London.

APPENDIX

My Fair Lady (1964). Audrey Hepburn stars as a poor, Cockney flower seller who is transformed into a lady of high society by an arrogant professor.

Notting Hill (1999). Hugh Grant and Julia Roberts star in this romantic comedy set in the London neighborhood of...you guessed it.

The Queen (2006). Helen Mirren expertly channels Elizabeth II in the days after Princess Diana's death. Its prequel, *The Deal* (2003), probes the relationship between Tony Blair and Gordon Brown.

Sammy and Rosie Get Laid (1987). An unconventional middle-class couple's promiscuous adventures expose racial tensions in multiethnic London.

Shakespeare in Love (1999). Tudor-era London comes to life in this clever, romantic film set in the original Globe Theatre.

Sherlock (2010-). Holmes (Benedict Cumberbatch) and Watson (Martin Freeman) are excellent in this BBC-TV update of the detective's story, set in present-day London.

Tinker, Tailor, Soldier, Spy (2011). There's a Soviet mole inside Britain's MI6 and retired agent George Smiley is summoned to ferret him out in this adaptation of John le Carré's 1974 espionage thriller.

To Sir, with Love (1967). Sidney Poitier grapples with social and racial issues in an East End inner-city school.

Upstairs, Downstairs (1971-1975). This TV series follows an aristocratic family and their servants in their new home at 165 Eaton Place.

Waterloo Bridge (1940). This Academy Award-nominated romantic drama recalls the lost love between a ballerina (Vivien Leigh) and a WWI army officer.

Victoria (2017-). PBS Masterpiece Theatre drama series chronicles the rise and reign of Queen Victoria (Jenna Coleman).

Conversions and Climate

NUMBERS AND STUMBLERS

- Some British people write a few of their numbers differently than we do: 1 = 1, 4 = 4, 7 = 7.
- In Europe, dates appear as day/month/year, so Christmas 2019 is 25/12/19.
- What Americans call the second floor of a building is the first floor in Britain.
- On escalators and moving sidewalks, Brits keep the left "lane" open for passing. Keep to the right.

- To avoid the British version of giving someone "the finger," don't hold up the first two fingers of your hand with your palm facing you. (It looks like a reversed victory sign.)
- And please...don't call your waist pack a "fanny pack" (see the British-Yankee Vocabulary list at the end of this appendix).

UNITS OF MEASUREMENT

Britain uses the metric system for nearly everything, but imperial units are still used in a few situations.

Metric Conversions

Britain uses the metric system for nearly everything. Weight and volume are typically calculated in metric: A kilogram is 2.2 pounds, and one liter is about a quart (almost four to a gallon). Temperatures are generally given in Celsius, although some newspapers also list them in Fahrenheit.

1 foot = 0.3 meter	1 square yard = 0.8 square meter
1 yard = 0.9 meter	1 square mile = 2.6 square kilometers
1 mile = 1.6 kilometers	1 ounce = 28 grams
1 centimeter = 0.4 inch	1 quart = 0.95 liter
1 meter = 39.4 inches	1 kilogram = 2.2 pounds
1 kilometer = 0.62 mile	32°F = 0°C

Imperial Weights and Measures

Driving distances and speed limits are measured in miles. Beer is sold as pints (though milk can be measured in pints or liters), and a person's weight is measured in stone (a 168-pound person weighs 12 stone).

1 stone = 14 pounds
1 British pint = 1.2 US pints
1 imperial gallon = 1.2 US gallons or about 4.5 liters

CLOTHING SIZES

When shopping for clothing, use these US-to-UK comparisons as general guidelines (but note that no conversion is perfect).

Women: For pants and dresses, add 4 (US 10 = UK 14). For blouses and sweaters, add 2. For shoes, subtract 2½ (US size 8 = UK size 5½)

Men: For clothing, US and UK sizes are the same. For shoes, subtract about ½ (US size 9 = UK size 8½)

APPENDIX

LONDON'S CLIMATE

First line, average daily high; second line, average daily low; third line, average days without rain. For more detailed weather statistics for destinations throughout Britain (as well as the rest of the world), check www.wunderground.com.

J	F	M	A	M	J	J	A	S	O	N	D
43°	44°	50°	56°	62°	69°	71°	71°	65°	58°	50°	45°
36°	36°	38°	42°	47°	53°	56°	56°	52°	46°	42°	38°
16	15	20	18	19	19	19	20	17	18	15	16

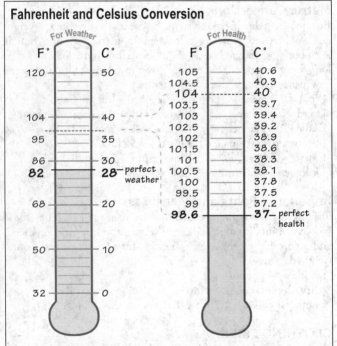

Fahrenheit and Celsius Conversion

Europe takes its temperature using the Celsius scale, while we opt for Fahrenheit. For a rough conversion from Celsius to Fahrenheit, double the number and add 30. For weather, remember that 28°C is 82°F—perfect. For health, 37°C is just right. At a launderette, 30°C is cold, 40°C is warm (usually the default setting), 60°C is hot, and 95°C is boiling. Your air-conditioner should be set at about 20°C.

Packing Checklist

Whether you're traveling for five days or five weeks, you won't need more than this. Pack light to enjoy the sweet freedom of true mobility.

Clothing

- ❏ 5 shirts: long- & short-sleeve
- ❏ 2 pairs pants (or skirts/capris)
- ❏ 1 pair shorts
- ❏ 5 pairs underwear & socks
- ❏ 1 pair walking shoes
- ❏ Sweater or warm layer
- ❏ Rainproof jacket with hood
- ❏ Tie, scarf, belt, and/or hat
- ❏ Swimsuit
- ❏ Sleepwear/loungewear

Money

- ❏ Debit card(s)
- ❏ Credit card(s)
- ❏ Hard cash ($100-200 in US dollars)
- ❏ Money belt

Documents

- ❏ Passport
- ❏ Tickets & confirmations: flights, hotels, trains, rail pass, car rental, sight entries
- ❏ Driver's license
- ❏ Student ID, hostel card, etc.
- ❏ Photocopies of important documents
- ❏ Insurance details
- ❏ Guidebooks & maps
- ❏ Notepad & pen
- ❏ Journal

Toiletries Kit

- ❏ Basics: soap, shampoo, toothbrush, toothpaste, floss, deodorant, sunscreen, brush/comb, etc.
- ❏ Medicines & vitamins
- ❏ First-aid kit
- ❏ Glasses/contacts/sunglasses
- ❏ Sewing kit
- ❏ Packet of tissues (for WC)
- ❏ Earplugs

Electronics

- ❏ Mobile phone
- ❏ Camera & related gear
- ❏ Tablet/ebook reader/media player
- ❏ Laptop & flash drive
- ❏ Headphones
- ❏ Chargers & batteries
- ❏ Smartphone car charger & mount (or GPS device)
- ❏ Plug adapters

Miscellaneous

- ❏ Daypack
- ❏ Sealable plastic baggies
- ❏ Laundry supplies: soap, laundry bag, clothesline, spot remover
- ❏ Small umbrella
- ❏ Travel alarm/watch

Optional Extras

- ❏ Second pair of shoes (flip-flops, sandals, tennis shoes, boots)
- ❏ Travel hairdryer
- ❏ Picnic supplies
- ❏ Water bottle
- ❏ Fold-up tote bag
- ❏ Small flashlight
- ❏ Mini binoculars
- ❏ Small towel or washcloth
- ❏ Inflatable pillow/neck rest
- ❏ Tiny lock
- ❏ Address list (to mail postcards)
- ❏ Extra passport photos

BRITISH-YANKEE VOCABULARY

For a longer list, plus a dry-witted primer on British culture, see *The Septic's Companion* (Chris Rae). Note that instead of asking, "Can I help you?" many Brits offer a more casual, "You alright?" or "You OK there?"

advert: advertisement

afters: dessert

anticlockwise: counterclockwise

Antipodean: An Australian or New Zealander

aubergine: eggplant

banger: sausage

bangers and mash: sausages and mashed potatoes

bank holiday: legal holiday

bap: small roll

bespoke: custom-made

billion: a thousand of our billions (a million million)

biro: ballpoint pen

biscuit: cookie

black pudding: sausage made from dried blood

bloody: damn

blow off: fart

bobby: policeman ("the Bill" is more common)

Bob's your uncle: there you go (with a shrug), naturally

boffin: nerd, geek

bollocks: testicles (used in many colorful expressions)

bolshy: argumentative

bomb: success or failure

bonnet: car hood

booking: reservation

boot: car trunk

braces: suspenders

bridle way: path for walkers, bikers, and horse riders

brilliant: cool

brolly: umbrella

bubble and squeak: cabbage and potatoes fried together

builder: construction worker

bum: butt

candy floss: cotton candy

caravan: trailer

car boot sale: temporary flea market, often for charity

car park: parking lot

cashpoint: ATM

casualty: emergency room

cat's eyes: road reflectors

ceilidh (KAY-lee): informal evening of song and folk fun (Scottish and Irish)

cheap and cheerful: budget but adequate

cheap and nasty: cheap and bad quality

cheers: good-bye or thanks; also a toast

chemist: pharmacist

chicory: endive

chippy: fish-and-chip shop; carpenter (see also "joiner")

chips: French fries

chock-a-block: jam-packed

chuffed: pleased

cider: alcoholic apple cider

clearway: road where you can't stop

coach: long-distance bus

concession: discounted admission

concs (pronounced "conks"): short for "concession"

cos: romaine lettuce

cot: baby crib

cotton buds: Q-tips

council estate: public housing

courgette: zucchini

craic (pronounced "crack"): fun, good conversation

(Irish and spreading to England)

crisps: potato chips

cuppa: cup of tea

curry: any Indian meal flavored with curry, popular with Brits

dear: expensive

dicey: iffy, risky

digestives: round graham cookies

dinner: lunch or dinner

diversion: detour

donkey's years: ages, a long time

draughts: checkers

draw: marijuana

dual carriageway: divided highway (four lanes)

dummy: pacifier

elevenses: coffee-and-biscuits break before lunch

elvers: baby eels

engaged tone: busy signal

estate car: station wagon

face flannel: washcloth

faff: bumble (about)

fag: cigarette

fagged: exhausted

faggot: meatball

fairy cake: cupcake

fancy: to like, to be attracted to (a person)

fanny: vagina

fell: hill or high plain (Lake District)

first floor: second floor

fixture: sports schedule

fizzy drink: pop or soda

flat: apartment

flutter: a bet

football: soccer

force: waterfall (Lake District)

fortnight: two weeks

fringe: hair bangs

Frogs: French people

fruit machine: slot machine

full Monty: whole shebang; everything

gallery: balcony

gammon: ham

gangway: aisle

gaol: jail (same pronunciation)

gateau (or gateaux): cake

gear lever: stick shift

geezer: dude (slang for young man)

ginger-haired: redhead

give way: yield

glen: narrow valley (Scotland)

goods wagon: freight truck

green fingers: green thumbs

grizzle: grumble, fuss (especially by a baby)

grotty: unpleasant, lousy

gutted: deeply disappointed

half eight: 8:30 (not 7:30)

hash sign: pound sign, as on a phone

heath: open treeless land

hen night: bachelorette party

High Street: Main Street (in a generic sense)

hire: rent, as in a car or bike

hire car: rental car

hob: stove burner

holiday: vacation

homely: homey or cozy

hoover: vacuum cleaner

ice lolly: popsicle

interval: intermission

ironmonger: hardware store

ish: more or less

jacket potato: baked potato

jelly: Jell-O

Joe Bloggs: John Q. Public

joiner: carpenter (see also "chippy")

jumble sale: rummage sale

jumper: sweater

just a tick: just a second

kipper: smoked herring

knackered: exhausted (Cockney: cream crackered)

knickers: ladies' panties

knocking shop: brothel

knock up: wake up or visit (old-fashioned)

ladybird: ladybug

lady fingers: flat, spongy cookie

lady's finger: okra

lager: light, fizzy beer

left luggage: baggage check

lemon squash: lemonade, not fizzy

lemonade: lemon-lime pop, fizzy

let: rent, as in property

licenced: restaurant authorized to sell alcohol

lie-in, having a: sleeping in late

lift: elevator

listed: protected historic building

loo: toilet or bathroom

lorry: truck

mac: mackintosh raincoat

main: entrée

mains: electrical outlet

mangetout: snow peas

Marmite: yeast paste, spread on sandwiches

marrow: summer squash

mate: buddy (boy or girl)

mean: stingy

mental: wild, memorable

mews: former stables converted to two-story rowhouses (London)

mince: hamburger meat

mobile: cell phone

moggie: cat

M.O.T.: mandatory annual car safety certificate

motorway: freeway

naff: dorky

nappy: diaper

natter: talk on and on

neep: Scottish for turnip

newsagent: corner store

nought: zero

noughts & crosses: tic-tac-toe

O.A.P.: old-age pensioner, retiree

off-licence: liquor store

on offer: for sale

one-off: unique; one-time event

panto, pantomime: fairy-tale play performed at Christmas (silly but fun)

pants: (noun) underwear, briefs; (adj.) terrible, ridiculous

paracetamol: acetaminophen, Tylenol

pasty (PASS-tee): crusted savory (usually meat) pie from Cornwall

pavement: sidewalk

people mover: minivan

pear-shaped: messed up, gone wrong

pensioner: senior citizen, retiree

petrol: gas

pillar box: mailbox

pissed (rude), paralytic, bevvied, wellied, popped up, merry, trollied, ratted, rat-arsed, pissed as a newt: drunk

pitch: playing field

plaster: Band-Aid

pram: baby carriage

publican: pub manager (old-fashioned)

public school: private "prep" school (e.g., Eton)

pudding: dessert in general

pull, to be on the: looking for love

punter: customer, especially in gambling

pushchair: stroller

put a sock in it: shut up

queue: line

queue up: line up

quid: a pound (money)

randy: horny

rasher: slice of bacon

redundant, made: laid off

Remembrance Day: Veterans' Day

return ticket: round-trip

revising; doing revisions: studying for exams

ring up: call (telephone)

rocket: arugula

roundabout: traffic circle

rubber: eraser

rubbish: bad

salad cream: mayo, mustard, and vinegar dressing

Sat Nav: GPS device

sausage roll: sausage wrapped in a flaky pastry

Scotch egg: hard-boiled egg wrapped in sausage meat

scrumpy: type of hard cider

self-catering: accommodation with kitchen

Sellotape: Scotch tape

services: freeway rest area

serviette: napkin

settee: couch

shag: intercourse (cruder than in the US)

shandy: lager and 7-Up

silencer: car muffler

single ticket: one-way ticket

skip: dumpster

sleeping policeman: speed bumps

smalls: underwear

snogging: kissing, making out

sod: mildly offensive insult

sod it, sod off: screw it, screw off

soda: soda water (not pop)

solicitor: lawyer (a.k.a. barrister)

spanner: wrench

sparkie: electrician

spend a penny: urinate

stag night: bachelor party

starkers: buck naked

starters: appetizers

state school: public school

sticking plaster: Band-Aid

sticky tape: Scotch tape

stone: 14 pounds (measurement of weight)

stroppy: bad-tempered

subway: underground walkway

suet: fat from animal rendering (sometimes used in cooking)

sultanas: golden raisins

surgical spirit: rubbing alcohol

suspenders: garters

suss out: figure out

swede: rutabaga

ta: thank you

take the mickey: tease

tatty: worn out or tacky

taxi rank: taxi stand

telly: TV

tenement: stone apartment house (not necessarily a slum)

tenner: £10 bill

theatre: live stage

tick: a check mark

tight as a fish's bum: cheapskate (watertight)

tights: panty hose

tin: can

tip: public dump

tipper lorry: dump truck

top hole: first rate

top up: refill a drink

torch: flashlight

towel, press-on: panty liner
towpath: path along a river
trainers: sneakers
Tube: subway
twee: quaint, cute
twitcher: bird watcher
Underground: subway
verge: grassy edge of road
verger: church official
way out: exit
wee (adj.): small (Scottish)

wee (verb): urinate
Wellingtons, wellies: rubber boots
whacked: exhausted
whinge (rhymes with hinge): whine
wind up: tease, irritate
witter on: gab and gab
yob: hooligan
zebra crossing: crosswalk
zed: the letter Z

INDEX

MAP INDEX

Explore Europe

At ricksteves.com you can browse through thousands of articles, videos, photos and radio interviews, plus find a wealth of money-saving travel tips for planning your dream trip. And with our mobile-friendly website, you can easily access all this great travel information anywhere you go.

TV Shows

Preview the places you'll visit by watching entire half-hour episodes of Rick Steves' Europe (choose from all 100 shows) on-demand, for free.

your travel dreams into affordable reality

Radio Interviews

Enjoy ready access to Rick's vast library of radio interviews covering travel

tips and cultural insights that relate specifically to your Europe travel plans.

Travel Forums

Learn, ask, share! Our online community of savvy travelers is a great resource

for first-time travelers to Europe, as well as seasoned pros. You'll find forums on each country, plus travel tips and restaurant/hotel reviews. You can even ask one of our well-traveled staff to chime in with an opinion.

Travel News

Subscribe to our free Travel News e-newsletter, and get monthly updates from Rick on what's happening in Europe.

Rick's Free Travel App

Get your FREE **Rick Steves Audio Europe**™ app to enjoy...

- Dozens of self-guided tours of Europe's top museums, sights and historic walks
- Hundreds of tracks filled with cultural insights and sightseeing tips from Rick's radio interviews
- All organized into handy geographic playlists
- For Apple and Android

With Rick whispering in your ear, Europe gets even better.

Find out more at ricksteves.com

Gear up for your next adventure at ricksteves.com

Light Luggage

Pack light and right with Rick Steves' affordable, custom-designed rolling carry-on bags, backpacks, day packs and shoulder bags.

Accessories

From packing cubes to moneybelts and beyond, Rick has personally selected the travel goodies that will help your trip go smoother.

Shop at ricksteves.com

Experience maximum Europe

Save time and energy

This guidebook is your independent-travel toolkit. But for all it delivers, it's still up to you to devote the time and energy it takes to manage the preparation and logistics that are essential for a happy trip. If that's a hassle, there's a solution.

Rick Steves Tours

A Rick Steves tour takes you to Europe's most interesting places with great

with minimum stress

guides and small groups of 28 or less. We follow Rick's favorite itineraries, ride in comfy buses, stay in family-run hotels, and bring you intimately close to the Europe you've traveled so far to see. Most importantly, we take away the logistical headaches so you can focus on the fun.

travelers—nearly half of them repeat customers—along with us on four dozen different itineraries, from Ireland to Italy to Athens. Is a Rick Steves tour the right fit for your travel dreams? Find out at ricksteves.com, where you can also request Rick's latest tour catalog. Europe is best experienced with happy travel partners. We hope you can join us.

Join the fun

This year we'll take thousands of free-spirited

See our itineraries at ricksteves.com

BEST OF GUIDES

Full color easy-to-scan format, focusing on Europe's most popular destinations and sights.

Best of France
Best of Germany
Best of England
Best of Europe
Best of Ireland
Best of Italy
Best of Spain

COMPREHENSIVE GUIDES

City, country, and regional guides with detailed coverage for a multi-week trip exploring the most iconic sights and venturing off the beaten track.

Amsterdam & the Netherlands
Barcelona
Belgium: Bruges, Brussels, Antwerp & Ghent
Berlin
Budapest
Croatia & Slovenia
Eastern Europe
England
Florence & Tuscany
France
Germany
Great Britain
Greece: Athens & the Peloponnese
Iceland
Ireland
Istanbul
Italy
London
Paris
Portugal
Prague & the Czech Republic
Provence & the French Riviera
Rome
Scandinavia
Scotland
Spain
Switzerland
Venice
Vienna, Salzburg & Tirol

HE BEST OF ROME

, Italy's capital, is studded with
n remnants and floodlit-fountain
s. From the Vatican to the Colos-
with crazy traffic in between, Rome
erful, huge, and exhausting. The
the heat, and the weighty history

of the Eternal City where Caesars walked
can make tourists wilt. Recharge by taking siestas, gelato breaks, and after-dark
walks, strolling from one atmospheric
square to another in the refreshing evening air.

Pantheon—which
dome until the
3,000 years old
ver 1,500).

athens in the Vat-
the humanistic

liators fought
her, entertaining

me *ristorante.*
t St. Peter's
ously.

ss in a coin

Rick Steves guidebooks are published by Avalon Travel,
an imprint of Perseus Books, a Hachette Book Group company.

Rick Steves books are available from your favorite bookseller.
Many guides are available as ebooks.

Credits

RESEARCHERS
To help update this book, Rick and Gene relied on...

Ben Curtis
Ben is a native of the Pacific Northwest, but he's lived in the UK, Germany, Spain, Norway, Hungary, and a few other countries besides. He's worked as a professor of history and politics, a tour guide, and an advisor to the British government. These days, home is wherever he can go for a hike, listen to some Beethoven, and write.

Cameron Hewitt
Born in Denver and raised in central Ohio, Cameron settled in Seattle in 2000. Ever since, he has spent three months each year in Europe, contributing to guidebooks, tours, radio and television shows, and other media for Rick Steves' Europe, where he serves as content manager. Cameron married his high school sweetheart (and favorite travel partner), Shawna, and enjoys taking pictures, trying new restaurants, and planning his next trip.

Robyn Stencil
Robyn credits the origin of her love affair with London to the Thames, supporting her motto "where there's a river, there's a run." Her ideal English adventure involves the call of gulls, plenty of flat whites, and friendly people from rocky coastline to green hills. When she's not researching, trapezing, or pursuing the perfect burger, Robyn calls Everett, Washington home and works as a tour product manager for Rick Steves' Europe.

PHOTO CREDITS

Front Cover: © SIME/eStock Photo
Title Page: London Schoolboys © Dominic Arizona Bonuccelli
Additional Photography: Dominic Arizona Bonuccelli, Rich Earl, Barb Geisler, Jennifer Hauseman, Cameron Hewitt, David C. Hoerlein, Lauren Mills, Pat O'Connor, Gene Openshaw, Sarah Slauson, Robyn Stencil, Rick Steves, Gretchen Strauch, Bruce VanDeventer, Wikimedia Commons (PD-Art/PD-US)
Additional Credits: p. 137, Tomb of Queen Elizabeth, Angelo Hornak/Alamy; Lady Chapel, Jon Arnold Images Ltd/Alamy; p. 141, Steve Vidler/Alamy; p. 169, Monet-Gare St. Lazare © National Gallery, London/Art Resource, NY; p. 178, Charles II © National Portrait Gallery, London; p. 187, Princess Diana © National Portrait Gallery, London (Bryan Organ, artist); p. 227, Lindisfarne Gospels © The British Library Board/The Granger Collection, New York; p. 228, Lindisfarne Gospels © The British Library Board/CPA Media Co. Ltd.; p. 229, The Gutenberg Bible, North Wind Picture Archives/Alamy; p. 229, Magna Carta © The British Library Board/The Granger Collection, New York; p. 234, Keystone Pictures USA/Alamy; p. 264, The Choir and High Altar © Johnny Greig/istockphoto.com, p. 269, John Donne, Angelo Hornak/Alamy; p. 285, crown jewels © ImageState/Alamy; p. 352, Cutty Sark © Cutty Sark Trust; p. 522 Horatio Nelson © The Granger Collection, New York

Photos are used by permission and are the property of the original copyright owners.